ALSO BY HOWARD M. SACHAR

The Course of Modern Jewish History

Aliyah: The Peoples of Israel

From the Ends of the Earth: The Peoples of Israel

The Emergence of the Middle East

Europe Leaves the Middle East

A History of Israel: From the Rise of Zionism to Our Time

The Man on the Camel

Egypt and Israel

Diaspora: An Inquiry into the Contemporary Jewish World

A History of Israel: From the Aftermath of the Yom Kippur War

A History of the Jews in America

Farewell España: The World of the Sephardim Remembered

A History of Israel: From the Rise of Zionism to Our Time
(revised and updated)

The Rise of Israel: A Documentary History (edited, 39 volumes)

Israel and Europe: An Appraisal in History

DREAMLAND

*Europeans and Jews in the
Aftermath of the Great War*

DREAMLAND

Europeans and Jews in the
Aftermath of the Great War

Howard M. Sachar

Alfred A. Knopf • New York • 2002

THIS IS A BORZOI BOOK
PUBLISHED BY ALFRED A. KNOPF

Copyright © 2002 by Howard Morley Sachar
All rights reserved under International and Pan-American Copyright
Conventions. Published in the United States by Alfred A. Knopf,
a division of Random House, Inc., New York, and simultaneously in
Canada by Random House of Canada Limited, Toronto. Distributed
by Random House, Inc., New York.
www.aaknopf.com

Knopf, Borzoi Books, and the colophon are registered
trademarks of Random House, Inc.

Library of Congress Cataloging-in-Publication Data

Sachar, Howard Morley.
Dreamland: Europeans and Jews in the aftermath of the Great
War / Howard M. Sachar.—1st ed.
p. cm.
Includes bibliographical references (p.   ) and index.
ISBN 0-375-40914-9
1. Jews—Europe—History—20th century. 2. Jews—Europe—
Social conditions—20th century. 3. Europe—Ethnic relations.
4. Europe—History—1918–1945. I. Title.

DS135.E83 S28 2002
940'.04924—dc21   2001038471

Manufactured in the United States of America
First Edition

For Jordan and Maya

If there were a sympathy in choice
War, death, or sickness did lay siege to it,
Making it momentary as a sound,
Swift as a shadow, short as any dream,
Brief as the lightning in the collied night,
That, in a spleen, unfolds both heaven and earth,
And ere a man hath power to say, "Behold!"
The jaws of darkness do devour it up;
So quick bright things come to confusion.

A Midsummer Night's Dream

Contents

MAPS

Foreword

If a "proud tower" had fallen in Europe, a new and better one was anticipated in its place. The carnage of 1914–18 had been the "war to end all wars," the war to "make the world safe for democracy." Dynamic new successor states were rising from the debris of expired autocracies. Political revolution was wresting the social terrain from once privileged elites. Had a climate of authentic freedom and justice for the Continent dawned at last?

There was a sure and certain indicator. It was the Jews. No people ever had experienced more of the Old World's underside, its legal, vocational, and physical repression. If the worst of the prewar inequities and anachronisms were now to be stripped away, the Jews would be the first to know. Indeed, with their uniquely survivalist commitment to peace and freedom, it was inevitable that they should be the first to hurl themselves into the Continent's explosive new chain reaction of political, economic, and cultural transformations.

Thus, in Eastern Europe, the Jews, long a people unto themselves, would press the cause of ethnic "self-determination" to its farthest linguistic and communal dimension. In both Eastern and Central Europe, for that matter, political messianists among them would lead the struggle for a classless, even utopian society. And in Central and Western Europe alike, Jewish liberal intellectuals would function at cutting-edge political and cultural *engagés*.

Neither before nor since that postwar era has the fate of Europe's Gentile majority and its Jewish minority been entangled as intimately, as passionately, as contentiously—as ferociously. Was the symbiosis in the end a productive one? Was the dream of an ongoing entwinement of destinies a puerile illusion or a visionary, even heroic ideal? Students of history will draw their own conclusions, as this historian has drawn his.

*   *   *

In the preparation of this work, I have benefited from the generous observations and suggestions of colleagues and friends. They can only be listed here, with my warmest appreciation. For Poland and the Ukraine: Professor Antony Polonsky of Brandeis University, Professor Ezra Mendelsohn of the Hebrew University of Jerusalem, and Professor Muriel Atkin of George Washington University. For Rumania: Professor Leon Volovici of the Hebrew University and Ms. Eva Gover of Tel Aviv, formerly Lecturer at the University of Bucharest. For Hungary: Mr. Charles Fenyvesi of Dickerson, Maryland, journalist and author.

For Czechoslovakia: Ms. Paula Zeigova of Prague, historian and teacher, and Professors Hugh Agnew and John Heins of George Washington University. For Austria: Dr. Stephen Beller of Washington, D.C., scholar and author. For Germany: Professor Henry Friedlander of the City University of New York, president of the German Studies Association, and Professors Mary Beth Stein, Andrew Zimmerman, Peter Rollberg, George Steiner, and Nathaniel Comfort of George Washington University. At the university's Gelman Library, for access to publications in a wide variety of sites: Dr. David Ettinger, Research Director, International Relations and Social Sciences; Mr. Glenn Canner, Associate Director of Inter-Library Loans; and Ms. Kim Tohuyen, Director of Consortium Borrowing.

Ms. Jane Garrett and Mr. Melvin Rosenthal of Alfred A. Knopf, my editors and close friends, have collaborated as intimately in this project as in our numerous earlier joint ventures. Eliana Steimatzky Sachar, my wife and tireless proofreader, has remained an indispensable partner in these endeavors for thirty-eight years. My father, Dr. Abram L. Sachar, the pioneering author of *Sufferance Is the Badge* (also published by Knopf, in 1940), was the inspiration for a work on Europeans and Jews in the aftermath of the Great War. No longer with us, he remains that inspiration.

H.M.S.
Kensington, Maryland,
May 14, 2001

DREAMLAND

Europeans and Jews in the
Aftermath of the Great War

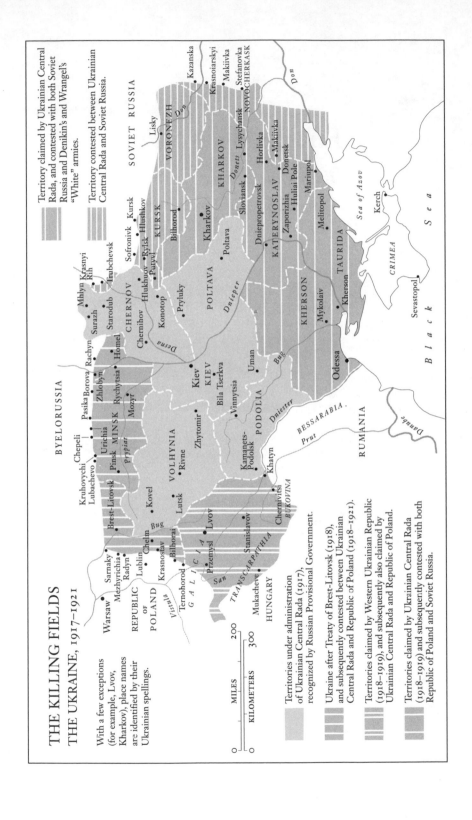

THE KILLING FIELDS
THE UKRAINE, 1917–1921

With a few exceptions
(for example, Lvov,
Kharkov) place names
are identified by their
Ukrainian spellings.

Territory claimed by Ukrainian Central
Rada, and contested with both Soviet
Russia and Denikin's and Wrangel's
"White" armies.

Territory contested between Ukrainian
Central Rada and Soviet Russia.

Territories under administration
of Ukrainian Central Rada (1917),
recognized by Russian Provisional Government.

Ukraine after Treaty of Brest-Litovsk (1918),
and subsequently contested between Ukrainian
Central Rada and Republic of Poland (1918–1921).

Territories claimed by Western Ukrainian Republic
(1918–1919), and subsequently also claimed by
Ukrainian Central Rada and Republic of Poland.

Territories claimed by Ukrainian Central Rada
(1918–1919) and subsequently contested with both
Republic of Poland and Soviet Russia.

I

A MURDER TRIAL IN PARIS

A Prosecution Begins

At 10:00 a.m. on October 18, 1927, the gates swung open to the Assize Court of the Seine, the fourth of five courtrooms in the Palace of Justice's stately complex. Some fifteen hundred persons, who had clogged the entryway since early morning, pressed forward to a chamber whose wood-paneled galleries accommodated barely four hundred spectators. Nearly half of them were journalists, many from other countries. They had come to witness a murder trial. Although both the victim, Simon Petliura, and the accused, Sholem Schwarzbard, were natives of the former tsarist empire, the crime had been committed in Paris a year and a half earlier.

Upon taking his seat on the dais, Presiding Judge Georges Flory informed the twelve jurors that French law permitted simultaneous criminal and civil actions. Accordingly, the victim's widow, Olga Petliura, and his brother, Oskar Petliura, were sharing in the prosecution. Judge Flory then turned to the prisoner in the dock. Sholem Schwarzbard, thirty-nine, was a pale and diminutive man, yet with the muscular physique of a bantamweight boxer. He listened impassively while the judge defined the various charges of premeditated homicide, as listed in Articles 294–298 and Article 301 of France's Criminal Code. Flory explained that all carried the death penalty. How did the defendant plead? To each charge, Schwarzbard responded with an emphatic "not guilty." Hereupon the judge invited Public Prosecutor Chrétien Reynaud to present the case for the state. The ensuing trial would continue for eight days.

The basic facts of the defendant's life by then had been extensively described in the world press. Schwarzbard's hometown was Balta, a predominantly Jewish community in the former tsarist province of Podolia, where his parents owned a tiny grocery store. Balta's Jews intermittently were victimized by pogroms. In one of these, Schwarzbard's pregnant mother was killed. The surviving four children endured lives of acute hardship. Sholem Schwarzbard as an adolescent was apprenticed to a watchmaker in a neighboring village. During Russia's "Octobrist" Revolution of 1905, the seventeen-year-old youth was imprisoned for participating in an antigovernment demonstration. Upon his release three months later, he and his younger brother Meir fled Russia, working and often begging their way through Europe, before finally settling in Paris in 1910. There they opened a watchmaker's shop.

Although the brothers soon married and assumed family responsibilities, their reaction to the outbreak of war in 1914 was characteristically uncompromising. Both immediately enlisted for military service, and both were assigned to the French Foreign Legion. Afterward, both suffered wounds in the Somme campaign, and both were awarded the Croix de Guerre. It was during his convalescence in a military hospital in February 1916 that Sholem Schwarzbard first learned of the immense tragedy that had befallen his people in Russia the year before. In December 1914, as the German army launched its offensive on the eastern front, Russia's supreme military commander, Grand Duke Sergei, classified the dense Jewish population in the tsarist borderlands as a potentially subversive element. These people, he decreed, should forthwith be transferred away from the principal battle zones. Thus began, in March 1915, a systematic expulsion of Jews from Russian Poland, Lithuania, and Courland. Ultimately, some half-million men, women, and children were uprooted and driven into the Russian interior. Wherever transportation was provided, the exiles were packed into freight cars and dispatched to inland villages on a waybill. But scores of thousands of others were indiscriminately herded eastward without a fixed destination. Often they subsisted in wagons, boxcars, even in open fields. At least sixty thousand Jews died of starvation and exposure during the vast expulsion. Hundreds of thousands of others suffered economic ruin.

In March 1917, even before receiving his medical discharge from the army, Schwarzbard learned of yet another upheaval in Russia. This one was political. The nation had undergone revolution, the tsar had abdicated, a liberal new regime had been installed. Thrilled by the news, Schwarzbard immediately sought permission from the French government to return to his homeland and seek out his family. His request was granted. Thus, in August 1917, accompanied by his wife, Schwarzbard departed by ship for Russia, and in September he rejoined his father, brothers, sisters, and stepmother in Balta. In Balta, too, he resumed his vocation as a watchmaker.

Yet Schwarzbard's civilian career endured less than a year and a half. Following a second, Bolshevik, Revolution, Russia fell into the throes of civil war. In January 1919, Schwarzbard was conscripted into the Red Army and thrown into battle against the "White" counterrevolutionary forces. After participating in the Bolsheviks' defense of Odessa, he was transferred in late spring to the struggle for Russia's Ukrainian provinces. Here the battle was waged first against the rebel Ukrainian Republican army, then against General Anton Denikin's "White"—counterrevolutionary—army. Another year would pass before Schwarzbard was released from military service. Exhausted by eighteen months of war and privation, he returned then with his wife to France (p. 14).

A Nation Is Reborn

These were the essentials of Schwarzbard's life, as recounted in the trial by his defense attorney. Normally, the little watchmaker's sacrifices on behalf of his adopted motherland would have warmed the heart of even the iciest French cynic. But Madame Olga Petliura's civil attorney, César Campinchi, offered another picture of the defendant. Schwarzbard was a professional revolutionary, Campinchi insisted, who had worked in league with Russia's Bolshevik regime. Here Campinchi cited Schwarzbard's youthful activities as a radical, his imprisonment during the 1905 Revolution, his arrest as a thief for stealing food while passing through Vienna in 1909. For the Ukrainian émigré groups that funded Campinchi's prosecution, meanwhile, the trial offered more than simply the opportunity to convict a murderer. There was a national record to put straight. Schwarzbard and his partisans were "desecrating" the facts of the Ukrainian people's struggle for freedom.

That struggle had continued intermittently throughout modern history. During the seventeenth century, it took the form of an uprising against the ruling Polish Commonwealth. In later years, following the eighteenth-century partitions of Poland, the Ukrainians had staged periodic revolts against both the governing tsarist empire and the Polish landowning aristocracy. By 1914, the Ukrainians numbered some 25 million, and if they remained a peasant and largely illiterate population, their nationalists, like those of Poland, still awaited their window of opportunity. It opened with the Russian Revolution of March 1917. The Russian provisional government, under the prime ministry of Prince Georgi Lvov, expressed sympathy for a certain limited Ukrainian autonomy within a Russian-dominated federation.

The Ukrainian nationalists were unimpressed. Rejecting the autonomist formula as vague and pallid, they encouraged Ukrainian conscripts to desert the Russian army en masse and form their own military units. Subsequently, in November 1917, exploiting the chaos engendered by Russia's second, Bolshevik revolution, the Ukrainians formally proclaimed their own autonomous republic. Establishing a central Rada—a parliament—in the Ukraine's historic capital city of Kiev, they appointed Mikhail Hrushevsky as the nation's first president and Simon Petliura as its minister of defense. Over the ensuing weeks, the Ukrainian Rada issued "Second and Third Universal Declarations," successively enlarging its ambit of governmental jurisdiction.

In Petrograd, meanwhile, the Bolshevik leader Vladimir Lenin was alarmed. Deeming the Ukraine's vast agricultural bread basket, and its naval ports and army bases, to be of critical economic and strategic importance to beleaguered Russia, Lenin insisted on a more limited version of Ukrainian autonomy. He was rebuffed. The rift between the two governments soon became irreconcilable. Indeed, in January 1918, the Ukrainian Rada and its Executive proclaimed the republic's full independence. For Lenin, therefore, the provocation demanded a frontal response. Two weeks later, detachments of Red Army troops occupied Kiev. Yet, even then, the Ukrainians were not without recourse. That same January, Major General Otto von Hoffman, Germany's plenipotentiary at the (ongoing) Brest-Litovsk peace negotiations, signed a separate treaty of "recognition and peace" with the Ukrainian separatists. Soon afterward, in early February of 1918, the German army pushed forward into the Ukraine, sending the Russians fleeing, and restoring the Ukrainian Rada to office in Kiev.

The "restoration" was a sham. The Rada functioned entirely by sufferance of the German army. Worse yet, the treaty the Ukrainians had signed at Brest-Litovsk committed them to deliver a million tons of grain and livestock to the Central Powers. The burden soon proved insupportable. In the summer of 1918, as Ukrainian resistance to these shipments stiffened, the Germans lost patience with their client regime. Dispersing the Rada and its Executive, they installed a puppet *hetman*—military commander—of their own, a functionary who set about fulfilling the delivery quotas with obsequious zeal.

For the Jews, the Ukrainian nationalist struggle proved a trauma of agonizing dimensions. It always had. A Jewish presence in the Ukraine traced back at least to the fourteenth century, when tens of thousands of Jews, fleeing massacres in German-speaking Europe, began pouring as refugees into the Ukrainian and Lithuanian territories of the Kingdom of Poland. Henceforth, under Polish royal protection, the Jews served the landowning aristocracy as estate managers and as rent collectors from the Ukrainian peasantry. The Ukrainians bitterly resented this double servitude. In their folklore, the Jews were not merely Antichrists. They were economic allies of the Poles. In the mid-seventeenth century, therefore, when the Ukrainian Cossack leader Bogdan Chmielnicki led his people in an explosive revolt against Polish oppression, his campaign was directed against Jews and Poles alike. Before the slaughter ended, in 1654, as many as fifty thousand Jews may have perished. In ensuing centuries, the Ukraine's periodic anti-Polish and anti-Jewish outbursts consumed possibly another fifty thousand Jewish lives.

Nevertheless, whether under Polish or—subsequently—tsarist rule, a Jewish nucleus in the Ukraine over the centuries managed to survive intermittent persecution and even to achieve a rather formidable demographic base. By the Russian census of 1897, Jews living in the Ukrainian regions numbered 1,927,000—almost 10 percent of the total population, and the largest concentration of Jews in the tsarist empire altogether. Most were town-dwellers. "Infidel," urban, commercial, this was an alien minority all but preordained to suffer majority xenophobia. In turn, with their long exposure to that hostility, the Jews reacted to the wartime separatist movement with profound trepidation. In the spring and summer of 1918, to be sure, under the brief, de facto rule of "civilized" Germany, they appeared to be at least physically safe. But when the German presence in Eastern Europe deteriorated in the autumn of 1918, Ukrainian nationalist forces moved to seize effective control of their ancient homeland. In preparing for independence, the Ukrainian Rada established a new administration, an executive Directorate of five men. The Directorate's president was Simon Petliura.

Born in Poltava in 1879 to an impoverished cab driver, Simon Vassilievich Petliura was precocious enough as a youth to be admitted to a Russian theological seminary, and tenacious enough to maintain his Ukrainian cultural identity during ten years of educational Russification. In common with most of his countrymen, the young man revered as his heroes Bogdan Chmielnicki, the seventeenth-century "Ukrainian Cromwell," and Taras Shevchenko, the great nineteenth-century Ukrainian poet. Yet Petliura had become more than a passionate nationalist. For him, a free Ukraine would become a land of social justice and equality for all nationalities, spared the hateful tsarist incubus of anti-Polish or even anti-Jewish bigotry. In pursuit of that dream, the young man eventually left the seminary (without graduating), and returned home to become active in the underground Ukrainian Social Democratic party.

When the World War began, Petliura avoided direct military service in the tsarist army by enlisting in a Red Cross medical unit assigned to Ukrainian detachments. Three years later, immediately following Russia's Bolshevik Revolution, he set about mobilizing a Ukrainian brigade to protect his people's newly proclaimed autonomy. In March 1918, the Ukrainian Rada confirmed Petliura as its minister of defense. The timing was less than propitious. By then the Germans were in effective occupation of the Ukraine. They chose to keep Petliura under house arrest in East Prussia.

Yet it was the Central Powers' last gasp in Slavic Europe. By early autumn of 1918 their contingents in the Ukraine were in retreat. Petliura was released. In November 1918, when the Ukrainian Executive was revived as a five-member Directorate, the thirty-nine-year-old Petliura was selected as the nation's *ataman*, its president. Thereafter it was

Petliura—a slight man of less than middle height, given to wearing a flamboyant yellow cockade and a richly bemedaled blue uniform—who would
direct the Ukrainian national struggle. Then, too, the Jews would come to
know him well.

Testimony on a Murder Victim

Nine years later, in Paris, Sholem Schwarzbard's defense attorney characterized the assassination of Petliura as an act of "moral justice." This was
not the view of Ukrainian expatriates in the West. Petliura's reputation had
become synonymous with their nation's honor. To define and defend that
honor, Public Prosecutor Chrétien Reynaud called a succession of Ukrainian émigrés to the witness stand. Under Reynaud's questioning, they
described the former ataman as a patriotic hero. As early as July 1917,
they reminded the court, the newborn Ukrainian Rada had made a point
of guaranteeing full civil rights and communal autonomy to all non-
Ukrainian ethnic minorities. Russians, Poles, and Jews henceforth could be
represented in the Ukrainian government by their own "undersecretaries."
Indeed, in November 1917, when the Ukraine first broke away from Russia's new Bolshevik regime, the Jews were guaranteed not less than fifty
delegates to the Rada. Abram Revutsky was appointed minister for Jewish
affairs. Solomon Goldelman was appointed the Ukraine's minister of labor.
Altogether, the witnesses testified, the last year of the war represented a
"honeymoon" between the Ukrainian and Jewish peoples.

The "honeymoon," at best an uneasy one, would not endure. It was supplanted in the spring of 1918 by the German puppet administration. While
protecting Jews physically, the occupation regime effectively canceled their
communal autonomy. And, once the Germans pulled out of the Ukraine in
the autumn of 1918, and as Petliura remobilized his army, there appeared
to be no further leeway for pluralistic niceties. The Ukrainian people soon
faced a new danger to their hard-won independence. In February 1919, the
Soviet Red Army launched an offensive into the Ukrainian regions from
the east, even as a White counterrevolutionary army under General Anton
Denikin pushed into the Ukraine from the south. Compressed into a
shrinking territorial enclave, Petliura's troops fell back to the west. By
spring, they were reduced to a tatterdemalion force of barely twenty thousand regulars. So it was, throughout 1919 and 1920, in the march and
countermarch of rival armies, that the Ukrainian Republic collapsed in
pandemonium, and soon in pillage and anarchy. Nearly a decade later, during the Schwarzbard trial, the civil prosecution's co-counsel, Albert
Willms, paraded his own long retinue of Ukrainian witnesses who testified
to the chaos and misery of those years, the depredations suffered by

Ukrainians, Poles, and Jews alike. If Jews were attacked, the witnesses insisted, it was simply because they were Bolsheviks, or had vacillated in their loyalty to the Ukrainian cause.

Schwarzbard's attorneys gave this argument short shrift. Leading the defense team was a prominent Jewish advocate, Henri Torrès. Thirty-nine years old, a decorated war hero, and one of the most successful criminal lawyers in Europe, Torrès was the grandson of Isaiah Levaillant, who had founded the League for the Defense of Human and Civil Rights at the time of the Dreyfus Affair. Like his grandfather, Torrès nurtured an intense solicitude for the victims of persecution. Lately he had visited Rumania to study that nation's rampant antisemitism, and upon his return had organized a protest campaign against the Bucharest government. With equal thoroughness, in his current preparations for the Schwarzbard trial, Torrès had sent his assistant to the Ukraine to interview Jewish survivors. With the financial help of American Jews, he brought several of these witnesses to Paris.

It was their testimony now that provided a grim insight into the years 1919–20. Ukrainian army units, demoralized and enraged by their defeat at the hands of both the Red and White armies, had redressed their losses by victimizing unarmed local Jews. In the recollection of Solomon Goldelman, the former Ukrainian minister of labor, "[n]ot a single Jewish city or town escaped a pogrom, robbery, or an [extortion] levied against it." Indeed, at least half a million Jews were reduced to destitution, and tens of thousands of others were murdered outright, or were mutilated or raped by Ukrainian military and guerrilla forces. The worst atrocities evidently were committed by Ukrainian Cossacks. Thus, in March 1919, Cossacks marched into the densely inhabited Jewish community of Proskurov. Upon reaching Alexandrovskaya Street, testified one survivor,

> they divided into groups of five to fifteen men and swarmed out into the adjoining streets, which were inhabited exclusively by Jews. . . . [Entering the] houses, [they] drew their swords and began to cut down the inhabitants without regard to sex or age. They murdered old men, women, and infants at their mothers' breasts. They were not content with killing, but thrust their victims' bodies through with bayonets. . . . The Jews were dragged out of the cellars and lofts and murdered. Hand grenades were thrown into the cellars, and [thus] entire families were put to death.

In Zhitomir province, the neighboring peasantry shared in the slaughter, and then in the frenzied spoliation of Jewish property. The killing and looting continued through the spring of 1919, from town to town—Uman,

Dubovo, Talnoie, Kristinovka, Ladyzhenka, Byasovok, Mankovka, Ivanka, Buki—precisely where organized Ukrainian military resistance was collapsing. Marauding guerrillas often compelled Jews to dig their own graves before shooting or bayoneting them. Between December 1918 and March 1919 alone, possibly thirty thousand Jews perished in the first wave of violence. A second, far larger wave of pogroms, beginning in the late spring, would continue well into 1920 (p. 14).

These were the desperate circumstances in which Jews by the thousands turned to the invading Red Army. Years later, in the Schwarzbard trial, the prosecution made note of that collaboration. "We indignantly protest against the massacres of Jews," acknowledged Albert Willms, ". . . [but] we add that . . . very often . . . it was the very attitude of the Jews which provoked the pogromist movements." A vigorous dissent came from a renowned Russian-Jewish attorney, Arnold Margolin, who insisted in his account of the Jewish ordeal in 1919–20 that the Ukrainian military leadership had created a self-fulfilling prophecy, and "[u]nder these conditions, to combat and kill Jews was synonymous with fighting against Bolshevism." Ukrainian nationalists simply found "Jewish Bolshevism" an effective pretext for mobilizing popular support.

Had Petliura cynically invented the charge of "Jewish Bolshevism"? The prosecution's retinue of Ukrainian witnesses insisted that the opposite was the case—that the ataman had made every effort to curb anti-Jewish atrocities. A few witnesses submitted photographic facsimiles of Petliura's declarations to his army. These were read aloud:

> Officers and Cossacks! . . . The army, which brings fraternity, equality, and freedom to all peoples of the Ukraine, must not pay attention to the provocateurs and adventurers thirsty for blood. The army shall not be an instrument of mischief against the Jews. Anyone who tolerates the crimes against them is an enemy of our fatherland and must be rejected as such from the human family.

Petliura then warned that "the penalty of death is instituted for those who will be involved in pogroms." Arnold Margolin himself recorded not a few of these executions, and they were confirmed by the American Jewish Congress (p. 33). The ataman unquestionably appreciated the need for Western Jewish goodwill. In July 1920, two members of an American Jewish relief mission in the Ukraine, Dr. Israel Friedlander and Rabbi Bernard Cantor, were waylaid and killed—apparently by local irregulars. Petliura reacted with evident indignation and sought (unsuccessfully) to have the murderers tracked down.

In the Ukraine of 1919–20, nevertheless, few Jews discerned evidence of the ataman's solicitude. Testifying for the defense at the Schwarzbard trial, Professor Elias Tcherikower, research director of the Jewish Scientific Institute ("YIVO"), presented a vast accumulation of data taken from Jews and Ukrainians alike. It revealed that Petliura evinced only a perfunctory interest in the fate of the Jewish minority. Thus, informed of an impending pogrom in Kiev, the ataman refused to block the violence. "Don't make me quarrel with my army," he protested to a delegation of Kiev officials, who feared the economic consequences of unrest in their city. "The army saved the Ukraine." In March 1919, when the threat of a pogrom loomed at Zhitomir, Petliura declined to receive a concerned local Ukrainian delegation, and the pogrom afterward unfolded without interference. Indeed, Petliura later elevated Petrov, the officer whose troops committed the attack, to minister of war. As the ataman passed through the village of Yaruga, a group of local Jews implored him to end the wave of recurrent pogroms. "Well, this is nothing," he replied. "The soldiers must amuse themselves." By Tcherikower's testimony, Petliura's role in the notoriously gruesome massacre of Proskurov was incontrovertible. Two days before the pogrom, on February 13, 1919, the ataman dispatched a telegram to General Semesenko, his area commander. It stated:

> Secret and important. All efforts of the Jewish population to organize a Bolshevik uprising should absolutely be suppressed severely with an armed force, so that no treacherous Jewish hand in [the province of] Podolia should dare to raise itself against the independent Ukraine.

There were non-Jewish witnesses who similarly verified Petliura's complicity. Henryk Pszankowski, the local Ukrainian representative of the Danish Red Cross in 1919, recalled General Semesenko boasting to Petliura that the army distributed leaflets of incitement in advance of the Proskurov massacre. On the witness stand in the 1927 trial, Professor Paul Langevin, vice president of the League for the Defense of Human and Civil Rights, declared: "After attentive study of the public documents, I have no doubt of the abomination which took place in the Ukraine. . . . There is even less doubt that at least half of these pogroms were the work of regular Ukrainian troops through the orders of their chief." Langevin held his ground under the prosecution's vigorous cross-examination. Defense Attorney Torrès then summarized the case against Petliura:

> There were some pogroms in all the armies in the Ukraine. . . . But Petliura, the Ataman General Petliura, under whose government the pogroms had been organized by the chiefs themselves, by the regiments, with their colonels in charge, by the squads with their [unit]

atamans in charge, without any of these superior officers or generals
being punished, without any of them who had transmitted orders for
pogroms being chastened—that is the terrible and blood responsibility of Petliura.

A Triangular Horror

In rebutting the avalanche of testimony, the prosecution managed to register a single but not ineffective demurrer. It was to contrast the ordeal of the
Jews under Petliura's Ukrainian army with their fate at the hands of General Denikin's White army. Anton Ivanovich Denikin, a professional officer
in the imperial Russian command, served briefly as Russian chief of staff
after the first, March 1917 Revolution, but soon afterward was imprisoned
for conspiring to overthrow the liberal government of Aleksander Kerensky. Following the Bolshevik Revolution of November 1917,
Denikin managed to escape southward to the Don region and in April
1918 to emerge as generalissimo of White forces in southern Russia. A
resourceful commander, Denikin swiftly regained military control of the
former tsarist Caucasus, and in May of that year he launched a major offensive into the Ukraine. By the summer of 1919, his army had cleared the
region both of Petliura's tatterdemalion rear guard and of isolated Bolshevik units.

Unlike Petliura, who still hoped to enlist Western support, Denikin felt
no need to maintain even a pretense of liberal moderation. He remained
an unregenerate disciple of the late tsar. Thus, in August 1918, periodic White assaults on Jews—always favored scapegoats under the tsarist
empire—burgeoned into mass pogroms. Even the turn in the tide of battle,
as the Red Army's larger manpower reserves pressed Denikin's forces back
to the southeast, brought no respite to the Jews. In their frustration, the
Whites descended with vindictive fury upon the surviving belts of Jewish
towns and villages. Anathematizing the Jews as Bolsheviks and Antichrists,
Denikin's troops often burned and buried their victims alive or drowned
them in wells, and raped and mutilated their women and children. Estimates of casualties vary, but none assessed the number of dead at less than
eighty thousand. Until World War II, the Ukrainian horror ranked as the
widest-ranging massacre of Jews in modern history.

It is of interest that Denikin himself escaped retribution of any kind.
Upon leading the remnant of his army into the Crimea, he transferred his
command to another White officer, General Piotr Wrangel, and then
departed Russia. Eventually Denikin made his way through Turkey to the
United States, where he lived quietly, if modestly, as a pensioner of the
émigré White Russian community. He died of natural causes in Ann Arbor,
Michigan, in 1947.

By the spring of 1919, meanwhile, Simon Petliura was facing his own moment of truth. With his troops overwhelmed by the numerically superior Red Army, the ataman grudgingly accepted the need for an accommodation with the oldest of his people's enemies, the Poles. In the late-eighteenth-century partitions of Poland, the defunct kingdom's southwesternmost region, Galicia, with its mixed Polish-Ukrainian population, had been awarded to Habsburg Austria, thereby becoming Austria's easternmost province. Then, a century and a quarter later, in the autumn of 1918, as the Austrian Empire itself disintegrated, Ukrainian troops in the Habsburg army deserted en masse to proclaim the eastern sector of Galicia as the "West Ukrainian Republic"—and a few months later to negotiate a federation with Petliura's Independent Republic of Ukraine, with its capital in Kiev.

The Poles would have something to say about this grandiose Ukrainian scheme. In late 1918, their political leadership similarly had declared the independence of Poland and then had celebrated their new statehood by launching an invasion of East Galicia—the "West Ukrainian Republic"—and claiming the region as part of Greater Poland. In ensuing months, Polish troops drove steadily ahead under the command of their national hero, General Jozef Pilsudski (pp. 20–21). By autumn of 1919, the hapless Ukrainians were caught in a pincers. In the west, Pilsudski's armies battered steadily ahead, investing almost the totality of the "West Ukrainian Republic." In the east, the Red Army was inflicting its own hammer blows on Petliura's exhausted troops.

At this point, in September 1919, Petliura in his desperation struck a deal with Pilsudski, the Polish leader. The Ukrainians would renounce their claim to East Galicia—the "West Ukrainian Republic"—if the Poles would allow Petliura carte blanche in the far larger terrain of eastern—integral—Ukraine. In April 1920, therefore, under Pilsudski's strategic command, the two armies embarked on a joint offensive into eastern Ukraine. They enjoyed early success. The Reds, still heavily engaged with Denikin's White forces to the southeast, were obliged briefly to evacuate Kiev. Within six weeks, however, the Soviet commander, General Mikhail Tukhashevsky, succeeded in regrouping his forces and launching a powerful counterattack on his own, not halting until his army reached the outskirts of Warsaw. Yet here Tukhashevsky finally outran his supply lines. Whereupon, in August, reorganized by a French "adviser," General Maxime Weygand, Pilsudski's Polish troops managed to hurl the Russians back.

By then, however, Poles and Russians alike had reached a state of exhaustion. Both sides expressed interest in negotiating a peace. In April 1921, after months of wrangling and periodic interruptions, a formal treaty was signed in Riga. By its terms, the Poles accepted the restoration of

Russian domination over integral—eastern—Ukraine. Polish rule in turn was recognized over the territory of Galicia, including the doomed "West Ukrainian Republic." Indeed, Poland now reemerged as a territorial behemoth, the single largest country in Eastern Europe, after Soviet Russia. By the same token, the Treaty of Riga left the new republic engorged with millions of ethnic minority subjects, among them, Ukrainians, Byelorussians, Lithuanians, Germans, and Jews (p. 44).

Betrayed by their erstwhile Polish ally, the Ukrainians had paid a grim price in their four-year struggle. Their casualties, military and civilian, may have reached three-quarters of a million. But the Jews had endured a proportionately far greater rictus of terror and loss. In the final Ukrainian offensive—and subsequent retreat—of 1919–20, Simon Petliura relinquished virtually all control over his troops' "extracurricular" activities. Whether coming or going, the Ukrainian army paid its characteristic respects to the Jews. It was an orgy of murder and pillage, a swath of horror that claimed possibly sixty thousand additional Jewish lives. If the Ukrainian people in future years enshrined Petliura as a nationalist hero, those Jews who survived the ataman's ministrations preserved their own assessment of the man. For them, ever after, Petliura was the "ataman from hell."

A Quest for Belated Justice

In early 1919, Sholem Schwarzbard, who had returned to Balta two years earlier, was mustered into the Red Army and into battle against the Ukrainian and White forces (p. 5). It was in the midst of this combat that he personally witnessed the depredations wrought on Ukrainian Jewry. In March 1920, he learned as well that Ukrainian guerrillas had slain his father and stepmother. Stoically, Schwarzbard continued his military service with the Bolsheviks for three additional months. Finally, demobilized in June, he departed Russia for the last time, returning to Paris with his wife and daughter. There, he reopened a tiny watchmaking shop on rue Menilmontant. There, too, in his free time, he contributed articles on Ukrainian Jewish issues to several Yiddish-language newspapers published in New York.

Others would depart Russia in this same period of Bolshevik triumph. By the spring of 1926, France had become the home of some 400,000 White Russian émigrés. Possibly half the taxi drivers in Paris were veterans of one or another of the Russian and Ukrainian armies. Former generals peddled newspapers or worked as hotel doormen. Their wives sold embroidery or waited on tables in run-down cafés. And in Paris, too, in the spring of 1926, lived Simon Vassilievich Petliura. After first taking refuge in Warsaw, the former ataman had moved on to Switzerland in 1924, and from there to Paris a year later. Among the Ukrainians in the French capital was a galamorphy of political factions—monarchists, Social Revolutionaries, Social Democrats, even separatists favoring a revived "West Ukrainian Republic." Petliura was intent on uniting these dissident groups. From the modest Left Bank walk-up he shared with his wife and daughter on rue Thenarde, he embarked on the publication of a small tabloid, *Tryzub*. It was suffused with anti-Russian and antisemitic invective. Although funds were chronically short and publication frequently was interrupted, Petliura began to make some headway in establishing a rudimentary Ukrainian "government-in-exile."

It was in September 1925 that news reached Schwarzbard of Petliura's arrival in Paris. From then on, the little watchmaker was a man possessed. Feverishly, he sought out Petliura's address and itinerary. In May 1926, he came up with a vital clue. Petliura often took lunch in a working-class restaurant, the Chartier, on rue Racine. In the early afternoon of May 25, therefore, Schwarzbard departed for the Chartier. In advance, he dispatched two express letters from a local post office. The first was to his wife. "My dear Anna," it said. "I am performing a duty for our poor people. I am going to avenge all the pogroms, the blood, the hatred of the Jews. Petliura . . . must pay with his blood. As for you, conduct yourself heroically. Accuse no one. I alone am responsible. . . . God bless you, Sholem."

The second letter was mailed to Henri Torrès, the Jewish lawyer who was widely identified with human rights issues. Schwarzbard was uninterested in becoming a martyr. In Berlin five years earlier, he knew, a young Armenian refugee, Solomon Teilirian, had assassinated Mehmet Talaat Pasha, the wartime Turkish minister of the interior and one of the authors of the 1915 Armenian genocide. In the ensuing trial, Teilirian had been acquitted; his deed was proclaimed an act of historic justice. In Lausanne, in 1923, a fugitive White Russian, Maurice Conrad, assassinated a Soviet diplomat, Consul Vorovsky, and based his defense on Bolshevik atrocities in Russia. A Swiss court acquitted Conrad on the same grounds of historic justice. Schwarzbard manifestly was anticipating a similar defense for himself.

At 1:00 p.m. of May 25, he waited on the sidewalk outside the Chartier restaurant as Petliura approached. Leaning forward, Schwarzbard asked: "Are you Petliura?" Instantly sensing his danger, the Ukrainian lifted his cane. Schwarzbard then pulled a revolver from his pocket. "Defend yourself, dog!" he shouted. Firing five times at point-blank range, he continued shouting: "For the pogroms! For my brethren!" Petliura lay groaning on the sidewalk for several moments, then fell silent. Immediately, bystanders seized Schwarzbard, who made no effort to escape. When gendarmes arrived, he handed over his empty pistol. "I have killed a great murderer," he declared. Commandeering a taxi, the gendarmes rushed Schwarzbard to a nearby police station.

Within days, a public debate began in the French press. Editorials, discussions, and interviews argued the legitimacy of an individual administering "historic justice" on his own. For Ukrainian émigré newspapers both in Europe and in North America, the issue was much clearer. Petliura was a martyr for his people, and Schwarzbard was an agent of Bolshevism whose pistol "dripped with the blood of the Torah." The Jews saw matters differently, of course. From thousands of anonymous Jews throughout the world, money poured in for a Schwarzbard defense fund. Jewish public figures, among them the Socialist leader Léon Blum, the philosopher Henri Bergson, the scientist Albert Einstein, the Zionist statesman Chaim Weizmann, volunteered their testimony on behalf of Schwarzbard. So did the renowned non-Jewish writers Sinclair Lewis, H. G. Wells, Romain Rolland, and Vicente Blasco Ibañez.

Meanwhile, during the year and a half preceding his trial, Schwarzbard from his cell in Paris's ancient Prison de la Santé busied himself dispatching letters to friends and relatives, to Yiddish-language newspapers in Europe and the United States. "I was too generous with this assassin," he wrote, typically, to New York's *Fraye Arbayter Shtime*. "I have opened a new chapter in our somber and bloody history. Enough of slavery, enough outpouring of tears, an end to supplication, crying, bribery. Lifting our heads, sticking out our chests, we demand herewith our right, that of living equal to all!" From beginning to end, Schwarzbard would maintain this defiant stance.

Moreover, when the trial began on October 18, 1927, Schwarzbard in the prisoner's box insisted upon chronicling in fullest detail his people's long and historic ordeal in the Ukraine. Only near the end of his four-hour testimony did he focus on the specific horrors of 1918–20. Disdaining to base his defense on mental stress, Schwarzbard touched only briefly on the fact that he himself had lost some two dozen relatives to the massacres. It was Judge Flory who at last brought the testimony to a halt. Had the defendant intended to kill Petliura or not, he asked, and did the defendant in fact commit the killing? Here Schwarzbard made his single concession to the French criminal code, and more specifically to the jury's moral requirement of a loophole for exoneration. He pleaded "not guilty" on all counts.

On October 26, the last day of the trial, Albert Willms presented a two-hour summation for the civil prosecution. While acknowledging the Jews' suffering, he rejected the manipulation of their ordeal as a moral defense. "[W]e feel . . . the same indignation . . . about the massacres of Christians," he argued. "And we add that it . . . was the very attitude of the Jews which provoked the pogromist movements." Schwarzbard's entire life history,

Willms insisted, was a tangle of anarchist associations and service in the Red Army. Only the Bolsheviks stood to benefit from this "odious crime." Willms's colleague, César Campinchi, was a Corsican whose summation was rather more florid, even more harshly accusatory. "And you, Schwarzbard, who are you?" he declaimed. "Your hands, are they clean? An 'idealistic anarchist,' someone has said. Perhaps. But your idealism started with burglary and ended with assassination."

For the defense, Henri Torrès, a dominant presence, six feet tall, with the physique of a wrestler and a booming voice, delivered his own summation. Beginning at 5:00 p.m., at a time when the participants and the courtroom's thousand or more spectators were approaching exhaustion, Torrès shrewdly limited his remarks to forty minutes. He also ignored the French criminal code. Instead, he preferred to remind the jury of France's "noble" tradition of justice, its protests against Russian pogroms as far back as 1903 and against Turkish atrocities in 1915. Schwarzbard's service to France, Torrès emphasized, had been characterized by patriotism and heroism, and the fate of his family was one of personal tragedy. Moreover, the ample testimony of witnesses revealed not only the magnitude of the Ukrainian horror but Simon Petliura's culpability in tolerating it. Torrès then recalled that other defendants, Solomon Teilirian and Maurice Conrad, had been acquitted for acts of "moral justice." "Gentlemen of the jury, I am done," he concluded. "[A]cquit Schwarzbard because you have compassion. Gentlemen, today you are responsible for the prestige of our nation and for the thousands of human lives that depend on the verdict of France."

Hereupon Judge Flory, in his final instructions to the jurors, once again tersely emphasized that they were limited to consideration exclusively of intent and consequence. Had Schwarzbard premeditated the deed, had he actually fired the shots, and by firing the shots had he caused the death of Petliura? No other matter was relevant. The jury then retired to deliberate. It was 5:50 p.m. Schwarzbard was led back to his cell. Three squads of special police kept order as a large, restive crowd milled about outside the Palace of Justice. Suddenly, only fifteen minutes later, a clerk rushed through the gates to announce that the jury had reached a verdict. Incredulous, the crowd began to edge back into the courtroom, while judge, attorneys, and Schwarzbard himself resumed their former places.

At Judge Flory's invitation, the jury foreman rose to declare that, on the first count, of firing the shots that struck Petliura down, the jury found Schwarzbard "not guilty"—and consequently there was no need to address the remaining counts. Hereupon the courtroom erupted in prolonged applause and cheering. Journalists and spectators alike joined in shouting: "Vive la France!" Schwarzbard's family members and friends tearfully embraced. Even Judge Flory could not suppress a smile as he announced that the defendant had been acquitted and therefore was to be released forthwith.

Throughout the Western world, news of the verdict was given front-page newspaper coverage and widespread editorial praise. Exoneration, however, did not guarantee Schwarzbard's personal safety. In Paris, as Ukrainian émigrés gathered in spontaneous meetings, they left no doubt that the final judgment on Schwarzbard had yet to be rendered, and that it was they who would execute it. At the suggestion of the police, therefore, Schwarzbard went into seclusion for several days. Never again did he return to his watchmaker's shop. Rather, in March 1928, he and his family departed France altogether. His first choice of refuge was Palestine, but British colonial authorities denied him a visa. Eventually Schwarzbard settled in Chicago. Yet here too he did not resume his vocation, and instead eked out a precarious livelihood contributing articles to the Yiddish press and addressing Jewish audiences. Ten years later, while on a lecture tour in South Africa in the spring of 1938, Schwarzbard died suddenly of a heart attack, at the age of fifty. The Cape Town Jewish community gave him a hero's funeral.

Sholem Schwarzbard's acquittal offered the Jewish people only meager post-factum satisfaction. The trial had revisited the most traumatic event in modern Jewish history. The death by exposure and hunger of 60,000 Russian Jews in the forced exodus of 1915 was superseded by the Ukrainian massacres of 1918–20, a slaughter that annihilated possibly 150,000 additional Jewish lives and orphaned at least twice that many children. Those Jews who resided in free Western democracies needed little reminder of their helplessness to protect their kinsmen in the East. Russia had been a member of the wartime Entente, yet none of the Allied governments had dared intercede with the tsarist regime on the Jewish issue. In the Ukraine, despite occasional circumspect assurances of goodwill to the Jews, Simon Petliura manifestly had been indifferent to the fate of this despised and exposed minority race. And since the 1921 Treaty of Riga, the circumstances of the surviving Jewish population in the Ukraine, as in the Soviet federation at large, would be determined by a hair-shirt Bolshevik cabal that sustained no meaningful line of communication with the West.

As early as 1918, for that matter, it was the consensus of Western Jewish leaders that all diplomatic efforts in behalf of East European Jewry should logically be focused on the Paris Peace Conference. Here, the assembled Allied prime ministers and foreign ministers would determine not only the future of the defeated Central Powers but also the fate of a host of successor states—the Baltic republics, Czechoslovakia, Poland, Yugoslavia, even "successor" Rumania. Beyond the inaccessible, Bolshevik-ruled Eurasian landmass, these were the nations, old and new, that encompassed the largest reservoir of European Jewry. All of them presumably would be bound by the constraints and guidelines imposed by Allied statesmen at the Peace Conference. It was in Paris, therefore, birthplace of the Declaration of the Rights of Man, that Jewish spokesmen from the Western democracies anticipated a unique and historic diplomatic opportunity. Here, at long last, they would safeguard their tormented people's future on the European Continent.

II

A MINORITY "BILL OF RIGHTS"

Jozef Pilsudski's Empire

The outbreak of war in 1914 found the Polish people, numbering approximately twenty million, divided among three great empires, and accordingly fractured in their political loyalties. The Poles of Habsburg Galicia and German-ruled Posen and Pomerania vaguely favored a victory of the Central Powers. With that triumph, the quasi-autonomous status they enjoyed under Austrian rule conceivably might be extended to the far greater number of their kinsmen living in tsarist Russia. By contrast, most of the Poles living in the Russian-dominated regions were intrigued by a promise issued by Grand Duke Nikolai, supreme commander of the tsarist armies, a commitment to a reunited Poland "free in religion, in language, and in self-government . . . under the scepter of the Tsar." Thus, in Warsaw, Roman Dmowski, an influential nationalist spokesman for the "Russian camp," assured his fellow Poles that allegiance to Russia's Entente partners, France and Britain, was their best guarantee of postwar freedom.

As it happened, neither a pro-German nor a pro-Russian orientation appealed to Jozef Pilsudski, and it was Pilsudski who emerged as the single most charismatic and influential champion of Polish nationalism. Born in 1867 in the Lithuanian province of the former Kingdom of Poland, and himself the scion of an aristocratic Lithuanian family, Pilsudski as a teenager had studied medicine at the Russian-language University of Kharkov. There, caught up in student revolutionary activity, the young man was arrested and condemned to five years of Siberian exile. It was in Siberia, the "university for revolutionaries," that Pilsudski became an ardent convert to the Socialist branch of the Polish freedom movement. Upon his—probationary—release from captivity two years later, after settling in Lodz, he rose swiftly in the ranks of the Polish Socialist Democratic party. Then, in 1901, serving as editor of the party newspaper, Pilsudski was arrested again and convicted for sedition. This time, by disbursing bribes among his guards, he managed to escape over the border, to Habsburg Galicia. And it was consequently in this Polish-inhabited province that Pilsudski, with Austrian government approval, set about organizing a "Polish Legion," a reserve force to be mobilized in the event of war with Russia.

Accordingly, when hostilities began in late July and early August of 1914, Pilsudski wasted no time in leading his modest, four-thousand-man detachment across the Russian frontier, and advancing some one hundred miles inland. Yet, at the same time, he pressed Berlin and Vienna for their commitment to a fully independent Poland. The Central Powers were unresponsive. They had a rather less grandiose scenario in mind. It was the "liberation" exclusively of Russian Poland. In July 1917, therefore, unwilling to be put off any longer, the embittered Pilsudski resigned his command. The Germans in turn placed him under immediate "house confinement" in Prussia's Magdeburg Fortress. There Pilsudski remained until the end of the war. There, too, in March 1918, he learned that Germany and Austria under the Treaty of Brest-Litovsk had amputated a major slice of Poland from Bolshevik Russia, and transformed the region into an occupied satellite. For the Poles, this shattering manifestation of Central-Power imperialism resolved their competitive political loyalties. Henceforth, their nationalist leadership, Pilsudski and Dmowski alike, placed their hopes exclusively in the Western democracies. Soon afterward, Dmowski surfaced in Paris as the spokesman for a "Polish National Committee," and was given instant recognition by the Allied governments.

On November 8, 1918, only three days before Germany's surrender, Jozef Pilsudski was released from his Magdeburg internment. Hastening back to Warsaw, he took it upon himself to proclaim the reunion of all Poland's divided sectors—Russian, Austrian, German—as an independent Republic of Poland. Whereupon all Polish factions, nationalists and Socialists alike, transferred their powers to Pilsudski, as the republic's "chief of state." To present the nation's best face to the world, moreover, both parties then designated the renowned pianist Ignacy Paderewski as prime minister. The constellation of leadership—Pilsudski, Dmowski, Paderewski—evoked immediate resonance in the West. Yet it was Pilsudski who remained the uncontested star of that constellation. The man radiated charisma and dynamism. Even non-Poles fell under his spell. After visiting him in May 1919, the American jurist Arthur Goodhart described the fifty-two-year-old chief of state as "an extremely tall man, powerfully built and looking every inch an athlete. His shaggy eyebrows, aquiline nose and long black moustache are typical of the daring soldier of fortune he has actually been."

Pilsudski's aura reflected his nation's. No liberated people ever entered the postwar years with a deeper reservoir of Allied goodwill. The partitions inflicted on their country in the eighteenth century, the gallantry of their successive revolts in the nineteenth century, their heroism in the recent war, all evoked their belated reward. In his January 1918 State of the Union address to the United States Congress, President Woodrow Wilson unequivocally committed the Allies to a restored and self-governing Poland. Subsequently, the immediate post-Armistice period became a moment of exhilaration and limitless hopes for this emancipated nation.

It was significant, however, that Wilson made no mention of Poland's future borders. These remained indeterminate. At the Peace Conference, France's Foreign Minister Stephen Pichon won Allied support for a Polish western frontier that would include former Prussian Posen and Silesia, as well as a substantial measure of Austria's former Galician possessions. But it was the issue of the eastern frontier that proved more difficult. The Allies were prepared to award West Galicia to the Poles; but East Galicia, substantially Ukrainian in population, was claimed not only by Pilsudski's Poland but by Petliura's Ukraine and Lenin's Russia (p. 13). With the Russians not present at the Peace Conference, the Allied leaders could do little more than tinker with a rough ethnographic division of the disputed territory. Ignoring Ukrainian claims altogether, they segmented East Galicia between Poland and Russia along the Bug River. This was the so-called "Curzon Line," named for the British diplomat George Curzon, who chaired the commission that produced the formula.

It was not Pilsudski's idea of a settlement. Early in 1920, in tandem with Petliura's Ukrainian army (p. 13), the Polish chief of state launched a major offensive that drove some one hundred miles beyond the Curzon Line. Within a month, the combined Polish and Ukrainian forces occupied the historic Ukrainian capital of Kiev. Then, six weeks later, the military balance in the Ukraine shifted yet again, as a powerful Soviet army suddenly cracked the Polish-Ukrainian lines and drove westward toward Warsaw. Finally, in August, with the help of General Maxime Weygand's French military mission, Pilsudski launched his troops on a "counter" counterattack of their own (p. 13). It was successful. The overextended Red Army fell back in disarray, and the Poles pushed forward into the Ukraine.

This was the state of mutual Polish and Russian exhaustion that produced the Treaty of Riga in April 1921. The new demarcation line, extending irregularly between thirty and forty miles beyond the Curzon Line, split the Ukraine essentially between Poland and Soviet Russia. If the Poles did not achieve the totality of their irredentist ambitions, Pilsudski's two-year struggle for a "Greater Poland" nevertheless won considerable success. But the costs were heavy. Much of the World War itself, after all, had raged back and forth over Polish soil. Following the Armistice of November 1918, the ensuing two years of ongoing conflict along Poland's eastern frontiers had simply compounded the ruination suffered by Poles and Ukrainians alike. And still another people experienced the full impact of Ukrainian, Polish, and Russian nationalism.

The Price of Vulnerability

It was the Ukrainian upheaval of the mid-seventeenth century, and the Polish government's political dysfunctionalism in the eighteenth century, that critically undermined the Jews' physical security and economic viability in Eastern Europe (p. 5). So, even more decisively, did the partitions of Poland among the three great central-eastern monarchies in the late 1700s. Claiming the lion's share of the defunct Polish Commonwealth—and of its extensive majority and minority populations alike—tsarist Russia subsequently imposed a harsh grillwork of restrictions on the territory's nearly one million Jews. Feared and despised by the Russians as a mercantile and infidel people, the Jews henceforth were confined by tsarist imperial rescript to a "Pale of Settlement," a vast geographical ghetto comprising essentially the areas of their former Polish-Ukrainian habitation.

It was under tsarist rule, too, that this Jewish population continued to grow exponentially, reaching perhaps three million by the mid-nineteenth century, and well over five million by the time of the 1897 Russian census. Ironically, the demographic upsurge proceeded in tandem with economic atrophy. By the early twentieth century, marginalized still further by the Russian and Austrian industrial revolutions, the Jews no longer could fulfill their historic role as artisans and small traders—either in the tsarist Pale of Settlement or in Habsburg Galicia. Their very economic redundancy, in turn, further inflamed Polish and Ukrainian judeophobia. In a classic profile of displaced nationalism, these two subject nations preferred to direct their political frustrations against the most vulnerable and despised of their own minorities.

The chauvinist fury reached its apogee in the era of the Great War and the early postwar years. From 1917 on, we recall, it was Ukrainian irredentism that took the grimmest toll on Jews. But the Poles, too, in their burgeoning imperialism, nurtured a comparable malice against this seemingly indigestible Jewish presence. As early as 1912, Polish antisemitism was exploited during the election campaign for the imperial Russian Duma. When the Jews of Warsaw expressed an interest in the candidacy of Jan Kucharzewski, a Polish moderate and an opponent of Roman Dmowski's right-wing "Endek"—National Democratic—party, the Endeks encouraged anti-Jewish riots throughout tsarist Poland, in tandem with an economic boycott of Jewish businesses.

Almost as soon as war broke out in 1914, moreover, several of the leading Polish newspapers accused the Jews of spying for the Germans, of sabotaging the tsarist army's route of march. The charges were fake. Nevertheless, in late 1914 the Russian government made its decision to uproot some half-million Jews from the critical border regions (p. 4). Little wonder that the Jewish populations of this intermingled terrain—of Central Poland, Western Ukraine, Lithuania, and Byelorussia—welcomed German military occupation in the years 1916–18. They anticipated more civilized treatment. From its headquarters in Warsaw, General Erich Ludendorff's eastern military administration protected Jewish personal safety and communal autonomy, even appointed four Jews to serve in its— essentially puppet—"Polish Council of State." It was a less than idyllic existence. The Germans restricted, requisitioned, and confiscated among Poles and Jews alike. Even so, the Jews' experience of German rule at least was incrementally more tolerable than their ordeal under the Russian tsar.

The interlude ended with the collapse of the Central Powers. At first, on November 7, 1918, declaring the independence of a "free, democratic" republic of Poland, the Polish National Council offered its assurances of political and civic equality for all its future citizens, regardless of origin, religion, or nationality. The declaration unquestionably expressed the intention of Jozef Pilsudski. In one of his first acts as chief of state, the Polish leader invited a delegation of Jewish political spokesmen to his office and reiterated to them his personal commitment to their people's well-being and communal autonomy.

But Pilsudski, the lifelong Socialist, with his pluralistic vision of Poland as a federation of nationalities, was not necessarily speaking for his people. The average Pole viewed with horror the very notion of living on a basis of political and communal equality with millions of non-Poles—with Ukrainians, Lithuanians, Byelorussians, Germans, or, worst of all, with Jews. In the warning of Roman Dmowski and his Endek party, the Jews, the most alien of minority peoples, infidels in a land of Christians, merchants in a land of farmers, should be apprised instantly and decisively of their second-class status in a newly independent Poland. The Endeks ensured that their views were disseminated widely among Polish soldiers and civilians alike.

In truth, Pilsudski himself bore more than a little personal responsibility for anti-Jewish violence. Early in November 1918, as he launched his war of "reunification" through Eastern Galicia and Lithuania, the chief of state was too preoccupied with military issues to constrain an upsurge of successor-state chauvinism. Thus, even as Polish troops battled Ukrainians for supremacy in the border regions, they found time to launch their own assaults against local Jewish communities. In November 1918 alone, Polish soldiers and armed civilians attacked, pillaged, beat, and occasionally murdered Jews in Lvov, Kielce, Lublin, Lida, and some one hundred other, smaller towns. Local police often collaborated. Informed of these atrocities, Pilsudski sternly condemned them. Yet, as the military campaign raged on throughout East Galicia—"Western Ukraine"—he was unable to exert direct control over his forces. The number of Jews actually slain at the hands of Poles did not exceed four or five hundred, and their ordeal surely could not be equated with the raw genocide committed by Petliura's and Denikin's armies in eastern, "integral" Ukraine. But it was violence committed by the darling of the Western Allies, a country that was flaunted as the glittering symbol of revived and heroic nationhood.

At the Paris Peace Conference, meanwhile, the assembled statesmen unanimously agreed that further desecration of that symbol could not be permitted. In the major cities of the West, Jewish mass meetings already were issuing resolutions of protest and supplication to the Allied governments. The Allies in turn raised the issue of Jewish mistreatment with Poland's Prime Minister Paderewski. Paderewski took the warnings seriously. At his urgent intercession, the worst of the anti-Jewish violence appeared to ebb by February 1920. But in the late spring of the same year, the Red Army launched its mighty counteroffensive in the Ukraine, eventually pushing deep into integral Poland, to the very gates of Warsaw. During their headlong retreat, Polish troops in their frustration and rage inflicted a more extensive series of assaults on the Jewish populations of Minsk-Mazowiecki, Siedlice, and other, smaller towns. Kangaroo court-martials ordered the execution of alleged Jewish "spies." In Plock, a local rabbi was shot for "directing Bolshevik fire from his balcony." Survivors recalled that the worst of the excesses were committed by General Jozef Haller's "Blue Army," a fifty-thousand-man force made up of expatriate American Poles. Returning to their former homeland, these transplanted inhabitants of Chicago, Pittsburgh, Cleveland, Buffalo, and other American industrial cities evidently were determined to be "more Catholic than the Pope." It was the "Blue Army" that doubled the number of casualties suffered by Jews throughout the earlier year and a half.

At the same time, other Americans were taking the lead in marshaling a response to the renewed wave of violence. These were the Jews of the United States.

An American Patron

It did not escape Jewish, Ukrainian, Byelorussian, Lithuanian, and other victims of Pilsudski's military campaign that the Poles were seeking to reincarnate their empire under the aegis of Wilsonian "self-determination." The American president, after all, was the first Western statesman to extend recognition to Poland's provisional government, in December 1918. In that same month, Wilson authorized the appointment of Hugh Gibson, the American consul in Warsaw, as minister to the new Polish Republic. At Wilson's behest, too, the Allied leaders granted the Poles "Associate" status at the Peace Conference—a gesture extended to no other successor nation. It was specifically this American influence and prestige that the Jews were intent on mobilizing in behalf of their traumatized kinsmen in Eastern Europe.

Although numbering less than four million on the eve of the war, the Jews of the United States even then were approaching the threshold of economic security and of a certain modest political influence. In 1914–15, they wasted no time in springing to the relief of hundreds of thousands of East European Jews caught in the zone of conflict between Russia and the Central Powers. Within months, they succeeded in establishing the American Jewish Joint Distribution Committee—known ever after simply as the "Joint." No philanthropic instrument, not even the Red Cross, proved more effective than the Joint in raising funds and dispensing supplies to victims of these eastern war zones. When the war ended, the relief effort for East European Jews steadily broadened, and all the more during the military campaigns in the Ukraine. By 1920, the Joint maintained a network of some five hundred soup kitchens and clinics throughout integral Poland and the Ukrainian battle areas.

By the same token, the Joint's personnel were the first to witness and assess the magnitude of Jewish vulnerability and suffering in the East. Arriving often within hours of pogroms committed by Polish military forces, they shared their information immediately with Jewish leaders in the United States. In turn, the most influential component of that leadership was the American Jewish Committee, a group of affluent and acculturated Jewish "veterans" whose antecedents lay principally in German-speaking Central Europe. On November 16, 1918, Louis Marshall, the Committee's president, dispatched an urgent letter to Woodrow Wilson, entreating him to warn Poland's government that its "aspirations for a new Poland cannot receive sympathetic consideration" unless it behaved with the "spirit of justice and righteousness." Wilson's response was cautious. He preferred to await the Peace Conference, he explained to Marshall, when "I shall deem it a privilege to exercise such influence as I can."

Yet, even before the Peace Conference began, the State Department was making its own discreet inquiries about anti-Jewish violence in Poland. Early in December 1918, William G. Sharp, United States ambassador to France, discussed the Jewish question with Roman Dmowski, the Endek leader who functioned as chairman of the Polish National Committee in

Paris. Dmowski in turn insisted that reports of pogroms were "greatly exaggerated," and mere "organized propaganda" by Jews in Poland and Russia. Some of these Jews, he added darkly, were secret agents of Bolshevik Russia. In reporting Dmowski's observations, Sharp offered no comment or rebuttal.

The reaction was not uncharacteristic of American officials in Europe. In a long cable to Washington in May 1919, Minister Hugh Gibson in Warsaw explained that the Jews, as merchants, "had a practical monopoly of all trade, particularly in foodstuffs," and that this state of affairs created much hardship among the Poles. "If a Jew is injured," observed Gibson, "it is called a pogrom. If a Christian is mobbed, it is called a food riot," and Washington therefore should react skeptically to press accounts about "alleged massacres" in Poland. Gibson's and Sharp's bland responses infuriated American Jewry. On May 21, 1919, they gathered by the thousands at Madison Square Garden to ventilate their shock and outrage. The banking patriarch Jacob Schiff dispatched a lengthy cable to President Wilson (then in Paris) demanding firm American pressure on the Poles. The United States Senate felt impelled to issue a resolution against the pogroms.

A week earlier, on May 16, 1919, Louis Marshall and his colleague Cyrus Adler, in Paris to defend Jewish interests at the Peace Conference, had secured an interview with the president. After discussing the question of treaty guarantees for Jews in Poland and other East European states (pp. 35–36), the two Jewish emissaries also pressed Wilson for an official mission of inquiry into anti-Jewish atrocities and economic discrimination. The president complied immediately. That same afternoon, he directed Secretary of State Robert Lansing to compile a list of prospective members for the investigative group. Within the week, Lansing came up with a panel of names. Indeed, his recommendation for the chairmanship was an authentic brain wave. It was Henry Morgenthau.

A real-estate millionaire of German-Jewish background, a major Democratic party financial contributor, and a former United States ambassador to Turkey, Morgenthau seemingly possessed ideal credentials for reassuring American Jews and impressing Polish officialdom. He would be bracketed by two "objective" professionals, Brigadier General Edgar Jadwin, an army engineer with much reconstruction experience in Eastern Europe; and Homer B. Johnson, a California attorney with an extensive record of public service. The mission's proposed legal adviser would be Arthur L. Goodhart, a distinguished scholar of jurisprudence, a future Master of University College, Oxford, and the second Jew in the entourage. The four men dutifully accepted their nominations. Morgenthau in fact was eager to regain the limelight he had enjoyed as ambassador to Constantinople.

On July 13, 1919, the Americans arrived in Warsaw, where they were greeted by Minister Gibson and ushered to their headquarters at the luxurious Raczynski Palace Hotel (partly owned by the Paderewski family). The American presence in Poland would continue for two months. From the outset, Morgenthau and his colleagues set about diligently querying Polish and Jewish representatives. Each side vied to make its case. Thus, Pilsudski, Paderewski, and numerous other eminences and aristocrats wined and dined the Americans, warmly proclaiming their nation's goodwill toward the Jews. If there were "occasional petty excesses" (Pilsudski's phrase), these often could be attributed to the Jews' propensity for Bolshevism or economic exploitation. But the sixty-one-year-old Morgenthau was hardly a novice in diplomatic negotiations. Although rather wizened and deceptively frail in appearance, the ex-ambassador vigorously, even aggressively dunned his interlocutors for evidence. In turn, reports of Morgenthau's "stubbornness," his "obdurateness," much offended Poland's right-wing press, which soon branded him as "Wilson's Jewish servant."

Less than a week after their arrival, Morgenthau and his colleagues embarked upon a tour of the areas that had undergone the heaviest pogroms. Everywhere the awaiting Jewish inhabitants greeted their visitors with near-messianic expectations, with flowers, flags, and cheering, with Zionist boy-scout troops leading processions of welcome. For his part, Morgenthau listened sympathetically as Jewish communal spokesmen described the glowering hatred, the ongoing economic boycott, and the threat of violence still looming over them. Visiting the cities of Brest-Litovsk and Minsk-Mazowiecki, the Americans witnessed personally the devastation that lately had been inflicted on Jewish homes and shops. In Bialystok, it did not escape the team that Jews were fearful of speaking to them, as blue-uniformed officers of Haller's Army lurked ominously outside synagogues and Jewish communal offices. In Vilna, the Americans were shown scores of freshly dug graves, heard accounts of wholesale murder, of mass looting that palpably had left thousands of Jews on the edge of destitution.

In the following weeks, nevertheless, Morgenthau's judgment could not remain untinctured by his personal ideology. In the recollection of Boris Bogen, the "Joint's" field director in Poland, and an unofficial adviser to the mission, Morgenthau on one day would promise to intercede vigorously with the Warsaw government in behalf of afflicted Jews; then, on the next day, he would swallow whole the official Polish line that the Jews needed instruction in good citizenship. It was not credulity alone that produced the chairman's ambivalence. Although an identified Jew, Morgenthau was profoundly seized of his people's obligation to adapt to the mores

of their respective host nations. He rejected the proposition that Jews anywhere should insist upon a separate language, a separate communal structure or school system. Ultimately, these were the acculturationist
certitudes that informed the "Morgenthau Report," when it was officially
submitted to President Wilson in October 1919, and published as United
States Senate Document No. 176, in January 1920.

Not incorrectly, the report attributed recent anti-Jewish outbursts to
"the chauvinist reaction created by [Poland's] sudden acquisition of a long-
coveted freedom." It went on then to provide a clinical account of the eight
most recent and explosive anti-Jewish episodes. Yet the report was austere, even antiseptic, in apportioning responsibility for the "excesses," and
made only cursory reference to the far-reaching Polish economic boycott
inflicted on Jews and other minorities. It openly characterized ethnic separatism as a barrier to Polish national liberation. Polish Jewry, the report
concluded, would do well to emulate Jews in the United States, who lived
in peace and security with their fellow Americans not least because they
refrained from ethnic overassertiveness. Maurice Samuel, an American
army private who served the mission as its Yiddish-language translator,
years later described Morgenthau's pieties as "driveling optimism" and "a
kind of senile gravity."

In the end, however, the mission did more good than harm. It palpably
enhanced Jewish morale in Poland. In whichever community the Americans visited, Jews lifted their heads again and made a holiday of their presence. It was a presence that registered on the Poles, as well. In Boris
Bogen's recollection, the Morgenthau visit functioned as a warning from
the United States: " 'An end to these outrages, if you desire the good opinion of America.' " The physical abuse of Jews in fact soon diminished
(although economic and political discrimination continued in full force).
Most decisively of all, however, the mission fortified American Jewry's
emerging role as preeminent defender of European Jewish minority rights.

Louis Marshall and the Rise of American-Jewish Diplomacy

During the war, thousands of Jewish immigrant families in the United
States shared in mass meetings and fund-raising campaigns on behalf of
their kinsmen in Poland and the Ukraine. Nevertheless, it was the more
affluent and acculturated board members of the American Jewish Committee who maintained their traditional leadership as patrons and protectors
of East European Jewry. The Committee's president, Louis Marshall, was
typical of these patricians. He was the son of German-Jewish immigrants.
Born in Syracuse in 1856, attending and completing Columbia Law School
in an unprecedented single year, Marshall soon achieved a reputation as a

peerless appellate lawyer. Ultimately he would argue more cases before the United States Supreme Court than any private attorney of his time. As a partner in the distinguished New York firm of Guggenheimer and Untermeyer (and marrying an Untermeyer niece), Marshall early on became a member of the German-Jewish upper crust that included Schiffs, Strausses, Warburgs, Seligmans, and other doyens. Intellectually, he was their star. Rather owl-like in appearance, stocky, balding, and bespectacled, Marshall was a giant the moment he became a negotiator. His clarity of analysis and powers of gentle persuasion established him almost instantly as first among equals on the board of the American Jewish Committee.

In his defense of Jewish interests, Marshall, like the other patriarchs, normally favored discreet, behind-the-scenes contacts with government officials. Yet he was capable of adjusting his method to the need. In 1911–12, as tsarist Russia maintained a ban on visits by American Jews, Marshall did not hesitate to go public, mobilizing press and politicians alike to block renewal of the Russian-American Commercial Treaty. In 1915, when Russia's Grand Duke Nikolai ordered the mass evacuation of hundreds of thousands of border Jews, Marshall helped organize public meetings, even congressional resolutions of protest against the tsarist government. And in the last months of the war, shifting his attention to the victims of Ukrainian and Polish atrocities, Marshall led the American Jewish Committee in formulating a strategy for the Peace Conference.

In turn, the Polish National Committee sensed the usefulness of heading off a Jewish diplomatic campaign. Visiting New York in September 1918, Ignacy Paderewski, soon to become his nation's prime minister, requested and secured an interview with Louis Marshall. The pianist-diplomat listened respectfully as Marshall ventilated his concerns about Polish Jewry. Sobered, but intent on winning American Jewish goodwill, Paderewski arranged a meeting the following month between Marshall and Roman Dmowski, the militant Endek leader and chairman of the Polish National Committee, who had arrived in the United States several weeks earlier for discussions with President Wilson and Polish-American leaders.

The conference took place at Dmowski's suite at New York's Plaza Hotel. It began equably enough, but when Marshall raised the issue of the recent pogroms and the Endek party's appeal for an anti-Jewish boycott, the conversation became tense. Dmowski responded that the Jews' predilection for commerce inevitably produced "a struggle for existence" with the Poles, an agrarian people. The nation's sheer poverty was an even more fundamental source of friction, he insisted. Would it not behoove the Jews of the United States and of other Western nations, Dmowski asked then, "in the interest of their own brethren . . . to furnish capital with which to develop commerce and industry in Poland . . . [which would help] create a feeling of friendship and unity"? There was a long moment's silence. Appalled at Dmowski's thinly veiled effort at extortion, Marshall was hard put to maintain his composure. He replied finally that there would be time enough later to discuss American Jewish investment; but the Polish government would first have to guarantee its minorities equal treatment.

To that end, and despite the unpromising initial encounter, Marshall arranged a dinner meeting for Dmowski with the board of the American Jewish Committee. But this second confrontation went no better than the first. Pressed on the anti-Jewish boycott, Dmowski refused to give assurances that economic discrimination would end unless the Jews "loyally and faithfully served Poland . . . [in its] struggle for unification and independence. . . ." The exchange then became heated, and finally collapsed in recriminations. Later Dmowski wrote: "When my sojourn in the United States came to an end, I knew . . . that during the Peace Conference we would have in the Jews the most vehement enemies of our cause." Dmowski was not wrong, if the "cause" was to foster an unremittingly nationalist, unicultural Poland. On November 7, 1918, Louis Marshall dispatched the first in a long series of memoranda to Woodrow Wilson. Calling the president's attention to Polish pogroms and boycotts, he urged that Poland not only adhere to specific frontier limitations, but also accept a minority "Bill of Rights" as the sine qua non for its acceptance into the family of nations.

In this correspondence, Marshall laid his finger on one of the most intractable problems to be confronted at the forthcoming Peace Conference. As the Allied diplomats wrestled with the task of establishing a chain of successor nations out of the debris of the former Russian, Austrian, German, and Turkish empires, they would soon grasp that frontier lines for the emergent new states could not effectively be "gerrymandered" to preclude enclaves of minorities. Rather, these ethnic communities, numbering some thirty million souls, ultimately would represent nearly one-fourth of the populations of Central-Eastern Europe altogether. It was an archipelago of races and nations that demanded the right not only of civil and political freedom but of national "self-determination," at the very least of cultural "self-determination." Could Wilson, Lloyd George, and Clemenceau ignore their clamor? And if not, by what juridical device could the Allied statesmen give satisfaction to these insecure and often contentious subcommunities? No European diplomat needed a reminder that earlier peace conferences—at Vienna in 1815, The Hague in 1831, Paris in 1856, Berlin in 1878—had failed to define the rights of minorities with legal exactitude, or to provide mechanisms for enforcing their security. And in none was the unique vulnerability of the Jews addressed more than superficially. By the autumn of 1918, Louis Marshall was intent on resolving these lacunae.

In the process, Marshall was obliged to reacquaint himself with some of the unique complexities of East European Jewish history. Well into the nineteenth century, the Jews of the Austrian and Russian empires had functioned traditionally as separate "corporations." Notwithstanding the hardships imposed by ghettoization, that corporate status invested them at least with extensive control over their own communal affairs. But in later years, political changes throughout Central-Eastern Europe presented the Jews with a new dilemma. Should they involve themselves in the various nationalist struggles—Polish, Ukrainian, Czech, Slovak, Serb—against Habsburg or tsarist rule, or should they link their political hopes to the suspect and endlessly delayed perfectibility of the imperial regimes? In fact, the largest numbers of Russian Jews, and many Habsburg Galician Jews, preferred neither of these two alternatives. Rather, they would opt for a third way. This was to fuse their struggle for civil rights with a parallel campaign for Jewish national-autonomist rights. Those rights obviously could not be territorial, given the Jews' geographic diffusion and fragile demography. They could, however, take essentially a linguistic, cultural, and communal form.

The notion of cultural-communal nationalism hardly originated among the Jews. In his *Studies in Religious History (Études d'histoire religieuse)* and *Essays on Morality and Criticism (Essais de morale et de critique)*, both published in the 1860s, the French historian-philosopher Ernest Renan first mooted the proposition that "spiritual-cultural" nationalism transcended "mere" territorialism. In 1902, the Austrian Socialist Karl Renner (p. 176) published a volume, *The Battle of Austria's Nationalities Within the State (Der Kampf der Österreichischen Nationen um den Staat)*, proposing that the Empire might sustain its viability as a federation of autonomous nationalities rather than accept disintegration into separate territorial entities. Renan's and Renner's cultural-nationalist formula was an imaginative one, and no people seized upon it with greater alacrity than did the Jews. Thus, over the turn of the century, the Russian-Jewish historian Simon Dubnow organized a "Folkspartei" to advance the cause of national-cultural autonomy for the Jews in Russia.

Although Dubnow's program was doomed by the counterrevolution that followed Russia's Octobrist uprising of 1905, most of the tsarist empire's Jewish political parties, including the Socialist Bund, eventually incorporated autonomist planks into their platforms. Even the Zionists agreed that a vibrant Jewish national-communal life should not await a possibly indeterminate redemption of the Land of Israel. As late as 1917, in the aftermath of the Balfour Declaration, with its endorsement of a Jewish

National Home in Palestine, Zionist delegates from throughout Europe gathered in neutral Denmark to issue a "Copenhagen Manifesto," reaffirming the importance of "national autonomy, cultural, social and political," for the Jewish populations of Central-Eastern Europe.

In fact, during the larger part of the war, the principal focus of this nationalist program no longer was to be found among the beleaguered Jews of the Eastern battlefields. It had shifted to the free and open United States. Here the immigrant kinsmen of Russian, Polish, Lithuanian, Rumanian, and other East European Jews could raise funds and engage in political agitation in behalf of their extended families overseas. And in the United States, too, it was specifically this immigrant confederation that was rapidly losing patience with the self-anointed spokesmanship of America's German-Jewish "establishment." Louis Marshall, Jacob Schiff, Cyrus Adler, and their fellow mandarins of the American Jewish Committee were known to regard the Jews exclusively as a religious community, whose political and even cultural loyalties belonged unreservedly to the nation-states of their residence. Yet for East European immigrant Jews, the formula was unacceptable—and altogether unthinkable for their captive relatives in the Old World. To make their case, the immigrants began pressing now for a more representative forum of their own, one that would respond to the existential requirements of postwar European Jewry. Their demand was for a democratically elected American Jewish "Congress."

Initially, the "veterans" caviled at the notion. But after protracted and often exhausting negotiations, the two "communities" finally reached agreement, and elections for an American Jewish Congress eventually took place in June 1917. Some 300,000 Jews participated, most of their votes going to the various Zionist and other cultural-autonomist factions. The Congress itself was not convened until the end of the war. But in December 1918 the delegates gathered in Philadelphia's Lee-Lu Temple, an opera house. The neighborhood, largely immigrant Jewish, was festooned with blue-and-white Zionist banners reflecting the impact of Britain's recently issued Balfour Declaration. The pro-Zionist formula that was hammered out by the Congress similarly reflected the thrilling vision of revived Jewish nationhood, and so did a series of resolutions favoring Jewish communal and cultural autonomy in Eastern Europe.

The Committee patriarchs accepted the new formula with good grace. In an interview with an Anglo-Jewish newspaper on December 28, Louis Marshall acknowledged

> that we are dealing with conditions unique to Eastern Europe, not those that prevail in the United States, in Britain, France, and Italy, whose populations are homogeneous and where the word "national"

applies to a political unit, not to an ethnic unit. . . . It is not for us in the United States to judge the wisdom of this conception.

A nine-man delegation then was selected for the Congress mission to Paris. Its chairman would be Julian Mack, a Harvard-educated federal judge of German-Jewish ancestry. Marshall would attend as a vice president—but in practical fact as the group's senior and most prestigious eminence. The two men would work together closely at the Peace Conference.

The Jewish "Lobby" at Paris

In early 1919, as the Allied statesmen gathered in the French capital, issues of national frontiers were given priority. Little attention at first was devoted to the fate of "residual" minorities. It was the Jews who would raise this issue, and with vigor and imagination. Indeed, they raised it even before the American Jewish Congress delegation embarked for Paris. On March 2, 1919, Marshall and Mack led a group of colleagues to the White House to present their Jewish "Bill of Rights" proposal to Woodrow Wilson. The president had briefly returned to Washington from his initial sojourn in Paris. When Marshall and his associates expressed the hope that a "Bill of Rights" on behalf of minorities could be incorporated into the very constitutions of the East European successor states, Wilson's response was affirmative, if somewhat vague. "Every one of the groups and peoples that is intolerant of the Jews is an applicant to us for something," he assured his visitors. ". . . In every one of the arrangements to be entered into with these new countries . . . I mean to insist that the thing we are discussing shall be written into the new covenant that is to be made with every one of them. . . . There will be hell to pay if they are not."

The following week, Marshall and his colleagues themselves departed for the Peace Conference. Once in Paris, their first priority was to formulate a common stance with the various European Jewish delegations. This was no easy task. While agreeing to share in a "Comité des delegations juives," the veteran spokesmen for French Jewry and Anglo-Jewry, like Marshall and his fellow patriarchs in the United States, had long functioned as intercessors and spokesmen on behalf of oppressed Jews in other lands. Their objectives, too, were distinctively "acculturationist." The venerable Alliance Israélite Universelle, a group of highly assimilated French Jewish "veterans," traditionally had made it their priority to "Gallicize" no less than to protect the large communities of North African and Middle Eastern Jews who lay within the French imperial sphere of influence. In that effort, the Alliance worked closely with the French foreign ministry.

Rejecting the very notion of Jewish "national" rights—either in Palestine or in Poland—the Alliance board and its executive-secretary, Jacques Bigart, fully endorsed the injunction of Eugène Sée, a senior foreign ministry official, that "[t]he business of the [Peace] Conference is to create a sovereign state for Poland, not for the Jews."

As for Britain's Jewish delegation at Paris, its membership included representatives of the two-century-old Board of Deputies of British Jewry and the more recent, but even more acculturated Anglo-Jewish Association. The two groups worked in tandem as the informally titled "Conjoint Committee." Under the direction of its much respected secretary-general, Lucien Wolf (pp. 36–37), the Conjoint was prepared to go incrementally further than its French counterpart in support of Jewish civil and political rights in Eastern Europe, even of cultural and educational autonomy. Like the Alliance, however, it flatly rejected the notion of Jewish "national" rights.

Notwithstanding the differences of nuance and emphasis between its own members, the American Jewish Congress delegation soon emerged as primus inter pares among the various Jewish lobbying organizations. Marshall himself was elected chairman of the pivotal human rights sub-committee within the "Comité des délégations juives." The assignment reflected not only the prestige of the United States, but specifically of the Jews of the United States. Louis Marshall, Julian Mack, and several others of their colleagues had developed numerous contacts with Woodrow Wilson. Henry Morgenthau and Oscar Straus were members of the president's entourage in Paris. Indeed, the adroit and gracious Marshall on his own probably would have emerged as the liaison of choice between the Jewish and Allied delegations. He had achieved his first and immediate rapport with the "Inquiry," a collection of scholar-advisers attached to the United States delegation in Paris, and specifically with David Hunter Miller, the "Inquiry's" expert on international law, and with the latter's deputy, Manley O. Hudson. Both men were much impressed by Marshall's invocation of Wilsonian "self-determination," and the uniquely American concept of a Bill of Rights. Not least of all, as Marshall invoked the formula of both civil rights and communal autonomy, he was shrewd enough to press his moral claim on behalf of all the residual minorities of Eastern Europe, not only of the Jews.

It was the confluence of these approaches that induced Miller to recommend to Secretary of State Lansing the formation of a committee to deal exclusively with the issue of minority peoples. The secretary liked the idea, and so did the president's political adviser, Colonel Edward House, who vetted it to Wilson. Accordingly, on May 16, 1919, the president received Marshall and Mack at his Paris apartment at Place des États Unis. It was a time when anti-Jewish pogroms in Eastern Europe were much in public consciousness, and it was at this meeting that Wilson agreed to dispatch an investigative body—the future Morgenthau Mission—to Poland (p. 27).

Marshall and his colleagues, however, were asking for much more than an investigation. They wanted presidential approval for the totality of the American Jewish Congress program, even assurance that Jews and other minorities would enjoy a direct right of appeal to Wilson's envisaged League of Nations. On both these issues, the president's response was typically cordial, but this time distinctly equivocal. He lent his fullest support to the concept of civil and religious rights for minorities. Yet, like Clemenceau and Lloyd George, the president wished no limitations placed on the new Poland's sovereignty and viability; and here he gently observed that a Jewish right of direct appeal to the League of Nations could be inimical to that objective (p. 41).

Remarkably, Marshall did not appear discountenanced by Wilson's qualified response. "No lover of mankind will ever forget [the president's] notable contribution to the cause of liberty and righteousness," he would write later. There was reason for Marshall's forbearance. He already had received more than half a loaf. On April 19, a full two and a half weeks even before receiving the American Jewish Congress delegation at his Paris apartment, the president had reviewed Lansing's and House's proposal—in effect, Marshall's proposal—for a special "Committee on New States and for the Protection of Minorities," and had approved it. Two days later, Clemenceau and Lloyd George similarly acquiesced. It was this committee that would be charged with drafting the "Bill of Rights" that presumably then would be incorporated into formal, binding treaty documents. It also was understood that the guarantees, if not all-encompassing in their autonomy provisions, would be extensive. The coup was a significant one for the Jews, indeed, for all the "residual" minority peoples of Central-Eastern Europe.

The Diplomacy of Compromise

Thus far, the accomplishment had been the work principally of Marshall and his American Jewish colleagues. But in the same spring of 1919, Lucien Wolf of the Anglo-Jewish Conjoint delegation also began to assume a decisive intermediary role. The son of Bohemian-Jewish immigrants, Wolf had been educated in Paris and Brussels, and subsequently became an erudite contributor to numerous British journals of international affairs. Well connected in government circles, elegant of manner and something of a fashion plate, Wolf in 1908 became an ideal choice as the Conjoint's first executive director. Afterward, he ensured that the organization functioned as a kind of shadow Foreign Office, conscientiously imitating Whitehall's methods and procedures. In this manner, he subtly pressed British diplomats to remain sensitive to Jewish circumstances in troubled areas.

Wolf also played a tough game of intramural politics. Tolerating no rivals among the Zionists or other Jewish nationalists, he preferred initially to concentrate on the issue of Jewish civil rights. Nevertheless, by the end of the war, confronting the hard evidence in Eastern Europe both of successor-state and Jewish nationalism, Wolf began tentatively shifting his position in favor of a certain limited Jewish cultural autonomy. The Foreign Office was not pleased. An old-boy network, its professional staff did not much care for Jews, and least of all East European Jews, whose alleged vices presumably were compounded in wartime by pro-Germanism. More fundamentally, J. M. Headlam-Morley, director of Whitehall's East European desk, wanted no limitation on the functional sovereignty of Poland or any other successor state. In any case, the Foreign Office regarded Zionism as the key to its "Jewish" policy, and Chaim Weizmann, the Zionist leader, as its preferred interlocutor.

By the spring of 1919, however, the upsurge of anti-Jewish violence in Poland (let alone the Ukraine), coupled with Woodrow Wilson's growing preference for more extensive minority guarantees, registered on the Foreign Office. The evidence of Polish-Jewish ethnicity also registered on the British diplomat Esmé Howard, then in Poland as a member of an inter-Allied commission. Howard's inquiries persuaded him that, beyond civil rights, the Jews should also be permitted their own Yiddish-language school system. Headlam-Morley did not demur this time. Neither did Sir Robert Cecil, the foreign undersecretary, who assured Wolf that he, Cecil, was "determined to do his best to make the [Minority] Treaties a real living charter of liberties for the Jews." With the support of the Foreign Office, Wolf in turn pressed the other Jewish delegations to accept the compromise autonomy program.

And here at last, Jacques Bigart and France's Alliance delegation grudgingly abandoned their objections to the program's "maximalism." So, too, did Marshall and Mack to the program's "minimalism." For them, ironically, Wolf's and Cecil's pragmatic emphasis on civil and communal autonomy failed to meet the fullest autonomist requirements of East European Jewry. Nevertheless, in addition to basic civil rights, the formula at least confirmed the freedom of each minority to administer its own linguistic, educational, religious, and social institutions. Marshall and Mack would live with the compromise.

In the first week of May 1919, the "New States and Protection of Minorities Committee" began its discussions under the chairmanship of

Philippe Berthelot, director of political affairs at the French foreign ministry. Italy and Japan also were represented. So too, manifestly, was the United States, first by David Hunter Miller, later by Manley Hudson, who in turn would be replaced by Allen Dulles. But the most innovative participant was Britain's Headlam-Morley. Consulting intimately with Wolf, the Englishman then crafted the treaty's basic provisions. Between May 3 and December 9, 1919, the committee held sixty-four meetings, but its key decisions, on Poland, were reached in the first month.

The Polish document in fact consisted of only twelve articles and filled barely two pages. Yet its guarantees were unprecedented in the history of Western diplomacy. The first and most important of these awarded full civil, religious, and political rights to all citizens of the new Poland. The provision appeared foolproof. As they framed it, the committee members were quite aware that the term "citizen" had itself been a Pandora's box in earlier treaties, for unpopular minorities afterward simply had been excluded from citizenship in their native lands. Even after signing the Treaty of Berlin in 1878, for example, with its minority guarantees, Rumania had disfranchised its Jews by the ingenious device of categorizing them as "foreigners who are not subject to another power." To block similar perversions in the future, the Polish minorities treaty laid down far stricter guidelines, requiring simply that naturalization be extended to all persons either born or "habitually" resident in Poland.

Yet it was in its cultural-autonomist provisions that the document charted new terrain. Here for the first time appeared ironclad linguistic rights. The Polish government was barred from imposing restrictions on "the free use by any Polish national of any language in private intercourse, in commerce, in religion . . . in publications of any kind," and "adequate facilities"—that is, interpreters—were to be provided minority members who testified in their own language before the law courts. Of perhaps even greater significance, the document in its Article 9 recognized that linguistic rights interfaced with educational rights. In towns or districts with a "considerable portion" of minorities, the treaty obliged the state to establish primary schools offering non-Polish children instruction "through the medium of their own language."

In ten of its twelve articles, the treaty functioned as a guarantor for all the ethnic and religious minorities living in the enlarged new Polish state—Ukrainians, Lithuanians, Germans, Byelorussians, Russians, as well as Jews. All now were beneficiaries of the Jewish initiative. But the Jews of Poland owed to Marshall and Wolf two key treaty provisions designated for them alone. The special treatment was not gratuitous. Except in the Ukraine, whose fate would lie well beyond reach of the Peace Conference, in no other European state did Jews live in comparable numbers. Thus, the document's Article 10 specified that, wherever Jewish schools were eligible for state funding, committees of local Jews should themselves be authorized to allocate and distribute those funds. Article 11 exempted Jews from "performing any act which constituted a violation of their Sabbath [Saturday]." Neither would the Polish government conduct national elections on the Jewish Sabbath.

The Allies made plain, finally, that they would brook no equivocation on the minorities treaty. In the document's very prologue, the Western statesmen "confirmed their recognition of the Polish State." The Polish government, in turn, "desiring . . . to give a sure guarantee to the inhabitants of the territory over which she has assumed sovereignty . . . [has] agreed as follows: . . . ." The quid pro quo was all but explicit. Even more so was Poland's obligation to incorporate this "Bill of Rights" into its very constitution, and to accept the League of Nations as international guarantor of the treaty (p. 41).

It was well understood that, except for its two specifically "Jewish" provisions, the Polish minorities treaty would serve as a model for similar treaties to be imposed on the other successor states, as well as on the former enemy nations of Central-Eastern Europe. For this reason, on May 31, 1919, there occurred a "Revolt of the Small Powers," the spokesmen for Rumania, Serbia, Greece, and Hungary, who protested the impending "infringement" of their nations' sovereignty. In fact, the Poles themselves organized the revolt. On May 22, Prime Minister Paderewski and his colleagues appeared before the New States and Minorities Committee to vent their indignation. No similar minorities provisions were being inflicted on the "Great Powers of Europe," noted the prime minister acidly, not even on defeated Germany, which after all would retain several million "residual" Poles. As for the treaty's two "Jewish" articles, Paderewski warned that any attempt to grant the Jews "special privileges" would only exacerbate the Jewish problem.

The Polish prime minister encountered a stone wall. Speaking for Britain, Headlam-Morley rebuffed Paderewski with all the fervor of the newly converted, and with a moraine of documentation (provided by Marshall and Wolf) on Polish antisemitic excesses. Meanwhile, Jacques Bigart and the French-Jewish delegates enlisted the support of Baron Edmond de Rothschild in Paris to monitor possible last-minute deviations within the French foreign ministry. There was none. At Louis Marshall's behest, finally, Henry Morgenthau wrote a personal letter to President Wilson. Whether these various efforts were decisive or redundant, Allied statesmen gave short shrift to Polish, Rumanian, and other protests. It was significant that Prime Minister Georges Clemenceau, the most committed Allied champion of a large and viable Poland, dispatched a flinty letter of rebuke to Paderewski on June 20, 1919. After inviting the pianist-statesman to consider that Poland owed its very independence to Allied sacrifices in the war, the French premier observed meaningfully that "[t]he information [at the disposal of the Allies] . . . has led them to the conclusion that . . . special protection is necessary for the Jews in Poland."

Woodrow Wilson was even more plainspoken. On May 27, upon receiving bitter reproaches both from Paderewski and from Rumanian Prime Minister Ioan Bratianu (p. 77), the American president reminded his Allied colleagues that they could not afford to guarantee the territorial integrity of the emergent successor states without first neutralizing potential threats to the peace. One of the gravest of those threats, Wilson noted, was the potential resentment of the minority peoples. Was not such resentment a factor in precipitating the recent Great War? The allusion to the South Slavs and the assassination in Sarajevo required no embellishment.

On June 24, 1919, therefore, only minutes after German and Allied representatives signed the Treaty of Versailles, with its relinquishment of Germany's former Polish territories, Paderewski and Dmowski were ushered into the Hall of Mirrors. There, in cold silence, the two Polish leaders affixed their signatures to the minorities treaty. Except for its two "Jewish clauses," virtually identical documents would be signed in ensuing months by Czechoslovakia (September 10, 1919), Yugoslavia (September 10, 1919), Rumania (December 9, 1919), Greece (August 10, 1920), and Armenia (August 10, 1920). Special minority provisions also would be incorporated into the peace treaties subsequently imposed upon defeated Austria (Saint-Germain), Bulgaria (Neuilly), Hungary (Trianon), and Turkey (Sèvres).

Louis Marshall's Hour of Vindication

Paderewski's resentful warnings to the Allies were almost immediately vindicated. Hardly was the ink dry on the Polish minorities treaty than the instrument was revealed as the most imperfect of diplomatic documents. Even the knotty question of citizenship, which had consumed scores of hours, was left riddled with loopholes. Ostensibly, the treaty was to give full citizenship to all residents on Polish soil. But during the war thousands of Jews, Germans, Ukrainians, and other minority members had fled the Polish battle zones, or themselves had served in one of the three imperial armies. Returning home, these non-Polish elements now pleaded for their 1914, prewar, residency to be accepted as the guideline for citizenship. The Poles refused, using November 11, 1918, as their criterion. In this fashion, many hundreds of thousands of non-Poles who had not yet returned before the Armistice Day cutoff were barred from citizenship.

Neither did these peoples win meaningful "federalist" autonomy, even those among them who had qualified for "valid" citizenship. Rather, they were given the legally innocuous title of "Polish nationals who belong to racial, religious or linguistic minorities." For the Jews, the designation foreclosed the possibility of establishing a National Council. It was a painful setback. So it was for the other minorities, but they at least had the psychological security of powerful "brother" states nearby, to champion their cause in the League of Nations and in other forums. Not the Jews.

Possibly more ominous yet was the ambivalent role to be fulfilled by the League of Nations as the minority treaty's enforcement mechanism. Under the document's guarantee clause, Article 12, the Council of the League was empowered to deal with treaty violations and to "take such action and give such direction" as needed. But Article 12 did not authorize the minority peoples themselves to appeal directly to the League. Only those Great Powers whose representatives actually sat in the Council were entitled to present complaints, or to raise issues, on behalf of distressed minorities. The procedure was dilatory and captious. It depended on the goodwill and initiative of states whose course of action was almost certain to be determined by self-interested Realpolitik. Marshall and Adler had raised the issue with Wilson at their May 16 meeting in Paris. But the president was not sympathetic to "the right of a minority in a given country to appeal [directly] against its government . . . [for] the whole policy would be fraught with disturbances." Possibly unspoken in Wilson's response was concern lest such disruptive claims eventually be adopted by Japanese, even blacks, in the United States.

It was during the same May 16 interview, rather, that Wilson offered his visitors a far older diplomatic alternative. It seemed preferable to him "that the Jews of America and England would keep a close watch over the affairs of their brethren in Eastern Europe, and if there were any infractions of the treaty they would have the right to bring them to the attention of their [own] governments, and through their governments to the League of Nations." The president's genial suggestion, that Western Jewish lobbyists continue to function as guardians and supplicants on behalf of their people in Eastern Europe, was profoundly distressing to Lucien Wolf. It smacked of retrograde nineteenth-century "intercessory" diplomacy, and the Conjoint secretary-general was angered that Marshall apparently was prepared to accept Wilson's formula. Indeed, an acrimonious exchange of letters between the two Jewish diplomats followed, and it ended their collaboration at the Peace Conference. It also led to a continuation of precisely the intermediary role Wolf had feared. In ensuing years he himself would be obliged to resume and even enlarge upon his prewar function as Western Jewry's vigilant spokesman on behalf of the East Europeans (pp. 87–88, 114, 118).

But not everyone shared Wolf's reservations. The Americans remained almost uniformly enthusiastic. In a letter of July 11, 1919, to Boris Bogen, the Joint's field director in Europe, Marshall assured Bogen that the treaties "will enable the Jews as well as all other minorities to live their own lives and to develop their own culture." In his view, the Jews of Poland should be counseled to "forget the past" and take the lead in establishing "cordial" relations with their Gentile fellow citizens. Upon Marshall's return from Europe, moreover, the American Jewish Congress led a broad array of Jewish organizations in tendering him a congratulatory welcome at Carnegie Hall on July 28, 1919. The affair overflowed with tributes and encomia for the renowned advocate's "unprecedented" diplomatic triumph. Taking the rostrum, Marshall disclaimed any credit:

> You, my friends, are celebrating an event which the Almighty in His wisdom willed. . . . It is, however, but natural that we of the House of Israel should unite in joyous thanksgiving. For the first time, the nations of the world have recognized that, in common with all other peoples, we are entitled to equality in law. . . . It has now become an established principle that any violation of the rights of a minority is an offense not only against the individuals but against the law which controls all of the civilized nations of the earth.

And then, in the precise and measured cadences of a veteran statesman, Marshall issued a cautionary note to the Jews of Eastern Europe:

> I am confident that I speak for every true Jew when I say that henceforth the Jews of Poland . . . [and other East European states] will vie with their fellow citizens in an effort to establish but one standard of civilization and to cultivate friendships and brotherhood. Let us forget the nightmare of the past. Let us be swallowed up by the brilliancy and glory of the dawning of a new day.

The audience of three thousand was itself overwhelmingly of East European extraction. These were the Jews who presumably knew their Poles, Ukrainians, and Rumanians. Nevertheless, as Marshall concluded his epiphany, these were also the first to leap to their feet in a thunderous crescendo of applause and cheering. The acclamation may have been less one of thanksgiving than of overwrought, even frenzied and prayerful hope.

III

IN SEARCH OF A CONGLOMERATE IDENTITY

The Wages of Conquest

In March 1921, upon signing the Treaty of Riga with Soviet Russia, Poland ended its two-and-a-half-year "Battle of the Frontiers." The reborn nation in its geographical amplitude now extended well beyond even the generous dimensions mandated by the Paris Peace Conference. Its population, augmented from some 20 million at the end of the World War to nearly 29 million only two and a half years later, had become the sixth largest in Europe. It was also one of the poorest. The sacrifices of almost uninterrupted conflict had taken their toll. Half of Poland's bridges and power stations, one-fifth of its buildings, three-fifths of its factories were destroyed. Some 11 million acres of agricultural land were ruined, as well as approximately 40 percent of Poland's prewar livestock.

There were even longer-range costs of the nation's putative victory. Before the World War, 85 percent of Poland's farm and industrial output had been absorbed by its three ruling empires. Now Russia and Austria took none of these exports, and Germany barely 10 percent. Surrounded by powerful revisionist enemies, the country was obliged to devote a third of its meager budget to national defense. These costs, and the still heavier ones of reconstruction, were complicated by the economic integration of Poland's enlarged territories, with their 10 million Polish and non-Polish inhabitants and their patchwork of inherited laws, administrations, civil services, and currencies. Little wonder that the nation's budget deficit in 1921 was 91 percent, and its inflation rate, 50 percent.

Poland's resources were hardly meager. Before the war, the regions of densest Polish habitation possessed significant quantities of coal, lumber, oil, and zinc. Far larger reserves were taken over with the expanded postwar frontiers, together with the Polish "Corridor's" valuable new maritime outlet to the Baltic. But few of these advantages were intelligently exploited. Well into the 1930s, Poland's landowning squirearchy, comprising less than 1 percent of the population, maintained its grip on 38 percent of the country's soil. Some three million Polish farmers continued to support their families on plots averaging less than five acres. The nation's per capita income in 1930, barely $100, remained among the lowest in Europe.

Political dysfunctionalism compounded economic infirmity. Poland's constitution was modeled on that of France. Its electoral system, operating by party lists, was based on proportional representation rather than on a victorious party's automatic majority control of the legislature. If the arrangement did not work well in postwar France (or Weimar Germany), it proved even less effective in a nation of Poland's social fragility. The epic rivalry between Jozef Pilsudski, the pluralist, and Roman Dmowski, the chauvinist, polarized the country's interwar politics. Dmowski's Endeks (National Democrats) and Pilsudski's Social Democrats were obliged to negotiate deals with a host of smaller parties—an almost predictable consequence of proportional representation. Government accordingly was reduced to precarious coalitions that were endlessly collapsing under the blackmail of marginal political factions.

Territorial insecurity further exacerbated the nation's legislative immobilism. Poland lay between Germany and Russia, each Great Power nurturing a revanchist grievance against this apparently voracious successor state. For Pilsudski, German and Russian irredentism could best be defanged by a more forbearing, federalist approach to the nation's German, Russian, Ukrainian, and other minorities. For Dmowski, the single, logical approach to the minorities was one of enforced "amalgamation." Non-Poles should be obliged to accept, even internalize, the demographic and cultural preeminence of the ethnic Polish majority. Nor did ideology alone, or even military vulnerability, animate Dmowski's fervid imperialism. Economics also played a role. Throughout the annexed, eastern territories, most of the bigger landlords were Poles. The peasants, whether sharecroppers or smallholders, tended to be Ukrainians, Byelorussians, or Lithuanians. A government adopting Pilsudski's federalist-reformist strategy would have allowed these soil-bound peoples a more equitable share of the gentry's large estates. All but reflexively, then, the squirearchy (if not the hereditary aristocracy) chose to give their support to Dmowski and the Endeks.

And so did other, even less affluent elements of the population. There appeared to be at least a subliminal consensus that the non-Polish minorities were a threat to national security. No other European state, after all, successor or otherwise, encompassed so large a proportion—fully 33 percent—of minority peoples. In the immediate postwar, the Ukrainians comprised 13 percent of the country's population; the Jews, almost 10 percent; the Byelorussians, 4 percent; the Germans, 3 percent; with the Lithuanians and other, even smaller communities totaling 4 percent. On July 31, 1919, five weeks after signing the minorities treaty, the Polish Sejm grudgingly ratified the document, and in March 1921, under heavy international pressure, the legislature similarly ratified a constitution, assuring Poland's minorities "the full and free development of their national characteristics by means of autonomous minority unions recognized under public law." But the series of guarantees proved hollow from the very outset. With Dmowski's Endeks comprising 40 percent of the Sejm's membership in 1919–22, no government dared ignore this powerful, chauvinist bloc and its priority agenda of "amalgamation."

Thus, the Lithuanians, a peasant people numbering barely 76,000, were obliged during the 1920s to accept Polish as the language of instruction in their—feeble—network of primary and secondary schools. The Byelorussians, comprising approximately 1 million, and sustaining essentially a pre-capitalist society, remained hardly less vulnerable than the Lithuanians to an "amalgamationist" offensive. By mid-decade, the government had almost entirely suppressed the Byelorussian school system, and had managed to dissolve any Byelorussian political party venturing to protest the campaign of educational deracination. The pretext was "insurrectionism."

The Germans and Ukrainians, on the other hand, represented a more authentic challenge to imperial Polonization. Concentrated in the nation's western borderlands, the Germans, a middle-class community numbering approximately 770,000 in 1921 (and 1.1 million a decade later), enjoyed the diplomatic support of the most formidable of Poland's neighbors. During the 1920s, Gustav Stresemann, Germany's foreign minister, actively cultivated their irredentism. In an endless farrago of accusations against Poland, Stresemann and later German foreign ministers organized congresses of German minorities and systematically invoked the minorities treaty to denounce Poland for mistreating its German subjects.

Were Berlin's charges exaggerated? Frequently they were, but some of the accusations were not without substance. As early as 1919, the Warsaw government dissolved the German Evangelical and Catholic Church associations, sponsors of over five hundred German-language schools in Poland. Fifteen years later, within the German-inhabited areas, only eleven German-language secondary schools remained on Polish soil, although German was taught as a separate language in hundreds of Polish-language schools. The Warsaw government maintained a close police surveillance of German social and cultural institutions, German religious youth organizations, German sports and hiking clubs. It imposed restrictions on the sale of Polish land to German farmers, and occasionally confiscated German property for alleged violation of administrative regulations. By the early 1930s, at least sixty thousand German farmers had been squeezed off Polish soil. The intimidation campaign eased only in 1934, when Poland entered into a pact of "friendship and non-aggression" with Nazi Germany (p. 67).

The ordeal of the Ukrainians was even harsher. Numbering at least

4.5 million in 1921, they constituted the largest minority in Poland, and their population would increase to nearly 6 million by 1939. Concentrated in former East Galicia, they were a people of small, desperately poor farmers. Their economic marginality was the consequence not only of battle devastation during the recent war, but of blatant Polish oppression. State subsidies, available for Polish agricultural cooperatives, were denied to Ukrainians. Ukrainian farmers were barred from increasing their individual landholdings; the principal unoccupied tracts in East Galicia were reserved for veterans of the Polish army. Evading the constraints of the minorities treaty and the 1921 Constitution, the government denied state or local funding to Ukrainian-language schools. In their dire impoverishment, the Ukrainians on their own could make only a feeble effort to develop an indigenous educational network. At that, the government ensured that Ukrainian school textbooks were purged of any Ukrainian historical material.

This was not a people willing to accept compliantly Poland's economic and cultural onslaught. When Soviet appeals on their behalf in the League of Nations Council produced no result, the Ukrainians engaged in mass protest demonstrations, even in occasional acts of sabotage against Polish farms and factories. In turn, Warsaw intensified its campaign of "pacification" in East Galicia, arresting hundreds of Ukrainian political activists and closing down scores of Ukrainian churches and chapels. As the *Manchester Guardian* correspondent noted in October 1930: "The Polish terror in the Ukraine is now worse than anything that is happening anywhere else in Europe. . . . [It is] not directed against individuals, but against a whole people."

The observation could have been made with even greater exactitude of Warsaw's campaign, official and unofficial, against the Jews, the single most vulnerable of reborn Poland's heterogeneity of minorities.

A Jewish Bill of Rights in Polish Action

It was a grim irony that the Poles should have inflicted the heaviest of their physical violence on Jewish civilians well after their government had signed the minorities treaty, on June 28, 1919. During the ensuing two years of the Russo-Polish War, General Haller's "Blue" Army and other Polish military units wreaked the worst of their havoc on the Jewish communities of the Ukraine, Byelorussia, and Lithuania (p. 25). Even as late as the summer of 1922, Jews scarcely dared appear on the streets at night in these regions, and in the summer of 1923 the mayor of Lodz appealed for government help in protecting his city against an imminent pogrom.

In truth, the minorities treaty had not been devised to cope with indiscriminate violence but with the narrower juridical issues of political status and cultural and communal autonomy. Yet on these issues, too, the document soon was exposed as toothless. If the Jews, a mercantile, "infidel" people, represented but 1 percent of the population in Germany, 2.5 percent in Russia, 4 percent in Czechoslovakia, 4.7 percent in Rumania, 6 percent in Hungary, 8 percent in Lithuania—in Poland they made up not less than 9.6 percent in 1921, and fully 10 percent by 1931. In their urban concentration, they offered a uniquely exposed and identifiable target. Thus, in Warsaw, Jews comprised almost 30 percent of the population; and in Lodz, Vilna, Bialystok, and Brest-Litovsk, nearly 40 percent.

In the renewed antisemitic onslaught, it was once again Roman Dmowski's Endeks who set the nationalist tone. They would consent to the ingestion of Ukrainians and Byelorussians, so long as these people of "lower civilization" accepted cultural Polonization. But the Jews could never be assimilated—nor should they be. As early as 1903, Dmowski in his *Political Testament* insisted that "[i]n the character of this race so many different values, alien to our moral constitution and harmful to our life, have accumulated that assimilation with a larger number of [Jews] would destroy us."

Could any steps have been taken to forestall a new wave of intimidation and delegitimation? The early years of constitution-building would have been precisely the time for Jozef Pilsudski, as head of state, to have spoken out with vigor against antisemitic excesses. He did not. By late 1922, sensing the fulminance of the nation's chauvinism, Pilsudski even muted his traditional federalism. Although his close political ally Gabriel Narutowicz was elected as first president of the Polish Republic in December 1922, the political right savagely denounced Narutowicz as "President of the Jews." Indeed, barely a week after taking office, Narutowicz was assassinated by a nationalist fanatic. In the ensuing government coalition, patched together in May 1923, the Endeks bulked even more formidably than before, and their party pronunciamento advocated "a government formed only by Poles," a proportionate "just share" for the Polish majority in all government contracts and employment, and containment of the influence of "unwelcome foreign elements."

With or without these guidelines, antisemitism remained a central feature of public policy. The issue of citizenship was an early harbinger. In Poland's successive peace treaties with the defeated Central Powers, and later with Russia, an identical commitment appeared:

Poland admits and declares to be Polish *ipso facto* and without the requirements of any formality, German, Austrian, Hungarian, and Russian nationals habitually resident at the date of the coming into

force of the present treaty in territory which is or may be recognized
as forming a part of Poland.

But of all the peoples in the newly acquired territories, Jews possessed the
least official proof of "habitual" residency. They had been driven from pil-
lar to post, first by the tsarist government in 1915–16, then by the march
and countermarch of Polish, Ukrainian, White Russian, and Soviet armies
in the eastern borderlands. Now, as half a million bedraggled Jewish fugitives sought to return home, they came without funds or chattels, and
assuredly without formal documentation.

In its inflamed nationalism, the Polish government needed little pretext
to confine these refugees to a juridical no-man's-land. Lacking official
"recognition," the Jews found themselves bereft of legal protection for
commercial contracts or even for home ownership, let alone the right to
vote or hold office. It was only grudgingly, under repeated appeal and
extensive international publicity, that the ministry of the interior began
authorizing a sequential naturalization, category by category, district by
district, town by town. Most of the cases were not settled until 1928, and
small pockets of Jews remained in a state of bureaucratic limbo well into
the early 1930s.

Under almost immediate attack, too, was the minorities treaty's elabo-
rately crafted provision for Jewish schooling. Article 9, it is recalled,
obliged the Polish government to fund Jewish schools in districts with substantial Jewish populations. The guarantee was stillborn. The early postwar era was a hard time for all Poles, years when some half-million Polish
children could not afford to attend school altogether. As the government saw it, subsidies for Jewish schools were an unaffordable luxury. Yet
the ministry of education might still have accepted, even encouraged, private Jewish funding. It did not. Rather, under various pretexts, it set
about harassing, even periodically closing Yiddish- and Hebrew-language
schools, often merely because alternate, Polish elementary schools were
available in the area. Although several large private Jewish school networks continued to function, by the early 1930s scores of Jewish primary
schools had become inoperative for "administrative" or "safety" or "financial" reasons.

Meanwhile, the government's campaign of vocational restriction against
Jews operated at all age levels. The rationale was Jewish overcrowding in
commerce and the professions. Statistics in fact bore out the charge. In
1922, Jews comprised 52 percent of Poland's tradesmen and owned 48 percent of the nation's retail shops (albeit most of these were tiny holes-in-
the-wall). In the liberal professions, Jews constituted a—bare—majority of
attorneys in the larger cities, and in the medical profession they ranked

proportionately second only to the Germans. Indeed, Jews altogether constituted a far higher percentage of the white-collar class than did any other
element, Polish or non-Polish. In its determination, therefore, to preempt
most of these middle-class sectors for Poles, the government in 1922
set about taking "remedial" measures. The first of these involved the civil
service, a sector in which Jews had been quite prominent in prewar Habsburg Galicia. Within two years, virtually all Jewish employees had been
squeezed out of government and municipal service. Afterward, denied
meaningful relief in public works programs, unemployed Jews were left
almost entirely to the care of their own, Jewish welfare organizations, particularly the Joint (p. 26).

The government adopted still other methods for displacing the Jewish
presence in white-collar vocations. One was fiscal. Ranking third as a
source of national income, commerce was subject in 1929 to the nation's
highest proportionate rate of taxation; and as a practical consequence, Jews
soon were paying 40 percent of all direct taxes in Poland. By the same
token, the new republic's official program of *etatism*—state capitalism—
also fell heaviest on the Jews. To jump-start Poland's ravaged economy, the
government in the 1920s set about establishing new industries under its
own direction or nationalizing private businesses already in operation.
These enterprises included public transportation and power utilities, the
salt, tobacco, liquor, paper, and match industries, even import-export and
agricultural brokerage offices—all vocations and services that historically
had been pioneered, managed, and extensively staffed by Jews. The policy
was by no means animated exclusively by antisemitism. Yet it was significant that Jews, who had been virtually synonymous with these sectors,
were promptly dismissed and their positions were given over to Poles. In
this fashion, with the anti-Jewish campaign shifting from physical pogroms
to "administrative" discrimination, its inroads upon the minorities treaty
eventually became even more debilitating.

In the United States, meanwhile, witnessing the collapse of their painfully achieved Peace Conference diplomacy, Louis Marshall and his American Jewish Committee colleagues entreated their government contacts to
intercede with Warsaw. To no avail. Under the Harding and Coolidge
administrations, the United States had opted out of European affairs.
Instead, throughout the 1920s, Lucien Wolf and the Anglo-Jewish Conjoint group bore the principal burden of Jewish international diplomacy.
Yet the results were hardly more impressive. The issue of Jewish rights was
not a priority for the British Foreign Office. Nor was it for a single Western government. As Wolf noted despairingly in a 1928 letter to his friend
Leonard Stein, the Jews within the space of a decade had devolved from
the single most effective of the various minority lobbies to the single least

effective. Lacking a "brother state," or at least a Woodrow Wilson, to press their cause, the Jews alone of Europe's ethnic minorities were almost entirely bereft of diplomatic leverage.

The Politics of Ethnicity

Was political leverage available? East European Jews in fact were veteran practitioners of intramural politics. For many years even before the Great War, they had expressed their various ideological views—Zionist, Socialist, or Orthodox-religious—on a party basis in regional and local Jewish communal councils. Afterward, their wartime experience of communal autonomy under German occupation (p. 24), and their subsequent postwar exposure to the ravages of Ukrainians, Poles, and Russians, merely fueled their passion for self-governing political status within the Polish Republic. So did the initial success of Jews in achieving wider autonomist privileges in the tiny Baltic successor states of Lithuania and Latvia.

But in Poland the most far-reaching of Jewish autonomist aspirations were blocked. On November 12, 1918, it is recalled, Jozef Pilsudski, newly arrived in Warsaw from his internment in Germany, granted an audience to a delegation of Jewish political and religious leaders. Courteously, he listened as his visitors made their case for political self-government, and for proportional en-bloc representation in the forthcoming Polish Sejm. And with equal courtesy, Pilsudski dismissed the proposal as too far-reaching. For all his tolerant federalism, the chief of state rejected any minority blueprint that extended beyond communal-religious autonomy. So did the Peace Conference (p. 35).

Once the grandiose objective of Jewish self-government was foreclosed, Jewish political leaders then began shifting their emphasis to the issues of civil, economic, and cultural rights. By the same token, they agreed to concentrate their efforts on the Sejm, Poland's dominant governmental institution. Here leeway apparently existed for a certain tangible minority representation. So it was that Jewish political parties, rather than prominent Jewish intercessors, or even minorities-treaty guarantees, henceforth became the chosen vehicles of Jewish group survival in Poland.

There were more than a few of these parties. Indeed, there was a veritable extravaganza of them. For one thing, each Jewish faction—of the right, left, or center—appeared to have its Orthodox religious doppelgänger. Additionally, party branches often tended to function on a semiautonomous basis within separate regions, in central Poland, the eastern "borderlands," East Galicia, and West Galicia. Amidst this welter of internecine contention and replication, however, it was Zionism that emerged as the dominant political force among Polish Jewry. The movement's prestige had been vastly enhanced by the recent establishment of a Jewish National Home in Palestine, even as the dynamism of Jewish nationalism was lent additional survivalist fervor by the wave of postwar pogroms. Thus, gaining control of the larger Jewish communal councils, the Zionists moved swiftly to develop Polish Jewry's most powerful youth groups, and the widest network of Jewish schools and mass-circulation newspapers.

With greater vigor than any other element, too, the Zionists prosecuted the political struggle for Jewish national and civil rights within Poland itself. Their dual role often produced tensions within the movement. Thus, the right-wing "Revisionist" Zionists—those who nurtured maximalist territorial claims on the Holy Land—were fixated on emigration to Palestine as the one and exclusive solution to Jewish minority vulnerability. But the General—"mainline"—Zionists refused to accept so doctrinaire a position. Had they ignored the domestic circumstances of the vast mass of Polish Jewry, they argued, to concentrate single-mindedly upon the transmigration of Jews to the Holy Land, they would have condemned Zionism in Poland to the political margins. Instead, their Zionism was obliged to function as an all-inclusive, autonomist variety of Jewish nationalism. It was a stance that best fitted the Zeitgeist of Polish Jewry.

Zionism was not without powerful rivals, to be sure. The most formidable was the Orthodox religionist bloc, the Agudat Israel party. Based on the great Chasidic—fundamentalist—dynasties of central and eastern Poland, Agudat Israel mobilized the loyalty of perhaps a fourth of Polish Jewry. In a historically pietistic community, the Agudists' grass-roots infrastructure of rabbinical and synagogue councils, of seminaries, religious schools, and social-welfare activities, offered the party a unique leverage, particularly among the impoverished, undereducated village Jews of the Ukrainian districts. Meanwhile, the Bund, the Jewish Socialist party, ranking third among Jewish voters, enjoyed plurality support among the substantial Jewish working classes. Committed equally to a democratic, egalitarian society and to the preservation of an autochthonous Yiddish culture, the Bund alone of the major Jewish parties was willing to make political common cause with its non-Jewish counterpart, the Polish Socialist party. Yet, whatever their ideological orientation, Poland's Jewish factions far transcended "conventional" politics. Their dense networks of ancillary youth and women's movements, their schools and social clubs, offered Polish Jewry an indispensable psychological defense in ethnic depth.

In the end, however, Jewish politicians could achieve credibility only to the extent that they made their people's case in the Sejm. The first elections to this parliament were scheduled for January 1919. Comprising almost 10 percent of the country's population, the Jews had anticipated "appropriate" proportionate representation in the Sejm. But in their initial—November 12, 1919—meeting with Pilsudski, they won no assurance on this point (p. 50). Neither did they from the Allied statesmen at Paris. Without these commitments, the Jewish parties' single remaining hope was to win an impressive parliamentary representation on their own. Yet that ambition, too, went unrealized. The Jews gained only 13 out of the Sejm's total of 444 seats—although, under the Sejm's convoluted procedure, 5 additional Jews eventually were appointed.

The Zionists at least would make the best of a bad bargain. Winning six of the "Jewish" seats, the General Zionists emerged as the dominant Jewish plurality in the Sejm. It was consequently they who took the initiative in organizing all thirteen of the Jewish delegates into a *kolo*, a "caucus," to speak with unanimity on behalf of common Jewish issues. The need for that collective spokesmanship could hardly have been more urgent. The Polish right (most of them Endeks) held an intimidating plurality in the Sejm. On numerous occasions, their deputies either left the Chamber or engaged in derisive shouting whenever Jews arose to speak in plenary session. Worse yet, the bitter infighting among the various Jewish parties themselves did nothing to fortify Jewish influence in the legislature.

The Politics of Illusion: The Minorities and the Ugoda

How then could these Jewish factions, comprising a pitiable 3–5 percent of the Sejm, protect the interests of some 2.75 million of their kinsmen in Poland? The General Zionists, largest of the Jewish parties, devoted their best energies to this question. And, in the process, the party leadership decided on a new, activist stance, one that rejected the historically "servile" Jewish formula of working through well-connected Jewish intercessors. Jewish pride was the Zionist raison d'être. Political muscularity would be its tactic. It was the General Zionist chairman, Yitzhak Grunebaum, who negotiated that tactic.

Born in Warsaw in 1875, trained as a lawyer, Grunebaum developed a thriving local practice before the war, largely among Jewish business clients. At the same time, as a passionate Zionist, he became a lifelong delegate to international Zionist congresses. Serving on the editorial board of several General Zionist newspapers, Grunebaum also was a major force in developing the Tarbut ("Culture") school network, the first Hebrew-language school system in the Diaspora.

Yet it was as a political negotiator among Jews and Poles alike that Grunebaum emerged as Polish Jewry's most respected statesman. It was he who organized the multi-party Jewish delegation to the Peace Conference.

And in January 1919, as one among the tiny group of Jews elected to the first Polish Sejm, Grunebaum was the principal organizer of the Jewish *kolo*, the caucus of Jewish delegates. Fluent in Polish, Yiddish, and German, courtly of dress and demeanor, his goatee always elegantly manicured, Grunebaum was an ingratiating figure both on the dais and as spokesman for the Jewish kolo in committee sessions. During his thirteen years in the Sejm, he evoked a grudging respect even from Polish nationalists for his dignity and tenacity on behalf of his people.

Above all, Grunebaum was a resourceful political tactician. It did not escape him that Poland's right-wing delegates, in formulating the 1921 constitution, had engaged in blatant "gerrymandering." Rural and urban voting districts alike were intentionally sculpted to the disadvantage of scattered minorities such as the Jews and (in some measure) the Germans. Grunebaum then shrewdly countered this subterfuge with a maneuver of his own. It was to negotiate a "Bloc of National Minorities," a united electoral list of all non-Polish peoples, with each ethnic group accorded its own appropriate proportion of Sejm seats. Grunebaum did not invent the formula. It sprang originally from the brow of Erwin Hasbach, one of the Sejm's German deputies. Yet it was Grunebaum who transformed the scheme into practical action.

The project was complex, and from the outset Grunebaum encountered much reluctance among the fiercely antisemitic Ukrainians, as well as among the Jewish Bund, whose leadership preferred to ally with the Polish Socialists. But with patience and a near-telepathic instinct for the self-interest of his interlocutors, Grunebaum eventually negotiated an alliance with most of the other factions. Indeed, the minorities bloc won an impressive success in the 1922 elections. Between them, the non-Polish nationalities returned 81 deputies to the Sejm, and fully 35 of these were Jewish! For Grunebaum and his colleagues, it appeared that the Jews at long last had become a force to be reckoned with in public affairs.

They were soon to learn otherwise. In their patriotism, members of the smaller Polish progressive factions hesitated to make common cause with the minorities bloc. Delegates of the Polish left, committed secularists all, rejected the very notion of state subsidies for minority schools, most of which operated under religious sponsorship. In one area only did Poland's Socialists and the minorities bloc cooperate. In December 1922, as the recently elected Sejm got down to business, the various joint delegations helped elect a liberal, Gabriel Narutowicz, as the nation's president. Yet even that single victory generated an upsurge of xenophobia so intense that it led to Narutowicz's assassination (p. 47). Deeply shaken, the Jewish kolo from then on was unprepared to risk cooperation with the other minority parties on any issue. Its members preferred instead to focus exclusively on Jewish national interests, even on individual Jewish party interests. This intramural parochialism may have been the most painful disappointment of all for Grunebaum. In 1923, exhausted by his people's immemorial contentiousness, he resigned as chairman of the kolo.

In the ensuing two years, between December 1923 and November 1925, Prime Minister Wladyslaw Grabski directed the nation's affairs as leader of a center-right government. For the Jews, Grabski's incumbency was hardly less than a disaster. A former economics professor and an Endek, the prime minister set about augmenting the earlier program of etatism—state capitalism—by nationalizing a still wider array of enterprises and vocations. Soon an additional 160,000 Jews became "redundant," deprived of employment in government-controlled corporations, excluded from membership in vital trade and industrial associations, restricted from engaging in commercial activities under a Sunday closing law, denied access to funding for their schools, or equal admission opportunities to universities. In their desperation, then, the members of the Jewish kolo in 1924 began evaluating a new political strategy.

It was the argument of Leon Reich, and a group of his fellow Zionist deputies in the Sejm, that the Jews and others of Poland's minorities nurtured entirely different agendas. The Germans were irredentist, and the Ukrainians and Byelorussians were obsessed with territorial autonomy. The Jews by the mid-1920s sought protection of their civil and cultural rights under the minorities treaty, nothing more. To ensure that objective, argued Reich, a direct Jewish approach to the government was warranted, a gesture of Jewish-Polish cooperation on issues that were specific to their own two peoples. In devising this strategy, Reich doubtless was influenced by his prewar experience as a citizen of Habsburg Galicia, where Jewish-Polish relations had been somewhat more equable.

It was a tradition Reich invoked now in his discussions with Prime Minister Grabski. Shrewdly, too, he reminded the prime minister that an accommodation with the Jews might prove useful in softening American Jewish mistrust of Poland. Grabski was listening. He was aware that Count Aleksander Skrzynski, the foreign minister, was soon to visit Western Europe and the United States in search of investment capital. In earlier years, seeking loans to help redeem the nation's wartime debts, Polish diplomats in London and New York had approached such prominent Jewish financiers as James de Rothschild, Henry Morgenthau, Otto Warburg, and Herbert Lehman. At the time, the overtures were rebuffed. Yet now, with the promise of support from the Sejm's Jewish bloc, Skrzynski would be better positioned to renew the effort. In late spring of 1925, moreover, he was visited in Warsaw by Lucien Wolf of the Conjoint. Once again the adroit Anglo-Jewish diplomat proved his worth as an intercessor. With his help, the Jewish bloc in ensuing months managed to negotiate a *ugoda*, a pact, with the Grabski cabinet.

Under the terms of the ugoda, the government would abrogate, or at least modify, the Sunday closing law; appoint a limited quota of Jews to civil-service positions; allow Jewish businesses to negotiate loans with the state credit bank, to bid on state contracts, and—in the case of certain larger enterprises—to enjoy a five-year moratorium from etatist nationalization. Additionally, Jewish schools would be offered a modest increment of funding. The Jewish numerus clausus would be eased for universities, and for the legal, medical, and other professional organizations. In turn, the Jewish delegation would cooperate with the Grabski cabinet on all matters of national welfare, and even support Poland's "hegemonic" control over the border populations. In negotiating the ugoda, then, had the Jews betrayed their former allies? Neither Lucien Wolf nor the Jewish kolo accepted this interpretation. The earlier minorities-bloc policy had proved bankrupt. Jews owed nothing to the other subject peoples, least of all to the Ukrainians, the virulence of whose antisemitism continued to exceed even that of the Poles.

Meanwhile, Foreign Minister Skrzynski, pocketing an apparently clean bill of health on the Jewish question, was able to sail off to the United States in high spirits. Upon arriving in New York, he made it his first order of business to inform a press conference that

[t]he Polish people have awakened to the realization that their antisemitism is a mistake. With sufficient capital there is room enough in Poland, as well as plenty of opportunities, for both Jews and Poles. The rights of the Jewish population in Poland will be secured by the fact that the Polish government will endeavor to stop the attacks on the Jews in the Polish press, and to mold public opinion on calmer and more favorable lines.

During his subsequent goodwill tour throughout North America, Skrzynski's meetings with Jewish financiers and communal leaders were equable.

They were also unproductive. Tangible evidence of the Polish government's change of heart was meager. No legislation was passed to activate the ugoda, except for such essentially cosmetic gestures as the acceptance of Yiddish and Hebrew as "official" languages in the Polish postal-telegraph system. Prime Minister Grabski's own party press maintained its snide anti-Jewish commentary, admonishing Jews to be "loyal." It is possible that the prime minister and foreign minister meant well by the Jews. But the issue was moot. In the winter of 1925, before Grabski could act

meaningfully on Jewish rights one way or the other, his government was
out of office.

A Republican Dictatorship

Since proclaiming its independence in November 1918, the Polish Republic had undergone 118 changes of government in less than eight years and
had swooned into a virtual administrative catatonia. In May 1926, as the
nation's politicians set about restructuring yet another center-right coalition, Jozef Pilsudski had seen enough. The soldier-statesman had with-
drawn from political life three years earlier. Retaining only command of
the army, he had declared his intention never again to assume civic responsibilities. But with the country in political disarray, the old marshal saw no
alternative but to restore at least a semblance of order. Hereupon he turned
to the veteran senior officers of his wartime Polish Legion to unseat the
current government. The response of these veterans was immediate. Their
coup was bloodless. Indeed, it was supported by most of the nation's political left and center.

Pilsudski in fact was uninterested in returning to the presidency. The
pomp and trappings of office held no appeal for him. Rather, he would
exercise power behind the scenes as minister of war, installing loyal tech-
nocrats as his handpicked protégés. His choice as president accordingly
was Professor Ignacy Moscicki; and for prime minister, Professor Kazi-
mierz Bartel. Neither man had been active in political life. Neither did Pilsudski formulate a tendentious political agenda for the country, other than
"moral regeneration." The Sejm interposed no difficulties. Thoroughly
intimidated, the legislators transferred key powers from themselves to the
president, then supinely allowed rigged elections to "endorse" Pilsudski's
personal choices. At first, civil liberties were not restricted. But in 1930,
as social restiveness mounted with the onset of the world depression
(p. 59), Pilsudski became more ironfisted. He began ordering the internment of recalcitrant politicians.

Like others of Poland's minorities, the Jews reacted to the Pilsudski
coup with muted optimism. Despite his brutal military campaign for the
eastern territories, the old soldier had always been a sympathetic federalist.
The recent ugoda with the government in any case was proving ineffectual,
and its leading advocate, Leon Reich, had been obliged to step down in
1925 as chairman of the Jewish kolo. In Reich's place, regaining his former leadership of the kolo, Yitzhak Grunebaum expressed his own warm
support for the new government changeover. Initially, too, Grunebaum's
hopes appeared to be vindicated. Prime Minister Bartel promised scrupu-
lously to respect the terms of the minorities treaty, and as a token of "good
faith" he appointed a joint monitoring committee of Jews and Poles.

Moreover, the government ensured that its "good faith" registered in the United States. In 1928, Poland's consul in New York, Mieczyslaw Marchlewski, shrewdly cultivated the "Landsmannschaft [fraternal consociation] of Polish Jews in America," and its president, Benjamin Winter, a real-estate tycoon. Marchlewski's vision, as he explained it to Winter and other Jewish contacts, was for American Jews to invest more heavily in Poland's Jewish cooperatives, to improve credit facilities for Jewish businesses in Poland, to increase Polish-Jewish manufacturing exports to the United States. These undertakings could only redound to Poland's wider economic advantage. In that effort, Marchlewski even organized a "Polish-Jewish Goodwill Committee" and launched its opening meeting with an elaborate series of publicity releases in the New York press.

However well intended, Marchlewski's grand scheme was vitiated by developments in Poland throughout the late 1920s. Its façade of republicanism notwithstanding, the government had become a military quasi-dictatorship, with numerous liberals and Socialists quietly disappearing into "internment." Thus far, most Jewish delegates in the Sejm had not been affected by the "cleansing" of the liberal-left. With the Jewish kolo divided, however—Reich's group favoring and Grunebaum's group opposing further cooperation—government pressure reduced the numbers of Jewish deputies and senators in the Sejm from forty-seven in 1923 to twenty-two by 1929. Few among this shrinking delegation were prepared to speak out in opposition to the Pilsudski regime. Although the estimable Grunebaum himself was the key exception, he had lost most of his—briefly revived—support in the kolo. Even his own General Zionist party dropped him as its spokesman. And by the early 1930s, the number of Jewish delegates in the Sejm dropped to six, in effect, to a political nonpresence.

A Hermetic Society

Was all gall and wormwood for Polish Jewry? They remained a substantial demographic element, after all, listed at 3.1 million in the 1931 Polish census, fully 10 percent of Poland's entire population, and 31 percent of the population of the nation's four largest cities—Warsaw, Lodz, Cracow, and Lvov. Moreover, in the smaller townships and villages of central and eastern Poland, Jews maintained routine business relations with their Polish neighbors. In state primary schools, attended by not less than 70 percent of Poland's Jewish children, the common Polish language of instruction permitted a certain functional contact between the two peoples. Although the Jews produced few prose writers of eminence in the Polish language, a number of their poets achieved a respectable audience among Poland's intelligentsia, particularly Julien Tuvim, Antony Slonimski, Franciszka Arnsteinow, Henryk Balk, Mieczyslaw Braun, Julia

Dickstein-Wielcznska, Juliusz Feldheim, Zuranna Ginczanka, Bruno Jasielski, and Cezary Jellanta.

Nevertheless, social interaction between Poles and Jews remained essentially minimal. Jewish workers and businessmen conducted their activities in separate organizations, in their own unions, their own merchants' and artisans' associations, their own credit cooperatives, health insurance programs, and relief agencies. From secondary school onward, the younger generation of Polish Jews participated exclusively in their own student associations and sports clubs. Their political parties remained unregenerately ethnocentric. Should it have been concluded, then, that ethnic separation necessarily implied cultural ghettoization? Here the evidence was mixed. Enjoying almost total freedom in their own communal and cultural affairs, Jews published an extraordinarily wide range of newspapers and journals. Whether in Yiddish, Polish, German, or Russian, the Jewish press by 1922 constituted 14 percent of all the newspapers and journals published in Poland altogether. It was a strident and polemical journalism. Reasonably free of government censorship, its outpouring of editorials did not hesitate to engage in sharp, often ferocious criticism of both Polish and Jewish political policies.

The vitality of this communal self-expression has led some historians to question whether Polish Jewry's straitened circumstances could be traced mainly to antisemitism. Was not the crisis of Jewish privation more intimately related to the economic underdevelopment of Poland itself? For that matter, in the first postwar decade, were the Jews of Poland necessarily more poverty-stricken than their Polish neighbors? Manifestly, they were not—surely not more than the vast underclass of Poland's rural majority. The growth rate of the Jewish population was testimony to this people's sheer life force, climbing at a rate of 7 percent a year. As late as 1931, moreover, six out of every ten persons employed in business were Jews.

Yet if the government trumpeted these statistics, it ignored still others: that a majority of Jewish "businesses" were tiny market stalls or nondescript hole-in-the-wall operations. Between 1921 and 1931, too, the number of Jews employed in manual labor began to edge ahead, from 58 to 60 percent. Nor were these workers destined for Poland's larger factories. Discriminatory hiring practices gradually reduced the number of Jews even in the great textile mills of Lodz and Warsaw, where they had been heavily concentrated in earlier decades. Rather, "manual" work for Jews in the 1920s and 1930s was confined principally to small workshops, essentially to cottage enterprises that earned little profit and offered no health or unemployment-insurance benefits. If the Jewish working class was growing in size, it was also growing in social displacement.

It may be questioned whether this "cold pogrom" was dictated by Poland's wider economic requirements. The nation, after all, possessed abundant natural resources (p. 43). Its vast stretches of arable soil would easily have supported the country's entire rural population had the government introduced the kind of modest land redistribution adopted by neighboring Czechoslovakia during the 1920s. But the Polish squirearchy was uninterested in relinquishing even the minutest fraction of its proprietorship. Indeed, the Catholic Church, the country's single-largest landowner, gave the sanction of religion to the economic status quo (pp. 61–62).

A Shift to Political Fascism

From 1929 on, shattered by the world depression, Europe's successor states responded to shrinking markets with a frantic imposition of tariff hikes and import quotas. Yet the struggle for economic autarchy proved futile, even counterproductive. Poland was a dramatic case in point. In late 1929, the national per capita income of France (by the measurement of Polish zlotys) had fallen to 2,000; of Germany, to 2,500; of Britain, to 4,200. In Poland, per capita income dropped to a starvation-level 600. In the Polish countryside, destitution became so acute that cases were not rare of parents selling their children for adoption.

So it was, for the first time since the pogroms and boycotts of the Polish-Ukrainian war era, that the economic misery of Jews in Poland approached the desperation of their Gentile neighbors. It was then, too, that public discrimination took its heaviest toll. Etatism remained one of its most painful features, for Minister of Finance Stefan Strzynski in 1932 coopted a still wider area of the economy for nationalization, and specifically in the commercial and banking sectors. The number of business licenses issued by the government declined from 466,000 in 1928 to 344,000 in 1932, with the principal decrease found among Jewish enterprises.

It was not a plight the government was intent on ameliorating. Jews who became unemployed by the tens of thousands encountered a bureaucratic stone wall. Public-works jobs, credit banks, and other forms of government relief almost invariably gave preference to non-Jews. Pilsudski himself doubtless was uninterested in exacerbating the Jewish condition; but the "cold pogrom" of the early 1930s reflected public frustration and bitterness no less than government policy. The Endek bloc of course was not slow to exploit the mood of helpless rage. Its circulars, with photographs of starving families, bore the caption: "Every Jew in business drives a Polish family to the wall." As in the early postwar period, the slogan was universally repeated: "Will you permit this to happen to patriotic Poles?"

In 1931, under the pressures of the depression, of etatist "redundancy" and popular antisemitism, nearly a third of Poland's working-age Jews were without steady employment income. Three years later, one-fourth of

Polish Jewry had become partially or completely dependent on philan-thropy. By 1936, the Jewish charity rolls approached two-thirds, and some 300,000 Jewish schoolchildren were estimated to be suffering from malnu-trition. In Vilna, four-fifths of Jewish schoolchildren were diagnosed as anemic. In Warsaw, tens of thousands of Jewish families clustered for shel-ter in single rooms. Once again, as in the war and immediate postwar periods, it was the Joint that functioned as the indispensable source of communal relief. Between 1920 and 1935, the mighty American phil-anthropy disbursed $117 million in charitable aid throughout Poland, maintaining scores of clinics, X-ray stations, infant-care dispensaries, and *casas*—small-credit funds for businesses and workshops. Yet these relief measures were the barest palliatives in a catastrophe so dire that it appeared incapable of becoming worse.

Politically, however, it did worsen. The process was gradual. Jozef Pil-sudski's initial military coup of May 1926, although authoritarian, was based at least on no particular totalitarian agenda. Labeling itself the Sanaya—the National Camp—the military cabal was essentially techno-cratic, and flaunted the virtues of discipline and efficiency. In contrast to the Endeks and other factions of the political right wing, Pilsudski and his associates tended to refrain from populist chauvinism. But once the depression struck, the "liberals" in the marshal's original entourage lost their influence. By 1930, the brunt of the junta's intimidation was directed less against Roman Dmowski's rabble-rousing constituency than against trade unions and rural cooperatives—and then, increasingly, against the nation's ethnic minorities. The transformation was characteristic of many a well-meaning elitist regime that proved incapable of solving economic crises. Demagoguery would buy time. In April 1935, to preempt interfer-ence with their flailing authoritarianism, Pilsudski's associates—he himself was quite ill—bullied the Sejm into enacting a new constitution. This one introduced severe voting restrictions and left to the president broad areas of "nomination."

One month later, in May 1935, Pilsudski died. Recalling the marshal's early goodwill toward them, the Jews of Poland mourned his passing. Some one hundred Jewish delegations marched in his funeral procession. Their grief may also have been premonitory. Soon afterward, the Sanaya's far-rightists took over the government. Their éminence grise, Colo-nel Edward Rydz-Smigly, dictated policy to the aging president, Ignacy Moscicki, and to the prime minister, Marian Zyndram-Koscialkowski. Those directives in any case accomplished nothing to reverse the deepen-ing economic emergency. In its turmoil and confusion, the colonels' junta moved increasingly toward Fascist populism.

An initial step on this route was Rydz-Smigly's decision to genuflect to the Endeks, still the nation's most intimidating party. The reorientation actually had begun even before Pilsudski's death, and reflected foreign-policy considerations no less than domestic pressures. In September 1934, Soviet Russia became a member of the League of Nations. Alarm bells immediately began ringing in Warsaw. Once the Soviets took their seats in the League Council, it was certain that they would raise the chronic issue of Poland's mistreated Ukrainian minority. Within the same week, in antic-ipation of this danger, the Polish foreign minister, Jozef Beck, formally renounced the minorities treaty. "The . . . system of minority protection," he argued, "has proven to be a complete failure. The minorities themselves gain nothing from it, while . . . the spirit of the treaty . . . has . . . become the tool of a slanderous propaganda directed against the States bound by it." The government did not formally repudiate the minority provisions within the 1921 constitution itself. Nevertheless, the auguries were omi-nous. Was a new wave of officially sanctioned chauvinism in the offing?

An "Ideological" Isolation

It was. Among the country's subject peoples, moreover, the Jews once again were the first to experience the cutting edge of political reaction. Indeed, from 1934 on, the status of Poland's Jewry emerged as arguably the single most ulcerated issue in the nation's political consciousness. It was not xeno-phobia alone that singled the Jews out. The Church played a central role in shaping public opinion and government policy. Throughout the 1920s and 1930s, in parochial schools, religious periodicals, and pastoral sermons, denunciation of Jews and Judaism achieved a new and unprecedented ferocity. Throughout the 1920s, the Church had stigmatized the Jews essentially as deicides. But as the depression widened, and with it the threat of social radicalism, the Catholic hierarchy put its emphasis on Jews as Bol-sheviks, as purveyors of moral corruption, as a people to be categorized with "the louse, the bedbug, the locust, the typhus bacillus, and the cholera and plague bacillus." In the words of the *Przewodnik Katolicki* of March 1933: "Wherever something is taking place which is harmful to our coun-try, just scratch around a little and you will find a Jewish culprit." "A terri-ble gangrene has infiltrated our body," editorialized *Przeglad powsrechy*, another Catholic monthly, "and we . . . are blind!"

By the mid-1930s, clerical antisemitism no longer was a matter simply of school instruction or journalistic execration. It had become ecclesiastical policy. In a pastoral letter of May 1936, Cardinal August Hlond, the Pri-mate of Poland, laid down an official guideline on the Jews:

It is a fact that Jews oppose the Catholic Church, are steeped in free-thinking and represent the avant-garde of the atheist movement, the Bolshevist movement, and subversive action. . . . It is true that

Jews commit fraud, usury, and are involved in [white slavery]. . . .
[T]he influence of Jewish young people on their Catholic peers is
generally . . . a negative one. . . . [Consequently] one does well to prefer his own kind in commercial dealings and to avoid Jewish stores
and Jewish stalls in the market, although it is not permissible to
demolish Jewish businesses.

Together with the Church, Poland's white-collar class emerged as a
major factor in the anti-Jewish assault, and particularly the bourgeois
"intelligentsia"—doctors, lawyers, and engineers, university and high-
school faculty members, and mid-level government bureaucrats. It was
their professional organizations that led the anti-Jewish campaign, among
them the Association of Social Workers, the Association of Chartered
Accountants, the Association of Christian Dentists, the League of Insurance Appraisers, the Polish Union of Physicians, the Polish Bar Association. In 1938, the Union of Polish Catholic Lawyers, the Union of
Catholic Writers, the Coordinating Committee of Academic Corporations, and the Union of Technicians and Engineers issued a joint statement. It declared forthrightly that

[d]epriving the Jews of earning money means that they will be forced
to leave Poland. This is the only radical solution of the Jewish question. . . . [W]e urge all Christians not to sell to Jews any land or
houses, not to buy from Jewish stores, not to employ Jewish lawyers,
physicians, engineers, architects, artists, or any other professional
men.

In June 1935, shortly after Pilsudski's death, Endek partisans in the
town of Grodno staged a series of anti-Jewish attacks, destroying and looting shops in the principal Jewish business quarter. Five months later,
another assault was launched on Jewish shopkeepers in Odrzywol, again
with extensive destruction and looting. Killings were less typical of this
violence than in the immediate postwar years, but smashed stalls and physical beatings were altogether characteristic. In 1936 and 1937, the gravely
depressed Bialystok region experienced serious anti-Jewish outbursts.
Here youthful Endek members mounted over three hundred separate
attacks on Jewish businesses and homes. The assault of May 13, 1937, in
the city of Brest-Litovsk, continued for sixteen hours and produced
unprecedented destruction and pillage. Similar assaults occurred in Minsk-
Mazowiecki, Przytyk, Bresc, Bugiem, and Czestochowa. In Czestochowa, a
pogrom of June 1937 continued for three days without police intervention,
and produced four deaths and several hundred wounded.

Special-interest groups alone, or even the Church hierarchy, could not have orchestrated a campaign of this range and intensity. The violence was endorsed by a widening spectrum of political parties. Since the 1920s, the Endeks had shifted their emphasis from a broadly diffused anti-minority chauvinism to a more tightly focused antisemitism. In 1937, the party executive stated bluntly that the time had come for the Jews, "a vicious people," to be deprived of all political rights, including the right of citizenship. Jews henceforth should be expelled from the universities, the army, the press, the theater, and from the economy of all cities and towns. In its essence, the new platform replicated that of the Nazis, intermingled with a few Polish variations and local adaptations. An Endek splinter youth group, the Nara—National Radical—Camp, endorsed the fullest measure of Nazi-style brutality. Its members henceforth took the lead in organizing anti-Jewish riots and beatings.

Beyond the Endeks and Naras, members of several "respectable" factions also were prepared to adopt anti-Jewish platforms. These included the socially prestigious Conservative party. Monarchist, clerical, and funded substantially by landowning gentry, the Conservatives at their annual convention of December 1937 approved the formula read off by their chairman, Prince Janusz Radziwill. "We accept the injunctions issued by . . . Cardinal Hlond," it declared, "which, while condemning feelings of hatred, regard it permissible to fight against Jewish influence in the economic and moral spheres." Even the nation's first prime minister, Ignacy Paderewski, who in earlier years had been a key liaison between Poland and American Jewish leaders (p. 30), felt obliged now to endorse an anti-Jewish stance for his new Stronnictwo Pracy (Camp of Labor). At its founding congress in January 1938, the party declared its intention to "fight for the complete elimination of Jews from industry, trade, and business . . . [to] support . . . a complete cultural separation from the Jews. . . . The party regards as the best solution of the Jewish problem a mass emigration of the Jews."

Although the Socialists and Populists disdained to embrace a flagrantly anti-Jewish program, these left-liberals were far outnumbered in voting strength by the combined forces of the right, all of whose parties favored elimination of the Jews from the nation's economic life. If there was disagreement, it related only to method. In Sejm debates of the mid- and latter 1930s, no other domestic issue took precedence over the "Jewish question," as legislators gave increasing attention to a variety of exclusionist proposals, from stripping Jews of civil rights to "encouraging" Jews to depart the country altogether.

From Popular Siege to Official Policy

As the antisemitic furor gained in momentum and decibel power, the government's response for some years remained ambivalent. On the one hand, the military cabal denounced the Nara's gangster methods. On the other, the sheer scope and venom of Jew-hatred had become a fact of political life that could hardly be ignored—or remain unexploited. The first intimation of a shift in the government's approach came in 1934, during Pilsudski's last full year of life. In an effort to lower prices, Prime Minister Leon Kozlowski announced that "all possible steps" should be taken against trade brokerage. Kozlowski's proposal required little decipherment. Brokerage traditionally was a Jewish vocation. That same year, a government decree ordered the mechanization of bakeries. This initiative too represented an economic death blow. Denied access to a government credit line, Jewish bakers could not meet the costs of modernizing their plants. Similarly, in 1935, the ministry of commerce declined to renew the licenses of Jewish wine merchants. The vocation was pronounced "overcrowded."

It was in the following year, however, that the government revealed its ulterior purpose in the form of a seemingly innocuous, even "humane" bill introduced in the Sejm. This one would have imposed limitations on *schechita*, the slaughter of animals in Jewish abattoirs in accordance with Jewish dietary law. Terming schechita "a cruel practice," the government plainly hoped to inflict the coup de grâce on Jewish religio-cultural identity, and thereby to encourage mass Jewish departure. Hereupon even nonreligious Jews rallied, mobilizing their contacts among Poland's Socialists and liberals to block the measure. But the government would not relent. With the support of all the country's rightist factions, it persisted in introducing and reintroducing anti-schechita legislation. Debates on the issue continued without pause in the Sejm. Indeed, they consumed almost half the parliament's sessions between 1936 and 1939. And, bit by bit, in a succession of initiatives, the Sejm by March 1939 finally approved a climactic bill, prohibiting schechita entirely—although the ban was not scheduled to take effect until 1942 (by which time other matters had obtruded).

In February 1937, meanwhile, the colonels' regime set about fortifying its ideological base by establishing a new mass organization, the Camp of National Unity, best known by its Polish acronym OZON. In principle, OZON welcomed all citizens who accepted its principles of "moral austerity and nationalism." Yet the Camp was barred to Jews, "for they do not belong to the Polish nation." Wrapped in the flag of integral Polonism, OZON soon achieved its purpose of diverting national attention almost exclusively to the Jewish issue, to the "just struggle for the economic self-sufficiency and cultural purity of the Polish people." Government ministers then vied with each other in characterizing the Jewish presence as the insurmountable barrier to Polish cultural greatness and political stability. In March 1938, the prime minister, General Felicjan Slawoj-Skladkowski, informed a press conference that the economic battle against the Jews was "O.K." ("owszem"), so long as violence was avoided. Mordantly, Jews soon took to describing the regime as the "O.K. government." In May of the same year, OZON went rather further, adopting a thirteen-paragraph resolution in support of mass emigration as the one and only solution to the Jewish question.

For a literate, non-agrarian people like the Jews, it was the issue of education possibly more even than economic opportunity or communal autonomy that defined their vision of survival in Poland. Even as late as 1928, Jews constituted 53 percent of Poland's lawyers, 40 percent of Poland's doctors, 36 percent of Poland's dentists and dental technicians. Whatever their political insecurities, Jewish families in the 1930s still nurtured the dream of a higher education for their children, and with it a future of economic self-sufficiency, The illusion was one of the first to be punctured. For Poles, a university degree represented hardly less than a title of minor nobility. It was unthinkable that Jews should be permitted equal access to the honor. As far back as 1923, the government submitted a bill to institute a numerus clausus for non-Poles in higher education. But the minorities treaty was still fresh in public awareness, and the reaction from Western capitals was sharp. The Polish government then expediently withdrew the proposed legislation.

Nevertheless, in practical fact, if not in public law, a Jewish numerus clausus soon came into effect within the faculties of medicine and dentistry. Poland of course was not unique in this regard. But discrimination in Polish higher education possibly was more flagrant than in any other area of the country's life. In 1921–22, government statistics indicated that, of Poland's 34,266 university students, 8,426 were Jews. By 1938–39, of the nation's 49,967 university students, only 4,613 were Jews. Study abroad offered Jews little respite. University graduates who returned home with professional degrees were obliged to wait not less than five years for licenses to practice in their fields.

Meanwhile, for the shrinking minority of Jews remaining in Polish universities, student life became a harsh, even grim ordeal. In 1922, Gentile classmates "encouraged" Jews to live in their own dormitories, which local Jewish communities then were obliged to provide at their own expense. Throughout the 1920s, Jews were harassed out of all extracurricular student societies. The atmosphere darkened far more ominously in the 1930s.

Nara student groups began agitating for the official segregation of Jews in classrooms. At first, the government did not respond. Whereupon, pressing the issue of segregation over the next few years, the militants disrupted university teaching schedules by mounting campus demonstrations and interrupting classroom lectures. Soon physical attacks on Jewish students mounted with such ferocity that, in April 1937, Minister of Education Jozef Ujejski broadcast an appeal for the nationalist groups at least to avoid using life-threatening weapons. In return, he promised, the government would reconsider the issue of segregation.

Five months later, "for the maintenance of peace," Ujejski's successor, Wojciech Swietoslawski, authorized the rector of the University of Warsaw to allocate the left side of classrooms for Jews. Special benches would be made available for them. The directive soon was extended to other universities, even to technical high schools. On October 19, 1937, in galled response to this humiliation, leaders of the various Jewish political parties organized a mass meeting in Warsaw's Jewish quarter. For six hours, all Jewish businesses and newspapers closed as a gesture of solidarity. In the universities themselves, however, resistance was continuous. Ignoring the "ghetto benches," Jewish students leaned against the wall or sat on the floor throughout all their lectures, day after day.

There were Poles who shared Jewish outrage. At the University of Lvov, the rector, Professor Stanislaus Kulczynski, resigned his office. Scores of academicians and other intellectuals wrote letters of protest to newspapers and to the government. At the University of Warsaw, Professor Tadeusz Katarbinski, an elderly man, became known as the "standing professor" for insisting upon delivering his lectures on his feet so long as Jewish students were not seated as equals. Professor Theodor Miller at the Warsaw Commercial College declared that the Nara hooligans should also move the crucifix, "for Christ, too, belongs in the ghetto" (a remark for which Miller was immediately dismissed). But the majority of professors and other university officials did not protest. Neither did a single member of the nation's Church hierarchy.

The Diplomacy of Redundancy

By the latter 1930s, virtually all the government's "Jewish" policies were directed toward large-scale Jewish departure. These programs included government subsidies for the transfer of Polish merchants from the western to the eastern borderlands, as replacements for Jewish merchants; the ghetto-bench program, coupled with silence on the mounting physical assaults against Jewish university students, even against Jewish women and children in public parks; and, perhaps most invidiously, the widening economic boycott of Jewish enterprises and workers, and the legislative program against Jewish ritual slaughter.

The timing of this multitiered campaign was inspired not only by ideological or even political factors. As in the case of the Ukrainians (p. 61), foreign policy also played a role. In January 1934, fixated as always by the Russian menace, Jozef Pilsudski in one of his last public acts entered into a ten-year nonaggression pact with Nazi Germany. Inevitably, the pro-German orientation began to exert its influence on domestic policy. Following Pilsudski's death, the marshal's successors leaned over backwards to propitiate their Nazi ally. For his part, Hitler shrewdly exploited the Jewish issue for his "eastern" strategy. On September 22, 1938, the führer confided to Poland's Ambassador Jozef Lipski his, Hitler's, intention to deport the Greater Reich's Jews to overseas colonies. He then intimated his willingness to include Polish Jewry in his plan. In response, Lipski promised that his government would erect a magnificent monument to the führer if this undertaking were put into effect.

The ambassador hardly exaggerated. By 1938, Poland's colonels' regime had embraced the goal of large-scale Jewish emigration as official policy. "This surplus of Jews," declared *Polska Zbrojna*, a mouthpiece of the government, "hangs like a millstone around the neck of Poland and exercises a most fatal influence on the economic development of our country." In January 1938, OZON—the Camp of National Unity—publicly endorsed mass Jewish emigration in the fourth of its published "Thirteen Theses." "The solution to the Jewish problem in Poland," it stated flatly, "can be achieved above all by the most considerable reduction of Jews in the Polish state." On January 23, 1939, responding to a petition from the Sejm's 116 Endek deputies, Prime Minister Slawoj-Skladkowski affirmed that his administration "would do all in its power to obtain outlets for [Jewish] emigration by international action."

In fact, "international action" had been under government exploration for several years. In 1937, the foreign ministry's consular bureau, directed by Wiktor Drymmer, began formulating a detailed program for "encouraging" Jewish departure. Under this scheme, all remaining Jewish employees would be dismissed from state-controlled or state-subsidized cultural institutions—from music, theater, and the arts. The numerus clausus in the practice of law, medicine, dentistry, engineering, and accountancy would be tightened almost to the point of closure. Most fundamentally, the new guidelines for Polish citizenship would be redefined to disenfranchise major categories of Jews, specifically those who had been absorbed into the nation since the early postwar period. In February 1938, Foreign Minister Jozef Beck accepted these proposals. From then on, the government's commitment to mass Jewish departure superseded the efforts of earlier years to seek out investment funds from Jews abroad.

The policy alteration was revealed on November 7, 1938, in a meeting between Dr. Grushka, Poland's consul-general in New York, and several prominent American Jewish financiers, among them George Backer, Alexander Kahn, and Morris Waldman. The Polish government no longer could accept Jewish investment funds devoted to "constructive work in Poland," Grushka explained. Rather, if Jewish leaders wished to underwrite large-scale Jewish emigration, this help alone would strengthen the "non-antisemitic elements" in Poland. Backer and his colleagues reacted to the proposal with abhorrence. They would have no part of it. But neither would the Warsaw government countenance any other option. In March 1939, Poland's ambassador to the United States, Count Jerzy Potocki, reiterated to the State Department that no further American Jewish investment funds would be accepted unless they were linked to substantial Jewish emigration.

Between the wars, some 430,000 Jews actually managed to emigrate, principally to North and South America, to Western Europe and Palestine. The numbers plainly would have been far larger but for immigration restrictions in other lands. In 1921, the United States began closing its doors to East and South European immigrants, and other nations somewhat erratically followed the identical course. The onset of the world depression in 1929 produced an even more remorseless tightening of immigration quotas. In response to Arab pressures, Britain's Colonial Office during the 1930s was severely limiting Jewish immigration to Palestine. For the Polish government, therefore, the critical issue manifestly no longer was the choice or means by which to drive Jews to mass departure, but the acquisition of potential destinations for them. Indeed, long before, and entirely unofficially, individual Polish diplomats had become intrigued by exotic alternative outlets for Jews. In 1926, Count Chlapowski, Poland's ambassador in Paris, sounded out Marcel Olivier, France's governor-general of Madagascar, on that island's availability as a haven for substantial numbers of Polish Jews. The response, equally informal, was courteously negative.

Ten years later, Poland's Foreign Minister Beck returned to the Madagascar proposal, this time in discussions with France's Prime Minister Léon Blum. Voicing no objection in principle, Blum referred the query to his colonial minister, Marius Mouter. Mouter in turn cautiously acknowledged that a limited immigration might be feasible, provided others could supply the necessary funding. Whereupon, in May 1937, with Mouter's approval, the Polish government dispatched a commission of Polish and Jewish experts to Madagascar, led by Major Mieczyslaw Lepecki, president of the International Colonization Society, and including Solomon Dyk, a Jewish agricultural engineer then living in Tel Aviv, and Leon Alter, executive-director of the Polish branch of the Joint.

The Lepecki Commission spent thirteen weeks evaluating Madagascar's absorptive capacities. Although Lepecki himself expressed mild optimism on the island's potential, the two Jewish members evidently were less impressed. Tropical diseases and native opposition struck them as insurmountable barriers. Whether or not the commission report actually was completed, it was never published. Yet, by late 1939, the Polish government had forged on to establish three new emigration bodies. These were the Committee for the Promotion of Jewish Pioneering and Colonization in Madagascar and Kenya; the Committee for Promoting [Jewish] Emigration to Africa and Australia; and the Committee for Jewish Colonization. The first two groups were chaired by Poles, the third by a Jew, Professor Moses Schorr. The committees had scarcely begun their discussions before the outbreak of World War II.

In any case, the Warsaw government always had taken a much keener interest in Palestine, a site that offered the advantage of its "official" designation as a Jewish National Home. In the 1920s and 1930s, Pilsudski himself expressed a warm sympathy for Zionism, presumably not least for its emigrationist usefulness. For the same reason, other Polish leaders often had cooperated with the Zionist leadership. As far back as March 1926, Prime Minister Aleksander Skrzynski wrote the veteran Zionist diplomat Nahum Sokolow: "The Polish Government is following with interest the progress made by the Zionist Organization in its effort to resurrect the national individuality and culture of the Jews in Palestine." And in 1929, Poland concluded an agreement with the Executive of the Jewish Agency, the Jewish quasi-government in Palestine, to facilitate money transfers for emigrants to the Holy Land.

Similarly, the Polish government became a consistent supporter of Jewish diplomatic claims to Palestine. In 1933, the right-wing Zionist leader, Vladimir Jabotinsky, was permitted to broadcast Zionist appeals on Polish state radio. From 1936 on, Jabotinsky held several meetings with Foreign Minister Beck. In lengthy and exceptionally cordial discussions, both men sought ways to encourage widespread Jewish departure for Palestine. For his part, Beck repeatedly entreated the British government to admit a larger number of Jews into Palestine. His appeals were unavailing, of course. In May 1939, the British Colonial Office issued its White Paper on Palestine, a policy declaration that in effect barred future Jewish immigration to the Jewish National Home.

It is of interest, too, that the mainstream Zionist leadership had always condemned the Beck-Jabotinsky negotiations. The cause of Jewish emigration, they insisted, should not be allowed to compromise the legitimate rights of Jews in Poland. Indeed, years before, they had won that assurance from Pilsudski himself (p. 24). Yet the OZON government was a different animal. It had baldly proclaimed its focus on emigration beyond all other solutions to the Jewish question. And Jabotinsky, fixated on the achievement of a Jewish state in Palestine, would not say the Polish government nay.

By the early 1930s, at least one other prominent Zionist had reached the conclusion that his people's future no longer could be salvaged in Poland. Like Jabotinsky, Yitzhak Grunebaum discerned certain "objective" causes of antisemitism. Some of these related to the history and sociology of the host nations. But at least one acknowledged the anomalous social and economic structure of Polish Jewry (a charge that so offended Grunebaum's followers that in 1931 they dropped him as chairman of the General Zionist party). And even that structure, Grunebaum intimated, was the unavoidable consequence of minority status in an irredeemably chauvinist successor state.

Like Jabotinsky, Grunebaum already had made his commitment to another land. Although still a member of the Sejm, in 1933 he emigrated to Paris, then went on to Palestine, where he accepted a position in the Executive of the Jewish Agency. Intermittently, to be sure, Grunebaum paid return visits to Poland, where he still carried weight among his former disciples. Otherwise, he remained in the Jewish Homeland, a white-haired eminence of somewhat diminished political vitality. When the State of Israel was established in 1948, Grunebaum became its first minister of the interior. His mandate was immigration. By then, however, his "clients" were the meagerest remnant of the people to whom he had devoted a lifetime of heroic but ultimately futile rearguard struggle.

IV

HOSTAGES OF "LATIN" CIVILIZATION

The Wages of Peculation

Among admirers and detractors alike, he was known as "the Sphinx." Ioan—"Ionel"—Bratianu, chairman of Rumania's powerful National Liberal party, dominated his nation's political life throughout the first quarter of the twentieth century. In 1878 Bratianu's father, Ion, had played a decisive role in transforming the Danubian principalities of Wallachia and Moldavia into the Kingdom of Rumania, and in selecting Prince Carol, a member of the Hohenzollern-Sigmaringen dynasty, as the nation's first monarch. Yet Ionel Bratianu, eldest of the kingmaker's three sons, surpassed his father in sheer manipulative genius. Even among a people frequently execrated for their Ottoman legacy of deviousness, Ionel Bratianu gained a foxlike reputation for political cunning.

Personal charisma only added to the younger Bratianu's arsenal of weapons. Well into middle age, he was an impressive figure of a man, with brown eyes blazing in a leonine head adorned with curly, silvery hair and a carefully trimmed Vandyke beard. A charming conversationalist and something of a womanizer, Bratianu had married twice, and both times expediently. His second wife, Elise Stirbei, was well connected. She had herself been married earlier to one of Bratianu's major political rivals, and her personal wealth and extensive social contacts among the upper gentry only fortified Bratianu's "noble" lineage as a boyar, a landowning aristocrat.

Born in 1864, Ionel Bratianu was trained as an engineer, but chose to continue his family's political vocation by winning election to the Chamber of Deputies in 1895. As heir apparent in the dominant middle-class National Liberal party, he rose swiftly through a succession of cabinet posts, becoming foreign minister in 1901, minister of the interior in 1907, and prime minister in 1909, the year he was elected chairman of the National Liberals. If by then the party had become a Bratianu fiefdom, so had much of the kingdom itself. Ionel Bratianu vastly increased the considerable wealth he inherited from his father. Through brazen influence-peddling, he laid his hands on much of Rumania's extensive natural resources in timber and oil. No stigma attached to him on this account. Among Rumanians, he simply evoked admiration as a master of his craft.

Yet it was in his wartime diplomacy that Bratianu's opportunism became most dramatically evident. As late as July 1914, Rumania was a "junior" member of the Triple Alliance, linked to Germany, Austria-Hungary, and Italy. The connection reflected the logic of the European chessboard. Rumania depended on Great Power support for its irredentist claims on 2.4 million ethnic Rumanians living in Hungarian Transylvania, in Bukovina, the Banat of Temesvar, the Dobrudja, and other sectors of the Habsburg Empire; for the half-million scattered through Bulgaria and elsewhere in the Balkans, and most important, for the 3 million living in tsarist Bessarabia. With its prewar population of 7 million, Rumania was too weak to liberate these kinsmen on its own. A link with the German-speaking Powers appeared to be the most promising strategy for achieving "unification."

Once hostilities began in 1914, however, Bratianu and the Liberals opposed a precipitous move into war. Instead, during the ensuing two years, the prime minister characteristically played each set of belligerents against the other "like a pedlar in an Oriental bazaar," contemptuously recalled French Foreign Minister Paul Cambon. In the end, it was not the Central Powers but the Entente that came up with an unrefusable offer. Under the terms of the Treaty of Bucharest, signed in August 1916, Rumania would declare war on the Habsburg Empire; sever diplomatic relations with Germany, Bulgaria, and Turkey; and at all costs refrain from concluding a separate peace. In return, the Allies would support Rumania's territorial annexation of Habsburg Transylvania and Bukovina, assure expanded autonomy for the Rumanians of tsarist Bessarabia, and award Rumania Great Power status at a future peace conference. It was an impressive coup for a third-rate Balkan backwater.

Considerably less impressive was the nation's military performance. The moment Bratianu's government declared war on Habsburg Austria and prepared to move against that empire's eastern frontiers, it faced the army of Austria's mighty German partner; and in the autumn of 1916, the German Reichswehr launched a counteroffensive that effectively destroyed the hapless Rumanian expeditionary force. Indeed, by December 1916, half of integral Rumania, including its capital, Bucharest, was in enemy hands. In ensuing months, then, and in disregard of his treaty obligations to the Allies, Bratianu conducted formal peace discussions with the Central Powers. And here again the wily Rumanian leader made the best of a bad bargain. Although he was obliged to accept a virtual satellite status for his country under Austrian and German hegemony, Bratianu in March

1918 also managed to wheedle a substantial territorial concession from the Central Powers, this one at the expense of Bolshevik Russia. It was the province of Bessarabia.

Then, in the summer of 1918, with the United States fully engaged in the war, the Western democracies seemed poised at last to turn the military tide. Would the Allies forgive Rumania its recent sellout to the enemy? Apparently they would. With Bratianu only too eager once again to betray his German and Austrian overlords, France's Prime Minister Clemenceau urged his partners to allow Rumania to reenter the war as an Allied "cobelligerent." In September 1918, they agreed. Hereupon, Bratianu immediately set about pressing his nation's territorial demands as if it had been a key partner in the unfolding Allied victory.

Breaking and Entering at Paris

The posture was repugnant to the Western leaders, even to Clemenceau. Before Bratianu could present Rumania's case at the Paris Peace Conference, he was kept cooling his heels until January 31, 1919. Even then, the prime minister's avariciousness served only to alienate the Western statesmen. He brazenly presented them with a territorial fait accompli. In the weeks since the collapse of the Central Powers, Rumania's army had crossed into all the regions—Transylvania, Bessarabia, the Banat, and Bukovina—that the Allies initially had promised in the original 1916 Treaty of Bucharest. Bratianu described the move simply as a response to "demonstrations for union" by the local Rumanian populations. Lloyd George and Clemenceau were not having it. Unless Rumanian troops were promptly evacuated, they warned, military force would be employed against them. Bratianu remained adamant. In a tense meeting with the Western leaders, he insisted that Hungary's agitation "along Bolshevik lines" necessitated the presence of Rumanian troops to protect southeastern Europe against "a serious and contagious disease."

Once again, the wily prime minister had found his interlocutors' soft spot. By early spring of 1919, Bela Kun's Communist regime in Hungary (pp. 110–11), and the threat of Bolshevism elsewhere in Central Europe, weighed increasingly heavily on the Allied statesmen. Responding to the transformed diplomatic climate, Clemenceau then muted his objections to Rumania's "preemptive" moves. In April 1919, Bratianu was able to ensconce his troops even more deeply in the neighboring territories, until they occupied almost the entirety of Transylvania and Bessarabia.

Then, on August 2, 1919, Hungary's Communist government collapsed. Bratianu hereupon lost his pretext of guarding Central Europe against "Bolshevism." With sublime effrontery, nevertheless, the Rumanian prime minister continued to stake his territorial case on wartime treaty promises, and even sent his army directly into Budapest. For the ensuing months of the Peace Conference, Bratianu fended off all Allied demands to withdraw his occupying forces. And once again, sheer gall paid off. By late 1919, conceding the possible ongoing usefulness of an anti-Bolshevik "cordon sanitaire" in Central-East Europe, the Allied leaders grudgingly acquiesced in the full spectrum of Bratianu's territorial demands. Only then, in mid-November, did the Rumanian prime minister order his troops out of Budapest. Three weeks later, on December 9, 1919, as Bratianu affixed his signature to the Austrian and Hungarian peace treaties, his Rumanian "Old Kingdom" added to its demesne the neighboring territories of Bessarabia, Transylvania, Bukovina, the Dobrudja, and most of the Banat, together with their vast natural resources. A prewar state of 80,000 square miles and a population of 7.2 million now encompassed 176,000 square miles and a population of 16.6 million.

The demographic revolution was also an ethnic one. The Old Kingdom's population had been 92 percent Rumanian, with a shared language that could be traced back to the territory's status as Dacia, a colony of the ancient Roman Empire. The annexed provinces now brought with them some 4.5 million inhabitants whose origins were distinctly non-Latin. The largest minority consisted of 1.9 million Hungarians. Other populations included 1.1 million Ukrainians, 340,000 Germans, 290,000 Bulgars, 200,000 Turks, Great Russians, and Gypsies—and fully 760,000 Jews. As in the case of Poland, it was the metamorphosis of an essentially homogeneous population into a complex mosaic of racial, cultural, and linguistic ethnicities that would determine both the state's future diplomacy and much of its domestic politics.

A Jewish Legacy

During the half century before 1914, the circumstances of the 280,000 Jews living in Rumania's Old Kingdom were not significantly less precarious than in tsarist Russia. On the one hand, a small number of Jews had become influential business and professional men. Jews owned several of Bucharest's largest newspapers, and two of its important banks. In the cities, Jews all but monopolized the practice of law, medicine, and dentistry. They found time as well to maintain a vibrant Jewish culture. In addition to hundreds of synagogues and scores of venerated rabbis, Rumanian Jews nurtured Europe's first permanent Yiddish theater and one of its earliest and most powerful Zionist movements. If the quality of their intellectual life was less evolved than that of their kinsmen in Central and West European countries, Jews as Rumania's quintessential liberal professionals contributed significantly to the nation's cultural and artistic life. The author of the first Rumanian grammar, the compiler of the first Rumanian dictionary, and several of the country's outstanding writers and composers were Jews.

Yet this protean minority hardly was typical of the Old Kingdom's wider Jewish population. Most Rumanian Jews were refugees, or the children of refugees, who had fled the tsarist Pale of Settlement in the late nineteenth century. A majority of the newcomers settled in the villages and smaller towns of the border province of Moldavia, where they subsisted as proprietors of tiny market stalls. Thoroughly parochial, isolated in their Yiddish-speaking culture, they were feared and reviled by the surrounding peasant population as infidels, aliens, economic leeches. The Rumanian government for its part wasted little time in marginalizing this unwelcome Jewish minority. It barred from citizenship all but a small economic elite, tightly limited their property rights, restricted their access to the law courts for commercial or even for elementary physical security. Jews henceforth remained at the caprice of local officials, who extorted them often to within an inch of their lives, and only intermittently protected them from local assaults and pillage.

It was the 1878 Congress of Berlin, following the Russo-Turkish War, that offered the little people their first glimmer of hope. As the assembled European diplomats turned their attention to the reconstruction of the Balkans, the Rumanians sought full and formal recognition of their national sovereignty. In turn, the powerful Jewish banking families of Bleichröder and Rothschild discreetly suggested to the Congress's central figures, Bismarck and Disraeli, that the quid pro quo for that recognition should be guaranteed equal rights for Rumanian Jewry. The statesmen agreed, and the Rumanians were obliged to acquiesce. Thus, Article 44 of the Treaty of Berlin proclaimed that religious differences no longer would bar individuals from "the enjoyment of civil and political rights, admission to public employment, functions, and honors, or the exercise of the various professions and industries in any locality whatsoever." But only a year later, the Rumanians characteristically "redefined" that commitment. Under Article 7 of their new constitution, non-citizens might be naturalized only by vote of both houses of Parliament. In the ensuing decades before 1914, among the scores of thousands of Jewish applications for citizenship, a grand total of 361 were approved.

Indeed, the mantle of disabilities was significantly enlarged. Lacking political or civil rights, Jews could gain entrance to merchant or professional "guilds," or purchase homes or other real property, only through the well familiar practice of bribing local officials. Popular antisemitism meanwhile reflected the nation's seething nationalist irredentism. In the last years before 1914, antisemitism penetrated every echelon of Rumanian society, and became something of a European scandal. In France, Georges Clemenceau publicly condemned Rumanian behavior as "une monstrosité au point de vue international," and added in a private letter to Luigi Luzzatti, an Italian Jewish former prime minister, that "Rumanian Jews are the last serfs still existing in Europe."

In Rumania as elsewhere in Eastern Europe, the Great War generated a renewed frenzy of xenophobia. A military staff order of August 1916 declared that "[a]ll Jews must be placed in the front line at the beginning of an attack." Another, of the same period, warned:

> Jews cannot be tolerated in the hospitals for wounded or sick. There must be no humanitarian feelings or sentimentality displayed toward them. It has been proved that, approaching our wounded with a mask of pity and the innocence of boy scouts, [Jews] are in fact spies.

Although there were no Russian-style mass evacuations, Jews were exposed to random pogroms, to widespread governmental confiscation of food and chattels, and to bouts of forced labor.

As in Poland and the Ukraine, it was German military occupation that offered a brief respite. Importuned by German-Jewish communal leaders, the military administration obliged Rumania's rubber-stamp parliament to bestow citizenship on all Jews who had been born or were domiciled in the country, or who had served in the army. But the concession was essentially toothless. It offered nothing to tens of thousands of Jews in Russian Bessarabia, who already had won equality from the Bolshevik government, and who now were to be annexed to Rumania (p. 73); or to the tens of thousands of Jewish refugees who had been flooding in from the war zones of Galicia and Podolia. In any case, soon after Germany and Austria surrendered, the puppet legislature was dissolved, and the Bratianu government wasted little time nullifying all the laws enacted by the Central Powers. For Jews, the single hope of meaningful emancipation would lie with the Western Allies, at the impending Peace Conference.

Others of Rumania's new heterogeneity of annexed minorities similarly awaited protection, among them Transylvania's sizeable enclave of 1.9 million Hungarians. But the Jews, their numbers swollen to 760,000—two-thirds of them also living in the newly "appropriated" regions, and constituting Rumania's third-largest minority—well understood the historic uniqueness of their vulnerability. So did Wolf, Bigart, Marshall, Luzzatti, and other Western Jewish spokesmen. Experienced intercessors, they now regarded it as indispensable that Rumanian territorial claims be linked to a definitive and foolproof minorities treaty. Thus, in Washington, during a lengthy interview with Secretary of State Robert Lansing on

November 25, 1918, Louis Marshall cited chapter and verse of Bucharest's unsavory record on the Jews. Did not the impending Peace Conference offer a matchless opportunity, he asked, to impose an "iron-clad obligation on Rumania . . . in terms which cannot be evaded?" The argument registered on Lansing, as it did on Wilson, Lloyd George, and Clemenceau. Indeed, once committed to the principle of minorities treaties, the Allied statesmen were prepared to force the issue with the detested Rumanians even more unrelentingly than with the Poles.

But on the status of the Jews, as on territorial questions, the Western leaders were dealing with the guileful Bratianu. Surpassing his father, Ion, who had openly and flagrantly circumvented the "Jewish" provisions of the original 1878 Treaty of Berlin, the younger Bratianu exploited his own, even more resourceful bag of evasions and obfuscations. In December 1918, he issued a preemptive "decree," ostensibly extending blanket citizenship to Rumanian Jewry. The edict was a fake. The prime minister ensured that its naturalization provisions were limited exclusively to those Jews who could prove that they had been born in the Old Kingdom and had never been subjects of another government.

The Allied leaders were not taken in. Their warnings to Bratianu were stiff. Accordingly, in May 1919, elusive as an eel, the prime minister adopted yet another stratagem. The new provision admitted to citizenship all Jews who simply filed a declaration affirming that they had been born in Rumania and owed allegiance to no other country. And this maneuver, too, was a hoax. As Wolf and Bigart noted, it required that all applications be approved by the Rumanian judiciary, a process that would mire naturalization efforts in the courts as interminably as in the prewar era. Concurring, the Western statesmen rejected Bratianu's "qualifications" out of hand.

In late May, finally, sensing that he was cornered, the Rumanian leader shifted his approach 180 degrees. Taking the offensive, he launched into an indignant denunciation of the very notion of a minorities treaty. The Allies were attempting to "segregate" nations into various categories of sovereignty, he insisted, and were palpably infringing upon Rumanian honor and dignity. Therefore, he, Bratianu, would sign such a document only if all the major European Powers made the identical commitment. It was Woodrow Wilson then who provided the Allied response to Bratanu's cri de coeur. In an open letter to the Rumanian prime minister three days later, Wilson observed that Western military sacrifices alone had made possible Rumania's territorial enlargement. There could be no guarantee for that settlement if such "disturbing elements" as the oppression of minorities remained to threaten the peace. The president's reply was a useful debating point. Could it be translated into a binding Rumanian commitment?

In June 1919, the Poles were the first to sign the prototype minorities treaty. The Rumanians managed to hold out much longer, and not without result. Although the communal-autonomist features of the Polish treaty all duly appeared in the Rumanian version, the "compromise" document Bratianu eventually accepted, on December 9, 1919, contained neither of the Polish treaty's two "Jewish articles." Its one specifically "Jewish" reference, Article 7, provided only that "Rumania undertakes to recognize as Rumanian nationals ipso facto, and without the requirement of any formality, Jews inhabiting any Rumanian territory, who do not possess another nationality." Upon ratifying the document, to be sure, the Rumanian parliament formally incorporated its principal articles into its 1923 constitution. Nevertheless, from beginning to end, and more flagrantly even than in the case of the Poles, the Rumanians would sabotage their minorities commitment both in letter and spirit.

Postwar Realities, Rumanian-Style

As Rumania entered the postwar era, its amplitude extended well beyond the vast enlargement of its territory and population. The country now was all but awash in new resources: in dense, alluvial topsoil and a luxuriance of forests; in a subterranean cornucopia of oil, iron, coal, lead, zinc, copper, mercury, bauxite, aluminum, salt, and graphite. Yet, for all its largesse, the inheritance would devolve essentially into the hands of Rumania's economic and political elite. As elsewhere in the Balkans, the peasants, comprising the overwhelming majority of the nation's population, barely eked out a subsistence as tenant farmers or as proprietors of dysfunctional miniplots. Even as Rumania vegetated as a rural poorhouse, however, cursed by excess population, illiteracy, and low productivity, its outpouring of surplus agricultural labor to the cities produced a sure and certain recipe for political unrest.

In the early postwar years, each of the nation's parties, not excluding the Socialists, accused "foreign elements" of dominating the country's economic life. There was some truth in the charge. Throughout the 1920s, at least 70 percent of Rumanian capital investment was provided by ethnic non-Rumanians, essentially in the annexed provinces. Among these "foreigners," Hungarians and Germans maintained their former preeminence in the oil and banking sectors, and accordingly became choice targets for political retaliation. Ignoring its treaty obligations, Bucharest denied funding to Hungarian- and German-language schools, imposed punitive taxes on Hungarian and German businesses, and inflicted administrative "corrections" that all but squeezed non-Rumanians out of the civil service.

None of the ethnic minorities, however, was persecuted as brutally as the Jews, or demonized as the principal source of the nation's manifold economic ills. But none other was as uniquely "infidel," urban, or mercantile a presence among a devoutly religious and overwhelmingly agrarian population. Jew-hatred plainly had been endemic to the Old Kingdom long before the war. After 1918, however, Rumanian chauvinism focused on the dense Jewish populations in the annexed territories with a revived and unique malevolence. In Bessarabia, with its exotically pietistic Chasidic communities, popular revulsion exacerbated culture shock. In Transylvania and Bukovina, whose middle-class Jewish enclaves traditionally had functioned as extensions of German culture, antisemitism evinced the regions' long-suppurating Rumanian irredentism. Thus, any Western illusions that the minorities treaty would be honored toward the Jews, of all peoples, were almost instantly dispelled. As Foreign Minister Alexandru Voievod murmured to an aide, upon signing the treaty in December 1919: "The Allies have written the treaties, but we Rumanians will know how to interpret them."

Ironically, when the "citizenship" articles of the document were incorporated into the new Rumanian constitution, on March 29, 1923, several prominent Jewish spokesmen were heartened by the development. Adolphe Stern, scion of a veteran Rumanian Jewish family and a member of the national parliament, waxed jubilant as he wrote the Italian Jewish statesman Luigi Luzzatti: "Dear Master and Friend: I am performing a duty to you, noble champion of religious freedom, and eloquent defender of the Jews in Rumania, in communicating . . . the news that those whom you called 'the last slaves of Europe' are finally free! And . . . the very government of Bratianu, whose party has created and fed on the 'Jewish question' in Rumania for half a century, has done the job!"

The "job" Bratianu had accomplished, however, was far from the one Stern apotheosized. As in the case of earlier false commitments, the constitution's citizenship provisions were interpreted exclusively on behalf of "veteran" Jewish inhabitants of the former Old Kingdom regions. The far more numerous Jewish populations of the annexed territories would again have to achieve their naturalization through special legislation. Scores of thousands of Jews who believed that they had automatically become Rumanian citizens now found themselves to limbo once more. In February 1924, under heavy Western pressure, the Rumanian parliament agreed to enact a "liberalized" naturalization bill. Yet, even in its modified version, the law required "proof" of residence for ten years prior to December 9, 1919, the date when the minorities treaty was signed. That "proof," often in the form of testimony by Rumanian officials or neighbors, did not come cheap.

In the spring and summer of 1924, an investigative commission sponsored by the "American Committee on the Rights of Religious Minorities," an ad hoc Jewish "front" organization, affirmed that some thirty thousand Jewish families in annexed Bukovina alone lacked naturalization, and scores of thousands of others scattered through Bessarabia and Transylvania similarly remained without a country and without passports. Living in a juridical no-man's-land, these noncitizens were barred from registering their children in public schools, from negotiating business contracts, even from owning land in their own names. Subject to eviction at any moment, they paid off local Rumanian police officials simply to remain where they were—as squatters. The committee noted, too, that the cultural-autonomist provisions of the minorities treaty were neither evaded nor subverted. They were simply ignored. Even in the schools funded by Jews themselves—the great majority—government accreditation was limited to schools providing instruction in the Rumanian language.

Economic discrimination was as integral a feature of Rumanian policy as juridical delegitimation. In December 1919, the government dismissed all former Habsburg civil servants in Transylvania in favor of ethnic Rumanians. Income taxes throughout the entire country were assessed on a graduated basis, the lowest rate to be paid by ethnic Rumanians, the highest by non-Rumanians in the annexed territories. These measures by and large did not distinguish between the various minority peoples, whether Hungarians, Germans, Ukrainians, or Jews. The Sunday closing laws did. So did yet another innovation, the characteristic successor-state program of etatism—state capitalism. Once the government set about nationalizing match, tobacco, salt, and liquor production, the Jews who formerly predominated in these fields were summarily dismissed.

Was there a political lifeline for this beleaguered subcommunity? Unlike Polish Jewry, with its centuries-old tradition of communal self-government, the Jews of Rumania were a comparatively recent population. In the Old Kingdom, as fugitives from tsarist Russia, they had enjoyed little opportunity to develop their own, indigenous political traditions. Indeed, the opposite was the case. Eager to achieve political equality, Jews in prewar Rumania had made a conscious effort to work through existing Rumanian political parties, even to cooperate with Bratianu's National Liberals. By contrast, the Jews of the annexed regions—of Transylvania, Bukovina, the Banat, and Bessarabia—represented a politically unknown commodity. Newly fallen under Rumanian domination, they remained a world unto themselves in their communal, linguistic, and cultural institutions. Thus, the Jews of Transylvania continued to use the Hungarian language; those in Bukovina, the German language; while in Bessarabia, Jewish private and public activities were conducted almost exclusively in Yiddish.

In 1919, therefore, leaders of the Union of Rumanian Jews, organ of the acculturated Jewish establishment, pressed their recently annexed kinsmen to maintain the veterans' prewar tradition of voting for existing Rumanian parties. And the Jews of the new provinces, in their vulnerability and insecurity, were prepared to adopt these guidelines. Yet it availed them little. In parliamentary elections later that same year, none of the Rumanian parties took a favorable stance on the Jewish question. With some chagrin, therefore, the Union reversed itself at the last moment and recommended simply that Jews withhold their votes entirely. This they did. Moreover, in 1920, facing the implacable hostility of the government, the Union itself was tempted to join with the powerful Zionist movement in structuring a single Jewish list of candidates for new elections. The experiment foundered. Not a single Jew was returned to Parliament. For the time being, then, the Union reverted to its traditional position of cultivating individual Rumanian parties.

Not so the much larger Jewish population of the annexed territories. In their frustration and bitterness, they ignored the Union's guidelines and set about organizing a "National Jewish" party. In 1928, four of the fledgling party's candidates actually managed to win seats in Parliament. Almost immediately, these delegates set about emulating their kinsmen in the Polish Sejm by organizing themselves into a Jewish kolo. In 1930, moreover, responding to an upsurge of antisemitic violence, Jews even in the Old Kingdom agreed to organize a forthrightly Zionist "Jewish party" (Partidul Evreesc). Under the party's aegis, the number of Jewish representation in Parliament modestly increased—to five delegates in the elections of both 1931 and 1932. Yet their lot was not easy, particularly in the enveloping racism of the depression era (pp. 90–96). When they attempted to address the Chamber, they faced a barrage of hoots and threats, even occasional physical assaults. After 1933, in any case, as Rumania turned increasingly Fascist (pp. 92–93), not a single Jew ever again was elected to Parliament.

The Foundations of Political Racism

In its nineteenth-century gestation, romantic nationalism in the Balkans oscillated between political liberalism and reactionary ethnicity. For the Rumanians, the orientation was never in doubt. Invoking the mythos of a common "Latin" ancestry, even the nation's more progressive intellectuals tended to characterize minorities such as Greeks, Jews, and assorted varieties of Slavs as threats to the nation's cultural homogeneity, and thereby to its future economic and political independence. From 1870 on, moreover, with the growing influx of Russian Jewish refugees, the basis already was being laid for a virulent political Jew-hatred.

The animus was shared by Rumanians of all backgrounds, from peasants who drew their imagery from medieval stereotypes of Jews as deicides, to white-collar employees whose economic insecurities and nationalist irredentism focused on Jews as "bloodsuckers" and perennial aliens. "Antisemitism in Rumania is more than just an idea," French Ambassador André Henry reported to Paris at the turn of the century. "It is a passion common to politicians of all parties, to the Orthodox Church, to all the peasants." It was a passion, too, that later would be aroused and all but institutionalized by Rumania's postwar territorial enlargement, by the tripling of its Jewish population, and by the identification of Jews with Russia's Bolshevik Revolution. The minorities treaty succeeded only in compounding these raging emotions.

In Rumania, as elsewhere in Europe, it was the intellectuals who emerged as the standard-bearers of antisemitism. In the nineteenth century, their ideologues included several of the nation's most prestigious cultural figures, among them the writers Vasile Aleksandi, Ioan Slavici, and Mihail Eminescu. Yet, by the twentieth century, Nicolae Iorga won widest recognition as spokesman for the new racist doctrines circulating in Germany, Austria, and France. A professor of Rumanian history at the University of Bucharest, and a prolific author of scholarly books and articles, Iorga was the founding president of several important Rumanian cultural institutions and societies. With the poet Octavian Goga, he was also a cofounder in 1909 of the right-wing Democratic Nationalist party—LANC (from its Rumanian acronym)—and in the postwar years he went on to serve in Parliament, then as a government minister, and even briefly as prime minister (p. 94).

In these multiple roles, Iorga refined his concept of a national "mystique" as an amalgam of the countryside's romanticized folk values. It was a mythologization he shared with other nationalist prophets, with Goga and Mihail Eminescu, and with France's Edouard Drumont and Charles Maurras (pp. 288–89). Like each of these apotheosists of nostalgia, Iorga made much of the threat posed by non-Rumanians to the nation's rustic "purity." No populist rabble-rouser, he rejected all appeals to violence. Neither did he focus his animus exclusively on the Jews. Iorga's preference simply was for a gradual, peaceful removal of all "alien" elements from key sectors of Rumanian life.

Rather, it was another academician, Alexandru Cuza, who ensured that Rumanian xenophobia concentrated specifically on the Jews. A professor of political economy at the University of Jassy, Cuza in his best-known work, *Nationality in the Arts* (1908), made the case that Jews, "as strangers belonging to another race, having different laws and [alien] cultural principles," should be purged from the nation's press, theater, music, and literature, and from all the major sectors of Rumania's economic life. Indeed, Cuza went much further than Iorga not only in singling out the Jews but in mobilizing against them the new Central European terminology of racism. For him, "the Jews had as their father the Devil, 'the slayer of men and the father of lies.' "

In the early postwar era, moreover, the professor updated his anti-Jewish crusade, relating it to new political circumstances, stigmatizing Jews as traitors, spies, Bolsheviks. Vigorously supporting the numerus clausus in universities and professional societies, Cuza insisted that even an anti-Jewish quota should be regarded merely as "a form of transition to the next, logical, and definitive phase: the numerus nullus." By the early 1920s, projecting himself as the high priest of Rumanian intellectual anti-semitism, Cuza decided that "the only feasible solution of the Jewish question is the elimination of the *yids*, which implies immediate action, in all fields . . . on the basis of a clear program designed for this necessity." The declamation resonated widely throughout the country. Moreover, Cuza, like Iorga, was no "mere" intellectual. In 1922, as a charter founder with Iorga and Goga of the racist LANC, he served both as a parliamentary delegate and as president of Rumania's Chamber of Deputies.

Yet, even Cuza began falling behind the times. By the latter 1920s, some of his younger followers, attracted to the dynamism of Italy's Benito Mussolini, preferred to transfer their allegiance from a "philosophic old gentleman" to a more activist and dynamic leader. In Corneliu Zelea Codreanu they found their man.

The Emergence of Fascist Populism

Born in Husi, a town in northern Moldavia, Codreanu was a hybrid. His mother was a Swabian German. His father, a prewar immigrant from Bukovina, at first bore the unmistakably Polish name of Zelinski. Determined to be more Catholic than the Pope, however, Zelinski-Codreanu became a passionate disciple of Alexandru Cuza and transmitted his nationalist fervor to his own son. Thus, when the war began, the seventeen-year-old Corneliu Codreanu abandoned his studies for the Orthodox priesthood to seek acceptance into his father's regiment. Underage, he was sent home. Before he could reapply on his eighteenth birthday, the Germans knocked Rumania out of the war. In 1919, with the Soviet Red Army threatening to return to Bessarabia, young Codreanu gathered several friends around him to prepare at last for battle. Again, none developed.

Only then did Codreanu proceed on to the Moldavian district capital of Jassy, enrolling at the local university to study law. There too he was swept

up in a particularly virulent new wave of antisemitism. One impulsion was
the opportunity at last to vent his raging nationalism. Another was the discovery in Jassy of thousands of "new" refugee Jews, most of them spilling
over from war-torn Bessarabia. And still another was Codreanu's exposure
to the single-minded Jew-hatred of the renowned Professor Cuza. Here at
last, the young man discovered his guru—and his raison d'être. He had
already given serious thought to the threat of Bolshevism, and the need to
rescue his impoverished nation through an alternative variety of "Christian" populism. To this redemptionist vision, he could now link Cuza's
favored strategy. It was to save Rumania's "soul" by purging the country of
its vast new Jewish population. Thus, in 1922, when the aging Cuza
assigned him the task of organizing LANC's student groups, Codreanu
eagerly accepted the challenge and swiftly put together an impressive network of youthful followers.

Codreanu may have been destined for the role of populist messiah. Tall,
handsome, eloquent, he captivated his listeners equally in conversation
or on the soapbox. Unapologetically, too, he cultivated their youthful
bloodlust, exhorting crowds of fellow students to intimidate their Jewish classmates, to hound them out of the lecture rooms by threat or by
actual violence. For young Codreanu, as for Professor Cuza, the Jewish
issue was one of evil against good, of atheistic Communism against the
unspoiled peasant, of Semitic alienism in a nation struggling to achieve
cultural homogeneity.

Within a matter of months, Codreanu's youth movement was given
an unanticipated stimulus. Early in 1923, Parliament approved the new
constitution, with its incorporated minorities treaty provisions (p. 79).
Infuriated by this "capitulation" to Western Jewish pressures, Codreanu
promptly drew up a list of deputies who had voted for the constitution, and
targeted them for murder. At the last moment, however, a police informant
divulged the plot. Codreanu and his fellow conspirators were arrested and
placed on trial. All but one of them were promptly acquitted. The single
exception was Ion Mota, a part-time law student, who had managed before
the trial to shoot the police informant dead. But in a second trial, even
Mota was acquitted. Immediately, Codreanu appointed Mota to lead an
elite shock unit of LANC, "The Brothers of the Cross." Aping Italy's new
Fascist duce, Benito Mussolini, the two young men "poeticized" death in
the cause of Christian nationalism:

> *Brother, do not fear*
> *That you will die too young,*
> *For you die to be reborn,*
> *And are born to die.*

The cult of mysticism also exerted a powerful attraction for a nation steeped in the traditions of Orthodox Christianity, even as appeals to "direct action" evoked a particularly eager response among "romantic" youth, among students and lumpenproletariat alike. Moreover, Codreanu did not hesitate to activate that "romanticism" by personal example. In 1923, when police dispersed one of his antisemitic demonstrations at the University of Jassy, he filed suit against the local police prefect, Manciu, for unwonted brutality. A court hearing exonerated Manciu. Enraged, Codreanu then took it upon himself to exact justice. He shot Manciu dead. For Rumania, the episode became a political turning point.

The government put Codreanu on trial. It was wasted effort. So inflamed was public fervor on behalf of the young messiah that the trial venue was shifted from Jassy to Turnu-Severin, at the far western side of the country. Yet even in Turnu-Severin, thousands of young men, wearing the LANC emblem, arrived from across the nation to demonstrate their support. And, once more, as in Mota's trial months earlier, the jury needed less than an hour to exonerate the defendant. Codreanu's trip back to Jassy subsequently burgeoned into a triumphant procession of over thirty thousand jubilant LANC partisans. The entourage was deluged with flowers from town to town.

For its part, the Bratianu government regarded the orgy of violence with mounting concern. If the mayhem continued, Rumania's already tarnished image and damaged credit rating would be further besmirched. Whereupon the minister of the interior sent word to Codreanu that it would be "safer" if the young man departed the country for an extended period. The death threat was barely veiled, and Codreanu then agreed to register for "postgraduate studies" at the University of Grenoble.

But only three years later, in 1926, fearing that his crusade would expire without him, Codreanu ventured a discreet return. The government was preoccupied by then with other political and economic difficulties (p. 90) and decided not to risk a confrontation with the LANC. Codreanu accordingly made his way home from France without incident and immediately reclaimed personal control over the populist movement. This time his agenda far transcended mere violence. With full support from the aged Cuza, the twenty-nine-year-old repatriate announced that he was acting on a "vision" he had experienced during his brief, earlier stint of imprisonment. The Archangel Michael had appeared to him and had enjoined him to guide the nation to moral resurrection.

To achieve that resurrection, Codreanu now set about organizing the "League of the Archangel Michael," a fellowship of patriots that would counteract Rumania's corruption and decay by hard work, discipline, and mutual loyalty. "Enough of politics, enough of talk," declaimed Codreanu.

"We want to build, from the smallest to the greatest . . . even villages, even cities, even a new Rumanian state." The response was instantaneous. Wearing the obligatory green shirts (signifying rural virtues), thousands of unemployed young men flocked to Codreanu's banner, eager to join him in a program that combined such unobjectionable public projects as road-building and hospital and school construction with the dynamic of the leadership principle, with military-style drills, public parades, and raucous demonstrations against the "Jewish menace."

As in earlier years, Codreanu envisaged his paramilitary legionnaires—soon to be known as the Iron Guard—as the nucleus of a revived political movement, "All for the Fatherland," that would transcend Cuza's original LANC faction. If there were few ideological differences between the two parties, "All for the Fatherland" had the advantage of Codreanu's personal leadership, a role he no longer was prepared to share with the aging Cuza. Indeed, the younger man wasted no time in moving to the offensive. In the 1928 national elections, his followers won an impressive 15 percent of the popular vote. Both as a party and as a paramilitary force, Codreanu's crusade apparently was emerging as a serious alternative to Rumania's established political alignments, even to its right-wing parties. By the late 1920s, it had burgeoned into a nakedly Fascist movement.

A Porous "Diplomatic Umbrella"

In Rumania no less than in Poland or in most of the other postwar successor states, the minorities treaty from the outset was honored mainly in the breach. Few of its provisions for communal-cultural autonomy ever materialized. In the case of Rumania, moreover, the minority crises that took priority for the Jews were visceral, survivalist ones of civil and political rights, of individual liberties, of plain and simple physical security. The status of Jewish students was revealing. It was specifically at the universities, the venue of Nicolae Iorga, Alexandru Cuza, and Corneliu Codreanu, that Jew-hatred achieved its most "focused" postwar virulence.

In the late teens and early 1920s, Rumanian students, even those without political affiliations, made a point of hounding their Jewish classmates out of their dormitories, forcing them into their own living quarters, then pressing—with eventual success—for an administrative numerus clausus that drastically limited the presence of Jewish students altogether. At the University of Bucharest, with a student enrollment of some 17,000, the number of Jews was reduced from 4,200 in 1920 to 1,500 by 1928. By 1928, too, the medical school, traditionally enrolling the largest number of Jews, no longer accepted a single Jewish applicant. Yet hardly less than the numerus clausus, it was physical intimidation that drastically reduced student enrollment. Encouraged unofficially by the ministry of the interior and frontally and flagrantly by Codreanu and his followers, "demonstrations" and physical beatings periodically drove Jews from attending classes, and from taking examinations.

Throughout the 1920s, Jewish communal leaders entreated the government for at least minimal compliance with the provisions of the minorities treaty, and the nation's own constitution. In this effort, no individual was more unflagging in his exertions than Wilhelm Filderman. A "veteran" of the Old Kingdom, the Bucharest-born Filderman had earned a doctorate in law at the Sorbonne in 1912 and then developed a flourishing practice in the Rumanian capital. With the outbreak of the war, volunteering for the army, he was one of the rare Jews granted officer status. In the early postwar period, as chairman of the Union of Rumanian Jews, Filderman maintained a dignity and courtliness in his meetings with government figures that won occasional reprieves from bureaucratic discrimination. Doubtless his contacts with Bratianu's Liberal party served him well in this effort. In 1927, Filderman won election to Parliament as a member of the Liberal list. It was likely that he could have achieved even higher personal status—and professional reward—had he accepted a role as the government's "show Jew." The notion did not cross his mind. Filderman's entire public life was devoted to his people's struggle for breathing room.

Yet, in the end, that struggle depended far more extensively on the help of outsiders. Once more it was Anglo-Jewry's Lucien Wolf who proved the key intermediary. In a respectful communication to Bucharest of October 1925, the Conjoint executive-secretary proposed a series of government measures against antisemitic hooliganism. The reply from Foreign Minister Ion Duca arrived several weeks later, via the Rumanian minister in London, Nicolae Titulescu. Its dissimulation was characteristic:

> The Roumanian Government [stated Duca] . . . intends to ensure to all the [religious communities] the free exercise of their religion and, while disapproving the outrages on this great and fundamental principle, our representatives will always take all the necessary measures to order that this principle shall be respected. . . . Mr. Wolf knows the sentiments which animate the Roumanian government.

Wolf knew them only too well. Nevertheless, he soldiered on, courteously expressing his personal goodwill, but urging Bucharest "to take some practical steps."

And then, in January 1927, after a particularly brutal series of attacks on Jewish university students, Wolf removed his gloves to address a sulfurous protest to Titulescu. Notwithstanding all Foreign Minister Duca's assurances, Wolf insisted, "during the last six months the agitators have redoubled their efforts against the Jews, applauded and encouraged by eminent politicians, professors, and other persons of authority." Here Wolf cited demands by Rumanian parliamentary deputies for a complete repudiation of the minorities treaty, for a total expulsion of Jews from the country and the sequestration of their property. From Paris, the following month, Jacques Bigart of the Alliance Israélite Universelle dispatched a near-identical complaint to Bucharest.

The Rumanian government briefly was given pause. In London, Titulescu felt obliged to enter into more extended discussions with Wolf. Nevertheless, in May 1927, the detailed response Titulescu conveyed from his country's new foreign minister, Ion Mitilineu, echoed an old refrain. It assured Wolf that these "unfortunate incidents" had "an absolutely local character and have been tendentiously exaggerated." "There have never been any pogroms in our country," the message continued, only "incidents and individual quarrels which the authorities have examined in an objective spirit, while taking . . . care that order should be respected by all." This time Wolf's counterresponse made no genuflection to diplomatic niceties. It was an extensively documented chronology of anti-Jewish outrages, most of these concentrated in the Transylvanian, Bessarabian, and Moldavian provinces. The account provided details of verbal incitements, of physical attacks in universities, in railroad stations, in the streets, acts of thuggery coupled with pillage and random vandalism—all encouraged variously by student groups, by paramilitary organizations, even by government and church officials, including the Rumanian Orthodox patriarch, Dr. Miron Cristea.

During the same years of the mid-1920s, Louis Marshall in New York maintained his own intercessory vigilance. In December 1925, it happened that Nicolae Titulescu had been selected to lead Rumania's "Debt-Funding Commission" to the United States. In his search for Wall Street loans, Titulescu well understood the importance of defusing American Jewish resentment. Eagerly, then, he accepted Louis Marshall's invitation to a luncheon with a blue-chip group of Jewish luminaries. At the gathering, the Rumanian diplomat launched into his familiar bland assurance that his nation's minorities had no cause for complaint, except for "isolated instances." Marshall was hard put to await the end of Titulescu's remarks before delivering a terse and uncompromising bill of indictment, a pungent recitation of Rumania's violations of its minorities treaty, the "hateful discriminations" meted out to Rumanian Jewry. Marshall concluded then by warning Titulescu in plainspoken language that, insofar as it was within the power of American Jewry, "Rumania cannot expect moral or financial credit in the United States." As the audience erupted into vigorous applause, Titulescu remained silent.

Nor was Marshall finished. In January 1926, he fired off an extended memorandum to Titulescu—who had returned to his post in London—amplifying his charges in graphic detail. At the same time, in contact with Rumanian Minister Cretianu in Washington, Marshall updated his documentation on the circumstances of Rumanian Jewry. Yet the renowned Jewish advocate possibly should have grasped by then that private diplomacy of any kind with Rumanian officialdom was bankrupt. At the Paris Peace Conference, Marshall, as the "father" of the minorities treaties, had lobbied earliest on to provide the League of Nations with an effective mechanism for treaty enforcement. But in 1925, he spent part of the summer in Geneva to evaluate the League Council's method of fulfilling this guarantee role. He found little cause for optimism.

As early as October 1920, the League Council had itself devised a cumbersome, two-stage procedure for dealing with minority grievances. The first established the minority's right of petition to the secretary-general of the League. Upon receipt of the bill of complaints, the secretary-general was obliged to notify the offending state, giving it opportunity to respond. Once that response was in hand, the secretary-general might then forward the original petition (and the ensuing correspondence) to the full League Council. Even this initial process could drag on for months. Afterward, in still another "filtering" stage, the petition would require a Council member's sponsorship for additional investigation. Then only could the secretary-general appoint a "committee of investigation," consisting of three other members of the Council. In turn, the committee's first objective was to resolve the dispute "amicably" through mediation. And this process, too, could devour additional months, and in any case might produce no success.

Was it possible for the Council of the League of Nations simply to bypass the committee and reach a decision on its own? Not likely. The Council was a political body, not a juridical one. With national priorities of their own, its members were uninterested in embarrassing a fellow state whose goodwill they might themselves require later. In the event of an impasse, the League Minorities Committee at best might forward the complaint for adjudication to the Permanent Court of International Justice at The Hague. But here, too, there was little assurance that the accused state would accept the Court's jurisdiction, let alone its judgments. Altogether, then, the League of Nations offered only a ziggurat of vexations for Europe's minority peoples.

Whatever their disillusionment, the Jews were further shaken by their lack of even a "surrogate" spokesman. The Germans in Eastern Europe had Berlin to speak out on their behalf; the Ukrainians had Moscow; the Hungarians had Budapest. Virtually all other minorities possessed the championship of neighboring "brother" states. The Jews had no one. During the entire interwar period, they ventured a bare two petitions to the League. One appeal, on behalf of Hungarian Jewry, in 1925, achieved no formal resolution (pp. 118–19). The other, on behalf of Jews in German Silesia, in 1933, achieved a four-year respite from the introduction of Nazi racial legislation. Yet that outcome was principally a consequence of the Polish-German Treaty of 1922, assuredly not the result of League action. By the mid-1920s, with most of the successor states fighting the minorities treaties tooth and nail, the Jews of East-Central Europe all but gave up on the League of Nations.

Hostages of Civil Struggle

In 1928, unable to cope with Rumania's stagnant economy, the once indestructible Ionel Bratianu resigned as prime minister. Succeeding his center-right National Liberal party was the faintly more progressive National Peasant faction, under the premiership of Iuliu Maniu. A rarity in his nation's politics, Maniu was an honest man. Upon taking office, he launched into a conscientious attempt to democratize the regime, even to address minority grievances. His effort was only incrementally successful. The obstacle did not lie only in the nation's suppurating racism, or even in the endemic venality of the Rumanian civil service. It could be attributed, as well, to the anomalous status of the Rumanian monarchy.

Crown Prince Carol, born in Rumania in 1899, was the first "native" member of his dynasty. Well-educated, cultivated, even hard-working, Carol might have developed into a productive and respected national talisman. It was not to be. The royal heir was financially avaricious, and prone as well to extensive philandering. Public opinion conceivably might have overlooked these seigneurial peccadilloes, until Carol took up with Elena Wolff. Known variously as Elena Lupescu or—more commonly—as Magda Lupescu, she was the daughter of a baptized Jewish father and a non-Jewish mother. In 1923, hopelessly smitten by the divine "Magda," Prince Carol divorced his wife, Princess Helen of Greece, to settle in with his femme fatale. Hereupon, under church and government pressure, Carol was obliged to renounce his succession to the throne and to live abroad. A regency was duly formed until Carol's young son, Prince Michael, should reach his majority. But early in 1928, following the death several months earlier of King Ferdinand I, the new Maniu government decided to bring Carol home, as a symbol of domestic stability. In June 1930, therefore, following two more years of extensive political negotiations, the royal exile was ushered back to Rumania, duly to be proclaimed King Carol II.

A problem soon developed. The restored monarch had assured Prime Minister Maniu that he would not bring his mistress with him. Yet no sooner had Carol returned than "Magda Lupescu" also mysteriously reappeared, taking up residence in a Bucharest villa near the royal palace. The public's reaction to this development was unaccommodating. Ugly rumors began circulating that no state contract could be signed without a payoff to "Duduia" (Magda Lupescu), the "Jewish female serpent." Prime Minister Maniu, who after two years in office had failed to resolve the paralyzing impact of the depression, proved equally incapable of dealing with Carol, who soon revealed his intention not simply to reign but to rule in the manner of the much admired Mussolini government in Italy. Before 1930 was out, the premier was maneuvered into resignation, a departure that in effect spelled finis to Rumania's postwar democratic experiment.

Over the next three years, Carol similarly forced the resignation of Maniu's rather nondescript successor, Gheorghe Mironescu; then of Nicolae Iorga, the "pioneering" right-wing xenophobe (by then too enfeebled by age and royal scrutiny to develop an innovative antisemitic program); then of the rather anodyne Alexandru Vaida-Voeved, who had briefly stood in for Bratianu back in 1919; then, in November 1933, of Ion Duca (p. 92). Tightly supervised by the king, none of these ministers succeeded in mitigating the impact of the depression. And none, surely, managed to assert his "constitutional" authority over the monarch. Rather, by 1933, it was the populist racists who emerged as Carol's most implacable enemies. More than any other element, these were the agglomeration of petit-bourgeois and lumpenproletarian unemployed who gravitated to Corneliu Codreanu's Iron Guard.

Since 1927, it is recalled, when they were known as the League of the Archangel Michael, these green-shirted messianists had combined public-works projects with raucous antisemitic demagoguery and physical hooliganism. Proclaiming the need for "moral and racial purification," Codreanu and his cohorts were particularly effective in gaining new recruits throughout the annexed territories. Their crudely racist demonstrations may have offended "respectable" society, but no police chief dared move against a vigilantist movement that thundered its patriotism so extravagantly and menacingly. With its work camps, its building projects of schools, churches, bridges, and clinics, the Iron Guard by the early 1930s had become virtually a state within a state. For Carol, that was its danger.

Nevertheless, the king at first contemplated harnessing the movement to his own authoritarian regime. Discreetly, he even funded a number of Iron Guard projects from the royal treasury. But two years into his restoration, Carol sensed that he had a bear by the tail, that the Iron Guards were distinctly uninterested in functioning within royal guidelines. Indeed, Codreanu's "All for the Fatherland" party was becoming an effective political force on its own, returning five delegates to the new parliament in the November 1933 elections. These were the circumstances in which Carol asked a Liberal politician, Ion Duca, an ex–foreign minister, to set up a government. The king's terms were plainspoken. He expected firm action against the Iron Guard. And Duca for his part was quite prepared to cooperate.

Thus, upon assuming office in October 1933, the new premier ordered the arrest of several prominent Iron Guards as "terrorists." By this act, Duca also signed his own death warrant. On December 29, following a conference with Carol at the king's winter lodge in Sinaia, the prime minister was shot dead by Guardist snipers as he prepared to board his train for Bucharest. The police managed to round up fifty-three suspected plotters, but only three were convicted, and none was given more than a short prison term. Codreanu himself was briefly taken into custody as the alleged mastermind of the assassination, but was almost instantly released by order of the examining magistrate. He had become untouchable.

The murder of Ion Duca loosed an avalanche of renewed violence. Rumanian political life now became in effect an escalating civil war between the Iron Guard and King Carol. Mass Guardist demonstrations against the government, coupled with mounting hooliganism against Jews, set the tone of the mid-1930s. Even the veteran nationalist ideologues Alexandru Cuza and Octavian Goga came to regard Codreanu as a threat to their own rightist political leadership. Indeed, to cope with that danger, Cuza in 1934 agreed finally to merge his LANC party into Goga's National Christian faction. It was a not illogical marriage of political convenience. A Transylvanian, and an eminent poet of Rumania's national awakening, Octavian Goga had moved after the war beyond romantic nationalism to a virulent racism, even adopting the swastika as the talisman of his National Christian party. In exploratory discussions, he and Cuza found themselves ideologically compatible. In 1935, both men paid respectful visits to Adolf Hitler in Berlin, and proclaimed the führer to be their inspiration in the struggle against international Jewry. The German foreign ministry reciprocated by making known its support of the National Christians, whom it considered more "reliable" than the mystical, populist Iron Guard.

In their ensuing political rivalry, neither the Iron Guard nor the National Christians would be outdone in the competitive malevolence of their Jew-hatred. Thus, on June 23, 1935, addressing a National Christian rally of forty thousand farmers in northern Wallachia, Cuza urged the government to strip the Jews of all civil rights. To mobilize support for the project, the professor-politician then set about organizing the largest antisemitic congress in European history. Assembling in Bucharest in November, the conclave was attended by some 280,000 Rumanians of all backgrounds. The king chose not to block the event. Instead, regarding Cuza's and Goga's Christian Nationalists as a potential fire wall against the Iron Guard, Carol even directed that two thousand rail carriages be provided for the arriving pilgrims. But when unknown assailants among the delegates shot and gravely wounded Rumania's chief rabbi, Dr. Jacob Niemirower, the deluge of ensuing protests from Jewish and Western liberal sources gave the king pause. At his instruction, the foreign ministry issued a statement promising firm action against any future violence or incitement to violence.

The commitment went unfulfilled. In the malaise of economic depression and chauvinist frustration, Jews remained the target of choice for the nation's rightist factions. At its convention in June 1936, the National Soldiers Front ordered a "spiritual mobilization . . . against the vast Jewish plot [to cripple] Rumania's economy." In May 1937, the Federation of Rumanian Free Professional Associations requested that its constituent groups purge their membership of all remaining Jews. The Rumanian Cultural League, whose president was the former prime minister Professor Nicolae Iorga, appealed for an economic boycott of Jews. To this crescendo of anti-Jewish imprecations and accusations, the Rumanian Orthodox Church lent its spiritual endorsement. In June 1935, Ion Mota now the Orthodox Archdeacon called for drastic measures against the Jews along the lines of "the great master, Adolf Hitler." In a pastoral letter of August 1937, Grand Patriarch Dr. Miron Cristea declared:

> One feels like crying with pity for the good Rumanian nation, whose very marrow has been sucked from its bones by the Jews. To defend ourselves is a national and patriotic duty, not antisemitism. . . . Why should the Jews enjoy the privilege of living like parasites upon our backs? Why should we not get rid of these parasites who suck Rumanian and Christian blood? It is logical and holy to react against them.

It was in any case politic. By 1937, the cabinet, a coalition of Liberals and monarchist loyalists, had decided to steal the Iron Guard's thunder by drafting a bill to "revise" the constitution's citizenship provisions—in effect, to reverse the belatedly achieved naturalization of tens of thousands of Jews in the annexed territories. Moreover, under the draft of a new labor bill, at least three-quarters of all job openings in private businesses, even Jewish-owned businesses, henceforth would be reserved for ethnic Rumanians. The new legislation, if enacted, would have spelled disaster for the Jews. In their horror, Western Jewish organizations and prominent Western liberals alike then inundated Bucharest with protests. The unanticipated scope of this Western outrage evidently registered on the cabinet. It decided to postpone action on both measures until after the scheduled 1937 elections.

The ensuing vote offered little comfort to the Jews. Polling only 37 percent, Carol's handpicked "Government" party, although the nation's largest, was unable to maintain its de facto control of the administration. The Goga-Cuza National Christian party received only 9 percent. By contrast, Codreanu's rabid "All for the Fatherland" front, which until then had been regarded as a loose but essentially misfiring cannon, now achieved a stunning 21 percent of the vote, sending sixty-six delegates to the Chamber, and thereby emerging as the third-largest party in Rumania, after the National Liberals and the Government supporters. King Carol now found himself in a painful dilemma. The "conventional" parties may have been discredited by their years of ineffective governance. Yet the notion of bringing Codreanu and the Iron Guard into even a coalition cabinet was unthinkable. Their raging populism, the blatant incendiarism of their Jew-hatred, and, not least, their pornographic diatribes against Magda Lupescu, the king's mistress—all persuaded Carol to devise a stopgap solution. He would turn instead to the Goga-Cuza coalition, the (lately retitled) National Christian party. By appointing to the prime ministry a man like Goga, a verbose ideologue, co-leader of a tiny electoral minority, the king might still exercise a certain control over public policy.

The decision shocked the nation's dwindling residue of Socialists and liberals. Rumania was now to be led by a crypto-Nazi, essentially a fatter and somewhat duller version of Codreanu. Was there a gleam of hope that the man could be politically neutered by his obvious dependence on the king? In fact, the new government would be limited even more by its own ineptitude. Announcing his intention of establishing a "Rumania for the Rumanians, based upon Christ, King, and Nation," the exultant Goga rushed to patch together a right-wing "wall-to-wall" cabinet, including several of the country's most notorious chauvinists (but excluding the Iron Guard). The experiment fell flat. Goga's administration endured barely seven weeks, until February 1938, when its sheer incompetence brought Rumania to the brink of economic collapse. Stocks fell catastrophically, and capital fled to other lands.

Nevertheless, during his abbreviated tenure, Goga managed to keep a single promise, the one that had recommended him to the king as a fire wall against the Iron Guard. This was to lead Rumanian Jewry to the headman's block. The very day he entered office, the poet-premier issued a decree suppressing the country's three largest newspapers, all Jewish-owned, for "maintaining an attitude contrary to the interests of the nation." The last remaining Jews in the civil service were dismissed, and Rumania's theaters were obliged to drop their—still extensive—Jewish staffs. Even these measures were by way of preliminaries. Goga also proclaimed his intention of completing the predecessor government's "unfinished business." All postwar naturalizations would be "reviewed"—in effect reversed—thereby abrogating the citizenship of those tens of thousands of Jewish families that had come under Rumanian sovereignty in the aftermath of the Peace Conference, and ostensibly under the international protection of the minorities treaty.

Once more, the Jewish watchdog organizations in Britain, France, and the United States, and even the governments of those countries, registered their protests. From Washington, President Franklin Roosevelt let it be known that the American people were "anxiously watching developments." The Soviet government, monitoring Rumania's shift toward the Fascist Powers (p. 97), used the episode as the pretext to recall its ambassador from Bucharest. In the same weeks of January-February 1938, the World Jewish Congress, an international federation of Jewish defense agencies, sought the intercession of the League of Nations. Although Jewish spokesmen by then entertained little hope of meaningful League action, they anticipated that the publicity might give pause to King Carol's rubber-stamp cabinet. To some extent, it did. Goga then agreed to postpone the legislation for several months.

But, in fact, the prime minister required no legislation to put much of his Jewish agenda into effect. The government could annul any certificate of naturalization if the document had been obtained by "fraud" or "misrepresentation." Under this pretext, several thousand Jews in the late winter of 1938 had their citizenship reversed. At the same time, Rumania's peasantry did not forget Goga's earlier vow to expropriate the Jews and distribute their holdings among "good Rumanians." Inhibited by international pressure, Goga thus far had not moved on that promise. Yet the farmers themselves now forced the issue. In many smaller communities they began squatting on Jewish-owned tracts, even occupying Jewish homes and businesses. Terrified, thousands of Jewish village families began fleeing into the larger towns. In Bukovina, Moldavia, and Bessarabia, the congestion in traditionally Jewish urban neighborhoods soon became acute.

Little time passed before the Rumanians discovered that they too would pay a heavy price for the upsurge of punitive xenophobia. Driven to the wall, thousands of Rumanian Jews almost immediately resorted to a campaign of passive resistance. Closing their businesses and commercial offices, they left behind them a vacuum of crucial managerial experience.

Soon the shock of these Jewish closures began reverberating throughout the nation, jeopardizing Romania's already precarious credit reputation. Indeed, the king had seen enough. In February 1938, he dismissed Goga, appointing in his place a technocratic "Government of National Consensus" under the leadership of Dr. Miron Cristea, the Orthodox patriarch. For the time being, Rumania would function without parliamentary participation. Goga meanwhile departed office sullenly, ending his farewell address on state radio with the widely publicized sentence: "Israel, you have won."

Had the Jews actually won a respite? Miron Cristea conceded nothing to Goga, or even to Codreanu, in the depth of his antisemitism (p. 93). Nevertheless, at Carol's "suggestion," the patriarch dispatched a letter to Chief Rabbi Niemerower, asking Jewish cooperation in "restoring spiritual peace, unity, and brotherhood among all Rumanians." As a gesture of good faith, Cristea announced a further—official—postponement of the revisionist naturalization program. The display of moderation was purely tactical, as it happened. The rescissions of citizenship quietly proceeded, but under administrative subterfuges. Thus, in June 1938, it was announced that some twenty-eight thousand Jews in the annexed territories had failed to "prove" their claims to citizenship, and were thereby denaturalized. Facing the imminent loss of their livelihoods, these newly stateless Jews were reduced once more to paying off Rumania's officialdom. But even bribery offered no certainty of protection. In that same June of 1938, the order was issued that all denaturalized "residents" of Czernowitz, the capital of Bukovina, with its dense, middle-class Jewish population, were obliged to liquidate their businesses within a fortnight. Worse was to come.

Hostages of Realpolitik

Throughout the late 1930s, as Rumania's economy continued its free fall under the impact of world depression and governmental chaos, the ensuing public unrest was grist for the Iron Guard's mill. National support for the paramilitary "crusaders" widened from month to month. Yet if Codreanu sought to focus public bitterness first and foremost on the monarch (and Magda Lupescu), Carol fully reciprocated that animus. In the spring of 1938, the king at last decided to move forcefully against his nemesis. At his orders, Codreanu was arrested on a charge of criminal libel. Put on trial in an "administrative" (nonjury) court, the Iron Guard leader was sentenced to ten years' imprisonment. Subsequently, in the summer and autumn, the police managed to round up some three thousand Iron Guard activists, and place them under "administrative" detention in the nation's most brutal concentration camps.

Thousands of other Guards remained at large, however. Well protected by families and friends, they were not about to twist passively in the wind. If they could not strike back directly against the throne, there was always a convenient surrogate at hand. Thus, rampaging through outlying towns and cities, they attacked Jewish shops and homes, and beat and occasionally murdered Jewish householders. Non-Jewish liberals also were among the victims. One of those severely wounded was Professor F. Stefanescu-Goanga, the much-admired rector of the University of Cluj. The king had long been awaiting a pretext for retaliation, and with the assault on Stefanescu-Goanga, he found it. His response was swift and merciless. On November 30, 1938, Carol's elite bodyguard unit hauled the Guard's fourteen senior officials from their concentration-camp imprisonment, trucked them to a deserted road, shot them, and left their mutilated bodies unburied. One of the executed prisoners was Corneliu Codreanu.

The civil war—it was hardly less—was not quite over. Isolated groups of Iron Guards still managed to conduct terror attacks against Jews and Carol's partisans. In September 1939, they ambushed and murdered Armand Calinescu, the king's latest puppet premier. Nevertheless, by the end of the year, Carol had essentially fulfilled his objective. The Iron Guard was all but reduced to impotence. After eight years of implacable and ruthless effort, the king apparently had established himself as the nation's uncontested dictator. At long last he required no further political fire breaks, no tactical marriages of convenience with chauvinist elements. Henceforth, he would govern Rumania with order, authority—and venality.

Was there still time, then, for the nation's Jews to breathe more easily? The prognosis was bleak. For generations, Jew-hatred had been acceptable, even respectable, in all of Rumania's social strata and within all institutions of the state—in government, the universities, in professional organizations and the press. But it was during the postwar years that antisemitism burgeoned into as central a feature of public life in Rumania as in Poland, and pragmatically far more brutal in its extensive physical assaults against Jews. By 1939, moreover, Rumania's political future was rapidly being transformed by the shifting balance of European power. Throughout the 1920s, Rumania had been an enthusiastic charter member of the "Little Entente," the French-sponsored alliance of East European successor states, all of them presumably sharing a vested interest in the postwar territorial status quo.

Yet by the mid- and latter 1930s, France no longer appeared to be a reliable guarantor of that postwar map. It had remained passive as Nazi Germany successively repudiated the constraints of the Versailles

Treaty, launching a mass program of rearmament in 1935, reoccupying the Rhineland in 1936, swallowing Austria and the Czech Sudetenland in 1938. As the inheritor, then, of the former Habsburg Empire's extensive trading arena in Danubian Europe, the Third Reich by 1938 was in a position to draw the region's chronically impoverished successor states into its economic orbit. Not least of all, the sheer dynamism of Nazi antisemitism was proving irresistible to the Fascist movements of these xenophobic, multiethnic nations.

Accordingly, in 1937 and 1938, as Germany augmented its frontiers and economic leverage in Central-Eastern Europe, Rumania's far-rightist parties vied with each other in genuflecting obsequiously to the Nazi führer. Even King Carol, although still committed to the Little Entente, felt obliged to visit Hitler in Berchtesgaden in November 1938, to profess his friendship, and to express hope that Germany in its "Ostpolitik" would continue to respect Rumania's neutrality (Hitler blandly provided that assurance). In 1939 and 1940, completing his purge of the Iron Guard, Carol periodically dispatched reminders to Berlin that his struggle to maintain royal authority was entirely unrelated to issues of foreign policy, even of racist ideology. Thus far, Hitler's political advisers accepted the king's rationale.

By then, World War II was under way. Beyond maintaining Rumania's neutrality, Carol directed his efforts to the achievement of profit from his country's central position as "broker of the Balkans," a key black-market conduit for both sets of belligerents. Indeed, the king characteristically set about augmenting his own vast personal wealth as arbiter of that commerce. But in the summer of 1940, France surrendered and the Reich's domination of Europe appeared unchallengeable. Hitler's earlier assurances notwithstanding, Rumania was obliged now to make its own payoffs to Germany's entourage of allies and dependencies. The price Berlin extorted was a crippling one.

The Bucharest government was "directed" to return Bessarabia to Soviet Russia (Hitler's erstwhile ally since the Molotov-Ribbentrop Pact of August 1939), northern Transylvania to Hungary, and the southern Dobrudja to Bulgaria. If the Paris Peace Conference of 1919 had tripled Rumania's territory and doubled its population, so now, under German diktat, that initial territorial bonanza was amputated by one-third, that engorged population by one-fifth. And at last, on September 6, 1940, with his standing as guardian of Rumania's independence fatally compromised, King Carol himself was obliged to flee the country, and Rumania was transformed almost overnight into a groveling lackey of the Third Reich.

Until that moment, with the ruler's evident tacit compliance, the status of Rumanian Jews had remained frozen in a kind of juridical no-man's-land. Only their physical security had appeared to be somewhat better protected after suppression of the Iron Guard. But now the king, functioning at best as the Jews' indifferent and imperfect shield, had become expendable. His fate henceforth was the weathervane of their own.

V

——————

BELA KUN AND THE LEGACY OF UTOPIANISM

A Trajectory of Embourgeoisement

On March 21,1919, a police escort deferentially ushered Zsigmond Kunfi, Hungary's "interim" prime minister, into the high-security zone of Budapest's aging Marko Street prison. The man who awaited him in the corner cell, Bela Kun, thirty-three years old, was middle-sized and muscular of build. His skull was shaven. His face (in the words of a contemporary journalist) "was of the Tatar type, with strong cheek bones, a large mouth, and stump nose. The eyes were small: they appeared to be cunning and clever." As Kunfi explained to the prisoner, he had come on behalf of the outgoing prime minister, Count Mihaly Karolyi, and the cabinet. They wished to learn Kun's terms for helping to establish a new coalition government in Hungary. The proposal, the very meeting, approached the threshold of surrealism. Prime Minister Karolyi was a political centrist and a Magyar aristocrat. Prisoner Kun was a Communist and a Jew.

The interview in fact was the end result of Hungary's chaotic military and political circumstances. During the recent World War, the nation had suffered the deaths of not less than 660,000 soldiers, while another 740,000 had been wounded or captured by the enemy. Tens of thousands of military deserters of all Habsburg nationalities were in hiding, often begging and looting their way through the Hungarian countryside. In the city streets, starving workers were rioting. Count Istvan Tisza, the wartime premier, who had ordered troops to fire on peace demonstrators, had himself been assassinated. Finally, on November 3, 1918, the new prime minister, Count Karolyi, won cabinet approval to seek an armistice. In an effort, moreover, to dissociate the country from the "imperial warmongers" of Vienna, Karolyi and his fellow ministers proclaimed Hungary's independence. At the same time, the prime minister attempted desperately to restore some degree of social order in Hungary before confronting the Allies at the Peace Conference. To that end, he restructured his cabinet to include both moderate liberals and Social Democrats.

But Karolyi was ill served by the Allied governments. None evinced sympathy for his vision of a reconstituted Hungary made up of a confederation of former subject peoples. In the last weeks before the armistice, these subject nationalities—Serbs, Croats, Slovaks, Transylvanian and Bukovinian Rumanians—were breaking away, proclaiming their independence or their union with neighboring successor states. By January 1919, Hungary already had lost more than half its prewar population. Indeed, Allied pressure merely accelerated this disintegration. From his headquarters in Belgrade, where he served as France's military commander for Central-Eastern Europe, General Louis Franchet d'Esperey dispatched an emissary, Colonel Vyx, to the Hungarian capital. Arriving in Budapest on March 20, Vyx informed Prime Minister Karolyi that all Hungarian forces should be pulled back sixty miles from the eastern slope of the Hungarian plain, "pending conclusion of a final peace treaty." Karolyi instantly grasped the true import of Vyx's ultimatum. The "pending" frontiers assuredly were intended as Hungary's final borders. The nation in effect was being cut in two. In his horror and outrage, the prime minister refused to be identified with this preemptive amputation. He resigned that same day.

The decision was impelled by more than simple despair. Karolyi and his Social Democratic coalition partners were apprised that the Soviet Red Army, counterattacking into the Ukraine (p. 13), was approaching Hungary's Carpathian Mountain frontier. The government accordingly faced the Hobson's choice either of putting the nation at the mercy of the Western Allies or of exploring a possible military alliance with Bolshevik Russia. Preferring the latter alternative, the Social Democrats informed Karolyi that it was wiser to leave the cabinet to them, for Hungary's Communists were more likely to join a leftist government, and then to function as trusted intermediaries with the Russians.

Evidently no other choice was available. Hungary's workers' and soldiers' "soviets" (councils) in any case were proclaiming the dictatorship of the proletariat, seizing the larger neighboring estates, looting the granaries, expelling municipal officials at gunpoint, and demanding an alliance with Moscow. These, then, were the circumstances in which Karolyi finally resigned on March 20, and in which Zsigmond Kunfi, as interim premier, was authorized the next day to visit Bela Kun at the Marko Street prison. As chairman of Hungary's Communist party, Kun would be sounded out on his terms for a political alliance with the Social Democrats.

A Magyarized Jewry

The Jewish world that produced Bela Kun was a formidable one in the prewar era. It was also a comparatively recent one, for the Jews were the latest arrivals among the heterogeneity of Hungary's minority peoples. As late as the eighteenth century, not more than eighty thousand Jews lived in the country, most of these from the neighboring Habsburg province of Galicia. Over the years, they had settled principally in the northeast, where they functioned as estate agents and tax collectors for the local boyars. An early turning point in their demography, in both Hungary and Austria, came in 1782, when Emperor Josef II issued a qualified edict of toleration. Intent on transforming Jews into useful subjects, the emperor allowed a select number of them to rent dwellings and workplaces throughout the realm's cities and towns.

In turn, exploiting this new opportunity, Jews in far greater numbers began migrating to Hungary from neighboring Poland. By 1840, they had achieved a population of some 240,000. They also stood at the threshold of a decisive emancipation. Indeed, the political turning point for Hungarians and Jews alike was the Ausgleich, the constitutional "rectification" of 1867 that transformed the Empire into the Dual Monarchy of Austria-Hungary. Enjoying full internal self-rule under a common Habsburg dynasty, exposed to the winds of Europe's ascendant liberalism, Hungary soon emulated its western, Austrian partner in extending political and civil equality to all its minorities.

From tsarist Russia, then, as well as from impoverished Habsburg Galicia, the westward migration of Polish Jews became a flood. By 1910, the date of Hungary's last prewar census, Hungarian Jewry had achieved a critical mass of 910,000, approximately 5 percent of the nation's population. The 205,000 Jews of Budapest represented over one-fifth of the capital's 1 million residents—thereby becoming European Jewry's second-largest urban population, exceeded only by Warsaw's. They also emerged as Hungary's predominant mercantile and professional community. By 1910, it was estimated that 54 percent of Budapest's commercial firms were owned by Jews, as were 85 percent of all Hungarian banks and financial institutions, including the nation's largest, the Commercial Bank of Pest. Indeed, Jewish-owned banks played a decisive role in funding Hungary's commercial and industrial expansion—much of which also was pioneered by Jews. Hungary's sugar industry was dominated by the Hatvany-Deutsch family. In textiles, the Goldberger Works were the nation's largest. Manfred and Berthold Weiss owned the single largest munitions factory in the country, and later constructed the nation's first shipyard and several of its largest railroads.

As always, education provided the impetus for the Jews' central role in the professions. In 1913, Jews comprised 17 percent of all students in Hungary's secondary schools, 57 percent in the nation's commercial schools, and 46 percent of the student body at the University of Pest. By then, too, Jews made up 46 percent of Hungary's journalists, 50 percent of Hungary's lawyers, 62 percent of Hungary's private physicians. A significant minority of Jews became politically prominent, although most of these tended to be converts or the children of converts to Christianity. Between 1900 and 1918, twenty-six deputies of Jewish ancestry sat in Parliament, and at least twelve "ethnic" Jews served as cabinet ministers.

Grateful for their acceptance, Jews of all backgrounds fully matched the ethnic Hungarian majority in nationalist devotion. Their inner, religious life reflected this impassioned acculturation. By the twentieth century, the largest "trend" within Hungarian Judaism was Neologism, a moderate-centrist form of religiosity that countenanced the mixed seating of men and women, and prayers intoned in both Hebrew and Hungarian. Even Hungarian Zionism operated within the parameters of cultural Magyarism, for emigration to the Holy Land was projected as an option essentially for the Jews of Russia or Rumania, not for those of Hungary. With the outbreak of war in 1914, no element in the nation, or in the entire Habsburg Empire, greeted the conflict with a more fervent effusion of loyalty. Some 240,000 Jews served in the Hungarian armed forces, and at least 10,000 perished in combat. Twenty-five "ethnic" Jews were generals. One of them, Samu Hazay, served as minister of war from 1910 to 1917.

Yet Hungary's Jews also became scapegoats for the economic and social hardships of the war. Antisemitism plainly had not originated during the conflict. For several decades even before 1914, the animus had been simmering among the nation's increasingly déclassé minor nobility and its urban lower-middle classes. By early 1918, as the war shifted decisively against the Central Powers, and as the threat of starvation mounted in Hungary, so did charges of Jewish economic exploitation. These resentments were further exacerbated by culture shock, as tens of thousands of insular Galician Jews, many of them kaftan-wearing Chasidim, flooded in from the eastern battle zone. In late 1918, the right-wing Christian Socialist People's party based its appeal principally on the need to "crush Jewish rule" in Hungary. Antisemitic books and articles proliferated, with three new publishing houses actually specializing in antisemitica. Almost overnight, so it appeared, Hungary's most intensely Magyarized minority race suddenly found itself widely execrated as the source of the nation's misfortunes. It was a stigma, in turn, that decisively influenced Hungarian Jewry's political culture.

A Hungarian Lenin

Although Jews by and large were the archetypes of middle-class respectability, their political haven in Hungary by the late war years had become the Social Democratic party. Founded in 1889, and drawing its widest membership from the Hungarian and Swabian-German working classes, the party nevertheless attracted an unusually large number of Jews into its leadership cadres. Urbanized and literate, often members of the liberal professions, Jews gravitated to a movement that preached and practiced egalitarian virtues, that accepted them as equals at a time when the upper strata of Hungarian society jealously preserved conservative and Catholic values.

Thus, Oszkar Jaszi, a distinguished historian of imperial history, established the Social Democrats' Free School for Social Sciences. Functioning as the party's intellectual vanguard, the school's faculty included Max Adler, Iwan Bloch, and the renowned German Social Democratic revisionist Eduard Bernstein. By the early twentieth century, the party's coterie of Jewish intellectuals came to be known as the "Galilei Circle." Its chairman was the Jewish-born Erwin Szabo, who had thoroughly familiarized himself with Marxist theory at the University of Berlin.

Sharing the nation's widely diffused fear and hatred of tsarist Russia, Hungary's Social Democrats initially supported the government's decision to enter the war. By 1916, however, the trauma of military stalemate and food shortages affected Socialists everywhere. As in Germany and Austria, the party's left wing fell increasingly under the influence of radicals, and after November 1917 specifically of Russia's Bolshevik Revolution. In Hungarian factories, new workers' "soviets" began springing up as the preferred instrument of social deliverance. In January 1918, Party Chairman Erwin Szabo and another Jew, Sandor Osztereicher, chairman of the "inter-factory soviet," were arrested on charges of sedition, together with the entire revolutionary Socialist antiwar faction. Immediately, then, Otto Korvin-Klein and Jeno Landler, both former moderate-revisionists (and former Jews), assumed the party leadership. No less committed than their predecessors to revolution and a separate peace, Korvin-Klein and Landler continued vigorously organizing mass protest meetings and wildcat strikes.

By early summer of 1918, the police were helpless to deal with the unrest. Mutinies were spreading to the army. And in October, with the war essentially lost, the Social Democrats had become too powerful to be barred from Count Mihaly Karolyi's coalition government. Their price for entering the cabinet was high. It included universal suffrage and the secret ballot, full civil liberties and progressive taxation, and comprehensive land reform and the nationalization of the country's "major enterprises." Prime Minister Karolyi was obliged to sign on to this agenda.

Virtually none of the program, however, was translated into practical action. In the chaos of the initial postwar months, the prime minister was uninterested in projecting an image of Hungary as a hotbed of

"Bolshevism"—not at a moment when the Allies were sharpening their knives on the eve of the Peace Conference. In turn, exasperated by Karolyi's timorousness, the Communists and the Social Democratic left wing in January 1919 intensified their demonstrations and strikes. Karolyi dug in his heels. The Communist reign of intimidation must cease, he insisted. To make his point, on February 21 the prime minister ordered the arrest of some one hundred prominent Communists. Among them was the man whom Vladimir Lenin himself lately had appointed as the party's leader in Hungary.

Born in 1886 in the small Transylvanian community of Szilagycseh, Bela Kun was the son of a Jewish notary. Like most of the local Jewish population, the father was culturally Magyarized. His religious attachments were perfunctory, and those of his sons even more so. Attending Calvinist primary and secondary schools, Bela Kun shared in the freethinking atmosphere of the town's Jewish lower-middle class. After a brief, indifferent stint in law school, then as a part-time clerk in the Kolozsvar branch office of the Workers' Insurance Bureau, Kun in 1910 was taken on as a reporter for a local newspaper. Here he found his métier as a political journalist. Mingling with workers, attending trade-union meetings, Kun also swiftly established his ideological identity. He began participating in union educational programs, sharing in strike activities, even participating as a delegate to Social Democratic congresses in Budapest. In 1913 he was appointed managing director of the Kolozsvar Workers' Insurance Bureau. Twenty-seven years old, professionally secure, and recently married, he might well have settled down thereafter to a tranquil bureaucratic routine.

Instead, when the war broke out, Kun promptly enlisted in the army. Soon afterward he was selected (as a university graduate) for officers training school. Upon finishing his course in February 1915, Lieutenant Bela Kun was dispatched to Galicia, where for the next fifteen months he saw intermittent battle action. Then, in the late spring of 1916, overwhelmed by a massive Russian offensive, Kun and his entire company were taken prisoner and carried off for internment in the Omsk district of Siberia. In Omsk's archipelago of prisoner-of-war camps, a majority of the 207,000 captives were Hungarians. Although Kun was entitled to a special officer's billet, he found the privilege meager comfort; his fellow officers endlessly harassed him as a Jew. He preferred instead to join with a number of political soulmates in organizing a Marxist discussion group.

Altogether, in the great network of Austrian-Hungarian POW compounds throughout Siberia, the organizers of these "camp revolutions" were prewar Socialists. Hungarian Jews were prominent among them. Literate, often multilingual, they succeeded early on in establishing contacts with radical elements among the surrounding population. Thus, in

November 1917, with the outbreak of the Bolshevik Revolution, several of
these Marxist POW groups became local Red Guard auxiliaries. As leader
of the largest POW Bolshevik unit, Kun in December was dispatched from
Omsk to St. Petersburg. There he was interviewed personally by Lenin,
who appointed him editor of the Bolsheviks' Hungarian-language newspaper. So it was, with his proven reputation as a writer, propagandist, and
organizer, that Kun rapidly emerged as one of the most influential foreign
Communists in Russia. Indeed, he would soon be appointed president of
all the expatriate groups, POW and others.

It had not escaped Lenin and the Bolshevik leadership that Hungary
was a choice target for propaganda. Among the Central Powers, the Hungarians had suffered the most extensive battle casualties on the Russian
front, and in their war-weariness they were approaching the breaking
point. Moreover, Hungary's landowning boyars were among the most
reactionary in Europe, and peasant bitterness against them was becoming
increasingly inflamed. It was not a coincidence, therefore, that Bolshevism
had taken particularly strong root among the Hungarian POWs in Russia;
or that, of the twenty thousand emissaries dispatched by the Soviet leadership as propagandists abroad, Hungarians led the list, with four thousand.
Kun played the leading role in organizing this program. It was he who
designed its training courses and wrote its instruction manuals.

In March 1918, once Russia signed the Treaty of Brest-Litovsk and officially left the war, large numbers of POW revolutionaries were able to
return to their native countries. Yet it was not until Hungary surrendered,
in November 1918, that Kun himself ventured to make his way back.
Aware that he was already marked as a subversive, he arrived under cover of
a Red Cross medical unit. His fake passport listed him as an army doctor.
Upon reaching Budapest, however, he immediately flaunted a personal letter of endorsement from Lenin, a document authorizing him to assume
leadership of Hungary's Social Democratic left wing, and to transform this
faction into the Communist party.

The letter opened all doors for Kun in the radical camp. Within a single
week, he managed to set up a party office, establish a party newspaper, and
launch a campaign of demonstrations and strikes on behalf of worker rule
and land collectivization. Kun's operational base, the newly structured
Communist Central Committee, was divided equally between local former
Social Democrats and former POW Communists. Six of the committee's
eight members were Jews—all of them, typically, the products of higher
education, and doubtless of social discrimination.

The Bolshevik Revolution in neighboring Russia manifestly was a decisive factor in the Communist rise to power in Hungary. So was the return
of thousands of disillusioned POWs. But the catalyst unquestionably was
Kun himself. A Social Democrat, one Kassak, noted in his diary:

Yesterday I heard Kun speak. . . . It was audacious, hate-filled, enthusiastic oratory. . . . He knows his audiences and rules over them. . . . Factory workers long at odds with the Social Democratic Party leaders, young intellectuals, teachers, doctors, lawyers and clerks who came to his room . . . met Kun and [embraced] Marxism.

The man's dynamism never flagged. Nor did the effectiveness of his propaganda. Among the peasantry and the urban unemployed, among refugees, disabled veterans, and university students, Kun and his closest associates offered such tangible inducements as collectivized land, unemployment compensation, severance pay, subsidized housing, nationalized public industries and utilities.

On February 21, 1919, in a particularly belligerent gesture, a large band of demobilized soldiers and unemployed workers launched an attack on the editorial offices of *Nepazava*, an organ of the mainstream Social Democrats. The police then began to shoot, and in the mêlée some thirty persons were killed and wounded, including seven policemen. The provocation was too much for Prime Minister Karolyi. That afternoon he ordered Kun arrested, and Communist party offices closed. Yet, for the embattled premier, Hungary's ordeal was in no sense eased (pp. 100–101). The ongoing Allied economic blockage and diplomatic pressures merely compounded the internal chaos. These were the circumstances, on March 20, that impelled Karolyi to make his agonizing decision to resign, thereby allowing his interim successor, Zsigmond Kunfi, to visit the Marko Street prison and invite Bela Kun to assume a decisive role in forming a new government.

In fact, Kun did not leap gratefully to accept the offer. He insisted on laying down conditions of his own. These were harsh. The Social Democrats at best would "share" cabinet responsibility as a "United Socialist Party"—in effect, as a merged entity with the Communists—in which all major decisions would be made by Kun and his partisans; the country itself would be known as the Hungarian Soviet Republic, and a Marxist economic agenda would be adopted. At this point, Kunfi departed for hurried consultations with his cabinet colleagues. Several hours later he returned to accept Kun's terms. The two men jotted down the agreement on a single piece of notepaper, and signed it in the prison cell. Kun then was released, to be ushered out personally and obsequiously by the prison warden.

A Hungarian Soviet Republic

The newly formed cabinet consisted of thirty-three "commissars." Of these, seventeen were Social Democrats, fourteen were Communists, and two were non-party representatives. The proportions were deceptive.

Communists held the key portfolios. Kun himself, assuming the commissariat for foreign affairs, actually dictated both his government's foreign and its domestic policies. The public's initial response to this political transformation—indeed, revolution—was by no means one of unalloyed terror. Even the middle classes secretly hoped that the Kun experiment might bring relief to their mutilated country and foil the Allied statesmen at Paris. Moreover, exhilarated by the government's apparent commitment to "social progress," a wide array of intellectuals lent it their services. The composer Bela Bartok accepted a position in the commissariat of the interior, together with the physicist Todor von Karman and the film director Sandor Korda.

The mood was one of optimism. "To many," wrote the journalist-author Arthur Koestler, who was a student in Budapest in 1919, "on a continent in shambles, [Kun] sounded like the voice from Sinai." Koestler remembered the nation's first May Day celebration as a time of near-euphoria, with balloons festooning the public squares and colorful posters everywhere, some designed by the elite of modern Hungarian artists. Farmhands and workers circulated through the streets of Budapest, behaving with an unaccustomed self-confidence and dignity.

But the mood would swiftly change. The government promptly set about confiscating the nation's privately owned factories, its banks and savings institutions, its wholesale commercial houses and local transportation companies, its concert halls, theaters, cinemas, apartment buildings, even private furniture, private libraries, private art collections, jewelry, oriental rugs, stamp collections. However well-intentioned, Kun soon revealed himself as a clumsy Bolshevik doctrinaire, lacking the faintest imagination in administrating a planned economy or, indeed, any governing talent at all. His cabinet increased pensions for crippled veterans and the unemployed, then simultaneously cut taxes on the urban working classes. Little time passed before the treasury ran out of funds to support either the pensions or the tax benefits.

Worse yet, Kun and his fellow Communists proved extraordinarily inept in coping with the rural peasantry, the backbone of the population. Even as the Soviet regime decreed nationalization of the larger estates, it made no provision for dividing the land among the impoverished majority of small farmers, or for meeting their critical need for agricultural machinery. The entire scheme soon lay dead on the paper. Even one of its earliest and most popular features, collectivization of the Church's bloated landholdings, was blighted by the government's decision to confiscate the modest personal possessions of village priests. The peasantry were religious. Whatever their land hunger, they reacted in shock to these gratuitous excesses.

By early summer of 1919, still another ugly feature of the Kun government revealed itself. It was physical intimidation. Communist paramilitary "enforcement squads" were directed to round up suspected "counterrevolutionaries." Under the command of Jozsef Czerny and Tibor Szamuely, both former POWs in Russia, these vigilante-hoodlums fostered a reign of terror. Dressed in leather trousers and coats, wearing rifles and bandoliers of cartridges, they clung to the running boards of automobiles that careened through city and village streets at night with sirens blaring. One of the squads' favorite maneuvers was to break their way into middle-class homes, requisitioning "illegal" foodstuffs and chattels, then dragging the hapless owners off to local jails where they often were kept waiting for days before facing their revolutionary judges. At Kun's orders, revolutionary tribunals had been established on the Russian Bolshevik model and empowered to issue instant sentences, occasionally even death sentences.

The "Red Terror" in fact claimed relatively few victims, possibly not more than some 160 dead over the entire five months of its operation. Its impact was essentially psychological, and not least in its post-factum consequences for Hungarian Jewry. It was this people's gravest misfortune that their fellow Jews shared with such unique prominence in the intimidation campaign. Tibor Szamuely became commander of all paramilitary activities. Otto Korvin-Klein was Szamuely's counterpart as chief political prosecutor. Other Jews in disproportionate numbers served as judges and prosecutors of the revolutionary courts, as propagandists and leaders of Communist youth and women's auxiliaries. Bitter charges of a "Jewish conspiracy" were falling on receptive soil.

Ironically, no people suffered in greater proportion from the Communists' depredations than the Jews themselves. They were archetypical members of the bourgeoisie, after all. Of the 715 hostages seized by the paramilitaries, 164 were Jews, including a significant nucleus of leading industrialists and bankers. Among the 160 prisoners condemned to death by the supreme revolutionary tribunal, 44 were Jews. Yet the Hungarian middle classes and much of the agricultural population fastened on the sheer visibility of Jews in Kun's government. Even the working-class women who stood in endless lines for supplies cursed the "Jewish commissars." From Budapest in May 1919, the British historian-diplomat R. W. Seton-Watson wrote the Foreign Office that "[a]nti-Semitic feeling is growing steadily in Budapest, which is not surprising, considering that [many] of the whole Government . . . are Jews, and also a large proportion of the Red Officers. . . . Personally, I do not think that anything on earth can stop the anti-Semitic movement in Hungary." Seton-Watson was prescient.

Military Failure and Counterrevolution

Possibly even more fatal to the Kun regime than its Jewish associations was its sponsorship, and eventual abandonment, by Bolshevik Russia. As the chosen protégé of the Russian Communist leadership, Kun made it one of his first orders of business to seek a treaty of military alliance with Moscow. To his shock and dismay, the appeal went unanswered. In the midst of their own civil war, the Bolsheviks were hard pressed to maintain authority within their own frontiers. In Kun's view, then, it became all the more critical for Hungary on its own to inspire Communist uprisings elsewhere in Europe—if only to create a buffer against the capitalist Allied Powers. But the mass recruitment did not happen. Germany's Communists had shot their bolt the previous winter (pp. 227–29), and trade union demonstrations of support in Austria and Bulgaria proved largely cosmetic. Bela Kun's vision of a revolutionary chain reaction in Central-Eastern Europe turned out to be a pipe dream.

For their part, the Allies reacted to the Hungarian Soviet regime by grossly overestimating its capacity for harm. Withdrawing their missions from Budapest, they simultaneously adopted a more forbearing stance toward Rumania's expansion at Hungary's expense (p. 73). Kun soon was devoting his major efforts to the defense of his nation's territory, the one and exclusive reason that had induced Karolyi and the Social Democrats to bring him to power. Thus, on April 12, 1919, he wired the Allied leaders in Paris, assuring them that his government accepted the original armistice lines, but not the territorial amputation prefigured by Colonel Vyx's recent ultimatum (p. 101). Was there not room for some negotiation? The Allies then agreed to dispatch General Jan Christiaan Smuts, the South African member of Britain's War Cabinet, to determine the Kun regime's flexibility. Smuts arrived in Budapest on April 14. But the Allied formula he brought with him was unacceptable to the Hungarians. It offered little more than a "neutral" zone to be established on Hungarian soil between the armistice and Vyx lines. Two days of talks produced no agreement, and Smuts broke off negotiations and ordered his train to depart.

Kun's adamance may have been ill-advised. By refusing a demilitarized buffer, he gave the Rumanians their pretext for thrusting deeper into Hungarian territory. Without further delay, their army moved from its advanced bases in Transylvania across the Tisza River and directly into "integral" Hungary. By June 1919, Rumanian forces were sixty miles from Budapest. Hereupon, in a shrewd countermaneuver, Kun ordered his own troops to avoid the far more numerous Rumanians and instead to strike northwestward, into a sector of former Habsburg Slovakia inhabited exclusively by Hungarians. The move caught the Allies by surprise. At Clemenceau's request, therefore, the Rumanians temporarily pulled back to the Tisza River line to allow the Western statesmen leeway for exploring a "diplomatic" solution.

In late June of 1919, a compromise of sorts was reached. If Hungarian troops would evacuate Slovakia, the Allies would ensure that the Rumanians confined themselves to their principal emplacements behind the Tisza. Kun pondered the offer, then overrode the objections of his colleagues and accepted it as a kind of Hungarian "Brest-Litovsk," a tactical breathing space. This was his second and final mistake. On July 29, ignoring an agreement in which they had not acquiesced, the Rumanians on their own initiative resumed their drive across the river. In desperation, Kun then hurled his last army reserves against the invaders. To no avail. Within hours, the Rumanians shattered the outmanned Hungarian force at the southern frontier city of Szeged. Kun's credibility as the defender of his nation's heartland now expired altogether.

Here at last the Allies were able to impose their maximalist terms on Budapest. Kun must be removed from office, they insisted, and his Soviet regime dismantled in favor of a Social Democrat–middle-class coalition. In return, the Western Powers would ensure a Rumanian withdrawal and terminate their economic blockade. The proposal was acceptable to the Social Democrats. On August 1, they presented Kun with an ultimatum. The Hungarian Soviet Republic must be dissolved forthwith, they demanded, and all its powers given over to a caretaker—in effect, a Social Democratic—successor government. Kun was shaken, and helpless. With his army scattered, the Red dictator no longer could dictate. Agreeing to step down, he could only warn resentfully that "no one will be able to govern here," that "the international proletarian revolution" would soon be restored.

The following day, August 2, Kun and eight of his closest associates, among them Gyorgy Lukacs, Matyas Rakosi, Erno Gero, Jozsef Revai, and their families, departed Budapest by train. Under diplomatic immunity, they were allowed to cross the frontier into Austria, where the entire group was interned in a special annex of Vienna's Seinhof lunatic asylum. Less fortunate were the Communist ex-officials who remained behind in Hungary. Tibor Szamuely, the notorious terror-squad commander, traveled by automobile to the border, but was stopped by the Austrian frontier police. Before he could be turned over to the Hungarian "White" authorities, Szamuely shot himself. Nineteen others of Kun's commissars who had not been granted safe passage also remained behind in Hungary. All were arrested, most were imprisoned, and three, including Otto Korvin-Klein, the former commissar of the interior, were executed by the counterrevolutionary government.

A "White" Counterrevolution

By the time the train carrying Kun and his retinue left Hungary, a successor administration, composed exclusively of Social Democrats, was established in Budapest under the premiership of Gyula Peidl, a respected trade-union official. At this point, the Allies possibly would have honored their commitment to expel the Rumanians and lift their economic blockade. But on August 4, 1919, a delegation of Hungarian rightists led by Istvan Friedrich, a veteran boyar politician, secretly approached the Rumanian command and asked the invaders to move directly into Budapest in order to "make a complete end of the Bolshevik terror." The Rumanians needed little persuasion. Two days later, their regiments entered the defenseless Hungarian capital and replaced Peidl with Friedrich as token premier.

Hereupon the Rumanians launched into a nightmare of pillage. For the next four months, their troops systematically looted Budapest and other occupied cities. Stores, homes, business offices, even hospitals and churches, were stripped down to the bare walls. The vandals did not leave Budapest until mid-November, and then only under dire warnings of Allied military intervention (pp. 73–74). Friedrich would pay for his treachery. The Allies coldly denied recognition to his government and refused to lift their economic blockade while he remained in office. In the interim, to restore order in Hungary until a final peace treaty could be formulated in Paris, the Western Powers authorized still another military force to fill the vacuum of the departed Rumanians. This one, however, was native Hungarian, and its leadership was fully as authoritarian as that of the late Kun regime.

The origins of the new counterrevolutionary military force were to be found in Szeged. During the entire period of Kun's Soviet Republic, this middle-sized southern community had remained in the hands of a loose confederation of minor boyars and urban white-collar former Habsburg officials. Chauvinist and reactionary, the "caretakers" gravitated to the single remaining Hungarian military unit not directly under Communist control. The detachment consisted of some five thousand former imperial troops led by Vice-Admiral Miklos Horthy, the wartime commander of the Habsburg navy. Equipped by the French army, Horthy's force soon tripled in size, then began collecting taxes and functioning in and around Szeged as a skeletal "government in exile."

By November 1919, the Allies were impressed enough by Horthy's anti-Communist bona fides to made him a tempting offer. They would support his efforts to establish a national government on condition that it function "moderately," avoiding counterrevolutionary excesses. The admiral and his confederates needed less than a day to accept. In mid-November, bearing the new title of "commander-in-chief" of the Hungarian national army, and resplendently bemedaled astride a white steed, Horthy led his troops into Budapest. There he installed as prime minister Karoly Huszat, leader of the right-wing "Christian National Unity" party. At the same time, to placate the Allies, Horthy offered a token representation in the cabinet to several Liberals and Social Democrats. Reassured by these measures, the Western Powers in December 1919 granted recognition to the new government.

From the inception of the Horthy regency, its pose of moderation was a sham. Its key personnel were chauvinist reactionaries—military officers, minor gentry, mid-level clerics, and petty bureaucrats—who were identified with the Szeged "government-in-exile" and its ideological counterparts in other Hungarian cities. It was this ultrarightist constituency that lent its financial and moral support to the "Society of the Awakening Magyars," a collection of lumpenproletariat vigilantes. Even before Horthy organized his official government in Budapest, the Awakening Magyars, under the command of a wartime officer, Captain Gyula Gombos, launched into their "cleansing operation" by rounding up suspected "radicals," "Bolsheviks," and "national traitors." Once in power, the admiral then ignored his earlier commitment to the Allies and tacitly permitted Gombos's vigilantes to continue their campaign of repression. Indeed, the counterrevolution soon developed into a full-fledged "White Terror." In addition to suspected Communists, its victims included the staffs of liberal newspapers, trade unions, and Social Democratic party offices.

In the manner, however, of other regions that were swept up in the frustrations and xenophobia of the early postwar era—Ukraine, Poland, Rumania, Bavaria—the White Terror in Hungary concentrated with particular ferocity on the Jews. Plainly, the Jews had always constituted the most vulnerable of the country's ethnic minorities. But it was specifically the role played by Kun and other Jews in the late Communist regime that would not be forgotten or forgiven. Horthy personally was by no means a fanatical antisemite. From the moment he entered Budapest, however, he set the tone of the counterrevolution by promising a well-deserved punishment to "Bolshevik traitors"—a code phrase that required little popular clarification. In the first three months of the admiral's rule, an estimated three thousand suspected partisans of the recent Kun government were killed, and a majority of these were Jews. Throughout 1920, others would be hunted down and slain.

Although several hundred Jews were among the White Terror's victims in Budapest itself, their unique exposure was in the provincial towns and villages. Thus, in the district capital of Siofok, some 140 Jews were simply rounded up and gunned down in a nearby forest. In Kacement, a town renowned for its high proportion of Jewish war veterans, another 200 Jews were seized at random and executed. Their corpses were disposed of in nearby fields and streams. In April 1920, paramilitaries descended upon the local Jewry of Koba and massacred nearly 300 Jewish men and boys. The terror campaign produced not only death and imprisonment but financial ruination. The marauding bands of Awakening Magyars used the threat of pogroms to extort money from their victims—by some estimates over 3 million florins. In their anguish, Jewish communal leaders repeatedly invoked their people's exemplary record of patriotism and military service. Personal appeals to Horthy brought little relief. To every Jewish delegation, the admiral explained that he could not appear to have "sold himself" to the Jews. From January to June 1920, an estimated ten thousand terrified Jews rushed to convert to Christianity. The effort brought little noticeable alleviation of pogroms.

Jewish organizations in the West, meanwhile, were unremitting in their protests and entreaties. In Britain, seeking Foreign Office intercession, Lucien Wolf of the Conjoint quoted the atrocities listed in a White Paper that had been issued by Sir Joshua Wedgwood, M.P., chairman of a recent Labor Party investigation on Hungary. Unmoved, the Foreign Office declined to interfere in the internal affairs of another nation, particularly one that was suppressing Communism. In Paris, the efforts of Jacques Bigart and his Alliance colleagues to intercede with the French Foreign Ministry similarly were rebuffed. Hungary was laying down a "cordon sanitaire" against Bolshevism, after all.

In Washington, meeting with Secretary of State Frank Polk on May 20, 1920, the redoubtable Louis Marshall achieved a somewhat more forthcoming response. The secretary gave Budapest to understand that "American sympathy for Hungary will depend largely on fair treatment given [to] minorities. . . ." It is uncertain that Polk's discreet admonition was effective. Although the White Terror was beginning to ebb by spring 1920, some 27,000 legal proceedings still were pending against individuals suspected of "treason," 129 executions already had been carried out, and nearly 6,000 detainees had simply been murdered. In every category, the proportion of Jews loomed largest.

The "Stability" of Authoritarianism

Miklos Horthy, who had taken power in Hungary ostensibly as a "caretaker" until a permanent and presumably democratic government could be established, would become one of Europe's more enduring political figures. Born in 1868 to minor Calvinist gentry, Horthy as a teenager opted for a military career and spent four years at the Habsburg naval academy. Upon graduation, he swiftly achieved a reputation as a formidable officer. Later, during the course of the war, his tactical naval successes in the Mediterranean were crowned in 1918 by a spectacular victory over an Italian squadron in the Strait of Otranto. By the time of the armistice, Horthy had been promoted to vice-admiral and supreme commander of the— rather modest—Habsburg fleet.

Yet the man's accomplishments on the high seas were less decisive in his career than his earlier experience as military aide-de-camp to Emperor Franz Josef. The handsome and multilingual young officer became a trusted companion to the old monarch. He also managed to absorb something of Franz Josef's shrewd instinct for balanced compromise. Accordingly, in late 1919, emerging as his nation's de facto ruler, Horthy addressed Hungary's chaos and ruination by focusing on social stability rather than political democracy. To be sure, he authorized national elections for January 1920, even introduced the secret ballot and broadened the franchise. But the counterrevolution had not run its course, and its White Terror ensured the return of a "congenial" parliament. It was this new, distinctly rightist legislature that vetoed a republican form of government for postwar Hungary. When the Allies warned against a restoration of the Habsburgs, Parliament adopted the euphemism of declaring a "regency" for the nation, and in March 1920 elected Horthy himself to the position of "regent for life."

At Horthy's "suggestion," moreover, Parliament invested the regency with broad powers. These included supreme command of the armed forces and the right to dismiss Parliament and to rule by decree in times of "emergency." The strange, hybrid regime undoubtedly was flawed by Western, democratic standards. Nevertheless, it produced several useful results. Exercising the fullest range of his authority, the regent gradually put an end to the Awakening Magyars' terror campaign. In April 1921, he asked Count Istvan Bethlen, leader of the Unity party, to assume the prime ministry.

Bethlen, a Calvinist Transylvanian nobleman, devoted to the traditions of the defunct empire, shared Horthy's commitment to the wider objectives of restored economic health and social equilibrium. To achieve these goals, the new premier organized a reliable police force, dispensed with the secret ballot, and gradually raised the property qualification for the suffrage. Once his political control was assured, however, Bethlen then shrewdly rectified the "social balance" by restoring freedom of the press, allowing the opposition parties to resume their political activities, and extending a general amnesty to several thousand imprisoned leftists. In this fashion, with the political opposition essentially housebroken and the nation's economy tentatively stabilizing, Bethlen's "neobaroque edifice" would dominate Hungarian public life for most of the ensuing decade.

From the outset of his incumbency, too, the new prime minister had to wrestle with the consequences of the peace instrument the Allies lately had inflicted on his nation. Of all the Paris Conference's basket of peace settlements, the Treaty of Trianon was the single most punitive. Signed in June 1920, the pact amputated fully 70 percent of Hungary's territory, 60 percent of its population, and major portions of its natural and industrial resources—all principally in favor of Yugoslavia, Czechoslovakia, and Rumania. The nation's resulting strategic and economic vulnerability, in turn, exerted a profound influence on both its foreign and domestic policies.

Like Horthy, Prime Minister Bethlen grasped intuitively the importance of cultivating a "moderate" image on the world scene, of avoiding any provocation that might incur the terrifying possibility of a resumed Allied blockade. To that end, Bethlen in 1921 adroitly quashed a last, feckless effort by former Emperor Karl to regain his throne. Afterward, trusted by the West, the premier was able successfully to negotiate minor border rectifications with Yugoslavia, and in 1922 even to win approval for Hungary's entrance into the League of Nations. Two years later, Bethlen wangled a financial loan from the League, further stabilizing Hungary's economic recovery.

The "Bill of Rights" in Hungarian Action

As the most violent phase of counterrevolutionary fervor subsided, the circumstances of Hungarian Jewry similarly began to improve during the Bethlen era. The Jews were reduced in numbers, to be sure. Under the 1910 census, their population was listed as 910,000 in a nation of 21 million (p. 102). Following the Treaty of Trianon, however, once Hungary itself was reduced to a population of 8 million, large segments of the prewar Jewish minority also were sheared away: 182,000 going to Rumania; 231,000 to Czechoslovakia; 43,000 to Yugoslavia.

Yet, even with these excisions, the remaining "critical mass" of 454,000 Jews actually signified a proportional increase, from 4.64 percent of prewar Hungary's population to 5.92 percent in the postwar. Indeed, with the loss of its South Slavs and Rumanians, Hungary's remaining Jews now emerged as the nation's single largest ethnic minority. Their profile as Hungary's single most urbanized community also was enhanced, for the peace treaty's territorial amputations and the White Terror impelled even larger numbers of Jews to depart the provinces for the capital. Under the 1920 census,

246,000 Jews lived in Greater Budapest, fully 23 percent of the capital's population.

These were the circumstances that fortified the Jews' long-standing identification with business and the professions. In Budapest, by 1924, not less than 12,000 of the capital's 18,000 businessmen were Jews, as were 22,000 of its 46,000 professionals (p. 120). Jews had pioneered and still largely owned major sectors of Hungarian industry, including textiles, china, glass, brick, cement, lime, wood, chemicals, matches, leather, glue, soap, canning, vegetable oil, sugar, commercial milling, and oil-refining. As elsewhere in Central-Eastern Europe, however, a far larger percentage of Jews were small entrepreneurs. Indeed, they remained Hungary's, and Central-Eastern Europe's, small businessmen par excellence.

Hungary's Jews also entered the postwar era in a state of acute political vulnerability. The Kun interregnum was by no means the only factor. In the period before 1914, the Jews were one of many minorities—Rumanian, Ukrainian, Slovak, Croat, Serb, and others. After the Treaty of Trianon, as the one substantial minority remaining in a truncated nation, they would in any case have been uniquely exposed to nationalist frustration. In their renowned acculturation, to be sure, Hungarian Jewry evinced little interest in activating their "communal" rights (p. 118). But their newly accentuated distinctiveness was economic as well as ethnic. In the postwar era, scores of thousands of white-collar Hungarians who had functioned as civil servants or office employees in the amputated territories now suddenly became unemployed refugees in a rump Hungary. Their numbers were further swollen by new waves of university graduates holding advanced degrees. With the professions and commerce traditionally dominated by Jews, the reaction of the newly déclassé Hungarians perhaps inevitably took the form of an even more virulent antisemitism.

Early in the 1920s, the Christian Association of Builders and Engineers and its sister organization, "Hungaria," persuaded the government to establish an official Chamber of Engineers. The new "chamber" would operate entirely under control of the two groups' own membership. Almost immediately afterward, Jewish engineers found themselves barred from government contracts, and from all private corporate contracts except with Jewish-owned firms. The proportion of Jewish engineers then dropped from 40 percent in 1910 to 16 percent by 1937. In medicine, an identical exclusionist program forced Jews from Gentile-dominated medical associations, from government hospitals, clinics, medical-insurance services, and from university medical-school faculties. By 1925, the Jewish presence in these institutions had fallen by two-thirds from the prewar years.

In Hungary, as in Rumania and Poland, it was the universities that launched the most aggressive anti-Jewish campaign. Once again students were the vanguard. Their Jewish classmates offered a uniquely exposed target. In 1919–20, following the population transfers of the postwar period, Jews accounted for 25 percent of the nation's university student body, 35 percent of all law students, 41 percent of all medical students. The ratio was intolerable to Gentile students, who launched angry demonstrations in support of a rigorous Jewish numerus clausus. Faculty members tended to endorse their demand. So did the government. In July 1920, Istvan Haller, Hungary's minister of the interior, reclassified Jews as a "separate nationality." Haller's purpose became clear in September, when Parliament approved a new education law. Its key provision asserted that "the proportion of the youth belonging to an individual race or nationality should, as far as possible, approximate among the students the proportion of that race or nationality in the country." Under these guidelines, and based on the government's latest "nationality" figures, the proportion of Jews would be reduced to 6 percent of the student body.

The moment the numerus clausus went into effect, in October 1920, the Hungarian Jewish Council launched an emergency campaign for repeal. The effort produced no change in the government's position. In November 1921, therefore, Lucien Wolf and Jacques Bigart delivered an urgent appeal to the Council of the League of Nations, invoking Articles 56, 57, and 58 of the Treaty of Trianon, the self-contained addendum that functioned as Hungary's version of the minorities treaty. Indeed, for the League no less than for the Jews, the appeal represented the first important test case on a minorities treaty. Its fate may offer a useful insight into this summum bonum of Western Jewish diplomacy.

Once the secretary-general transmitted the Jewish petitions to the League Council, and the latter in turn delegated a three-member investigative committee (p. 41), the complaints were forwarded on to Budapest within the month. The Hungarian reply was duly sent back to the League in January of 1922. Issued over the signature of Prime Minister Bethlen, the response alluded to the overabundance of professional people who had been uprooted from Hungary's amputated territories. Provision had to be made for the thousands of these newly déclassé individuals, Bethlen explained, if only to avoid the horrors of the recent Kun revolution. Early in 1923, the prime minister himself traveled to Geneva in hopes of negotiating certain territorial modifications in the Treaty of Trianon. On that occasion, he took time to meet with Wolf, Bigart, and other Western Jewish representatives who had made the journey to Switzerland to interview him. The discussions, in the premier's suite at the Hôtel de la Paix, were courteous. But when Bethlen hinted that the treatment of Hungarian Jews would be influenced by the cooperation of Jews abroad in revising the Treaty of Trianon, the atmosphere became tense. Wolf and

Bigart cautioned Bethlen that political extortion would only exacerbate anti-Hungarian feeling among Western Jews and Western governments alike. The response startled the prime minister, who was accustomed to the more obsequious Jews of his own country. Yet he would not back down.

In July 1923, the League Council's investigative committee returned to Geneva from Hungary. Soon afterward it issued a report condemning the numerus-clausus law as a violation of the minorities addendum to the Trianon Treaty. And once again Bethlen's government held firm. The law was the consequence of an unjust treaty, it asserted. Once the shackles of that treaty were removed, the law would be modified. There the matter rested, with the League Council unwilling to take action beyond its leisurely and apparently endless correspondence with Budapest. Finally, in January 1925, exasperated by the sluggish pace of negotiations, Wolf and Bigart requested that the League submit the numerus-clausus issue for adjudication to the Permanent Court of International Justice at The Hague. In November 1925, after several additional months of temporization, the League Council acquiesced. Almost at the last moment, then, on December 19, Count Kuno Klebelsberg, Hungary's minister of education, appeared before the League Council to intimate that the "temporary" numerus clausus could be modified "as soon as the social and economic life of Hungary recovered its former stability." Gratefully, the Council members pounced on the minister's hint, agreeing to postpone their appeal to The Hague.

The Hungarian government still was in no hurry to act on behalf of the Jews. It preferred to await the outcome of the December 1926 parliamentary elections. Even after the voting took place, and the Bethlen coalition was reconfirmed in office, the prime minister bided his time, declaring that the moment for action was not yet propitious. But one moment was as unpropitious as another. In October 1927, when Bethlen finally declared his intention to have the quota law amended, his announcement stirred up a hornet's nest. University students held protest meetings. So did rightist politicians. One of these, Gyula Gombos (pp. 121–22), assured a convention of his Awakening Magyars that the proposed amendment would be blocked by force, if necessary.

The threat was gratuitous. The amendment Bethlen shepherded through Parliament in December 1927 was a fake. Ostensibly jettisoning racial and national quotas, the legislation went on to declare that "the total number of those admitted shall be adequately distributed among the various administrative districts of the country." Inasmuch as 60 percent of the nation's Jews lived in Budapest, the law merely substituted geographic for national quotas. It also instituted vocational quotas, by giving preference to the children of farmers, workers, and other distinctly non-Jewish categories. Little had changed. Thousands of Jewish students would still be obliged to seek their university opportunities in Austria, Czechoslovakia, and Western Europe. Nevertheless, after much soul-searching and discussion, Wolf and Bigart decided not to fight the issue any longer. The amendment at least did away with the one feature they, and the Hungarian Jewish leadership, found most repugnant. It was the categorization of the Jews as a separate "nationality."

Except for the numerus-clausus issue, Bethlen during his ten-year premiership actually offered the Jews a certain modest respite. The nation could hardly develop without their capital investment, after all. With Horthy's approbation, the prime minister was prepared to allow Hungarian Jews free rein in their economic activities. And, indeed, amid Hungary's wider economic recovery, they flourished handsomely. If most Jews remained small businessmen, the elite among them continued to forge well ahead of other Hungarians. Government surveys revealed that Jews maintained board control of 70 percent of Hungary's largest industrial enterprises, and of all four of Budapest's leading newspapers. As late as 1937, an extraordinary 83 percent of Hungary's millionaires were Jews, and the average Jewish per capita income was at least four times higher than that of non-Jews—most of whom were either farmers or urban workers.

Well into the 1930s, too, Jews remained possibly even more visible in the professions than they had been before the war. Notwithstanding discrimination at universities and in professional societies, Jews still constituted a fourth of all the doctors in Budapest, and nearly a third of the capital's lawyers. The principal Budapest theaters were owned by Jews, and their offerings for the most part were produced and directed by Jews. Sandor Hevai, director of the National Theater, was widely recognized as the "Max Reinhardt of Hungary," even as the Jewish-born Ferenc Molnar was the nation's most admired playwright. Pioneer Hungarian film producers, later to make their greatest mark in the West, included Sandor (Alexander) Korda, Adolph Zukor, and Joszef Pasternak. From Hungary, too, came the renowned Jewish scientists Leo Szilard, Jeno Wigner, Edward Teller, Janos (John) von Neumann, Todor von Karman, Gyorgy von Hevesy, as well as the psychiatrists Sandor Ferenczi and Franz Alexander (p. 186). Hungarian Jewry even produced an extraordinarily high number of Olympic athletes, the legacy of Europe's venerable tradition of ethnic sports clubs.

Yet no vocation was more quintessentially Jewish than journalism, and specifically political journalism. As late as 1935, nearly three-quarters of Hungary's political columnists were Jews, including the nation's single most influential political editor, Bela Zsolt. A wounded war veteran, Zsolt won great popularity as an incisive columnist for several liberal newspapers. From 1929 on, he edited a weekly journal of his own, *A Toll*

(The Pen), which became the principal liberal forum for Hungary's intellectual—heavily Jewish—middle class. Without exception, the newspapers and other publications of Hungary's Social Democratic party were edited and staffed principally by Jews.

During the 1920s, Jews in growing numbers ventured even more directly onto the political route, most of them as members of the Social Democratic party. In the 1928 Parliament, seven Jews sat in the Lower House, while a parliamentary amendment that year extended to Hungary's chief rabbis the privilege, enjoyed by other religio-communal leaders, of membership in the Upper House. Throughout the 1920s, "counterrevolutionary" antisemitism remained unrequited, even virulent. Nevertheless, it was an animus that no longer appeared capable of wreaking its initial, postwar havoc.

The Flowering of "Szeged" Fascism

The world depression, beginning in late 1929, was not felt immediately in agricultural East-Central Europe. Yet, within two years, its consequences in Hungary became increasingly painful, and soon acute. Destitution among both the agrarian and urban populations often approached the threshold of starvation. The collapse overwhelmed Istvan Bethlen. In August 1931, physically and emotionally exhausted, the premier resigned in favor of his close political associate, Count Gyula Karolyi (a cousin of the former prime minister, Count Mihaly Karolyi). Although a man of decent instincts, Gyula Karolyi was entirely unequipped to cope with the nation's escalating social unrest, its worker strikes and peasant demonstrations. Harsh police repression failed to suppress the tumult. In September 1932, Admiral Horthy dismissed Karolyi. Fearing a national revolution, the regent was persuaded to adopt the drastic measures of the immediate postwar years. Personally, he had only distaste for the right-wing populism of the former "Szeged" radicals. Yet Horthy also saw no alternative now but to appoint their leader, Gyula Gombos, to the prime ministry.

The son of German-speaking Swabian peasants, and a former Habsburg army captain, Gombos had emerged in 1919 as commander of the Szeged group's chauvinist-populist Awakening Magyars (p. 113). Over the next two years, he remained one of Horthy's most loyal counterrevolutionary hatchetmen, and his right-wing bona fides continued apparently undiminished throughout the mid-1920s. In 1928, even Prime Minister Bethlen felt it expedient to placate the army's chauvinist younger officers by appointing Gombos as his minister of defense. Yet Gombos for his part regarded the assignment as merely a stepping-stone. Vain and aggressive, he fancied himself another Mussolini, and even mimicked the Italian duce in uniform and demeanor. And now, in September 1932, elevated to the prime ministry, the thirty-eight-year-old Gombos did not discourage his adoring protégés from acclaiming him the prophet of a Fascist-populist renaissance.

The assumption was premature. In advance, the regent and Bethlen, the ex–prime minister, together with other, more traditionally conservative political eminences, imposed stiff safeguards on the premier-designate. Gombos was not to introduce populist economic reforms. He was not to appoint to the cabinet his Szeged radical cronies. He would not tamper with Hungary's parliamentary system. Finally, to preserve the nation's standing in the West, Gombos was not to allow excesses on the Jewish question. The latter proved a major concession. Although Gombos's wife was the adopted daughter of Jews, antisemitism had always been a central feature of his own chauvinist program. In his earlier, Szeged-based career, he had pressed unrelentingly for harsh official quotas on Jewish business and professional activities. In 1925, Gombos and his political ally Tibor Eckhardt convened a rather seedy "World Antisemitic Congress" in Budapest. As minister of defense, presiding in 1931 over a ceremonial gathering of the Hungarian Order of Heroes, Gombos denied admission even to the most impressively decorated Jewish war veterans.

Now, however, only a year later, on the threshold of the premiership, Gombos agreed to mute his Jew-baiting. He went so far as to dispatch an aide, Gabor Baros, to negotiate a secret deal with Samu Stern, president of the Budapest Jewish Council. As the assistant explained to Stern and to several other Hungarian Jewish leaders, Gombos had changed his mind on the Jewish question. He preferred now to concentrate on a program of "social justice." To that end, he would countenance no initiative against Jewish rights or interests—provided the Jews supported his "progressive economic policy" and raised no obstacles to the flotation of government loans (an implicit reference to foreign Jewish investment). The offer was accepted. An official "protocol" was duly formulated and signed by Gombos and Stern. Soon afterward, in October 1932, following his accession to the prime ministry, Gombos affirmed his new moderation in his inaugural address to Parliament: "To Jewry, in turn, I openly and sincerely declare: I have revised my position. That part of Jewry that throws in its lot with the Hungarian nation I wish to regard as brothers, as I do my Hungarian brothers."

The display of goodwill was fraudulent. In ensuing months, as his orthodox fiscal program failed to make headway against the depression, Gombos reverted to type. In 1934 he manipulated the election to ensure a pro-government majority. Soon afterward, he began replacing career army officers and civil servants with political cronies, until much of the state apparatus devolved under his personal control. In foreign affairs, moreover, Gombos almost from the moment of taking office publicly and fervently applauded the territorial revisionism of Mussolini and Hitler. Indeed, he became the first non-German head of government to visit Hitler, in July 1933, and in ensuing years he would pay repeated visits to the Nazi führer. With Germany in any case accepting the bulk of Hungary's agricultural exports, the smaller nation soon was drawn into the Reich's economic orbit.

Gombos's effort to ingratiate himself with the Nazi regime was only one of the developments that undermined his earlier protocol with Hungarian Jewry. The politics of division was even more critical. By 1935, with the economy in the doldrums, Gombos was prepared to countenance a wider array of antisemitic movements and political parties, including one that openly dubbed itself the Hungarian Nazi Party. A year later, when student riots against Jews flared up with an intensity not evident since the early postwar period, the government declined to intervene. Rather, almost at the same time, Gombos suggested that it would be useful for Jewish businessmen to give preference to non-Jewish employees. To encourage the process, he established a separate ministry of industry, directed by Geza Bornemisza, a former chairman of the radical-rightist Christian Association of Builders and Engineers (p. 117). Bornemisza promptly set about circulating questionnaires to all industrial enterprises, to ascertain the "religious identification" of their employees.

For the Horthy regency, as for the Jews, 1936 was a watershed. The original leaders of the rightist camp, both its conservative and its "Szeged" wings, soon were edged from the political scene. Undermined by Gombos, Bethlen lost his moderating leadership over the conservatives. And then Gombos, after a long bout with cancer, died in October of that year. Henceforth, as the ideological right gravitated almost inexorably toward chauvinist extremism, Horthy in his alarm sought a political stopgap, a new premier who would not compromise the nation irretrievably in the eyes of the Versailles Powers. His initial choice was Kalman Daranyi, leader of the National Unity Party. A magnate of impeccably conservative instincts, Daranyi nevertheless shared his fellow landowners' disdain for the vulgar race-baiting of the Fascist populists.

Yet, by then, Horthy and Daranyi alike failed to grasp the burgeoning strength of far-rightist extremism. Its most politicized faction, soon to be known as the Arrow Cross, had been growing during the months of Gombos's protracted illness into the largest of the nation's congeries of Fascist parties; and its leader, Ferenc Szalasi, a former army major, was evincing all of Gombos's demagogic chauvinism. Ironically, Szalasi himself did not meet his own self-defined qualifications of "pure" Magyarism. His father was descended from Transylvanian Armenians. His mother was of mixed Ruthenian-Slovak-Hungarian ancestry. Unlike Gombos, whose populism always had been fueled by a rich dose of political opportunism, Szalasi genuinely cared about the nation's poorer classes. Yet he cared no less for Hungary's amputated provinces, and consequently his social compassion was linked to a fiery, rather mystical pan-Magyarism. And on the all-devouring Jewish question, Szalasi was implacable. Although he was uninterested in actively persecuting Jews, he wanted them out of the country—without recourse to violence, if possible, allowing them to take their property with them, but expeditiously, and en masse.

By the latter 1930s, Szalasi plainly was emerging as the politician likeliest to fill the ideological vacuum left by Gombos. To his banner flocked thousands of "Gombos orphans," city-dwellers and farmers alike, junior military officers and even numerous former Socialists. For most of them, the Arrow Cross program offered a tantalizing alternative both to failed capitalism and to vapid liberalism. More crucially, Szalasi was known to be on excellent terms with senior German officials. Following Hitler's Anschluss with Austria in March 1938, all of Hungary's various nationalist factions sensed that a relationship with Germany offered the nation its single best opportunity to revise the Treaty of Trianon. Szalasi apparently was the best man to cultivate that relationship. Indeed, the Arrow Cross leader was known to have a plan. For him, the surest route to German support of Hungarian revisionism was a "congenial" domestic political agenda, that is, a total exclusion of Jews from all sectors of Hungarian economic and cultural life.

Yet the flagrant brutality of this pro-Nazi program was a source of alarm to Horthy and Daranyi. In their view, naked racism threatened the very texture of Hungary's much vaunted "European" civilization, and assuredly its remaining economic and diplomatic links with powerful Western capitalist democracies. It was thus to block the Fascists that the regent and the prime minister decided to initiate a political firebreak. They would produce their own agenda of "controlled," "prophylactic" antisemitic legislation, a program that would be structured on the Bournemisza "industrial survey" authorized by the late Gombos. In March 1938, alluding to these accumulated questionnaires, Daranyi informed Parliament that their data confirmed the overweening role played by Jews in the nation's economic and cultural life, and the consequent need to reduce their influence. To that end, Daranyi proposed

> that we create a just situation . . . [which] will remedy or eliminate the
> mentioned social disproportion and reduce the influence of Jews in
> the cultural and other areas of national life to a proper scale. Such [a

reduction] . . . will also redound to the benefit of Jewry itself, because it will . . . substantially mitigate antisemitism, and with it the spread of extreme intolerant movements.

In drafting the government's envisaged "Jewish Bill," Dr. Bela Imredy, president of the Hungarian National Bank, heeded the cautionary advice of Harold Bruce, a British financial adviser to the Hungarian National Bank, and of John Montgomery, the United States minister in Budapest. It was the suggestion of these Westerners that the shrewder approach would be to consult in advance with Samu Stern, president of the Budapest Jewish Council (p. 118), in an effort to draft a bill that—if inevitable—at least would be limited in scope. But as the legislation was formulated, it proved too draconian for Stern, for its provisions extended well beyond those of the 1920 academic numerus-clausus law. Moreover, the bill this time referred specifically to Jews by name, not (as in 1920) to all "nationalities," and actually went so far as to adopt the German precedent of identifying Jews by race. Under the new category, even those Jews who had apostatized to Christianity after the collapse of the Kun regime, in August 1919, were still to be designated as Jews.

In substance as well as in rationale, the proposed legislation was a killer. Employment quotas for Jews were established for the first time in such "chambers" as the press, theater, film, medicine, law, engineering, commerce, and white-collar office work, where "Jews can be admitted in numbers . . . only in such proportion that their number does not exceed 20 percent of the total chambers." Exceptions were limited to disabled war veterans, war orphans, or widows, or to those who had converted before August 1, 1919. Finally, salaries paid to Jewish white-collar employees were limited to 20 percent of the salaries paid "Hungarian" white-collar employees.

Whatever its Nazi-style characteristics, the Jewish Bill at least authentically reflected Hungarian public opinion. Except for the Social Democratic press, hardly a single newspaper editorialized against it. Moreover, the bill enjoyed the fullest support of the Hungarian Catholic hierarchy. From Cardinal Jusztinian Seredy down, Church officials agreed that the one and only solution to the Jewish question was either total assimilation or total emigration. The bill carried the title "For a More Effective Safeguard of Equilibrium in Social and Economic Life," and was tabled in Parliament on April 1938. It was passed five weeks later.

In the course of the parliamentary debate, Hungarian Jewish spokesmen invoked the usual litany of Jewish patriotism and military heroism. Yet, when Britain's Conjoint Committee and France's Alliance Israélite Universelle proposed an appeal for League of Nations intervention, it was

Hungary's own Jewish leadership that rejected the very notion. "Patriotism" precluded recourse to outside interference. In any case, world attention was focused more directly on the recent German Anschluss with Austria, and the Third Reich's unfolding terror campaign against Austrian Jewry. But if Hungary's Jews chose to mute their protests on the new law, Hungary's Fascists did not. They denounced it as too mild. By 1938, these far-rightists had coalesced almost unanimously around Szalasi's Arrow-Cross movement. In the space of a single year, their membership had risen from 20,000 to over 100,000, and their marches, demonstrations, and strident oratory mounted in scope and decibel level.

It was to ward off this burgeoning Fascist threat that Horthy in May 1938 decided on a change of prime ministers. He replaced the somewhat hesitant Daranyi with Bela Imredy, author of the Jewish Bill. More than a financial expert, Imredy had acquired a reputation as a decisive executive, presumably the sort of man who would react with firmness to right-wing provocation. And, initially, the regent's choice appeared to be vindicated. After only a week in office, Imredy banned state employees from membership in political parties, a measure clearly aimed at the Arrow Cross. At Imredy's orders, Szalasi was arrested for "subversive activity," and in August he was sentenced to a three-year prison term. But if the new prime minister was unwilling to tolerate political hooliganism, neither would he jeopardize the government's equable relationship with Nazi Germany. It was in September 1938 that Adolf Hitler blackmailed his way into the Czech Sudetenland. Two months later, in return for Budapest's "loyalty and understanding" on the Sudeten issue, the führer issued his first "Vienna Award," returning to Hungary a 6,500-square-mile strip along the Slovakian border, together with its nearly 1 million, predominantly Hungarian inhabitants.

Seventy-eight thousand of these new inhabitants were Jews. Although they had remained intensely loyal to Magyar culture during their years under Czechoslovak sovereignty, Prime Minister Imredy regarded their transference to Hungarian rule with unalloyed horror. For him, this was not the moment to exacerbate the nation's Jewish problem. Rather, Imredy decided to achieve multiple objectives in a single maneuver. He would cordon off the Jews—Slovakian and Hungarian alike—from the national economy, and in this fashion simultaneously ingratiate his government even further with Nazi Germany. In December 1938, therefore, the prime minister introduced a "Second Jewish Bill" in Parliament. This "Christmas present for the Jews," as Imredy described it, went considerably further even than its recent predecessor. For one thing, as overtly racist as Hitler's Nuremberg Laws, making no mention of baptismal "cutoff" dates, the new measure simply defined as a Jew anyone with at least one Jewish parent or two Jewish grandparents.

Imredy's economic provisions similarly moved close to the Nazi model. Whereas the first bill was aimed principally at white-collar employees and professionals, this one indiscriminately restricted Jewish participation in commerce—either as employees or as self-employed proprietors—to 12 percent of the working population; and in the professions, to 6 percent. No Jews at all would be represented in the civil service, in school faculties, in trade union offices, in the theater or the press. At the same time, Jewish householders were barred from purchasing or renting residential plots larger than (the equivalent of) nine hundred square feet. Those Jews who had acquired Hungarian citizenship after the outbreak of the World War would now be denaturalized. Altogether, the bill portended nothing less than economic ruination for the Jews.

By the same token, the program in its wanton brutality was unpalatable to Horthy and Bethlen, the former prime minister, and to their shrinking constituency of "moderate" conservatives. For them, the destruction of Jewish banks, factories, and other traditional financial enterprises would only place the Hungarian economy further under Hitler's thumb. If the measure could not be derailed, it had at least to be modified. Thus, with the regent's tacit approval, Bethlen and his colleagues explored ways of outflanking Prime Minister Imredy, who manifestly was becoming a loose cannon. For some months, as it happened, they had been checking into the "racial" bona fides of the nation's most sinister pro-Nazi, the Armenian-Slovak-Ruthenian mystic, Ferenc Szalasi. While the Arrow Cross leader was currently serving a term in prison (p. 126), he remained the gravest threat to the nation's political stability and diplomatic independence. Then, in February 1939, pursuing their genealogical investigation, Bethlen's researchers came across an unexpected discovery. This one related not to Szalasi, however, but to Imredy.

The prime minister apparently was descended from a racially dubious great-grandmother. Although no hard evidence was found that she was Jewish, it was noted that she had been baptized at age seven. Immediately, Bethlen took the documents to Horthy. The regent needed no further pretext to dispense with Imredy. Summoning the premier to his office, Horthy accused him of violating the constitution. Hereupon he produced Bethlen's documents. Imredy read them, paled visibly, even appeared to grow faint. Wordlessly, he nodded and left the office. That evening, on state radio, Imredy himself announced the discovery, and his resignation as prime minister. "It is inconsistent," he acknowledged, "under such circumstances that I should be identified with [the proposed anti-Jewish] legislation."

Horthy replaced Imredy with Count Pal Teleki, an old-style conservative who disliked the Nazi connection and detested mobocracy. Yet Teleki was not quite prepared to risk public contumely by blocking the Second

Jewish Bill. He assured the regent that the wiser course was to apply the measure "with restraint and discretion." Not without reluctance, Horthy finally acquiesced. Over the ensuing four months, the draft of the bill duly made its way through Parliament. In the final hours of the legislative debate, Jewish ex–military officers, wearing their war decorations, conducted a silent vigil outside the parliament building. The bill then achieved a solid majority and became law on May 4, 1939. Its consequences for Hungarian Jewry proved almost immediately ruinous, Teleki's assurances notwithstanding. Although some Jews managed to operate their businesses or professional activities through Gentile "fronts," at least half of the nation's Jewish breadwinners were stripped of any practical means of earning a livelihood. In the provinces, where Jewish identities could not be disguised behind a façade of any kind, entire Jewish communities soon began departing for the larger cities, abandoning homes, businesses, synagogues, and cemeteries. A proud and distinguished minority people now faced destitution.

The scope of the tragedy lay not least in Hungarian Jewry's absence of psychological defense. Unlike the Jews of Poland, and even of large sectors of Rumanian Jewry, Hungarian Jews had committed themselves to acculturation with a passion not exceeded by their nation's Gentile majority. Did they deserve such abasement, they queried rhetorically now in their letters to the press and in petitions to the government—they, a people whose only desire for more than a century had been to be Hungarian and Hungarian only? A people that had fought Hungary's enemies on so many battlefields and contributed so extensively to its economic and intellectual achievements? The lamentation was an old one, and in Hungary it would evoke the same practical resonance as elsewhere on the Continent.

A Utopianist Valedictory

On August 2, 1919, as Bela Kun fled over the border to Austria, he did not disguise his resentment toward the Hungarian working classes. They had neglected "to fulfill their historical mission of collective and spiritual emancipation," he insisted. It was a jeremiad that Kun would never abandon. But neither was he prepared to twist helplessly in the wind. Following nearly a year's confinement in various Austrian internment camps and hospital security-wards, Kun and his closest associates finally were permitted to depart for Soviet Russia on July 15, 1920. And once in Moscow, the expatriates were all given their due. Indeed, Lenin personally appointed them to positions of responsibility. Istvan Bierman became a member of the Ukrainian Communist Party Central Committee. Matyas Rakosi, Jeno Varga, and Kun himself were assigned to key advisory positions in the Comintern.

Within six weeks of his arrival, moreover, Kun, as primus inter pares among the émigrés, set off on a whirlwind of transplanted activism: organizing a national "educational" conference of former Hungarian POWs, addressing numerous ethnic congresses, writing articles for *Pravda* and other Soviet newspapers and journals. Envisaging himself above all as a man of "frontline" action, Kun pressed for a central role in Russia's ongoing civil war. Eventually, his request was granted. In late autumn of 1920, he was named political commissar of a Red Army division then engaged in combat on the Crimean front against General Piotr Wrangel's White Army (p. 12). Here Kun displayed considerable personal bravery. On a one-man mission through the White lines, he arranged a Bolshevik alliance with the Anarchist leader Nestor Makhno, whose troops otherwise might have joined the enemy.

But soon afterward, functioning as de facto political commissar for all Bolshevik forces in the Crimea, Kun revealed another facet of his character. The Soviet military command had promised a general amnesty to all White troops who voluntarily surrendered. Thousands did. Kun then took it upon himself to repudiate that commitment. At his orders, some ten thousand White prisoners were rounded up and summarily executed. Even hardened Bolsheviks were appalled that a foreigner and a Jew had presumed to commit this atrocity against Russian soldiers. The episode nearly terminated Kun's émigré career.

It was political patronage that saved him. In the early postwar period, the Comintern's senior figures, Gregori Zinoviev, Karl Radek, and Nikolai Bukharin, regarded Kun as precisely the man to carry out the Bolshevization of Germany's Communist party, which was in disarray following its abortive Spartacist revolt (pp. 228–29). In the spring of 1921, with Lenin's belated approval, the Comintern dispatched Kun to Berlin. He brought with him a team of ten German-speaking Hungarian colleagues, most of them former POW comrades, and all but two of them Jews. Upon arriving in Berlin, Kun and his entourage persuaded the militants among the party's leadership to organize still another nationwide general strike, even an armed insurrection. This they did, over the strenuous objections of Paul Levi, Clara Zetkin, and other party conservatives. The uprising began on March 1, 1921, and, like its predecessors of two years earlier (p. 229), the putsch failed miserably. Some 145 workers were killed, and another 3,470 were imprisoned.

Kun himself ignominiously fled the German capital for sanctuary in Riga, Latvia. From there he was returned by airplane to Moscow. In a private meeting with Lenin afterward (according to a Comintern insider), the Bolshevik chairman "breathed fire and flames" at the demoralized Kun, who subsequently fainted on the street after leaving Lenin's office. Once again, Kun's political career faced termination. And once again, it was the

Comintern Executive that extended his lifeline. Its leading members still regarded him as Hungarian Communism's "legitimist" representative in Russia. Yet Kun's status was becoming increasingly precarious. In 1922, Lenin sent him off to direct the agitprop department of the party's Ural bureau. There, in ensuing years, Kun functioned as little more than a glorified apparatchik. He still participated in the Comintern's various "ethnic" committees, but after Lenin's death his own career devolved into abject sycophancy. Reduced to joining with the Stalinist group against Trotsky, Kun ever after remained tremulously on the qui vive to determine the correct ideological stance of the moment.

During the late 1920s and early 1930s, meanwhile, still endlessly prolific as a writer, Kun managed to produce over two hundred articles, as well as Hungarian-language translations of the entirety of Lenin's collected works. He participated in innumerable committees and research teams. Yet most of these activities were of marginal influence. Kun's role in the Comintern steadily declined. With the political climate shifting ominously, his onetime patrons—Zinoviev, Bukharin, Radek—all were disgraced, and ultimately doomed. By the early 1930s, Stalin in his paranoia turned harshly against foreign elements in the Comintern. All their spokesmen were becoming expendable, particularly a Jew like Kun. Sensing that his days were numbered, Kun sank into depression and passed his time within a diminishing circle of fellow Hungarian expatriates. In 1936 he was dropped from his chairmanship of the Hungarian party in Russia and consigned to the directorship of a minor Communist publishing firm.

Kun's last chapter began in May 1937. He was summoned to a meeting of the Comintern Central Committee, where he was formally denounced for his "disrespectful and subversive attitudes" toward Stalin. As he sought to protest this "terrible provocation," two MKVD (internal security) men escorted him from the room. Several weeks later, Kun was arrested. In January 1938 his son-in-law, Antal Hidas, a member of the Soviet Writers Union, also was taken into custody. Kun's wife, Irena, was arrested in February. Years later, it was learned that Kun spent twenty-nine months at Moscow's Lefortovo and Butyrka prisons. Intermittently tortured, he refused to confess to charges of espionage and Trotskyite conspiracy. It was in this period, too, that nineteen of Kun's fellow Hungarian commissars were executed, together with untold numbers of lesser Hungarian Communists. On November 30, 1939, the fifty-three-year-old Kun was himself shot in the basement of Butyrka prison.

Irena was deported to Central Asia. The Kuns' daughter, Agnes, was dismissed from her job in a publishing house. Her husband, Antal, was dispatched to a concentration camp. All survived their ordeal, and after the war all returned to Hungary. Among the small number of others who returned, as fugitives either of Hungary's White Terror of the 1920s or of

Russia's Stalinist terror of the 1930s, were Erno Gero, Jozsef Revai, Gabor Peter, Mihaly Farkas, and Matyas Rakosi. Although supremely indifferent to the tatterdemalion remnant of their fellow Jews, these new Hungarian commissars from 1945 on would have much to say to the nation that had laid the collaborative groundwork for Hungarian Jewry's wartime deracination.

VI

THE PROFESSOR AND THE PROPHET

Imperial Prague and Jewish Memory

On June 11, 1924, eight days after his death at the age of forty-two, Franz Kafka was interred in Prague's Jewish cemetery. Less than two hundred mourners shared in the procession from the funeral hall to the grave site in the city's Straznice district. Among them were Kafka's family members, the companion of his final year, Dora Dymant, and his close friends, Max Brod, Hugo Bergmann, Oskar Baum, and Felix Weltsch. Kafka's passing evoked rather subdued local press comment. Only Milena Jesenska's tribute in *Narodni listy* was unrestrained, describing Kafka as "a German writer, little known among us," a soul of "extraordinary delicacy, intellectual refinement, and fierce refusal to compromise." If the appraisal reached the mark, it was not least for placing Kafka against the matrix of German, rather than Czech literature. Culturally, he was supremely a product of prewar, Habsburg Prague.

No other European city dominated its national hinterland more extensively than this ancient commercial and administrative capital. Residing in Prague his entire life, Kafka breathed in the mystery of a historic palimpsest. On one of its surrounding promontories loomed the vast castle-fortress of Hradcany. At the city's opposite end stood the mighty Vysehrad citadel. Between these two defining talismans, protected by the embankment of the River Moldau, lay Altstadt (Old Town), the heart of Prague's mercantile and small-handicrafts economy. On the Moldau's same embankment lay Neustadt (New Town). Founded as a residential settlement by Bohemia's King Charles IV, Neustadt gradually encroached upon the Altstadt; while across the river stretched Kleinseite (Little Side), a richly picturesque artery between the islanded west bank and the commanding slopes of the Hradcany Castle. In Prague's very center, finally, lay Josefstadt, named after Emperor Josef II. An enclave within the Altstadt enclave, it was Josefstadt that encompassed Prague's historic Jewish quarter.

Altogether, Prague was a kaleidoscope, its geographic diversity reflecting ethnic diversity, its ethnic diversity reflecting the economic and political development of the Empire itself. By the early 1800s, emerging as a major center for new industry, for mines, foundries, and factories, Habsburg Bohemia became the magnet for hundreds of thousands of immigrants from the eastern reaches of the Empire. Prague itself accordingly underwent a massive expansion. Between 1869 and 1900 alone, its population more than doubled, from 240,000 to 514,000. As the city became "Slavophied," its German population during these years similarly grew, from approximately 40,000 to 70,000. Yet the increase was deceptive. As a proportion of Prague's inhabitants, the German population dropped by more than half, from 13 to 6 percent.

The Jews, too, shared in the city's demographic transformation. Theirs was a venerable presence, extending back at least to the twelfth century, and growing almost imperceptibly afterward, decade by decade, as tiny rivulets of kinsmen arrived from the Balkans and Poland, from German Franconia and Bavaria. As late as the sixteenth century, the Jewish enclave did not exceed some one thousand souls. Nevertheless, within its Josefstadt ghetto, the little community was free to worship in its own Altneuschule synagogue and to conduct its affairs within the ambit of its traditional communal autonomy—even to erect its own town hall, replete with a tower clock on which Hebrew letters became the "numbers." Early in the twentieth century, wistfully regarding that exotic Jewish icon, the French poet Guillaume Apollinaire was moved to write:

> The hands of the ghetto clock run backward.
> You also creep slowly back through life
> Climbing to the *hradchen*, listening at twilight
> To Czech songs from the tavern.

In the sixteenth century, moreover, the Jews brought over from Italy an important Hebrew printing press, and ensuing years witnessed an impressive development of Jewish culture under the leadership of several notable rabbis. By 1600, Prague was the home of at least six thousand Jews.

The trajectory of their growth was not uninterrupted. Plagues ravaged their numbers in common with Prague's other inhabitants. In 1745, Empress Maria Theresa, fervid in her Catholic pieties, ordered a full-scale expulsion of the Empire's Jews. The ban would not endure, however, not in the Age of Enlightenment. In 1782 the empress's son and successor, Josef II, issued his celebrated Toleranzpatent, an edict of toleration, marginally easing residential and vocational restrictions on Jews. Finally, in 1867, under Emperor Franz Josef, a general political emancipation was extended to Jews throughout the entire Habsburg realm. It was this climactic benediction that opened the floodgates for an influx of village and small-town Jews, who now poured into the larger imperial cities. By 1880, some 20,000 Jews were living in Prague. By 1910, there were 34,000, in a total population of 443,000. The figure was deceptively modest. Those 34,000 Jews constituted over half the city's German-speaking minority.

Kafka's family odyssey reflected this demographic transformation. In 1874 young Hermann Kafka, Franz's father-to-be, departed his Bohemian village of Wossek to join the swelling Jewish migration to Prague. Characteristically, he settled in the city's Josefstadt ghetto, near the Altstadt Square. The congested encincture had devolved by then essentially into a slum for impoverished Christians and immigrant Jews alike. With its cheap dives and bordellos, Josefstadt in fact became a curious amalgam. "Cheek by jowl with the haunts of vice and debauchery," recalled one writer, "were the austere houses of believing Jews who locked their doors at nightfall, kept the Sabbath, and observed the high festivals in traditional style." Yet, as Prague's construction boom sustained its momentum over the turn of the century, Josefstadt gradually atrophied into little more than a shell. Most of the Jews by then had found better housing elsewhere, although still within the lower-middle-class Altstadt district. Hermann Kafka, moving his family from one dwelling to another, similarly remained within the Altstadt, less than one hundred yards from the crumbling Josefstadt ghetto.

For Franz Kafka, who lived with his parents almost two-thirds of his life, it was less the Prague of ongoing reconstruction that loomed in his creative memory than the city in its older, historic ambience. While he did not specifically identify its features by name, he conjured up an atavistic image of narrow lanes with immemorial houses and quaint little shops, all sparingly lit by gas lamps at nightfall. Old Prague was Franz Kafka's universe. Even upon assuming the physiognomy of a mythic city, it was the background for his relationship to the world, and for virtually all his writing.

For Jews, that world was infused with a special mystery. Its legends of the Golem persisted with such tenacity that even the radical journalist Egon Kisch (p. 178) once insisted that he had discovered the remains of the medieval creature in an attic of the Altneuschule, Prague's oldest Jewish house of prayer. The Hebrew word *Golem* means "lifeless, unformed matter," and the initial Golem legend is rooted in one of the earliest Cabbalistic—Jewish mystical—works, the *Yetzirah*, which describes possible ways of animating inert substance. Cabbalists believed that a person with the proper qualifications could bring to life not only golems, but also human corpses. One such individual was the sixteenth-century mystic Rabbi Liwa ben Bezalel, better known as Grand Rabbi Loew, whose grave can still be found in the Jewish cemetery. Recognized as a man with special knowledge of God's word, and presiding like a Solomon over his community, Loew was alleged to possess astonishing psychological powers to interpret and cure "disorders of the soul."

Our "authentic" description of the Golem was produced by Loew's son-in-law, Yitzchak ben Shimshon Cohen, who claimed to have assisted the rabbi personally in transforming the inanimate lump of clay into a man who would see, hear, and understand everything. The single function the Golem could not perform was speech. Otherwise, he chopped wood, swept floors, hauled up water from wells, and fulfilled other menial tasks. By Jewish tradition, the Golem manifestly was obliged to rest on the Sabbath, when Rabbi Loew "de-activated" his supernatural powers by removing from beneath his tongue the *Shem*, the ineffable name of God that most crucially gave him life.

On one Sabbath, however, the rabbi unaccountably neglected to remove the *Shem* from the Golem. Whereupon, in a fury, the creature began to hurl about him utensils, furniture, and other chattels. Terrified, people raced to the synagogue to inform Loew. The rabbi interrupted his prayers, rushed home, and finally succeeded in pacifying the Golem by removing the amulet. He also decided then to change the Golem back again to lifeless matter. Subsequently, the creature's remains were placed in the attic of the Altneuschule, where they lay forgotten for two hundred years. Even so, in all that time, Prague's Jews and Gentiles alike remained well versed in the Golem legend, and it continued to infuse its aura of mystery into the world that defined Franz Kafka's art.

If the ancestral legacy was inescapable for Prague Jewry, so were the advantages of identification with the Empire's enlightened civil administration and reigning German culture. Thus, Kafka's father, a rural Jew who spoke Czech in his native village, upon arriving in Prague immediately cast his lot with the city's German-speaking minority. These after all were the "aristocrats" who dominated politics, commerce, and the professions. If there was little social contact between the two peoples, the German enclave at least accepted the Jews as pragmatic allies against the Czech majority. For his part, Franz Kafka shared in Prague Jewry's devotion to the imperial connection. Together with virtually all the Altstadt's Jewish children, he attended the Deutsches Staatsgymnasium, and afterward the German section of Prague's Karl-Ferdinand University. By 1890, after all, no fewer than 40 percent of this institution's students were Jews, and only 1 percent of them were enrolled in its Czech section. Prague's Jews similarly tended to frequent specific "German" coffee shops in or near the Altneustadt district, to organize their own German political clubs, to read and often to contribute to the same German-language liberal newspapers (p. 136).

Indeed, beyond associating within the same concentric circles, Prague's

Jewish intellectuals altogether were emerging as the leading lights of the city's German culture. In German theater, the producers, directors, and patrons were overwhelmingly Jews. With the single exception of Rainer Maria Rilke, the most renowned German writers and poets of early-twentieth-century Prague, and of Bohemia-Moravia at large, were Jews. Max Brod, Franz Werfel, Egon Kisch, Oskar Bauer, Paul Kornfeld, Rudolf Fuchs, Ludwig Winder, Otto Pick, and Hermann Ungar figured prominently among these literary talents. The German newspapers of Prague, led by the *Prager Tageblatt*, whose chief editor was the former theater director Heinrich Tweles (later Sigmund Blau), were edited almost exclusively by Jews. A Jewish physician, Hugo Sallum, reigned as Prague's arbiter of German literary tastes. His second in command was another highly acculturated Jew, Friedrich Adler, who shared Sallum's Teutonic fervor and sedate literary tastes. Trained as a lawyer, Adler produced masterful translations from Czech into German. But a younger generation was rising to challenge these classic standards, and again, the new Prague rebels by and large were Jews. Of these, Kafka would prove the most enduring influence.

A Father's Son, A Loveless Functionary

The author's father, Hermann Kafka, son of a village butcher, had been reared in abject, even desperate poverty. Upon migrating to Prague as a young man, he had clawed his way through the classic (and despised) career of a "Jew-peddler" to become proprietor of a small retail gift shop. Undistinguished though the vocation was, it represented middle-class status for Hermann Kafka, a plateau he had reached through brute drive and a single-minded focus on "respectability." These were less than ideal qualities, however, for Hermann Kafka's subsequent role as father to his own brood of two sons and three daughters. A large, bull-necked man, he overwhelmed his children with truculent pressure to "make something" of themselves. No blows were ever struck, but the mood was continually one of intimidation. Moreover, as oppressive to Franz Kafka as his father's coarse philistinism was the hypocrisy of the man's Judaism. Hermann Kafka observed the principal Jewish holidays as little more than a socially expedient gesture to his middle-class Jewish neighbors.

Something of Franz Kafka's guilt-ridden sense of personal inadequacy appears in two of his better-known stories, "The Judgment" ("Das Urteil") and "The Metamorphosis" ("Die Verwandlung"), both published in 1916. The former is an account ostensibly of the protagonist's— Georg's—fatal neglect of a close friend, a dereliction that impels Georg's outraged father to pass a death sentence on his son. Yet, at the last moment,

Georg inflicts the punishment on himself, by drowning. In the longer, and far superior, novella "The Metamorphosis," Gregor, the protagonist and principal support of his aged, impoverished parents, finds himself suddenly transformed into a gigantic but helpless cockroach. The bizarre occurrence infuriates Gregor's father, who repudiates him. In his despair, Gregor resigns himself to extinction, again at the palpable wish of his father. "The Metamorphosis" ends with the vindictive, post-factum revelation that the father, with a secret nest egg of his own, has long been gratuitously sponging off his son's earnings.

Lest there were doubt about the poisoned filial substructure underlying much of Kafka's writing, the thirty-six-year-old author made his tension explicit in 1919. In an impassioned, sixty-one-page letter to Hermann Kafka, he upbraids his father for displaying only exasperation with his son's commitment to writing, and his son's failure to contract a "good" marriage and home of his own. "[I]n every trifle you convinced me . . . of my incapability," protests the aggrieved Franz. ". . . You created in me a nerve-destroying fear and sense of guilt." He adds, later: "I once wrote of someone, accurately: 'He is afraid the shame will outlive him.' " The reference is a telling one. It is the final sentence in one of Kafka's later and profoundest works, *The Trial (Der Prozess)*.

Kafka acquired much of the literary terminology for that guilt from his vocation. Entering the German section of Prague's Karl-Ferdinand University in 1901, he was drawn at first to the humanities. His father shot down the notion immediately. Jewish boys registered for such "practical" subjects as law or medicine. The son opted then for law. It was a deadening five-year ordeal for him. Even so, Kafka managed to acquire the requisite doctorate of jurisprudence in 1906. Eventually, through a university friend, he secured a bureaucratic position at the Workmen's Accident Insurance Institute. As a quasi-governmental body, the institute normally preferred to hire "Aryans." Kafka may well have been taken on as one of a handful of token Jews. The appointment in any case proved a blessing for him. His conscientious work ethic won the admiration of his superiors, who rewarded him over the years with numerous promotions, and eventually granted him the much-respected position of senior secretary. With a spacious office, a decent salary, and extended vacation and sick-leave benefits, Kafka remained on comfortably at the institute until 1922, in effect, until the end of his working life.

Of comparable, literary usefulness to Kafka were his duties within the institute's elaborate administration. These consisted essentially of classifying the work-safety conditions of Bohemia's larger industrial enterprises. The task gave him the opportunity to travel throughout the eastern Empire, studying the performance of its various mills and factories. He derived much from the experience. Like the labyrinth of jurisprudence and of other administrative bureaucracies, the operation of industrial machines provided Kafka with the raw data of his literary creativity. "The Penal Colony" ("Die Strafkolonie") was a case in point.

Written in two inspired weeks late in 1914, and published two years after that, the tale describes a prison camp on the model of Devil's Island, and an execution device that implacably destroys its condemned victims by incising their flesh with acid-dipped spikes. The clinically accurate details of engines, cogs, pulleys, wheels, and gears plainly were inspired by the machinery Kafka witnessed in his tours of factories, and afterward evaluated in reports for his office. The story itself bespoke the author's ongoing preoccupation with human cruelty—it was written following the outbreak of the World War—but even more with the source of his own guilt. As Kafka's diary entries and letters reveal ("miserable creature that I am"), it was he himself who stood exposed as the deserving object of punishment.

Yet Kafka's gnawing sense of culpability did not appear to derive exclusively from having "failed" his overbearing father. It may also have reflected his evident inability to make a definitive emotional commitment to women. Was he self-conscious of his ungainly figure, which shot up, awkward and ill coordinated, during his early adolescence? Photographs of Kafka even as a grown man display a rather spindulate frame, and a dark, brooding face rendered somewhat cadaverous by outsize ears. It is not unlikely that he distrusted his body and developed a fear of physical intimacy. If so, his inhibition was at odds with his aching need for the "settled structure" of marriage. When he was twenty-nine, he approached the very threshold of that relationship.

In August 1912, Kafka met a young Jewish woman, Felice Bauer, at the home of his friend Max Brod. Employed as a clerk for a dictaphone company in Neustadt, Silesia, Bauer was on a visit to her firm's Prague office. Although quite plain, she struck Kafka as cheerful, forthright, and thoroughly bourgeoise. Above all, to him, she signified normalcy and domesticity. Over the ensuing two years, Kafka wrote Bauer hundreds of letters and postcards. In the spring of 1914, the couple rented an apartment in Prague, and in June they became engaged. Then, five weeks later, Kafka suddenly broke off the engagement. It does not appear coincidental that, soon afterward, he began work on *The Trial*, the novel to which he gave his principal creative effort during the war years.

The book may subliminally have evoked Kafka's horror at the likely fate of millions of combatants. Yet it chronicled even more forthrightly the struggle of its protagonist, Josef K, to discover the nature of his own guilt, together with the identity of his judges and the logic of a sentence based on an apparently reasonless verdict. In some measure, K's transgression is the obtuseness of his lament, one that he never ceases voicing until shortly before the end, that a wrong has been done him. Only too late does he awaken to a likely source of his shame, that he has failed to evince compassion for others. His guilt, in short, is that of an inauthentic existence, a "vie manqué." Although K is put to death by two faceless officials, morally he is his own executioner.

By the time he completed *The Trial*, Kafka had also refined his unique literary style. His use of language, spare and clinical, was far removed from the lush and often fevered romanticism employed by Prague writers as proof that they were not mere "provincials," outside the mainstream of German literature. In Kafka's hands, prose became a hard-edged and rather glacial instrument with which to transform his direst nightmares into straightforward, even pedestrian realities. Moreover, befitting the elegiac, fatalistic mood of virtually all Kafka's writings, the atmosphere of *The Trial* and numerous others of his works is steeped in twilight. Thus, in *The Trial*, twilight suffuses K's office, his bedroom, floods its way into the courtroom, which thereby is transformed into a shadowy, tomblike chamber, until all illumination finally is extinguished by the night of K's execution.

A Professor of Moralism

It was also the twilight of Kafka's, and Prague Jewry's, final anchorage in Habsburg German culture. The moorage had always been a fragile one, characterized at best by a sense of caution, at worst by suspicion, and often distaste. Initially, Czech Jewry's passion for the German connection signified a commitment to political emancipation even more than to cultural sophistication. They owed everything to the Empire, after all, their civil rights, their economic and social mobility. And yet, by 1883, the year of Kafka's birth, Habsburg liberalism already had crested. The last progressive cabinet had fallen in 1879, to be replaced by the pietistic, conservative government of Count Eduard von Taaffe. Ethnic self-assertion, whether German or Hungarian, Czech or Serbo-Croatian, was emerging as the wave of the Empire's future—and of its ultimate demise. The society in which Habsburg Jews sought assimilation was crumbling.

Indeed, Theodor Herzl, the founder of political Zionism, was among the earliest to issue the warning openly. For him, the evidence was incontrovertible. Unless they apostatized, Jews were almost certain to be denied access to prestigious civil service appointments (p. 163). In academic circles, at the German section of Karl-Ferdinand University, the völkisch— "integral," racist—antisemitism of Georg von Schönerer was evoking interest and wider acceptance. Jewish students found themselves increasingly isolated, blackballed from student societies, subjected to mounting abuse and humiliation.

In Prague, moreover, the thirty thousand-odd Jews of Kafka's lifetime were buffeted by the rising tide of majority nationalism. This one was Czech. In Prague and Pilsen, as in Bohemia's and Moravia's smaller towns, Czech economic circumstances and political expectations fully matched the growth of the Czech population at large. The poets Karl Hynek Macha and Viteslav Halek, the novelists Bozena Nemcova, Karolina Svetla, and Alois Jirasek, popularized an extended range of nationalist themes, and so also did Czech literary associations, paintings, posters, exhibitions, music, and theater.

In the early and mid-nineteenth century, Czech cultural nationalists were ambivalent in their attitude toward Jews. The writers Karl Hynek Macha and Vaclav Nebesky, and the dramatist Jiri Kolar were open admirers of Jewish economic and intellectual vitality. But others were less forbearing. The essayist Karel Havlicek Borovsky was among the first to characterize Jews as opportunistic sycophants of the German ruling minority. In 1882, a year of economic depression, antisemitic riots in Prague culminated in the widespread pillage of Jewish shops and homes. Five years later, in still another anti-Jewish upsurge, Czech workers and teenagers in Prague joined in looting Jewish businesses and synagogues. Yet, of graver concern to the Jews even than random violence was the persistence of folkloristic antisemitism among the Czech population at large. Throughout the 1880s and 1890s, there had been periodic revivals of the hoary ritual-murder accusation, three in 1893 alone.

The charge was revived with particular intensity in 1899. In March of that year, a nineteen-year-old seamstress, Agnes Hruza, disappeared in the Brzina Forest near Polna, a Bohemian town near the Moravian provincial frontier. Her body was discovered soon afterward, on April 1, the day before Easter Sunday. An autopsy determined that Agnes had been stabbed and strangled (although not sexually molested). It appeared that her corpse had been dragged to the spot of discovery, for pieces of her clothing were found strewn elsewhere. Almost immediately, the rumor began circulating that Agnes was the victim of Jewish ritual murder, that her blood had been used for the Passover Seder. Within the week, a suspect was taken into custody. This was Leopold Hilsner, an unemployed Jewish shoemaker in his early thirties. A witness had seen a man running away from the body and had recognized him as Hilsner (an "identification" that was later punctured in courtroom cross-examination).

A search of Hilsner's lodgings revealed clothes that appeared to be covered with foliage and specks of blood. Confronted with the evidence, the disoriented Hilsner argued that the clothes were borrowed, and that he had not worn them for two years. Yet it was also established that he had known Agnes Hruza and had followed her home several times before. Hilsner had a shady past, was known to be aggressive with women, and once had threatened to kill a former girlfriend. Together with the tainted clothing, and the witness's initial testimony, Hilsner's record was suspect enough to get him indicted and put on trial in the circuit court of Kuttenberg. There he was represented by the local public defender, a nondescript country lawyer. The prosecuting attorney, Dr. Schneider-Svoboda, was the supreme counselor of the provincial court and a widely renowned bulldog.

The prosecution's case in fact appeared substantial, and Schneider-Svoboda presented it in fire and brimstone. No reference was made initially to ritual murder. That lacuna was filled, rather, by Karel Bax, a Prague attorney and counsel to the mother of the murdered Agnes Hruza, who worked closely with Schneider-Svoboda. After reviewing the prosecution's case, and noting that the victim had not been sexually molested, Bax declaimed:

> Then why, for what reasons, was Agnes Hruza murdered? . . . [The killers] wanted to murder a Christian person, an innocent girl, in order to get her blood. . . . We are confronted with a fact that has been proved, which cannot be refuted. . . . We must defend ourselves against the Ritual Murder tradition.

Only then did Schneider-Svoboda endorse the ritual-murder charge as an integral feature of the state's case. Indeed, he went on to cite various Jewish sources, even the Talmud, as "evidence" of this practice. On September 16, the jury found Hilsner guilty of murder. The judge then sentenced him to be hanged.

Newspapers throughout the Empire gave wide coverage to the Hilsner case. Without taking an editorial position, all devoted extensive space to scholarly and ecclesiastical views and counterviews on the ritual-murder charge. It was in the aftermath of the trial, moreover, that a forty-nine-year-old professor of philosophy in the Czech division of Prague's Karl-Ferdinand University produced an assessment of unique critical weight. The author was Tomas Garrigue Masaryk, a figure who lately had emerged as a renowned cultural icon among the literate middle classes of Bohemia and Moravia. It was not a career that would have been predicted. The son of a Slovak coachman and a Czech domestic, Masaryk by birth seemingly was destined for a life of menial service. It was his precociousness as a student that saved him. His succession of prizes and scholarships led to a University of Vienna doctorate in history and philosophy, and ultimately to a faculty appointment in Prague. In ensuing years, as a prolific author,

Masaryk distinguished himself for his richly tapestried volumes on the Czech Reformation.

Additionally, as a committed Czech nationalist, Masaryk in 1889 transformed one of the two scholarly journals he edited into a political-cultural review devoted to Czecho-Slovak patriotic themes. Three years later, his admiring countrymen elected him as one of their delegates to the Habsburg Reichsrat, where he became an eloquent and respected champion of their national cause. Yet Masaryk was not about to become a facile demagogue in behalf of Czech nationhood. He adamantly refused to tailor the facts of history to accommodate his political agenda. This point was made early on, in a lengthy essay Masaryk published in his own philosophical journal, proving that two ostensibly medieval Czech poems, widely hailed by his countrymen as Slavic counterparts of the German *Nibelungenlied*, in fact were mere patriotic forgeries by an early-nineteenth-century Bohemian poetaster. The article infuriated Czech ultranationalists, many of whom denounced the professor for his "treachery." Unrepentant, Masaryk replied forcefully that "[i]t is a deliberate and discerning love of our nation that appeals to me, not the indiscriminate love that assumes everything to be right and righteous merely because it bears a national label." It was also the approach he brought to the Hilsner case.

One of Masaryk's former university classmates, Sigmund Muntz, took it upon himself to send the professor a full account of the Kuttenberg trial. A senior editor of Vienna's *Neue Freie Presse*, Muntz was privy to details of the affair that he suspected Masaryk might not know. In fact, accusations of ritual murder were far from unknown to the professor. In his native Moravian town of Hodonin, similar rumors periodically had been directed at the few dozen local Jewish families. If Masaryk himself ever shared those suspicions, his attitude changed upon entering the University of Vienna. There, Sigmund Muntz was only one of a number of Jews he had come to know and befriend. He maintained those relationships over the years. It was true, however, that Masaryk had been on vacation in the Moravian countryside in September 1899, and thus had not followed the court proceedings of the Hilsner case.

Appalled at the ritual-murder accusation, the professor immediately responded to Muntz, providing a concise historical overview of the blood libel. With Masaryk's permission, Muntz in turn published the letter. It covered two full pages of the *Neue Freie Presse* and subsequently was reprinted in numerous Czech-language newspapers. Later, Masaryk used his own philosophical journal to publish an even more damning exposé of the blood-libel accusation both throughout history and in the current Hilsner case. In page after page, his indignation barely suppressed, the professor warned in apocalyptic language that "[i]t is blasphemy for a

Christian to state that ritual murder comes from the spirit of the Jewish religion." In a subsequent essay, Masaryk laid down a thunderous challenge: "I repeat what I have written on the blackboard for my students. The whole Polna trial and its exploitation from clerical and antisemitic quarters is an outrage against the healthy mind of humanity."

Although Masaryk's reputation alone could not have reversed the Hilsner judgment, it almost certainly assured the closest judicial attention upon appeal. In the late summer of 1900, the court of claims in Vienna overrode the verdict, then ordered a new trial. This one took place in Pisek, Bohemia, in October of the same year, and the issue of ritual murder no longer was raised. Instead, Hilsner simply was found guilty of acting as an accomplice in the murder of Agnes Hruza, and his sentence thereby was reduced to life imprisonment. Even then, the passions aroused by the trial did not subside. As late as 1907, anti-Jewish riots erupted in the Bohemian countryside, and in Prague's Josefstadt quarter. Only slowly did the worst of the antisemitic frenzy begin to ebb. Years later, in 1916, Emperor Karl, as one of his first acts upon assuming the throne after the death of Franz Josef, issued Hilsner a royal pardon. Leaving prison broken in health and mind, the Jewish carpenter never again was able to find employment. He died in 1925.

Meanwhile, for all his moral rectitude, Tomas Masaryk himself paid dearly for leaving the academic ivory tower to take on an unpopular cause. Much of the press and nearly all the Church hierarchy fell on him for "mixing" in a legal matter. When he turned up for class on November 10, 1900, following Hilsner's retrial, he was greeted by placards urging students to boycott the lectures of a man "who had taken up the cause of a Jew." Masaryk wrote later:

> At [the time of the Hilsner trial] . . . not only the student body but the whole [of Karl-Ferdinand] University was infected with the uncultivated virus of street antisemitism. I see the frightened faces of many of my acquaintances in front of me and remember how they evaded me. . . . I have taken part in many struggles, but the battle against antisemitism cost me the most in both time and pain.

A Statesman of Conscience

In the years following the Hilsner case, Masaryk gradually resumed his former status as the ideological spokesman for Czech and Slovak nationalism. Reelected to the Reichsrat in 1901, he served as leader of his own "Realist" party, committed to his people's self-determination within a pluralistic, federal empire. Soon, too, Masaryk achieved recognition as the preeminent champion of the entire Slavic opposition bloc in the Reichsrat, defending the cause of Serbs and Croats, as well as Czechs and Slovaks. And when the World War began in July 1914, he characteristically denounced the government for its punitive campaign against Serbia.

The professor's stance was not without its risks. Indeed, it was to avoid prosecution that Masaryk early in 1915 made his way to Western Europe. In Paris, with its local *sokol*—nationalist society—of some three thousand Czech expatriates, he won immediate French governmental recognition for his people's liberation movement, and for its expatriate representation (soon to be institutionalized as the Czech National Council). A year later, meeting with French Foreign Minister Aristide Briand, Masaryk and his close associate Eduard Benes appealed for diplomatic support on behalf of full Czecho-Slovak independence. Briand, in turn, although sympathetic, intimated that Czech claims would require a "pragmatic" as well as a moral basis. The hint was all but explicit. It was accordingly to secure that "pragmatic" leverage, following the overthrow of Russia's tsarist regime in March 1917, that Masaryk subsequently transferred his activities to St. Petersburg. His purpose was to organize a separate army unit of Czech and Slovak prisoners of war. Presumably these former Habsburg troops would be eager to join the Allies in a liberationist struggle for their homeland.

They were. Some 35,000 POWs were recruited and organized into a Czechoslovak Legion. Although they were blocked by the later Bolshevik government from direct access to the Western Allies, the legionnaires on their own carried out an arduous trek eastward across the vast breadth of Russia. From the port of Vladivostok, the troops later were transported by Japanese naval vessels to the United States, and eventually were shipped on to Europe, where they joined the hard-pressed Allies. The epic journey registered powerfully on the consciences of Western statesmen.

It was on the Americans, however, that Masaryk pinned his keenest hopes for a fully independent Czechoslovakia. His wife was American. During his visits to the United States in earlier years, Masaryk had come to admire the vibrant pluralism of American democracy. He also possessed an important asset in America's expatriate community of a million and a half Czechs and Slovaks, who evidently shared his vision of a united postwar Czechoslovakia. Moreover, in 1916 and again in 1918, Masaryk held several warm interviews with President Woodrow Wilson, and a mutually admiring relationship developed between the two men. It was not Masaryk's pro-Allied loyalty alone that bonded this friendship. His intellectual rectitude and personal charm unquestionably played a role, as well as the dignity and modulated charm with which he made his case in personal discussion. Years later, David Lloyd George acknowledged that

Masaryk was one of the three most persuasive diplomats of his experience at the Peace Conference (Greece's Eleutherios Venizelos and the Zionists' Chaim Weizmann were the other two).

The subsequent achievements of the Czech Legion merely fortified Masaryk's claim, and the self-determination of Czechoslovakia then became one of Wilson's objectives for the postwar peace settlement. Thus, in June 1918, when Britain's Foreign Secretary Arthur Balfour recognized Czechoslovakia as a sovereign ally, Wilson endorsed that recognition, as well as the frontiers that Masaryk projected for his multinational state. In November, following the surrender of the Central Powers, Masaryk returned in triumph to Prague. The Czech National Council had seized control in this ancient provincial capital on October 28, 1918. Two and a half weeks later, on November 14, the same body elected the sixty-eight-year-old statesman-scholar as president of their newly proclaimed Republic of Czechoslovakia.

Masaryk assumed office in a nation of approximately 8 million Czechs, 3 million Slovaks, 2.8 million Germans, 700,000 Hungarians, and 300,000 Poles. Approximately 270,000 Jews, too, were represented in the new successor state—90,000 in Bohemia, 38,000 in Moravia, 136,000 in Slovakia, and 7,000 in Silesia. In 1921, when the Allies belatedly awarded Ruthenia (Carpatho-Russia) to Czechoslovakia, the Jewish population was augmented by an additional 93,000. At this point, Masaryk's new republic contained the sixth-largest Jewish population on the Continent, outside the Soviet Union. They were also a disparate minority. Those who lived in Slovakia and Ruthenia were mainly villagers, either small merchants or artisans of modest circumstances. Their culture tended to be ethnocentric and Yiddish-speaking. By contrast, the Jews of Bohemia and Moravia tended to live in cities and towns and, with few exceptions, they were a quintessentially middle-class, German-speaking community (pp. 135–36).

In the last months of the war, however, as the Empire's various nationalities began preparing for full independence, Jews of all backgrounds explored ways of protecting themselves from the anticipated excesses of successor-state majorities. On October 14, 1918, the Zionist leadership of Austria, with their ideological commitment to Jewish peoplehood, took the lead in organizing an intercommunal Jewish conference in Vienna. Arriving from the principal cities of the collapsing Empire, the delegates elected a "Jewish National Council" and issued a policy statement that was intended essentially as a message to the Allied Powers. Whatever the Empire's fate, they expected to be awarded the identical civil and collective recognition—and thus the identical protection—extended to any other nationality.

To fortify that demand, a parallel Jewish National Council was appointed a week later, on October 22, for Bohemia-Moravia. Headquartered in Prague, and functioning under the chairmanship of Max Brod, the new body endorsed the Vienna agenda point by point. Six days after that, on October 28, when the Republic of Czechoslovakia was formally proclaimed, Brod and his colleagues personally resubmitted their program to the new government. They discerned no contradiction in accepting a Zionist agenda for protection as a "national minority." In their explanation to Masaryk, they reminded the president that their acculturation had been to an essentially Germanic empire, and not to a Slavic majority whose behavior toward their people was less than reassuring. And Masaryk, with his unique background, had every reason to understand the Jews' chronic insecurity.

The Good Zionist

In the prewar years, both as a scholar and as a deputy in the imperial parliament, Masaryk had carefully explored all facets of the European nationalities issue. With the Jews also figuring in his evaluation, he had concluded that Zionism was a vehicle less for Jewish emigration to Palestine than for Jewish dignity and pride in Europe. As early as 1899, in his essay "The Philosophical and Sociological Bases of Marxism," Masaryk rejected a purely economic interpretation of the Jewish issue, and adopted a proto-Zionist approach. "Marx does not want to see in the Jewish question the national, the racial question," he argued, "which it nevertheless is."

In this same article, Masaryk wrote of the need to regenerate the spirit of the Prophets: "One part of this work of regeneration I see in Zionism. I do not mean by that the migration of the Jews to Palestine . . . but they must understand that their moral condition is in need of reform." A year later, in an essay he contributed to Arthur Kronenberger's volume *Zionists and Christians (Zionisten und Christianen)*, Masaryk added: "The Zionist movement appeals to me a great deal. . . . In Zionism I see, to quote a well-known expression, 'a drop of oil of the Prophets.' " Insofar as Zionism fortified Jewish pride and self-reliance, Masaryk would lend the movement his fullest intellectual support and personal prestige.

Beyond these "objective" considerations, however, Masaryk appreciated the debt he owed the Jews. In a later volume, *World Revolution (Weltrevolution)*, he recalled his visits to the United States in 1907 and during his émigré wartime diplomacy in 1916 and 1918:

> Particularly in America the Jews helped me, and here I was more than compensated . . . for any part in the Hilsner affair. In 1907 the Jews of New York gave me a tremendous welcome and I had many

personal contacts with the representatives [both] of the Orthodox [and Zionist] group[s].

During the war period, one of those Zionist contacts was Supreme Court Justice Louis Brandeis, whose parents had immigrated from Bohemia in the nineteenth century. Through Brandeis, in turn, Masaryk secured his first interview with Woodrow Wilson. In subsequent discussions with Brandeis, with Louis Marshall, Judge Julian Mack, and Rabbi Stephen Wise, he learned too that "[i]n America the Jews are well treated in the press and it was very advantageous to have this force with us."

Masaryk was prepared to reciprocate. In late October of 1918, while still in the United States, he had participated in a "Congress of the Oppressed Nationalities of Central Europe," meeting in Philadelphia, and had won the conclave's support for the recently issued Balfour Declaration, with its promise of a Jewish National Home in Palestine. Before departing the United States, Masaryk reiterated to the Federation of American Zionists that "[t]he Jews will enjoy the same rights [in an independent Czechslovakia] as all the other citizens of our state." That assurance would cover the full plenum of "national-communal" as well as civil-political rights.

Accordingly, on December 31, following his return to Prague and his election to his nation's presidency, Masaryk received Max Brod, chairman of the Jewish National Council, and a leading Zionist, and emphasized once more that he, Masaryk, favored "recognition of the legitimate position of the Jewish nationality in the Czechoslovakian state." Several days later, the new president repeated this assurance to Jakob Landau, a correspondent of Prague's *Jüdische Telegraf*: "If a man tells me he is a German," the president explained, "I must accept it. If he declares that he is a Jew, then I must accept this, too. This develops from the right of self-determination which must find its application among the Jews."

It was specifically the promise of a free choice that the Jews were seeking. Their priority was not only collective self-expression but self-protection. As early as November 1918, units of the Czech Legion were sharing in the widespread pillage of Jewish shops and homes in Slovakia. Antisemitism in the eastern regions was further inflamed during the brief incursion of Bela Kun's Hungarian Red Army in the spring of 1919 (p. 110). For months afterward, hardly a Jewish community in eastern Slovakia escaped looting. The violence reached its peak in November 1919, but continued to flicker intermittently for nearly a year.

As early as October 1918, however, with an acute presentiment of the fulminant nationalism glowering around them, a group of Czech Jewish activists, led by Ludvik Singer, an eminent Prague lawyer, set about organizing the first "Congress of Czechoslovak Jews." Assembling in the Czech capital on January 4, 1919, the larger gathering unanimously endorsed a program of Jewish "national" rights, and then sent a delegation to the Peace Conference. The delegation members—Singer, Max Brod, Norbert Adler, and Hugo Bergmann—would serve as Czech Jewry's principal lobbyists in Paris.

Their interlocutor was Czechoslovakia's newly appointed foreign minister, Dr. Eduard Benes. Thoroughly steeped in the Western, liberal tradition, Benes required no encouragement to follow his president's "Jewish" guidelines. "The Jews as well as the other national minorities of this Republic will be given equal rights of citizenship and all minority rights," he assured Bergmann and Brod on April 5, 1919. The commitment was honored on September 10, 1919, when Benes signed the minorities declaration annexed to the Treaty of Saint-Germain, the Austrian peace agreement (which established the State of Czechoslovakia). Virtually identical to the minorities treaties signed by the defeated Central Powers (except for Germany), and by the other successor states, this declaration in turn was incorporated into the constitution of the Czechoslovakian Republic in February 1920.

Neither in the peace treaty nor in the constitution were specific nationalities mentioned, but a Jew could declare himself a member of the Jewish or any other of Czechoslovakia's ethnic communities. In common with these other nationalities, Jews were entitled to the full plenum of linguistic, communal, and educational rights incorporated in all other minorities treaties. Within the next few years, moreover, these guarantees were fulfilled in both letter and spirit. Thus, in Slovakia and Ruthenia, virtually all Jews opted for registration as a minority nationality, and for a separate school system of their own, with Yiddish as its language of instruction. The state funded these schools in their entirety. In Bohemia and Moravia, circumstances were different, but exclusively as a matter of Jewish choice. Here only 38 percent of the Jewish population listed themselves as Jews by nationality, and even then essentially as a safeguard for assured access to the League of Nations in the event of revived discrimination. The overwhelming majority of Jews still preferred to send their children to the public school system, where Czech was employed as the language of instruction.

But in whichever province, all Jewish communal institutions, all Jewish holidays, enjoyed full juridical protection. It was an impressive achievement, and a unique one. In contrast to the minorities treaties signed by Poland, Rumania, or Hungary, this one had not been wrested from a reluctant government as a consequence of Allied pressures. The award of Jewish national minority rights had been swift, forthcoming, and condign. If ever an individual set the tone for this benediction, it was the scholar-statesman in the Hradcany presidential castle.

A Prophet of National Identity

For the Jews, nevertheless, the transition from "collateral" membership in a ruling German patriciate to minority status among a politically dominant Czech majority was challenging, and often painful. Franz Kafka himself possibly made the transition more easily than did most of his fellow Jews. Well before the war, he had developed equable relations with the Czechs. Although he could not identify with their political nationalism, he respected their culture, possessed a good command of the Czech language, attended Czech theatrical performances, mingled with Czechs in their Czech Democratic Club. There is no evidence that he attributed the vulgarisms and periodic violence of Czech antisemitism to the Czech people at large.

Yet, like other Prague Jews, Kafka maintained his principal social contacts neither with the Czechs nor with the Germans, but with his own people, whether his most intimate friends, Max Brod and Franz Werfel (p. 161), or with such cordial acquaintances as Hugo Bergmann and Felix Weltsch. At first, it was exclusively an ethnic relationship. By the turn of the century, few of Prague's Jewish intellectuals shared more than a vestigial sense of religious traditionalism. As a youngster, Kafka routinely underwent bar mitzvah, although the invitation cards his parents sent out described the ceremony as "confirmation." Until his early twenties, he accepted his Jewishness matter-of-factly, if superficially.

Then, during his law studies, Kafka found himself drawn to the Bar Kochba Society. Conceived as a Zionist cultural group by the Viennese Jewish philosopher Martin Buber, Bar Kochba functioned essentially as a social outlet for Jewish university students. Nevertheless, the organization also periodically attracted interest with its lectures on Jewish intellectual themes. During the immediate postwar period, when various mystical and apocalyptic ideologies gained adherents among the distraught populations of the former Central Powers, Martin Buber himself became something of a Jewish cult figure. His neo-Chasidic notions of völkisch—"integral," "ethnic"—Jewishness, which he tended to identify with the "Ostjuden" of Galicia, apparently filled a certain emotional void among an impressionable minority of younger Jews.

Kafka, however, riven with emotional longings of his own, had begun navigating his way toward an "integral," spiritual anchorage well before the war. In 1910, curiosity drew him to the performance of a visiting Yiddish theater group from Lemberg (Lvov). The setting was Prague's rather drab Café Savoy, and the actors were amateurish and histrionic. Yet it was the very "authenticity" of these Jewish *Ur*-types that evidently touched a chord. When a second Galician troop visited Prague in the winter of 1911–12, Kafka attended its performances repeatedly. He also befriended one of its actors, Yitzchak Löwy, and pressed the young man for information on Galician Jewish life. Images of these insights would appear in several of Kafka's later writings. Afterward, too, he entered into a more detailed study of Chasidic legends and traditions.

Possibly something of the romanticized Chasidic influence appears in Kafka's 1917 story "A Country Doctor" ("Ein Landartz"). It becomes evident in this tale that the doctor is incapable of curing his afflicted patient, who requires a different, spiritual type of healing. Was this a veiled intimation that only a Chasidic rabbi could fulfill such a role? In his 1919 "Letter to My Father," Kafka similarly upbraids Hermann Kafka for engaging in a pedestrian "businessman's" Judaism. In later years, with the influx into Czechoslovakia of thousands of new Galician Jews, most of them fugitives from the war zones and the later, postwar Ukrainian massacres, Kafka would have occasion to study the Easterners' religious sociology even more intimately (p. 158).

Yet Kafka's need for a "spiritually" comforting Judaism was influenced not only by his cultural uncertainties. His physical deterioration also played a role. In September 1917 Kafka began spitting up blood. An examination revealed that he was suffering from laryngeal tuberculosis. Eventually the disease required increasing absences from work, and intermittent confinement in sanitoria. Racked by anxiety and a sense of helplessness, Kafka wrote comparatively little between 1917 and 1919. It soon became evident, too, that his illness exacerbated the psychic forebodings that had plagued his early career. His friend Albert Ehrenstein may have been right in suggesting that, like Chopin, "Kafka had been dying all his life."

In his last, postwar years, even in his physical infirmity and his "Jewish" preoccupations, Kafka made a point of developing closer associations with his Czech fellow workers, and attending meetings of the Czech National Democratic and Socialist parties. On one occasion, he entered into a romantic relationship with a vibrant Czech woman, Milena Jesenska, a literary critic who earlier had been married to a Jewish intellectual. It was Jesenska who sought Kafka out after reading and becoming entranced by his stories. With his permission, she translated several of his earlier works into Czech. Although their "affair" lasted barely seven months, and was entirely epistolary, Jesenska never regretted the experience. "A woman is punished when she shows too much initiative," she confided to a friend. Jesenska was more prescient than she knew. The conversation took place in a Nazi concentration camp, where she languished for four years as punishment for helping Jews and other "undesirables" to flee. She died there of malnutrition in 1944.

If Kafka and Prague Jewry at large escaped the uglier features of rampant postwar antisemitism, they could not be indifferent to the pogroms raging through Slovakia in 1919–20, in the aftermath of the Red Hungarian occupation. Several racist demonstrations erupted even in Prague. Kafka noted in a letter to Jesenska in November 1920 that "[t]he whole afternoon I am in the streets and bathe in Jew-hatred. Just now I heard someone call the Jews 'prasive plemeno' ['a mangy race']." Jewish archives were ransacked. A bonfire of Hebrew manuscripts blazed all day outside one of the medieval synagogues in the Altneustadt district. In his anxiety, Kafka noted "the absence of any firm Jewish ground beneath my feet." The loneliness inflicted by a ravaging illness, by a mordant vision of the human condition, could only have been intensified by the anomie of a Jew cast adrift in an unstable new society.

A later tale, "Josephine the Singer, or the Mouse Nation" ("Josephine die Sängerin, oder das Volk der Mäuse"), finished in 1924, seemingly reaffirmed Kafka's sense of isolation. Some critics have discerned the prototype for Josephine in an actress belonging to a prewar Yiddish theatrical troupe. Possibly Kafka himself appears in the tale, as a female mouse, a singer among a nation of mice (Jews?), who eventually become helpless, unable even to whistle as loud as the other mice. Kafka concludes his story with the observation: "Josephine, redeemed from earthly sorrows . . . will rise to the heights of redemption and be forgotten like all her brothers."

Although still nominally employed at the Workmen's Insurance Institute, Kafka by 1922 actually was spending the larger part of his time in sanitoria. He was also devoting his last reserves of energy to his longest novel, *The Castle (Das Schloss)*, a project on which he had been laboring since 1919. He would not complete it during his lifetime. Max Brod edited the manuscript only after Kafka's death, and published it in 1926. Even under these limitations, however, *The Castle* emerges as Kafka's most subtle and powerful creation. In the manner of his earlier fiction, *The Castle* takes the characteristic form of a dream-narrative. The real blends seamlessly with the surreal, and human effort flounders against an ill-defined implacability.

Arriving in a mythic village (possibly inspired by Wossek, the Bohemian hamlet of Kafka's paternal forebears), "K," a surveyor, seeks an interview with his putative employer, Count Westwind, who rules his domain from a neighboring castle. The account of K's doomed effort to gain access to the brooding, infinitely remote castle is one of endless disorientation, of pointless movement through deserted streets and cramped rooms, and confused encounters with cryptic villagers and enigmatic bureaucrats. The novel breaks off at a moment when K, finally reaching the castle and seeking entrance to the count's interior offices, confronts yet another blind alley. It is the castle's underground recesses—and a likely metaphor for death.

Interpretive literature on *The Castle* runs into many hundreds of articles and books. Some, like Max Brod's preface to the posthumous first edition in 1926, proclaim the novel a symbolic quest for divine grace. Other critics see the book as an allegory of impersonal bureaucratic power. Freudians tend to emphasize unconscious symbols. Sociologists have related the novel to the context of the time. Yet, with the prevailing theme incontrovertibly that of K's (most surely, Kafka's) alienation, the source of the author's estrangement could well have been manifold. It would have stemmed from his debilitating illness; his personal "intellectual" sensitivity, bullied by an overbearing father; his minority status as a German-speaker among a Czech majority. Virtually all critics agree, in any case, that Kafka's loss of anchorage was profoundly linked to his Jewishness. His diary entries in 1921 and 1922 reveal an endless preoccupation with the hopeless status of Jews in Prague, of his personal need to find a way "out of here." "K" is his precise analogue, whom *The Castle*'s villagers and functionaries alike regard as a hapless intruder. "May I pay you a visit one day?" K asks a schoolteacher, and receives a predictably ambivalent response: "I live in Swan Street at the butcher's."

A Belatedness of Recognition

On June 3, 1924, after six months of intermittent lapses into unconsciousness, Franz Kafka died in a sanitorium in Dierling, near Vienna. "He was little known among us," acknowledged Milena Jesenska, in her eulogy of Kafka two days later, in Prague's *Narodni listy*. It was an understatement. Nearly a decade would pass before the full measure of the writer's genius was recognized. More than any other, it was the devoted Max Brod, functioning as Kafka's literary executor, who ensured his friend's place in Europe's cultural pantheon. Himself a noted writer, Brod was particularly successful in blending Jewish, Czech, and German cultural elements in a series of well-received historical novels and essays on Jewish nationality.

During the war, Brod engaged in pacifist propaganda in Switzerland, then returned to become a Zionist spokesman for Jewish national rights (p. 147). In the early 1920s, he directed the Czechoslovak government's first press department, then served as theater and music critic of the German-language *Prager Tageblatt*. Beyond all his public and literary activities, however, Brod is most widely remembered as Kafka's soul mate and devoted sounding board throughout his friend's lifetime, and as editor, publicist, and pioneering interpreter of Kafka's posthumous manuscripts, including not only *The Castle*, but Kafka's diaries and later his assembled letters.

In Czechoslovakia, ironically, recognition of Kafka's talents came later than in Western Europe. Some of the obituaries in Prague even misspelled his name. It was not Brod but Milena Jesenska who first pressed Kafka's case among the Czech reading public. Jesenska's circle was of the left, and it was among these Socialist elements, who regarded him as a voice for "social justice," that Kafka acquired his first and posthumous readership in the Czech language. Even then, it was only with Paul Eisner's translation of *The Castle* into Czech in 1935 that this profoundest of Kafka's novels began to evoke resonance in the writer's native country. Czech intellectuals accepted Eisner's interpretation of Kafka as a surrealist, as the revealer of subliminal processes that defeated human understanding, as the discoverer of a new system of references, askew in their angle of vision but somehow piercingly on the mark in their appraisal of an alien world. Indeed, among Czech readers, that world came to be known by the slang term *kafkarna*.

Did Kafka's emergence as a literary icon in the 1930s prefigure a wider appreciation of the Jewish cultural leaven in this postwar successor state? Most of Czechoslovakia's intelligentsia, after all, accepted Eisner's dead-accurate characterization of Kafka's achievements as "a mixture of three races." The Jewish presence unquestionably was becoming as substantial a fact of life in Czechoslovak cities as it was elsewhere in East-Central Europe. The 1930 census revealed that Czechoslovak Jewry totaled approximately 360,000. Although this number represented only 2.4 percent of the nation's population, 80 percent of the Jews of Czechoslovakia lived in towns with over 5,000 inhabitants, and 60 percent in towns with over 50,000 inhabitants—Prague, Brno, Ostrava, Bratislava. Replicating their demographic pattern elsewhere in Europe, the Jews emerged as a disproportionately urbanized, and thereby disproportionately visible, element in the national landscape.

Their middle-class vocational pattern similarly remained as intact during the postwar era as it had under the late Habsburg Empire. In the areas of their greatest density, in backward Slovakia and Ruthenia, the profile was essentially lower-middle-class. But the rather more affluent Jews of Bohemia and Moravia-Silesia included a significant minority of dynamic entrepreneurs, mainly in the textile, food-processing, and wood-and-paper industries. Possibly 30 to 40 percent of the total capital invested in Czechoslovak industry in the 1930s was Jewish-owned. The firm of Petschek & Weimann played a key role in the development of mining in north Bohemia, and Jewish enterprise also was prominent in Ostrava's steel industry, and in Prague's private banks and insurance companies. During the latter 1920s, the government's characteristic successor-state shift to etatism—state capitalism—and its encouragement of large-scale cooperatives, marginally reduced Jewish leverage in industry and commerce. Nevertheless, the presence of Jews in the urban economy continued distinctly out of proportion to their modest numbers.

Throughout these same postwar years, moreover, Jews participated quite vigorously and extensively in the political life of the country. In underdeveloped Slovakia and Ruthenia, to be sure, many Jews still tended to give their votes to specifically Jewish factions. Yet, even in these regions, it was the major national—liberal—parties that claimed the lion's share of Jewish support. Throughout Czechoslovakia as a whole, most Jews in any case sustained their classical allegiance to the more progressive parties. Within these camps, several Jews shared in their respective parliamentary delegations. Alfred Meissner and Lev Winter played leading roles in the Social Democratic party. Ludvik Czech and Siegfried Taub were early activists in the "German" party, as was Julius Schultz in the "Hungarian" party. Rudolf Slansky and Viktor Stern were prominent Communists. As elsewhere in Europe, Jews were extensively represented in political journalism. At least half the editorial staff in the Social Democratic press were Jews.

The proportion of Jews in Czechoslovak medicine and law—approximately 25 percent in both categories—never quite matched that of early postwar (pre-Fascist) Hungary. A key factor in this "anomaly" was the uncharacteristic breadth of the non-Jewish middle class in Bohemia and Moravia-Silesia. For nearly a century, as the industrial heartland of the old Habsburg Empire, these regions had produced a substantial, well-educated Mittelstand. The tradition continued in the postwar years, and so did the large mixture of Sudeten Germans in all branches of the middle-class economy. But if Czechoslovakia's Jews bulked rather less formidably in medicine and law than elsewhere in East-Central Europe, they also encountered fewer barriers in their choice of professions. Indeed, they moved with quickening tempo to immerse themselves in the new majority culture.

The role of Jews in Czech literature offered a useful litmus test. In the immediate postwar period, Frantisek Langer emerged as the nation's most widely acclaimed "patriotic" novelist. Prague-born and a medical doctor, Langer had served on the Russian front in 1917, where he was captured and later released to become a surgeon in the Czech Legion. In the postwar era, serving as a colonel in the Czechoslovak army medical corps, Langer devoted his every spare moment to writing. He achieved fame initially in 1920, with the publication of *The Iron Wolf (Zelezny vlk)*, a collection of his memoirs in the Czech Legion. While other stories and novels followed rapidly, it was Langer's succession of dramas that established his international reputation. His most enduring play, *Periphery (Periferie)*, staged in 1925, was greeted with vast critical and popular success as a tragicomic variation of Dostoevsky's *Crime and Punishment*.

Meanwhile, Richard Weiner, a contemporary of Langer, served as the

Paris correspondent of the Czech daily *Lidov noviny* until shortly before his death in 1937. The author of several collections of poetry and books of shorter prose, Weiner often was compared to Marcel Proust, even to Kafka, in the subtlety of his interior explorations. Abandoning the traditional forms of grammar and syntax, his unique style distorted conventional word structures—and accordingly precluded the wider audience achieved by Langer. Nevertheless, literary historians came to regard Weiner as one of the authentic pioneers of European surrealism.

The most widely respected cultural figure in the early republic, however, more even than Langer, and surely more than Kafka, whose major works achieved translation into Czech only in the late 1920s and early 1930s, was Otokar Fischer. Born in 1888, the holder of degrees from both the German and the Czech divisions of Prague's Karl-Ferdinand University, Fischer joined that institution's faculty in 1919 as professor of German literature. From this vantage point, as scholar, dramatist, poet, essayist, translator, literary historian—altogether as a polymath of creativity—Fischer in his full maturity emerged as the literary doyen of postwar Czechoslovakia. An early convert to Catholicism, he acknowledged in his 1923 collection of poetry, *Voices (Hlasy)*, a tendency to "hear voices" that he had not heard or desired to hear before. "I feel an aversion toward the trial of a people [downtrodden]," he wrote, "and yet I am myself the desert through which Israel wanders." It was inevitable, in the light of Fischer's ethnic ambivalence, that the literary figure to whom he was most often compared was Heinrich Heine, the renowned nineteenth-century German-Jewish poet. Fischer himself produced a monumental two-volume work on Heine, and in later years acknowledged that, like Heine, he regarded his own apostasy as the most agonizing problem of his life.

Fischer, Langer, Weiner, and other Jewish literary figures of the 1920s and 1930s were extensively published in books, belletristic journals, and—above all—in the widely perused literary columns of Czech newspapers. Adaptability doubtless was the Jewish métier. Yet no minority people ever made the transition from one language to another, one culture to another, with greater alacrity or acuity. By the same token, no minority people anywhere could have placed greater faith in their vibrant, newly born postwar homeland.

A Premonitory Vision

Nor was any statesman in Europe more trusted, even more widely venerated, by the Jews than Czechoslovakia's founding president. Tomas Masaryk had risked his earlier academic career, his very physical safety, in puncturing the blood libel. He alone among the postwar leaders had not waited to be bullied into accepting minorities guarantees for his precocious young republic. No other statesman, surely, either in public or in private, had so uncompromisingly asserted and reasserted his friendship for the Jewish people, for their aspirations equally as Czech citizens, as Jews, and as Zionists. Throughout the fifteen years of Masaryk's incumbency, until his retirement in favor of Eduard Benes in 1935, the president's office remained as accessible to Jews as to any other of Czechoslovakia's ethnic representatives.

The nation's borders remained open, as well. During the war, some 35,000 Jews had arrived in Slovakia as fugitives from East European battle-fields and persecution. Following the armistice, Czechoslovakia in its early struggle for economic viability was hard-pressed to absorb these new-comers. Nevertheless, for the ensuing three years, the Masaryk govern-ment accommodated the refugees in military barracks, until some 20,000 of them gradually were returned to Poland, Hungary, or Austria, or to West European countries. In 1932, when the juridical status of approxi-mately 10,000 remaining Jews had not yet been determined (although they had long since been permitted to live and work in the country), Parliament accepted Foreign Minister Benes's recommendation and issued them a col-lective bill of naturalization.

There were other instances of governmental forbearance. Elsewhere in East-Central Europe, the 1920s and 1930s were the years of tightening admissions quotas for Jewish university students. The Masaryk govern-ment categorically rejected any notion of a Jewish numerus clausus. Indeed, thousands of Jews from Poland, Rumania, and Hungary, denied entrance at their own universities, managed to study at Czech institutions. Their presence did not go uncontested, to be sure. Students in the German section of Karl-Ferdinand University held intermittent protest meetings against the "alien presence." In 1922, their nationalist animus exploded when the faculty senate elected Professor Samuel Steinberg as univer-sity rector, thereby breaking a former Habsburg taboo against Jews in aca-demic administration. Launching a general strike, the students protested this violation of the university's "true German character." Several right-wing deputies in Parliament, Slovak as well as German, then joined in the clamor, pressing both for Steinberg's withdrawal and for an official numerus clausus on Jewish students.

It was significant, however, that neither proposal got out of Parliament's education committee. When Steinberg offered to forgo his rectorship, the ministry of education declined to accept his resignation. Six years later, in 1928, political rightists once again demanded a Jewish numerus clausus. And once again, the government majority in Parliament shot the notion down. In Prague, that same year, seven hundred delegates attending the annual convention of the Federation of Czechoslovakian Lawyers adopted a near-unanimous resolution in support of the government's position. The contrast with their professional counterparts in Rumania, Poland, and Hungary could not have been more vivid.

Notwithstanding the palpable vigor of Czechoslovakia's democracy, antisemitism was far from moribund in the postwar years, even in the more affluent and better-educated Bohemian, Moravian, and Silesian regions. Jan Neruda, the nation's uncrowned poet laureate, opposed political equality for Jews as a matter of Czech "cultural purity." Neruda's reservations were shared by Svatopluk Cech, another renowned poet-essayist. Well after Czechoslovakia's rise to independence, antisemitism remained an apparently ineradicable feature in much of the country's popular culture. It attained political expression through the right-wing National Union, founded by Jiri Stribrny in 1927; and through the Czech Fascist Community, led by the former army general Radola Gajda.

Nor was race-hatred exclusively an offshoot of the interethnic resentments surviving between Czechs and Germans, or between Czechs and Slovaks. The diabolization of Jews continued notably rampant among the country's more backward Slovakian and Ruthenian agricultural populations. Andrej Hlinka's Slovak People's Party, as militantly anti-Jewish as it was anti-Czech, emerged in the late 1920s as a powerful separationist force. And following the rise of the Hitler regime in Germany, in 1933, irredentist antisemitism flared up among the Sudetenland's 2.8 million Germans with a virulence not exceeded in the Third Reich itself.

For all his moral gravitas, therefore, and his personal commitment to a liberal and pluralistic nation, Tomas Masaryk remained entirely sentient to the political fragility of his multiethnic republic, and to the unique vulnerability of its Jews. It was an awareness that doubtless reinvigorated his support for Zionism. Earlier in the twentieth century, Masaryk had placed his emphasis on Zionism's capacity for "moral regeneration." "I do not mean by that the migration of the Jews to Palestine," he insisted. "The Jews may remain where they are, but they must understand that their moral condition is in need of reform." In his initial, December 1918 interview with the correspondent of Prague's *Jüdische Telegraf*, the new president again expressed his support for Zionism as a "moral" endeavor.

But during the latter 1920s, with anti-Jewish violence erupting in Slovakia and anti-Jewish demonstrations occasionally surfacing even in Prague, Masaryk went out of his way specifically to endorse the development of an economically and demographically viable Jewish homeland in Palestine. In 1927, he visited the Holy Land for the dedication ceremony of a forest named in his honor. It was the president's first trip outside Czechoslovakia since the war, and he undertook it as an eighty-year-old man. Did he know something? Fear something?

From the moment of Czechoslovakia's birth, the Jews of Prague, still extensively identified with German culture, received official encouragement to list themselves as Jews by "nationality." The government's initial purpose was to lure this middle-class element away from the German bloc. The Zionists plainly required no encouragement. It is recalled that, in Bohemia-Moravia, a substantial minority of Jews—38 percent—availed themselves of the choice, and among the Yiddish-speaking Jews of Slovakia-Ruthenia the figure was not less than 54 percent. Yet this "constitutional" identification was never translated into political action. The Zionist-sponsored "Jewish National party" rarely attained the minimum quota needed for parliamentary representation.

On the other hand, few even of Prague's middle-class Jews ever quite nurtured the illusion that they would be regarded as "authentic" Czechs. In earlier years, a significant nucleus of Prague's younger Jewish intellectuals was prepared to accept Zionism as an expression of cultural anchorage (p. 149). Among the Bar Kochba Society, Viktor Kellner then became the first member actually to settle in Palestine, in 1910. Another participant, Hugo Bergmann, migrated to Palestine late in 1924. A number of others subsequently departed to share in the establishment of Hefziba, a pioneering kibbutz in the Jezreel Valley. Although Max Brod, the most eloquent advocate of Zionism in the postwar era, did not uproot himself until the Nazi seizure of Czechoslovakia in March 1939, there was never a doubt that Palestine would ultimately be his destination. He and his wife settled that year in Tel Aviv.

Before the war, as a student and then as a fledging lawyer, Franz Kafka had listened in fascination as Martin Buber regaled the Bar Kochba group with his mystic, romantic version of Zionism. Kafka's exposure to the wave of "authentic," "folk-rooted" Galician Jewish refugees only fortified that interest. In his later, postwar correspondence with Milena Jesenska and Max Brod, he expressed a stereotypical Zionist evaluation of Western "assimilated" Jews, and of himself (self-lacerating as always) as a prime example of a *"krumme Westjude"* (a twisted—neurotic—Western Jew). Yet the appraisal also reflected Kafka's mordant conviction that Gentile xenophobia evidently was implacable. He personally was a witness to anti-Jewish riots, after all (pp. 150–51), in November 1920, and read the antisemitic tirades of the right-wing Czech press. Neither did his former German-speaking milieu offer much comfort. Prague's newspapers provided extensive coverage of the blatant, frontal antisemitism developing in postwar Germany and Austria.

Well before the end of the war, in 1917, Kafka gave fictional expression to this despairing "pogrom" Zionism in a pair of stories appearing in Martin Buber's journal *Der Jude*. Under the heading "Two Animal Tales" ("Zwei Tiergeschichten"), they were titled "Jackals and Arabs"

("Schakale und Araber") and "A Report to an Academy" ("Ein Bericht für eine Akademie"). The stories offered a harsh satire on Western Jewry. The jackal in fact was an accepted image for the kind of neurasthenic Diaspora Jew disdained by the Tolstoyan Zionist A. D. Gordon, as well as by hostile Gentiles. In Kafka's account, these cultural misfits similarly bear the "Jewish" trait of following "unserer alten Lehre"—"our old traditions"—and in preserving desiccated notions of messianism. In Palestine, an Arab country, they carry with them a rusty pair of scissors which they present to each traveler, entreating him to cut the Arabs' throats. Seeking an improvement in their condition, but lacking the self-reliance of "authentic" Zionists, they anticipate a messianic intervention to solve their problems.

Much of this sense of beleaguerment is evident in Kafka's second extended story, "A Report to an Academy," in which a guest speaker lectures a scientific body on "the life I formerly led as an ape." Captured on Africa's Gold Coast, the ape is transported to Europe in a cage too narrow for him to stand upright or to sit down. Despite these constraints, the creature manages to learn from his sailor-captors the rudiments of human behavior. It is they who give him the name "Rotpeter," suggested by the red scar on his cheek. The Zionist parables are unmistakable. The ape's home on the Gold Coast would be related not only to the myth of the Golden Age but also to the primitive vitality Western Zionists ascribed to East European Jews. The ape's wound suggests that, by contrast, Jews in Western society are maimed or disabled. Even the name, "Rotpeter," is a repellent one, comparable to the demeaning surnames assigned to Western Jews in the time of Emperors Josef II and Friedrich II.

Once he arrives in Hamburg, Rotpeter must choose between the zoo and the music hall. He rejects the former as still another ghetto and works feverishly to qualify for a theatrical career by undergoing a crash course in Europeanization ("die Durchschnittsbildung eines Europäers"). Swiftly emerging as a celebrity, Rotpeter persuades himself that he actually has become human. But of course his fame relates precisely to the fact that he is not human, and can never be regarded as human. He is an ape, nothing more, who has cleverly learned to imitate a human being.

It was in the postwar years that Kafka began to fantasize about settling in Palestine. Particularly appealing to him was A. D. Gordon's idealized "religion of labor," a concept that suggested both physical and spiritual recovery. By early winter of 1923, Kafka's own health had deteriorated alarmingly, and he permitted himself to be booked into a hotel-sanitarium at Müritz on the Baltic. Nearby, at a vacation camp maintained by Berlin's Jewish Kultusgemeinde, Kafka met one of the camp's staff members, Dora Dymant, a nineteen-year-old girl who had left a Chasidic home in Poland. Within days she and the doomed forty-one-year-old Kafka fell deeply in love. Uninterested in returning to Prague, the couple moved into a small Berlin apartment.

By then Kafka had formally retired from his position with the Workmen's Insurance Institute and was subsisting on a tiny pension. Nevertheless, the ensuing months were the happiest of his life. He and Dora read Hebrew texts together and attended lectures at the local Jewish Lehrhaus, an adult Jewish study center established by the philosopher Franz Rosenzweig. The two also laid detailed plans to emigrate to Palestine. It was an idyll of dreams and hopes, and it endured only a few months. Kafka's tuberculosis soon became terminal. In March of 1924, Max Brod arrived to help Dora bring Kafka back to Prague, and from there soon afterward to a sanitorium near Vienna. Kafka died three and a half months later.

In 1929, Dora Dymant married a prominent German Communist, by whom she had a daughter. The day after the Nazi takeover, in the winter of 1933, her husband fled to the Soviet Union. Eventually Dora and her child succeeded in rejoining him there. But later he was executed in the Stalinist purges. In 1939, Dora and her daughter finally managed to secure exit permits, and to reach England. There Dora died in 1942. As for Kafka's family, all but one escaped the Nazi dragnet, surviving to die in their own beds. The exception was Ottla, his younger sister and closest sibling. Some years after Kafka's death, she married a non-Jew and remained with him in Prague. Accordingly, in 1941, as the Germans rounded up Czechoslovakia's Jews for imprisonment and eventual liquidation, Ottla was granted exemption as the wife of an Aryan. Rather than take refuge as a "fraud," however, she divorced her husband. Thus, in August 1942, she was deported—albeit to the "privileged" concentration camp of Theresienstadt. Again, typically, Ottla would accept no exemptions. In October 1943, she volunteered to escort a children's transport to Auschwitz, understanding perfectly well the fate that awaited her.

Although Franz Kafka himself survives only in historical memory, ultimately he does so neither as a Zionist nor as a martyr to liberal humanism. Johann Bauer, one of Kafka's most astute biographers, has caught the essence and enduring significance of the man: "He always belonged to the intellectual underworld rather than to the light of day. . . . Kafka in Bohemia was always the great unknown: a Wandering Jew and a haunter of crooked alleys, a poet whose theme was the chaos and anxiety of civilization, a prophet of calamities to come."

VII

NOTES FROM A SHATTERED DREAM

The New Jerusalem

In the summer of 1909, Franz Kafka and Max Brod embarked on a hiking vacation in Switzerland. Accompanying them was Franz Werfel, a young friend whom Brod later described as "[r]otundly handsome at nineteen, carefully unkempt, vestigial baby fat turning into incipient flab, with a ravaged, childlike expression." The only son of a wealthy Prague glove manufacturer, Werfel already had displayed precociousness as a lyric poet of enchanting optimism. "O heart, rejoice!" he declaimed. "I have done a good deed. O earth, o evening, joy, o to be alive." Werfel's exuberant adoration of life and mankind, his wide-eyed belief in "the divine mystery and holiness of man," touched Brod deeply. Two years later, in 1911, he would arrange for Werfel's collection to be published and promoted under the title *The Friend of the World* (*Der Weltfreund*), and thereby gain the younger man instant acclaim as the golden voice of the new Expressionism. Certainly the contrast between the chubby, ebullient Werfel, splashing in tepid pieties, and the tortured, ascetic Kafka, pursuing his vision of alienation and catastrophe, could not have been more emphatic.

In 1914 Werfel moved to Vienna, where his lyrics rapturously expressed the progressivist certitudes of Central Europe. They would also express the hopes and dreams of a torrent of immigrant Jews even then pouring into the Habsburg capital from the Empire's outlying reaches. In 1910, Viennese Jewry numbered some 175,000 souls, approximately 9 percent of the city's population. It was a comparatively recent demographic base. Although a modest Jewish enclave had established itself in Vienna in medieval times, it had been interrupted by two full-scale expulsions, in 1421 and 1669. The small number of Jews who trickled back over the decades experienced lives of ghettoization and abasement. Initially, it was Josef II's Toleranzpatent, in 1782, that liberated Vienna's few hundred Jews from the heaviest of the "Jew taxes" and granted them access to improved neighborhoods and wider vocational opportunities. Emperor Josef plainly was no philanthropist. He intended to "productivize" and

"Germanize" his Jews, to ensure that they contributed meaningfully to the imperial economy.

The emperor's successors, Leopold II and Franz II, were less taken by this characteristic Enlightenment objective. Following the Congress of Vienna, in 1815, in the heyday of Metternichian reaction, Austria's Jews were denied the opportunity to buy new homes, to own land, to establish new synagogues, orphanages, or hospitals. Subsequently, the revolution of 1848 offered a flicker of hope to this modest community of some three thousand individuals, allowing them access to the imperial law courts; but in 1851 the new young emperor, Franz Josef, was persuaded to rescind that privilege. It was not until the 1867 Ausgleich, the "rectification" of the Empire into its two self-governing states of Austria and Hungary, that Jews at last were accorded the fullest measure of political equality, including the right to sit in the Reichstag. By 1890, fifteen Jews actually held parliamentary seats.

Responding to this progressive, if erratic, trajectory of emancipation, Jews from the Empire's provincial hinterlands began moving into its larger cities during the second half of the nineteenth century, migrating essentially from impoverished Moravia and Slovakia, later from Galicia, with their collapsing agricultural economies, and their surrounding populations of glowering, suspicious farmers. From the 1870s onward, it was the Empire's great administrative centers—Budapest, Prague, and, above all, Vienna—that became the European magnet for these Dorfjuden, these rustic village Jews. Ultimately, not less than three-quarters of the Jews of Austria would live in Vienna, most of them immigrants or the offspring of immigrants. While the elite minority of veteran Jews settled principally in the capital's upper-middle-class Alsergrund district, the newcomers congregated in the lower-middle-class Leopoldstadt quarter.

However diverse their backgrounds, by the turn of the century Vienna's Jews saw only hope in their future. Vienna was the epicenter of imperial benevolence. Here prosperity was growing. Here law and order prevailed. Here accident and health insurance coverage was second only to Germany's as a model for the rest of the world. Vienna provided, as well, an effulgence of internationally renowned theaters, concert halls, museums, boulevards, and parks. And over the vast extravaganza presided Emperor Franz Josef, a justice-loving, benevolent father to his people. Portraits of the revered monarch hung in thousands of Jewish homes, and many Jews named their first son after him.

Their gratitude was not misplaced, nor was their vision of progress and prosperity unrealized in the magnificent capital city. In Vienna it was almost exclusively Jews who embodied capitalism's "Protestant" ethic. The majority were classically Mittelstand—middle-class—either small merchants or salaried clerks, salesmen, or managers in Jewish-owned businesses and industries. But from their midst also came a significant minority of economic movers and shakers. In Austria, as in Hungary, Jews built the nation's steel mills and railroads, its textile, sugar-refining, and meat-packing industries, its leading banks, the largest number of Vienna's fashionable stores, and most of its great newspapers (p. 164.).

Here, too, as elsewhere in Central-Eastern Europe, the liberal professions were disproportionately and vibrantly Jewish. The German-Jewish novelist Jakob Wassermann discovered to his surprise that Vienna's cultural life, more even than his native Berlin's, appeared to be largely dominated by Jews. He recalled:

> The aristocracy would have nothing to do with such [cultural] things. . . . [T]hey not only maintained a respectful distance from intellectual and artistic life but feared and condemned it. The small number of untitled patrician families imitated the aristocracy. . . . The court, the lower middle class, and the Jews gave the city its stamp. And that the Jews, as the most mobile group, kept all the others in continuous motion is . . . not surprising. But I was amazed at the hosts of Jewish physicians, attorneys, clubmen, snobs, dandies, proletarians, actors, newspapermen, and poets.

Another renowned Jewish literary figure, Stefan Zweig, attributed the Jewish cultural phenomenon to the stigma of "mere" commerce. By transcending that blemish, Zweig suggested, the Jews as marginal men could achieve both protection against the bigotry of Gentile employers and social acceptance within the ambit of a much-revered "deutsche Kultur." To Jews decamping from the Slavonic hinterland, it was a culture that signified all that was liberal, just, progressive, in effect, "civilized."

Education provided the indispensable key to that civilization. Thus, by 1910, Jews represented one of every three students in Vienna's gymnasia, one in four at the University of Vienna. Academic credentials alone manifestly would not yet give Jews access to the more prestigious civil-service billets. Nevertheless, as early as 1880, a majority of Vienna's attorneys were Jews, and by 1900 Jews constituted nearly half of Vienna's physicians. As "liberal intelligentsia," Jews by 1910 had become a protean nucleus even among the university's teaching faculty (although rarely at the exalted rank of professor), most specifically in the law and medical schools, but also, increasingly, in the humanities. The emerging discipline of musicology was the creation essentially of Austrian (and German) Jews. Guido Adler held the University of Vienna's first chair in this field, and his most eminent protégés also were Jews—Ernst Kurth, Egon Wellesz, Karl Geiringer, Hans Gal, Paul Nettl, Paul Pisk.

In journalism, the preponderance of Jews was more overwhelming in

Vienna than in any other city in the world, even Berlin, even Budapest. By the turn of the century, much of the city's liberal press and virtually all its Social Democratic press were either Jewish-owned or heavily staffed with Jews. Their influence transcended even their proportions. Thus, of the city's extensive spectrum of newspapers, by far the most widely read and respected was the *Neue Freie Presse*. Such was the political influence of the *Presse*'s Jewish owner, Moritz Benedikt, that he was said to be capable single-handedly of making or breaking government ministers. The *Presse*'s music critic, Eduard Hanslick (a Jew, as were nearly all of Vienna's music journalists), similarly could make or break a musical production. The newspaper's predominantly Jewish drama and literary critics no less decisively ordained the fate of stage productions and new authors. The *Presse*'s only serious rivals were the *Neue Wiener Tageblatt*, founded and owned by Moritz Szeps, and the Social Democratic *Arbeiter Zeitung*, edited by Friedrich Austerlitz, both Jews. Vienna's three principal cultural journals similarly were published by Jews: *Die Zeit*, by Heinrich Kanner and Isidor Singer; *Die Wage*, by Rudolf Lothar; and *Die Fackel*, by Karl Kraus (pp. 173–74).

In a bio-bibliographical handbook, Harry Zohn, a distinguished historian of Central European Jewish culture, lists some 238 major Jewish literary figures who did their principal writing in early-twentieth-century Vienna. Of the twenty-three best-known authors within the Jung-Wien— "Young Vienna"—generation that largely dominated Austrian literature until 1938, at least sixteen were Jews. Within this constellation, in turn, none was more widely acclaimed than Arthur Schnitzler. Born in 1862, trained as a physician, Schnitzler for several years practiced in his father's successful Viennese nose-and-throat clinic. Then, in the late 1880s, abandoning medicine, the younger Schnitzler began to devote himself exclusively to writing, indeed, to the production of a seemingly endless flow of poems, stories, novellas, and dramas. By the turn of the century, Schnitzler's fictional output was the most extensive of any "serious" writer in Habsburg Austria, and unquestionably the most widely read. Possibly it was the physician's eye that accounted for his "diagnostic" insight into human motivations, which fully matched his lambent dialogue and surgical descriptive powers. Photographs of Schnitzler in his early forties reveal a delicately chiseled face, with deep-set eyes gazing out over an immaculately trimmed goatee. A bon vivant, something of a philanderer, the man simultaneously epitomized and captured the charm and cynicism of upper-class Viennese society in its last, prewar efflorescence. Until his death in 1931, at the age of sixty-nine, Schnitzler remained the doyen of Austrian authors of fiction. More than any man of his generation, it was he who "sang the swan-song of old Vienna."

If the sunburst of Austrian Jewish belletrists, musicians, scholars, lawyers, doctors, critics, academicians, and journalists played a decisive role in Viennese cultural life in the last Habsburg decades and beyond (pp. 182–83), the achievement also could be attributed to the patronage of Vienna's Jewish upper-middle class. "[N]ine-tenths of what the world celebrated as Viennese culture [at the turn of the century]," acknowledged Stefan Zweig—himself a major figure in that galaxy—"was promoted, nourished, or even created by Viennese Jewry." Jakob Wassermann confirmed that "whoever wished to 'put something through' in Vienna in the realm of culture was drawn instinctively to the benevolent embrace of the Jewish higher bourgeoisie." No other city in Europe was so endlessly fertilized by the inflow of talent, and, at that, of culturally voracious Jewish talent from the outer reaches of the Empire. And none other, not even Berlin, managed to produce a more coruscating Jewish intellectual elite. It was supremely the Jews, insisted Zweig, who "gave to what was Austrian, and Viennese [culture] its most intensive expression. . . . [They] renewed the city's universal fame."

The Poison in the Schlag

With this record, in this oldest and most distinguished of European empires, was not the solution of the equally historic Jewish question in sight at last? In fact, the opposite was the case. Whatever the Jews' ultimate contribution to Austrian life, the swelling influx of Ostjuden, in all their pungent and often exotic ethnicity, their hard-driving, desperation-rooted upward mobility, was a source not only of cultural effervescence but of culture shock and growing popular resentment. Moreover, by the turn of the century, Austria's struggling lower-middle class reacted with particular beleaguerment to the widening competition of Jewish small-businessmen and professionals.

It was accordingly in this fin-de-siècle era that Georg von Schönerer rose to public attention by exploiting völkisch—ethnic-racist— antisemitism for political purposes. The son of a prominent engineer and railroad planner, Schönerer managed only a haphazard education and an even less certain livelihood in the Austrian provincial bureaucracy before turning full-time to politics. Denouncing Jews, Slavs, and others of the Empire's ethnic nationalities, Schönerer organized a Pan-German party whose agenda favored a total dismantlement of the Habsburg realm and the reunion of its exclusively "Aryan" population with imperial Germany. In its contempt for Catholic universalism and parliamentary government, Schönerer's blueprint ultimately proved too draconian for "respectable" Austrian court and middle-class society.

But a somewhat more palatable alternative was offered by Karl Lueger. A man of proletarian background who had worked his way through university, Lueger was first elected to Vienna's municipal council in 1875, at the age of thirty-one. Eloquent and charismatic, the young politician soon found his métier in targeting Jews as the source of Vienna's endemic underemployment. Upon establishing the Christian Socialist party as his showcase, in 1890, Lueger proposed henceforth to create job opportunities for all "deserving" Christians through the imaginative device of extensive public-works projects, the dismissal of all Jewish municipal employees, and the transfer of municipal contracts from Jewish to Gentile providers. Unlike Schönerer, Lueger professed only respect for the integrity of the Empire. By the late nineteenth century, he emerged as a seemingly acceptable, even attractive, candidate for mayor of Vienna.

Indeed, Lueger actually was elected to the mayoralty three times—although on the first two occasions he was vetoed by the emperor, who feared his populism and antisemitism. In 1897, however, after eliciting Lueger's assurances of nondiscrimination, Franz Josef finally authorized him to take office. Throughout the entire fourteen years of his incumbency, Lueger proved to be an extraordinarily innovative and effective mayor. The quality of municipal services he provided was unprecedented until then in the capital's history. At the same time, he managed to keep his promise to the emperor, muting his antisemitism. "Wer ein Jude ist, bestimme ich," he joked with confidants. "I decide who is and is not a Jew." Nevertheless, Lueger's earlier years of racist campaigning already had done their damage. White-collar antisemitism, always socially acceptable, had now been institutionalized as politically respectable.

For their part, the Jews of Vienna responded to the upsurge of hostility with mixed emotions. The thousands of Ostjuden who had experienced authentically brutish Jew-hatred in their regions of origin were less than fazed. The reaction of the more acculturated Jewish veterans was somewhat more ambivalent. They argued that it was the influx specifically of these "uncouth" Easterners that was jeopardizing their own painfully achieved status. But in fact, public animus was directed against "respectable," acculturated Jews and tatterdemalion East European Jews alike. At the University of Vienna, Jews of all backgrounds were systematically excluded from student organizations, even were subjected to a widening gauntlet of harassment and physical abuse. One of these was Sigmund Freud's son Martin. Beaten so badly that he required facial surgery, the younger Freud was impelled to join the Zionist student group, Kadimah, where he was swiftly taught the art of self-defense.

Other routes were available for those seeking relief from the burdens of Jewish identity. A significant minority of Jews apostatized. Gustav Mahler converted to Roman Catholicism to ensure his appointment as director of the Vienna State Opera. Mahler's young admirer, Arnold Schönberg, similarly would undergo conversion (p. 270). Although the best-known of Austria's Jewish writers remained at least nominally among their own, they plainly shared the "soul malaise" of other Jewish intellectuals. Arthur Schnitzler was preoccupied not simply with the mores and foibles of Viennese society. As a young man, he too had been the target of antisemitic abuse. For many years afterward, he managed to avoid the Jewish question in his writings. By the twentieth century, however, he decided at last to confront the issue head-on in the form of a novel.

Completed in 1907, and entitled *The Road Is Open (Der Weg ins Freie)*, Schnitzler's book offers a penetrating typology of Austrian Jews floundering under the pressures of bigotry. They range from self-hating Jews and confused, ambivalent Jews, to "cosmopolitan" Jewish Socialists and vibrantly romantic Zionists. The novel takes no definite stand. The reader is left to determine his own private "road." Yet Schnitzler himself apparently had not yet exorcised the specter of antisemitism, for he devoted still another work to it, a drama, *Professor Bernhardi*. Completed and produced in 1912, the work was inspired by difficulties that Schnitzler's own father, Dr. Johann Schnitzler, had experienced in his medical practice.

Professor Bernhardi is the Jewish director of a private clinic. His position is undermined by the intrigues of several jealous colleagues, who accuse him of barring a priest from administering last rites to a dying young woman, when in fact Bernhardi's purpose was simply to leave the sedated patient unaware of her imminent death. The episode creates a scandal, and the Church swiftly inflames anti-Jewish rage. Eventually Bernhardi is charged with obstructing a sacred rite. Placed on trial, he is convicted on false testimony and sentenced to prison. In current literary perspective, *Professor Bernhardi* stands as a one-dimensional polemic. Yet, for its time, the work accurately reflected the Zeitgeist of Mayor Lueger's Vienna.

Schnitzler's drama offers an interesting subtext, as well. In one of *Professor Bernhardi*'s dialogues, Dr. Schreimann, a converted Jew, declares to Professor Bernhardi: "Had I been a Zionist, I should have had an easier time." It was a telling aperçu, and unquestionably it was Schnitzler's. He and Theodor Herzl had been university students in the same period, but had come to know each other only years later, when Herzl emerged as the founder of political Zionism. Herzl then had sought to lure Schnitzler into the movement. "Are you coming with us?" he inquired genially. Schnitzler was not. As he explained in an essay he published a year and a half before the war:

I would not want Zionism eliminated from the world's political scene of today, or from the soul-economy of contemporary Jewry. As a spiri-

tual element to elevate one's self-reliance . . . and especially as a philanthropic action of the highest rank, Zionism will always retain its
importance, even if it should someday prove to have been merely a
historical episode.

But Schnitzler made plain that he was a "German" writer, as were most of
his fellow Jews of the Jung-Wien group, and that Austria alone was his
Heimat, his homeland and "hearthland." Even Herzl had to agree, observing: "Schnitzler, he belongs here as much as Mozart and Schubert." Until
the outbreak of the war, and well after, Schnitzler's viewpoint remained the
prevalent one of Austria's Jewish "establishment."

A Voice from the Underground

Far more even than the "clinical" Dr. Arthur Schnitzler, it was Franz Kafka
whom intellectual historians have identified as the pioneering "psychoanalyst" of literature. Only Kafka himself rejected the characterization. "It is
no pleasure to busy oneself with psychoanalysis," he wrote Werfel, in
December 1922, "and I keep as far away from it as possible." Yet, in dis-
claiming identification with the provocative "new thinking," Kafka did not
question its therapeutic usefulness. If psychoanalysis had not approached
the threshold of full medical acceptance by the early 1920s, it was nonethe-
less achieving a far wider measure of intellectual credibility.

Sigmund Freud, founder of the "new thinking," was a quintessential son
of the Habsburg Empire. Born in 1856, in Freiberg, Moravia, of Galician-
Jewish parents, he was the oldest of eight children in the second brood of
Jakob Freud, his wool-merchant father. Jakob was forty-one; his new wife,
Amalie, was twenty-one. By his first marriage he had two sons. Emanuel,
the elder, already had made Jakob Freud a grandfather by the time Sigmund was born, so that the new arrival had a nephew older than himself.
By his own account, Sigmund experienced pangs of jealousy as a child of
two and a half, when he had to share his mother's warmth and love, this
time with his first sister, Anna. Given the tangled age-sex relationship in
his family, it was less than surprising that Sigmund Freud early on become
preoccupied with the riddle of sex.

Soon afterward, the family moved to Vienna, settling in the predominantly Jewish Leopoldstadt district. Although Jakob Freud's circumstances
were modest, he managed to provide his son with every educational opportunity, including his five years of medical school at the University of
Vienna. Upon receiving his degree in 1881, Sigmund Freud underwent
a four-year internship at Professor Ernst Brücke's celebrated Institute
of Neurology. In 1884, entering private practice, he divided his work each

day between paying patients and non-paying laboratory research. From the outset of his career, moreover, Freud displayed astonishing scientific skills: publishing important articles on the acoustic nerve, on the cerebellum, on aphasia, on the therapeutic properties of cocaine. It was a creative life, but a less than remunerative one. Year by year, Freud was obliged to put off his marriage to his fiancée. In 1886, he departed on a year's traveling fellowship at Professor Jean-Martin Charcot's renowned Salpêtrière Hospital for Neurological Diseases in Paris. Charcot was a famed specialist in hysteria, a subject that lately had claimed much of Freud's attention.

It is possible that Jewish considerations subliminally influenced the young researcher. Before Freud, hysteria and "neurasthenia" were classified as degenerative diseases, and were ascribed principally to heredity. Neurologists tended also to link these illnesses to specific ethnic groups, and most specifically to Jews. The view was shared even by a number of Jewish scientists, including Cesare Lombroso, the pioneering forensic psychiatrist, and Max Nordau, a Viennese physician whose 1892 book, *Degeneration (Entärtung)*, stressed the biological-hereditary nature of the disease. In France, too, the notion that the Jews were a race particularly susceptible to "degeneracy" was taken seriously in medical circles, not least by the great Charcot himself. It was an argument that racists like Edouard Drumont and—in Austria—Georg von Schönerer already were seizing upon with ferocious alacrity. During his residency at the Salpêtrière Hospital, Freud could not have avoided the political implications of these studies in "ethnic" hysteria.

Of more urgent importance to Freud than political or social theories was Charcot's innovative use of hypnosis on patients. The treatment appeared to ease certain hysterical symptoms, such as tremors and paralysis. Yet hypnosis was unable to eradicate symptoms permanently. Upon returning to Vienna in 1887, Freud gradually hit upon the technique of "free association," allowing the patient in a waking state to express whatever thoughts or memories came to mind, in this fashion gradually unlocking forgotten events, and thereby alleviating the patient's symptoms. Freud eventually dubbed the technique "psychoanalysis." Listening to his patients, Freud also began to discern certain vital clue-symbols to their forgotten traumas, particularly in the world of their dreams. He published his findings in 1900 in his single most important book, *The Interpretation of Dreams (Die Traumdeutung)*. Dreams were the method, Freud argued, by which emotional tensions—usually embedded memories of unfulfilled needs—were relieved through the hallucinatory language of symbols. The language of dreams, then, offered a key insight to the repressed memories that triggered such physical dysfunctions as hysteria.

Mentioning the Unmentionable

Beyond devising curative procedures, Freud was also exposing to the medical world a restive, heaving sea. He was not its lone discoverer. Belletrists such as Dostoevsky and Proust intuitively divined the atavistic role of irrational impulses. In the 1870s, the German philosopher Eduard von Hartmann formulated his own stratification of the human mind, and actually coined the term, "unconscious," that Freud later would use. Yet it was supremely Freud whose techniques of free association and dream interpretation opened a royal road to the hidden world of the unconscious. Perhaps most important, Freud in his close working association with the neurologist Wilhelm Fliess became even more acutely aware of the role of sexuality within that world. In 1905, publishing his observations in *Three Essays on Sexuality* (*Drei Abhandlugen zur Sexualtheorie*), Freud also drew extensively on a case history, one he shared with his colleague and friend, Dr. Josef Breuer.

In 1880, Breuer had treated a young woman, "Anna O," for hysteria. Her symptoms were classical ones—paralysis, neurasthenia, disturbance of vision and speech—and they appeared to become most acute while she was nursing her father through a serious illness. Breuer's initial therapy was hypnosis, and for a while Anna O's condition seemed to improve, although it never disappeared. The case remained an isolated and forgotten episode. But six years later, in 1886, upon witnessing Charcot's experiments in Paris, Freud recalled Breuer's treatment of his patient. In 1894, he and Breuer described it in a jointly published volume, *Studies in Hysteria (Studien über Hysterie)*, where they identified repressed memory as a source of trauma.

To Freud, however, the lingering significance of Anna O's case was its apparent confirmation that sexual crisis played a unique role in the hidden underworld of the unconscious. Indeed, he came increasingly to the conclusion that obsessional neuroses in Anna and other patients were associated with a pervasive sense of sexual guilt. At first, Freud suspected that the emotion was associated with a passive acceptance of a childhood seduction. Only some years later, performing an unprecedented feat of self-psychoanalysis, did he revise his theory with an even more revolutionary one. Far from childhood seduction, the repressed emotion was a jealous childhood sexual hunger for one's parent. Drawing from Sophocles' ancient Greek play *Oedipus Rex*, which focused on this primal incestuous sin, Freud labeled the phenomenon an "Oedipus complex," a concept that afterward he developed into a central feature of his theory of psychoanalysis.

Much of the immense biographical literature on Freud has sought to identify a hidden Jewish agenda in the great psychiatrist's work. In its most extreme expression, the argument is made that "Freud, consciously or unconsciously, secularized Jewish mysticism, and psychoanalysis can intelligently be viewed as such a secularization." Other versions regard his career as the expression of his "deep ambivalence about his Jewish origins." Freud personally rejected these speculations. Describing himself as an "absolutely irreligious Jew," he insisted that his discoveries should be regarded as universalistic. The renowned cultural historian Peter Gay shares this evaluation. "Freud was a Jew but not a Jewish scientist," he argues. There was no "elusive Jewish quality that somehow, mysteriously, informed Freud's work." Gay's appraisal may well be correct.

Yet the social circumstances of Freud's life as a Jew in modern Austria were entirely relevant to his intellectual career. His choice of a profession doubtless was influenced at least in part by a characteristic Jewish need to be self-employed. Alert to the slightest hint of prejudice, which he gallantly confronted head-on, Freud developed only limited friendships with non-Jews, either as a university student or in his later medical practice. His closest personal friends in his early career were Breuer and Wilhelm Fliess, both Jews. With only a single exception, his colleagues in the "Psychological Wednesday Evening Circle," which met weekly at his apartment at Bergasse 19, were all Jews (p. 186). And so were most of his early patients. Conceivably it was their febrile intelligence and "cooperability" that made them likely candidates for the "talking cure." As shall be seen (p. 205), "Anna O" was a particularly vivid example of these qualities. Indeed, his patients shared common circumstances with Freud himself, and with an entire generation of acculturated Central European Jews.

The most inescapable of those circumstances manifestly was anti-semitism. In Austrian medicine, prejudice barred Freud from a professorship. Notwithstanding his brilliant early record as a neurologist, the university medical school consigned him to the traditional "Jewish" rank of docent, in effect, an "adjunct." Almost certainly, a key factor drawing large numbers of Jews to psychiatry in its early decades was the field's sheer marginality. Often described as the "forensic specialization of deviate behavior," psychiatry was regarded as the virtual basement of Viennese medicine, and thus it remained one of the few medical areas in which Jewish physicians encountered no significant obstacles.

Still another reaction to prejudice, however, may have been the unconscious desire of Central European Jews, functioning on the vocational and social periphery, to unmask the emotional dysfunctionalism of an anti-semitic Gentile world. Even Jews who were not psychiatrists took pleasure in the "new thinking" and its potential for social retaliation. As early as

1910, Freud joined the B'nai B'rith Lodge of Vienna. Serving as an alternative to the professional societies that blackballed him, the international Jewish organization provided Freud with a guaranteed audience. In Vienna, its members delighted in listening to him air his theories at a time when the city's medical and ecclesiastical authorities yearned to see him behind bars. One of the most compelling of these "Jewish" circumstances, finally, may have been a peculiar talent evinced by members of a minority people, themselves afflicted by a dense mantle of personal and social insecurities, to empathize with the frustrations and neuroses of others. Few Jewish psychiatrists escaped these Jewish-rooted complexities. Even Freud, for all his tough-mindedness, was inhibited for decades from visiting Rome, a city that he identified (by his own later acknowledgment) as the very fount of his people's historic mistreatment.

But whatever the inner torments that impelled Freud through his pioneering exertions, he made astonishing headway. Displaying uncommon administrative skill, in 1908 he laid the foundations for the Vienna Psychoanalytic Society, which then held its first convention in Salzburg (p. 186). A year later, the first issue of the *International Journal of Psychoanalysis* was published. At the same time, disciples and patients—most of them still Jews—began making their pilgrimages to Freud from throughout Europe. Among these was Gustav Mahler, director of the Vienna State Opera. Overpowered by the amatory and social demands of Alma Schindler, his much younger Gentile wife, Mahler, a frail, sensitive genius, became impotent. During the summer of 1910, after making urgent inquiries, he arranged an emergency meeting with the great Freud. The two giants met in the Dutch town of Leyden. During the ensuing four hours of an intensive psychoanalytic interview, Freud divined that Alma needed a father figure, that Mahler was precisely the man for her, and therefore he need feel no further insecurities in their nuptial relationship. The analytic discussion evidently produced an effect. Mahler recovered his potency, and the marriage was a happy one until his death, which unfortunately took place only a year later.

The "World of Yesterday" Shatters

For the Jews of Central Europe, as for those of Eastern Europe, the outbreak of the Great War proved a double tragedy. Beyond the "normal" sacrifices of battlefield and home front, they experienced the overspill of wartime xenophobia. In Austria, the trauma was exacerbated by a vast new influx of Galician and Bukovinian Jewish refugees. By the war's midpoint, in 1916, at least seventy thousand of these fugitives had poured into Vienna, gravely straining the city's overburdened facilities as well as the locals' already exhausted cultural tolerance for the Ostjuden. Gentile resentments were not alleviated even by Austrian Jewry's unsurpassed battlefield performance and devout civilian patriotism.

Sigmund Freud was among these loyalists. "All my libido is given to Austria-Hungary," he commented to a friend. Two of Freud's sons served in the army. The elder, Martin, a lieutenant, won the Military Cross on the Italian front (where he was later briefly taken prisoner). Writing his friend Anton Kippenberg, Stefan Zweig acknowledged that "in spite of all my hatred and aversion for war, [m]y great ambition . . . is to be an officer with you in the [German] army, to conquer in France." To his joy, Zweig was conscripted in December 1914. Sharing in that initial exultation, Franz Werfel also was called to the army, and spent the first half of the war in an artillery regiment on the eastern front.

The euphoria did not long endure. Martin Freud soon experienced the hectoring antisemitism of his fellow officers. Stefan Zweig, who had welcomed the outbreak of hostilities with the cliché of the moment, "diese grosse Zeit" (the greatness of the hour), was dispatched to Galicia, where he first encountered the full horror of battle. In late 1917, by then a committed pacifist, he was allowed to visit Switzerland on a "goodwill" mission, and there he developed contacts with like-minded intellectuals, among them Fritz von Unruh, Hermann Hesse, and Romain Rolland. With them, Zweig signed petitions denouncing the war's brutalities, and subsequently he remained on in Switzerland until the armistice. Franz Werfel, similarly dispatched by the army to Switzerland on a propaganda/lecture tour in the spring of 1918, voiced his own developing pacifist sentiments. Fortunately for him, he suffered only a tough reprimand upon his return.

One who spectacularly ignored the risk of harsher consequences was the journalist Karl Kraus. The son of Bohemian Jews, Kraus studied briefly at the University of Vienna, then left to try his hand as an actor. Unsuccessful, he was taken on as a columnist for a small arts magazine. Here Kraus's formidable verbal talents registered almost immediately. In 1899 the mighty *Neue Freie Presse* invited him to become its chief satirical writer. Brashly declining the offer, however, the twenty-five-year-old Kraus preferred to use a family subvention to establish his own monthly journal, *Die Fackel* (The Torch). Although the *Fackel* initially published contributions by several of Kraus's literary contemporaries, after 1911 he himself did all the writing, until his death in 1936. From the outset, his targets were venality and hypocrisy, and he flayed the alleged perpetrators with uncontrollable fury—and often with a reckless lack of discrimination (p. 193).

Following the outbreak of the war, however, it was the chauvinism of the Central Powers that evoked Kraus's most impassioned moral crusade.

His journalistic technique was to create "scenes" based on actual quoted press statements by Austrian and German public officials. By citing these quotations, then by shrewdly juxtaposing two contradictory texts, the *Fackel* conveyed a frequently devastating verdict on the war and the nation's civilian and military leadership. Indeed, defying press censorship and threatened legal retaliation, Kraus also read out much of this material in lecture halls and cabarets. In published form, it appeared first in the wartime editions of the *Fackel*, then in a postwar compendium entitled *The Last Days of Mankind (Die letzten Tage der Menschheit)*.

The work is set in the streets of Vienna and Berlin, in government offices, military hospitals, churches, schools, and private kitchens. Throughout, scores of characters pontificate, including emperors, generals, editors, academicians, and clergymen. There is no apparent plot. Scenes range from one-line "blackouts" to impressionistic tableaux. There are wicked parodies of pompous bureaucrats and ultramilitant private citizens. As the tragedy careens toward its final Götterdämmerung, the epilogue is a searing rhymed recapitulation of the play's motifs. In the silence that follows, God's voice is heard declaiming the words uttered by Germany's Kaiser Wilhelm at the onset of the war: "Ich habe es nicht gewollt" (I did not wish this). Europe's humanists would regard Kraus as a fearlessly eloquent scourge of mindless chauvinism. German ultrapatriots would regard him simply as a traitorous Jew.

There was reason enough for social bitterness following the collapse of the Central Powers. On November 11, 1918, in horrified recognition of their impending isolation as a remnant nation, and confronted by an escalating series of workers' strikes, Austria's deputies in the Habsburg imperial Reichstag "accepted" the abdication of Emperor Karl, and declared "German Austria" a provisional "democratic republic" within the Greater Reich of neighboring Germany (a union that the Allies firmly rejected, then and later). A veteran Social Democrat, Karl Renner, assumed office as provisional chancellor. Three months later, in February 1919, the new republic held its first official elections. Although the Social Democrats emerged as the largest winners, they failed to gain an absolute majority. In consequence, they entered into a coalition with the right-wing Christian Socialists and with other, smaller nationalist factions, operating under Renner's chancellorship. It was a marriage of convenience that would soon prove unworkable.

At the Paris Peace Conference, the Allied statesmen turned their attention to Austria only after dealing with Germany. But in September 1919, they obliged the Renner government to accept a peace document, the Treaty of Saint-Germain, that stripped Austria not only of the entirety of the prewar Habsburg Empire but also of two-fifths of the German-speaking homeland itself. From a mighty conglomeration of 52 million inhabitants, Austria now was transformed into a hunchback republic of barely 7 million. The city of Vienna alone encompassed a third of the nation's entire remaining population, while its attenuated hinterland consisted of six tiny mountain cantons possessing few natural resources beyond attractive scenery. Before the war, the empire had boasted highly developed resources—Silesia's coal, Bohemia's steel, textiles, and quarries, Hungary's wheat, northeastern Italy's wharfage and maritime facilities—as well as a network of railroads and a huge administrative bureaucracy. Most of this vast reticulation now was gone. Worse yet, Austria was surrounded by former subject nations, a majority still hostile, and all intent on maintaining stiff tariff barriers against Austria's modest exports. The country was left threadbare and hungry, "too small to live, too large to die," as political commentators described it.

A year after signing the peace treaty, the Austrian parliament adopted a constitution. Drafted by Hans Kelsen, a Jewish law professor at the University of Vienna, the document established a powerful legislature elected by a party-list system, that is, by proportional representation. The arrangement proved counterproductive, hardening ideological lines and discouraging political compromise. Assuredly, it proved incapable of coping with the nation's postwar economic misery. This was the grim legacy with which the Social Democrat–dominated coalition now had to grapple.

The party itself had been established in 1888 and was largely the achievement of Jewish intellectuals. Viktor Adler was one of its earliest pioneers. Reared in Vienna's drab Leopoldstadt quarter, and educated at the University of Vienna, Adler took his degree in medicine. Afterward, devoting much of his practice to working-class families, the young physician was shaken by the poverty he encountered beneath Vienna's glittering surface. The experience drew him to Marxism. So, too, did the poisonous anti-semitism he had encountered since his university years, and which even an expedient conversion to Protestantism did not spare him. By his mid-thirties, Adler had all but abandoned his medical practice to devote himself to the cause of Social Democracy.

Thus, in 1889, at an early party congress, Adler formulated a compromise program that blended orthodox Marxism and moderate revisionism. Its agenda, focusing essentially on social welfare and international peace, was particularly attractive to Jewish professionals. Gravitating to Social Democracy in the last Habsburg decades, most of them came from the Germanized middle class, where in earlier years they had given their political loyalties to the Liberal party. They brought with them a minority people's vested interest in humanism and internationalism, ideals that the Liberals evidently had abandoned. One of these Liberal defectors was Otto

Bauer. The son of a prosperous Jewish textile manufacturer, Bauer in 1907 published a monumental volume, *The Nationalities Issue and Social Democracy (Die Nationalitätfrage und die Sozialdemokratie)*, essentially as a companion to Karl Renner's 1902 book, *The Struggle of Austrian Nationalities within the State (Der Kampf der Österreischischen Nationen um den Staat)*.

Both works advocated an enlightened federal-autonomist approach to the Empire's contentious non-Austrian peoples. With the outbreak of war, to be sure, the party leadership under Karl Renner agreed initially to support the national cause. But the ongoing horrors of the conflict soon obliged many of the Social Democratic leaders to reexamine their position. Here it was that Otto Bauer, returning from Russia in a prisoner exchange in September 1917, played the decisive role. At his initiative, the Social Democratic leadership agreed to identify with the peace camp and support de facto independence for the subject nationalities.

Following the end of the war and establishment of the Austrian Republic, it was Bauer and the Jewish intellectuals who remained the Social Democrats' most dynamic force. Although Karl Renner became chancellor of the beleaguered postwar coalition government, Bauer became foreign minister. Taking over from Viktor Adler, who died one day after the provisional republic was established, Bauer then rapidly transcended his portfolio by orchestrating a major part of the government's domestic agenda. It was essentially at Bauer's initiative that the subsequent two years of Social Democratic governance produced the most sweeping working-class legislation in the nation's history. The program included an eight-hour workday, paid holidays, prohibition of child labor and night work for women, and a vast increase in unemployment and health insurance. Ultimately, the program overreached itself. Financed by punitive taxes on business, it contributed to the nation's ruinous inflation. Nevertheless, Bauer and his colleagues at least had defined social goals that future governments could ignore only at their peril.

Rather more successful, even in the longer term, was the impact of Socialist (and doubtless Jewish) utopianism in the capital itself. Vienna's antiquated municipal government was given over largely to the administration of three remarkable public servants, Mayor Karl Seitz, Dr. Hugo Breitner, and Dr. Julius Tandler. With Seitz, a non-Jew, providing the political leadership, Breitner, who was Jewish, was entrusted with the city's financial affairs; and Tandler, a converted half-Jew, shouldered the task of reconstructing its welfare organizations. Their achievement was historic. A former bank director and something of an irascible genius, Breitner "progressivized" the city's tax system, then used an accumulated surplus to provide affordable electricity, water, and public transportation rates for Vienna's citizenry, and to construct sixty thousand affordable workers' apartments, together with a wide network of schools and playgrounds.

Equally impressive was Tandler's transformation of the city's welfare and public health services. A professor of anatomy at the University of Vienna Medical School, Tandler was a thickset figure, with a huge dark moustache, and an artist's broad-brimmed hat and neckerchief. The façade of stagy bohemianism was entirely deceptive. The man was a brilliant impresario. He it was who reorganized the hospitals and clinics to provide specialized care for the thousands of local children who were afflicted with tuberculosis and rickets. Tandler ensured, too, that youngsters from deprived families were provided with free school breakfasts and lunches. Under his direction, an extensive welfare program was established for pregnant mothers, offering them prenatal and postnatal medical attention, and rent vouchers and milk vouchers in case of need. Altogether, under the perennial control of the Social Democrats, Vienna developed the single most enlightened municipal administration in the world.

It was in the early 1920s, as well, that Austrian Jews of all backgrounds virtually completed the prewar shift in their political loyalties from the Liberals to the Social Democrats. The reasons were not arcane. Internationalism remained a key factor, of course. Yet, more than any other political faction, even more than the Liberals, Social Democracy had purged itself of its residual, class-based antisemitism. By contrast, the Social Democrats' principal rival, the Christian Socialist party—the "Christian Socials"—had been founded on a program of ideological antisemitism; and while this feature of its agenda had been muted during Karl Lueger's mayoralty (p. 166), the party maintained a close if unofficial relationship with the Catholic hierarchy. The political antipodes could hardly have been more dramatic. Indeed, the Jews' en bloc reorientation to the left was further underscored by their inescapable prominence in the upper echelons of the Social Democratic leadership. Among these were men of the caliber of Bauer, Breitner, Viktor and Friedrich Adler, Max Adler, Gustav Eckstein, and Rudolf Hilferding. Altogether, of the 137 "important" figures in Austrian socialism listed in Ernst Glaser's book, *The Hinterland of Austrian Marxism (Im Umweld des Austromarxismus)*, no fewer than 88 were Jews or part-Jews.

An Expiration of Political Accommodation

It was perhaps inevitable, then, in the parliamentary elections of December 1918, that the Christian Socials reverted to the demagoguery of their initial, nineteenth-century incarnation. They structured their political campaign almost exclusively around the "Jewish danger." On this occasion, the effort failed to produce an electoral victory, although it won the party a slot in the Social Democratic coalition cabinet. But in December 1920, the amputations produced by the Saint-Germain peace treaty, and the raging inflation, forced yet another national election. This time, once again exploiting antisemitism to the hilt, the Christian Socials now assumed the leadership of a restructured coalition.

Indeed, Ignaz Seipel, who replaced Karl Renner as chancellor, was a monsignor of the Catholic Church and a former professor of moral theology. He was also an experienced politician who had served in Emperor Karl's wartime provisional government and in the first postwar republican cabinet. Aloof and sophisticated, Seipel personally disdained rabble-rousing of any kind. His antisemitism was discreet. Insofar as he proclaimed it at all, his "Jewish" objective was simply to limit Jewish cultural and political influence in Austrian life. Otherwise, the new chancellor had more urgent preoccupations. These were to stop the treasury's printing presses, and then to negotiate a loan through the League of Nations. Seipel met these goals, but only through the draconian surgery of terminating numerous public welfare projects and laying off thousands of redundant civil servants. If his measures achieved a certain economic stability, the salaried, lower-middle class was the element that paid most heavily.

With or without the monsignor's approval, therefore, Christian Socialist politicians concentrated upon diverting these white-collar frustrations. In the effort, they found it a comparatively simple matter to identify Jews with the dangers of political radicalism. Evidence of the connection was not lacking. In Germany, Rosa Luxemburg had figured prominently in the recent "Spartacist" uprising. In quasi-autonomous Bavaria, a Soviet republic already was functioning under a Jew, Kurt Eisner; while the Hungarian Soviet Republic under Bela Kun and its dominant Jewish leadership was sending tremors of fear throughout East-Central Europe. In Austria itself, for that matter, as far back as October 1916, Friedrich Adler, a physicist and the frail, intellectual son of Viktor Adler, had shot and killed the Austrian prime minister, Count Karl von Stürgkh, as Stürgkh was dining with friends in a downtown Vienna restaurant. At his trial, the younger Adler defended his act as a protest against an oppressive regime that was destroying the Austrian people, soldiers and civilians alike. He was sentenced to death, but the imperial court in 1917 commuted the sentence to eighteen years, unwilling to risk worker unrest during a period of national crisis. Soon after the armistice, the provisional republic granted Adler a full pardon.

In the immediate postwar years, moreover, as funds and propaganda materials flooded into Vienna from Bolshevik Russia, local radicals embarked on putsch efforts of their own. Again, Jews played a central role. One of the best known was the Prague-born journalist Egon Kisch. On November 12, 1918, Kisch and several of his fellow "Red Guards" launched an armed raid on the offices of the *Neue Freie Presse*. Still Austria's most influential newspaper, the *Presse* remained a bastion of moderate liberalism, and thus a particular bête noire for Communists and other radicals. The assault was easily repelled, without loss of life. (Ironically, Kisch's brother Paul was one of the newspaper's editors. Legend has it that, as the Red Guards reached the *Presse*'s main entrance, Paul Kisch raised his finger menacingly. "Egon, turn back right now," he warned, "or I'll tell Mama!"). Yet the image of Jewish radicalism was not erased. It was to Jews that the Christian Socials attributed blame for the "punitive" taxes and social egalitarianism of "Red Vienna," and the widespread economic misery of the nation's déclassé white-collar elements.

Never before had this little people loomed so prominently in Vienna's life. In 1910, Jews numbered some 175,000 in a metropolitan population of 2,300,000 (p. 161). By 1923, although war losses and economic privation reduced the city's population to approximately 1,865,000, the Jews' demography by then had stabilized at about 200,000 (out of 240,000 Jews in all of Austria), an increase attributable to the wartime influx of Galician and Bukovinian refugees, almost half of whom stayed on in Vienna. Despite the rigors of war and the postwar years, moreover, Viennese Jewry remained an overwhelmingly middle-class element. As late as 1934, in their favored bailiwick of the professions, they still constituted 62 percent of the city's lawyers and 47 percent of its physicians and dentists. In business, at least 70 percent of the city's wholesale and retail trade remained in Jewish hands.

Again, the figures were deceptive. Embourgeoisement was by no means synonymous with affluence. The Galician Jewish refugees were quite poor, with most of their "businesses" little more than shoestring operations. Even the commercial and professional status of the "veteran" Jewish majority was the consequence largely of public and private antisemitic discrimination. Throughout the postwar years, of some 160,000 civil servants in Austria, less than 700 were Jews. Even fewer Jews secured employment in Gentile-owned businesses. Yet the typical Austrian Gentile knew only what he saw, and it appeared that, everywhere he turned, he saw professional offices and storefronts with Jewish names. Before 1914, in a comparatively prosperous empire, a vocationally elitist Jewish presence could be accepted or ignored. Not in the misery of the postwar era, and even less when that presence was further equated with the political radicalism of "Red Vienna," and with an infusion of culturally objectionable Galician refugees.

So it was, in the late teens and early 1920s, that a storm of "Judenhetze" acquired dimensions unprecedented in recent Austrian history. In 1919, verbal abuse was matched by a series of thuggish rampages through the commercial neighborhoods of the Leopoldstadt quarter, demonstrations that ended only after Jewish war veterans hastily organized a defense force. But in the autumn of 1920, when Albert Einstein accepted an invitation to lecture at the University of Vienna, police had to be summoned to cordon off the campus against threatened antisemitic violence. In the hinterland, the provincial legislatures of Upper Austria and Upper Tyrol limited visits by "outsiders"—a code word for Ostjuden—to three days, and many Austrian resorts now denied admission to Jewish guests altogether. Rallies and demonstrations against Jews became almost weekly occurrences. For two and a half years the wave of xenophobia endured, not subsiding until the early spring of 1923. It was Chancellor Seipel, finally, who insisted that the Christian Socials adopt a more subdued and respectable middle-class orientation. The party depended on business contributions, he reminded them, and the Austrian economy altogether was in urgent need of foreign investors and foreign markets.

Yet, if violence ebbed, the appeal for verbal moderation rang hollow. Austria's political landscape had taken definitive form by the early 1920s, and its lineaments were ugly. Beyond the lockstep of its electoral system, a graver danger was the emergence of paramilitary "defense" forces. One such private army, springing up in the provinces during the early postwar years, consisted essentially of veterans' groups, intent on protecting their family property against marauders, many of whom were also demobilized soldiers. By late 1918, the self-defense vigilantes had coalesced into the Heimwehr, a "Home Defense Force." Nominally apolitical, the Heimwehr almost from the outset was linked unofficially with the Christian Socials.

In turn, responding to the threat of an armed right wing, Julius Deutsch, the (Jewish) minister of defense in Karl Renner's coalition government, moved swiftly to organize a parallel defense force under Social Democratic auspices. This was the Schutzbund, the "Protective League." Thus, by 1920, two quasi-armies had emerged, both functioning outside official government control, with the Schutzbund maintaining its base in "Red" Vienna, and the Heimwehr winning its recruits mainly in the hinterland. The ominous polarization continued on into the 1920s—and well beyond.

The Malaise of the Intellectuals

For Jews, the social disruption of postwar Austria was movingly dramatized in a 1927 play by Franz Theodor Csokor. Entitled *3 November 1919* (best translated as *The Army That Did Not Return*), it depicts a colonel in the old imperial army who dies broken-hearted as he witnesses the disintegration of his multinational regiment. At the colonel's funeral, a representative of each of the unit's nationalities throws a shovelful of earth over his bier, say-ing "Earth from Hungary," "Earth from Poland," "Earth from Slovenia," and so on. When the shovel is handed to the regiment's Jewish doctor, he hesitates, and then with much uneasiness finally mutters: "Earth from . . . earth from . . . Austria."

Csokor's aperçu of Jewish ambivalence in the residual homeland may not have been immediately appreciated. Jewish communal life in Vienna and other Austrian cities remained extraordinarily vibrant throughout the postwar years. It was further enhanced by the infusion of some thirty-six thousand intensely ethnocentric Galician refugees (p. 179). The government continued to authorize Austria's Jewish Kultusverein—its official community council—to impose "taxes" on its constituents, thus ensuring subventions for a wide plenum of Jewish religious and welfare activities.

Moreover, Jews emerged even more prominently among the nation's cultural icons than before the war. Ludwig von Mises led the consortium of renowned, predominantly Jewish, economists who comprised the liberal "Vienna School." Jewish composers, conductors, and performing artists remained luminaries in the nation's musical life. Indeed, the legacy of Gustav Mahler, and the growing influence of Mahler's avant-gardist "pupil," Arnold Schönberg, produced a new genre of musical composition, the "Second Vienna School." In theater, the ascendancy of Jews as producers and directors was virtually unchallengeable. In 1924, Max Reinhardt returned from Germany, where he had single-handedly revolutionized the stage (p. 268), to assume direction of Vienna's famous Staatstheater, then to develop an annual summer drama "festival" in Salzburg. In journalism, the editorial staffs of Vienna's leading newspapers remained as overwhelmingly Jewish as in the prewar years. Even in sports, Austrian Jews managed to achieve the same notable visibility as in Hungary (p. 120). Fred Oberländer was Austria's reigning heavyweight wrestling champion during most of the 1920s; Willi Kurtz, its heavyweight boxing champion. HaKoach, the Zionist sports club, periodically won Vienna's field-hockey championship.

Yet it was the Jewish belletrists who grasped most intuitively the decisive shift in Austria's cultural template. Their elegy for the lost empire often assumed the dimensions of an idyll, a retrospective mythologization in which Jews as well as other peoples had shared in the benevolent pluralism of Habsburg rule. With terse understatement, Josef Roth offered a characteristically bittersweet evaluation of the moribund realm. As a Viennese journalist in the postwar years, the Galician-born Roth became obsessed with the helpless victims, the lost generation, of shattered Europe. In his 1924 novel *Hotel Savoy*, he offered a poignant account of one of those victims, a Jew returning from battle service to his hometown in Galicia. Hungry, ragged, and alienated, the victim only then senses that the prewar empire, for all its anachronisms and debilities, at least offered an anchorage against rootlessness and anomie. Roth embellished upon his theme of a lost generation in a series of novels throughout the 1920s and 1930s, and perhaps most effectively in his 1932 *The Radetzky March (Der Radetzkymarsch)*, a delicate and moving tribute to the late Franz Josef. In 1939, when Roth died as a refugee in Paris, at the age of forty-five, a descendant of the House of Habsburg ordered a wreath placed on his grave.

None of the prewar Jewish literary figures was immune to the wrenching transformations of the recent conflict, not even the ebullient Franz Werfel. In 1917, transferred from his artillery regiment on the eastern front to the War Archives in Vienna, the twenty-seven-year-old Werfel first met thirty-eight-year-old Alma Schindler. Widowed at the death of her first husband, Gustav Mahler, Alma had subsequently met and married the architect Walter Gropius. But with Gropius off at the front, Werfel now fell completely under the spell of this renowned femme fatale and entered into an affair with her. It was Werfel who probably fathered her fourth child, a stillborn. Soon afterward, Alma parted from Gropius, who granted her a divorce in 1920, and moved in with Werfel—although their relationship would not be formalized by marriage until 1929.

In the midst of these complex emotional developments, Werfel remained acutely sensitive to the far vaster trauma afflicting his fellow Austrians, and not least his fellow Jews. Indeed, early in the war, he captured an essential element of the Jewish tragedy in a short story, "Ein Uhlan," an account of an Austrian Jewish trooper driven insane when he learns that the first man he has killed in combat is a fellow Jew. An increasingly outspoken pacifist (p. 173), Werfel soon after the armistice joined Egon Kisch in the unsuccessful leftist effort to take over the *Neue Freie Presse* building, and for several days afterward remained in hiding before he could rejoin Alma.

The problem of revolution against militaristic capitalism continued to impinge on Werfel's subsequent writing career. The theme was evident in his lavish Expressionist allegories, *Mirror-Man (Spiegelmensch)*, *The Old Goat's Song (Der Bocksgesang)*, and "Comrade Weisse," all produced in the early 1920s. In each of these narratives, Werfel made plain his retrospective contempt for the dilettante intellectual—transparently modeled on Egon Kisch—the kind who provokes uprisings without staying power or a long-range program of moral reform. Even as Werfel embellished on the imponderables of revolution in later works of the 1920s and 1930s, including the dramas *Juarez und Maximilian* and *The Kingdom of God in Bohemia (Das Reich Gottes in Böhmen)*, he managed to provide no clear resolution of the issue. It was not until publication in 1933 of *The Forty Days of Musa Dagh (Die vierzig Tage des Musa Dagh)*, based on the 1915 Turkish genocide of the Armenians, that Werfel finally seemed to acknowledge the legitimacy of forthright resistance to oppression.

By contrast, Arthur Schnitzler, the doyen of the Jung-Wien constellation, was rather less interested than his literary colleagues in addressing the tragedy of the defunct empire. The ex-physician's preference still was for the exploration of individual motives. Portentous themes like the rise and fall of dynasties, even the fate of the Jewish people, no longer lay within his ambition, or perhaps within his reserve of energy. In the chaos of the postwar era, Schnitzler's very silence was eloquent. On the occasion of his sixtieth birthday, in 1922, his friend Stefan Zweig wrote in a Festschrift tribute:

> [T]he unforgettable types which he created and which one could see daily, only yesterday, on his fiftieth anniversary, in the streets, in the theaters, in the drawing rooms of Vienna, almost formed by his vision, have suddenly disappeared from real life, which has been transformed. Das süsse Mädchen [the sweet, unaffected, guileless young thing—almost a stock character in Schnitzler's plays] has become a prostitute; the Anatols [after a charming bon vivant of an early Schnitzler comedy] play at the stock exchange; the aristocrats have fled; the officers have become salesmen and agents. . . . Some of the problems with which Schnitzler dealt in such an intellectually animated . . . fashion have acquired a different and much more vehement mood, especially the Jewish problem and the social problem.

Stefan Zweig was himself the ideal commentator for a ceremonial tribute to a distinguished colleague. More than any individual of his generation, he was the quintessential man of letters, the definitive arbiter of literary taste, the paradigm of sophisticated European culture in its last, postwar efflorescence. Thirty-seven years old in 1914, Zweig had been the youngest member of the original Jung-Wien group. Although he had taken his university degree in law, it was literature that almost immediately became his one and exclusive avocation. In ensuing years, producing a string of well-received short stories, novels, and plays, Zweig achieved an even wider eminence as a biographer and interpreter of historic literary figures, from Shakespeare to Goethe, from Tolstoy to Proust.

By the latter 1920s, as polymath, historian, and critic, Zweig towered over almost every literary figure on the Continent. With the possible exception of Thomas Mann, no one in German-speaking Europe, and few literary personages in any culture, could match him in sheer range of erudition and fecundity of publication. With his works translated into nearly every European language, Zweig had become an international cult personality and was in continual demand before lecture audiences throughout the Continent. His substantial foreign royalties, moreover, enabled him to purchase an elegant home on the Capuchin Hill overlooking Salzburg. There, accumulating a vast private library, he reigned like a philosopher-king, hosting an endless stream of visitors from many countries. And there, too, as the consummate humanist, Zweig presided as Europe's major intellectual figure in the world peace movement. In that cause, he produced a deluge of articles, lectures, and personal correspondence with other cultural celebrities who shared his passionate internationalism.

Zweig's contemporary, the perennially acerbic Karl Kraus, had not for a single moment shared the sweetly reasonable illusion of European, and specifically Austrian, self-improvement. Even the brief postwar ascendancy of the Social Democrats did not alter Kraus's evaluation of Austrian politics as irredeemably corrupt, and the Austrian people as incorrigibly chauvinist. During the war, he had concluded his *Last Days of Mankind* with the premonitory warning: "More death and sickness will once again come into the world than was ever hinted at during the war." In August 1924, on the tenth anniversary of the outbreak of the war, Kraus issued a parody of the initial public reaction to August 1914, "In These Great Times" ("In dieser grossen Zeit"). Entitled "In These Petty Times" ("In dieser kleinen Zeit"), this one predicted that a new call to the colors would inflame vulgar chauvinism and produce the identical wartime horrors.

If Kraus, a Jew, offered a mordant commentary on the Austrian future, Hugo Bettauer, a Jewish convert to Protestantism, issued his own dire parable on the vulnerability of Austrian Jewry. Scion of a Galician merchant family, Bettauer before the war was employed in Berlin as a journalist for the Ullstein chain of newspapers, and he was twice imprisoned for slandering Kaiser Wilhelm II. In 1921, the Hearst chain hired him as their Vienna correspondent. By then, Bettauer had published several successful novels, but it was in 1923 that he produced his best-known work, *The City Without Jews (Die Stadt ohne Juden)*. The book was a cold-eyed portrait of contemporary Austria, of its turgid xenophobia and confused, dysfunctional Jewish minority.

As Bettauer's narrative unfolds, Austria's popular chancellor, Dr. Karl Schwartzfeger—transparently based on Vienna's renowned fin-de-siècle mayor, Karl Lueger—appears before Parliament to offer a solution for the nation's widespread unemployment. It is to expel the Jewish population. As Schwartzfeger explains:

> [T]he trouble is simply that we Austrian Aryans are not a match for the Jews. . . . With their uncannily keen intelligence, their worldliness and freedom of tradition, their catlike versatility and their lightning comprehension . . . they overpowered us, became our masters, and gained the upper hand in all our economic, spiritual and cultural life. . . . Either we, who make up nine-tenths of the population, must perish, or the Jew must go.

The cheering deputies then overwhelmingly approve the chancellor's bill to evict the nation's Jews, after a "merciful" six-month grace period. The public, too, reacts in a delirium of joy at the prospect of gaining access to Jewish businesses and apartments.

The response of the Jews, of course, is one of terror and chaos, as they rush frantically to liquidate their properties and estates. Except for a perfunctory interfaith love story, Bettauer treats these people less than sympathetically. But his sharpest barbs are reserved for the chancellor and the latter's constituents in Parliament, who become increasingly frustrated as their blueprint for economic resurrection flounders. Jewish holdings devolve into the hands not of Austrian Gentiles but of foreign banks. The sheer bureaucratic expense of administering the exodus depletes public resources. Meanwhile, bereft of the former galaxy of Jewish professionals, Vienna's courts, hospitals, theaters, concert halls, and museums cease to function. Indeed, public discontent with the entire operation ultimately leads to the fall of the government, and elections afterward produce a new parliament, which immediately reverses the law of expulsion. The nation's Jews thereupon return en masse to Austria, much to public jubilation.

In March 1925, a year and a half after publication of Bettauer's roman à clef, a youthful member of the Austrian Nazi party, Otto Rothstock, walked into the author's office and shot him fatally. At his trial, Rothstock insisted that his deed had been necessary to help save "deutsche Kultur" from degeneration. Rothstock's lawyer, Walter Riehl, himself a prominent Austrian Nazi, then persuaded the jury to find the young man innocent by reason of insanity. The judge in turn duly sentenced Rothstock to a mental institution—which twenty months later released him as sane.

A Prophet of Social Morbidity

Sigmund Freud's family had survived the war comparatively unscathed. His sons had returned safely from military service. The eldest, Martin, had been repatriated following his brief internment as a POW in Italy. The family's worst privations were the fuel and food shortages of the early 1920s, and even these were mitigated by the visits of foreign patients, bringing hard currency with them. Freud's pathbreaking theories of the unconscious were evoking steadily wider respect, both in medical circles and in the cultural world at large. Even the University of Vienna now belatedly had to recognize the impact of the "new thinking." In 1920, it promoted Freud from docent to professor. By then, he had assumed the quasi-religious status of a prophet.

He was a less than forbearing one. Few of his disciples presumed to modify his central thesis, of sexuality as the fundament of the unconscious, and the Oedipus Complex as the primal trauma of sexuality. Yet, shortly before the war, Alfred Adler, an early member of Freud's circle, was among the first to question that iron law, projecting the notion of "inferiority" and "superiority" complexes as alternate unconscious determinants. Enraged by this lèse-majesté, Freud promptly excommunicated Adler from his inner sanctum. There would be other rebels in future years. None, however, affected the prophet as grievously as the "crown prince" whom Freud had anointed to rescue psychoanalysis from its essentially Jewish identification.

Well into the early 1900s, the clinical center of psychiatric research in Europe was not yet Vienna, nor even Paris, but Zurich, and specifically the Burghölzli Mental Hospital, which functioned as a cantonal asylum as well as the psychiatric training hospital for the University of Zurich Medical School. Here, in 1900, Dr. Carl Gustav Jung, a twenty-five-year-old Swiss pastor's son, and himself a graduate of Zurich's medical school, had become assistant to the Burghölzli's renowned director, Dr. Eugen Bleuler. A brilliant researcher, Jung early on became aware of Freud's psychoanalytic methods, which he began applying to his own patients. In 1906, Jung's maiden publication, *The Psychology of Dementia Praecox* (an affliction later called schizophrenia), offered the first clinical confirmation of the role of sexuality in the unconscious.

That same year, Jung initiated a respectful correspondence with Freud, and the two began exchanging articles and observations. In February 1907, Jung and his wife visited the Freuds in Vienna. On one side, as Martin Freud recalled, there was Jung, tall, upright, clean-shaven, with a bullet head of close-cropped hair, the very model of a Nordic Siegfried. Freud, twenty years older, goateed and slight of build, was intense, animated, and ebullient. The discussion between the two men continued for thirteen hours, and was cordial, even warm.

Soon afterward, in 1908, under Freud's active supervision, Jung helped organize the first international gathering of psychoanalysts in Salzburg, and then produced the society's journal, the *Jahrbuch für Psychoanalytische und psychopathologische Forschungen*, with Jung himself as editor and president of the emergent society. When several members of the original Psychological Wednesday Evening circle complained to Freud that the presidency and editorship should be reserved for him alone, Freud demurred. He had written his colleague Karl Abraham, earlier: "[A]s a Christian and a pastor's son, [Jung] in his association with us . . . [spares] psychoanalysis the danger of becoming a Jewish national affair." Indeed, Jung by then had emerged as the most intimate member of Freud's entourage, even accompanying the prophet (and Sandor Ferenczi) to the

United States in 1909 for a Clark University symposium. On shipboard during the eight-day crossing, Jung and Freud analyzed each other's dreams.

Over the next few years, however, a hairline ideological rift between Freud and Jung gradually widened, as the younger man proved increasingly unwilling to accept the preeminent role of sexuality in the unconscious. In a series of papers, Jung even challenged the concept of the Oedipus complex as a prime factor in sexuality; and in a letter afterward he indelicately warned Freud to take "an objective view of our common endeavors." In the last two years before the war, relations between the two became increasingly tense, and Jung effectively terminated them in December 1912, by writing Freud:

> I would . . . point [out] that your technique of treating your pupils like patients is a blunder. In that way you produce either slavish sons or impudent puppets. . . . I am objective enough to see through your little trick. . . . Meanwhile, you remain on top as the father, sitting pretty.

Jung and Freud would never again resume even the basic civilities of personal contact. Two years later, the entire Zurich—that is, Jung—group voted to withdraw from the International Society. Freud by then had his own rationale for the schism. Writing an American colleague, James Putnam, he ascribed it to Jung's "brutality and antisemitic condescension towards me." Yet later, ironically, Freud noted to another friend, Lou Andreas-Salomé, that Jung was displaying "unveiled adherence to Bergson. So you see he has found another Jew for his father complex."

The reference to Bergson was significant. Henri Bergson, of Jewish parentage, and arguably France's single most influential philosopher of the prewar era, formulated and fervently advocated the notion of an élan vital, a "life force" that propelled all of mankind to its collective achievements (p. 284). Jung in the last years before the war appeared to be moving in the direction of a similarly atavistic dynamic, one he preferred to describe as the "collective unconscious." All humans, he insisted, were born with minds on which already were imprinted "archetypes," vestigial traces of the collective religious or ideological beliefs and social systems of their respective races. It was an inheritance, he would subsequently argue, that contained all the wisdom and experience of uncounted centuries. In making the case for "thinking with a nation's collective blood," Jung in later years would lend the specious veneer of intellectual respectability to European Fascism, even to European racism (pp. 199–200).

Yet Freud himself soon was engaged in social explorations that rested on equally fragile conjectures. Indeed, the problem of man in society would consume the last twenty years of his life. As early as 1907, he had begun producing a series of astonishingly erudite essays on Shakespeare's *Macbeth*, *Hamlet*, and *Richard III*, on Dostoevsky's *The Brothers Karamazov*, on Michelangelo's statue of Moses, all of which evinced a growing obsession with the human condition in its wider dimensions. In 1913, with the publication of his book *Totem and Taboo (Totem und Tabu)*, Freud shifted his emphasis more decisively from specific mental aberrations to mankind's collective behavioral patterns. In this short volume, building on James Frazier's theory that primitive society consisted of hordes of brothers led by a powerful father, Freud argued that the sheer generic force of the Oedipus complex—the most universal of human conflicts—impelled the sons to rise against the father and kill him. The structural order thereupon collapsed in a formless pandemonium. It was consequently the family's, and the tribe's, need for a powerful leader that led eventually to totemism, and later yet to more elaborate religious systems; for the totem and the deity in effect were the reincarnation of the murdered father-figure.

After the war, in 1921, shaken by mankind's propensity for mass destruction, Freud pressed further in his social inquiry with his *Group Psychology and the Analysis of the Ego (Massenpsychologie und Ich-analyse)*, then, in 1927, with his *Civilization and Its Discontents (Das Unbehagen in der Kultur)*. In both works, he elaborated on the need for an archetypical father-figure who would preside as the arbiter of social justice and thus as the indispensable linchpin of a tightly structured community—in effect, of civilization. It was a Hobbesian vision of society wherein Freud equated humanity's gravitation to strong leadership with a collective "superego." Possibly the concept was influenced by Freud's own Jewish middle-class family culture, with its venerated and awe-inspiring father.

It was rather more likely, however, that he drew his bleak assessment from a kind of intuition that the roots of totalitarianism lay more innately in democracy than in autocracy. As the 1920s progressed, and as authoritarian regimes gained power in one European nation after another, Freud's critique of social behavior focused less on the demise of representative government than on the wanton brutality of racism. To the end of his life, his lack of enthusiasm for "the masses" remained constant, and with it his disdain for the assumption that the wisdom of collective minds signified an improvement over the judgment of strong but enlightened individual leadership.

The Rise of Austrian Fascism

Nowhere was the fragility of the democratic experiment more apparent than in Austria itself. In July 1927, the simmering hostilities between the

Christian Socialists and the Social Democrats boiled over. Incensed when a district court acquitted several right-wing toughs who had been accused of murdering a number of striking workers, crowds of trade unionists attacked the ministry of justice. Before the police could restore order, eighty-five of the protesters had been killed and over a thousand wounded. From then on, the animus between the Austrian right and left remained lethal and unbridgeable.

The pressures of governing amidst this polarization ultimately became too much for Chancellor Seipel. In June 1929 the monsignor resigned, and in September so did his successor, Ernst von Streeruwitz. Over the ensuing two years, following the collapse of the New York stock market, the world depression ramified throughout the entirety of Central Europe. In May 1931 Austria's renowned Kreditanstalt chain of banks collapsed, and the little country's industrial production dropped by some two-thirds, even as its unemployment rate doubled. During these same intervening months, one Christian Socialist chancellor followed another in a frantic effort to cope with the metastasizing economic crisis. No help was forthcoming from the other parties. Otto Bauer, who served as ideological leader of the Social Democrats, flatly refused to share in "administering the affairs of a doomed capitalism."

In the parliamentary elections of 1932, therefore, the Austrian people decided to place their trust in yet another Christian Socialist government, this time under a charismatic new chancellor, Engelbert Dollfuss. A much-decorated war veteran with a rural, arch-conservative background, Dollfuss at age thirty-nine now became the youngest head of government in Europe. He was unquestionably the shortest, standing barely four feet eleven inches. In fact, the "duodecimo chancellor" proved to be a forceful government leader. By committing himself to strict observance of the 1919 Treaty of Saint-Germain, and its injunction against an Anschluss—a union—with Germany, Dollfuss won the trust of the Western democratic governments, as well as important trade concessions from Italy's Mussolini, who needed an independent Austria as the northern "buffer" for his own country.

The pro-Western stance was not an easy one for the chancellor. He faced stiff competition from other, avowedly revisionist elements. The most important of these was the Austrian Nazi party. During the 1920s, Adolf Hitler was a frequent guest speaker at Austrian Nazi gatherings, and by the time of his rise to power in Germany, in 1933, Austria's Nazis were dutifully parroting the führer's demand for an Anschluss. Dollfuss was not having it. Beyond their need for Western, and Italian goodwill, the chancellor and his fellow Christian Socials were ideologically wedded to the Church. They would not allow their little Catholic nation to be swallowed up by a largely Protestant German Machtstaat. In June of that year, Dollfuss banned the Nazi party. Immediately afterward, intent on creating a fire break against the party's revival, he entered into a marriage of convenience with the paramilitary Heimwehr organization.

The Heimwehr's commander, Ernst Rüdiger Prince von Starhemberg, the thirty-one-year-old scion of an aristocratic family, had lately transformed this onetime haphazard collection of regional militias into a national quasi-army of some ninety thousand well-trained, well-disciplined, uniformed paramilitary troops. In the process, the Heimwehr was emerging as a political force of intimidating dimensions. Indeed, to harness its latent power, Chancellor Karl Vaugoion, Dollfuss's immediate predecessor, appointed Starhemberg minister of the interior; and in early 1933, several months after assuming office, Dollfuss took the even more dramatic step of appointing Starhemberg vice chancellor. It was with this augmented strength on his ideological right, which soon would be restructured as the "Fatherland Front," that Dollfuss now prepared to fend off the looming Nazi threat to Austrian independence.

From their traditional base in Vienna, meanwhile, the Social Democrats regarded the new coalition with growing alarm. Indeed, their worst fears appeared to be realized as Dollfuss and the Fatherland Front set about imposing new authoritarian constraints both on Parliament and on local governments. Hereupon the Social Democrats reacted with drastic measures of their own. In February 1934, they launched a general strike in Vienna, paralyzing all public utilities. It was a calamitous miscalculation. The previous month, as it happened, Mussolini had issued an ultimatum to Dollfuss, warning that he, the duce, could not assure Austria protection against Nazi Germany unless the chancellor first broke the power of his country's Social Democrats. Still, Dollfuss had hesitated, unwilling to alienate the Western democracies.

But now, waiting no longer, Dollfuss ordered the police to break the strike. When the Social Democrats' own paramilitary force, the Schutzbund, fought back, the chancellor called up both the Heimwehr and the regular army. In the ensuing two days of battle, over 600 workers were killed and some 2,000 were wounded before their Schutzbund surrendered. Immediately afterward, Dollfuss had eleven Schutzbund leaders executed for "treason," and dissolved the Social Democratic party altogether. Henceforth, Austria would function under an undisguised Fascist dictatorship.

As the nation veered steadily rightward, its Jews needed little reminder that local Nazis remained their most dangerous enemies. Throughout the 1920s, as bands of swastika-wearing toughs rampaged through working-class districts, beating up union and Social Democratic party leaders, they managed to devote special attention to Jews. By the end of the decade, Austrian Nazis and other far-rightists had declared open season on Jewish shops in the Leopoldstadt quarter. Windows were broken, antisemitic epithets were painted on doors, Jewish bystanders were driven off the streets and occasionally beaten. Attacks on Jewish students at the university were an old story, predating the republic. Yet they achieved a special intensity in the depression years. At the medical school, Jewish students were obliged to seek the protection of the Bar Kochba and Kadimah Zionist societies and the HaKoach sports organization, which ushered them in "convoys" to and from their classes.

"Ideologically," however, it was the Christian Socialist leadership even more than the Nazis who set the tone on the Jewish issue. During the mid- and latter 1920s, Chancellor Ignaz Seipel normally had been moderate and controlled in his distaste for Jews. But upon retirement in 1929, living out his final years in a monastery, the monsignor permitted himself a more unrestrained antisemitism. It reflected that of the Austrian Catholic hierarchy. Alluding to the prominence of Jews in the upper cadres of the political left, Bishop Johannes Geföllner of Linz and Bishop Alois Hudal of Graz repeatedly denounced Jews for propagating the spirit of atheistic materialism.

Thus far, Chancellor Dollfuss himself offered little evidence of personal bigotry. Before assuming office in 1932, he socialized with a number of Jews and occasionally vacationed at the home of Berta Zuckerkandl, a wealthy Jewish matron. For some months even after becoming chancellor, he appeared to follow Mussolini's lead in rejecting Hitler's racial theories. In 1934, to be sure, *Die Reichspost*, the official organ of the Christian Socialists, expressed a certain editorial sympathy for Hitler's boycott campaign against Jewish businesses, and Dollfuss affirmed in a speech before a congress of the Fatherland Front that "the state must be built upon Christian, German, authoritarian lines."

On the other hand, Dollfuss had banned the Nazi party and had asserted his determination at all costs to forestall an Anschluss with Hitler's Germany. For this reason, not a few Jews rallied to the chancellor's side, among them Karl Kraus, who regarded Dollfuss as the one man capable of saving the nation from the Nazis. There was hardly a choice. Even the "shadow committee" of the banned Social Democratic party had decided to purge its highly visible and often abrasive Jewish eminences. Men like Bauer, Deutsch, Ellenbogen, Dannenberg, among many others, were accused of having contributed to the 1934 disaster. The flavor of antisemitism was distinctly apparent in these recriminations and accusations. Repudiated in their formerly elitist connection with the Social Democrats, Austrian Jews now confronted as racking a political dilemma as any in their modern history.

A Consternation of Self-Appraisal

It is worth recalling, on the other hand, that the Jewish experience in the postwar era was by no means one of unrelieved trauma. Well into the mid-1930s, most Jews still were earning a living. Most still believed themselves reasonably well acculturated into Viennese life. They had developed a rather impressive defense agency, the Union österreichischer Juden. With access to a wide pool of lawyers, the Union was quite willing to press through the courts issues of discrimination and harassment, particularly the mistreatment of university students. The Union's veteran Jewish "establishment" in any case sternly rejected an alternative route, one proposed by the Zionists and the Galician Orthodox. This was to appeal to the League of Nations under the rubric of the Treaty of Saint-Germain's minorities addendum (p. 40). They would have no part of a "remedy" implying that Jews were a separate nationality.

Even so, the very issue of the Jews' collective identity suggested an ongoing psychological ambivalence. There could be little doubt that the insecurities of the prewar era were infinitely exacerbated under the far graver tensions and frustrations of the 1920s and 1930s. That sense of exposure was shrewdly anticipated in Schnitzler's 1907 *The Road Is Open*. In a famous passage, the Gentile protagonist reflects: "Wherever he went, he met only Jews who were ashamed of being Jews, or others who were proud of it and feared people who might think that they were ashamed."

The theme appears years later in *Auto-da-Fé* (the "English" title used for *Die Blendung*), a 1935 novel by Elias Canetti, a Bulgarian-born Viennese Jew—and years later, a Nobel laureate. When the Jewish protagonist, Siegfried Fisherl, first meets a non-Jew, he is almost preternaturally anxious to determine whether the Gentile is an antisemite: How could one tell? The world was swarming with antisemites. A Jew was always on the lookout for deadly enemies. In truth, those "enemies" were not lacking even among Jews themselves. Canetti's Fischerl, a dwarfed, hunchbacked, hook-nosed swindler, could not have emerged a more grotesque caricature even from the pen of a Nazi.

It was a stereotype pioneered by Jews far more consumed with insecurities than was Canetti himself. The writer Arnold Zweig regarded "the so-called Jewish 'self-hatred' as a specific Austrian form of ego denial, [as a] Jewish *Weltschmerz*, Jewish doubt, the passionate drive to deny of one's own being." Long before, in 1903, Otto Weininger, twenty-three years old, a precocious Viennese philosopher, published *Sex and Character (Geschlecht und Charakter)*, a savage tirade against both women and Jews. Regarding Jews as afflicted with both feminist and materialistic "decadence,"

Weininger viewed the struggle between Aryan Christianity and Semitic Judaism as a battle between masculinity and feminism, in effect, between good and evil. The volume became an instant bestseller, going through twenty-eight printings. Yet its success proved inadequate to rescue its mentally unstable author. He committed suicide only a few months after the book's appearance.

Weininger's former schoolmate in gymnasium, Arthur Trebitsch, a tall, fair-haired young Jew, transcended even his late friend in developing Aryan racial theories comparable to those of Hermann Ahlwardt and Houston Stewart Chamberlain. Like Weininger, Trebitsch became deranged, although he was institutionalized before he could do away with himself. Less fortunate were his contemporaries, the chemist Max Steiner, the philosopher Paul Rée, and the poet Walter Calé, all of whom became delusional in their Jewish insecurities and committed suicide. Others survived their own variations of malaise and self-abasement to offer commentary on the Jewish people's debilities and transgressions.

None did so more unsparingly, however, than Karl Kraus, Central Europe's notorious journalistic Cassandra, and an early convert to Roman Catholicism. If moral hypocrisy, chauvinism, philistinism, arrivism, and sheer vulgarity were Kraus's bêtes noires, for him no people in Europe embodied those vices more quintessentially than did the Jews. And on no subject did he wax more acidulous. In 1897 Kraus's first published essay, "The Ruined Literature" ("Die demolierte Literatur"), evinced the author's contempt for the largely Jewish clique that congregated at the "literary" Café Griensteidl. Only a year later, Kraus's second brochure, "A Crown for Zion" ("Eine Krone für Zion"), heaped comparable scorn on Theodor Herzl and the Zionist movement. During all the thirty-seven years in which issues of Kraus's *Fackel* appeared, hardly any lacked a snide allusion to one variety or another of Jewish miscreants, whether the "effete" Jewish publishers of Vienna's "morally corrupt" newspapers and cultural journals, or the climbers and materialists who were the first to "wrap themselves in the flag of Habsburg patriotism once war began," or "pretentiously" assimilated veteran Jews, or "uncouth" Ostjuden— Kraus reacted to them indiscriminately as if they were his private gall and wormwood.

Franz Werfel's reaction to the accident of his Jewish birth bore no resemblance to the pathological vindictiveness of Weininger, Trebitsch, or Kraus. It was far more complex. His literary agenda in the postwar years evidently was dictated by his aging love goddess, the bloated Alma Schindler, who in 1929 finally agreed to marry him. Taking her "corpulent little Jew" in hand, she encouraged him to shift his efforts from poetry to novels and plays. The advice proved sound, both literarily and financially.

Werfel was a superb craftsman, with a dead-accurate sense of pace and style. His works sold handsomely. None more so than *The Forty Days of Musa Dagh*, his account of the heroic wartime resistance of a besieged Armenian community (p. 182). First published in 1933, and subsequently appearing in nineteen languages, the novel became Werfel's most spectacular success. Critics surmised that the work also revealed the author's unique empathy as a Jew for the fate of another beleaguered minority people. The speculation was misplaced. He was writing as a neo-Christian, not a Jew.

In January 1917, while in his twenties, Werfel published his confession of faith in a *Neue Rundschau* essay, "The Christian Program" ("Die christliche Sendung"). The work rhapsodized with the passion of an author who at last had found the true light after having "wandered as an exile from its shores." Unquestionably, Werfel experienced and repeatedly expressed a genuine solicitude for his Jewish forebears. Years later, his biblical play, *The Eternal Road (Der Weg der Verheissung)*, conceived in 1933 when Hitler came to power, then set to synagogue music by Kurt Weill and magnificently staged in New York in 1937 by Max Reinhardt, was hailed by some as the perfect artistic embodiment of the Jewish fate. Yet Werfel's subsequent novels, *Embezzled Heaven (Der veruntreute Himmel)*, published in 1939, and his 1942 *The Song of Bernadette (Das Lied von Bernadette)*, made clear his spiritual rapport with Roman Catholicism. Indeed, the formidable Alma left no doubt on this point. When Werfel died suddenly in August 1945, she arranged for him to be given a Catholic funeral by assuring ecclesiastical officials that he had formally undergone baptism. The assurance was mendacious. Baptism was a final step Werfel could never bring himself to take.

A rather less tortured odyssey was followed by the Vienna-born Arnold Schönberg. It is unlikely that Schönberg's widowed Jewish mother raised serious objections when her son converted to Protestantism in 1898, at the age of twenty-four. The move apparently was a careerist one and unrelated to "spiritual" influences one way or another. Serving as professor of composition at the Berlin Academy of Arts from 1925 until the Nazi takeover in 1933, Schönberg in his cultural interests appeared to be committed exclusively to music, and to the education of disciples like Anton Webern and Alban Berg in his revolutionary new theory of "atonality" (p. 271).

In fact the impression was no less facile than Schönberg's earlier perfunctory conversion. Exposure to the malevolence of postwar European racism evidently produced a crisis of conscience. During a vacation stay in Paris, in 1928, Schönberg discreetly allowed it to be known that he was resuming his affiliation with the Jewish people. Even earlier, in 1922, he had begun composing his drama, *The Biblical Road (Der biblische Weg)*, itself the forerunner of his later opera, *Moses und Aron*. In these works, Schönberg outlined his vision of a Jewish nation independent again, building the Promised Land anew. From the 1920s on, he never ceased to devote his most urgent thought, and many of his compositions, to Jewish themes.

As for Stefan Zweig, the quintessential European humanist, the interwar years represented an ongoing tidal wave of personal creativity. Yet these also were the years in which he was obliged to give far more serious thought to his Jewish heritage. Formerly "uncompromised" in his secular humanism, married (after an earlier divorce) to a Gentile woman, Zweig had long insisted that his only "political" cause was that of international peace. He had always been timorous about raising Jewish issues, and observed even after the rise of Hitler that "[w]e [Jews] must do nothing now that involves a personal political demonstration." Yet his genuflection to his roots, however belated, was authentic. In 1929, he had declared to Joseph Leftwich, a prominent British Jew:

> Ever since the giving of the Decalogue, the Jewish people has assumed service in the vanguard of humanity. Naturally, such an exposed position entails great danger, but this danger is an integral part of our task, because it is only in spiritual struggle that the individual becomes really alive and the community persists.

Zweig put his money, if not always his political efforts, where his convictions lay. The establishment of the Nazi Reich severely pauperized many of his closest Jewish friends, and he was unstinting in providing them with funds. Before he died by his own hand in Petropolis, Brazil, in 1942 (p. 203), Zweig left instructions that he be given a Jewish funeral. A rabbi and a cantor then presided over the final obsequies. At his directive, too, the stones both over his grave and over that of his non-Jewish wife were inscribed in Hebrew.

The Unflinching Prophet

It was the profoundest of ironies that Sigmund Freud, the intellectual whose identification with his fellow Jews was possibly the most steadfast of all his contemporaries, was also the most emphatic in his rejection of Judaism as a religion. Both elements of Freud's Weltanschauung, ethnic pride and irreligiosity, appeared to assume final definition following his break with Jung, the watershed crisis of his career. In July 1913, blaming himself for having forced his Vienna loyalists to accept "the blond Siegfried" as president of the International Psychoanalytic Association, Freud informed Sabrina Spielweiss, a former patient of Jung's, that he, Freud, was "cured of the last shred of my predilection for the Aryan cause. . . . We are and remain Jews. The others will only exploit us and will never understand or appreciate us." Yet it was also the break with Jung that impelled Freud to launch into his extensive cycle of volumes on the origins and development of religion. *Totem and Taboo* was the first consequence of this new focus (*The Future of an Illusion* [*Die Zukunft einer Illusion*], published in 1927, would be the second). It was a project, as Freud wrote Karl Abraham, that "would serve to make a sharp division between us and all Aryan religiosity."

At the same time, the undertaking would enable Freud to confront the ghosts of his Jewish ambivalence. His studies on Moses, beginning in 1914 with his essay on Michelangelo's statue of the great law-giver, fitted into this re-evaluation. "There is every reason to suppose," observed Ernest Jones, Freud's biographer and early collaborator, "that the grand figure of Moses . . . was of tremendous significance to [Freud]. Did Moses represent the formidable Father-image or did Freud identify himself with him? Apparently both, at different periods." Freud's ongoing appraisal of Moses's role in Judaism, the West's great parent religion, was given its final, perhaps inevitable impetus with the advent of Nazism, whose pagan and lethal Aryanism was the precise antithesis of Judaism. "Faced with the new persecution," Freud wrote Stefan Zweig in September 1934, "one asks oneself again how the Jews have come to be what they are and why they have attracted this undying hatred. I soon discovered the formula: Moses created the Jews."

Freud's explanation, *Moses and Monotheism* (*Der Mann Moses und die monotheistische Religion*), was the small volume he began in 1934 and which was published in 1939. One of the essay's two key theses was that Moses was not a Jew, but rather an Egyptian who developed his belief in monotheism under the influence of a prevailing Egyptian religious trend. A second, even more provocative argument was that Moses, the angry, overpowering leader, was slain by his rebellious followers—a natural thematic extension of the sons killing the father in Freud's earlier *Totem and Taboo*. It was this murder, in Freud's analysis, that became the source of an unconscious sense of guilt from which the Jews never managed to liberate themselves.

The concept was a shattering one, and over the years Freud intermittently procrastinated before finally bringing himself to complete the manuscript. Indeed, its central conclusion was not presented until the Fifteenth Congress of the International Psychoanalytic Association, which met in Paris in 1938. Too old and ill to attend, Freud sent his daughter Anna to read key extracts, and thus to "soften" the book's iconoclasm at a time when Nazism was threatening modern civilization, and most specifically the Jewish people. One of those extracts stated:

We know that Moses had given the Jews the exalted sense of being God's chosen people. By dematerializing God, a new valuable contribution was made to the secret treasure of the people. . . . The political misfortune of the nation taught them to appreciate the only possession they had retained, their literature, at its true value. . . . From now on it was the [Torah] and the intellectual effort applied to it that kept the people together.

In short, the Torah, five books structured about the Great Lawgiver, no longer was to be regarded as a crescendo of rage or compulsion. In Freud's interpretation, Moses and the Torah were to be identified with the "superego," in effect, with civilization, the force generated within the individual to keep him from pre-societal "instinctual gratification." As Freud saw it (and as Anna read to the Fifteenth Congress): "The hatred for Judaism is at bottom hatred for Christianity, and it is not surprising that in the German [Nazi] revolution this close connection of the two monotheistic religions finds such clear expression in the hostile treatment of both."

Once *Moses and Monotheism* was published—posthumously—in 1939, its underlying "spiritual-psychological" thesis was overshadowed by its shocking allegation of the murder of Moses. Even Freud had entertained second thoughts, regretting that he had chosen to produce the work in Jewry's most terrible hour. To Arnold Zweig he wrote in February 1938: "[N]ow that everything is being taken from them, I had to go and take their best man." Freud's pain reflected his own close, even principled commitment to his fellow Jews. The identification of course would never be confused with religiosity. From his earliest manhood, Freud had cast a baleful eye on traditional ritual (p. 198). Following his betrothal to Anna Bernays, he sought—not always successfully—to wean her of her "religious prejudices" and "foolish superstitions." Although he consented to a traditional Jewish wedding, afterward Freud countenanced no Jewish prayers or holiday observances in the family home. None of his sons underwent the bar mitzvah ceremony. Even so, Freud's professional and personal associations throughout his life remained overwhelmingly Jewish (p. 186). "I was born on May 6, 1856," he declared forthrightly at the opening of a brief autobiographical essay, "at Freiberg, Moravia. . . . My parents were Jews, and I have remained a Jew myself." His enduring respect for the Jews as a people doubtless was the mirror image of his personal self-respect.

Almost certainly it was pride that helped explain Freud's disdain for Jews who opportunistically accepted baptism, thereby manifesting a careerism that he regarded as hardly less than a pathology, even a form of treason against the Jewish people. In 1926, discussing with Professor Sandor Ehrmann the recent conversion of Albert Kovner, a prominent Polish Jewish intellectual, Freud rejected Ehrmann's suggestion that conversion was an entirely personal act, if it enabled one to "fulfill one's life's goal." Such an act was never a merely private one, Freud countered, for it "endangered the common interest." The identical moral adamance characterized Freud's reaction to Franz Werfel's literary flirtation with Christianity. The two met in 1926, and it was then that Werfel presented Freud with a copy of his new drama, *Paul Among the Jews (Paulus unter den Juden)*, which turned on the question of Paul's conversion. Freud's reaction was not sympathetic. Afterward, when Werfel sent him a passionate letter defending his own role "as a Jew," writing about conversion at a historic moment when one could still be both a Christian and a Jew, Freud suggested with cool reserve that Werfel was displaying little more than distrust of his own Jewish identity.

More even than self-respect influenced Freud's rejection of apostasy, however. At the turn of the century, as Karl Lueger's Christian Socialist antisemitism became a public issue, Dr. Max Graf, a colleague of Freud's, wrestled with the notion of expediently arranging his son's conversion. He sought Freud's advice. Sternly, Freud counseled against the step. "If you do not let your son grow up as a Jew," he warned, "you will deprive him of those sources of energy which cannot be replaced by anything else. . . . Do not deprive him of that advantage." Freud elaborated upon this "advantage" in his letter of thanks to B'nai B'rith, whose Vienna lodge in 1926 had formally celebrated his seventieth birthday: "Only to my Jewish nature," he wrote, "did I owe the two qualities which had become indispensable to me on my hard road. Because I was a Jew, I found myself free from many prejudices which limited others in the use of their intellect, and, being a Jew, I was prepared to enter opposition and to renounce agreement with the 'compact majority.' " He would make the same point to numerous colleagues and friends over the years. His letters to Karl Abraham asserted repeatedly that Jews found it much easier than Gentiles to accept "subversive" ideas, for Jews after all were possessed of "our ancient Jewish toughness."

It was almost certainly the emphasis on "toughness" and independence that evoked Freud's interest in Zionism. He became an early admirer of Herzl, and on one occasion actually dreamed of Herzl revealing himself as "an appearance filled with glory." Freud was pleased when his son Martin joined the Kadimah Zionist society at the university and shared the group's concept of "muscular Judaism" (years later, in 1936, Freud himself accepted an honorary membership in Kadimah). After the Great War, Freud also became an admirer of Chaim Weizmann, the Zionist elder statesman, and in 1925, when the Hebrew University was founded in Jerusalem, Freud accepted Weizmann's invitation to join its board. Writing Dr. Jacob Meitlis of Vilna, in 1938, Freud evaluated contemporary events against the matrix of Jewish history. "Once again our people is faced with dark times," he acknowledged, "requiring us to gather all our strength in order to preserve all culture and science during the present harsh storm." Josef Wortis, one of his former patients, recalled a conversation with Freud, in which he, Wortis, raised the frequent accusation of the Jews as over-intellectualized: " 'So much the better for psychoanalysis, then!' replied Freud."

A Prophet of the Abyss

Carl Jung plainly would not have agreed. In the aftermath of his break with Freud, in 1912, the former heir apparent set about fortifying his stature as an alternative prophet to Freud. He launched into the production of a formidable sequence of books, articles, and reviews. Throughout the 1920s and 1930s, traveling the world, he delivered papers at international medical and psychoanalytic congresses, and in 1933 he resumed teaching at the University of Zurich. By then, too, his own psychological-philosophical system was assuming clearer definition. Its underlying structure this time was based on far more than a mere rejection of sexuality and the Oedipus complex as the exclusive wellspring of unconscious motivation. Jung now refined his initial, tentative notion of a collective unconscious, of "the mighty deposit of ancestral experience accumulated over millions of years, the echo of prehistoric happenings to which each century adds." It was an elaboration that later produced important political ramifications.

In 1933, Dr. Marius H. Göring, a psychiatrist and a cousin of the Nazi leader Hermann Göring, set about reorganizing the German Medical Society for Psychotherapy. In the eyes of the Hitler regime, the society had been compromised by its Jewish origins and membership. A new president was needed, a man whose international credentials would evoke instant respect. To that end, Dr. Göring approached Jung and persuaded him to accept the presidency and the editorship of the organization's journal, the *Zentralblatt für Psychotherapie*. Although Jung later would claim that his acceptance was entirely pragmatic, to ensure the survival of psychoanalysis in German-speaking Europe, he could not have been oblivious of Göring's ideological agenda, to purge the movement of its Jewish "tribalism."

By then, in fact, Jung shared that agenda. As far back as 1918, explaining the divergence of Germanic psychotherapy from Freudianism, he explained in one of his papers:

As a rule, the Jew lives in amicable relationship with the earth, but without feeling the power of its subterranean impulses. . . . [T]his may explain the Jew's specific need to reduce everything to its material beginnings. . . . I can understand very well that Freud's . . . reduc-

tion of everything psychic to primitive sexual wishes and power drives
has something about it that is beneficial and satisfying to the Jew,
because it is a form of simplification. . . . But these specifically Jewish
doctrines are thoroughly unsatisfying to the Germanic mentality; we
still have a genuine barbarian in us who is not to be trifled with.

Twenty years later, upon accepting Göring's invitation, Jung launched
his editorship of the *Zentralblatt* with a brief foreword in its December
1933 issue, stressing the necessity henceforth of distinguishing between
German and Jewish psychotherapy. In the journal's ensuing issue, in January 1934, he followed with a much longer article, "The Present Situation of Psychotherapy." After drawing attention again to the differences
between Freud and himself, Jung went on to argue that

[t]he Jew, a cultural nomad, has never and probably will never create
his own cultural forms because all his instincts and gifts depend on [a]
more or less civilized host nation. The Aryan unconscious has a
higher potential than the Jewish; this is an advantage of a youthful-
ness which still is nearer to barbarism.

Warning his readers once more of Freudianism's tendency to devalue the
"creative forces" in the romantic Aryan soul, Jung insisted that Freud
"knew the German soul as little as [Freud's] . . . idolaters knew it."

In this respect, Jung's comments about his former friend probably were
accurate—Freud did not understand the Teutonic "soul." In 1930 he
assured the American ambassador in Berlin, William C. Bullitt, that "[a]
nation that produces Goethe could not possibly go to the bad." Evidently
Freud nurtured comparable illusions about the Austrians. As his own country turned Fascist, the aged prophet steadfastly resisted the entreaties of
friends and colleagues to leave Vienna and settle elsewhere. Then, in 1936,
his eightieth birthday was celebrated throughout Europe and the Western
Hemisphere. Festschriften were organized in many different capitals. His
home in Vienna was deluged with letters and telegrams of congratulation,
and some two hundred scholarly and literary delegations arrived to deliver
birthday greetings in person. Press accounts of these festivities were carried in the world's leading newspapers. Except for the Nazi Reich, however, Austria was the single nation in Europe whose press declined to take
more than perfunctory notice of the event.

A Danubian Farewell

Engelbert Dollfuss's decision in June 1933 to ban the Nazi party was vitiated by his ensuing brutal suppression of the Social Democratic uprising

in February 1934 (p. 190). Unwittingly, the chancellor had forfeited a key bastion of support against pressure for an Anschluss with the German Reich. That pressure was soon transformed into physical intimidation. Orchestrated from Berlin, the violence included bomb attacks on Austrian government facilities and assassination attempts against Austrian officials. The campaign of mayhem and destruction crested on July 24, 1934, when a band of Austrian Nazis forced its way into the chancellery building in Vienna, shooting and killing Dollfuss himself.

The attempted putsch failed. Austria's president, Wilhelm Miklas, immediately named another cabinet minister, Kurt von Schuschnigg, as acting chancellor. The Nazi death squad was captured and put on trial, and its five principal assassins were summarily executed. At the same time, Mussolini issued a stern warning to Berlin that the little Austrian Republic was under Italian protection. Disavowing the entire episode, the German führer then promised to respect Austrian independence.

Settling in as chancellor, the thirty-six-year-old Schuschnigg made plain that the rule of law, if not of democracy, would now prevail in Austria. In that stance, he appeared to have the support of the country's "respectable" middle class and rural population. Yet no one appreciated more than Schuschnigg that Austria's survival ultimately depended on the protection of Fascist Italy. Endlessly genuflecting toward Mussolini, the chancellor structured his government's authoritarian "corporativism" even more closely on the Italian model. But the tightwire gamble proved less than effective. By 1936, diplomatically isolated in the West as a consequence of his recent invasion of Ethiopia, Mussolini saw no alternative but to orient his foreign policy more closely toward Nazi Germany's. Schuschnigg in turn felt obliged to visit and negotiate an "understanding" of his own with Hitler in Berlin. Under the provisions of the agreement, the führer would respect Austrian sovereignty; while Schuschnigg for his part would appoint Austrian Nazis to key positions in his cabinet. From July 1936 on, a German sword of Damocles would dangle over the Austrian Republic.

Ironically, until these last years of Austrian political reaction, Jews had maintained their cultural preeminence. Of the four Austrian scientists who became Nobel laureates in the latter 1920s and early 1930s, three were Jews. Until the early 1930s, Vienna's Jewish physicians still attracted patients from throughout the world, and Jewish attorneys continued substantially to dominate the legal profession. Nor did Jews play less eminent a role as Vienna's orchestra conductors and concert performers, its theatrical producers and directors, its most influential journalists and cultural critics.

Even for these luminaries, however, the sands were beginning to run out. At Austria's universities, an unofficial numerus clausus was sharply limiting the enrollment of Jewish students. Student societies excluded Jews altogether. Chancellor Schuschnigg was far from a rabid antisemite. Yet, for reasons of political expediency, he too now authorized a number of segregationist measures. In September 1934, only six weeks after the Nazi putsch had been foiled, the ministry of education issued a directive requiring Jewish schoolchildren to be grouped in their own classes. The edict was a shocker, even for Austria. Its resemblance to government policies then developing in "backward" Poland (pp. 64–66) was rather too much for Austrian business circles, most of which still were concerned about the nation's image abroad. The directive was canceled.

The government found more subtle methods of isolating Jews, however, practicing antisemitism on "rubber-soled shoes." In November 1934, a new trade law authorized state economic corporations to license the nation's commercial enterprises. With Jews blackballed from membership in the corporations, the law simply became a crude device for delegitimating Jewish companies. Indeed, the party newspaper of Schuschnigg's own Fatherland Front quietly promoted boycotts of Jewish merchants by selectively accepting advertisements by "Christian merchants." With the support of the influential Catholic monthly *Schönerer Zukunft*, the ministry of justice issued a decree barring physicians from practice unless they had completed a minimum of one year's service in a hospital. On its face, the requirement of hospital internship was hardly unreasonable. Since 1933, however, Jewish physicians had been systematically forced out of Austrian hospitals, and the decree's effective consequence was simply to exclude young Jewish doctors from the practice of medicine altogether.

In the winter of 1938, finally, there began the sequence of events that led directly to the Anschluss with Nazi Germany. On February 12, Schuschnigg was summoned to Berchtesgaden, Hitler's vacation retreat in the Bavarian Alps, and ordered forthwith to link his nation's economy and foreign policy to the Third Reich's, and to give over his government to Austrian Nazis. Thoroughly intimidated, Schuschnigg promptly agreed to the ultimatum. But upon returning to Vienna and gradually regaining his nerve, the chancellor announced on March 9 that he was scheduling a national plebiscite in four days to determine if the Austrian people themselves really wished a functional union with Germany. It was Schuschnigg's instinct that his Catholic nation still would opt for independence, and the German government thereby would be stripped of any diplomatic pretext for an Anschluss. He did not know his Hitler. On March 11, the enraged führer sent his army into Austria to effect a "voluntary" union of the two countries. No resistance was offered, either by Western governments or by Mussolini, and assuredly not by the Austrian government or people.

If the Anschluss signified the end of Austrian independence, it plainly represented an end to all hope for the nation's quarter-million Jews. The campaign of persecution and terror that had long since operated in Germany now was visited upon Austrian Jewry with practiced efficiency and brutality. Even the approximately 160,000 Jews who managed to emigrate did not assure themselves of permanent refuge, for most fled to other European countries that would themselves be under the Nazi heel. Among the more fortunate émigrés were Franz and Alma Werfel. Seeing the handwriting on the wall, the couple departed in 1937, a year before the Anschluss. Moving to France, then to England, they traveled on eventually to the United States, where they lived comfortably in Los Angeles on Werfel's book and film royalties. Stefan Zweig and his wife did not enjoy that luxury. Following the Nazi occupation, the two would share the homelessness of most of their Jewish colleagues and friends. Zweig's extensive connections among intellectual figures in Western democratic nations proved no match for government bureaucracies. Although in 1934 he and his wife had lived briefly in England, they were unable to secure permanent visas to that nation—or to any other.

Eventually, in 1942, after wandering from country to country, the Zweigs achieved a precarious respite in Brazil, if only on temporary visas. For several weeks they subsisted in a tiny hotel in the city of Petropolis, vainly awaiting a renewal of their papers. At last, despairing of their future, and doubtless of European civilization altogether, the couple swallowed lethal doses of Veronol and expired on their hotel bed. Zweig's suicide note acknowledged that it was better "to conclude in good time and in erect bearing a life in which intellectual labor meant the purest joy and personal freedom [meant] the highest good on earth. I salute all my friends. May it be granted them yet to see the dawn after the long night. I, all too impatient, go on before."

Sigmund Freud adamantly refused to budge from his Viennese "Heimat" until after the 1938 Anschluss. Yet, by then, his colleague Ernest Jones already had begun taking steps that some three months afterward opened the route to Britain. Jones's friendship with Earl De La Watt, Lord Privy Seal, and with Home Secretary Sir Samuel Hoare, smoothed the way for the issuance of immigration permits. So it was that the eighty-two-year-old Freud and sixteen members of his family—wife, children, and grandchildren—were allowed to depart, although their belongings remained behind, and their modest bank accounts were impounded. Even at the last moment, the Gestapo insisted that Freud sign a disclaimer, affirming that he was leaving of his own free will and had not been mistreated. The old man's sense of humor had not left him. Signing the document, he added a wry postscript: "I can recommend the Gestapo to anyone."

In May 1938, the Freud entourage crossed the border of the Greater Reich for France. In Paris, United States Ambassador William Bullitt (a profound admirer of Freud and co-author with him of a psychoanalytic essay on Woodrow Wilson), escorted the family members personally to a Channel port, where they embarked by ferry for England. Relatives awaited them at Folkestone harbor to offer financial help and to provide comfortable lodgings in London's Hampstead district. In his last months, as he stoically awaited his death from jaw cancer, Freud lacked neither for personal security nor for respectful visits from numerous British cultural luminaries. He died in September 1939, without learning that his four aged sisters, who had remained behind in Vienna, had not yet received their promised British visas. Eventually, all would be shipped to various Nazi concentration camps, and to their deaths.

The old prophet's last thoughts may be gleaned from an extract of a letter to his son Ernst (already in England), written shortly before Freud departed Vienna. "Two prospects present themselves in these troubled times," he wrote, "to see you all together once more, and to die in freedom. Sometimes I see myself as a Jacob being taken by his children to Egypt when he was very old. Let us hope that there will not follow an exodus from Egypt." Then, alluding to "Ahasuarus," the euphemized Wandering Jew of modern German and French literature, Freud ventured the wishful conclusion: "It is time that Ahasuarus come to rest somewhere."

VIII

THE AGE OF THE ASSASSINS

Embourgeoisement and Feminism

We have few details about Freud's celebrated "Anna O" in the years immediately after she left her treatment with Dr. Josef Breuer. It is known only that she suffered occasional relapses, spent time in a sanitarium, traveled, and eventually regained her health. In 1889, Anna O moved from her native Vienna to live with her widowed mother in Frankfurt-am-Main, and remained there ever after. To protect her identity, Breuer and Freud avoided comment on her subsequent life. But once her case was described by Dr. Ernest Jones many years later, it was learned that Anna O's actual name was Bertha Pappenheim. If the former patient "sublimated" her lingering psychoses, apparently she managed the feat no longer through psychotherapy but through social activism. For Bertha Pappenheim in fact was nothing less than the founder and moving force of Jewish feminism in German-speaking Europe.

It appears not unlikely that the achievement was itself an outgrowth of Pappenheim's emotional vulnerability. In the years of her early convalescence in Frankfurt, the young woman remained acutely sensitive to the "infirmity" of social injustice, whether inflicted on her personally or on those close to her. No injustice was less tolerable for her, as it happened, than the grillwork of public and private constraints imposed on her gender. Until 1908, German women were barred from political activity in all but two of the Empire's Länder, its constituent states. By tradition, if not by law, women were denied access to business proprietorship or the practice of the free professions. With few exceptions, charitable work— normally associated with a local church—remained the single "creative" outlet even for the most ambitious and talented of women.

These barriers proved more disquieting yet for Jewish women, members of a people who in any case had long functioned within an attenuated civic orbit. It was not until 1871 that the newly created German Empire followed Prussia's lead in extending the franchise even to Jewish men, some twenty years after this benediction had been extended to German males at large. Neither did the "Jewish question" in Imperial Germany disappear with political emancipation, no more than it did in Habsburg Austria. By unspoken understanding, Jews of both sexes remained excluded from important areas of government service. Until the outbreak of war in 1914, it was exceptionally difficult for an unbaptized Jew to gain a diplomatic appointment, a commission in the German army, or a university full professorship.

Public or social discrimination hardly created an insuperable barrier to economic security, of course, whether in Germany or elsewhere in Central Europe. Numbering approximately 510,000 by the early twentieth century, Jews in the German Empire characteristically belonged to the middle class and earned their livelihoods in business and the professions. Here they forged ahead even more rapidly than did their Gentile counterparts. By 1910, Berlin's 120,000 Jews, comprising 5 percent of the capital's population, paid 31 percent of the city's municipal revenues. Nearly 25 percent of the board members in ten major branches of German industry and banking were Jews. Jews occasionally were even granted access to the imperial court. Thus, Kaiser Wilhelm II, although not troubling to disguise his private antisemitism, was open to the financial advice of such business tycoons as Albert Ballin of the Hapag-Lloyd (Hamburg-America Packetboat) Company, Max Warburg of the M. M. Warburg Merchant Bank, Carl Fürstenberg, Germany's "cotton king," and Walther Rathenau of the mighty AEG electricity conglomerate.

Yet, for Jewish women, it was their people's very economic success that exacerbated the "normal" frustrations of gender inferiority. Concentrated in cities and towns, enjoying the leisure of household help and labor-saving devices, Jewish women by the turn of the century were also Germany's first religio-ethnic group to practice birth control widely. More than others of their sex, they possessed the time and energy to devote to larger public causes, to the very movements that remained beyond their reach. Bertha Pappenheim was well seized of this anomaly. She was herself one of its victims. Her earlier, personal trauma could only have been compounded by laws and traditions that denied her access to a university education, to employment worthy of her superior intellect, or even to equal status with men in German-Jewish communal life. She had long been an avid reader of the German feminist journal *Die Frau*, and a "spiritual" disciple of Mary Wollstonecraft, Britain's pioneering eighteenth-century feminist. In 1889, Pappenheim translated Wollstonecraft's famous book *A Vindication of the Rights of Women*, and that same year published a play, *Women's Rights*.

It was in the late 1890s, moreover, working as a volunteer in a Frankfurt soup kitchen for East European Jewish refugees, that Pappenheim gave close attention to the careworn and bedraggled circumstances of immigrant women, particularly those who had arrived from the congestion and poverty of Habsburg Galicia. In 1902, visiting this Polish region, she grasped even more acutely the economic despair that impelled Jewish women westward. Thus, two years later, Pappenheim launched into the establishment of a Bund der jüdischer Frauen, a League of Jewish Women. By the early postwar era, the Frauenbund would encompass fifty thousand members, nearly one-fourth the adult Jewish female population of Germany. The measure of the organization's growth lay not alone in the care it provided for impoverished girls (an old story for all women's philanthropies, Jewish and non-Jewish), or even the creative social outlet it offered middle-class Jewish matrons. Rather, one of Pappenheim's key objectives was to address the crisis of the "socially fallen," that is, of East European Jewish prostitutes.

There were several thousand of these desperate creatures, and many also had brought their illegitimate children with them. Pappenheim was not the first to identify their plight. Several years earlier, in England, the social cancer of Jewish immigrant prostitution had led to the establishment of the Jewish Association for the Protection of Girls and Women; and, in the United States, of the National Council of Jewish Women. The crisis nevertheless had developed earliest in Central Europe. Between 1871 and 1904, some 2 million Galician and Russian Jews passed through Austria and Germany in their flight westward. Most of these Ostjuden continued on to North and South America. But at least 150,000 of them remained on the Continent; and, of these, nearly 70,000 settled in the German Empire. The number would double still again in the war (p. 242). The government's response to the influx was not congenial. Under Germany's federal structure, Land (state) and even local bureaucrats exercised almost unlimited power over immigrants, and these officials tended to judge each new arrival on the basis of "economic usefulness." Most of the refugee Jewish men were petty merchants. Categorized as less than economically "useful," they were shunted off from one German state or town to another. The treatment of immigrant prostitutes was still harsher.

The "fallen women" came mainly from Galicia. Indeed, by Bertha Pappenheim's estimate, not less than 30 percent of Galicia's prostitutes altogether were Jewish girls. It was the atomization of East European Jewish families that created their plight. With fathers departing for the West, often leaving wives and children to be sent for later, "white slavers"— procurers—moved swiftly and ruthlessly to exploit the ensuing social chaos. They lurked everywhere, awaiting vulnerable young Jewish women at ports, in railroad stations, on trains, often posing as clergymen, as social workers, or even as promised "marriage partners." For Pappenheim, the care of these vulnerable and exploited immigrant women was a moral imperative for German Jewry.

The response was full-hearted and efficient. The Bund der jüdischer

Frauen developed an extensive literature (in Yiddish) to warn Jewish women of the dangers awaiting them as they traveled westward. From 1910 on, the Frauenbund's representatives and hostels were available at all the principal railroad stations and harbors. Even earlier, in 1907, Pappenheim succeeded in opening a hostel at Neu-Isenberg, outside Frankfurt, the first institution in Europe to provide "endangered or morally sick" Jewish girls and unmarried mothers with compassion and care, as well as training in "home economics," dressmaking, and other modest vocations. Neu-Isenberg became a model for similar, non-Jewish projects in Europe and the United States.

In their redemptive effort, however, Pappenheim and her colleagues were impelled by more than feminism, or even sheer compassion. Jewish "white slavery," they knew, was further inflaming a German xenophobia that itself was fueled by East European Jewish immigration. The influx of Ostjuden manifestly was not the only or even the principal stimulus of German antisemitism in the last prewar decades. But the mass immigration offered still another pretext for racists like Heinrich von Treitschke, who found it useful to execrate the "filth and degradation" carried into Germany by these "Asians." (Years later, Julius Streicher's Nazi journal, *Der Stürmer*, would gleefully quote Pappenheim's own statistics on Jewish white slavery.)

For members of the veteran Jewish "establishment," therefore, the East European immigration in its pungent ethnicity and frequent uncouthness, and assuredly in its susceptibility to prostitution, represented more than a human tragedy. It was becoming a threat to their own painfully achieved social and cultural status. In an article, "Hear O Israel" ("Höre Israel"), written for the liberal journal *Zukunft* in March 1897, a Jewish patrician, Walther Rathenau, expressed an elitist's characteristic revulsion at

> [a]n Asian horde on the sandy plains of Prussia . . . forming among themselves a closed corporation, rigorously shut off from the rest of the world. Thus they live half-willingly in their invisible ghetto, not a living limb of the people, but an alien organism in its body. . . . So what is to be done? . . . The goal of the process should be, not imitation Germans, but Jews bred and educated as Germans.

The Eastern Connection

Eastern Jews added considerably more to the German amalgam than "Asian alienism," or Gentile antisemitism, or even veteran-Jewish insecurity. From the Polish and Russian newcomers came a fortified political activism, including a quite unique tradition of women's political activism.

As far back as the 1863 Polish insurrection against tsarist Russia, the dynamic role of women as comrades-in-arms actually gave the uprising its title, the "Women's War." The Polish revolution failed, as it happened, but the ongoing momentum of women's political and social radicalism continued. In ensuing decades, young men and women alike, most of them students, many of them sons and daughters of middle-class families, worked together in the Polish revolutionary underground.

The image of the woman rebel was an indelible feature of Rosa Luxemburg's formative years. She was eight years old in 1879 when Vera Zasulich walked into the office of General Tryupov, military governor of St. Petersburg, and shot him at point-blank range. She was ten when Sophia Perovskaya, herself the daughter of a Russian general, was executed for participating in the assassination of Tsar Alexander II. When Luxemburg graduated from gymnasium, the twenty-one-year-old Maria Bohusz, a leader of the first Polish workers' party, Proletariat, died in Siberian exile. Siberian exile was the fate also of Aleksandra Jentya, daughter of a Jewish physician and cofounder of Proletariat. Indeed, it was in the battle for social revolution even more than for Polish independence that Jews achieved their greatest visibility. By the late nineteenth century the very term, Socialism, betokened a new era of elementary human justice for all the downtrodden of the earth, worker and peasant, man and woman, Jew and Gentile. Rosa Luxemburg early on was caught up in that ferment.

The youngest of five children of a middle-class Jewish timber merchant, Rosalia Lukksemburg was born in 1871, in Zamosz, a small Chasidic town in Lublin province. Her family, atypically, was Polish-speaking and secular. Traveling often to Germany on business, her father insisted on sending his three sons to Berlin for their high school education, and in 1873 he moved to Warsaw to escape Zamosz's suffocating obscurantism. Yet, even in Warsaw, Rosa Luxemburg's life was painfully constricted. When she was five, a hip ailment was inaccurately diagnosed as tubercular (the malformation proved to be genetic), and she was confined to bed in a cast for nearly a year. The experience left her with one leg shorter than the other, and with a permanent, dwarflike gait. It also left her exposed to continual taunting by schoolmates. Characteristically, she became an overachiever. Upon finishing at the top of her class, she won acceptance under the minuscule Jewish quota to a prestigious state gymnasium. Here again she overcame the derision of Gentile fellow students to graduate first in her class.

As it happened, Luxemburg in her teens also had become thoroughly immersed in the revolutionary Socialist movement. Under continual police surveillance, she too risked the imprisonment suffered by innumerable other young revolutionaries of her era. Whereupon, terrified for her safety, her parents arranged for her to be smuggled across the Austrian frontier. It was a useful move. Upon reaching Vienna, Luxemburg managed to support herself as a governess for the children of a Jewish family, and within a year and a half saved enough to travel on to Switzerland. Here it was, at the age of nineteen, that she enrolled in the department of social sciences of the University of Zurich. The new world that opened out to her was one not only of intellectual discovery, but of social equality among male and female students. In the 1890s, the city of Zurich was a hotbed of émigré Socialists, including such East European luminaries as Georgi Plekhanov, Uri Martov, and Vladimir Lenin. Polish Jews, men and women, students and non-students alike, were prominent members of this vibrant nucleus.

Rosa Luxemburg's most intimate attachment among them was to Leo Jogiches. Three years older than she, Jogiches was the son of a prosperous and cultured Vilna Jewish family. Shortly after finishing gymnasium, he became chairman of the Vilna branch of the revolutionary-terrorist Narodnaya Volya (People's Will) party. He paid with jail time. Upon release from his second confinement, in 1889, the young man departed for Switzerland. There he joined the flood of other expatriates registering at the University of Zurich. In Jogiches's case, matriculation was the barest formality. Almost from the moment of his arrival in Zurich, he hurled himself with characteristic zeal into Socialist activism. Initially, he joined Plekhanov's Marxist circle, the "Emancipation of Labor." But less than a year later he broke with Plekhanov, whose authoritarianism fully matched his own, and used his personal family funds to establish a Polish-language Socialist review, *Sprawa Robonicza*.

Luxemburg soon joined Jogiches's personal coterie, and with him in 1892 founded a new offshoot, the SDKP, the "Social Democratic Party of the Kingdom of Poland and Lithuania." It was a far-leftist faction that rejected the "official" Polish Socialist party (which ultimately would fall under the leadership of Jozef Pilsudski) for its "diversionary" role in linking Socialism to "particularist" nationalism. Other members of Jogiches's entourage tended also to be assimilated Polish Jews, often from middle-class families whose cultural background generally was more German than Russian or even Polish. Operating outside the norms of "respectable" society, these youthful expatriates maintained a political stance that was both unregenerately antinationalist and anticapitalist.

For Rosa Luxemburg, ideology was fortified by tough-minded intellectual historicism. In the dissertation she would eventually present for her doctorate in 1897, *The Industrial Development of Poland (Die industrielle Entwicklung Polens)*, the young woman provided solid evidence that the economic growth of Russian Poland had always been indissolubly linked to the vast Russian market. All the more reason, she argued, for Russia's Polish provinces not to be "artificially" pried loose from their surrounding

Russian hinterland. It was significant, too, that Luxemburg's internationalism offered no greater tolerance for Jewish than for Polish "particularism." Years later, she would write to a friend, Mathilda Wurm:

> What do you want with this particular suffering of the Jews? The poor victims on the rubber plantations in Putamayo, the Negroes in Africa with whose bodies the Europeans play a game of catch, are just as near to me. . . . I have no special corner of my heart reserved for the ghetto. I am at home wherever in the world there are clouds, birds, and human tears.

In her future life, the Jewish facet of Luxemburg's background would play no part whatever in her political agenda.

The young woman's ideological bond with Jogiches soon took on a new, emotional dimension. In 1892 the two began living together. Despite her unprepossessing physical appearance, Luxemburg evidently overwhelmed Jogiches by sheer intellectual brilliance and moral strength. For her, in turn, his ideological passion, his ascetic face, burning eyes, and temperamental aloofness made him a kind of Dostoevskian hero, the one man able to engulf both her mind and her heart. She worshipped him. Her letters to Jogiches when they were apart are suggestive. Enclosing the draft of an article she had written, she would implore: "Help, for heaven's sake, help. . . . I know you'll pick up the main thread immediately and add the finishing touches. . . . Just give me a few new ideas." More passionately: "I feel the way you do. I dream about being near you, my only love. I struggle with myself, struggle hard, and I still need you. . . . My golden one."

In organizational acuity, however, Luxemburg far transcended the mood-ridden, pathologically secretive Jogiches, who never managed to earn a single degree, or even successfully to develop his own SDKP faction. It was she who became a dynamic and respected voice within the Socialist world at large, particularly among German Socialists. They flocked to hear her as she addressed her fellow delegates at Socialist conferences in Switzerland and Germany. Indeed, for German Social Democrats, Luxemburg was a revelation: as a student, a Pole, a Jew, a woman. The party's leading figures, Wilhelm Liebknecht and August Bebel, soon brought her into their inner circle. Accordingly, in 1897, upon receiving her doctorate, Luxemburg made the decision to move on to Germany. The heartland of European Socialism, the home of Europe's first, best-funded, and most solidly organized Social Democratic party, Germany offered a matchless arena for her talents. Separation from Jogiches plainly was not an easy step for her, yet it was their mutual agreement that he would join her "presently."

The legalities of resettlement in Germany presented greater complica-

tions. Still a citizen of the Russian Empire, Luxemburg was vulnerable at
any time to extradition as a political radical. Her best hope of security was
to acquire German naturalization, or at least permission for an extended
German residency. Yet, when all her efforts in this direction encountered a
bureaucratic impasse, Luxemburg turned to a more direct route. She
would marry a German, thereby acquiring her husband's nationality. The
designated partner was one Gustav Lübeck, a son of German Socialist
friends living in Zurich. Jogiches countenanced the move. The marriage
then duly took place in April 1898 in the Basle city hall, and for all practical
purposes ended immediately afterward. The "newlyweds" separated on the
steps of the building, never to see each other again. It would take Luxemburg another five years to secure a divorce, but the charade was worth the
bureaucratic ordeal. In May 1898, "Dr. Rosalia Lübeck" departed Switzerland for Germany, to enter a world with dramatically extended political
vistas.

"Red Rosa" in Germany

Upon arriving in her new German domicile, Luxemburg was initially dispatched on her Social Democratic career with a modest assignment as
party organizer among Polish-speaking workers in Posen. Typically, she
hurled herself into the task with energy and passion. Within months she
became the party's recognized authority on East European affairs. In fact,
Luxemburg's influence soon extended well beyond the Social Democrats'
"Polish" section. Admired for her doctoral credentials, her brilliant mind
and linguistic fluency in German, Polish, and Russian, she became a much-
sought-after contributor to party newspapers and lecturer before party
audiences. Altogether, the young woman's intellectual originality was
hardly less than dazzling. Thus, in 1899 she formulated the term "imperialism" even before John Hobson officially invented the word to describe
the global shift in world politics.

   Luxemburg's influence soon played a role even on Social Democratic
policy decisions. By the turn of the century, Eduard Bernstein's famous
revisionist articles had been widely circulated, advocating a reconciliation
between Socialism and capitalism. For Luxemburg, the very notion of a
reconciliation was heresy. Riposting to Bernstein with an eloquent series of
articles in 1898 and 1899, she skewered revisionism as "doctrinal compla-
cency." The indictment provided vital ammunition to August Bebel and
Wilhelm Liebknecht, the Social Democrats' senior eminences, in keeping
the party officially committed to the goal of revolution. Indeed, Luxemburg herself was achieving recognition as one of those eminences. By the
early twentieth century, she had become a perennial in her party's delegation to international Socialist congresses.

Thus, in 1904, Luxemburg joined Bebel and Liebknecht at the biennial Congress of the Second International, meeting in Amsterdam. And from Amsterdam, returning to Germany, she was ushered forthwith to jail. The year before, Luxemburg had been convicted for "insulting the kaiser" in one of her speeches. She had appealed the court judgment, but the appeal had been rejected. Now she would serve her six-week sentence. Ironically, the imprisonment only fortified Luxemburg's "revolutionary" bona fides. Upon being released, she was scarcely able to meet the vastly enlarged demand for her speeches and articles.

At the same time, Luxemburg's growing fame took its toll on her love affair with Jogiches. During her initial years in Berlin, the couple had maintained an intense and devoted correspondence. Jogiches sent her money and "instructions," as well as commentary on her work and personal lifestyle. She accepted them all gratefully. She also accepted his assurances that he would shortly join her. The promise was not kept. Fending off her repeated pleas, Jogiches insisted on remaining in Zurich for an additional two years, immersing himself in endlessly convoluted stratagems and conspiracies on behalf of his SDKP party in Poland. It was not until 1900 that he reluctantly gave in to her entreaties and moved to Berlin. There the couple took up a clandestine existence.

With the passage of time, however, the arrangement began to falter. Jogiches at thirty-four chafed at his subordinate role, functioning all but clandestinely in "Red Rosa's" shadow, lacking a profession or even a persona to compare with hers. In his frustration, he became increasingly irascible. Finally, in 1902, he departed again, this time for tsarist Poland, where he intended to assume direct leadership of his party. Luxemburg's devotion to Jogiches at all times remained intact. Yet her patience with the logistics of their relationship was fraying.

Their affair was terminated by Russia's 1905—Octobrist—Revolution, and its concomitant "Walewska" revolution in the Polish regions. Unable to resist the challenge of personal participation, Luxemburg departed for Poland in late December. Arriving in Warsaw frozen and exhausted, she nevertheless immediately set about haranguing crowds of workers to maintain their wildfire of strikes, assuring them that a proletarian revolution would follow. But it did not. In March 1906, Luxemburg was herself arrested and jailed. Fortunately, she managed to establish contact with one of her brothers, who raised "bail" (bribe money), enabling her to return safely to Germany.

From then on, however, despairing of her ability to influence the course of events in tsarist Poland, Luxemburg confined her efforts to Germany. Jogiches meanwhile was tracked down and jailed in Warsaw only four months after her own brief incarceration. Convicted of treason, he was sentenced to eight years of hard labor in Siberia. Yet he too managed a dramatic escape—this one without recourse to bribery—and eventually returned to Germany in April 1907. But the sequence of conspiracies, hairbreadth rescues and flights, and extended separations left Luxemburg emotionally drained. She would not take Jogiches back.

The years between 1907 and 1914 became Luxemburg's most intellectually productive. She published two volumes on political economy and churned out a seemingly endless torrent of articles for party newspapers and journals. In this period, nevertheless, her ideological influence may have begun to wane. Luxemburg, after all, was an unremittingly orthodox Marxist. Yet, even as the Social Democratic leadership continued to pay lip service to the Marxist goal of a class revolution, the party rank and file were accommodating to Germany's prosperity and patriotism. Few members saw the need to opt for more radical solutions. The purists who stood with Luxemburg in maintaining the revolutionary faith were a respected but diminishing group.

Several of this shrinking circle were non-Jews, including the distinguished Social Democratic leaders Karl Kautsky and Karl Liebknecht (son of Wilhelm). But many others were of Jewish descent, among them Laura Lafargue, Marx's daughter and keeper of her father's literary legacy; and the renowned party attorneys and Reichstag members Paul Levi and Kurt Rosenfeld. Even Luxemburg's closest friend, Clara Zetkin, a non-Jew and the director of the party's women's division, was the wife of the Russian-Jewish Osip Zetkin.

The Marxist utopianism of Luxemburg and of other transplanted Jewish "Easterners," politically oppressed and economically redundant, might have been predictable. Less so was a sudden shift to the political left by a growing minority of native-born German Jews. Most of these young men and women were products of "respectable" middle-class families, and even former loyalists of the National Liberal party, which traditionally had represented Germany's business and professional Mittelstand. What could have accounted for this ideological transformation?

A Revived Political Vulnerability

One factor was the "treason" of German political liberalism. The middle class was coming to terms with the kaiserian Machtstaat. Anchored to a vast and open trading arena, the resplendent new Reich was generating unprecedented material prosperity. German business elements in turn were reevaluating, and increasingly abandoning, their traditional identification with the National Liberals. Not all Jewish business and professional men joined them in their exodus. Indeed, two Jews, Eduard Lasker and Ludwig Bamberger, played influential roles in the National Liberal leadership. A number of prominent Jews even were approached to become party candidates for election, including Walther Rathenau and Albert Allen (although neither accepted). By the early twentieth century, nevertheless, it was becoming apparent that the National Liberals themselves were passively accepting an accommodation with the authoritarian imperial regime.

Moreover, in these same years, ideological rightists began to grasp the political usefulness of antisemitism as a device for luring white-collar and even working-class voters away from the parties of liberalism and Socialism. At their Tivoli convention in 1892, the Conservatives for the first time adopted an anti-Jewish plank, deprecating "Jewish influence" in national affairs. Over the turn of the century, the term "Verjudung"— "judaization"—was applied increasingly to the "disproportionate" role played by Jews in economic, cultural, even political life. The accusation might have remained unrespectable so long as it was trumpeted by demagogues like Adolf Stöcker, the royal chaplain and founder of the marginal Christian Social Workers party. But once it was invoked by the aristocratic Conservative party, the charge came to be parroted openly by Germany's cultured elite, not excepting the monarchy.

Kaiser Wilhelm II personally would take no steps to deprive Jews of their rights. Yet he hardly disguised his reservations on Jewish public visibility. "Jewish influence in the press . . . is increasing steadily . . ." he observed in 1913. "In it, Jewry has found its most dangerous scene of action. . . . Our efforts must indeed be directed against restricting as far as possible [that influence] in artistic and literary activities." Wilhelm's chancellor, Theobold Bethmann-Hollweg, agreed that "the Jewish spirit has contributed especially to the degeneration of the freedom of the press." The strictures already were evoking practical consequences (p. 206). The issue of Jewish political and social equality was emerging as a subject of open discussion—in the press, in the Reichstag, and in the Land diets.

If the National Liberals did not embrace this resurgent antisemitism, neither did they openly reject it. Jews of all backgrounds, as a result, tended to appraise the Social Democrats as an alternative political haven. Nor were even the Social Democrats entirely free of antisemitism. Several of the party's early leaders, even the great-spirited Karl Kautsky, were critical of Jewish capitalism, and the view unquestionably was shared by German workers. Nevertheless, more than any other faction, the Social Democrats unambiguously defended Jewish rights and condemned discrimination at all levels. So it was that a growing minority of Jews began to appear among the party's candidates for the Reichstag. Eight Jewish Social Democrats were elected in 1898, twelve in 1912, and thirteen after a by-election that same year. From the early twentieth century on, approximately 10 percent of the party bloc in the Reichstag were Jews. They were a better-educated group than the trade unionists who comprised the party's largest membership. Most of them were lawyers. In Reichstag committee work, their legal and economic expertise often was unmatched. In the last decade before the war, the largest numbers of Social Democratic publicists and journalists were Jews. Heinrich Braun, brother-in-law of Austria's Socialist leader Viktor Adler, founded the respected party journals *Neue Gesellschaft* and *Jahrbuch für Politik und Arbeiterbewegungs.* Josef Bloch edited the *Socialistische Monatschrifte.*

Like their non-Jewish colleagues, a majority of Jewish Social Democrats gravitated toward the party's moderate-revisionist center. But a smaller number attached themselves to the purist, revolutionary faction. Predictably, these were the Jews singled out by the antisemites, who dubbed them "Russian buffalo-Jews." Rosa Luxemburg was the most visible figure in this group. Other Jewish radicals, whom conservatives indiscriminately tarred as "Easterners" or "Asians," included the Reichstag delegates Hugo Haase and Ludwig Frank. Both men were native-born, as it happened, and both were renowned idealists who commanded much respect among their colleagues. Haase, a Baden lawyer who for years had provided his services pro bono to workers, was elected deputy party chairman in 1911, and cochairman (with Friedrich Ebert) upon the death of August Bebel in 1913. Whether of the party's moderate or its left wing, however, the Jewish minority within the Social Democrats was emerging not only as an influential party avant-garde, but as a convenient bête noire for the vindictive German right.

War and the Politics of Polarization

On August 4, 1914, Germany's Social Democrats betrayed their movement's historic commitment to international peace. A party caucus voted to support the government's war budget. Only a tiny handful among the party leadership opposed the majority decision. One of these was Karl Liebknecht. The other was Rosa Luxemburg. Their defection initially availed little. Indeed, Luxemburg's political isolation was compounded by her legal vulnerability. In September 1913 she had declared to a party audience: "If the government thinks we are going to lift the weapons of murder against our French and other brethren, then we shall shout: 'We will not do it!' " Immediately she was arrested for incitement and sentenced to a year's imprisonment, to which could be added an indeterminate period of "protective custody." The appeal process stayed Luxemburg's incarceration for thirteen months, but in February 1915 she was rearrested and dispatched to Berlin's Alexanderplatz prison to serve her term.

Luxemburg's treatment was far from unbearable. She was allowed reading material, given leave to correspond freely and to accept food parcels from friends. She managed even to engage in political writing. Thus, in December 1915, she produced the first comprehensive antiwar pamphlet to come out of Germany, *The Crisis of German Social Democracy (Der Krise der Sozialdemokratie)*. Bearing the signature "Junius," the polemic has retained its fame to this day. It raised the banner of resistance to war and imperialism, to capitalist "exploitation," to the "swindle of national self-determination." Yet it was also bitterly critical of the "craven" Social Democratic party itself—"shamed, dishonored, wading in blood and dripping with filth." For Europe's beleaguered Marxist purists, Luxemburg's Junius pamphlet was a breath of fresh air.

The schism among the Social Democrats had widened much further with Germany's invasion of neutral Belgium. When asked in late 1915 to approve an extension of war credits, a far larger minority, 44 of the party's 110 Reichstag delegates, voted against the request. And in April 1917, Karl Kautsky, Hugo Haase, and even the famed revisionist Eduard Bernstein created their own minority of 18 deputies, breaking off from the Social Democrats entirely and organizing a new, antiwar faction, the "Independent" Social Democratic party. Yet the Independents were not prepared to disgorge Germany's recent military gains. Only one group was. A year earlier, a tiny splinter faction within the Social Democrats assumed the title Spartacus League (Spartakusbund). Named for the leader of the Roman slave rebellion of antiquity, and inspired by Luxemburg's "Junius pamphlet"—and her ongoing succession of defiant prison letters—the Spartacists gathered in Luxemburg's own vacant Berlin apartment to endorse her uncompromising commitment to peace and social revolution.

In April 1916, when her one-year sentence expired, Luxemburg was released from prison. Immediately she hurled herself again into the propaganda campaign to end the war, and to repudiate all territorial annexations. Several weeks later, she joined Liebknecht in organizing a mass demonstration in Berlin on behalf of "peace, bread, and freedom," and exhorted the army to lay down its weapons. Ten thousand people attended. In reaction, the government promptly stripped Liebknecht of his Reichstag seat and sentenced him to prison. Three months later, in July 1916, Luxemburg also was put under "protective custody," this time without trial. Carried off to Berlin's women's prison on the Branimstrasse, she was subsequently transferred to Wronski prison, near Posen, far to the east. She would not know freedom again until the end of the war.

As in her original imprisonment, Luxemburg's circumstances at first were not inhumane. She was allowed to correspond (subject to military censorship) and to receive food parcels. Her most devoted intermediary still remained Leo Jogiches. Now working underground and incognito in

Germany, Jogiches was in his element as a conspirator of revolution. Love between the two had long since vanished, but their mutual respect had not flagged, nor their commitment to a shared goal. Then, in March 1918, Jogiches was himself arrested and imprisoned. With an identical stoic devotion, Luxemburg promptly instructed her correspondents to send Jogiches every parcel of food they had intended for her. In March 1918, when the Brest-Litovsk Treaty officially ended the war with Russia, she entreated her Polish Socialist comrades to "save Leo."

Meanwhile, Luxemburg's initial reaction to the Bolshevik Revolution was one of almost inexpressible joy. With her Spartacist colleagues, she exhorted the Social Democratic leadership to give unstinting support to the Communist experiment. Yet, as the weeks passed, so did her reservations about Lenin's emergent dictatorship. "Freedom only for the supporters of the government," she wrote in one of her smuggled articles, "only for the members of one party—however numerous they may be—is no freedom at all." Since the summer of 1917, moreover, there had been other, more personal difficulties to give Luxemburg pause. Until then, she had reacted against the boredom and drudgery of prison life by endless reading and writing. But in July 1917, she was transferred from Posen to the town prison of Breslau. Soon her confinement became more rigorous, her letters more closely monitored. At times she was reduced to sending her messages on the torn pages of French poetry books. Her secret "ink" was her own urine. Her health worsened. In the last year of her imprisonment, at the age of forty-seven, Luxemburg's hair turned completely white.

The Politics of Patriotism

During this wartime period, the emergent image of Jews as radical subversives might logically have been eclipsed by the far more tangible evidence of their patriotism. Once hostilities began, German Jewry's various Gemeinden, their religio-communal councils, appealed to all Jews to "devote your resources to the Fatherland above and beyond the call of duty! . . . All of you—men and women—[must] place yourselves in the service of the Fatherland through personal help of every kind and through donations of money and property." "I foresee a great victory for Germany and Germanism," exulted Jakob Wassermann in his diary entry in August 1914. "Germany is becoming a world power." For the renowned Judaic philosopher Hermann Cohen, the Jews bore an obligation "piously to respect Germany, their spiritual home." When Britain entered the war against Germany in August 1914, the German-Jewish poet Ernst Lissauer immediately whipped off a doggerel, "Hymn of Hatred against England" ("Hassgesang gegen England") containing such verses as:

Never is our hatred going to abate.
Hatred on the sea, hatred on the land.
Hatred of the head, hatred of the hand. . . .

Once a Lutheran organist set the piece to music, its stanzas immediately were on everyone's lips, and the kaiser personally bestowed a medal on Lissauer. In the spring of 1915, in a pronunciamento entitled "Memorandum of the Six Federations," ninety-three of the nation's most distinguished public figures supported the legitimacy of Germany's invasion of neutral Belgium and denied the widely circulated accounts of army brutality against Belgian civilians. Among the signatories were the renowned Jewish scientists Fritz Haber, Richard Wilstätter, and Paul Ehrlich.

Years later, German Jewry's national Kultusverein published statistics on the Jewish war record. These revealed that over 100,000 Jews had served in Germany's armed forces and 12,000 had died in combat. Civilian contributions were no less formidable. In numbers unimaginable before the war, Jews were recruited for key public positions. Albert Ballin of Hapag-Lloyd was charged with the establishment of a central acquisition agency, Reichsinkauf, for the purchase of crucial civilian supplies. The economist Julius Hirsch directed the regulation of food prices. The industrialist Eduard Anhold organized coal supplies through the Reichskohlenamt. The renowned immunologist August von Wassermann produced his tetanus vaccine essentially as a treatment for war wounds. Fritz Haber developed the poison gas that became one of Germany's deadliest weapons (even as Richard Willstätter invented the gas mask as a defense against the same threat). Altogether, Haber became the single most important organizer of science in wartime Germany. A brilliant administrator, he mobilized some 150 leading scientists and aggressively coordinated their efforts to meet the nation's military and civilian requirements. In addition to poison gas, Haber's Kaiser Wilhelm Institute adapted his own 1908 process for synthesizing nitrogen to the production of nitric acid, a vital ingredient for both military explosives and agricultural fertilizer.

No civilian contributed more to the war effort, however, than did the industrialist Walther Rathenau. Nor did any other figure embody more of the contradictory legacies of the modern German Jew. Although horrified by the outbreak of hostilities, Rathenau promptly endorsed the goal of a full and decisive victory. In December 1914, he urged Chancellor Bethmann-Hollweg to project as Germany's war aim the "complete political and economic reduction of France and England," and "important changes on the map and massive indemnities." In 1917, Rathenau even proposed that tens of thousands of Belgian laborers be forcibly imported to Germany. Yet there was a counterpoint to the man's apparent nationalist implacability. In

these same war years, Rathenau outlined a broadly compassionate economic agenda for cooperation between labor and management (p. 221),
thereby revealing himself as a paradigm of both his people's driving meritocracy and its minority sentience to the perils of a skewed society.

Rathenau's father, Emil, the owner of a small iron foundry in north
Berlin, became a successful manufacturer of steam engines. In 1881,
attending the Paris Exhibition, the senior Rathenau witnessed Thomas
Edison's new lightbulb. On an impulse, and with borrowed money, he purchased the German patent rights to the invention, and two years
later founded the company that became the Allgemeine Elektrizitäts
Gesellschaft—AEG. Under Emil Rathenau's vigorous initiative, the
undertaking flourished, eventually to become the German equivalent of
America's General Electric Company. Walther Rathanau, born in 1867,
was all but programmed by his father for the responsibilities of industrial
leadership. After studying chemistry and electrical engineering at the
Universities of Berlin and Strasbourg, he was sent off for managerial
apprenticeship in AEG's provincial factories at Neuhausen and Bitterfeld.
Returning to Berlin ten years later, at the age of thirty-two, he joined
AEG's executive board.

The younger Rathenau's relations with his imperious father were not
easy; but upon the death of a brother in 1903, and Emil Rathenau's progressive incapacitation, Walther Rathenau became de facto chairman of
the AEG board. Indeed, well before Emil's death in 1915, the son had
developed a legendary expertise in negotiating merger and trust agree-
ments. Under his direction, AEG by 1909 had become one of the world's
largest industrial conglomerates, interlocked with eighty-four German
firms and twenty-four foreign companies. In the last decade before the war,
the government respectfully consulted Walther Rathenau on economic
issues of key importance to the Empire.

He lived his role. In his palatial winter and summer homes, Rathenau
entertained in appropriately royal style. A lifelong bachelor, cultured and
charming, he made his way through society as purposefully as in business.
Nor was his sense of his own worth ever modest. Edvard Munch's famous
portrait of Rathenau accurately reveals a tall man (over six feet), his countenance fine-boned over an elegant goatee, standing haughtily in evening
dress, cigar in hand. The Austrian novelist Robert Musil, who based his
novel *The Man Without Qualities (Der Mann ohne Eigenschaften)* on Rathenau, explained his hero's social success:

> Surrounded by the magic glitter of his wealth and the rumor of his
> importance, he dealt with men who occasionally surpassed him in
> their fields of expertise but who found him sympathetic as a layman
> [who was] surprisingly knowledgeable in these fields.

Rathenau was no mere social dilettante, however. Artistically gifted, fluent in several languages, he much enjoyed corresponding with the leading writers of his time, men of the caliber of André Gide, Hermann Hesse, Rainer Maria Rilke, Stefan Zweig, and Gerhart Hauptmann. He also cultivated an image as a literary figure on his own account. Producing numerous journal articles on social and cultural themes of the day, Rathenau subsequently published these collections in ten books, one of which, commonly translated as *In Days to Come (Von kommenden Dingen)*, sold over 100,000 copies. Collectively, Rathenau's writings projected his vision of a "just" society in which "the equalization of property and income is a commandment of morality and economics," as he wrote in *In Days to Come*. He anticipated a Germany that would encourage workingmen to become better educated and raised in dignity, and an economy to be organized around nonprofit foundations. Rathenau offered no fiscal mechanism to achieve this utopian goal. Altogether, his writings constituted a rather vanilla exhortation to economic man: be good. But if unfriendly critics dismissed Rathenau as the "prophet in a dinner jacket," few could doubt that he transcended most of his fellow tycoons in social compassion and public-spiritedness.

The qualities Rathenau brought to the war crisis, however, were those of single-minded patriotism and cold-eyed economic efficiency. Focusing his attention on the Empire's supply needs, he swiftly grasped that Britain's naval blockade required Germany to adopt emergency measures toward the accumulation of critical raw materials. When he pressed the issue with his government contacts, the war ministry authorized him to establish a Raw Materials Department. Initially, the office operated with a skeletal staff of a single lieutenant-colonel and three junior civilian assistants. But in ensuing months the personnel swelled to over a hundred, as Rathenau developed his list and extensively commandeered widening quotas of vital supplies extending from metals and chemicals to wool and rubber. Nothing of value to the war effort was left to the disposal of individual businessmen. Masterfully orchestrating the allocation of the nation's resources, Rathenau kept the German war economy functioning at least a year longer than its resources otherwise would have permitted.

At the same time, he nurtured few illusions about public reaction to his war service. Rathenau was a Jew, after all. Stefan Zweig recalled of him: "Rarely have I sensed the tragedy of the Jew more strongly than in his personality which, with all its apparent superiority, was full of a deep unrest and uncertainty." "[S]omewhere within him he felt fear lurking as his basic instinct," wrote his friend Count Harry Kessler. "In those very years which were decisive for his future career, this lack of self-confidence was deepened by . . . the fact that he was a Jew and [by] the harshness of the world." Rathenau himself on occasion would exaggerate his awareness of this vulnerability. Several years before the war, when Foreign Minister Bernhard von Bülow first met Rathenau (as Bülow wrote long afterward), "[Rathenau] approached with a bow as flawless as his dress. . . . 'Your Highness,' he said in his pleasant-sounding voice, 'before I am honored by the favor of being received by you, I must make a statement that is at the same time a confession.' He paused briefly and then, winningly: 'Your Highness, I am a Jew.' "

If Rathenau tended to react eccentrically to his own Jewishness, his evaluation of other people's Jewishness was equally reserved. The behavior of the Ostjuden, it is recalled, evoked his 1897 critique "Hear O Israel." By the same token, Rathenau often apotheosized Germanness in ways that appeared to contrast it invidiously with Jewishness. Early in 1914, he was moved to write an epiphany of love for the "northern spirit" of Germany:

> *Blood and steel-blue corn and air*
> *Blessed lakes the eyes of heaven*
> *Wooded vaults of dark fir*
> *Spindrift of pale dunes. . . .*
> *Country, my Country, thou, my love.*

The love went unrequited. At the outset of the war, to be sure, the government moved to transcend ethnic and sectarian divisions, banning or censoring the more inflammatory anti-Jewish publications, recruiting Jews at every level of government, even calibrating its foreign policy with an eye to Jewish sensitivities. Thus, intent on enlisting Jewish support for its territorial conquests in Eastern Europe, Berlin organized the "German Committee for the Liberation of the Jewish Nation of Russia." The project did not get far. Most German Jews were repelled by the very notion of redefining the Ostjuden as an autonomous nationality. For the same reason, the government's belated genuflection to Zionism in 1918 evoked little response among German Jewry. Well before then, they had more than enough to worry about at home.

Antisemitism was resurgent. By the winter of 1915–16, with the war frozen in stalemate and public opinion vaguely turning against draft dodgers and war profiteers, unrest focused increasingly on the Jews. Indeed, the war ministry soon was inundated with denunciations of Jewish treachery and malfeasance, with charges that Ballin, Rathenau, and other governmental Jews were "taking over" German institutions. "The greater the number of Jews killed at the front," lamented Rathenau to a friend in August of that year, "the better their enemies will be able to prove that they all remained in the rear, getting wealthy like the usurers they are. Hatred will double and triple."

His pessimism was well grounded. From the onset of hostilities, the Reichshammerbund (Imperial Brotherhood of the Hammer), a chauvinist cabal led by Theodor Fritsch—later a prominent Nazi official—pressed for a Judenzählung, a census to determine if Jews were making their "fair share" of sacrifices. Fritsch enjoyed support in high places. In December 1915, a discreet conference of other major agitators, including the future Nazis Count Reventlow and Adolf Bartels, similarly approved a research survey for a work to be titled *The Jews in the Army (Die Juden im Reichswehr)*, and subsequently to be distributed among officers and students. For Fritsch, Reventlow, Bartels, and other far-rightists, the ulterior purpose of a Judenzählung was to undermine the moderate Bethmann-Hollweg government with evidence that Jews were being allowed to shirk military service, or to serve in disproportionate numbers behind the lines, or to figure too prominently in the various wartime supply corporations—like Rathenau's.

Although the government would have no part of a Judenzählung, it could not stop the army from conducting its own survey. Within the Reichswehr, the éminence grise in this project was a key member of General Ludendorff's staff, Lieutenant Colonel Max Bauer, cofounder of a xenophobic fringe group, the Alldeutscher Verband, and a politician manqué who had been instrumental in maneuvering Ludendorff's recent appointment as quartermaster-general. To their consternation, Jewish soldiers were obliged now to fill out a questionnaire that pressed for details of where, how, and when they were fulfilling their actual military service. A number of senior officers even began transferring Jews under their command to frontline duty simply to avoid accusations of pro-Jewish favoritism.

Before long, the military inquiry produced civilian imitators. Only a week after the Judenzählung was ordered, Matthias Erzberger, chairman of the Catholic Center party, demanded a Reichstag committee investigation of Jews employed in the offices and agencies of the war economy. No Reichstag action was taken, nor were the results of the military survey ever made public until after the war, when it was revealed that the number of Jewish casualties and medal recipients actually was far out of proportion to Jewish numbers in Germany at large. But the impact of these surveys and accusations on Jewish morale was devastating. Rabbi Dr. Hermann Cohen spoke of a "stab in the heart." "We have become marked men," agonized Hugo Haase, the former Social Democratic Reichstag deputy, now serving as an army lieutenant, "second-class soldiers." In shock, Ernst Simon, who had enlisted in 1914, noted two years later that the Judenzählung evidently "reflected genuine popular attitudes." No Jewish combatant could ignore the painful evidence of military distrust and pervasive civilian antisemitism.

Jewish civilians had not awaited the humiliation of the Judenzählung to reevaluate their attitude to the war. When hostilities began, few Jews were outright pacifists, except for a tiny nucleus within the Social Democratic left wing. But if the vast majority of German Jews were not exempt from the patriotic euphoria of 1914, they recovered from it possibly more rapidly than did other Germans. Many prominent Jewish liberals, and virtually all Jewish—and non-Jewish—Social Democrats refused to endorse the pugnacious "Memorandum of the Six Federations" of spring 1915, with its chauvinist apologetics. Some Jews drafted counter-petitions, urging a peace of compromise. Jewish names appeared with growing frequency in organizations devoted to a moderation of German territorial demands. Of the largest Jewish-owned newspapers, the *Berliner Tageblatt*, the *Vossische Zeitung*, and the *Frankfurter Zeitung* were editorializing by 1917 in favor of a compromise peace and internal political democratization. The evidence was compelling that wide numbers of Jews at large shared in this moderationism.

It was a stance that evinced more than a dispersed and exposed minority's vested interest in international brotherhood. Jewish patriotism had been challenged. The old prewar suspicions had been fanned into renewed xenophobia. Accordingly, in vivid contrast to Jews in the Habsburg Empire, German Jews by and large welcomed the popular revolution that ended the war. They anticipated a better relationship with the "new" Germany.

A Valedictory for "Red Rosa"

In the last weeks of hostilities, Germany achieved through military defeat, as it never had in peacetime, its first significant movement toward authentically democratic government. Antiwar protests had gained momentum following Russia's Bolshevik Revolution, and had continued with growing frequency until November 1918, when they were massively augmented by mutinying sailors and soldiers. On November 9, tens of thousands of these protesters converged on the royal palace, demanding nothing less than dissolution of the monarchy and an immediate end to the war. At this point, Friedrich Ebert, chairman of the Social Democratic party, "suggested" to Prince Max of Baden, the current chancellor, that the government forthwith be turned over to the Social Democrats. Caving in, Max promptly resigned in favor of Ebert himself. For all practical purposes, the monarchy had expired. Within the day, Kaiser Wilhelm and his family boarded the cream-and-gold-encrusted royal train and departed for exile in the Netherlands.

In response then to public demand, and in preparation as well for negotiations with the Allies, Ebert felt obliged to broaden his coalition by including the far-left Independent Socialists. The latter in turn laid down their own conditions. For the time being, they insisted, political power should be vested in workers' and soldiers' "soviets," and cabinet members must be entitled "People's Commissars." Again, Ebert agreed. The new "Soviet of People's Commissars" thereupon included three Social Democrats and three Independents. Yet the chancellor and his colleagues would not be pushed to the brink of Communism. They excluded the Spartacists from the government coalition. Moreover, to present a moderate, "respectable" face to the West, Ebert acceded to Prince Max's earlier appointment of Matthias Erzburger, chairman of the Catholic Centrist party, to lead the armistice delegation to the Allies on November 11.

Ebert and his associates moved further yet along the path of moderation. On December 1, when the Social Democrats convened a "Reich Congress of Workers' and Soldiers' Soviets" in Berlin, they chose voluntarily to renounce the powers unexpectedly thrust into their hands by the revolution. Rather, the congress approved elections the next month for a National Assembly, which then would duly formulate a constitution for the new republic. The decision left the radicals stunned. Indeed, outraged at this "abject surrender" of revolutionary authority, a Spartacist contingent of sailors and civilians on December 13 launched a break-in of the chancellery building.

The assault was stopped in its tracks. Earlier, Ebert had won the support of the military leadership by promising to avoid any "radical" innovations. Now the army command kept its part of the bargain. Exploiting its still impressive reserves of firepower, it killed and wounded scores of the assailants and sent the rest fleeing. Hereupon, denouncing the "brutality" of the repression, the Independents left the government coalition—and Ebert promptly filled their positions with his own Social Democrats. Except for ending the war, therefore, and ushering in a democratic republic, the Socialist revolution apparently was liquidating itself.

It was a nightmare that Rosa Luxemburg, Karl Liebknecht, and other Spartacists had most feared. Their League had been founded, after all, as a direct outgrowth of Luxemburg's celebrated "Junius" pamphlet (p. 217). Its purpose was classically and unequivocally Marxist, to "fuse the proletariat of all countries into one living revolutionary force." Until the end of the war, while both Luxemburg and Liebknecht remained in prison, the League maintained its revolutionary agitation under the direction of Franz Mehring, Clara Zetkin, and Leo Jogiches (until his own imprisonment). But the Spartacist leadership, and thousands of common working people, well understood that Luxemburg and Liebknecht remained the heart and soul of their movement.

Thus, on November 9, 1918, the day the new governmet declared a general amnesty for political prisoners, a huge crowd of revolutionaries thronged the gates of the Breslau Citadel to usher Rosa Luxemburg out to freedom. Although frail and ill, her eyesight still uncertain in the autumn sunlight, the tiny woman did not so much as await her return to the capital before addressing a mass meeting in Breslau's town square. The revolution must now be carried to its logical climax of a classless society, she declaimed to uproarious cheering. There could be no return to the exploitative capitalist order. Then Luxemburg was brought back to Berlin. Here she was awaited at the Zoogarten railroad station by two other newly released prisoners. They were Liebknecht and Jogiches. Gaunt and sunken-cheeked, Jogiches clasped her to him. Their embrace was tearful—and elegiac.

Luxemburg's followers had provided lodgings for her in a modest hotel suite. Office facilities were made available in a commandeered right-wing publishing plant. Here she immediately set about producing a Spartacist newspaper, *Die Rote Fahne*. Working at white heat, as if there had been no two-year interregnum of deprivation and illness, Luxemburg churned out articles and editorials, entreating her readers to organize a Red Guard, to expropriate hereditary wealth and absentee property, and above all to convene an "authentically revolutionary" soviet to replace Friedrich Ebert's "fraudulent" Soviet of People's Commissars.

In fact, Luxemburg's program, while fiery on the printed page, was less than draconian. It sternly repudiated the kind of Bolshevik regime then operating in Russia. Alluding to developments in the east, Luxemburg warned in her editorials that Lenin's dictatorship was

> worse than the disease it was supposed to cure. . . . Socialism by its very nature cannot be dictated [or] introduced by command. . . . Without general elections, without unrestricted freedom of press and assembly, without a free exchange of opinions, life dies out in every public institution and only bureaucracy remains active.

"The Bolsheviks," Luxemburg stated to Lenin's personal emissary, Karl Radek, "are welcome to keep their tactics for themselves."

This was a bittersweet period for "Red Rosa." With Jogiches once again at her side, it appeared that they were starting over together. Politically, they were. If romantic love between them had long since disappeared, so had resentment and rancor. Henceforth their single priority was to overthrow a "traitorous" semibourgeois government, to deliver all power "to the masses," to "the workers' and soldiers' soviets," as she declared repeatedly in her editorials, and to avoid a Leninist-style dictatorship. It was a precarious ideological tightwire, and not without risks to Luxemburg's personal safety. Although remaining at her editorial office in Berlin, she was obliged to move from hotel to hotel to avoid possible right-wing murder attempts. On street corners and billboards, in newspapers and leaflets, she was denounced as a Bolshevik, a Jew, a devil, bent on destroying Germany. On one occasion a Freikorps—paramilitary—attempt to kidnap Luxemburg and Liebknecht was repelled only at the last moment by her watchful Spartacist bodyguards.

Throughout December 1918, anti-government violence flickered periodically in the capital and other German cities. On December 6, when Spartacists and Independents joined forces in a protest demonstration, they were met by machine-gun fire, leaving 187 dead. In ensuing weeks, exchanges of volleys between troops and striking workers claimed additional scores of lives. These were the circumstances that persuaded Liebknecht and several other Spartacist leaders that their only remaining alternative was to negotiate a closer relationship with Soviet Russia. As the first step in this direction, they argued, the Spartacus League itself should be transformed into an openly identified Communist party.

Luxemburg and Jogiches opposed the move. It would lead inevitably to a Bolshevik-style, elitist revolution, they insisted, and the masses in Germany needed more indoctrination before they were ripe for that kind of upheaval. But on December 31, a Spartacist conference voted by two to one to transform the faction into the "Kommunist Partei Deutschlands" (although the title "Spartakusbund" was maintained in parentheses). Immediately, then, the pace of revolution was accelerated beyond Luxemburg's control. On the night of January 5–6, 1919, a joint committee of Communists and Independents followed Liebknecht's initiative, summoning workers to a general strike in preparation for a takeover of the government itself.

Upon being informed that Liebknecht had embarked on the revolution without careful preparation or organization, Luxemburg cried in protest: "How could you? What about our program?" Yet, once the struggle began, she and her staff at the *Rote Fahne* were left with no alternative but to support it with all possible energy. "Act quickly," she editorialized. "The revolution demands it." The appeal was wasted. On January 8, the government launched a full-scale counteroffensive. Ebert's defense minister, Gustav Noske, himself a veteran Social Democrat, had long been chafing to settle accounts with the "Bolshies" who were maligning the name of honest workers. To that end, he relied extensively on the paramilitary Freikorps. Numbering about 250,000 nationwide, these déclassé right-wing war veterans functioned under regular army command. In Berlin, heavily armed with automatic weapons and even some artillery, they turned on the revolutionaries with a vengeance. By the time the four-day battle ended, on January 12, over a thousand rebels lay dead, with thousands of others wounded, and both Freikorps and army troops were in firm command of the capital.

Two days later, Luxemburg's final *Rote Fahne* editorial rolled off the mimeograph at a secret hideaway in Berlin's middle-class, largely Jewish Wilmersdorf district. It was a poignantly defiant affirmation that "the revolution marches on—over the graves, not yet filled in, over 'victories and defeats'—toward its great task." By then, Luxemburg and Liebknecht had been making their separate ways from one hiding-place to another. On January 15, both took shelter in the apartment of old friends, the Marcussohn family. It was precarious sanctuary. Defense Minister Noske had put a price of 100,000 marks on their heads. That very evening a neighbor informed police that strangers were in the building, and at about 9:00 p.m. a Horse Guard military unit broke into the apartment and arrested the two fugitives.

The Horse Guards had made their headquarters in the Hotel Eden, near the zoo, and there Luxemburg and Liebknecht were brought in for questioning. Both were savagely beaten. When the "interrogation" ended, Captain Waldemar Pabst made a show of arranging for the two captives to be transferred to the Moabit prison. Liebknecht and Luxemburg then were dragged separately out a side exit. As Liebknecht stumbled into an awaiting car, he was clubbed senseless. Afterward, carried off into the darkness, he was shot and his body was dumped in an alley. At the Hotel Eden, meanwhile, a second automobile awaited Luxemburg. She was already unconscious as she was pulled into its backseat. When the vehicle drove off, one of its occupants, Lieutenant Kurt Vogel, put a pistol to Luxemburg's head and shot her. The drive continued to the Liechtenstein Bridge, where the dead woman was thrown into the Landwehr Canal. Several hours later, a government news release stated that Liebknecht had been shot "while attempting to escape," and that "Red Rosa" had been seized by an "angry crowd" and her current whereabouts were unknown.

Only Jogiches entertained no illusions about Luxemburg's fate. On January 15, maintaining a hardened revolutionary's stoic demeanor, he dispatched a cryptic telegram to Lenin: "Rosa Luxemburg and Karl Liebknecht have carried out their ultimate revolution." The day before, Jogiches himself had been arrested, but had managed to escape without being identified. From his hideaway in a secret flat, taking over sole leadership of the Spartacus League, he was determined to carry on its work. But there was little time to regroup. Elections for the National Assembly took place only a few days later, and the delegates subsequently proceeded to Weimar to debate a new constitution under the very guns of the Freikorps (p. 241).

Jogiches and his colleagues then moved rapidly to launch one final strike, on March 3, 1919. There must not be violence, Jogiches insisted, no provocation that would enable Noske to repeat the massacres of January. But again the leadership lost control. The Communists had cached substantial quantities of weapons and they promptly began attacking Berlin's police stations. As in January, Noske was ready and waiting. His Freikorps troops this time were equipped with artillery, tanks, flamethrowers, even airplanes. Two days of carnage followed, with over six hundred of the rebels left dead. One of them was Jogiches. He was seized on March 10 while paying a return visit to Luxemburg's apartment, in search of her papers. Carried off to the Alexanderplatz police headquarters, he was beaten senseless, then shot.

Nearly three months later, on May 31, 1919, a partly decomposed corpse was spotted in one of the locks of the Landwehr Canal. It was retrieved, then taken to the city morgue, where it was promptly identified as Luxemburg's. Informed of this development, Noske ordered that the body be removed from the morgue and buried secretly. But the press already had picked up the news. Paul Levi, who had assumed leadership of the Communist party after Jogiches's murder, "officially" identified the dead woman's remains and arranged for Luxemburg to be ceremonially buried in the Friedrichsfelde cemetery. On the day of her interment, June 13, 1919, mourners in seemingly endless thousands filed by to pay their respects both to Luxemburg and to Jogiches, whose body had been reinterred by hers. Seven years later, on June 13, 1926, a memorial was unveiled to commemorate their last resting place.

Meanwhile, as far back as the summer of 1919, at Paul Levi's orders, the Communists abandoned the weapon of political strikes. All efforts henceforth were to be devoted to a resurrection of the *Rote Fahne*, under the editorship of Josef Borenstein, and to a peaceful reconstruction of party cadres. It was only in the late 1920s, after years of comparative political quiescence, that all factions of the ideological left began giving retrospective attention to Luxemburg's career. The initial evaluation was that she had lent her powerful intellect and acerbic pen to a precipitous and senseless revolution. This interpretation, fostered during the Stalin era, has largely been dispelled by modern scholarship. So, too, has the image of Luxemburg as a sulfurous political virago. The publication of several small volumes of her letters, entirely personal and of a touchingly human and often poetic beauty, are enough to destroy the legend of a bloodthirsty "Red Rosa." She was a sentimental woman, a passionate lover of Jogiches, a bird-watcher and flower-cultivator, a woman to whom guards at her prison bade goodbye with tears in their eyes.

Luxemburg's alleged "political ruthlessness" in fact was mobilized less on behalf of an abstract dialectic than for world peace and the common people. Not for her the Leninist vision of war as the indispensable catalyst of revolution. The very notion of mass death and destruction, of a Bolshevik-style dictatorship, she regarded as intolerable. Today, Rosalia Lukksemburg emerges as a courageous if single-minded personality, who embraced the Marxist cause doubtless with historical naïveté but also with unique moral courage against the prevailing nationalist trends even within the Socialist world. And in a life of self-sacrifice, she paid her ultimate dues.

The Wages of Jewish Radicalism

At 9:45 a.m. on February 21, 1919, Kurt Eisner, minister-president of Bavaria, Germany's second largest "Land," departed his Munich office on foot to attend the opening session of the newly elected Landtag, the state parliament, two blocks away. Preceding him on the Promenadenplatz were two bodyguards and two political aides. None looked backward. Unnoticed, a young man then walked up softly behind the minister-president and fired two pistol shots into his back, killing him instantly.

Eisner's death was preceded by that of Bavaria's monarchy. It was only upon entering the newly established German Empire, in 1871, that Bavaria took belated and reluctant steps toward parliamentary government. Still allowed to maintain its own dynasty, the House of Wittelsbach, the southern kingdom did not become a constitutional monarchy until 1912. Even Bavaria's Social Democratic faction represented the party's most cautiously moderate branch. Altogether, before 1918, this formidable citadel of Catholic conservatism tolerated no politically progressive movement of any kind. All the more ironic, therefore, that Bavaria emerged as the first of Germany's Länder to become a Socialist "republic," and remained in the grip of authentic political radicalism longer than any other German state.

It was in early November 1918, after more than four years of heavy military casualties and painful civilian austerity, that revolutionism burgeoned as dramatically in Bavaria as in Prussia and other German states. From the outset, the process was guided by the far-leftist Independent Socialists. Their leader was an even unlikelier political phenomenon. Kurt Eisner was not a Bavarian. Assuredly, he was not a Catholic. Born in Berlin in 1867, he was the son of a Jewish shopkeeper. Upon graduation from the capital's Friedrich Wilhelm University, he found his vocation in journalism. Subsequently, as a political columnist for the *Frankfurter Zeitung* and other newspapers, Eisner staked out his ideological home in Social Democracy. His acerbic political essays spared no vested interest, neither the aristocracy, nor the great money lords, nor even the kaiser. In 1897, he was convicted and given a three-month jail sentence for lèse-majesté.

The brief incarceration actually became Eisner's stroke of fortune. It won him the admiration of Wilhelm Liebknecht, the "grand old man" of German Social Democracy. Upon Eisner's release, Liebknecht appointed him to the editorial board of *Die Vorwärts*, the senior Socialist newspaper in Europe. Within three years, Eisner rose to the position of managing editor. His fall was almost as rapid. Despite his hostility toward the royal court and the economic barons, Eisner was no less opposed to violent revolution. In 1905 he refused editorial endorsement of a mass sympathy strike on behalf of Russia's Octobrist Revolution. His moderate revisionism offended old Liebknecht, who fired him.

Out of work and out of favor with the party, with a wife and five children to support, the thirty-eight-year-old Eisner soon was obliged to earn his bread as a freelance writer in the "provinces." In 1910, leaving his family behind, he decided to try his luck in Munich. This proved a useful move. Eisner's reputation as a fearless critic of "Prussianism" won him appointment as political editor of the *Münchener Post*, the organ of Bavarian Socialism. Soon he was back in his element. His coterie of admirers swelled. Physically, Eisner was less than impressive, a small, thin man of sallow complexion, with wispy hair, a full reddish beard already streaked with gray, and thick, steel-rimmed glasses. Morally, however, he achieved larger-than-life dimensions with his uncompromising editorials against imperial chauvinism and the rising spirit of Junker militarism.

When war began in 1914, Eisner at first avoided a doctrinaire condemnation. "Now that tsarism has attacked Germany," he wrote, "we have no choice. There is no looking back." But within the year he changed his mind again. Horrified by Germany's invasion of neutral Belgium, he urged an end to the conflict. For his efforts, he was dismissed from his newspaper and once again reduced to freelancing. Yet, upon departing the Social Democratic line, this time moving to the left rather than to the right, Eisner did so in full force. He began organizing demonstrations against the war. In 1917, as a founding member of Germany's breakaway Independent Socialist party, he became chairman of its Bavarian branch. In the spring of 1918, leading a protest strike against Germany's punitive dismemberment of Russia under the Treaty of Brest-Litovsk, he was arrested, convicted for incitement, and confined for eight and a half months in the Stadelheim Citadel. The episode became even more of a defining moment for Eisner than his earlier, youthful imprisonment. As Bavarian Socialism's first major political martyr, he acquired a legendary aura among fellow "progressives."

Eisner was set free in the last week of October 1918. By then, Munich was in political chaos, with Socialists of all colorations demanding an end to the war and the eradication of both monarchies, Bavaria's Wittelsbach and Imperial Germany's Hohenzollern. Eisner and his fellow Independents took the lead in this campaign, organizing massive demonstrations on behalf of peace and republicanism. On November 7, factory work stopped throughout Bavaria's principal cities. Thousands of mutinous troops began mingling with the striking workers, brandishing red flags, spontaneously forming joint "soviets." Hereupon, with breathtaking audacity, Eisner decided the course of the uprising on his own. Escorted into the Bavarian Landtag on November 8, he informed the assembled legislators, "in the name of the Soviet of Workers and Soldiers," that the Wittelsbach dynasty was ended, that Bavaria now was a republic, and that all power henceforth was invested in the "Soviet" over which he himself would preside as provisional minister-president and foreign minister. No other political spokesman dared say Eisner nay, not even the Social Democratic moderates, who then agreed to join his coalition government.

Several hours later, in the same Landtag auditorium, Eisner addressed the self-coopted Soviet, promising to achieve "a peace of understanding" and free and democratic elections for a Bavarian Constitutional Assembly. In the interim, he would appoint a cabinet divided equally between his own Independents and mainstream Social Democrats. It was a mirror image of the Ebert-Haase government then being established in Berlin. Moreover, during the first weeks of November, Eisner enjoyed extraordinary prestige. His "revolution" was accepted by all the major political parties in Bavaria. With the Provisional National Soviet authorizing the cabinet to govern by temporary decree, military discipline and bureaucratic order appeared to reign once again.

There was a fly in the ointment. No one in the Eisner government possessed meaningful executive experience. If the Bavarian Soviet experiment functioned without opposition, it also functioned without significant reform. Its only "Socialist" innovation was a blandly welfarist eight-hour day, improved factory working conditions, and an increase in unemployment insurance. Otherwise, the minister-president and his colleagues, even his Independent partners, displayed no willingness to tamper with the great landed estates, with industrial cartels, or with major public utilities. In Munich, as in Berlin, these issues were postponed to a vague and indefinite future. With little real understanding of economics, Eisner acknowledged that "authentic" Socialism would have to wait until most of the world's other democracies had also been socialized.

No less than ideological moderation, it was Realpolitik that determined the minister-president's timorousness. Eisner well understood that his Bavarian Socialist regime was isolated in Central-Western Europe. To ensure lenient treatment from the Allies, it would have to distance itself from the warmongering reputation of the former Reich, and if possible even from "greater" Germany altogether. Yet, when Eisner visited Berlin on November 23, 1918, and submitted to Ebert his proposal for an autonomous Bavarian foreign policy, the German chancellor all but exploded at this "act of treachery." In turn, shaken and bitter, Eisner hurried back to Munich to announce that his government was "severing diplomatic relations" with Berlin. The move was both impulsive and futile. It evoked no special, forbearing treatment from the Allies, who maintained their blockade against the totality of Germany. In Bavaria as in the nation at large, the economy was facing collapse.

Meanwhile, with the date of January 12, 1919, set for elections to their Landtag, the Catholic Bavarians began to reappraise a government that was not only Socialist and ineffectual, but substantially Jewish. Eisner himself was far from an observant Jew (although he had never distanced himself from his people). But the Bavarian citizenry knew only what they saw. Besides Eisner, they saw Gustav Landauer and Erich Mühsam sitting in the six-man "Central Soviet," as well as other Jews who were prominent in various factions of Bavarian Socialism (pp. 235–37).

Indeed, not a few Bavarian Jews of middle-class background were distressed at this visibility. The industrialist Sigmund Fränkel addressed an open letter to the Jewish leaders of the successor "Soviet Republic" (p. 235), imploring them to forgo their radicalism and thus spare Bavarian Jewry a rising tide of antisemitism. The president of Bavaria's Jewish Kultusgemeinde felt impelled to publish a statement in the *Münchener Neuste Nachrichten* in February 1919, insisting that those Independent Socialists and Communist leaders who bore Jewish names "have long ago ceased to be Jews and stand completely outside the Jewish community." The mood of Jewish alarm was entirely justified. As the election campaign gained momentum, so did accusations and recriminations against Eisner and his government: "Out with the Israelite devil!" "We want a Bavarian!" Rumors circulated that Eisner's real name was Salamon Kuchinsky, that he was an agent of Lenin, that he was in league with the "Elders of Zion" (a mythical cabal, described in a widely circulating antisemitic screed of the postwar period).

Over three million Bavarians voted in the Landtag election of January 12, 1919. The outcome proved a disaster for Eisner and his partners. The mainstream Social Democrats received the largest plurality of votes, and were followed by the various Catholic "confessional" parties. Eisner and his fellow Independents won only three seats, one more than the tiny Communist faction. For another month and a half, the minister-president trimmed and maneuvered, seeking frantically to reconstitute his precarious coalition. To no avail. So it was, at 9:45 a.m. on February 21, that Eisner set out from his foreign ministry office for the Landtag to tender his government's resignation. With his short and tubby frame, his goatee, and trademark huge black hat, he was an easily recognizable figure. It was then that the youthful assailant crept up behind him and fired the lethal pistol shots into his back.

Eisner's bodyguard in turn shot and wounded the assassin. The police then rushed the young man to a hospital, where surgeons managed to save his life. It soon emerged that the murderer's name was Anton von Arco auf Valley. He was twenty-one years old, a lieutenant of the Royal Bodyguard, and a count, indeed, the son of Count Maximilian von Arco auf Valley, whose family could trace its patent of nobility back to the twelfth century. But he was also the son of Fräulein Emma von Oppenheim, and thus was a half-Jew. Several days of police investigation produced the motive for young Arco's act of homicide. He had applied for membership in the Thule Gesellschaft, an ardently racist society named after a legendary Nordic *Ur*-kingdom, which lately had made a point of recruiting intellectuals such as Dietrich Eckhardt and Alfred Rosenberg, and promising junior officers such as Rudolf Hess. Its emblem was the swastika. Once Anton von Arco was discovered to be a *Jüdling* ("Yid")—as the society's president, Rudolf van Sebottendorf, explained later—he was immediately and comtemptuously rejected. Later, Sebottendorf added, Arco in his bitterness and frustration "evidently wanted to show that a half-Jew could perform such a deed."

During the last weeks of his life, Kurt Eisner had been humiliated at the polls, ridiculed in the press, vilified as a "foreigner" and above all as a Jew. Now, on his death, he suddenly emerged as the "noblest" Bavarian of them all, as a folk hero. The assassination site was transformed into a makeshift altar, adorned by scores of wreaths. Within hours of Eisner's death, flags were flying at half mast on government buildings. The Munich working proletariat set up framed copies of his portrait, and all who passed by were "asked" by rifle-carrying soldiers to remove their hats. The day of Eisner's funeral, February 27, was proclaimed a day of offical mourning throughout Bavaria. As a vast memorial procession made its way to the Landtag, church bells rang incessantly (over the objections of the Bavarian Catholic hierarchy). In the Landtag hall, Eisner's body lay in state, with thousands of mourners filing by. Bruno Walter, director of the Munich State Opera and himself a Jewish convert to Catholicism, conducted Beethoven's *Leonore Overture.* Afterward, at Eisner's interment, his friend Gustav Landauer pronounced the final eulogy. No *kaddish* was intoned.

Nearly a year later, in January 1920, when Arco finally was brought to trial after the last of Bavaria's post-revolutionary unrest had subsided, the court listened to extensive defense testimony that the young man had consummated "a noble deed." Whether the three judges agreed or not, on January 16 they sentenced Arco to death, then promptly commuted his sentence to life imprisonment. Arco's confinement in Landsberg fortress proved to be hardly more than an inconvenience. He was released in April 1924 to make room for another prisoner, one Adolf Hitler, and received a hero's welcome home. Soon afterward, Arco gained a high position in the newly established Lufthansa airline. In 1941, the Nazis proclaimed him an "honorary Aryan."

The Aftershocks of Revolution

On February 21, 1919, in the uncertainty immediately following Eisner's assassination, the original Central Soviet—the makeshift cabinet—declared a state of martial law. To alleviate public misgivings, the government promised that the newly elected Landtag would be called into session "as soon as conditions permit." But it was not until March 1919 that the parliament was allowed to convene. Its first act was to grant full legal authority to a new cabinet, functioning under the chancellorship of a veteran—mainline—Social Democrat, Johannes Hoffmann. At its opening session, the Hoffmann government in turn agreed (however grudgingly) to accept the newly formulated Weimar Constitution (p. 241). Bavaria thereupon ceased to be an autonomous nation, and became a Land, in the manner of Germany's other states.

Yet the Hoffmann administration soon proved as ineffectual as the recent Soviet had been in coping with Bavaria's massive unemployment and raging inflation. Over the next weeks, the Independent Socialists and other far-leftists conferred urgently and angrily, demanding the immediate establishment of an "authentic" soviet and a new "people's army"—in effect, a new revolution. The time was propitious, the radicals believed. Spartacist uprisings continued to flare up in Berlin, while the Bela Kun Communist regime lately had assumed control in Hungary. On April 4, 1919, a mass meeting of radical leftists gathered in Munich's Löwenbrau beer hall to press their claims for an "authentically" Socialist government. Three days later, political power shifted almost by default to a far-leftist council of some one hundred men, who thereupon proclaimed a "Soviet Republic of Bavaria." Immediately breaking off diplomatic relations with Berlin, the council then sent the Hoffmann government fleeing to the town of Bamberg, in the northern part of the state.

The guiding spirits of the new Red regime were Gustav Landauer, Erich Mühsam, and Ernst Toller. None of them was Bavarian. Rather, they were Jewish intellectuals from elsewhere in Germany, idealists whose unquestioned humanism was almost entirely vitiated by lack of governmental experience, or even of a coherent governmental vision. Landauer, forty-nine years old, was the most broadly cultured of the three. Son of a prosperous Karlsruhe merchant, he had become an ardent Socialist while a student at Berlin's Karl Ferdinand University. Restraint did not figure in his ideology or his tactics. As editor of an Anarcho-Socialist newspaper, demanding an end to political oppression and economic exploitation, the young man was given an eleven-month prison sentence in 1893 on a charge of incitement. After serving his term, and upon being denied readmission to the university, Landauer then worked as a freelance journalist. In 1899 he resumed his "incitement" and was imprisoned once again, this time for six months.

Shortly after his release, Landauer divorced his wife, married the poetess Hedwig Lachmann, and eked out a modest livelihood publishing books and articles on literary themes. As always, his "extracurricular" writings were devoted to the Socialist cause, and two of his prewar books, *Die Revolution* and *An Appeal for Socialism (Aufruf zum Sozialismus)*, laid out a utopian program for "cooperative" living, wherein the proletariat somehow would govern "by example," above politics and above party. At war's end, Landauer gravitated to Munich. There, quite suddenly and unpredictably, he emerged as one of Bavaria's most admired radical intellectuals. With his luxuriant head of hair and full beard, and a recently developed forensic dynamism, he also suddenly became the most widely recognized and widely caricatured member of the new leftist "triumvirate."

His close associate, Erich Mühsam, eight years younger, shared Landauer's messianic vision of a classless society. A Berliner, son of a pharmacist, Mühsam attended university, studied pharmacy, and briefly practiced the profession with his father before turning full-time to his chosen avocation as poet, dramatist, literary critic, and political journalist of "Anarcho-Syndicalism." Joining Landauer in postwar Munich, the youthful writer modulated his radicalism sufficiently to be taken on as a publicist for the brief Eisner government. But after Eisner's death, waiting in the wings during the Landtag interregnum, Mühsam became a charter member of the April 7 Bavarian Soviet Republic and served as the new regime's "commissar" for planning.

Mühsam was surpassed in sheer charisma, even in intellectual firepower, by the youngest member of the trio, the twenty-five-year-old Ernst Toller. Born in Posen to impoverished Polish-Jewish parents, Toller shared his family's devoted German patriotism. When the war began, he volunteered for the army and for thirteen months served on the western front, where he was twice wounded. By the time he was invalided out, in 1916, Toller had become a committed pacifist and "ethical" Socialist. He was also emerging as an Expressionist poet-dramatist of considerable reputation. Tall, strikingly handsome, and charismatic, he rapidly became an influential presence among his fellow Socialists. As in 1914, he was prepared to sacrifice himself for his beliefs. For his role in organizing a strike in Munich's Krupp armaments works in January 1918, he was reconscripted and dispatched to a military prison.

In the general amnesty following the November 1918 revolution, Toller was invited to serve as Eisner's deputy. Holding this position until the minister-president's assassination, the young man then stayed on in the Provisional Soviet until the newly elected Landtag convened. No hair-shirt Bolshevik, Toller personally was uninterested in further radical experiments. But when the "Soviet Republic of Bavaria" was proclaimed on April 7, 1919, he agreed somewhat hesitantly to serve the insurrectionist regime as "commissar for public instruction." Years later, in his autobiography, Toller professed to have discerned the ineptitude of the "Coffee-house Anarchists" from the outset. Edicts were issued proclaiming the arming of the workers, the regulation of all food supplies, the nationalization of the press and even the confiscation of all homes possessing more than three rooms. Toller himself briefly got into the utopianist spirit by decreeing tuition-free admission to Munich's Ludwig Maximilian University. "This Soviet Republic was a foolhardy *coup de main* on the part of the bewildered workers," he subsequently acknowledged, "an attempt to salvage the lost German Revolution. What would it achieve?"

In fact, it survived barely a week and a half. Food and fuel were swiftly exhausted, and the regime's orders and edicts soon were ignored by the confused and frightened citizenry. The commissar for foreign affairs, Dr. Franz Lipp, fecklessly appealing to Berlin for help, complained that the late Hoffmann—Social Democratic—government had gone so far as to "abscond with the key to the ministry bathroom." An adventure that had begun as opéra bouffe was to end in tragedy. On April 17, 1919, with the support of the Red Militia, a small junta of "pure" Communists confronted Landauer, Mühsam, Toller, and other members of the Soviet leadership to announce that the "pseudo-Soviet" was finished, and that the "real" Soviet now would begin. When Landauer and Mühsam protested, they were clapped in jail. So commenced the third, and final, metamorphosis of Bavarian Socialism.

Like their predecessors, none of the leading putschists was a Bavarian, and their credentials even as Germans were uncertain. But they were all Jews. One of them, Tovia Axelrod, thirty-two years old, was a Russian citizen and a close friend of Lenin. He had come to Germany following the Treaty of Brest-Litovsk as an assistant to Adolf Joffe, the first Soviet Russian ambassador to Imperial Germany. When Joffe was expelled from the country for propagandizing, Axelrod remained on and made his way to Munich, which by then was under the new Eisner government. The other two "Bolsheviks" also were of mixed background. Max Levien, a tall, blond thirty-four-year-old, was the scion of a Jewish merchant family whose nationality was part Russian and part German. He had lived in Moscow until the age of twenty-one, then had fled tsarist antisemitism to study in Germany. Returning home afterward, Levien was arrested for revolutionary activity and sentenced to a Siberian lead mine. Instead, he bribed his guards, "escaped," and made his way back to Germany. There he served briefly in the Reichswehr during the war before undergoing a brief military imprisonment for Spartacist incitement.

Eugen Leviné, at thirty-six the oldest of the three "Russians," was born in St. Petersburg. He also had come to Germany before the war to study. Returning home following Russia's 1905 Octobrist Revolution, he was obliged to flee the tsarist counterrevolution four years later and to make his way back to Germany. With the outbreak of the war, Leviné was conscripted into the German army. Like Levien, he became a Spartacist, but—almost miraculously—suffered only a military discharge for his activities. In fact, his passion and commitment had much impressed Rosa Luxemburg. Shortly after the war and only two weeks before her own death, Luxemburg delegated Leviné to represent the German Communist (Spartacist) party at the first meeting of the Communist International in Moscow. When the German government blocked him from crossing the frontier, Paul Levi, Luxemburg's successor as party chairman, sent Leviné to Munich. There, in April 1919, he joined Axelrod and Levien in directing the Communist putsch.

Upon seizing power after the fall of the "Coffeehouse Anarchists," the "Bolshevik Triumvirate" launched into a climactic program of Red terror, filling Munich's Stadelheim prison with hostages from middle-class and aristocratic families alike. Schools were closed, opposition newspapers were banned, and a Bavarian Red Army was organized out of some twenty thousand militiamen who had remained on from the various predecessor leftist governments. Initially, the putschists asked the much-admired Ernst Toller to serve as commissar of defense. He declined. Neither the portfolio nor the regime was congenial to him. Yet, unwilling to let the government fall into the hands of counterrevolutionaries, he agreed to command a local battalion for the Munich area.

The defense effort in any case was too late. On April 20, the Hoffmann "government-in-exile" turned to Berlin for help. Hoffmann himself traveled north to meet with the German war minister, the redoubtable Gustav Noske. Noske in turn agreed to dispatch a substantial contingent of Freikorps troops, provided there was no further nonsense about Bavarian separatism. Hoffmann agreed. In late April, a thirty-thousand-man force, commanded by General von Epp, a professional Reichswehr officer, launched its drive over the Bavarian frontier.

At Munich's outskirts, Toller, who had rounded up ten thousand loyalists, fought a pitched battle with the local counterrevolutionaries and succeeded in driving them back. The respite lasted all of two days. When Epp's army arrived, on April 30, it embarked on a carefully coordinated, entirely professional offensive against Munich, blasting the defenders with heavy artillery and aerial bombardment. The rebels held out for three days, but on May 2 the Freikorps successfully occupied the city. At this point, on their own initiative, Epp's troops embarked upon an indiscriminate White Terror, combing Munich for "Reds," whether hard-core Communists or Socialist moderates. At least a thousand people were slaughtered within a six-day period. On May 13, the Hoffmann émigré government was permitted to return from Bamberg, and the Freikorps regiments thereupon departed Munich. Yet, even afterward, the hunt for suspected radicals continued. Axelrod was the first to be apprehended—and released. Moscow warned that he possessed diplomatic status, a holdover from his assignment to the Joffe Mission. Within the week, Axelrod was allowed to return to Soviet Russia.

Other leaders, however, both of the Soviet Bavarian Republic and of the earlier Socialist regimes, were less fortunate. They were systematically hunted down. Erich Mühsam, captured at the outset of the Freikorps invasion, was placed on trial and sentenced to fifteen years' imprisonment. Although he would be amnestied after six years, he served his time at the notorious fortress of Niederschönwald, where he was continually singled out for "special" treatment." The "special treatment" left him deaf in one ear and with a grave heart condition. Upon his release, Mühsam embarked on the publication of a small, eccentric journal of his own, *Das Fanal* (The Signal), and became something of a hero among the "progressive" younger generation. His respite was brief. In March 1933, the Nazis seized him in their roundup of left-wing intellectuals. After systematically torturing him, they shot him in July 1934. Gustav Landauer meanwhile was among the first to be hunted down in the White Terror of May 1919. The Freikorps troops who captured him in the apartment of a friend promptly beat him to death. Eugen Leviné's fate was barely more dignified. Captured after ten days of hiding, he was tried and convicted of high treason, and promptly shot.

Summary execution might also have been the fate of Ernst Toller, but he managed to remain in hiding until the initial fury of the White Terror passed. Some months later, he too was discovered and placed on trial. Yet his defense attorney, Hugo Haase, the renowned Independent Socialist and cabinet minister (in the early Social Democratic–Independent coalition), secured a comparatively lenient, five-year sentence for his client. In prison, spending months in and out of solitary confinement, Toller managed to use his isolation creatively, writing the Socialist and pacifist dramas that won him an enormous following in the outside world. Among these plays were *The Machine Wreckers (Die Maschinenstürmer)*, about the Luddite movement in England; and the even more renowned *Masses and Man (Masse Mensch)*, reflecting his personal dilemma as an advocate of nonviolence caught up in revolution. By the time of Toller's release from prison in 1924 (a day early to protect him from waiting right-wing assassins), he had become the most famous German playwright of the early postwar era.

In ensuing years, no longer in politics, Toller continued to protest injustice through his leftist dramaturgy. When the Nazis assumed power, he was away on a lecture tour of Switzerland, and thereby almost certainly avoided sharing Mühsam's fate. Departing for London, Toller rented a house, married a young German actress, wrote more plays, contributed articles to the anti-Nazi press, visited Republican Spain during the Civil War, and raised money for the Spanish Loyalists in Britain and the United States. In 1939, Toller settled in New York. In May of that year, his wife left him. Unable to earn a livelihood and mired in depression, he booked a room in the Mayflower Hotel and hanged himself.

In Bavaria, as in Germany at large during and after the upheavals of the early postwar years, the reactionary press focused its accusations on the Jews. All the violence, it was alleged, whether in Soviet Russia or in Hungary, in Prussia or Bavaria, could be attributed to a vast Jewish-Bolshevik conspiracy. Little distinction was to be drawn between the hard-edged Communism of Levien and Leviné, the vigorous but antiviolent messianism of Rosa Luxemburg or Paul Levi, the progressive leftism of Kurt Eisner, or even the anodyne welfarism of Hugo Haase and Otto Landsberg, who sat in Friedrich Ebert's neo-Centrist Social Democratic cabinet. In Germany's public consciousness, the Jews were a people to be linked reflexively and irredeemably with the terrifying perils of alien radicalism.

The Wages of Jewish Respectability

On January 19, 1919, the very week following suppression of the Spartacist uprising in Berlin, thirty million Germans went to the polls for their first postwar election. Their ballots produced a solid triumph for Friedrich Ebert and the Social Democratic moderates. With a dominating plurality of 163 deputies (out of 421), Ebert anticipated that the National Assembly would write a new constitution for the emergent republic. Accordingly, he shifted the National Assembly's venue away from Berlin, which then still was flickering with intermittent political violence, to sedate, provincial Weimar, with its humanistic memories of Goethe, Schiller, and Herder. In Weimar, on February 10, four days after gathering in the town's dignified old National Theater, the delegates formally elected Ebert president of the new German Republic. Ebert's close associate, Philipp Scheidemann, was elected chancellor of the left-center coalition government. A brief Spartacist uprising in Berlin temporarily interrupted the Assembly's proceedings. But in the first week of April, with order restored, the Weimar conclave finally approved the draft of a new constitution. Only then did the legislature reconvene in Berlin, as a normally functioning "Reichstag" (p. 244).

Three months later, on June 28, 1919, in the Hall of Mirrors at Versailles, a German delegation signed a peace treaty with the Allies. The document was not forbearing. Besides stripping Germany of its overseas empire, and the provinces of Alsace-Lorraine, the Treaty of Versailles established a "Polish Corridor" across eastern Germany, "demilitarized" the Rhineland, and imposed heavy reparations obligations upon the German government. In its apparent implacability, moreover, the treaty evoked such rage and frustration among the German people at large that in March 1920, a group of disgruntled nationalists, led by Dr. Wolfgang Kapp, a former official of the imperial foreign ministry, launched its own putsch against the government, taking over the chancellery building. This time the army and the Freikorps refused to intervene; the revered General Erich Ludendorff was one of the conspirators. The Kapp insurrection guttered out after a few days, as it happened, but only when Germany's labor unions mounted a nationwide strike that effectively paralyzed Kapp's efforts to run the economy.

Ebert, Scheidemann, and the Social Democrats now had their first great chance after the Kapp fiasco to carry out long-promised reforms: to liberalize the army command and civil service; and to break up the vast Junker estates and industrial cartels. Nevertheless, fearing to open the door once again to "Bolshevism," they declined to take any of these steps. Their fear soon became a self-fulfilling scenario. Exploiting the vacuum of political leadership, the hard-core Communists rose as if from the dead to mount a final disruptive offensive. In the Ruhr Valley they put together a militia of some fifty thousand workers, a "Red Ruhr Army," to assault military posts and police stations throughout the entire industrial basin.

And once again, with the approval of the Social Democratic government, the Freikorps struck back with cold ferocity. This time over a thousand workers—men, women, Red Cross nurses—were mowed down. The Communists would not recover. But neither would the Social Democrats. In the Reichstag elections of June 1920, their party lost sixty seats. Their smaller allies, the Centrists and Democrats, also lost badly. By contrast, the two main conservative parties doubled their strength. Socially polarized, Germany had created a political monster, a Reichstag that henceforth would live on without a pro-democratic majority. The Weimar Republic would not overcome the crippling legacy of its birth.

Neither would the nation's Jewish minority. They had faced the turmoil of the postwar era with a gnawing presentiment of their own vulnerability. Their numbers unquestionably had grown, to 565,000 (under the 1925 census). The influx of nearly 70,000 East European refugees had more than compensated for war losses and a limited postwar emigration. Yet Jews still constituted less than one percent of the German population; and it was specifically for that reason that their role in the early postwar economy loomed even further out of proportion to their modest numbers. Three-quarters of the Jewish work force congregated in middle-class occupations, with over 60 percent of these in commerce. As late as 1930, Jews owned almost half of Germany's textile companies, a quarter of all wholesale food companies, some two-thirds of Germany's larger department stores and chain stores. At least half of Upper Silesia's industry, including its largest steel conglomerate, was either owned or managed by Jews.

Moreover, nearly half the nation's private banks were owned by such renowned Jewish families as the Mendelsohns, Bleichróders, Schlesingers, and Warburgs (although private banks were losing out by then to the more powerful corporate banking houses). In the publishing sector, Jews easily maintained their historic leadership. The two largest German publishing houses, Ullstein and Mosse, were Jewish-owned (p. 257), and Jewish journalists remained exceptionally prominent in the liberal and left-wing press. Elsewhere in the professions, Jews by 1933 represented 11 percent of Germany's doctors, 16 percent of its lawyers and notaries—and more than 50 percent of the lawyers in Berlin (p. 257).

Affluent luminaries hardly were typical of the Jewish majority, however, not even of the middle-class majority. Throughout the early postwar period, some 15 percent of all German Jews either were refugees or the children of refugees from Eastern Europe. Impacted into the nation's commercial and industrial centers, helpless to protect themselves against the complicated and protracted naturalization regulations of individual German Länder (p. 207), the newcomers remained subject to chronic unemployment and sporadic official harassment. At least three-quarters even of the "native" Jewish Mittelstand were proprietors of small, often quite modest retail establishments, and thus were uniquely vulnerable to larger competitors. Together with the Gentile white-collar population, they were badly hurt, often ruined, during the postwar inflation. By late 1923, Berlin's Jewish Kultusverein maintained nineteen soup kitchens and seven shelters for destitute Jews. And later yet, when the world depression struck, the sixty thousand Jewish unemployed (in 1932) represented essentially the same proportion as among non-Jewish unemployed.

By the same token, if German-Jewish demography was middle-class, Jewish social values similarly reflected those of the wider German Mittelstand. Patriotism was one of these. Horror-stricken at the territorial losses inflicted by the Versailles Treaty, the largest majority of Jews in the eastern, amputated Polish Corridor regions aligned themselves with the German cause, both for reasons of pro-German sentiment and for fear of the notoriously antisemitic Poles. Some Jews actually joined the clandestine Freikorps units that fought to keep the eastern lands German. In the Rhineland, Jews demonstratively shunned all contact with the occupying French army; and upon the liberation of this territory from French military rule, in 1930, Rabbi Max Dinemann delivered a sermon at Offenbach-am-Main, comparing the event to the deliverance of the ancient Hebrews from their wanderings in the desert.

At all times, too, the immersion of Jews in German life remained full-hearted. Registration of their children in the public school system was hardly less than the marque of their patriotism (and doubtless of their growing secularism). Of 194 private Jewish elementary schools that had functioned in Prussia before the war, only 99 were left in 1927. In Bavaria, during the same period, less than half the prewar era's 84 Jewish schools survived. Not all Jews welcomed this intensified acculturation, to be sure. The East Europeans' tradition of cultural ethnicity persisted—and in turn stiffened the resistance of "veteran" Jews to Polish-Jewish immigration. On the one hand, the "veterans" dutifully maintained a wide spectrum of philanthropic services for the wartime refugees. In the early postwar period, however, they tended to share the public and official conviction that the nation's shattered economy required a closure of the eastern borders.

It was thus a Prussian Jew, Fritz Rathenau, a cousin of Walther, who drafted the 1920 edict of the Prussian ministry of the interior, sealing that Land's frontiers against East European immigrants. The action met with widespread Jewish approval. "[I]f impoverished Germany cuts off immigration from the East for economic and political reasons," declared Berlin's Rabbi Felix Goldmann, "that is a decision that has nothing whatever to do with a specifically Jewish viewpoint. It has to do with purely political and economic issues, and today it is the best Jews who speak out as Germans against immigration into Germany."

And yet, these credentials of Jewish patriotism and "respectability" notwithstanding, the upheavals of the immediate postwar years had imprinted the image of Jewish radicalism indelibly in the German mind. This was ironic. Even into the 1920s, a majority of German Jews continued to vote for liberal, middle-class parties. Politically, their major port of call remained the Democratic party (Deutsche Demokratisches Partei—the

DDP), an amalgam of the venerable National Liberal and Progressive parties that had claimed Jewish allegiance in the last decades of the Empire (pp. 214–15). Jewish businessmen and professionals still continued to exercise important roles in the DDP, contributing their funds and energies as well as their votes, and thereby earning for the DDP the sobriquet "Judenpartei."

It was a Jewish jurist, moreover, Hugo Preuss, who emerged as arguably the party's most significant intellectual influence. A professor of jurisprudence at the Berlin Handelshochschule (College of Commerce), Preuss in the prewar era already had become one of Germany's most prolific and respected authorities on public law. No mere closet scholar, Preuss was continually recruited to serve on various Land and other public commissions, and he lost no chance vigorously to press his case for governmental democratization. Thus, immediately after the fall of the empire, the fifty-year-old Preuss published a carefully reasoned article in the *Berliner Tageblatt*, warning against the resuscitation of an authoritarian regime, whether of the right or of the left. Only a day and a half later, Cabinet Chairman Ebert invited Preuss to his office, appointed him deputy minister of the interior, and asked him to proceed forthwith to draft a constitution for the new German Republic.

The urgency of the assignment did not intimidate Preuss. He had given thirty years of thought to an appropriate basic law, and accordingly managed to complete his first version in time for the opening of the National Assembly in Weimar on February 6, 1919. The delegates set to work on the document at once. In negotiating the final draft with them, Preuss exhibited flexibility and imagination (for example, keeping the term "Reichstag"—Imperial Parliament—for emotional reasons). With only minor exceptions, the "Weimar Constitution" proved in its time to be possibly the most liberal public law ever formulated in Europe—if one of the least durable.

Although there is no precise record of Jewish voting statistics in the republican period, one estimate suggests an average for the 1920s of approximately 65 percent for the Democratic party, 30 percent for the Social Democrats, with the rest scattered. But if a majority of Jewish voters continued to give their votes to the Democrats at least until the mid-1920s, the visibility and influence of Jews in the leftist factions soon appeared overwhelming. Among the Communists, it is recalled, even after the deaths of Luxemburg and Jogiches, the party's chairmanship devolved upon the fiery trial lawyer Paul Levi. Jews also played their well-familiar roles as party activists, editors, and theorists. For that matter, a substantial contingent of Communist deputies in the Reichstag bore such names as Rosenberg, Rosenbaum, Schwarz, Katz, Scholem, and Eppstein. Only by mid-decade, after Joseph Stalin's protégé Ernst Thalmann took over leadership of Germany's Communist party, was the Jewish presence on its central committee and its parliamentary delegations phased out.

It was in the latter 1920s, meanwhile, as Germany's liberal-center parties began veering steadily to the right, that the Social Democrats consolidated their position among possibly a majority of German Jews. Even before the war, Jews had emerged as a highly visible and dynamic element in the party, most of them identified with its moderate, "revisionist" majority. Afterward, in Friedrich Ebert's first postwar government, Otto Landsberg served as Social Democratic "commissar" in the "Council of Commissars," while another Jew, Hugo Haase, represented the Independent Socialists in the same cabinet (the two wings would reunite in 1922). In the coalition cabinet formed under Philipp Scheidemann after the National Assembly elections of January 1919, Landsberg and the Independent Socialist Emanuel Wurm served as government ministers. Rudolf Hilferding was finance minister in the first Stresemann coalition cabinet of 1923 and in the later Müller cabinet of 1929.

In 1925, Jews provided 10 percent of the delegates to the Social Democratic party congress. Of the sixty Jews who served intermittently in the Reichstag from 1919 to 1928, thirty-five were Social Democrats, while the rest either were Democrats or Communists. Beyond the central government, there was additional evidence of a decisive Jewish political reorientation leftward. Paul Hirsch, a Jewish Social Democrat, served as the first minister-president of Prussia in 1919–20; while Ernst Heilmann, the "uncrowned king of Prussia," was the longtime chairman of the Social Democratic delegation in the Prussian Landtag. And, as always, Jews served in disproportionate numbers at all levels of the Social Democratic party as economists, lawyers, journalists, educators, and technical experts.

Yet the leftward repositioning of Jewish political loyalties was accompanied by another, not unrelated development. This was a perceptible diminution of Jewish political visibility altogether. Indeed, the postwar sunburst of Jewish political leadership, whether in revolutionary or elected governments, proved a notably evanescent phenomenon. After Curt Joël, a nonparty appointee, held the Republic's justice portfolio in 1931–32, no Jew ever again served as a minister in the national government. Similarly, the number of Jews in Land governments continued to shrink after 1922, as did the Jewish membership of Reichstag delegations. Fourteen Jews sat in the first Reichstag of 1920. In 1932, there was one. The two developments—the Jewish ground-level shift to the political left and the atrophy of Jewish political visibility at the upper levels of government—were intimately linked. Both reflected an exponential upsurge of political and popular antisemitism.

"Knallt ab den Walther Rathenau"

It was specifically in the economic and political chaos of 1919–23 that Jew-hatred acquired a virulence unprecedented in modern German history. The venom drew its sustenance from multiple sources. The most obvious, even the most simplistic, was the highly visible role of Jews in the left-wing extremism of the early postwar years. Another was the historic anti-Jewish bias of Germany's religious denominations, particularly its Evangelical Church, long a supporter of authoritarian government. Still another was the venerable class stratification of aristocratic and court circles, not excluding the kaiser himself, who stereotyped the Jews as a "toadstool on the German oak." Nor was any adherent of Pan-Germanism inclined to minimize the role of Jews as "internationalists" and "treasonous pacifists."

The conservatives of the prewar empire had found it useful to stigmatize liberalism as Jewish. Now, in the postwar era, far-rightists devised the strategy of characterizing the Weimar experiment as nothing less than a "Jew Republic." In that effort, they orchestrated their antisemitic campaign with authentic German efficiency. Before the war, the nation's aggregation of far-rightist parties, leagues, and minigroups had never managed a coordinated effort. But in February 1919, gathering in Hamburg as an "Anti-Revolutionary Convention," a wide spectrum of these factions laid the groundwork for a German People's League for Protection and Defiance (Deutsch-völkisch Schutz-und-Trotzbund). In ensuing months, the league in turn served as a nucleus for the Community of German People's Unions (Gemeinschaft deutschvölkische Bunds). By 1922, the "Community" had grown to 250,000 members in 250 branches and had distributed some 7.6 million pamphlets, 4.7 million prospectuses, and 7.9 million propaganda stamps. All focused on the Jews: as subversives, malingerers, and profiteers during the war; as economic parasites and political radicals immediately after the war; and, above all, as the éminences grises behind the Weimar Republic.

It was during the postwar years, too, that "Aryan" racism acquired a new and highly politicized intensity. The pseudoscience extended well back to the nineteenth century, to the writings of Wilhelm Marr, who first coined the term "antisemitism," and applied it in 1879 in his best-selling apocalyptic pamphlet, "The Victory of Judaism over Germanism" ("Der Sieg des Judenthums über das Germanenthum"). Afterward, the ex-Socialist Eugen Dühring gave the "racial struggle" against Jews a consistent ideological foundation. The renewal of German culture, Dühring argued, demanded a forthright repudiation of Jewish religious ideology and Jewish social mores—both characteristic of the "Semitic mind," and both thereby inimical to "Aryan civilization."

The composer Richard Wagner was only one of the many German cultural icons who eagerly subscribed to the new racist ideology. In the last prewar decades, the Aryan myth became particularly attractive to the lower-middle class, those clerks, pensioners, and small shopkeepers who felt themselves deeply threatened by the juggernaut of modern capitalism, an "alien" force that presumably was subject to manipulation by an "alien" race. And in the havoc of the postwar period, the concept of Aryanism appealed with especial poignancy to the identical Kleinbürgertum, the element most thoroughly deracinated by the inflation of the 1920s, and thus most prone to take compensatory solace in their own "superior" racial pedigree.

As elsewhere in postwar Europe, a prefiguration of this white-collar vindictiveness was to be found among Germany's university students. Plain and simple fear of Jewish professional competition unquestionably was a factor in their animus, and so was völkisch, post-adolescent romanticism. In the Weimar Republic, universities were forbidden to adopt a numerus clausus. Discrimination consequently took a more social form. Jews were excluded from student societies and mercilessly hazed in university dormitories. Jewish professors occasionally were harassed. Even Albert Einstein found his lectures at the Kaiser Wilhelm Institute periodically hectored by völkisch student groups. Evincing a cultivated distaste for Jewish "modernism," "leftism," and—increasingly—racial "levantinism," faculty members in large numbers similarly gravitated to the political right.

Germany's Jews for their part could have survived an antisemitism that remained essentially verbal and social. As late as 1923, the entire antisemitic vote, including ballots cast for the ultrarightist Nationalist party (by no means a one-issue faction), never exceeded 8 percent. Physical attacks on "private" Jews still were comparatively rare. Then, in 1923, as the French army occupied the Ruhr to compel German reparations payments, and as the German mark collapsed, rage suddenly boiled over. On November 5, thousands of impoverished and infuriated Germans, blue-collar and white-collar alike, descended on Berlin's Scheunenviertel district, where numerous East European refugee families lived and operated tiny shops. For the ensuing day and a half, hundreds of Jews were beaten and nearly a thousand Jewish stores were ransacked before police managed to end the violence and looting.

Thuggery and pillage were by no means the only—nonpolitical—aberrations committed by a traditionally law-abiding people. More ominous, in the revolutionary and counterrevolutionary hatreds of the early postwar era, was the growing frequency of political assassination. The Heidelberg historian E. J. Gumbel has calculated that 376 political homicides were carried out in Germany between 1918 and 1922, and overwhelmingly by the ideological right. Eminent Gentiles among the victims included, in

August 1921, Matthias Erzberger, the Catholic Centrist statesman who had signed the armistice. Yet the majority of these "executions" were committed against Jews. Most were leftist Jews: Luxemburg, Jogiches, Landauer, Mühsam, and even Hugo Haase, the Independent Socialist who cochaired the Ebert cabinet. In 1922, however, Maximilian Harden, editor of the moderate-progressive journal *Die Zukunft*, was beaten nearly to death by two rightist strong-arm men. He survived, but was left paralyzed. When the assailants were brought to trial, they argued that Harden had been disloyal to Germany as a writer of unpatriotic articles; and that, as a Jew who had changed his name from Witkowski, Harden had gotten no more than he deserved. The jury evidently agreed. It returned a verdict of "battery without intent to kill," and the court sentenced the defendants to one-year prison terms.

The assault on Maximilian Harden may have appalled even German ultraconservatives. Yet the deepest shock was evoked by the fate of a personage who embodied nearly every virtue of public-spirited German patriotism. As the war neared its end, Walther Rathenau had pleaded with the chancellor, Prince Max of Baden, to save the Empire by rushing through a program of far-reaching constitutional reforms. When the revolution no longer could be stayed, however, Rathenau accepted the birth of the new republic philosophically. Still in his early fifties, he was too restless and engagé to withdraw from national affairs. For the first (and last) time, he contemplated running for the new National Assembly as a candidate of the Democratic party—until the distrustful party leaders sabotaged the notion by assigning him a low, essentially unelectable slot on their list of nominees.

The man plainly remained an ambivalent figure in public consciousness. Even "respectable" conservatives pigeonholed him as a rich Jewish intellectual manqué, while Social Democrats typed him merely as a successful industrialist of kindly instincts. Returning to his base at the AEG conglomerate, the chastened Rathenau for the while expressed his national concerns exclusively in writing. In December 1918, on the eve of the Peace Conference, he published an "Open Letter to Colonel Edward House," President Wilson's closest adviser. "If vindictiveness [to Germany] prevails . . . ," he warned, "then . . . a horde of [Bolshevik] desperadoes will be encamped before the doors of Western civilization." In 1919, Rathenau found time to produce two small books, *Apologia* and *Der Kaiser*, in which he deplored the polarization of German political life.

In 1920, he gradually was drawn back again into public service. Josef Wirth, a member of the Catholic Center party and finance minister in the Social Democrat–dominated coalition government, consulted Rathenau with growing frequency. Both men had been trained as engineers; both were lonely bachelors and workaholics. They soon became warm friends. In July 1920, Wirth persuaded Rathenau to help him grapple with the burning reparations issue. Like all Germans, they regarded this feature of the Versailles Treaty as gratuitously punitive. Nevertheless, Rathenau supported an honorable effort to fulfill its terms. Only through "Erfül-lungspolitik," he contended, the punctilious observance of national obliga-tions, could Germany regain Allied trust, and thereby win a possible future revision of the payments schedule. Wirth reacted well to the suggestion.

Then, in May 1921, Wirth himself became chancellor of a new, Centrist-dominated coalition government. One of his first acts was to appoint Rathenau "minister of reconstruction," in effect, minister for repa-rations. Taking leave of his business affairs, Rathenau promptly hurled himself into a tireless round of negotiations with the Allied governments, seeking a formula for easing the reparations burden. Over the months, his diplomacy made a certain headway. By December, Britain's Prime Minister Lloyd George seemed receptive to a more flexible approach to Germany's economic problems.

Rathenau's functional role as diplomat soon would be institutionalized. In early spring of 1922, Wirth asked him to accept the portfolio of foreign affairs. It was an act of rare courage on the chancellor's part, for he was ten-dering the government's pivotal ministry to a Jew. Rathenau consented, although he understood rather better than Wirth the depth of Germany's seething nationalist passions, the ideological and personal attacks he was likely to face. His mother was altogether shaken by his acceptance (he had not dared inform her in advance). When he lunched with her the next day, both sat in long silence until she could bear it no longer and said: "Walther, why have you done this to me?" "I really had to, Mama," he replied. "[T]hey could not find anyone else." The explanation was accu-rate. Rathenau alone appeared free of political affiliations; his appointment did not affect the cabinet balance. More important, he was trusted by the Allies.

That faith soon would be put to the test. In April 1922, Rathenau as foreign minister prepared to accompany Chancellor Wirth to Genoa for a conference on European economic reconstruction. The meeting was a crucial one. Not only would Western European leaders be present, but a Russian delegation also would attend for the first time since the Bolshevik Revolution. Following the end of the war, German foreign ministry offi-cials had explored two lines of approach to Soviet Russia. One group favored the Western Allied policy of a diplomatic quarantine. Others advo-cated a cautious rapprochement with Moscow. Rathenau himself remained open-minded. In April 1919, at his own expense, he had sent a personal aide to Russia to gather information about the new Leninist regime. Soon afterward, he led a small group of industrialists in organizing a study commission on Russia. In late 1919 and early 1920, he twice visited the imprisoned Karl Radek, who had participated in the abortive Spartacist uprising. In Radek's Berlin cell, the two men cautiously explored the notion of increased trade between Germany and Russia.

As late as April 1922, Rathenau still believed that a reconciliation with the Western Allies deserved priority. But once in Genoa, he sensed that his hopes of Allied forbearance on reparations were premature. For five days, as discussions on general European issues plodded on, Rathenau repeatedly and vainly sought a private audience with Lloyd George. Could the Western statesmen themselves be conducting secret meetings with the Russians, he wondered, plotting a deal at Germany's expense? Then, at 2:00 a.m. on April 16, Ago von Maltzen, director of the foreign ministry's Russian department, appeared in Rathenau's hotel room with unexpected news. Soviet Foreign Commissar Georgi Chicherin had just telephoned to invite the Germans to a private meeting later that day in Rapallo, a nearby resort town. Still in his pajamas, Rathenau immediately moved to Chancellor Wirth's suite next door. After much discussion, both men agreed that Rathenau should meet with Chicherin and "play the Russian card."

The German and Russian foreign ministers accordingly conferred that same afternoon. By 6:30 that evening they had signed the "Treaty of Rapallo." The document provided for a mutual repudiation of claims for war costs and damages, mutual trade relations on a most-favored-nation basis, and the immediate establishment of diplomatic relations. The understanding thus ended each nation's economic and international isolation, and allowed each a substantial new maneuverability vis-à-vis the Western Allies. Yet, for all the Rapallo agreement's potential advantages to Germany, its immediate consequence was to strip the Wirth government of the confidence it had begun to elicit among Western statesmen, and to preclude its much-coveted alleviation of reparations. The consequence for Rathenau personally was even graver. Long outraged by the very notion of "Erfüllungspolitik," his rightist enemies now could denounce him not only as a Jew, a defeatist, and a traitor, but as a Bolshevik and a Russian agent.

On the evening of June 23, 1922, Rathenau held a lengthy dinner meeting with one of his most implacable critics, Dr. Karl Helfferich, a former minister in the imperial government and currently a member of the Reichstag's far-rightist Nationalist delegation. The discussion was exhaustive, as each man sought to find a limited common ground with the other, and it continued until the early hours of June 24. Rathenau thus slept somewhat later the next morning, not leaving his home in Berlin's Grünewald suburb until 10:45. He was seated in the back of his open limousine as his chauffeur pulled out of the driveway onto the main road. On a side street nearby, others were lying in wait.

The previous April, a seventeen-year-old gymnasium student, Hans Stubenrauch, had confided his intention of assassinating Rathenau to a classmate, Hans-Martin Günther. The son of a retired Reichswehr general, Stubenrauch was a member of the ultranationalist League of the Upright (Bund der Aufrechten). Upon Rathenau's return from Genoa at the end of May, the two youths discussed their intention with a twenty-five-year-old ex–naval officer, Erwin Kern, and the latter's friend, Hermann Fischer, also twenty-five. Both Kern and Fischer were members of Organization Consul, a terrorist society formed out of the Freikorps' notorious Eckardt Brigade, and a group fully sharing Stubenrauch's hatred of Rathenau. It was Organization Consul that popularized the imprecation:

> *Knallt ab den Walther Rathenau*
> *Die gottverdammte Judensau.*
> *(Liquidate that Walther Rathenau*
> *The goddamned Jew-pig.)*

Through Fischer, Kern contacted yet another likely partner from Organization Consul. This was Ernst-Werner Techow, twenty-one, the son of a deceased Berlin magistrate. The young men then set about formulating a plan for the murder.

On the evening of June 18, Kern, Günther, Fischer, and Techow, together with Techow's younger brother Gerd, age sixteen, and still another chauvinist romantic, Ernst von Salamon, twenty-two, who had been recruited at the last moment for his expert knowledge of getaway routes—all met at the home of Techow's widowed mother to plot their ambush. Finally, on the morning of June 24, the six conspirators parked their automobile on a side street of the Königsallee. It was their good luck that the foreign minister was personally contemptuous of danger and had steadfastly refused all police protection. Britain's Ambassador, Viscount Edgar d'Abernon, recalled that Rathenau had "often told me he is sure to be assassinated," but had seemed almost eerily fatalistic about the prospect.

Rathenau's presentiment was not mere poetry. In late May, Chancellor Wirth received a visit from the papal nuncio, Monsignor Eugenio Pacelli (later Pope Pius XII). Without revealing names, Pacelli stated only that a priest had divulged to him a plot against the foreign minister. Wirth later gave Count Harry Kessler an account of the conversation:

> [Pacelli] informed me simply and soberly in a few sentences that Rathenau's life was in danger. I could not question him: the interview took place in absolute privacy. . . . Then Rathenau himself was called in. I implored him . . . to give up his resistance to increased police protection . . . [but] he stubbornly refused. . . . With a calm such as I

have never witnessed in my life . . . he stepped up to me, and putting both his hands on my shoulders, said: "Dear friend, it is nothing. Who would do me any harm?"

He got his answer at 10:45 a.m. on June 24.

As Rathenau's automobile reached the Königsallee, it slowed to cross a pair of streetcar tracks. Here it was that young Techow, driving the assassins' vehicle, pulled up beside the foreign minister's open limousine, aimed his pistol carefully at close range, and fired off a quick succession of shots. Rathenau fell back. Fischer then stood up and threw a grenade into the car. It exploded a few moments later, after the murderers' vehicle had sped off. Rathenau's chauffeur raced his automobile to a nearby police station, and a woman who had witnessed the scene jumped into the backseat and tried to help. She was a nurse. But it was too late. By the time a doctor arrived, Rathenau was dead.

Meanwhile the assassins had abandoned their car and fled Berlin for the Baltic port of Warnemünde, where they expected to book passage to Sweden. But with no vessel available, they purchased bicycles and turned back southward. For almost a month, Kern and Fischer hid in an abandoned castle in a dense, rarely traveled forest. But at last, in July, they were located and cornered in their shelter. As the police closed in, Kern was slain in an exchange of fire. Fischer then shot himself. The thirteen surviving conspirators, active and marginal, eventually underwent a trial. All were found guilty of murder or of being accessories to murder. The court sentenced Techow to fifteen years in prison, a term that later was commuted to seven years. In fact, he served only four years, then went back to school and became a lawyer. Salamon served five years in prison and eventually became a screenwriter. After World War II, he wrote the immensely popular novel *Fragebogen*, satirizing Allied efforts to de-nazify Germany. The other defendants received even shorter sentences. In July 1933, eleven years after the deaths of Kern and Fischer, the Nazis mounted a parade to their graves, where Heinrich Himmler gave a memorial address.

By noon of June 25, 1922, when news of Rathenau's death became generally known, workers streamed out of the factories and began marching through the streets. Harry Kessler recalled: "Four deep, they marched in their hundreds of thousands, beneath their mourning banners, the red of Socialism and the black-red-gold of the Republic, in one endless disciplined procession, passing like a portent silently along the great thoroughfare lined by immense crowds, wave after wave, from the early afternoon until late into the June sunset." Addressing a stunned Reichstag that same day, Chancellor Wirth denounced both the assassins and their supporters. "The real enemies of our country are those who instill this poison into our people," he declared bitterly. "We know where . . . to seek them. The enemy stands on the right [Der Feind steht rechts]." On June 26, the funeral service was conducted in the Reichstag gallery. The orchestra of the State Opera played the "Coriolanus Overture" and Siegfried's funeral march from Wagner's *Götterdämmerung*. President Friedrich Ebert delivered the oration. Afterward the cortege, with an honor guard and a rolling of drums, proceeded through the Brandenburg Gate to the Rathenau family plot. As at Kurt Eisner's funeral three and a half years before, no *kaddish* was intoned.

Later in 1922, during the trial of the conspirators, it happened that Techow's mother, the widow of a respectable magistrate, was subjected to insults on the streets and in the shops. When Rathenau's mother learned of this indignity, she wrote Frau Techow a famous letter:

In grief unspeakable I give my hand to you, the most pitiable of women. Tell your son that I forgive him, as may God forgive him, if he makes a full and frank confession before earthly justice and repents before heavenly justice. If he had known my son, the noblest man whom earth ever bore, he would rather have turned the murder weapon against himself than against him. May these words give peace to your soul.

Every year on June 24, over the next decade, elaborate ceremonies were conducted throughout Germany, sponsored by the Democratic League, the Republican ex-Soldiers League, and other Social Democratic and liberal organizations. It was the custom for solemn poetry to be read, addresses to be delivered, orchestral dirges to be played. Converted into a museum, Rathenau's town house became the headquarters for the Walther Rathenau Society. There was also a Walther Rathenau Foundation devoted to studies on his life and career. "In the twenties," astutely wrote one of his biographers, "the prewar Rathenau, the social climber, the imperialist, the businessman and the metaphysician dropped out of sight to be replaced by Rathenau the peacemaker, the European, and the realist, or else by Rathenau the traitor and appeaser."

German Jewry manifestly shared in the canonization of Rathenau. Choosing to overlook his earlier, notorious article "Hear O Israel," they apotheosized him as a man who "proved to his country and his times more forcibly than anybody else that there is no contradiction between complete loyalty to the German state and pride in Jewish faith and tradition." This for a man who all his life refused to join the Jewish Kultusverein. Rathenau might appropriately have been taken at his own word when he insisted: "I am a German of Jewish descent. My people is the German people, my fatherland is Germany, my religion that Germanic faith which is above all else religious."

The self-appraisal was characteristic of a significant minority within the Jewish population, from Rosa Luxemburg and a vast skein of Jewish leftist idealists, whose Socialist humanity transcended issues of ethnicity (p. 211), to the formidable Rathenau himself whose "Jewishness" was little more than a contemptuous refusal to apostatize. Germany was their Heimat, their homeland, their "cradleland," virtually their secular religion. Reflecting on that Heimat during his imprisonment, Ernst Toller expressed its heartbreaking elusiveness as well as any:

> [I] thought of the first day of the war and my passionate longing to prove that I was a real German by offering my life to my country: of my writing from the Front to the [Jewish] authorities to say that they could strike my name from the list of the Kultusverein. Had it all been for nothing? Had it all been wrong?

IX

MINERVA'S OWL AT WEIMAR'S TWILIGHT

Weimar in Cultural Memory

When one thinks of Weimar Germany, suggests Peter Gay, the renowned historian of modern European culture, one thinks of Expressionism in art, literature, and music, of libertinism against old-fashioned moralism. Yet Gay reminds us that much of Weimar's avant-gardism was conceived in the last decades of the Empire and was gestating vigorously well before the fall of the kaiser. The Republic merely liberated ideas and movements that already were structurally in place. Moreover, even as the brassy, iconoclastic Weimar style predated the Republic itself, so Weimar culture transcended the frontiers of geographical Germany. Virtually all the famed German Expressionist artists had studied or worked in other countries, particularly in France, Italy, and the Netherlands. Many of the greatest German writers of this period—Werfel, Kafka, Freud, Kraus, Stefan Zweig—were citizens of other countries or fulfilled their careers outside Germany. All contributed to the Weimar "style," to its toughness of fiber, its unselfconscious internationalism, its contempt for chauvinism.

That style, insolent and astringent, came to be associated primarily with Berlin, a city that achieved its edgiest resonance during the post-armistice years. A representative constellation of European intellectuals either gravitated to Berlin or oriented their work to the Berlin tempo. Thus, Kurt Tucholsky, living in Paris, wrote his affectionate ditties and nostalgic sketches about Berlin. Willy Haas, Prague-born and living in Berlin, where he edited the literary magazine *Literarische Welt*, acknowledged his admiration for the German capital, its "delightfully understated, cool . . . ambience, [its] indescribable dynamic, [its] work ethic, [its] vigor, [its] willingness to accept hard blows and carry on." Stefan Zweig, professing to find Berlin a corrupt Babylon, actually was fascinated by the city and alluded to it repeatedly in his writings. The symphonic conductor Bruno Walter recalled Berlin in the mid-1920s as "electric" with its literature and cabarets, its theaters and concert halls, its extravagance of books, journals, and newspapers. Not least of all, as the poet Gottfried Benn acknowledged in his autobiography, Berlin's culture—Weimar culture—consciously or unconsciously was forever identified with the Jews.

The linkage was an irony of sorts, for the Jews were by no means principally responsible for Weimar culture or for many of its most impressive achievements. The left-wing plays of Bertolt Brecht were much better than those of Ernst Toller. No Jewish novelist was as great as Thomas Mann. Nor was the composer Paul Hindemith or the architect Walter Gropius less controversial or creative than their Jewish counterparts, Arnold Schönberg and Erich Mendelsohn. In intellectual creativity as in business and politics, Jews in their middle-class status typically were inclined toward the behavior and tastes of German society at large. Even so, Jewish cultural eminence, if not predominance, already had become a central fact of life in the last years of the Empire. In 1913, the critic Moritz Goldstein noted with some concern that "German cultural life seems to be passing increasingly into Jewish hands. . . . We Jews are administering the spiritual property of a nation which denies us our right and our ability to do so."

Goldstein's anxieties notwithstanding, Jews soon were contributing even more vibrantly to the diversity and effervescence of Weimar culture than they had to the intellectual life of the Wilhelminian era. It was the Republic, after all, that offered a traditionally suspect minority people vocational opportunities unmatched in any other major continental nation. Those openings were still erratic. After the brief interregnum of revolutionary upheaval, Jewish political eminence faded rapidly. Teaching opportunities in universities were not substantially more abundant for Jews during the 1920s than in the prewar decades. Indeed, university faculties and student bodies alike were even more poisonously antisemitic than before the war (p. 215). It was nevertheless during the Weimar years that a coruscation of Jewish academics achieved international recognition. In science, five of nine Nobel Prizes won by Germans went to Jews—two for medicine, three for physics. In the humanities and social sciences, Jews produced such heavyweights as the philosophers Ernst Cassirer and Edmund Husserl, the historians Ernst Kantorowicz, Gustav Mayer, and Erwin Panofsky, the sociologists Karl Mannheim and Franz Oppenheimer.

Moreover, in their sentience to the fragility of the new democratic experiment, Jewish social scientists displayed an almost feverish obsession with the interpretation of contemporary political and social issues. At their initiative, the study of government ("political science" in the United States) became fashionable during the Weimar period, although less within the curriculum of established universities than in "parallel" or "associated" institutes. With Jewish funding, and with a predominantly Jewish faculty, the German Higher School for Politics (Deutsche Hochschule für Politik) opened in 1920, and by 1932 its two thousand students—many of them journalists and some of them diplomats—were attending a full program of lecture courses. Similarly, the Institute for Social Research (Institut für Sozialforschung) was underwritten by private Jewish money and staffed principally with Jews, most of whom tended to be liberal or leftist in their political ideology. The institute's first director, Carl Grünberg, was a veteran Socialist, as was his successor (in 1932), Max Horkheimer; and so were its most eminent faculty members, Otto Kirschheimer, Leo Löwenthal, Herbert Marcuse, Friedrich Pollock, Felix Weil, and Theodor Adorno. A scintillating group, they produced a series of volumes that were unsurpassed in their analysis of contemporary political and social developments, both in Germany and in the institute's post-Weimar incarnation in New York.

The Jewish presence in the legal profession, meanwhile, continued to bulk formidably large. In the mid-1920s, not less than a quarter of the lawyers practicing in Prussia were Jews, and over half the lawyers in Berlin (p. 242). More palpable yet was the Jewish role in Weimar journalism. The network of liberal and Socialist-oriented newspapers—most affiliated with various political parties—was the largest in Germany, and their staffs, often known as the "linke Intellektuelle," were heavily Jewish. Even Germany's most respected non-"affiliated" newspaper, the mighty *Frankfurter Zeitung*, whose superb coverage touched on virtually everything in modern political and cultural affairs, was owned by the Sonnemann family, and its editorial staff also was largely Jewish. Another Jewish family, the Mosses (p. 242), owned the *Berliner Tageblatt*, Germany's most widely read liberal newspaper. Again, with few exceptions, the *Tageblatt*'s editorial staff was Jewish.

Yet even the Mosses could not quite approach the journalistic influence of the Ullstein family, owners of the single largest publishing conglomerate in Europe. In addition to its extensive book and magazine divisions, the House of Ullstein published four daily newspapers in Berlin alone, including the *Berliner Morgenpost*, with the single largest mass press circulation, 1.8 million, in the German-speaking world. Beyond its publishing empire, Ullstein revolutionized newspaper publishing in Germany by employing hundreds of foreign correspondents, by establishing its own wire service, its own photographic agency, even its own travel bureau. Under the direction of Dr. Franz Ullstein, senior among five brother-partners, the nominally apolitical House of Ullstein in practical fact adopted a liberal and internationalist stance in public affairs.

For moderate-left intellectuals, however, the most influential galaxy of "progressive" journals in early Weimar Germany included *Das Tagebuch*, a weekly founded in 1920 by Stefan Grossman and Leopold Schwarzschild; Karl Kraus's *Fackel* (which enjoyed a wider readership in Germany than in its native Austria), and supremely Maximilian Harden's renowned *Zukunft*. Yet once Harden was forced into early retirement by paralysis, the consequence of a near-fatal beating by right-wing assailants (p. 248), his *Zukunft* was rapidly supplanted by *Die Weltbühne* as Germany's preeminent left-liberal journal. Thereafter, for the nation's progressive idealists, with their large Jewish quotient, the *Weltbühne* more than any other political-cultural publication became an ideological home. Established in 1904 under the early editorship of Siegfried Jacobsohn, the *Weltbühne* achieved its fullest resonance only after 1926, when Kurt Tucholsky became its editor and intellectual guide.

The son of a middle-class Berlin Jewish family, Tucholsky had spent the largest part of the war in battle action on the eastern front. The experience transformed him into a committed pacifist. Although trained originally as a lawyer, he turned to journalism and launched his professional writing career in 1918 as a contributor to the *Weltbühne* and a defender of Germany's Socialist revolution. It was not a political stance that endured. As the months passed, witnessing the murder of Luxemburg and Liebknecht and the re-entrenchment of the old imperial military and civil service establishment, Tucholsky tended increasingly to parody the Weimar experiment as a "Scheindemokratie," an "illusory democracy." Later, as editor of the *Weltbühne*, he shared columns with ideological soulmates, although few of them could match his caustic brilliance. Emphasizing caricature and satire rather than straightforward political analysis, the journal under Tucholsky's editorship soon developed into the very conscience of Germany's liberal-left.

And by the same token, the *Weltbühne*'s editorial staff became an object of rage for political reactionaries, not least because Tucholsky and so many of his "nest of traitors" were Jews (although, for careerist reasons, he himself had converted to Protestantism as a young man). Ironically, Tucholsky soon became an unwitting ally of this anti-republican camp. In his eyes, the Social Democrats and other progressives were as legitimate a target for his scathing derision as the political right. They had "betrayed" the revolution, after all. In 1929, despairing of Germany's political future altogether, Tucholsky departed in voluntary exile for Sweden. It was in Sweden, in 1933, following the Nazi takeover at home, that he committed suicide. Decades later, Professor Golo Mann (the son of Thomas Mann) and other liberal historians criticized Tucholsky and the "*Weltbühne* Circle" for playing into the hands of reactionaries with their acerbic maximalism, thereby helping to sabotage the Weimar Republic. The evaluation survives historical scrutiny.

A Mastery of the Volkswesen

For the Jews, a passionate embrace of Germany's Volkswesen, its "cultural essence," had never been a matter simply of facile linguistic mimicry or verbal pyrotechnics. They internalized the German language as an act of reverence. Even for the recent wave of East European refugees, the transition from Yiddish to *Mauscheln* (Yiddish-inflected German) to Hochdeutsch was extraordinarily rapid. As for the veteran Jewish population, command of the German literary tradition had long since become a defining feature both of their acculturation and of their patriotism. Claiming that tradition as their own, ardently caressing it for its every hidden facet and dormant nuance, Jewish belletrists soared almost without warning into contemporary Germany's literary firmament.

Jakob Wassermann may have been their doyen. Born in Fürth, a product of Franconia's deeply traditional Jewish community, Wassermann gained his widest reputation in the early postwar years with his psycho-historical sagas *The Jews of Zirndorf (Die Juden von Zirndorf)*, *Caspar Hauser*, and above all his grandiose two-volume epic of prewar Europe, *The World's Illusion* (the best-known translation of its German title, *Christian Wahnschaffe*). If these works did not quite sustain their moral gravitas beyond the interwar years, neither were they ever exceeded in sheer technical virtuosity. Wassermann's style palpably derived from Balzac and Hugo, and his central theme, the achievement of toleration and brotherhood through the pangs of suffering, was worthy, even noble. In hewing to that moralistic road, Wassermann doubtless was encouraged by the vast popularity of his 1928 novel, *The Maurizius Case (Der Fall Maurizius)*, based on an actual false accusation of financial peculation launched against a Jewish business executive. The book's commercial and critical success prompted Wassermann to deliver lectures on the future adventures of his principal character, Erzel Landergast, before adoring crowds that included the cream of Germany's liberal intelligentsia.

Arnold Zweig, son of a Silesian Jewish shopkeeper, earned his way through university as a precociously successful novelist and playwright. Volunteering for military service in 1914, he survived four years of trench warfare on the western front. Afterward, in a characteristic profile of other Jewish intellectuals, Zweig resumed his literary career as a committed pacifist and Socialist. These were the ideals that animated his best-selling novel, *The Case of Sergeant Grischa (Der Streit um den Sergeanten Grischa)*, published in 1927. One of Germany's two or three most effective war novels, it chronicles the fate of a recaptured Russian prisoner of war. After a long bureaucratic wrangle among the German military command, the hapless Grischa is illegally executed merely for the sake of preserving troop "morale" on the eastern front. The book's runaway acclaim induced Zweig to continue with an ongoing cycle of antiwar novels. None of them quite matched *Grischa* in critical or popular success. In 1933, following the Nazi takeover, Zweig migrated throughout Europe, eventually reaching Palestine in 1940. After the war, destitute and exhausted, he settled in

East Berlin, where he was honored and pensioned by the Communist authorities.

It was Alfred Döblin, however, who emerged as possibly the single most widely read German author of the Weimar period. His output included short stories and novellas, half a dozen full-scale novels, a volume of theater reviews, another of literary criticism, several collections of political essays and satires, an account of his travels in prewar Poland, and still another chronicle of his flight through Paris in 1940—as well as plays and radio and film scripts. Döblin's literary technique, of precise, "clinical" naturalism, reflected his training. The son of a Polish-Jewish tailor, he worked his way through the medical school of Friedrich Wilhelm University, then served as an army doctor during the war. The experience confirmed Döblin's hatred of militarism and Prussian autocracy. It also honed his literary instincts. With the guns thundering in nearby Verdun, Döblin managed during brief intervals at the field hospital to produce two sulfurously anti-militarist novels, one based on the career of Albrecht von Wallenstein, the imperial generalissimo of the Thirty Years War; the other, a political parable set against a Chinese backdrop.

Following Germany's surrender, Döblin as a matter of moral conviction settled into an essentially pro bono practice on behalf of working-class patients in Berlin's grim Alexanderplatz district. There, too, he devoted his every spare moment to writing. Nonpolitical and nonreligious (he renounced Judaism in 1917), denigrating Communism as no less crude and simplistic than right-wing chauvinism, Döblin based his ethical *engagement* on plain and simple humanism. His close friend, Ludwig Marcuse, remembered him as "a cheerful, impetuous jack-in-the-box . . . a [charming] quarreler who was always contradicting everything and who thought heads were meant for running into walls with." Döblin was in his forties when he set to work on his masterpiece, *Berlin Alexanderplatz.*

Published in 1929, the docudrama is an epic impressionistic collage of Berlin's mayhem and terror during the revolutionary postwar years. It has survived also as a classic aperçu of big-city life, of the lonely individual caught up in the pandemonium and anomie of the metropolis. Widely praised as much for its steely prose as for its social and political insights, the novel became an immense critical and popular success. It was also Döblin's last major work before the Nazis came to power. In 1937 he fled to Zurich, and later to the United States. With handouts from friends, he barely kept body and soul together until the end of the war. Afterward, returning to Germany, Döblin spent his last years doing hackwork for the Bundesrepublik's ministry of education.

Lion Feuchtwanger may have been the most forthrightly Jewish of Weimar's literary heavyweights. Born into a prosperous Bavarian Orthodox Jewish family whose nine children all became noted professionals, Feuchtwanger in 1907 earned a doctorate in philology and philosophy at Munich's Ludwig Maximilian University. Soon afterward he became literary editor of the widely read magazine *Der Spiegel*. With the outbreak of the war, shocked by Munich's atmosphere of xenophobia and antisemitism, Feuchtwanger set about writing a series of antiwar articles. Remarkably, he was neither imprisoned nor drafted. Following the armistice, it was specifically the hatred directed at Walther Rathenau, and Rathenau's assassination, that inspired Feuchtwanger's greatest novel, *Jüd Süss*, published in 1925.

A reworking of the career of the famed seventeenth-century court Jew Joseph Süss-Oppenheimer, who was hanged for his role as adviser to the Duke of Württemberg, *Jüd Süss* movingly captured the tragedy of Jewish eminences who presumed to ascend the pinnacle of German political and social life. Widely praised, the novel became a best seller, and was even made into a German silent film. Feuchtwanger followed this triumph with other novels on Jewish and political themes. One of these, *Success (Erfolg)*, a biting account of early Nazism in Feuchtwanger's native Bavaria, also won much critical and popular acclaim. Then, with the accession of Hitler, Feuchtwanger fled, initially to France, where later he was briefly imprisoned following the German conquest, and eventually to the United States in 1941. He remained in the United States, living in moderate comfort, and intermittently contributing articles to the German émigré press, until his death in 1958.

Ultimately, it was Carl Zuckmayer, possessing the keenest instinct among his contemporaries for the popular market, who emerged as the financial "star" of Weimar's literary galaxy. A Rhinelander, born in 1896 of a Jewish mother but raised as a Catholic, Zuckmayer during the war served as an officer on the western front. Although trained as a lawyer, from 1919 on he devoted himself exclusively to playwriting. It was in 1925, after several false starts, that he found his métier with a comedy, *The Joyful Vineyard (Der fröhliche Weinberg)*. Inventively witty and perfectly attuned to audience tastes, it was a spectacular popular success. Four and a half years later, Zuckmayer produced his most celebrated hit, *The Captain from Köpenick (Der Hauptmann von Köpenick)*. Loosely based on an actual episode of 1906, the play was a hilarious spoof of Prussian militarism and arguably the best comedy ever produced in Germany. Performances of the work ran for more than three years. In 1931, Zuckmayer also managed to adapt Heinrich Mann's novel *Professor Unrat* into the scenario for the motion picture *The Blue Angel (Der blaue Engel)*. With the renowned actor Emil Jannings in the lead role, *The Blue Angel* made a young ingenue, Maria Magdalene (Marlene) Dietrich, an instant star. By then, too, Zuckmayer's comedies and screenplays had made him a millionaire, and Germany's most "bank-able" playwright.

The career and personal fate of Else Lasker-Schüler could not have represented a starker contrast. The daughter of a prominent Elberfeld merchant banker, Lasker-Schüler chose to follow her own muse. Twice married and twice divorced, the mother of an illegitimate child, she lived the Expressionism she published, dressing in pantaloons like an oriental potentate, entitling herself "Jussuf, Prince of Thebes," embellishing her exoticism with pitch-black hair and coal-black eyes. In 1902, after Lasker-Schüler published her first volume of poems, *Styx*, the Catholic poet Peter Hille dubbed her "the Hebrew poetess . . . her creative spirit a black diamond . . . the black swan of Israel."

The "Hebrew poetess" characteristically professed much affection for Eastern Jews and their "wonder rabbis," one of whom she extolled in her story "Der Wunderrabbiner von Barcelona" (1921). Her first novel, *My Heart (Mein Herz)*, appeared in 1913. Some of Lasker-Schüler's fervid prose was autobiographical, notably *The Day of Atonement (Der Versöhnungstag)*, recollections of the Yom Kippur commemoration in her parental home. Yet her outstanding achievement was her lyric poetry. This too was devoted principally to Jewish themes, including her best-known collection, *Hebrew Ballads (Hebräische Balladen)*, published in 1913. Throughout the 1920s and early 1930s, Lasker-Schüler continued to produce verse of rare distinction, winning prizes and commissions and reading her work throughout Europe.

Tragically for her, Lasker-Schüler's dazzling talent and unsurpassed fecundity often were overshadowed by the calculated bohemianism of her lifestyle. The Berlin Jewish establishment was embarrassed by her eccentricity. She in turn shunned respectable society as "philistine." Living in cheap rooming houses, she ate her meager fare in equally plebeian cafés and gave away her money to those even poorer than she. Upon fleeing to Switzerland when the Nazis seized power in 1933, she spent her first week sleeping in a park until she was arrested as a vagrant and public attention was drawn to her. It was not until the Swiss Jewish community came to her rescue that she was able to rent a room and continue her writing. Although in ensuing years Lasker-Schüler produced more "revolutionary" poetry and befriended political radicals and fellow literary émigrés, no local publisher would touch her work, for the Swiss government exercised its right of vetoing foreign writers to avoid offending mighty Germany. Finally, in 1938, Lasker-Schüler made her way to Palestine. There, too, however, she lived a life of desperate poverty. Begging her bread from café to café, she subsisted on the edge of chronic starvation. She died in Tel Aviv in 1945, just short of her seventy-sixth birthday.

Lasker-Schüler's fate was not significantly kinder than that endured by numerous other Jewish writers of her generation. Walter Benjamin, a prolific Berlin philosopher and drama critic, emigrated to Paris when the Nazis assumed power. In 1940, following the German conquest of France, Benjamin was among the thousands of refugees who fled to the Vichy zone. From there, in September of that year, he joined a throng of other fugitive Jews who made their way through the Pyrenees. When the Spaniards would not admit them, Benjamin swallowed the morphine tablets he had acquired in advance, and perished. Ernst Weiss, a respected German-Jewish novelist, a friend of Kafka and a student of Freud, slashed his wrists in his Paris refuge the day the Germans entered the city. The poet and playwright Walter Hasenclever swallowed a lethal dose of Veronal in the Vichy internment camp of Les Milles, near Aix-en-Provence. Carl Einstein, possibly Germany's leading interpreter of modern art, drowned himself in a river near Bayonne to avoid falling into the hands of the Gestapo.

A Transmutation of the Volkswesen

I. SCREEN

No facet of Weimar's intellectual and artistic prodigality was more striking than its film and theatrical world. In motion pictures, the stylistic inventiveness of Ernst Lubitsch was a benchmark of that originality. The sheer range of Lubitsch's cinematic art was unparalleled, whether in farce, comedy, satire, drama, fantasy, tragedy, or spectacle. Born in Berlin in 1892, fourth son of a struggling Polish-Jewish tailor, Lubitsch as a youngster was obliged to leave school to augment the family's income. To the despair of his father, he chose the "disreputable" vocation of acting. Worse yet, Lubitsch's initial roles were as a comic buffoon, taking pratfalls in vaudeville, cabarets, music halls, or other beer-sodden fleapits. In 1911, however, the great director Max Reinhardt (pp. 267–69) discerned potential in this ungainly nineteen-year-old and brought him into his famous Deutsches Theater. There Lubitsch played minor roles, essentially in Shakespearean comedies, all the while soaking up his trade like a sponge.

At the same time, moonlighting as an apprentice at the primitive Bioscope film studio, Lubitsch also developed a knack for motion pictures. Three years later, another Jewish impresario, Paul Davidson, who had become a film producer to service his chain of fifty theaters, hired Lubitsch as a comic actor in his Berlin company, UFA (Universum Film Aktiengesellschaft). Lubitsch's early role was that of "Meyer," a slapstick Jewish caricature, for one-reelers. Soon, however, he began concocting his own farces, and eventually he was allowed to write and direct his own films. But the young artist also yearned for more imaginative comedies. With friends at cafés at night, he set about developing the genre of sharp-edged kidding and roguish horseplay, the renowned "Lubitsch touch" that he soon introduced into his films. He applied that "touch" in 1917 when he directed the Polish actress Pola Negri in her first film, *Vendetta*. A commercial success, the production established Lubitsch's reputation in German cinema.

Ironically, when revolution and inflation followed in the aftermath of the war, motion pictures flourished as never before in Germany. Whatever the daytime violence and economic misery, at night people flocked to the cinemas, spending their increasingly worthless marks on cheap, escapist entertainment as if there were no tomorrow. Lubitsch in turn sensed that the moment was risk-free to discard trash for more serious experiments. Persuading Davidson to back the production of *Carmen*, he directed the picture with Pola Negri in the title role. On UFA's back lot in Berlin's Tempelhof district, Lubitsch thereupon created a masterpiece of fiery realism, a film that became a sensation in the United States as well as in Europe. Indeed, beyond any other single work, *Carmen* put German cinema on the map. In the ensuing years, Lubitsch went on to direct even more lavish drama-spectacles, establishing his reputation as the "Reinhardt of motion pictures." As early as 1921, he was also brought occasionally to Hollywood to direct films for Paramount, thus becoming the first of the great European directors to make his mark in the United States.

More than any of their contemporaries in other countries, for that matter, more even than the American D. W. Griffith, film directors in Germany were the earliest to marshal the entire visual sphere of artistic techniques, including Expressionist settings, experimental lighting, unorthodox cinematography, and crowd choreography. Fritz Lang may have been the most imaginative pioneer in this avant-gardist genre. Like many of the artists who achieved their widest breakthrough in Germany, Lang was an Austrian, born in Vienna in 1890 to a Jewish mother and a Gentile father. Following in the footsteps of his architect father, he studied at Vienna's College of Technical Sciences, acquiring an artistic training that later influenced the distinctive visual style of his films. In his teens, however, breaking from parental control, young Lang traveled extensively throughout Europe and the Orient. He returned to Vienna only when the war began, to join the Habsburg army. In battle action on the eastern front, he was repeatedly wounded and repeatedly decorated.

It was during Lang's hospital convalescence in 1916 that a fellow patient introduced him to Josef May, a Jewish producer-director of film detective thrillers and romantic period dramas. Upon discharge from the army, Lang wrote two original stories for May, and soon was taken on as a scenario-writer for Decla, May's Berlin studio. In 1920, Decla in turn was purchased by UFA, Germany's largest film company. Emerging as UFA's chief scenario-writer, Lang subsequently persuaded May and Erich Pommer, the company's (Jewish) senior producer, to allow him to direct his own scripts. The experiment proved as successful with Lang as with Ernst Lubitsch. Brilliantly adapting the new art of Expressionism, Lang displayed a unique stylistic elegance in translating postwar Germany's sense of helplessness and paranoia to the screen. His unorthodox use of exotic architectural settings was particularly notable for accenting his films' brooding atmosphere of underlying menace.

Ironically, Lang's most pathbreaking work, *The Cabinet of Dr. Caligari*, (*Das Kabinett des Dr. Caligari*), was one on which he collaborated only in preliminary discussions and story lines. Yet it was his influence that was plainly discernible in the final version. The film's history is intriguing. On a visit to Berlin soon after the war, a young Czech Jew, Hans Janowitz, made the acquaintance of a young Austrian Jew, Carl Mayer. Both suffered from private nightmares. Janowitz recalled witnessing the murder of a little girl in a Hamburg slum. Mayer had memories of his own father, so mentally depressed upon going bankrupt that he shot himself. The two young men talked endlessly about writing a film script that somehow would combine—perhaps exorcise—Janowitz's recollections of the Hamburg murder and Mayer's resentment of the psychiatrist who had failed his father.

The basic plot eluded them, however, until they went to a fair on the Kantstrasse one evening and, among the sideshows, saw a man perform great feats of strength while apparently in a hypnotic trance. That same night, Janowitz and Mayer began writing their scenario. In its final version, it deals with a mysterious Dr. Caligari who travels with a somnambulist, "Cesare." At night, Cesare wanders about in a trance, murdering anyone who has incurred Dr. Caligari's wrath. Eventually, after Cesare kills a young girl (and then mysteriously expires), Caligari is pursued to an insane asylum, where he is revealed to be not a patient but the asylum's director. Once his double life is exposed, moreover, he himself ends up raving in a straitjacket. The young authors envisaged *Caligari* not simply as a horror film but as a kind of revolutionary allegory, with Caligari personifying the insane evil of unlimited state power, and Cesare representing the common man who is unthinkingly trained to kill and be killed.

Erich Pommer purchased the script from its authors and assigned it first to Lang, then, at the last moment, to another young Jewish director, Robert Wiene. Intent on producing an "artistic" film, Wiene and Pommer hired a distinguished cast, engaged three Expressionist painters to design the sets that are still a marvel of insane distortion, with crooked windows, tilting chimneys, and eerie mixtures of light and shadow. Released in 1926,

Caligari was the first of Germany's "art films," the first to be made entirely inside a studio, the first to exploit the possibilities of a mobile camera. It achieved worldwide success.

As the pioneer of cinematic Expressionism, meanwhile, Lang continued to refine his techniques throughout the 1920s and 1930s. They were evident in his subsequent ventures, among them *Sleepy Death (Der müde Tod)*, *Metropolis*, and perhaps most important, in 1930, *M*. A memorably sympathetic portrait of a tortured child-murderer, "M" is pursued by the police, but eventually is trapped by Berlin's criminal underworld, whose denizens regard him as a threat to their own "honorable" activities. With few exceptions, Lang's social dramas reflected the nightmarish conditions of postwar Germany through the allegorical use of sinister characters, minimalist dialogue, inventive manipulation of light and shadow, and shrewd editing. Upon arriving in Hollywood as a refugee in 1934, Lang was immediately signed up by Metro-Goldwyn-Mayer as one of the great studio's premier directors. He soon became one of its most successful.

II. STAGE

Lang's good fortune in the United States was not characteristic of most of Germany's other émigré Jewish theatrical geniuses. Max Reinhardt might have been the greatest of these. In a diary entry of October 12, 1930, the peripatetic Count Harry Kessler offered a widely shared appraisal of Reinhardt's work at its apogee in Berlin:

> In the evening [I] saw Reinhardt's new production of *A Midsummer Night's Dream* at the Deutsches Theater. Sheer enchantment. The dreamlike setting is divided between a festive chamber and a forest lit by stars. . . . [The actors' movement] dissolves into the airiness of ballet. . . . Deliberate artificiality and yet vibrant imaginative insight. The loveliest performance of the *Dream*, and the nearest in spirit to Shakespeare, that I have ever seen.

Neither Kessler nor other culturally au-courant Germans would have missed a major theatrical performance. The dazzling effulgence of German stage productions between 1918 and 1933 was unmatched in any other country. And even as theater was the queen of Weimar culture, Reinhardt was its king.

Like so many other facets of its national culture, the origins of the golden age of German drama extended back at least to the 1890s, when starkly naturalistic productions of Ibsen and Hauptmann were staged in Berlin, and their most influential producer-director was Otto Brahm. The son of a Hamburg Jewish merchant, Julius Abrahamsohn, Otto Brahm (who changed his name as a young man) attended Karl Friedrich University in Berlin, earning a doctorate in literature. Initially working as a drama critic for the mighty *Vossische Zeitung*, Brahm chafed at the shortcomings he discerned in the capital's ample theatrical productions. In 1889, therefore, organizing a small group of like-minded writers and directors into a Freie Bühne—a Free Stage—Brahm set about producing the works of Hauptmann, Ibsen, and other contemporary playwrights in a more "modern" style, without artificial romanticism. Soon other "free" theater clubs sprang up, emulating Brahm's approach. Brahm himself, in 1893, became director of the great Deutsches Theater, Berlin's preeminent stage; and in 1904 he moved on to its sister institution, the equally prestigious Lessing Theater. From this stage, as from its predecessor, he consolidated the triumph of "modernism" in German drama.

One of the actors who worked in Brahm's Deutsches Theater ensemble was a talented youth who went by the name of Max Reinhardt. He was the oldest of seven children born to Wilhelm and Rosa Goldmann. The father, a business failure, moved the family from Baden to Vienna, where the son left school at age fourteen to help put bread on the table. For three years, the youth worked as a factory apprentice, then as a bank clerk. At age eighteen, he began indulging his passion for the stage by performing in a suburban student drama group. In 1893, changing his name to Reinhardt, he was working at the municipal theater of Salzburg, Austria, when Otto Brahm sat in on a performance. Impressed, Brahm engaged Reinhardt for the Deutsches Theater. It was there, for the next eight years, that Reinhardt developed into a consummate character actor and an avid student of every aspect of contemporary stagecraft.

There, too, in this same period, the young man grew increasingly restless at Brahm's penchant for bleakly "objective" naturalism. Even in his early twenties, Reinhardt sensed the theater's potential for a more "fluid," even a more physically spectacular entertainment. To exploit that potential, he recruited several colleagues and organized cabaret and resort theatricals during summer vacations, developing productions that offered a more audacious use of visual and acoustic dynamism. In 1903, a large contingent of Brahm's Deutsches Theater ensemble shifted its allegiance to Reinhardt, joining him in establishing a "Little Theater" troop. In rented facilities, their first effort was a highly imaginative version of Maxim Gorki's *The Lower Depths*. The production created a sensation and transformed Reinhardt himself literally overnight into the premier man of theater in Berlin.

With borrowed funds, the young genius then purchased a second house, the Neues Theater, where he soon expanded his repertoire to include contemporary classics. Visiting London, meanwhile, to study the work of a renowned theatrical scenic designer, Gordon Craig, Reinhardt also began adapting Craig's innovative use of color and brilliant lighting. Soon he went further yet, transcending the limitations of the proscenium by moving his actors through aisles and balconies. Music, dance, pantomime, architecture and engineering—with runways, bridges, revolving stages, aprons, spotlights, a phantasmagoria of staircases—all gradually were incorporated into Reinhardt's productions. Beyond his imaginative use of light and space, and the perfection of nuance he evoked from his actors, Reinhardt developed a mastery of crowd scenes that transformed his productions into breathtaking spectacles as much as high art. During his visits to London, Reinhardt had been stimulated by the freer British style of producing Shakespeare. In 1904, therefore, he brought to Berlin his own first production of *A Midsummer Night's Dream*. It was a decisive moment. With that magical production, Reinhardt became the preeminent theatrical figure in Europe.

Indeed, Reinhardt's drama revolution swept Otto Brahm from his pedestal. The older man was dropped from his directorship of the Deutsches Theater, and the position was given to Reinhardt. Within six months, after aggressively organizing an investment company, Reinhardt purchased the Deutsches Theater outright (and later also the Lessing Theater). Henceforth he would produce and direct as he pleased. In the theater's ensuing "Reinhardt" quarter-century, drama "mattered" as never before. "You sat [at a Reinhardt production]," recalled the novelist and playwright Bruno Frank, "in thrall to the world Reinhardt had created." Soon, too, the great man brought his wider spectacles, including *Oedipus Rex* and *The Miracle*, to Russia, to England, to the United States—all to unprecedented crowds and rapturous public and critical acclaim. With the outbreak of war, the German foreign ministry found it useful to dispatch Reinhardt and his company as cultural propagandists to Europe's neutral countries.

It was the war, however, and Germany's defeat and economic collapse, that inevitably took their toll on Reinhardt's more ambitious productions. Audiences found it easier, and cheaper, to seek entertainment and psychological escape in neighborhood cinemas. While continuing to stage his productions in his personal showcases, Berlin's Deutsches Theater and Lessing Theater, Reinhardt gradually shifted his focus to Austria. There, exploiting the incomparable natural setting of Alpine Salzburg, he launched into an annual series of festivals, all structured on the classic Jedermann—"Everyman"—theme. Once again the great director's instincts for showmanship paid off. Crowds arrived from throughout the world to witness these annual spectacles. Moreover, the financial rewards of the Salzburg festivals eventually permitted Reinhardt to retrieve his fortunes in Berlin. He enlarged his Berlin theaters and added to their number by opening smaller and less expensive playhouses throughout the city. Under the astute business direction of his brother Edmund, the "Reinhardt Organization" at various times operated at least ten theaters in Berlin and Vienna. Virtually all the great theatrical artists of Europe performed in Reinhardt productions. Many of the Continent's future producers and directors became his students and protégés.

As in the case of so many other cultural giants, however, Reinhardt's triumph began to crumble even before the advent of Nazism. The great depression of 1929 was the initial blow. In Reinhardt's case, it was exacerbated by the death that year of Edmund, his financial guardian angel. The Reinhardt empire soon became mired in debt. It still mounted famed performances, still produced the majestic Salzburg Festival, but these could not keep a rudderless ship afloat. Hitler's accession to power in 1933 was the coup de grâce. Fleeing Germany, Reinhardt lost his operational base and most of his possessions. He sought asylum initially in tottering Austria, then in 1934 moved on to the United States.

There, the triumph in California of his fourteenth production of *A Midsummer Night's Dream* won Reinhardt a three-picture contract with Warner Brothers. But he did not find the film milieu congenial. He never matched the "touch" of one of his earliest performers, Ernst Lubitsch. In his desperation, Reinhardt established a drama school in Los Angeles. It did not succeed. He directed two successful productions of *Die Fledermaus* in New York, but after that no further opportunities came his way. When Reinhardt died in New York in 1943, friends took up a collection to pay for his funeral.

III. MUSIC

In the postwar era, Germany for the first time surpassed truncated little Austria as the musical center of Europe. Notwithstanding military defeat, revolution, and economic chaos, the nation's dense orchestral and operatic infrastructure remained intact. Throughout the war and postwar years, hardly a day passed without performances in one or another of Germany's concert halls, opera houses, or music festivals. Berlin's symphonic conductors were the standard of Europe. The music courses of the Preussische Akademie der Künste, taught by internationally renowned figures, were regarded as the standard of the world. It was at this same Academy of Arts, in 1925, that the fifty-one-year-old Arnold Schönberg took up his assignment as director of three master classes in musical composition. He was behind schedule. His directorship had been confirmed only after months of agitation against him led by Alfred Heuss, editor of the monthly *Zeitschrift für Musik*. As Heuss saw it, the Schönberg appointment, coming not long after that of another Jew, Leo Kestenberg, represented a frontal assault on everything "true" Germans held sacred in art. In Schönberg's case, his revolutionary concept of atonality was even more flagrantly alien to the Wahrheit—the "central truths"—of German musical tradition.

Geographically, Schönberg doubtless was an Ausländer, a foreigner, even twice over. He was born in Vienna of Jewish "provincials," parents who themselves recently had migrated to the Austrian capital from the Czech and Slovak hinterlands. Otherwise, his life's experience was culturally Germanic. Reared in Vienna's middle-class Leopoldstadt district, young Schönberg was only halfway through his intermediate school when his father died, and he was obliged to enter the workforce at the age of sixteen. Employed as a bank clerk, the youngster nevertheless managed to attend every concert and opera performance he could afford. He also taught himself the fundamentals of piano and violin, and the essentials of composition.

At the age of twenty-one, after losing his position at the bank, Schönberg found employment as a conductor for a metalworkers' choral society, then took on "piece work" as an arranger of operettas and popular songs. In the process, the young man churned out some six thousand pages of commercial orchestrations. The hackwork was not wasted. It taught Schönberg to put his own musical thoughts on paper with all the efficiency of a court stenographer. By the turn of the century, he was producing compositions of increasing complexity and sophistication. Several of his works were performed at the Vienna Court Opera.

It was in 1900 that Schönberg first moved to Berlin. He had been offered a remunerative position as choral director of the Buntes Theater, one of the city's largest. In the German capital, for the next four years, the young man supplemented his income by orchestrating numerous works for the popular composer Richard Strauss. Evidently he was making all the right career moves. He even converted to Protestantism. Upon returning to Vienna in 1904, Schönberg married a Gentile woman of aristocratic background, and his brother-in-law Alexander von Zemlinsky, a noted Austrian court conductor, put him in touch with Alban Berg and with the incomparable Gustav Mahler. With Mahler's help, several of Schönberg's compositions were performed not long afterward by local and provincial symphony orchestras. In the last years before 1914, as one of Vienna's most highly paid musical instructors and program composers, Schönberg was comfortably ensconced in the Austrian musical establishment.

The war years took their inevitable toll. Schönberg's best-paying students were conscripted into the army. His family knew privation. Accordingly, in 1921, in his early middle age, Schönberg concluded that even inflation-ravaged Germany offered likelier economic potential than did attenuated little Austria. In Berlin, too, he would seek wider recognition for the project to which lately he had been devoting his best talents. This was a new approach to tonality. It was Schönberg's intention to extend "his" harmonic scale from eight to twelve tones, which then could be manipulated either in their original position, or inverted, or reversed, to produce an entire composition. The purpose of his "dodecaphony," Schönberg explained, was nothing less than the creation of a new harmonic system to replace classical melody.

For his listeners, however, the revolution was difficult to grasp, and conductors and instrumentalists resented the imposition of a far more complex set of tonal rules. Earlier performances of Schönberg's experimental music in Viennese concert halls had elicited hissing and booing, and sent audiences fleeing for the exits. His "Chamber Symphony" was nicknamed the "Chamber-of-Horrors Symphony." When Schönberg arrived in Berlin, the critic Walter Dahme proposed taking up a collection to send him back to Vienna. Nevertheless, in Weimar's new experimentalist atmosphere, Schönberg's dissonance and "atonality" gradually won a coterie of supporters among music critics and even among several conductors. Once he achieved "respectability" with his 1925 appointment to the Academy of Arts, his compositions were performed by the City Opera Company and by Radio Berlin. By 1933, when the Nazis dismissed Schönberg from the academy, and he departed Germany, his innovations had become irreversibly incorporated into the modern musical vocabulary.

It is of note, however, that the earliest and widest impetus for atonal experimentation came less from Berlin's great concert halls than from its cabarets and popular theaters. Indeed, the cabaret perhaps more than any other setting became the seedbed of avant-garde Weimar culture. In the chaos of postwar Germany, and notably in cynical, worldly-wise Berlin, it was on the tiny stages of these often hole-in-the-wall nightclubs that recitations and reviews produced a cacophony of new expressive forms. As Peter Gay has observed, if much of the cabaret life in the early postwar ran riot in escapist debauchery, not all of its offerings were nudity, homosexuality, or honky-tonk. Kurt Tucholsky's biting aphorisms were performed in several of the "better" cabarets in Berlin, particularly in the Chat Noir, owned by Tucholsky's friend Rudolf Nelson (né Lewisohn). So were the mordant satires of Karl Kraus, who "performed" in Berlin and other German cities even more frequently than in his native Vienna. And from the German cabarets, most decisively of all, Kurt Weill provided European popular music with the kind of harsh, astringent dissonance that Schönberg was pioneering in the concert halls.

Born in the venerable Jewish community of Dessau in 1900, Weill was the third son of a synagogue cantor. As a youth in gymnasium, he shared in patriotic choral performances, and often conducted the school orchestra. In 1918, rejected for military service as an asthmatic, young Weill went on to acquire a solid musical training at Berlin's Hochschule für Musik. Afterward, upon returning home to the economic chaos of the postwar years, he helped support his family by playing the organ in the local synagogue, by private tutoring, and by conducting local orchestras and choral societies. In 1920, Weill then fulfilled his life's dream, winning a scholarship to Berlin's renowned Preussische Akademie der Künste (p. 269). Thus, in Berlin, for the next three years, he underwent a rigorous training in classical musical composition.

It was also in this period, however, that Weill was seized of the modernist and distinctly nonclassical cultural explosion occurring in postwar Berlin. Expressionism had become all the vogue in music, as in art and literature. In Berlin's concert halls, the genre's preeminent exponents were Igor Stravinsky, Darius Milhaud, Paul Hindemith, and Arnold Schönberg. Weill drank in their performances at every opportunity. Yet he did not neglect the cabarets. It was on their stages that young performers—most of them amateurs and political leftists—adopted a brassy, irreverent atonality that was emerging as the virtual hallmark of Weimar's popular musical culture. Weill approached the new effervescence cautiously. By 1923, as an acknowledged master of classical musicianship, he was earning a solid reputation and a comfortable income producing a torrent of compositions, most of them on commission for ballet-pantomimes, for string quartets and concertos. Although he continued to explore the new avant-gardist genre with mounting interest, his own experiments in it remained private.

Then, in 1924, Weill came under the influence of Georg Kaiser, a forty-six-year-old philosopher-playwright. Kaiser not long before had written a war drama that deeply engaged its audience by its selective and restrained use of Expressionism. As Kaiser explained to Weill, the identical fastidiousness should be applied to musical drama. Avant-gardism for its own sake was a waste. Rather, it had to be linked purposefully to social *engagement*. In that endeavor, Kaiser then persuaded Weill to join him in producing a musical drama. The relationship was fruitful, if brief. For one thing, it was through Kaiser that the frail, bespectacled Weill met a hoydenish young Viennese soubrette, Lotte Lenya, whom he eventually married, and who starred in numerous of his later works.

The Kaiser-Weill collaboration also produced an Expressionist one-act musical drama, *The Protagonist*. Completed in 1925 and set in the time of Shakespeare, it was a work of "black nihilism," in which the artist—the protagonist—is betrayed equally by life and art. Kaiser's story line was compelling, and Weill's music was an almost perfect blend of lush melody and caustic atonality. Performed in Dresden, *The Protagonist* evoked instant acclaim, and soon was taken up by light-opera houses throughout Germany. For Weill, the experience was defining. He had found his métier. Fired by audiences' enthusiastic response to "useful" atonality, he collaborated with Kaiser on two more one-act operas in the new style, each displaying impertinent political overtones and witty repartee.

Nevertheless, Weill on his own vaulted ahead even more daringly, experimenting with still other techniques: among them harsh syncopation, dance-music rhythms, jazz-band instrumentation, and a ferocious intensity of declamation. In 1927, contemplating a kind of satirical quasi-jazz *Rosenkavalier,* he had the good fortune to encounter a talent fully equal to his own. This was Bertolt Brecht. Born into a comfortable Bavarian Catholic family (and married later to a Jewish actress, Helen Weigel), Brecht had served in the war, an experience that turned him into a pacifist and a Communist. By the early 1920s, Brecht also was emerging as a dramatist of exceptional talent and imagination, the precocious author of *Drums in the Night (Trommeln in der Nacht)* and *Edward II.*

Yet Weill responded with particular enthusiasm to Brecht's harshly abrasive ballads and poems. The two men soon agreed to collaborate, and in 1927 Weill set to music Brecht's *Mahagonny* libretto. Produced in 1930 as the *Rise and Fall of the City of Mahagonny (Aufstieg und Fall der Stadt Mahagonny),* the work drew its inspiration from the political theater pioneered in Berlin's cabarets through the readings of performers like Tucholsky and Kraus. It was an electrifying blend of libretto and offbeat musical dissonance, and the production was significantly enhanced by the collaboration of an inspired Jewish designer, Caspar Neher, who subsequently would create the sets and costumes for all the team's joint ventures. In the history of German musical theater, the late 1920s came to be known as the "era" of Brecht-Weill-Neher.

The collaboration actually reached its apotheosis in its first joint stage venture, in 1928. This was *The Three-Penny Opera (Die Dreigroschenoper),* an updating of John Gay's eighteenth-century *Beggar's Opera,* which lately had been in and out of production in postwar Europe. The catalyst for the work was Ernst-Josef Aufricht. Of the same generation as Brecht, Weill, and Neher, Aufricht was the son of an affluent Silesian-Jewish wood merchant. Long fascinated by the theatrical world, in 1927 he used his comfortable inheritance to lease an ornate little Berlin theater and then to set out in quest of suitable new plays. Approaches to established dramatists like Ernst Toller and Lion Feuchtwanger were unproductive. But with Brecht and Weill, already working on a version of the *Beggar's Opera,* Aufricht hit pay dirt.

A caustic satire on bourgeois society, the adaptation of Gay's work was completed in less than a year. With Lotte Lenya playing the female lead, the production opened in August 1928 and became the most spectacular success in the history of twentieth-century German musical theater. Indeed, within a week of its opening, *The Three-Penny Opera* was booked into over fifty houses across the country, and by the end of the year it was playing all over Europe. When recording companies from throughout the world signed contracts, Brecht and Weill became household names, the very incarnation of Weimar culture in current and historical perspective.

There were other collaborations between Weill, Brecht, Neher, and Aufricht, but none of them, not even *Mahagonny*, approached the bombshell of *The Three-Penny Opera*. The world depression struck particularly hard at Germany's cultural sector. Subsidies to state theaters and orchestras were cut. Although several of Brecht's and Weill's important works still lay ahead, after *Mahagonny* none of these was to be produced in Germany. Once the Nazis assumed power, it was "Goodbye to All That," to the partnership and the theatrical genre that, more than any other, would be enduringly identified with the sunburst of the Weimar years.

IV. "JUDENPHYSIK"

As in the realm of "higher" culture, the foundation for Weimar's ongoing scientific and technological achievements was laid during the Wilhelminian Empire. Even in those last prewar decades, the "special calling" of science was obliged to make room for a new race of Jewish overachievers. Indeed, at its upper levels, German science was almost unique in its pluralistic creativity, its incremental willingness to allow Jews to share in the nation's rise to scientific greatness. Jewish participation still was won at heavy psychic cost, to be sure. In his volume, *Einstein's German World*, Fritz Stern has elegantly characterized this dilemma by tracing the parallel careers of two Jewish geniuses, Fritz Haber and Albert Einstein.

In 1918, Haber, a chemist, was awarded the Nobel Prize for devising the technique of fixating ammonia from hydrogen and nitrogen. Even earlier, his towering scientific reputation made him the logical choice to direct the University of Berlin's mighty Kaiser Wilhelm Institute of Physical Chemistry and Electrochemistry. Haber's conversion to Protestantism as a young man doubtless eased the way for his future advance. Beyond vocational careerism, however, his personal obsession ever after was to serve his beloved German Fatherland. Thus, when hostilities began in 1914, Haber responded to the crisis in a near-paroxysm of patriotism.

It soon veered to chauvinism—in common with that of possibly a majority of other German academicians and scientists. When the Reich-wehr's invasion of neutral Belgium aroused international condemnation, ninety-three of Germany's most renowned cultural figures signed the notorious manifesto approving the invasion, denying charges of atrocities against Belgian civilians, and even characterizing the enemy as "Russian hordes allied with Mongols and Negroes unleashed against the white race." Together with the Jewish Nobel laureates Paul Ehrlich and Richard Wilstätter, Haber was one of the signers of the "Manifesto of the Ninety-Three" (p. 219). More pragmatically, Haber's services to his nation's military effort were unsurpassed, for he became in effect the organizer-in-chief of science in wartime Germany. Thus, under his direction, techniques were perfected for the manufacture of nitric acid and synthetic saltpeter, ingredients of critical importance for military explosives and agricultural fertilizer. Conversely, among Germany's enemies, Haber was identified as the "evil genius" whose researches had made poison gas feasible, and who had pressed assiduously for its use as a military weapon. His name was placed on the Allied list of war criminals to be extradited for trial (after the war, the charge eventually was dropped).

On the other hand, as director of the Kaiser Wilhelm Institute, Haber played the decisive role in bringing Albert Einstein to Berlin in 1914. Like Haber, Einstein was the product of a veteran, middle-class German-Jewish family. His childhood in Ulm, near the Swabian Alps, was in every respect unprecocious. If it was also untraditional in its Jewish identifications, Einstein at least shared the characteristic Jewish fixation with a higher education. Thus, in his teens, unprepared to contest the Jewish numerus clausus at German universities, Einstein followed the entirely typical Jewish path of proceeding on to Switzerland—in this case to Zurich's Polytechnical Institute. There, in 1901, he received his undergraduate degree in physics. In Switzerland too, afterward, frustrated in his efforts to secure a teaching position at a German gymnasium, Einstein accepted employment as a technical expert for the Swiss Federal Patent Office. Opting for Swiss citizenship, he also continued his graduate studies at the Polytechnical Institute, and eventually earned his doctorate in physics, in 1904.

It was in these same years, under the influence of a renowned Jewish physicist, Hermann Minkowski, that Einstein was drawn increasingly to the study of electromagnetism and its relationship to space, an issue that lately was shaking the traditional Newtonian-mechanical theory of the universe. In 1905, immersing himself in this promising new field, the young patent inspector published a series of six concise scientific papers, each of which was original enough to assure him a place in the textbooks. The third and most important of the papers, appearing in Germany's *Annalen der Physik* and entitled "On the Electrodynamics of Moving Bodies," introduced the theory of relativity. At the age of twenty-six, Einstein had come up with the shattering notion of a cosmos in which stars and entire galaxies moved in relation not to space but exclusively to each other. Soon afterward, in 1907 and 1908, two articles by Hermann Minkowski gave mathematical resonance to Einstein's dazzling but purely physical theory of relativity; and a year later, in 1909, the German physicists Max Planck and Max Born published their own papers, which similarly buttressed Einstein's theories.

Only then did the young man's professional career begin to flourish. In 1909, the University of Zurich appointed him associate professor of theoretical physics. Two years later, he departed to accept a full professorship at the German section of Prague's Karl-Ferdinand University (p. 135). And two years after that, at the initiative of Fritz Haber, Einstein achieved the summum bonum of his dreams, appointment as professor and first director (at a munificent salary) of the department of physics at the Kaiser Wilhelm Institute in Berlin. The appointment produced ambivalent consequences, however. When the war broke out, Einstein was appalled by the indiscriminate nationalist fervor of his academic colleagues. Nor did he disguise his appraisal of the German people altogether as frenzied chauvinists. In May 1915, when a German U-boat sank the *Lusitania*, Einstein was one of the first to condemn the act, and to characterize the German government as a lunatic asylum. Through intermediaries, he also maintained close contacts with fellow scientists in England and France, and with fellow pacifists in Switzerland. It was a record German nationalists would not forget.

Early in 1916, Einstein expanded his initial theory of relativity in a longer, fifty-three-page article for the *Annalen der Physik*. Entitled "The Foundation of the General Theory of Relativity," the thesis explored in greater detail the concept of "space-curvature," the renewed claim that light did not move in straight lines, and that the universe could be viewed from the earth only through the distorting—that is, relativistic—spectacles of gravity. It was not possible, however, to test the theory except during an eclipse, to learn whether light from the stars was deflected when passing through the gravitational field of the sun. But in November 1919, astronomers studying an eclipse off the coast of Africa confirmed the theory. Einstein thereupon became the single most famous scientist in the world, and in 1921 the recipient of the Nobel Prize for Physics.

In that eminence, he also became one of Weimar Germany's most important assets. His frequent visits abroad throughout the 1920s helped reduce anti-German hostility by focusing attention on the achievements of German culture and science. Einstein willingly cooperated in the effort. The harshness of Allied policies toward defeated Germany shocked and disillusioned him. Repeatedly, he signed petitions imploring the Western Powers to save the famished German people from starvation, and thus to encourage the new and democratic Weimar Republic. If Einstein's views on the Germans were in a process of continual change, the one constant in his attitude was his pacifism and internationalism, his touchingly naïve advocacy of a universal world government.

In fact, Einstein was courting disaster. Although in some circles he was the most loved and admired Jew in Germany, in others he was one of the most hated. Within the academic community, memories of Einstein's pacifism were long. Some colleagues even attacked his scientific credibility. In 1920, his efforts to defend his theory of relativity at a meeting of the German Association of Scientists met an uproar of protest. The reaction perhaps was not unlike the outrage provoked by Schönberg's music. Both innovations evidently robbed the German public of the categorical absolute vital to their Volkswesen, their "national essence." In the seismic transformations of the postwar years, Germans felt above all else the need to cling to das Altbewährte—their "old home truths." For them, Jewish intellectuals altogether were to be regarded as inveterate troublemakers and Querulanten—provocative question-askers—of a nonstable society.

The physicist Philipp Lenard, himself a 1905 Nobel laureate, led the pack. Lenard had done pioneering research on the photoelectric effect before Einstein explained it in quantum-mechanical terms. An incipient Nazi, Lenard as early as the 1920s produced such observations as "the Jew conspicuously lacks understanding for the truth, in contrast to the Aryan research scientist with his careful and serious will to truth." In September 1922, moreover, when Einstein was invited to address a convention of German scientists in Leipzig, Lenard threatened to disrupt the meeting, and in advance had a circular distributed, signed by nineteen German scientists, denouncing relativity as "alien to the German spirit." For Professor Ludwig Bieberbach, Einstein was "an alien mountebank"; while Professor Wilhelm Müller denounced the theory of relativity as a bid for "Jewish world rule." Well after Einstein's theory was proven and the Nobel Prize awarded him, he felt the poison of antisemitism. "The yellow press and other halfwits are at my heels to the point where I can scarcely draw breath," he told an associate, "let alone do any really decent work." His original instincts about the German intelligentsia were being confirmed.

Yet Einstein's relationship with Haber survived apparently intact. Their differences over wartime policy notwithstanding, the two remained the closest of friends, with Haber continually vigilant lest Einstein be lured away by one of the many professional offers flooding in on him. The two worked together energetically in the postwar years to ensure that German participants were not excluded from international scientific congresses. But, once again, they began to diverge on issues of government policy. As indiscriminate as always in his German patriotism, Haber feared the impact of the Versailles Treaty's disarmament clauses. It is possible that, upon renewing his contacts with the military, he became involved in secret deliberations on armed collaboration between Germany and Soviet Russia. His own Kaiser Wilhelm Institute, meanwhile, experimenting with pesticides, had developed Zyklon B, the poison gas of whose future use Haber could have had no intimation. Nor could he have anticipated the radical transformation his own life was to undergo. He learned within weeks of Hitler's accession to power, of course, when a new law dismissed all "non-Aryans" from Germany's civil service, including the Kaiser Wilhelm Institute.

Even afterward, it was characteristic of Haber that he sought to enlist aid for his dismissed fellow scientists, and in May 1933 he wrote Einstein, who had departed Germany shortly before the Nazi takeover. Einstein responded generously, but could not resist observing: "I can conceive of your inner conflicts. It is something like having to give up a theory on which one has worked one's whole life. It is not the same for me because I never believed in it in the least." The remark was entirely forthright. From the outset of his career in Germany, Einstein had displayed far more insight than Haber into the nation's—and specifically its universities'— endemic chauvinism. In 1927, when the Prussian Student Organization took a poll of its members on the question of admitting Jews, three-quarters of the responses were in the negative. The evidence is compelling that the largest number of university academicians during the Weimar era were political right-wingers, as were members of the nation's professional classes at large.

During the 1920s and early 1930s, meanwhile, as antisemitism gained renewed virulence in Germany, Einstein's Jewish and Zionist commitments acquired sharper definition. He helped Chaim Weizmann raise funds for the Hebrew University during an American tour shared by the two men in 1921. In 1923, Einstein visited Palestine and proclaimed his experience the "greatest event of my life." Although remaining an entirely nonobservant Jew, Einstein on one evening in January 1930 appeared in a Berlin synagogue, wearing a skullcap and playing his violin to help raise contributions for a new Jewish community center. If the project availed little for German Jewry by then, it provided the great scientist his opportunity for an ethnic reaffirmation. He had long since identified the source of his ultimate loyalties.

A Perversion of the Geist

In his autobiographical *My Life as German and Jew (Mein Weg als Deutscher und Jude)*, the novelist Jakob Wassermann recalled:

If anyone were to ask me among what people I had found the greatest understanding, encouragement, response, and support, I should have to reply: among Jewish men and women. If the same question were put to any writer or artist of non-Jewish origin the answer would . . . be the same. . . . Jews were their discoverers, their receptive audience, their heralds and their biographers. Jews have been and still are the caryatides of almost every great name.

There were not lacking others to corroborate that, in Germany, as in Austria during the interwar years, the Jewish role in the cultural firmament far transcended the achievements of individual geniuses. Among these "witnesses," Thomas Mann acknowledged that

Jews "discovered" me, Jews published and propagated my reputation; they performed my impossible plays. . . . And when I go out into the world, and visit cities, it is almost always Jews, not only in Vienna and Berlin, who welcome, shelter, dine and pamper me. . . . It is a fact that simply cannot be denied that, in Germany, whatever is enjoyed only by "genuine Teutons" and aboriginal *Ur*-Germans, but scorned or rejected by the Jews, will never really amount to anything, culturally.

When Heinrich Mann was asked whether he would endorse either the mass baptism of Jews or their forced emigration to Palestine, he countered: "But what is to become of the so-called host people, already suffering from spiritual undernourishment, if the Jews were now also to fail them?"

Yet, by the same token, if Weimar culture was unthinkable without the Jews, it was similarly the Jews who limited its appeal and all but assured its political impotence. Their visibility amid Weimar's avant-garde effervescence played into the hands of reactionaries. So, even more, did their visibility among the left-wing intelligentsia (not to mention the left-wing political leadership). Indeed, for rural and urban white-collar elements, Weimar was nothing less than the "Jew Republic" (p. 247). With Jewish Marxists promoting a revolutionary agenda, on the one hand, and Foreign Minister Rathenau advocating "Erfühlungspolitik," on the other, the evidence of that Verjudung—that "judaization"—appeared compelling for those seeking it out. The sheer proliferation, finally, of Jewish journalists and academicians questioning the central verities of Deutschtum, Jewish composers and physicists undermining the "old home truths," Jewish theatrical and film directors ostensibly transforming drama into a form of "mass hypnosis" and "sexual excitement"—all convinced German traditionalists that popular culture had become the chosen instrument of Verjudung.

The Weimar years produced numerous versions of the "judaization" theme. It was in the confused postwar era that grotesque works like Artur Dinter's 1918 novel, *The Sin against the Blood (Die Sünde wider das Blut)*, could win a mass audience. A leader of early Thuringian Nazism, Dinter in his novels and pamphlets produced an entire philosophy of "spiritual racism." Jews were the physical embodiments of deeply fallen souls, he argued. In the *Ur*-time of creation, they had chosen egoism and materialism as their spiritual direction. If race were the vessel through which this Geist—this spirit—was transmitted, then Jews under no circumstances could be admitted to the Aryan Blutsgemeinschaft, the fellowship of Aryan racial purity.

In his 1930 tract, *The Nordic Soul (Die nordische Seele)*, L. F. Clauss argued that external appearance actually was not the essential hallmark of Aryanism. It was rather the "race-soul," the fount of all creativity, which Nordic blood alone produced. Racial types, suggested the influential "scientific" racist Dr. Hans F. K. Gunther (later to be professor of "racial science" at the University of Jena), could be regarded essentially as physical representations of an inner nature. In this convenient fashion, anthropological and metaphysical categories of beauty and soul converged. And more than in any other realm, during the Weimar period, they converged in the realm of culture.

The Response of Sweet Reason

With an ardor surpassing even that of the empire's last years, German Jewry in the early Weimar period claimed that it was the sheer depth of their acculturation that set them apart from all other Jews in the world, and specifically from the Jews of Eastern Europe. German Jews, they insisted, had absorbed a culture, a blend of moral and aesthetic values, that epitomized the proudest Enlightenment traditions of German history. These were the traditions, after all, that had become synonymous with the city of Weimar, and its revered archetypes of Goethe, Lessing, and Herder. In March 1919, Eugen Fuchs, president of the jüdische Kultusverein, offered a characteristic appraisal of the new Republic's historic significance for German Jews. Weimar meant nothing less, he insisted, than the end of militarism and authoritarianism, the end of ruling-class intolerance, an end to oppression of the "true" German spirit. Most decisively of all, it meant the end of antisemitism, a vestige of medievalism "under attack by Reason in all political parties."

But while they expressed faith in the Republic as a broom likely to sweep away the last of the old detritus, even the most acculturated of Jewish "veterans" could not remain indifferent to the need for continued vigilance. As far back as 1893, a number of prominent German Jewish businessmen had founded their own Committee for Defense against Antisemitic Attacks (Kommittee zur Abwehr gegen antisemitischer Angriffe). Soon afterward, the committee was subsumed under the aegis of the newly formed Central Association for German Citizens of the Jewish Faith (Kultusverein für deutsche Staatsburger jüdischen Glaubens), which had been established initially to enable Jews to conform with the earlier Prussian (and later imperial) Religious Law of 1869. Little time passed before antidefamation evolved into one of the Kultusverein's principal functions.

Manifestly, it was not the only function. The Weimar years represented a period of immense communal and intellectual vitality for German Jews. Both within and outside the Kultusverein, renowned Jewish scholars— Hermann Cohen, Ismar Elbogen, Martin Buber, Franz Rosenzweig, Simon Dubnow (a temporary resident in Berlin)—significantly enlarged the cultural horizons of the vibrant Jewish minority. Impressive networks of Jewish community centers, hospitals, and senior-citizen homes, of study centers and lecture, theatrical and musical programs, even a distinguished Jewish publishing house, were sustained and continually enlarged during the Weimar years.

Nevertheless, to the dismay of the senior Jewish establishment, it was specifically antidefamation that had to be worked overtime almost from the earliest years of the Republic. Throughout the 1920s and early 1930s, "defense by education" remained the Kultusverein's instrument of choice. Its deluge of publications endlessly cited the contribution of Jews to Germany's military struggle, to the nation's political resurrection, to its economic and cultural life. The Kultusverein produced formidable lists of statistics on the role of Jewish financiers, industrialists, and scientists in war and peace alike. Between 1929 and 1933, even as antisemites of various hues produced at least seven hundred books on the "Jewish Question," Germany's Jews in their turn more than doubled this number as they engaged in acrobatics of self-definition and self-justification.

Apologetics were fortified by rationalization. While the Kultusverein in no sense was prepared to discount the ugliness of Nazism, it tended to interpret Nazi electoral gains simply as the most recent variation of an antisemitism that had come and gone earlier in German history. As late as 1931, editorials in the Kultusverein's *Zeitung* insisted that the overwhelming majority of Germans still rejected Hitler and antisemitism. Had it not been for "the accident of economic problems," argued the *Zeitung* in its 1932 New Year's issue, and the schism within the liberal and leftist political parties, "the majority of the German people would continue along the democratic path." As late as April 1933, in the midst of the Nazi government's initial wave of antisemitic legislation, the Kultusverein would repeat its conviction that "Germany and Germans will [not] abandon [our common national goals] and forget us."

Actually, the German people did not. In his 1931 autobiography, the renowned sociologist Franz Oppenheimer felt impelled to affirm that

> I have been fortunate to have been born and educated in the land of Kant and Goethe, to have their culture, their art, their language and their knowledge as my own. My Germanism is as sacred to me as my Jewish forefathers. . . . I combine in me the German and the Jewish national feeling.

More than they knew, or wished, the non-Jewish citizens of twentieth-century Germany had become a mirror image of Oppenheimer's self-appraisal. For them, the scholarship, art, literature, music, and science—in effect, the cultural "essence"—of the nation's protean Jewish minority had become no less inseparably, no less ineradicably their own.

X

IN SEARCH OF LOST SWANNS

Monsieur Proust Enters Society

On October 27, 1927, the last day of Sholem Schwarzbard's trial for the assassination of Simon Petliura, the prosecuting and defense attorneys delivered their summations. Maître Henri Torrès, representing Schwarzbard, concluded his defense with an emotional appeal:

> No, it is no longer you, Schwarzbard, who is the [defendant] here. It is the pogroms. . . . Gentlemen of the jury . . . with [the defendant] there are the multitudes of the tortured, and [also] the voices of the giants of the French Revolution and the French tradition of liberalism. The Abbé Grégoire, Rabaud Saint-Étienne, Mirabeau, Gambetta, Victor Hugo, both the dead and the living, plead with you to acquit him, this man who bears on his forehead, like a terrible seal, all the tragedy of a people. . . . Gentlemen, you are responsible today for the prestige of our nation and for thousands of lives which depend on the verdict of France.

But Judge Flory's directive to the jurors gave short shrift to Torrès's peroration. They were, he warned, to limit their consideration specifically to the intent and consequence of Schwarzbard's deed, nothing more. Did he willfully murder Petliura or not? On this issue, could a jury of Frenchmen ignore a judge's instructions, and feign blindness to the cold evidence of retributive assassination?

It could. Only twenty-five minutes were needed for the jury to pronounce a verdict of not guilty (p. 17). The courtroom erupted in pandemonium. In their euphoria, the eight hundred spectators shouted "Vive la République! Vivent les jurés français!" It was an emotion widely shared by the press. With few exceptions—almost exclusively on the far right—newspapers headlined the vindication less of Schwarzbard himself than of French "honor," French "humanity," French "nobility." Within the month, the French National Assembly passed a series of laws relaxing the naturalization process for political refugees. The economy was reviving. A gesture of self-indulgent magnanimity did not seem out of place.

Plainly, the Jews of France were the first to acclaim Schwárzbard's acquittal. They were a middle-sized community. Although their numbers had doubled since the war (p. 290), their entire critical mass as recently as 1914 had not exceeded 130,000. Of these, two-thirds had settled in Paris, with the rest divided essentially between Alsace-Lorraine in the northeast and Provence in the southwest. As late as 1914, too, most Jews were ensconced comfortably in the middle ranks of the bourgeoisie. Their political status appeared equally secure. With the liquidation of the Dreyfus Affair, the Third French Republic evidently had broadened its anchorage in secular egalitarianism. Although bigotry and xenophobia doubtless had not vanished in that "Belle Époque," between 1899 and 1914, at least the champions of royalist and clerical reaction no longer represented a credible political force.

So it was that Jewish upward mobility continued unimpeded in these golden years of economic and cultural efflorescence. Some Jews, then and earlier, even had become titled aristocrats, counting among their numbers such renowned financial dynasties as the Rothschilds, Camondos, Cahen D'Anvers, Pereiras, Königwarters, Menasches, De Hirsches, and D'Almeidas. There were Jewish deputies and senators in Parliament, Jewish officers in the army (including the redeemed and promoted Dreyfus). In cultural life, Jews in university faculties and student bodies, in scholarship, literature, music and theater, included such luminaries as the playwright Henri Bernstein, the actress Sarah Bernhardt, the composer Maurice Ravel, the artists Camille Pissarro, the sociologist Émile Durkheim, the anthropologist Claude Lévi-Strauss, the political economist Bernard Lazare, the poet André Spire.

In *Creative Evolution (L'Évolution créatrice)*, the best known among his numerous volumes, the philosopher Henri Bergson provided his countrymen with moral assurance that the élan vital, the "dynamic spark" latent in individuals and nations alike, could be invoked to transcend all obstacles and setbacks—a proposition some of his countrymen applied even to the humiliation of the 1870 Franco-Prussian War. The crowds attending Bergson's lectures at the Collège de France came to hear not a scholar but a prophet of limitless human and collective indomitability.

In the manner of their German Jewish cousins during these same prewar years, French "Israélites" envisaged their religious affiliation as a matter purely of "cultism," subordinate to their broader national loyalties. Since the French Revolution, acculturation had become the very marrow of their patriotism. Jews would pray together, frequently would socialize together, but the veterans among them no longer separated themselves by neighborhoods, nor did they so much as contemplate engaging in political affairs as a separate bloc. Often living in Paris's most exclusive faubourgs and mingling increasingly with Gentiles, they expressed their residual Jewishness by "civilizing," "Gallicizing" the widening immigrant community of their East European coreligionists, and by demonstrating in their own careers that Jews were exemplary citizens.

Some among them had become socially quite fashionable. Marcel Proust even became something of a parlor adorability. In 1889, when he had just turned eighteen and registered for his compulsory military service, the army file described him as five foot six in height, possessing "an oval face with chestnut hair, dark chestnut eyebrows, low forehead, medium-sized nose and mouth and a round chin." Photographs suggest that Proust's features bore a resemblance to those of his mother, Jeanne Weil. She was the daughter of a wealthy Jewish stockbroker, Nathé Weil, and through her mother, Adèle Berncastel, was the great-niece of Isaac Adolphe Crémieux, who had served as minister of justice in the Second French Republic. Proust's father, Dr. Adrien Proust, a distinguished physician, was a Catholic. In fact, marriages between well-connected Jewish and Gentile families were not uncommon in the latter decades of the nineteenth century.

Marcel Proust, born in 1871, was a frail child, who throughout his life would suffer acutely from asthma. In his condition, he demanded and received the major share of the distraught mother's attention. (Biographers have speculated that Proust's homosexuality may have been rooted in his mother-fixation.) In Paris, attending classes at the best private schools, and associating with boys of his own station, many of them also the children of wealthy Jewish or part-Jewish families, Proust soon revealed himself as a youth of astonishing literary sensibilities. When his six-month army term was up, he immediately enrolled at the Sorbonne, placating his parents by studying the "practical" subjects of law and political economy. Upon graduation, however, Proust put his degree to no "practical" use. By then he was committed to the life of a writer. His parents acquiesced. When he accepted a position as "adjunct associate" at the Mazarin Library, essentially as a non-paying façade for his writing career, his father subsidized the young man's ample living expenses.

The investment was not wasted. Notwithstanding his recurrent asthma attacks, Proust soon established himself as a marvel of creativity. From the mid-1890s on, he produced an uninterrupted series of reviews and essays for literary supplements and journals, even founded his own literary journal, *Le Banquet*, which attracted contributions from talents as diverse as Anatole France, Alphonse Daudet, and the young Léon Blum. Proust's own belletristic writings were based almost without exception on the mores of the haut monde, the salons along the Faubourg Saint-Germain, where the rich and elegant consorted. Many of the latter were Proust family friends (p. 287). Others simply were mandarins who were taken by Marcel Proust's personal charm, "[his] extraordinary voice," recalled the Marquise de Clermont-Tonnère, ". . . caressing, pleasing, charged with a thousand gracious inflections . . . [uttering] phrases you are not used to hearing—'I hope you are not angry,' 'Your goodness toward me,' 'He is so kind to me.' " "He sometimes exaggerated his affability as flattery," wrote another acquaintance, Fernand Gregh, "but always intelligently; and we had even created among ourselves the verb *proustify* to express a slightly too conscious attitude of geniality. . . ."

The high society of Proust's leisure hours encompassed Jews or part-Jews as well as Gentiles. Indeed, the first salons Proust attended, and later described, were those of his great-uncle's Jewish mistress, Laure Hayman, and of Mme Arman de Caillavet, née Léontine Lippmann. Mme Arman's guests included a galaxy of eminent cultural figures, among them Alexandre Dumas *fils*, Guy de Maupassant, and Anatole France. Jacques Bizet's Jewish mother, Geneviève Halévy, also was a perennial of that social scene. At the age of twenty, she had married the composer Georges Bizet, a former student of her father, Jacques Fromental-Halévy, who was a professor of composition at the Conservatoire de Musique. After Bizet died, the formidable Geneviève let fourteen years pass before she married Émile Straus, a Jewish lawyer said to be an illegitimate half-brother of the three barons Rothschild, who employed him. The Strauses resided luxuriously in the Boulevard Haussmann. Young Proust was a frequent visitor. Possibly the most important woman in his life, after his mother, was the middle-aged Geneviève Halévy Bizet Straus, whose salon also attracted many of the best and brightest of the day, artists, diplomats, writers.

As a central feature of Proust's existence, the extended family of Jewish relatives and friends played a decisive role in the initial publication of his masterpiece, *À la recherche du temps perdu* (most recently translated as *In Search of Lost Time*). In 1912, upon completing *Swann's Way (Du côté de chez Swann)*, the first volume of his multiplex masterpiece—it would eventually comprise eight volumes—Proust set about finding a publisher for his distinctly unconventional manuscript. In February 1913 he wrote René Blum, Léon's brother, who was friendly with Bernard Grasset, a brilliant young publisher known for his interest in avant-gardist works. Whether owing to Blum's intercession or Proust's willingness to underwrite the costs, Grasset agreed to publish *Swann's Way*.

Appearing in bookstores in 1914, Proust's maiden novel revealed more imaginatively than any of his earlier, shorter pieces his ability to revive an unconscious memory and record it with phenomenal precision. The feat may have reflected his infirmity as an asthmatic, retreating in daylight hours to his famous cork-lined room, and allowing thought processes to compensate for an atrophy of physical capacity. "My present unconscious memory," he acknowledged, "fundamentally ignorant of the circumstances and surroundings . . . was sending [me] memories in floods." At the risk of confusing his readers, Proust allowed his narrative to flow from one time to another, one place to another. As in dreams, the dead are revived, as one phase of Swann's/Proust's life blends into another without transition. The young author in effect was replicating Freud's technique of free association.

The work's social significance, meanwhile, was its incomparable insight into haut-monde Parisian society, as Proust reconstructed its minutest details. From beginning to end, its "Jewish" dimension is critical to Proust's entire magnum opus. *In Search of Lost Time* accordingly is structured on three principal Jewish characters: the actress Rachel; the aggressive, unsympathetic Albert Bloch; and the assimilated Charles Swann, a member of the exclusive Jockey Club. All are the unwitting victims of a false, even fatally bigoted society, whose values, Proust tells us, are an imposture, an embrace of all that is vulgar and base. Eventually, reflecting his creator, Swann discovers his own authentic identity when he takes up the Dreyfusard cause during the "Affaire." "I was the first Dreyfusard," Proust himself later claimed proudly, if inaccurately, "for it was I who went to ask Anatole France for his signature" on the famed Pétition des Intellectuels. Proust's distant relatives, the two Halévy brothers, together with Jacques Bizet and the latter's close friends, all set to work collecting signatures—and all thereby consciously imperiled their social standing.

Ironically, until the army's case against Dreyfus began to collapse, Proust had been on equable terms with the anti-Dreyfusards Charles Maurras and Léon Daudet (pp. 288–89). Yet in one of his novel's episodes, Swann appears at the reception of the Prince de Guermantes during the bitterest period of the Affaire. Rather than avoid its consequences, he takes pains to warn his erstwhile Gentile friends against making antisemitic remarks in his presence.

The Belle Époque at Twilight

Once the Affaire wound down, to be sure, a substantial minority among the "Gallic" haut monde revived their Jewish associations. But could the old geniality be restored? The Belle Époque may have been a period of unsurpassed bourgeois—and Jewish—upward mobility; but the resentments festering beneath the political surface were not trivial. From 1898 on, the newly elected Radical Socialist government, heavily stacked with

Freemasons, launched into its retaliatory campaign against the political right, blocking the promotion of Catholic military officers, closing schools and other institutions operated by Catholic religious orders, and in 1905 formally terminating state subsidies to religious bodies altogether. These measures often were carried out with such gratuitous heavy-handedness that Catholic traditionalists set about organizing their own countercampaign.

Édouard Drumont, the journalist who had sparked the initial anti-Dreyfusard onslaught, may have been a politically crippled figure long before his death in 1917. But others were not lacking to pick up the torch of nationalist reaction. Thus, coining the phrase, "integral nationalism," Maurice Barrès invested the ideology with a new and mystical resonance, emphasizing the "spiritual" character of France's blood and soil. It was Charles Maurras, however, more than Barrès or any other of France's ultraconservatives, who transformed ideological reaction into an inflammatory xenophobia. In the spring of 1899, as the Affaire reached its dénouement, a group of self-styled "philosophical traditionalists" led by Maurice Pujo and Henri Vaugeois organized a Comité d'Action française, dedicated to a reestablishment of the old "verities." Maurras joined the committee a year later and swiftly became its leader and driving force.

Charles Marie Photius Maurras, born in a small Mediterranean fishing village in 1868, the son of a provincial tax collector, had anticipated a career as a naval officer. But upon being rejected by the naval academy for reasons of partial deafness, he entrained for Paris, where his parents registered him in a Catholic lycée. It was the youth's first exposure to an authentically cosmopolitan city. The extensive presence in the capital of Jews and other "non-Gallic" types quite shocked him. Nine years later, as a twenty-six-year-old fledgling literary critic for the right-wing newspaper *La Cocarde*, Maurras gave a name to these elements. For him, they were "métèques," that is, aliens, a term he borrowed from the ancient Athenians and which later he enlarged to include Protestants and Freemasons. By the turn of the century, retrieving the mantle of the discredited Drumont, Maurras and his colleagues of the Action française had formulated a program to resuscitate a monarchial France. In their idealized vision, the Paris-dominated government once again would be decentralized, all the old provinces would be restored in their autonomy, together with the medieval Provençal dialect. Most decisively of all, the nation would be purged of Jews and other "métèques."

In the aftermath of the Dreyfus Affair, Maurras and his closest soul mates in the Action française, among them the renowned nationalist historian Jacques de Bainville and the literary critic Léon Daudet (the son of Alphonse), set about refining their political strategy. It frankly envisaged the use of force. "The crowd," Maurras insisted, "always follows." To mobilize the "crowd," Maurras in 1905 set about transforming the original Comité de l'Action française into a "ligue," an ideological consociation. In the process, the former café intellectual revealed himself to be a dynamic and imaginative politician. Under his guidance, branches of the Action française were swiftly organized among a wide diffusion of anti-Dreyfusard and other antisemitic elements.

In 1908, the ligue established its own newspaper, also titled *L'Action française*. With Maurras setting editorial policy, it was the managing editor, Léon Daudet, who guided the paper to financial solvency. Like his father, Daudet was neither a first-class novelist nor a first-class polemicist. But he demonstrated an infallible instinct for public relations (he later served briefly in the postwar Chamber of Deputies) and for revenue-generating. Some of the funds came from his own and his wife's family estate, but more were raised from other wealthy contributors and advertisers, who ensured the paper's solid economic base. It was thus from the densely packed, garishly headlined pages of *L'Action française* that a torrent of xenophobic abuse poured out. "The métèques are our foreign guests," Maurras editorialized, "domiciled or recently naturalized. . . . The Jews are foreigners settled in France for a longer or shorter period of time." Jews were not only masters of high finance and international connections (the old Drumont accusation), they also were foreigners, aliens, with a characteristically alien disdain for national traditions or ideals.

In the last years before the war, exploiting the putative threat of alienism rather than the more traditional bête noire of republican parliamentarism, the Action française corraled widening support from military, aristocratic, and petit-bourgeois elements. Its youth organization, a collection of toughs dubbed Camelots du Roi (literally, "the king's street vendors"), disseminated anti-Jewish wall placards, attacked performances by Jewish musicians and artists, broke up Henri Bernstein's plays at the Comédie Française, and organized chauvinistic parades on Joan of Arc's Day. In this fashion, acting out the gospel of "integral nationalism" more frontally than Maurice Barrès or even Edouard Drumont could have imagined, the Action Française emerged by 1914 as the cutting edge of a potential right-wing revival.

Wartime Trauma, Social Recovery

Together with their Gentile countrymen, France's veteran Jews responded to the outbreak of the Great War in an orgy of patriotism. Even the prospect of tsarist Russia as an Entente ally did not dampen their loyalty. In 1915–16, French Jewry attempted to downplay the mass evacuation of

Russia's borderland Jews (p. 4) by attributing reports of this horror to German propaganda. It was rather more difficult to ignore the mistreatment of Russian-Jewish immigrants in France itself. Upon being conscripted into the army, these newcomers initially were thrust into the Foreign Legion, where they were brutalized by their fellow soldiers (many of them common criminals). Not until 1917, after repeated appeals by the Alliance Israélite Universelle, were immigrant Jews transferred out of the Legion into the regular army. Except for this aberration, in any case, Jewish recruits and Jewish civilians alike were regarded as compatriots in the struggle against a common enemy. Barrès and even Maurras were prepared to deliver good-conduct certificates to Jewish fighting men. "It is civic unity that matters," they acknowledged. ". . . Our antisemitism consists in not being willing to let the Jews govern France. This firm resolve can coexist with the just recognition of merit."

Following the armistice, however, the nationalist passions that had blazed during the war would not be instantly extinguished, or limited to the former German enemy. The costs of victory had been too high. Devastated territories had to be revived, destroyed industrial plant to be replaced, pensions paid to widows and wounded veterans. Then, in 1923, the Germans defaulted on their scheduled reparations payments, and the French in their exasperation marched their own troops into the Ruhr Valley to compel the Germans to pay up. The effort failed. The value of France's currency all but collapsed—ultimately to a bare 15 percent of its prewar value. The impact of the devaluation was particularly shattering for white-collar workers and their families, whose life savings were all but liquidated in the process. As in Germany, it was this embittered petite bourgeoisie that subsequently would become fertile soil for the xenophobic right.

Remarkably, even in the worst of its economic crises the French government kept the nation's doors open. Between 1919 and 1929 it permitted the immigration of nearly three million foreigners, most of these from Eastern and Southern Europe and the Near East. It was the largest postwar influx of foreigners accepted by any Western nation, including the United States. The apparent disjunction between economic fragility and open immigration lay in France's catastrophic battlefield losses, and the country's urgent military and economic need for demographic revival. Thus, by 1936 (well after free immigration had been stopped), over 11 percent of France's work force was composed of foreigners. They included 720,000 Italians, 244,000 Spaniards, 195,000 Belgians, and 435,000 East Europeans—most of the latter from Poland, the Ukraine, and Rumania. Among these, in turn, 185,000 were Jews. Indeed, by 1936, East European Jewish immigrants constituted fully 60 percent of the Jews in France.

The largest numbers of the Jewish newcomers settled in Paris, mainly in the Right Bank's lower-middle-class Marais quarter. Here they formed the nucleus of the capital's apparel industry. They also constituted a distinctly ethnocentric, Yiddish-speaking community, maintaining their own synagogues, religious schools, and (more frequently) their own ardently left-wing Bundist-Socialist societies. It was a pluralism that offended and alarmed the acculturated Jewish veterans, for whom "Gallicization" remained French Jewry's moral imperative. At the Paris Peace Conference, it was after all the Alliance Israélite Universelle that had resisted Louis Marshall's efforts to assure "national-cultural" autonomy for the Jews of Poland (pp. 34–35). Jewish ethnocentrism in France itself was all the more unthinkable.

French Gentiles, meanwhile, regarded the strident leftism of the Jewish newcomers with even greater abhorrence. For them, it was a mirror image of Jewish prominence in the Bolshevik Revolution—a disaster that had pulled Russia out of the war, threatened France's military survival, and repudiated the massive tsarist bond debt to French creditors. Even the vigorously liberal Georges Clemenceau, in a November 1917 interview he granted the journal *L'Homme enchaîné*, did not disguise his alarm:

> Without patriotism, how can there be a homeland? What is a people that no longer has a homeland? . . . Alas, we see it in this mob of German Jews who, unable to keep the land of their ancestors, appeared at the instigation of their brothers in Germany to derussify Russia.

Clemenceau would soon recover his generosity of spirit. Upon assuming the premiership a few days later, he appointed a Jew, Georges Mandel, as his chef de cabinet—in effect, as his executive director—in a government with three other Jewish chefs de cabinet.

But in the postwar years, far-rightists no longer hesitated to pounce on their favorite bêtes noires. Maurice Barrès warned that "Russia is disappearing because it is infested with Jews. Rumania is disappearing for the same reason. . . . [T]he Jews are the masters in the United States and in England." Charles Maurras, in his fanatical hatred of Germany, managed ingeniously to combine Germany, Jews, and Bolshevism in the same camp. After 1918, he stigmatized Germany as the center of world revolution, the "stem and root" of Russian Bolshevism, inasmuch as German Jews were "the masters in Moscow." Even "respectable" conservatives in the Chamber of Deputies shared in the denunciation, attacking the "cosmopolitan madmen and the traitors who seized power [in Russia]." The Catholic journals *Documentation catholique* and *Revue internationale des sociétés* branded Jews as fomenters of atheistic Bolshevism worldwide, as a "gigantic boa whose constricting coils are tied around an agonizing world, squeezing it, crushing it."

In May 1920, a series of strikes in Paris escalated into a riot. Three workers were killed and some one hundred police and Gardes Républicains were injured. The violence in turn evoked an explosion of press attacks against "Jewish radicalism." In clerical and traditional rightist circles, accusations were circulated of "Bolshevik terrorism" as the instrument of "Jewish associations." For Charles Maurras and Léon Daudet, the political climate seemed ideal for intensifying their campaign equally against the older target of a "Judeo-German financial syndicate" and the newer menace of a "Judéo-Bolshevik" conspiracy. The Consistoire Israélite, French Jewry's official "ecclesiastical" administration, reported in July 1920 that antisemitism in senior military circles was approaching the level of the Dreyfus Affair. Many Jewish officers felt compelled to apply for early retirement.

The upsurge of postwar xenophobia began to ebb only in the mid- and latter 1920s. A new spirit of diplomatic relaxation with Germany apparently was ushered in with the signing of the Locarno Treaty in 1925, while a rescheduling of German reparations payments under the "Dawes Plan" allowed for a gradual economic improvement in France. With the insecurities and aftershocks of the war slowly easing, the nation evinced a certain modest social stabilization. So, accordingly, did the political and psychological circumstances of French Jewry. And so too did public reaction to the jury verdict on Sholem Schwarzbard.

Well before mid-decade, for that matter, Marcel Proust was approaching the zenith of his intellectual reputation. The second segment of his Swann narrative, *In the Shadow of Flower-Bedecked Girls (A l'Ombre des jeunes filles en fleurs)*, had been published in 1919. Even more than its predecessor, the narrative is complex, moving in cycles and epicycles, with familiar characters materializing in and out various chapters. Demanding much of its readers, the book was not an instant popular success. Yet its critical reception was overwhelming. After a year, the volume was awarded the nation's highest literary accolade, the Prix Goncourt. In late 1920, Proust also was awarded the rosette of the Legion of Honor. Several months afterward, there appeared still another installment of *In Search of Lost Time*, this one entitled *The Guermantes Way (Le Côté de Guermantes)*.

Set in the Paris of the Dreyfus Affair, the new installment matches, even exceeds, *Swann* in capturing the rich tapestry of haut-monde society. This time the central figure is a non-Jew, the Duchesse de Guermantes, a product of the Faubourg Saint-Germain's irredeemably reactionary soirées. In the midst of a pageantry of set pieces, in and out of Paris, in and out of upper-middle-class and aristocratic dining rooms, the interaction of Gentile and Jew is drawn with the same piercing acuity as in Proust's earlier segments. There are few heroes. One of its set figures, Bloch, is a caricature of a Jewish nouveau riche, as vulgar in his arrivism as in any antisemitic caricature. But Swann himself, who appears and reappears throughout the succession of soirées, emerges by contrast (and notwithstanding his baffling marriage to Odette, the courtesan) as the epitome of unself-conscious authenticity.

Proust's critical success, his Prix Goncourt and other honors, produced no radical change in his lifestyle. Ensuing segments of his mighty epic—*Sodom and Gomorra, The Captive, The Vanished Albertine,* and *Time Regained*—emerge as the most transparently autobiographical of his volumes, and display Swann leading a life virtually indistinguishable from Proust's own. He, Proust, still worked on steadfastly in his cork-lined bedroom. But his occasional nocturnal forays in and out of salons and restaurant-dinner parties were confined now to a select group of friends, to those whom he regarded as "worthy" of his company. He made the conscious choice henceforth to drop even the most aristocratic of his former acquaintances. Beyond his homosexual companions, those friends tended to be fellow succès d'estime—Igor Stravinsky, Sergei Diaghilev, Pablo Picasso, James Joyce, André Gide. By the time of Proust's death, of pneumonia, in 1922, at the age of fifty, his friends had become almost exclusively a meritocracy. Like Swann himself during the trauma and denouement of the Dreyfus Affair, he appeared no longer to have need of merely fashionable companionship.

A Paralysis of Republicanism

The aura of egalitarianism was fleeting. One of the consequences of the war was the dysfunctionalism it aggravated in the nation's political structure. Government in France, with its proportional representation and its multitude of splinter parties, was all but tailor-made for bedlam. Between 1876, when a constitutional assembly established the Third Republic by the margin of a single vote, and 1920, there had been fifty-nine governments. From 1920 until 1939, there would be another forty-one. Political instability in turn exacerbated the nation's deeper social lesions. These were substantial. Beyond their Catholic-traditionalist social values, the politicians of France's nationalist right spoke for private property, for the preservation of a notoriously inequitable tax structure. Their greatest fear was of the possible "Bolshevization" of the nation's laboring classes.

Sharing in their concerns was France's largest "swing" party, the Radical Socialists. The title was a misnomer. With Clemenceau, the "Radicals" had emerged out of the furor of the Dreyfus Affair as champions essentially of secular republicanism. Otherwise, based on peasant proprietors and on small businessmen, the party adopted a cautiously "moderate" approach to political and economic issues. It offered no vision of fundamental economic reform, nor any effective political barrier to elitist vested interests. And following Clemenceau's resignation as premier in January 1920, it was essentially the right-wing National Bloc that dominated French politics throughout most of the ensuing decade.

A united Socialist party in these years might still have made its impact on public policy. During the war, in common with other factions, the Socialists had joined in the government of "sacred union." Yet, afterward, they vowed never again to participate in a "bourgeois" cabinet. Throughout the greater part of the 1920s, therefore, no meaningful reforms were instituted in the nation's tax structure or industrial working conditions. It was not until June 1932, following the onset of the world depression, that a new election produced a certain rickety, arm's-length parliamentary cooperation between Radicals and Socialists. The policy alignment lasted barely six months and accomplished nothing, except to frighten the political right. Indeed, from 1933 onward, fearful that even the bland Radicals might open the floodgates of leftist extremism, France's conservative parties evinced a growing susceptibility to crypto-Fascist ideology. By then, after all, much of the Continent had gone that route, from Italy and Germany to a majority of France's "Little Entente" allies in Eastern Europe.

As elsewhere on the Continent, the targeted enemies of France's ultra-right were not simply the Socialists who threatened the elite's economic and nationalist certitudes, but Jews and other "non-Gallic" elements who grated on the nation's religious identity and cultural sensibilities. The baggage of Italian and German Fascism unquestionably appealed to these reactionaries. Yet they also drew much of their inspiration from native sources, from such intellectual predecessors as Arthur de Gobineau, Georges Sorel, Édouard Drumont, and, not least, Charles Maurras. Well into the early 1930s, it was Maurras who remained primus inter pares among the nation's prophets of reaction. Exploiting the frustrations of the early postwar period, Maurras and his closest Action française associates, Daudet and Bainville, organized lectures and demonstrations throughout the country, invoking the well-familiar perils of a resurgent Germany and of a Bolshevik, "non-Gallic" France.

Meanwhile, the ligue's newspaper, the *Action française*, with its densely upholstered coverage of political and cultural affairs, continued to attract tens of thousands of readers of all social backgrounds. These included the poet T. S. Eliot, and a significant minority of Jews, Marcel Proust among them. At the same time, the ligue's core constituency of rightists enjoyed the paper's editorial emphasis upon discipline, hierarchy, and authoritarianism. By the early 1930s, Maurras was shifting away from abstract royalism to Fascism of the Italian model, and to Mussolini as a Bonapartist "in spirit"; while Daudet praised Fascism as a "national, unitary system."

By the early 1930s, too, the Action française had been joined by numerous other Fascist or crypto-Fascist imitators, most of them sharing a common frustration with "effete" parliamentarism, an instinctive preference for a strong leader, and a growing receptivity to violence. Among them were such Italian-style squadristi, more noisome than numerous, as Marcel Bucard's Francisme, Antoine Redier's Solidarité française, and General Noël de Castelnau's Ligue des Patriotes. A rather more serious competitor for ultraright-wing loyalties was the Jeunesses patriotes. The movement's founder, Pierre Taittinger, the son of a devoutly patriotic Lorrainer family, had entered the war as a sergeant and emerged as a twice-wounded, much-decorated captain. With his formidable military record, Taittinger was promptly elected to the Chamber of Deputies in 1919 as a member of the rightist Bloc National, then reelected throughout the 1920s and early 1930s. A dynamic overachiever, Taittinger also used his wife's ample inheritance to pyramid his business fortune into some twenty commercial enterprises, including the champagne company that still bears his name. An ardent admirer of Mussolini, Taittinger in 1924 funded and organized the Jeunesses patriotes and subsequently nurtured its youthful membership into the single most militant of all France's paramilitary ligues. Conducting their marches and demonstrations in full military panoply, with uniforms and torchlights, the putative squadristi emulated their counterparts in Italy, brawling with Communists and Socialists alike, attacking trade-union offices, breaking up workers' strikes.

Yet Taittinger's Jeunesses patriotes and even Maurras's Action française ultimately were eclipsed in sheer critical mass by the Croix de Feu (The Fiery Cross). Launched in 1927 exclusively as a veterans' organization—in effect, a French version of the American Legion—this nominally apolitical ligue achieved major salience only in 1931 when its command was taken over by Lieutenant Colonel (Count) Casimir de la Rocque. A renowned war hero who had served on Marshal Foch's staff on the western front, de la Rocque subsequently had been attached to the French military commission that "advised" Poland in its defense of Warsaw against the advancing Red Army (p. 13). His early confrontation with the Bolsheviks was a defining moment for the colonel. Although a law-abiding man who initially espoused no tendentious political doctrine, he soon grasped the urgency of "national vigilance" against subversion (that is, leftist, alien) influences.

Uniformed and highly disciplined, the Croix de Feu under de la Rocque's command engaged in massive parades and torchlight pageants.

Eventually its partisans even included non-veterans. Some of these were members of Catholic youth organizations, others were simple lumpenproletariat. All, however, were committed to de la Rocque's stance of "national vigilance." "If necessary," promised the colonel, "we shall descend into the street . . . to help the army and the police establish order by any means." If the threat was ominous, so was the ligue's sheer emergent bulk. By 1934, with a membership estimated at 130,000, and enjoying the tacit approbation of numerous senior army officers, the Croix de Feu had become the largest and most prestigious of all France's paramilitary organizations.

The "Events" of February 1934

The moment for these and other crypto-Fascist ligues to flex their muscles came in the winter of 1933–34. Mired in depression, the French people witnessed nothing but governmental ineptitude in dealing with the economic crisis. Since the 1932 election, the Radicals and Socialists had enjoyed a comfortable majority in the Chamber of Deputies. Yet they failed to agree on an economic agenda. The Radicals preferred a cautious deflationary approach. The Socialists advocated "reflation" and public spending. Each faction blocked the other's program. The results were five governments between 1932 and December 1933 alone, and public outrage approaching the threshold of conflagration. The spark was provided on Christmas Eve of 1933.

It was then that a certain Tissier, who managed the municipal pawnshop of Bayonne, a southwestern port city, paid a visit to the subprefect of his district to acknowledge an act of malfeasance. Two years earlier, Tissier and a group of business partners had sold 200 million francs' worth of two-year credit bonds without meaningful collateral. They assumed that there would always be time to cover repayment by milking "other resources." But now the two years had expired, and there were no "other resources." Losing his nerve, Tissier felt obliged to confess. As his crestfallen admission emerged, however, it became apparent that he was merely a small cog in a far larger operation. Its arch-manipulator was Alexandre Stavisky.

Thirty-eight years old, a dapper bon vivant, "Sasha" Stavisky posed as a master of high finance. Sporting a chauffeured limousine and displaying a taste for the company of the rich and famous, he became a familiar figure in trendy watering places from Cannes to Deauville. To the police and judiciary, however, Stavisky was nothing more than "a gentleman among gangsters, and a gangster among gentlemen." Born in Kiev, he had been brought to France with his Jewish immigrant parents as a small boy. His father, a dentist, opened an office in Marais, the Jewish quarter of Paris, and soon developed a practice comfortable enough to provide his son with quality schooling. But if young Stavisky acquired a certain cultural varnish in his expensive private lycée, he also fell in with a group of sybaritic classmates. Sharing their taste for fast living, he dropped out of school to set up in business as a precocious "theatrical entrepreneur." The enterprise served as a front for prostitutes and loan sharks.

When the war begin in 1914, Stavisky unhesitatingly volunteered for the army, but soon was discharged for undisclosed medical reasons. His activities afterward are uncertain, but evidently he got by for a while as a gigolo for wealthy women. Journalists subsequently described Stavisky's "anthracite eyes, circled with green penumbra, drooping ears, pinched little moustache," his "lustrous profile." In 1921, "le beau Sasha" managed to become a "financier" again. On one occasion he was arraigned for counterfeiting; on another, for forgery; on another, for stock fraud. In each instance, he mysteriously disappeared just before the trial began. By 1926, when Stavisky was arrested (and released) yet again, this time for defrauding a stockbroker of 7 million francs, the press began describing him as "the king of crooks." That same year, Stavisky's father committed suicide.

In the late 1920s and early 1930s, Stavisky began developing contacts with parliamentary deputies and assistant cabinet ministers. By offering munificent salaries, he lured several of these unsuspecting eminences onto the boards of his "investment companies." One of his first ventures was the municipal pawnshop of Orléans. Purchasing a significant bloc of stock in this semipublic corporation, Stavisky then floated additional shares at vastly inflated prices. When funds had to be repaid, he was already well launched on other bond issues for other municipal pawnshops, using new funds to redeem older bonds. For a while, the elaborate Ponzi-style operation worked smoothly. But le beau Sasha's crowning achievement was the Bayonne Affair. Gaining control of the pawnshop soon after it was established, he hired others to seek out investment funds for his newest bond issues. Among these associates were Tissier, the pawnshop manager; Leonhard Cohen, its assessor; and Marcel Grabat, mayor and parliamentary deputy of Bayonne. With their collaboration, and with a board of well-paid municipal officials serving as window dressing, Stavisky was able to sell bonds carrying a face value of 200 million francs. But finally, in the autumn of 1933, the affair blew open when Stavisky could not produce the funds needed to cover a maturing issue. It was then that Tissier lost his nerve and made his Christmas Eve visit to the subprefect.

Hereupon the Sûrêté Générale was brought in, and the record of Stavisky's earlier pawnshop swindles was uncovered. A summons went out for his arrest. He was nowhere to be found. It soon developed that, on

December 23, aware that his operation was about to be exposed, Stavisky obtained a passport at the local police prefecture under the name—actually his bodyguard's—of Miemancrenko. Further investigation revealed that "Miemancrenko's" passport had been stamped at the Swiss frontier, then restamped when the subject reentered French territory. This was the clue that ultimately brought French police to Chamonix, a border village in the French Alps. At Chamonix, on January 9, 1934, Stavisky was traced to a local villa. The police knocked at the villa's door. At that moment, inside, Stavisky fired a bullet into his head. Only 33,000 francs were found on his body, and it was assumed that the rest of his absconded funds had been deposited in a Swiss bank account. Stavisky also left a suicide note for his son, begging forgiveness. This was the official version.

But few people in France believed a word of the official version. It was the consensus of political leaders of all parties, and of most of the press, that the police had murdered Stavisky to prevent the revelation of his many connections among public figures. Predictably, it was the *Action française* that milked the scandal for all it was worth. Did not the "Affaire Stavisky" expose the bottomless corruption of Parliament and of its "respectable" politicians? the newspaper editorialized. Was this not evidence that Stavisky (to whose Jewish antecedents the paper devoted a full issue) and his Jewish cronies held France's politicians in thrall? Soon the *Action française* had even juicier grist for its mill. Beyond Parliament, important government officials evidently had been corrupted by Stavisky's operations. The revelation became public when an assistant government prosecutor was rushed to the hospital after taking poison, and when a deputy minister of agriculture cut his throat in Fontainebleau Forest.

If doubt remained of Stavisky's link with senior government functionaries, it was dissipated by the fate of Judge Prince, former director of the finance department of the public prosecutor's office, and the official directly responsible for fraud investigations. On January 20, 1934, Prince's mangled body was found on a railroad track near the town of Dimon. It developed that he had sought to shield the public prosecutor against charges of incompetence; and the public prosecutor, Maurice Pressard, happened to be the brother-in-law of Camille Chautemps, who was none other than prime minister of the current Radical Socialist government.

Shaken by the revelations and accusations, Chautemps promptly authorized a full inquiry, to be conducted by a highly respected senior police official, Inspector Guillaume. Guillaume's investigation unearthed much evidence of incompetence and negligence among high government officials, but nothing to impugn either Pressard, or the late, unfortunate Prince, or least of all Prime Minister Chautemps. Could the premier then declare the case closed? Not a chance. The political right smelled blood.

On January 9, 1934, the *Action française* headlined its editorial "Down with the Thieves" and urged "the people of Paris to come in large numbers before the Chamber of Deputies . . . to clamor for honesty and justice." In fact, demonstrations outside the Palais Bourbon, home of the Parliament, had been mounting for at least a week before the *Action française*'s call to action. Nor were the mobs of demonstrators limited to followers of Maurras and his Action française. All the rightist paramilitary ligues now sensed that the moment was ripe for a decisive blow against the Chautemps government, and thereby against the shaky cooperation between the Radicals and Socialists.

On January 13, the *Action française* issued a second appeal for mass demonstrations. This one produced larger crowds, and growing violence. So did a third summons on January 22. The protests mounted steadily, on January 24, 27, and 28. Beleaguered on the right, and given only tepid support by the Socialists, Prime Minister Chautemps had had enough. He submitted his government's resignation on the 28th. For the first time in the history of the Third Republic, a parliamentary majority government had capitulated to a mob. Even then, the appetites of the rightist organizations had only been whetted. Their riots picked up momentum, day after day.

Meanwhile, the president of the Republic, Albert Lebrun, sought out an acceptable compromise figure among the Radical majority to replace Chautemps. His choice fell on Édouard Daladier. Daladier was a decorated war veteran and a practicing Catholic, and it was assumed that these credentials might spare him the obloquy of the rightist ligues. To win over Socialist participation in a broadly based cabinet, on the other hand, Daladier in early February announced his intention of sacking Paris's right-wing prefect of police, Jean Chiappe. Instead, the maneuver served only to enrage the political right. On February 5, Maurras and other ligue spokesmen called upon their supporters to demonstrate "in force" before the Palais Bourbon the next evening, February 6, when Daladier was scheduled to submit his proposed cabinet to the Chamber of Deputies.

Even as the paramilitaries mobilized their followers, they achieved little coordination among them. With the exception of the Action française, most of the ligues—the Jeunesses Patriotes, the Solidarité française, the Ligue des Patriotes, the Croix de Feu—seemed uninterested in restoring the monarchy, as in the era of the Dreyfus Affair. Rather, they were intent simply on rioting, on intimidating, to ensure a more rightist parliamentary orientation, even a more authoritarian government. But if few displayed any immediate interest in overthrowing the Republic, their escalating "demonstration" of February 6 unquestionably threatened the popularly elected Chamber of Deputies. As many as ten thousand partisans and hangers-on converged at the Place de la Concorde, near the bridges that would carry them across to the Left Bank, to the Palais Bourbon. Bitter clashes with the police and the Garde Républicain continued throughout the evening.

Finally, about 11:30 p.m., heavy reinforcements of police began to push the crowds back. Their success was not entirely their own. The Croix de Feu, largest of the rightist paramilitary organizations, happened also to be the most disciplined. Its commander, Colonel de la Rocque, satisfied that the demonstration had made its point, ordered his units to pull back. Others followed their lead, and the worst of the threat to the Chamber of Deputies eased. Yet, by then, 14 rioters had been killed and 236 seriously injured, while police casualties included 1 killed and 92 seriously injured. Property damage came to some 10 million francs.

Moreover, the aftershocks of demonstrations continued. In the Chamber, throughout the late afternoon of February 6, Premier-designate Daladier eventually won a majority, this time with the help of the Socialists. Yet he would derive little comfort from this "victory." The next morning, February 7, Marshal Louis Lyautey, one of the nation's most renowned military figures and an arch-rightist, warned President Lebrun that if Daladier did not resign, he, Lyautey, would order the Jeunesses Patriotes to march on the Chamber. Other rumors were circulating of a plan to establish a rogue "provisional government" at the City Hall. The prospect of civil war left Daladier appalled. On the afternoon of February 7, he tendered his resignation. For the second time in ten days, a duly elected government had fallen victim to right-wing intimidation.

Hereupon President Lebrun cast about for a prime minister to organize a "safe" caretaker government of "national union." He found his man in old Gaston Doumergue, a leader of the Radical Socialists' "conservative" wing. For the while, the ligues decided to bide their time. All the more so as the Doumergue cabinet fell increasingly under the thumb of such rightist veterans as Minister of State André Tardieu. Another arch-conservative, Marshal Henri-Philippe Pétain, was appointed minister of war, while still another rightist, Pierre Laval, became foreign minister. And within a few weeks, deserted by his Radical Socialist cabinet members, Prime Minister Doumergue himself resigned. This time an even more unregenerately conservative government was patched together under Pierre Flandin. In June 1935, Flandin in turn would be succeeded as premier by Pierre Laval. So it was, from February 1934 on, that the forces of reaction were entrenching themselves in France. Their cutting edge was a comminution of Fascist and crypto-Fascist paramilitary ligues. The Third Republic, its survival presumably guaranteed by the dénouement of the

Dreyfus Affair less than thirty-five years earlier, now once again appeared in mortal peril.

An Unlikely Champion

As the violence raged on the evening of February 6, 1934, and as both rightists and Communists howled down Édouard Daladier in the Chamber of Deputies, the premier-designate found his only source of support among the Socialists. This was an irony. Daladier and the Socialist leader Léon Blum had long been political, even personal, enemies. Yet it was "Blum alone," Daladier later admitted, "who advised me to remain in office and fight back." Moreover, bravely facing down the demonstrators, Blum remained at his post when the angry mob threatened to invade the Palais Bourbon at any moment, and possibly lynch him and other Socialists. Who, then, was this thin, bespectacled man, with his reedy voice and foppish necktie and lapel flower, who courageously stood his ground at a moment of grave political and personal danger?

Born in 1872, Léon Blum was one of five sons of an Alsatian Jewish family that had settled in Paris in the mid-nineteenth century. The father, Auguste Blum, opened a silk-ribbon factory. In the quickening growth of the women's fashion market, the business flourished and eventually become the largest silk-ribbon company in France. After the father's death in 1921, Blum Frères was managed by three of Léon Blum's four brothers, until the 1929 depression and a change in women's fashions ended its success. The reputation of great wealth that clung to Léon Blum in later years was always a myth.

In his youth, Blum's family life was warm. He and his brother Lucien were particularly close. At lycée, both were precocious students of classical literature. Léon Blum would carry that interest furthest. Even as he studied law at the university, his literary passion remained undiminished. Attending cultural salons, he made the acquaintance of Gide, Valéry, Proust (p. 286), and other renowned literary figures. Indeed, during these student years, Blum himself contributed essays to French literary magazines. A collection of his articles, appearing in book form when he was twenty-two, quite astonished readers with its erudition and insights.

Upon receiving his law degree in 1894, Blum chose to forgo a routine business practice in favor of public service. He became an "auditeur"— a citizens' representative—at the Conseil d'État, France's chancery court, dealing with issues of equity appeal against the government. Here Blum proved to be a skilled and conscientious advocate on behalf of petitioners. At the same time, he was able to give over his evenings and weekends to intellectual and social interests. It was the era of the Dreyfus Affair, and inevitably those interests turned to public issues. They also turned to Socialism, for it was in 1898 that Blum came to know Jean Jaurès, the charismatic parliamentary leader of France's Socialist party.

Thirteen years younger than Jaurès, Blum almost immediately became the great man's protégé and devoted friend. In 1904 he accepted a position as deputy editor of the Socialist newspaper, *L'Humanité*. The party's appeal to Blum was both intellectual and moralistic. "Socialism wishes to bring social justice into accordance with reason," he explained, in a fin-de-siècle review of Anatole France's *Crainquebille*, "to line up positive institutions with rational convictions." With this typically cerebral approach, Blum shared Jaurès's determination to achieve "reasoned" compromise among the various Socialist factions. Like Jaurès, he rejected the alternative of a violent class revolution.

The two friends divided only on issues of military preparedness. For the older man, Socialism was pacifism, and there could be no compromise on this principle. Indeed, Jaurès's adamance ultimately cost him his life; on the eve of the war, he was assassinated by a demented superpatriot. Blum, on the other hand, although bitterly mourning his friend's death, was quite prepared to join other party revisionists in supporting the national cause against Germany. When three Socialists—Jules Guèsde, Albert Thomas, and Marcel Sembat—agreed to become ministers in a government of "sacred unity," Blum himself accepted appointment as Sembat's chef de cabinet in the ministry of public works. The experience proved invaluable for him. By the time Blum left the government, upon Sembat's departure in 1917, he had acquired a penetrating insight into the operation of the public bureaucracy.

Some months later, it was Russia's Bolshevik Revolution that opened a fault line in France's Socialist movement. By the end of the war, a majority within the party was prepared to move decisively to the left. Indeed, by March 1919, when the Soviets organized the "Third International," France's working classes already had veered markedly to the camp of radicalism. The full extent of their ideological transformation became evident in December of that year, when the Socialist party held its national congress in Tours. As chairman of the party—a role he all but inherited upon the death of Jaurès—Blum issued an impassioned appeal to the delegates to avoid the Communist "trap" of unconditional membership in the Comintern, of accepting the "false god" of a proletarian dictatorship. "You will not make the revolution," he warned, "by consorting with gangs that run after any man on horseback." Yet Blum's cri de coeur proved unavailing. The congress voted overwhelmingly to join the Third International. A telegram then arrived from Gregori Zinoviev, chairman of the Comintern, demanding that all "dissenters" be expelled from the party. After the ensuing purge of "right-wingers," Léon Blum among them, the remaining left-wing majority became the French Communist party.

For his part, Blum immediately set about reconstructing the remnants of the original—mainstream—Socialist party. Here it was that the former dandy, the littérateur, the urbane salon conversationalist, revealed formidable political skills and ideological tenacity. Relying upon a solid nucleus of 30,000 out of the former 180,000 members of the pre-Tours Socialist movement, he worked unremittingly to rebuild the party's cadres. In the process, as a member of the Chamber of Deputies (since 1919), Blum also established a legendary personal reputation for intellectual and moral integrity. Even Maurice Barrès, his former literary "mentor" and current political adversary, wrote of Blum in the 1920s: "I am touched that the revolutionaries [sic] have chosen Blum and [Paul] Boncour. These intellectuals . . . elevate the tone of the gangster-like discussions. . . . They are civilizers as well as destroyers." So formidable was Blum's reputation among deputies of all parties that the Chamber would fill up whenever he was due to speak. Although he was a less than charismatic figure, with his drooping moustache, pince-nez spectacles, and frail voice, Blum's speeches were masterpieces of Cartesian logic and stylistic polish.

Throughout the 1920s, too, as Russia's Bolshevik regime proved fully as brutal as Blum had warned, and as bread-and-butter unionism gained momentum under a revived Socialist-dominated trade union confederation, Blum was able gradually to reconstruct his party. By 1932, the Socialists had more than regained their pre-Tours strength. In the elections of that year, they returned 105 deputies, nearly twice as many as the Communists. In some measure, Blum accomplished the feat by ideological integrity, by refusing to accept a marriage of convenience with the petit-bourgeois Radicals. The party would enter no coalition with any other faction until the Socialists themselves governed that coalition and determined its legislative agenda.

But with the events of February 6, 1934, everything changed. In the tumultuous eight hours of that day, as Daladier frantically scrambled to put together a new government, Blum promised his support. "In the battle now engaged," he declared, "we claim our place in the front line. . . . The Fascist reaction will not pass." Blum then made Daladier an unprecedented offer. The Socialists would agree to participate in a Radical-led government. Yet the gesture came too late. Daladier's nerve was gone. The new government, when it was formed several days later under "Papa" Doumergue, was predominantly of the right. Blum, in turn, horrified by the new political configuration, decided on a bold step. It was to guide the Socialists in another direction. On February 12, he appeared with

Maurice Thorez, chairman of France's Communist party, in a joint public rally against "Fascism." An unlikely political phenomenon was in the making.

It was to be led by an even unlikelier one—Blum himself. The man's intellectualism was the least of his "apolitical" burdens. In earlier years, Jews had participated only intermittently in politics. During the Orleanist monarchy, Benjamin David was elected a parliamentary deputy in 1834, and sixteen years later the banker Michel Goudchaux briefly held the portfolio of the finance ministry. Following the 1848 revolution, Isaac Adolphe Crémieux served as minister of justice in the Second Republic, and Achille Fould as minister of finance. Fould's three sons, and his grandson, subsequently were elected to the Chamber of Deputies. Leo Frankel, a political refugee from Hungary, became minister of labor in the Paris Commune of 1870. Under the Third Republic, David Raynal was appointed minister of public works in Léon Gambetta's government of 1881, and later minister of the interior. Throughout the nineteenth century, the modest role of Jews in French political life apparently did not evoke much interest one way or another.

Then came the trauma of the Dreyfus Affair. In the resulting explosion of antisemitism, the opportunity for Jews to share in public life appeared all but foreclosed. Several years afterward, however, with the evident triumph of French liberalism, the number of Jews in government service resumed its slow, earlier increase. Georges Mandel served as Clemenceau's wartime chef de cabinet, even as Blum served as Sembat's. Louis Klotz and Édouard Ignace became ministers in the same cabinet; and Klotz also was one of France's signatories of the Versailles Treaty. In the 1920s, Abraham Schrameck, formerly governor of Madagascar, became minister of the interior, then minister of justice in the leftist confederation, the "Cartel des Gauches," and Maurice Bokowsky served as minister of commerce and industry during the same period.

Yet it was also in the postwar years that the full impact of reawakened xenophobia focused on the Jews, and with particular ferocity on Léon Blum. In truth, Blum was no stranger to obloquy, even before embarking on his political career. In 1907, his provocative little volume *On Marriage (Du Mariage)* evoked howls of outrage for its attack on the "double standard" of premarital sex. Unrequited anti-Dreyfusards promptly denounced the book as "Jewish pornography," as a "Jewish-Masonic and secularist" plot "to dishonor all the women of France." Even "civilized" conservatives resented Blum's presumptuousness in tampering with Gallic values. After dining with Blum in 1914, André Gide recorded in his diaries that "the virtues of the Jewish race are not French virtues. . . . [T]hey speak with greater ease than we because they have fewer scruples." Later that same year, as Blum entered the war cabinet, even a fellow Socialist—and a fellow chef de cabinet—Hubert Bourgin, described him as

> nervous, feverish. . . . His eyes shone with a prodigious gleam . . . his moustache revealed a sensual mouth which seemed to be savoring the taste of a voluptuous prey. . . . It seemed to me that I was watching the unfolding of this superior and strange person, this admixture of messianism and Jewish prophetism adopted to the modern age, of Oriental passion, of Asiatic frenzy.

These reservations were the merest prelude to the avalanche of postwar denunciations. In December 1920, Léon Daudet, the erstwhile friend of Proust, warned his readers in *L'Action française* that "a simian little *youtre* [yid] like Blum is utterly indifferent and even hostile to French interests." In Blum's initial parliamentary years, he underwent ad hominem taunting even during his most brilliant speeches in the Chamber. "There's room only for Frenchmen here," heckled a royalist deputy, Magne, on one occasion in January 1923. Léon Daudet trumped Magne by shouting: "To Jerusalem!" Another far-rightist, Jean Ybarnegary, then characterized Blum as a "Protestant Jew." Rumors were circulated about Blum's personal life, his alleged vast personal wealth, which presumably included a fabulous silver collection (he lived in a comfortable but unpretentious Right Bank apartment). As Blum successfully rebuilt the Socialist party, Charles Maurras would write of him in 1928: "There is a man who should be shot, but in the back." Another rightist, Pierre Gaxotte, called Blum a "Palestinian mare" and suggested that he and other Jews be sent to a concentration camp in Madagascar. A January 1934 issue of *La Solidarité*, journal of the Jeunesses Patriotes, carried a full-page photograph of Blum, overlaid with the caption: "Public Enemy Number 1."

Blum's response to this litany of abuse was instructive. In common with the pallid cultism of most veteran Jewish families, his own religious observance had been perfunctory. He and his brothers underwent the bar mitzvah ceremony, but afterward rarely attended synagogue. Nevertheless, Blum stood on his heritage with unflagging dignity, making plain that he regarded his ancestry as a source of "nobility," of "generosity." In later years he would claim (possibly factitiously) that his "religion of justice" had led him to embrace Socialism. The sentiment he expressed in delivering the eulogy for his friend, the writer Bernard Lazare, doubtless evinced a sense of his own self-respect: "He had within him a Jew of a great race, of a prophetic race, of the race which says 'a just man' where others would say 'a saint.' "

During the parliamentary episode of January 1923, as he was vilified by

Magne, Ybarnegary, Daudet, and other ultrarightists, Blum responded in the ensuing tumult:

> I am in fact a Jew. . . . I shall allow no one to remind me of the race into which I was born, and I have never renounced it, and toward it I maintain only sentiments of recognition and pride. . . . I was born in France, I was raised in French schools. My friends are French. . . . I have the right to consider myself perfectly assimilated. Well, I nonetheless feel myself a Jew. And I have never noticed, between these two aspects of my consciousness, the least contradiction, the least tension.

To emphasize the point, Blum intermittently attended public Jewish functions. In 1929, identifying with the Zionist cause, he accepted Chaim Weizmann's invitation to participate in the founding session of the Jewish Agency for Palestine, and assured his fellow delegates that he was proud to participate "both as a Socialist and as a Jew in a venture that merits the admiration not only of Judaism but of all humanity."

Ironically, Blum's forthrightness often gave concern less to his political enemies than to the veteran Jewish leadership, which would have preferred that he adopt a lower political profile (pp. 310–11). Blum reacted to this timorousness with contempt. In 1935, publishing his *Memoirs of the [Dreyfus] Affair*, he recalled: "The rich Jews, the Jews of bourgeois means, the Jewish [officialdom] feared engaging in the battle for Dreyfus, exactly as they fear today the battle against Fascism. . . . They did not understand then any better than they do today that no precaution . . . could protect them from being victimized by anti-Dreyfusards any more than by triumphant Fascism." In November 1938, addressing the Ligue international contre l'Antisemitisme, he voiced the identical scorn for "establishment" Jews who feared too large an influx of Jewish refugees. "I would not see anything in the world as dolorous and as dishonorable," he insisted, "as seeing French Jews applying today to close the doors of France to Jewish refugees from other countries. Let them not imagine that they are thus preserving their tranquility, their security." The warning was prescient.

An "Anti-Fascist" Crusade

The simultaneous rise and fall of the Daladier government on February 7, 1934, represented a supreme moment of vindication for the rightist paramilitary organizations, and specifically for the Croix de Feu, the most disciplined and "respectable" of the ligues. The organization's membership climbed to 130,000 by the summer of 1934, and to 160,000 by early 1936. It was the mounting threat of a Fascist coup, in turn, that impelled France's political left into urgent action. Thus, immediately following the "events" of February 6–7, the Confederation Générale du Travail, the Socialists' national labor organization, ordered a general strike for February 12. Hereupon, for the first time since the schism of Tours in December 1919, the parallel federation of Communist-dominated unions decided to share in the procession. The event did not quite yet represent a political alliance. Maurice Thorez, the Communist party chairman, was not interested in defending a "rotting" republic.

By the late summer of 1934, however, alarmed at the prospect of a rearmed Germany, the Soviet leadership in Moscow began to shift their own position. Hints were dropped in Soviet publications of the possible usefulness of a Communist joint stance with other anti-Fascist elements, even with the hated Socialists. In France, therefore, Maurice Thorez dutifully called for negotiating a "unity-of-action" pact with the Socialists. Although wary, Blum and his colleagues agreed to enter into discussions with Thorez and the latter's associates. In the spring of 1935, after months of intensive and often abrasive negotiations, a formula eventually was agreed upon for the parliamentary elections scheduled for April 1936. Both parties would cooperate to defeat the forces of reaction. Those candidates of either party who scored highest in the first round of voting would be given joint support in the second, decisive round.

It was not the Socialists and Communists alone who signed on to the pact. Early in 1935, fearful lest his own party be marginalized by the left's new political configuration, Édouard Daladier of the Radicals persuaded his colleagues to enter into the alignment, which would be entitled the Popular Front. The leadership of the three factions thereupon cobbled together a cautiously progressive, Social Democratic–style agenda. The program called for enforcement of the rights of trade unions, rejection of clerical participation in the public school system, reversal of the current government's deflationary policies, enactment of a wider national unemployment insurance system, and an extensive public works program. Only the foreign-policy plank remained deliberately ambiguous. On the one hand, it favored collective security under the League of Nations. On the other, it called for a gradual reduction of armaments, and nationalization of privately owned munitions factories.

Campaigning began in the late autumn of 1935. Amply funded, the rightist parties conducted a vigorous public-relations offensive, systematically invoking the threat of Bolshevism. By contrast, the parties of the Popular Front appeared unable to overcome their lingering intramural suspicions. Their cooperation was intermittent and undisciplined. But an event of February 13, 1936, suddenly remobilized the Popular Front effort. On that day, Léon Blum was being driven home from his office by a colleague, Georges Bonnet, and Madame Bonnet. En route, their automobile was halted in the Boulevard Saint-Germain by a huge funeral procession. The deceased was none other than Jacques de Bainville, the venerated royalist historian and polemicist of the Action française. Uniformed lines of Camelots du Roi, the Action française youth group, formed a guard of honor.

Suddenly members of the crowd recognized Blum. Howling with rage, they mobbed the Bonnets' car, smashing its windows. Blum was dragged out and savagely beaten, then left on the street, bleeding heavily. The Bonnets pleaded with the concierge of a neighboring building to open the gate for Blum. She refused. Eventually several construction workers and two policemen intervened to carry the Socialist leader into another apartment building. Soon afterward, he was transported to a hospital, where the severed vein in his neck was sutured.

Three days later, half a million marchers participated in a mass rally to protest the assault, and Prime Minister Albert Sarrault, a Radical presiding over a fragile coalition government, issued a decree ordering the dissolution of the Action française. Shortly afterward, a magistrate sentenced Charles Maurras to a four-month prison term for incitement to murder. Blum himself, meanwhile, suffering from shock and loss of blood, was obliged to remain in the hospital for nearly two weeks, then to convalesce in southern France throughout the entire spring election campaign. Yet the widespread sympathy he evoked unquestionably helped the Popular Front cause. For a brief moment, like Dreyfus at the turn of the century, Blum emerged as a symbol of the Republic itself.

The first round of voting, on April 26, 1936, resulted in a solid, if unspectacular, victory for the Popular Front. It was the second round, on May 6, that produced an authentic triumph. The National Front (as the combination of right-wing groups styled itself) received 4.5 million votes; but the Popular Front parties received 5.6 million. As a coalition, the Popular Front brought in 375 deputies, 153 more than the National Front. Socialist jubilation was tempered somewhat when the Communists announced that their own deputies would support the new government in the Chamber of Deputies, but would refrain from actually participating in a "bourgeois" cabinet. Blum and the Socialists as a result would share executive responsibility with the Radicals alone. Nevertheless, as the single largest party in the Chamber, the Socialists at long last would exercise decisive leadership. And Léon Blum in consequence would become the first authentically Socialist prime minister in French history.

His election of course represented an even more stunning innovation.

None of the ultrarightists allowed the nation to forget Blum's Jewish identity. On the one hand, antisemitism even during the 1930s was less central an issue in French public life than during the Dreyfus Affair. In the years of that earlier trauma, it would have been unimaginable for a Jew to be elected premier. But the lesson learned during the Dreyfus years, that antisemitism could be transformed into a political weapon against liberal democracy, was put to far more systematic use in the late 1920s and 1930s. It was supremely the depression era that fused antisemitism with paramilitary Fascism. Thus, while the Jew-hatred of the Action française was an old story, others of the ligues now picked up the antisemitic refrain. The Solidarité française stigmatized the Popular Front leadership as

> the Blums, the Kaisersteins,
> the Schweinkopfs, and the Zyromskis, whose very
> French names are a whole pogrom.
> Patriots, these are your masters!

In previous years, Colonel de la Rocque had not overtly identified himself with antisemitism. Well into the 1930s, he accepted Jewish war veterans in his Croix de Feu. By mid-decade, however, the colonel was sharing in the denunciation of "left-wing Jews," particularly foreign refugees who were exploiting the "hospitality of France . . . the sweetest of adoptive mothers."

Ultimately, it was Blum's leadership of the Popular Front that gave far-rightist elements their supreme opportunity. Georges Suarez, editor of a xenophobic screed, *Gringoire* (after a villainous character in Victor Hugo's *Notre Dame de Paris*), popularized the phrase: "That man is not from here." Ligue spokesmen and editors now vied with each other in diabolizing Blum. "Here is a man to shoot down," repeated Maurras in 1934. "Human detritus should be treated as such." An excerpt from a 1934 essay, "The Three Enemies of France: the Freemasons, the Jews, and the Métèques" ("Les trois ennemies de la France: les franc-maçons, les juifs, et les métèques"), by Ismar Gibelin, a leader of the paramilitary Faisceau, claimed:

> The Abominable Kike, the traitorous Léon Blum, leader of the Socialists (capitalists in rabbit fur), has renounced the social and French direction of [Jean] Jaurès. An unassimilable Jew, Léon Blum, has dishonored Socialism. . . . For Léon Blum dreams of one day becoming the "Bela Kun" of France.

Caricatures in the right-wing press depicted Blum in various guises: as a sinister androgyne, a degenerate sophisticate, with his white handkerchief, drooping moustaches, and effete manner; as a jackal; as a forest creature, spittle dripping from his fangs.

Not even Blum's election as prime minister could assure him the minimal respect traditionally accorded his office. On June 7, 1936, the day he presented his government to the Chamber of Deputies, Xavier Vallet, a one-legged war veteran and stalwart of the far right, solemnly advised Blum: "Your advent, M. le Premier, is without question a historic date. For the first time this ancient Gallo-Roman land is to be ruled by a Jew. . . . To govern this peasant nation of France, it would be better to have someone whose origins, however modest, lie deep in our soil, rather than a subtle Talmudist." (The Chamber then erupted in a bedlam of taunts and counter-taunts.) A year later, a rightist publicist, Marcel Jouhandeau, author of the recently published *Le Péril juif*, invented a new genealogy for Blum as an "Asiatic" of East European ancestry, a fiction that was republished in an apolitical, thoroughly respectable business journal, *Les Nouvelles économiques et financières*, which stated as a fact that Blum's name actually was Karfunkelstein. "Leon Karfunkelstein," it wrote, "known as 'Blum,' was born in Vidine [Bulgaria] in 1872 and came to Paris in 1874 with his parents."

The *Action française*, meanwhile, described Blum's inauguration into office as "the *youtre*'s revenge." "The Jewish ship adrift," "the Jewish revolt sings its victory." Blum's cabinet would become "the cabinet of the Talmud." In one fifty-line article, Maurras succeeded in calling the new premier a camel sixteen times, with the rest of Blum's cabinet described as idiots, fanatics, deserters, crooks, traitors, prostitutes, pederasts. Blum's exaggerated "sexuality" became a favored theme for Maurras, who adverted repeatedly to the prime minister's "sinuous," "sensual" mannerisms. Earlier, in January 1936, Maurras had described Blum as a sadist and inveterate pederast, a polymorph. This theme too was taken up by other enemies.

If Blum himself remained unintimidated by the campaign of vilification, the Jewish leadership failed to match his stoical dignity. It was hardly a secret that French Jews over the years had voted overwhelmingly for either the Socialists or the Radical Socialists. As in the case of German and Austrian Jews, minority insecurity dictated their politics. Yet in the immediate aftermath of the Popular Front electoral victory, *L'Univers israélite*, a publication of the Jewish Consistoire, ventured only the insipid observation that "France gives to the world an example of fraternity, of concord, and of harmony." *La Tribune juive Strasbourg-Paris*, organ of the venerable Alsatian Jewish community, offered the worshipful reminder that "[w]e consider it a privilege to belong to France. The world knows that there are no better patriots than French Israelites." The *Tribune* then went on to exhort

French Jewry to display a "sagacious restraint" in their reaction to Blum's election. "Jews do not express their joy by crying 'hosanna,' " it cautioned its readers. "They do not manifest any particular enthusiasm at the accession of M. Léon Blum to the premiership."

Jacob Kaplan, Grand Rabbi of Paris, went rather further in adopting a stance of "sagacious restraint." In a private communication, he gently suggested that Blum forgo the premiership altogether. In return, Rabbi Kaplan confided, a group of affluent French Jews would arrange for him to receive the equivalent of a premier's life pension. There was no response. On the day following Blum's accession to office, therefore, Rabbi Kaplan felt it appropriate to conduct a commemorative service at the Temple Victoire dedicated to the Croix de Feu! De la Rocque and the colonel's senior associates participated, as did Baron Robert de Rothschild, president of the Consistoire Israélite of Paris, and other members of the Consistoire and rabbinate. Using the occasion to repudiate all charges of Jewish separatism and parochialism, Kaplan once again asserted French Jewry's unequivocal devotion to their country.

A Premier's Agenda

Sixty-four years old as he prepared to assume office, tall, lean, and entirely recovered from his neck wound, Léon Blum assured the French public that he was in fullest possession of his physical and intellectual powers. Others saw whatever they wished to see. One political journalist, Jean Lacouture, remembered the premier-elect more poetically:

> [Blum's] silken moustache and his long hair were beginning to gray. His height and his build . . . made him stand out in a political world . . . of . . . stocky men with potbellies. . . . Behind the glasses that made them glitter, his gray-blue eyes maintained their sometimes satiric gaiety. The voice . . . remained fragile, but sometimes, when emotion did not make it crack, it took on surprising depth. . . . [H]e rests his very white face, divided by the bridge of his Modigliani-like long nose which makes a sharp angle with his jutting chin, on a very long and delicate hand which surrounds his face like a cloth of the Pietà.

The journalist Alexander Werth wrote: "[W]hen you see Blum, you sometimes imagine that Marcel Proust's Swann would have rather looked like him in his old age."

The new premier faced a challenge to that Proustian "delicacy." In mid-May 1936, only two weeks after the election, a series of massive industrial work stoppages all but paralyzed the nation's economy. Spreading from factory to factory, the strikes eventually "immobilized" over 1 million workers. The unions' purpose in fact was not to undermine the new government, but to send Blum a message, to ensure that he would not become simply another expedient manipulator of the status quo. Blum's response was energetic, even preemptive. On June 4, he entered into urgent triangular discussions with the Manufacturers Association and the trade union confederations, although he was not scheduled to assume office until June 7. Within a few hours, he negotiated an agreement. Strongly weighted in favor of the workers, it gave them their principal objectives, of union recognition, collective contracts, significant wage increases, and Blum's commitment to provide labor with a legislative "bill of rights."

Upon assuming office, the new premier honored his commitment in letter and spirit. The agenda he submitted to the Chamber of Deputies in the summer of 1936 called for a forty-hour workweek, collective bargaining, paid vacations, reform of the tax system in favor of the working classes, introduction of national unemployment insurance, a far-reaching public works program, enlargement of free, compulsory schooling, nationalization of the private munitions companies, and emancipation of the Bank of France from the grip of some two hundred powerful families. In launching this vast social transformation, moreover, Blum acknowledged that he was inspired by the American New Deal. At times he actually referred to his program as a "French New Deal." And like Roosevelt's celebrated "one hundred days," Blum's "new social charter" won massive parliamentary approval in record time—in this case, within sixty days.

France's political opposition was not chastened. The national Chamber of Commerce declared war on the forty-hour workweek. So did most of the—traditionally ultraconservative—professional associations, led by the legal and medical societies. The army command, following the lead of Marshal Pétain and General Weygand, publicly opposed the government's commitment to the League of Nations and international disarmament. Neither did the Church hierarchy react congenially to the Popular Front. In October 1936, France's five cardinals warned that the "closed fist"—the Communist salute—was too prominent among the government's political supporters. It was among the ultraright, however, the "integral nationalists," that fury at Blum and his supporters became particularly uncontrollable. Their rage was all but foreordained by one of the new government's initial decrees, in June 1936. Although the Sarrault government earlier had dissolved the Action française, after the February 13 physical assault on Blum, other paramilitary ligues had remained intact. But now these too were officially banned.

They were not about to go quietly into the night. Thus, upon being terminated as a ligue, the Croix de Feu immediately and ingeniously reconstituted itself as a political party, the PSF—the "Parti social français." The transformation was a sham, of course. As a harsh critic of parliamentarism, Colonel de la Rocque was uninterested in engaging in national elections. Rather, he anticipated that his following eventually would bulk as a potential alternative to the parliamentary system altogether. Possibly he was right. By 1938, in its disciplined muscularity, the PSF's membership was estimated at 600,000. Its rolls included 3,000 mayors, some 1,000 municipal councilmen, and a dozen parliamentary deputies.

Close behind the—transformed—Croix de Feu in decibel power and public visibility was the Parti populaire français. A late bloomer, the PPF was organized ab initio as a party in 1936. Its founder, Jacques Doriot, actually had begun his career as a Communist, but in 1934 he underwent a crise de conscience and discerned true salvation for France in the authoritarian models of Mussolini and Hitler. Initially, Doriot gravitated into the Croix de Feu; but in 1936, losing confidence in de la Rocque's "moderation," he established the PPF for those who shared his eagerness for "decisive" action. By 1938, Doriot's party may have accumulated as many as 170,000 members.

Other former ligues meanwhile regrouped themselves under various façades, among them the Association Marius Plateau, the Institut Action française, the Institut royale. Whatever their secret agenda, or the military and police contacts that helped provide them with weaponry, the threat these reconstituted ligues and cabals represented possibly was less military or even political than psychological. In their incendiary anticommunism, their antiparliamentarism and antisemitism, they fanned the internecine hatreds that enfeebled the nation's diplomatic and military resolve at a moment of growing European crisis.

A Political Demise

Even as ideological and political reaction mounted in the Popular Front era, its fulminance could also be attributed to the complexities of France's foreign relations. In Spain, in July 1936, a right-wing military junta launched an uprising against the nation's left-leaning "Frente Popular" government. Blum had been in office only a month when the news reached him. He and Spain's Prime Minister José Giral were old comrades within the Socialist International, and Giral now was appealing to Blum as a friend for the immediate delivery of airplanes, artillery, and assorted small arms. Blum did not hesitate. He assured Giral that the matériel would be made available immediately and directly from France's own military stocks.

Yet Blum made his decision in the very period that France was undergo-

ing a major realignment of political viewpoints on foreign affairs. Until late
1934, the nation's right wing consistently preached the need for vigilance
against Germany's revival as a Great Power. It was the left that advocated a
more general, universal disarmament, and reliance on the League of
Nations to preserve European peace. Throughout the 1920s and early
1930s, no one championed this stance of classically Socialist internationalism more avidly than did Léon Blum himself. In common with his late
mentor, Jean Jaurès, and with millions of his war-weary countrymen, Blum
feared the revival of militarism in France, and a diversion of the country's
resources from the vital priorities of social reforms.

By 1935, however, each side of the French ideological spectrum began
to modify its position. The right, endlessly on guard against social change,
adopted a companionable attitude not only to Italian Fascism but, increasingly, to German Nazism. In both movements, it discerned an antidote to
trade unionism and "Bolshevism." By contrast, French Socialism was shifting incrementally away from doctrinaire pacifism. For Blum, the move was
still tentative. He continued to favor international disarmament, support of
the League of Nations, and accommodationist diplomacy. In June 1936,
receiving the German economics minister, Dr. Hjalmar Schacht, the premier opened the conversation with the observation: "I am a Marxist and a
Jew . . . but we cannot achieve anything if we treat ideological barriers as
insurmountable."

Neither was Blum prepared to jeopardize France's close diplomatic
relationship with Britain. Thus, on July 23, 1936, he was given pause by
an appeal from Stanley Baldwin, Britain's Conservative prime minister.
France must not provide overt support to Spain's leftist government, Baldwin insisted; the move would only strengthen world Communism. Hardly
less sobering was an urgent entreaty from Blum's political partners, the
Radicals, to avoid provoking the Fascist Powers. The right-wing parties, of
course, were death on the very notion of extending help to the "Communist butchers" of Madrid. To circumvent this diversity of pressures, therefore, Blum and his foreign minister, Yvon Delbos, initially formulated a
subterfuge. They began dispatching the promised military supplies "unofficially," in clandestine shipments from French "private parties."

Yet, within a fortnight, news of this secret replenishment effort leaked.
Protests began flooding in from Rome, Berlin—and London. Of still
greater danger to the Blum government was the political reaction in
France itself. The Radicals threatened to pull out of the cabinet. On the far
right, an avalanche of calumny was directed against the premier. As always,
Maurras's *Action française* led the pack, with *Gringoire*, *Je Suis Partout*, and
other neo-Fascist newspapers following. "It is as a Jew that one must see,
hear, fight, and destroy this Blum," wrote Maurras. "This man is anything

but French." In the same period, the French ultraright had recourse to a phrase heard only intermittently before the Spanish Civil War: "Better Hitler than Blum."

In his diplomatic and political isolation, Blum now felt obliged to support an alternative, British, proposal for a "Non-Intervention Committee," an agreement to cooperate in embargoing the shipment of weaponry to both sides in the Spanish conflict. Yet, from its inception in August 1936, the agreement proved entirely toothless. Mussolini and Hitler continued to provide the Spanish Fascists with large quantities of military equipment, and then, increasingly, of military "volunteers." For Blum, the consequences of diplomatic equivocation soon became politically crippling. Furious at the premier's "betrayal" of the Spanish Republicans, his Communist parliamentary supporters turned against him. By late autumn of 1936, the Popular Front was openly splintering.

Blum's domestic program similarly was placed in jeopardy. Since the promising legislation of June–July 1936, not a single important new reform had been adopted. By autumn, as French industrial productivity continued its downward spiral under its heavy social burdens, the flight of capital from the country increased. Even a devaluation of the franc did not help, and early in 1937 Blum was obliged to decree a "pause" in public spending. Then, on March 16, a sudden crisis erupted in the Paris industrial suburb of Clichy. At a local theater, a rightist meeting of the PSF—the political incarnation of the Croix de Feu—clashed with a counterdemonstration of trade unionists. In the mêlée, police fired on the workers, killing and wounding some two hundred of them. Blum happened to be attending the opera that night. Alerted by an aide, the prime minister rushed straight to Clichy in his dress suit and top hat. Upon arrival, he was jeered by thousands of onlookers, most of them workers and their families. In ensuing days, the leftist press execrated Blum as "the assassin of Clichy."

It was the death agony of the Popular Front. Industrial strikes multiplied uncontrollably. In June 1937, almost out of gold reserves, the Blum government in its desperation asked Parliament for "emergency powers" to ban free trading in gold. Hereupon the Senate, traditionally a bastion of conservatism, rejected the measure. Possibly Blum might have called new elections, but he feared arousing popular passions any further. On June 21, he submitted his resignation, asking only that his fellow Socialists participate in a new government, this one under the Radical Socialist leadership of Camille Chautemps. Blum would serve as vice-premier in a cabinet he still gallantly titled a "Popular Front" government.

But after nearly thirteen months in office, the authentic Popular Front experiment was over. The Chautemps cabinet reversed its predecessor's course, raising taxes and retrenching on various scheduled public works projects. The French ultraright meanwhile was gaining a renewed momentum. Hooded "Cagoulard" thugs were setting off bomb explosions outside Socialist and trade union offices in Paris. De la Rocque's putative PSF movement continued to grow. And on the left, during the autumn and winter of 1937, a series of factory strikes were directed mainly at the government's nonintervention policy in Spain. With the Communists no longer prepared to support the restructured Popular Front government, Chautemps's cabinet fell in mid-January 1938. Once more, then, Blum was called upon to form a coalition. But his efforts to pick and choose among a spectrum of parties failed. So did his reserves of personal strength. That same January, Blum's wife, Thérèse, died of cancer. A successor government, again under Chautemps, was organized, but this time without Blum—or any other Socialist. The cabinet was made up exclusively of Radicals.

There was a final postscript. In March 1938, Chautemps revealed his ineffectuality during Hitler's Anschluss with Austria. His government collapsed. Once again, Blum was called upon to form a cabinet. In fact, on this—third—occasion, the Socialist leader managed to organize a tentative coalition resembling the one he had originally fashioned with the Radicals in May–June 1936. He even succeeded in negotiating through the Chamber his domestic agenda of increased family pensions. But the Senate did him in once more, vetoing the legislation. He promptly resigned, this time refusing to serve as deputy prime minister under Édouard Daladier and the Radicals. Léon Blum's latest and last premiership had endured all of three weeks.

Reassessing the Jewish Presence

Barely a month passed before the Daladier cabinet set about burying the achievements of Blum's Popular Front experiment altogether. Dismantling the forty-hour workweek, the new government eviscerated the remaining public works programs, and crushed workers' strikes in mines and railroads under the rubric of "military emergency." Daladier's management of foreign affairs proved even more disastrous. The man obsequiously collaborated in Britain's two-stage sacrifice of Czechoslovakia to Nazi Germany in September 1938 and March 1939.

Unrecognized at the time, Daladier's foreign and domestic policies in fact were intimately linked. International crises gave him the pretext both for reversing social reforms and restricting civil liberties. Thus, in September 1939, exploiting public outrage at the Nazi-Soviet Non-Aggression Pact, which had been signed only the month before, Daladier closed down the Communist press, and later outlawed the Communist party altogether—even locking up forty-four Communist parliamentary deputies. As the prime minister saw it, a harsh stance toward the political left also would help placate Hitler and Mussolini. So would a harsh stance toward "non-nationals." Almost predictably, then, the Jews were the first "non-nationals" to bear the brunt of the government's sharp swing rightward.

France's economic doldrums alone would have compounded Jewish vulnerability. In the depression-ridden 1930s, some fifty-five thousand new Jewish refugees poured into France, more than two-thirds of them fugitives from the Nazi Reich and East-Central European Fascist regimes. By their "invasion" of the capital's Marais quarter, the newcomers represented more than the well-ventilated Jewish threat to Gallic culture. They were competition in the labor market. Nor was it only the usual aggregation of Fascists and crypto Fascists who denounced the recent arrivals for taking "the bread out of French mouths." As in other Western countries, entirely reputable associations of doctors and lawyers joined in the appeal for stricter curbs on immigration. The allusion to Jews would have been gratuitous.

To Frenchmen of all backgrounds, finally, the Jews, immigrants and established residents alike, threatened to embroil the nation in complications with Nazi Germany. France's mood in the 1930s was still one of peace at almost any price. Even right-wing veterans organizations persuaded themselves that Hitler as an ex-soldier was uninterested in another war. Shrewdly cultivating that illusion, the German government bought up a collection of small-circulation French newspapers and news agencies, which then duly parroted Berlin's assurances of goodwill. In 1935, the Nazis also founded and subsidized the Comité France-Allemagne under the chairmanship of Count Fernand de Brinon, a closet Fascist. In ensuing years, the committee made shrewd use of local antisemitism. During the last months before the outbreak of war in 1939, a confidential, and entirely apolitical, police report on antisemitic activity in the Paris region provided sixty-six pages of data on "specialized" hate organizations whose one and exclusive motif was antisemitism. Citing names, addresses, membership, and biographies of leaders, the report left no doubt that each of these covens was intimately enmeshed with Germany, and often accepted German guidance in promoting the line that the Jews alone were manipulating France into war.

In their propaganda effort, the Nazis enjoyed the active support of the former ligues. Immediately following the Munich crisis of September 1938, Colonel de la Rocque, Charles Maurras, Marcel Déat, and Jacques Doriot issued public testimonials in praise of the Daladier government for "keeping the peace." Afterward, as the Polish crisis burgeoned out in the spring and summer of 1939, Déat on May 4 could emblazon an admonitory query across the front page of his party newspaper, *L'Oeuvre:* "To Die for Danzig?" The notion plainly was unthinkable. Even less imaginable was the prospect of dying for the Jews. Throughout 1938 and 1939, other ultrarightist newspapers—*L'Action française, Candide, Gringoire, Je Suis Partout*—insisted that Jewry alone was fomenting the series of war scares. In his editorial, "Attention les Juifs!," Maurras spoke for all these factions with his warning that the Jews would pay dearly for their war-mongering, for their effort to "deliver the world to Bolshevism."

As early as 1937, another talented writer, the forty-three-year-old Louis-Ferdinand Céline, pressed the Jewish "war-monger" line in a sensational novel, *Trinkets for a Massacre (Bagatelles pour un massacre)*. Born Louis-Ferdinand Destouches to lower-middle-class parents, the author had fought in the World War, where he suffered a head wound. Upon receiving his military discharge, he attended and completed medical school. His career as a physician did not flourish. He was dismissed from his first two clinics—in both instances, he would claim, at the initiative of hostile Jewish superiors. By the 1920s, in a sharp career change, "Céline" (as he now called himself) devoted his principal efforts to writing.

Céline's narratives, racy and flamboyant, were peopled with grotesque Jewish caricatures. By the time *Trinkets* appeared, antisemitism had become the consuming obsession of the author's life. Indeed, for Céline, international Jewry represented the seedbed not only of Bolshevism and financial parasitism but of war-mongering. "Above all, war must be avoided," he insisted. "For us, war . . . means the end of the show, the final tilt into the Jewish charnel house," and it was therefore incumbent upon the French people to display "[t]he same stubbornness in resisting war that the Jews display in dragging us into it. . . ." Acknowledging that "I don't want to go to war for Hitler," Céline made equally plain that "I don't want to go against him, for the Jews . . . I'd prefer a dozen Hitlers to one all-powerful Blum." An astonishing popular success, *Trinkets* ultimately sold seventy-five thousand copies.

The Jews of France meanwhile displayed a characteristically ambivalent reaction to the "new" antisemitism. The animus now, after all, was linked increasingly to the nation's fear of war. Even as late as November 1938, in the aftermath of Kristallnacht, the Nazi mass destruction of synagogues and Jewish shops throughout the Greater Reich, the Consistoire Israélite remained punctiliously circumspect. From their consistorial pulpits, the rabbis of France lamented the persecution of members "of all faiths by the enemies of religion." Yet, together with the Rothschilds and other lay spokesmen of the veteran Jewish community, the rabbinate discouraged all appeals for boycotts or public demonstrations against Germany.

Thus, from the "Rothschild Temple," on rue de la Victoire, Rabbi Julien Weil advised his congregants that sorrow at the fate of German Jewry should not lead French Jews to oppose a Franco-German rapprochement. "No one sympathizes more [than I] with the pain of six hundred thousand German Israelites," he declared. "But nothing appears to me more precious . . . [or] more necessary, than maintaining peace on earth." It was a sentiment publicly endorsed by General Jacob-Léon Weiller, the most senior of French Jewish army officers. In a special press release, Weiller insisted that French Jews did not seek war with Germany. Other members of the Jewish establishment similarly rejected all "provocative" suggestions for a Jewish self-defense organization within France itself. The immigrant Jewish community might take over such a venture, they warned.

The patricians' concern was justified. The East Europeans in any case had never accepted the authority of the Consistoire or the Jewish lay leadership. In common with most Jews, in 1936 they had voted eagerly and overwhelmingly for the Popular Front, and had made no secret of their admiration for Blum, both as a Socialist and as a proud Jew. Moreover, with their own bitter memories of East European antisemitism, the immigrants had responded to the threat of Nazism earlier and more forthrightly than had the veterans. In 1935, when the Hitler government passed the Nuremberg (racial) laws, it was these transplanted Russian, Polish, and Rumanian Jews who had pressed vigorously, if vainly, for an anti-German boycott. And by the summer of 1939, as war drew nearer, immigrant Jews all but deluged recruitment offices. Unlike their forebears of World War I, many of whom recoiled at the prospect of an alliance with the Russian tsar, the Easterners' passion now to fight Nazi Germany transcended all earlier political ideologies. In disregard even of the recent Nazi-Soviet Pact, *Die Naye Presse*, the newspaper of France's Yiddish-speaking immigrant Communists, called upon Jews of all backgrounds to register for military service.

From the government, however, these protestations of Jewish loyalty evoked a chill response. Only years later was it learned that the Radical Socialists were secretly instituting a major policy shift on immigrant and minority issues. Unknown to the public, the ministry of the interior from 1933 on was quietly assembling "Carnet B," a list of persons to be arrested in the event of war. At first, the list consisted mainly of native Fascists. By the mid-1930s, however, almost half the names on the list were foreign-born Jews suspected of Communist affiliations. By then, too, the government had begun imposing a numerus clausus on the proportion of foreigners allowed to practice medicine and pharmacy. Restrictions abated somewhat during Blum's Popular Front government. But in 1938, with Daladier as prime minister, the anti-immigrant policy regained its momentum. Hitler's Anschluss with Austria unquestionably exacerbated the refugee crisis, as thirty-nine thousand new Jewish fugitives crossed into France. "[We have] reached the saturation point," explained Henri Béranger, France's delegate to an international conference on refugees meeting at Évian-les-Bains in July 1938. ". . . [It] does not permit receiving any more refugees without tipping the social balance." Béranger doubtless voiced a national consensus.

By the time of the Évian Conference, in fact, the French government was considering an alternative solution to the Jewish immigration problem. This was the resettlement of refugees in Madagascar. Ironically, it was a solution that the Polish government in recent years had been seeking for its own "redundant" Jewish population (pp. 68–70). Now, suddenly, Madagascar emerged as a possible dumping ground for France's own "redundant" Jews. During a visit to Washington in October 1938, Foreign Minister Georges Bonnet actually raised the idea in talks with Undersecretary of State Sumner Welles. Could the United States help underwrite such a transmigration of refugees? Although the proposal never achieved practical form, it prefigured a scheme, "the Madagascar Plan," that Hitler himself later would explore—and then finally discard in favor of a more draconian solution.

In September 1938, facing the Sudeten crisis and the possibility of revived social and political tensions at a moment of acute national peril, the Daladier government instructed the police to impose tighter surveillance on foreigners. Henceforth, prefects of frontier departments were authorized to expel aliens on their own responsibility. The government was quite aware that refugee Jews could not simply be repatriated to Nazi-controlled territory. Instead, it offered an interim palliative. The newcomers would be transferred from the over-congestion of Paris to remote corners of the provinces, where they could be carefully monitored. From late 1938 on, therefore, refugees found themselves often in limbo between deportation or quasi-internment in designated provincial enclaves. In November 1938, too, the Daladier government issued a decree of authentically sinister implications. This one announced that French nationality might be stripped even from those foreign-born persons who already had been officially naturalized, should they be judged "unworthy of the title of French citizen." Jews were not specifically mentioned in this measure, any more than in earlier ones. They did not have to be.

Léon Blum's Last Trial

For six months after war began in September 1939, the French army vegetated in its Maginot Line redoubts, anticipating that serious conflict could be avoided along the western front. The "phony war" ended in March 1940, of course, as the Germans launched their blitzkrieg through the Lowlands, and into northern France. Here it was that the demoralized and discredited Daladier was replaced as premier by Paul Reynaud, a member of the centrist Parti Alliance-Démocratique. For the sake of national unity, Reynaud included three Socialists in his cabinet—although not Léon Blum, whose presence was regarded as potentially divisive. As the German offensive gained momentum, however, Reynaud soon felt compelled to reshuffle his cabinet. He gave the ministry of the interior to the Radical Socialist Georges Mandel, a Jew who had served as Clemenceau's chef de cabinet in World War I (p. 291). As "the Tiger's cub," helping Clemenceau stamp out defeatism in the trenches, Mandel ever after enjoyed a legendary reputation for Jacobin energy and determination.

Yet Reynaud inadvertently neutralized the Mandel appointment by bringing in Henri-Philippe Pétain as vice premier. Despite his mythological status as the "hero of Verdun," the old marshal was an arch-reactionary, and now an arch-defeatist. He would not bestir himself to save a dying republic. Soon after the government fled to Bordeaux, it was Pétain who took over the prime ministry to seek a "soldier's peace" with the onrushing Germans. The rightist political veteran Pierre Laval subsequently joined Pétain as vice premier, and soon would emerge as the latter's éminence grise.

Nevertheless, some French politicians nurtured the hope that France could fight on in its overseas empire. Léon Blum was one of these. In late June 1940, he was among the thirty parliamentary deputies authorized to depart by special train for Porto-Vendres, near the Spanish border. From there, a naval cruiser was assigned to carry them off to Casablanca, where they anticipated joining a government-in-exile. At the last moment, however, Blum decided to travel to Porto-Vendres by automobile, stopping at Toulouse en route to visit with his daughter-in-law and granddaughter (his son Robert was then serving in the army). The detour was a fateful one. It caused Blum to miss the sailing date, and the cruiser departed without him. Worse yet, the government did not uproot itself from France. Conceivably, Pétain and his associates had planted the false account of a government-in-exile to lure the more ardent resisters out of the country.

From then on, Blum rejected the pleas of friends to attempt an escape to England. For him, the decision to remain on French territory was a matter of honor. After the surrender at Réthondes on June 22, 1940, the entire government transferred itself from Bordeaux to the modest southwestern resort town of Vichy. As a member of Parliament, Blum shared in the move. Lodging at the Vichy home of a friend, Isidore Thivrier, the former premier nurtured the lingering hope that his shrunken Socialist bloc in the

transplanted Chamber might yet sustain a democratic flame, however feeble. It was an illusion. Controlled by reactionaries, Parliament swiftly gave
Pétain near-dictatorial powers. The few remaining Socialists then wilted.
Ignoring Blum's appeals, they set about pandering to the Pétain-Laval government.

It was Pierre Laval henceforth who discerned the opportunity for a
campaign of retribution. His targets were the vulnerable and isolated former leadership of the Popular Front, those who had "fecklessly and suici-
dally" made anti-Fascism "the foundation of all our domestic policy and all
our foreign policy." Thus, in July 1940, the Vichy government pushed
through a bill denying membership in Parliament to anyone "who has not
been a Frenchman for many generations." No one could doubt whom
Pétain and Laval had in mind. Ironically, even under these guidelines,
Blum would still have qualified as a deputy. But with the handwriting
clearly on the wall, he prepared to seek passage for Morocco. And once
more, a change in plan obtruded. En route to the Mediterranean coast,
Blum learned that his son was a war prisoner of the Germans. Refusing
then to depart the country until he could learn of his son's whereabouts,
Blum immediately moved in again with friends in Toulouse.

It was thus in Toulouse, on July 28, 1940, that the sixty-eight-year-old
Blum was arrested by the Vichy police. Carried off to the town of Bourassel, he was imprisoned, together with seven other former government
figures, among them Daladier, Reynaud, Mandel, and the ex–military
chief of staff, General Maurice Gamelin. The charge against them was
responsibility both for France's unpreparedness for war and for the nation's
"unconstitutional" entrance into the war. The prisoners then were subjected to months of harsh pretrial interrogation. Yet the trial date itself was
unaccountably postponed, month after month. Finally, on October 15,
1941, the court announced that it had rendered a "preliminary verdict." All
eight men, including Blum, were found guilty and condemned to life
imprisonment. Under the bizarre procedures of Vichy law, however, the
prisoners then were allowed to prepare their defense, to "appeal" the verdict. After vegetating in prison for yet another four months, Blum and his
fellow defendants were brought to court on February 19, 1942, to submit
their "appeal" personally—in effect, to undergo their trial.

The proceedings, in the town of Riom, would consume twenty-four
public sessions over nearly two months. All the prisoners vigorously
defended their records. In Blum's case, it was a defense of the entirety of his
1936–37 Popular Front government. Firmly and defiantly, in day after day
of testimony, the seventy-year-old former premier retraced the history of
his administration. He denounced his accusers for acquiring their "information" from hangers-on of the former paramilitary ligues and other
right-wing groups. "These are the men who should be in your dock," he

insisted. "These are the ones who are responsible for this misery, this suffering." In Blum's testimony, the Popular Front was nothing less than a crusade on behalf of the laboring classes, people who had lived too long in poverty. "Dreams! Fantasies!" he scoffed at the charge of having tolerated a progressive military disarmament. Was he not the first prime minister since the end of World War I to launch France on a serious effort of military preparedness? It was a bravura performance.

Indeed, on April 14, 1942, under pressure from Otto Abetz, Germany's ambassador to Vichy, the Pétain government suspended all further court hearings. They had become an embarrassment. Vichy had managed simply to provide Blum with an effective forum. Reports of the trial had gotten out to the West. By the time the defendants were returned to their fortress-prison in Bourassol, Blum had become the object of hundreds of letters of support from admirers abroad. In New York, American trade unions organized a rally in his honor. Eleanor Roosevelt signed a telegram of congratulations, which actually reached Blum in his cell.

The satisfaction was purely moral. The prisoners faced the possibility of life imprisonment, or conceivably worse. Jews by the thousands were being carried off in cattle trains from Drancy, outside Paris, for an unknown destination (later discovered to be Auschwitz). One of the deportees, in September 1942, was Blum's brother René. He would not return. In November 1942, the German army crossed over into Unoccupied France—the Vichy zone. From then on, Blum was a captive not only of Pétain but of Hitler. His prison circumstances worsened. All visitors and mail deliveries were stopped. Subsequently, in March 1943, he was carried off from Bourassel to the German concentration camp of Buchenwald, together with Daladier, Reynaud, Mandel, Gamelin, and several others.

At first, the prisoners were treated with a certain deference, and allowed to live together in a common house. Blum even was permitted to marry a distant cousin, Jeanne Levy, the divorced wife of the famed lawyer Henri Torrès, the defender of Sholem Schwarzbard (p. 17). She joined her husband in Buchenwald, and shared his room. Physical conditions remained tolerable, but the psychological pressure mounted suddenly, in July 1944, when Georges Mandel was separated from the other prisoners and taken away. It later developed that Pierre Laval, the Vichy vice premier, had reminded the Germans that Mandel had been a scourge of France's native Fascists. Accordingly, the prisoner was transported back to Paris and placed in the custody of the collaborationist French milice, who promptly shot him.

If Blum and his wife were spared this fate, it was due only to a combination of near-miracles in the last, surrealistic weeks of the war. On April 3, 1945, as Allied forces penetrated deeper into Germany, Léon and Jeanne Blum suddenly were evacuated from Buchenwald. The Gestapo drove them through the country, to Ratisbon, then, several days afterward, to Munich, where they were imprisoned in the concentration camp of Dachau. A week later, the Blums were carried off yet again, this time to the Dolomite Mountains of Italy. Here it was that a German officer, a Captain von Alvensleben, suddenly disarmed the troops guarding the Blums and arranged for the prisoners to be transported to the American lines. On May 8, the day Germany surrendered, an American military airplane flew the Blums to Naples. There they were driven to the headquarters of the Mediterranean area commander, Field Marshal Sir Harold Alexander, who ensured that they received immediate medical treatment and comfortable lodgings. On May 14, another American transport plane flew the couple back to Paris. There Blum's closest aides, his son Robert (recently freed from German captivity), and other members of the Blums' families awaited them at Orly Airport.

France had been liberated the summer before. Yet, by then, of the nation's prewar population of 300,000 Jews (some 40,000 had fled before the Nazi conquest), a total of 90,000 had perished. Of these, in turn, 76,000 had lost their lives in Auschwitz and other Polish death camps; the remaining 14,000 died in Occupied and Vichy France as a consequence of detention camp conditions or spot executions. Approximately a third of the 90,000 dead were French citizens, the rest were foreign refugees. It is noteworthy that the largest numbers of victims had been delivered into the hands of the German SS by the French police and French milice. Their homes and businesses had been taken over by French Gentiles.

Upon regaining a measure of his strength, Léon Blum devoted his every public hour to the reconstruction of his beloved Socialist party. In that effort, he consented to deliver the keynote address at the party's first postwar congress, on August 13, 1945. As the tumultuous cheering of three thousand delegates died down, the former premier addressed his constituents. Beginning his speech with the poignant observation, "I am a man who has been given time to think," he went on to share with his fellow Socialists the lessons he had learned:

> What is important [he insisted] . . . is to go beyond the economic and social liberation of the individual, which is not the final goal, but the means, the necessary [preliminary] . . . for the transformation of the human condition. . . . Our real aim, in the society of the future, is to make humans not only more useful, but happier and better and, in this sense, Socialism is more than a conception of social evolution or social structures; it is a universal doctrine, a doctrine which must impregnate hearts and minds, transform ways of life and thought and mores.

Even now, following a career of ample exposure to the romanticized egalitarianism of his fellow citizens, and with more than a little time to reflect on the wider implications of the "human condition," Blum stood before his countrymen as a reanointed elder statesman, gallantly to reprise the cherished idyll of an immemorial concatenation of European Jewish dreamers.

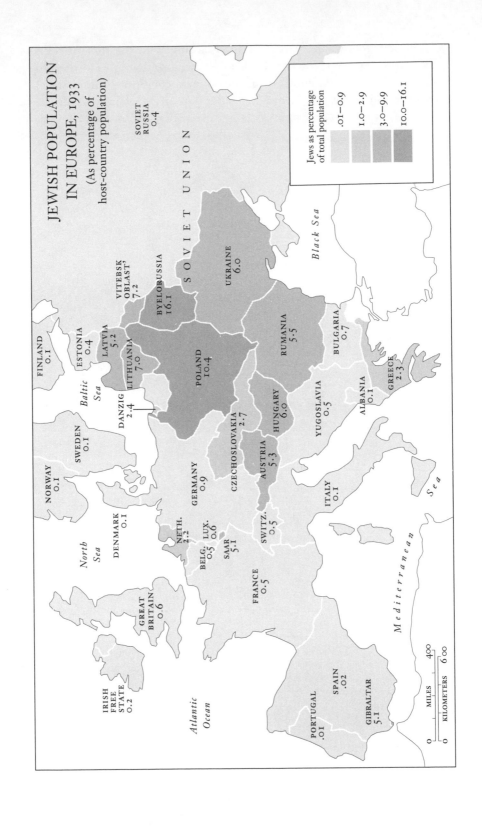

JEWISH POPULATION
IN EUROPE, 1933
(As percentage of
host-country population)

Jews as percentage
of total population

.01–0.9
1.0–2.9
3.0–9.9
10.0–16.1

SOVIET
RUSSIA
0.4

SOVIET UNION

Black Sea

VITEBSK
OBLAST'
7.2

BYELORUSSIA
16.1

UKRAINE
6.0

FINLAND
0.1

ESTONIA
0.4

LATVIA
5.2

LITHUANIA
7.0

POLAND
10.4

RUMANIA
5.5

BULGARIA
0.7

Baltic
Sea

DANZIG
2.4

SWEDEN
0.1

HUNGARY
6.0

YUGOSLAVIA
0.5

ALBANIA
0.1

GREECE
2.3

NORWAY
0.1

DENMARK
0.1

GERMANY
0.9

CZECHOSLOVAKIA
2.7

AUSTRIA
5.3

ITALY
0.1

North
Sea

NETH.
2.2

BELG. LUX.
0.5 0.6

SAAR
5.1

SWITZ.
0.5

IRISH
FREE
STATE
0.2

GREAT
BRITAIN
0.6

FRANCE
0.5

Mediterranean   Sea

Atlantic
Ocean

PORTUGAL
.01

SPAIN
.02

GIBRALTAR
5.1

0   400
MILES
0   600
KILOMETERS

Notes

I. A MURDER TRIAL IN PARIS *(pp. 3–19)*

8 A "honeymoon" between the Ukrainian and Jewish peoples: Hunczak, Taras. "A Reappraisal of Syman Petlura and Ukrainian-Jewish Relations, 1917–1921," *Jewish Social Studies*, Vol. 31, no. 3, 1963, pp. 166, 169.

9 "[N]ot a single Jewish city or town escaped": Goldelman, Solomon I. *National Autonomy in the Ukraine, 1917–1920.* New York, 1972, p. 115.

9 "And [thus] entire families were put to death": Heifetz, Elias. *The Slaughter of the Jews in the Ukraine in 1919.* New York, 1919, p. 42.

10 Thirty thousand Jews perished in first wave of violence: Friedman, Saul S. *Pogromchik: The Assassination of Simon Petlura.* New York, 1988, pp. 74–79.

10 "The very attitude of the Jews which provoked the pogromist movements": Friedman, op. cit., p. 319.

10 "To combat and kill Jews was synonymous with fighting against Bolshevism": Margolin, Arnold. *The Jews of Eastern Europe.* New York, 1936, p. 130.

10 "Jewish Bolshevism" an effective pretext for mobilizing popular support: Szajkowski, Zosa. "Symon Petliura and Ukrainian-Jewish Relations, 1917–21: A Rebuttal," *Jewish Social Studies*, Vol. 31, no. 3, 1963, pp. 190–91.

10 "Must be rejected as such from the human family": Desroches, Alain. *The Ukrainian Problem and Simon Petlura (The Fire and the Ashes).* Chicago, 1970, p. 42.

10 "Death is instituted for those who will be involved in the pogroms": Ibid., pp. 42–43.

10 Executions . . . were confirmed by American Jewish Congress: American Jewish Congress. *The Massacre and Other Atrocities Committed against the Jews of Southern Russia.* New York, 1920, p. 61.

10 Petliura . . . sought (unsuccessfully) to have the murderers tracked down: Lichten, Joseph. "A Study of Ukrainian-Jewish Relations," *Annals of the Ukrainian Academy of Arts and Sciences in the United States*, Vol. 5 (1956), *passim.*

11 "The army saved the Ukraine": Szajkowski, op. cit., p. 193.

11 "The soldiers must amuse themselves": Ibid., p. 193.

11 "Should dare to raise itself against the independent Ukraine": Ibid., 194.

11 Semesenko boasting . . . that the army distributed leaflets of incitement: Ibid.

11 Langevin held his ground under cross-examination: Friedman, op. cit., pp. 147–50.

11–12 "Terrible and blood responsibility of Petliura": Ibid., p. 230.

15 "I alone am responsible. . . . God bless you": Ibid., pp. 66–67.

15 Solomon Teilirian had been acquitted in Berlin: Sachar, Howard M. *The Emergence of the Middle East, 1914–1924.* New York, 1969, p. 251.

16   "[D]ripped with the blood of the Torah": Friedman, op. cit., p. 72.

16   "I was too generous with this assassin": Ibid., pp. 86–87.

17   Only the Bolsheviks stood to benefit: Ibid., p. 310.

17   "And you, Schwarzbard, who are you?": Ibid., p. 314.

17   "Gentlemen of the jury, I am done": Ibid., pp. 324–38.

18   A slaughter that annihilated 150,000 additional Jewish lives: Szajkowski, op. cit., p. 211.

II.   A MINORITY "BILL OF RIGHTS"   *(pp. 20–42)*

21   "The daring soldier of fortune he has actually been": Goodhart, Arthur L. *Poland and the Minority Races.* London, 1920, p. 119.

24   [Pilsudski] was too preoccupied . . . to constrain upsurge of successor-state chauvinism: Korzec, Pawel. *Juifs en Pologne: La Question juive pendant l'entre deux-guerres.* Paris, 1980, p. 110.

24–25   Polish troops attacked Jews in big cities, some one hundred smaller towns: Cohen, Israel. *My Mission to Poland, 1918–1939.* New York, 1951, p. 379; See also Morgenthau, Henry. *All in a Lifetime.* New York, 1922, p. 14.

25   Local police often collaborated in attacks on Jews: Korzec, op. cit., p. 75.

25   Informed of atrocities, Pilsudski condemned attacks on Jews: Ibid., p. 79.

26   Joint Distribution Committee shared information on Polish atrocities with American Jewish leaders: Adler, Cyrus, and Aaron M. Margalith. *With Firmness in the Right: American Diplomatic Action Affecting Jews, 1840–1945.* New York, 1946, pp. 156–57.

26   With the "spirit of justice and righteousness": Best, Gary D. *To Free a People: American Jewish Leaders and the Jewish Problem in Eastern Europe, 1880–1914.* Westport, Conn., 1982, p. 216.

26   "I shall deem it a privilege to exercise such influence as I can": Ibid., p. 218.

27   Dmowski said some Jews were agents of Bolshevik Russia: Adler and Margalit, op. cit., p. 150.

27   Washington should react skeptically to reports about "alleged" massacres of Jews: Ibid., p. 154.

27   Schiff demanded that Wilson put pressure on Poles: Best, op. cit., p. 219.

27   Marshall, Adler demanded official commission of inquiry into anti-Jewish atrocities: Adler, Cyrus. *I Have Considered the Days.* Philadelphia, 1941, p. 315.

28   Polish press branded Morgenthau "Wilson's Jewish servant": "Survey of Jewish Conditions in Poland," *American Jewish Yearbook*, Vol. 22 (1920), p. 286.

28   Polish looting left Jews on edge of destitution: Goodhart, op. cit., pp. 107–108.

28   Polish official line that Jews needed instruction in good citizenship. Bogen, Boris. *Born a Jew.* New York, 1930, pp. 210–11.

29   Morgenthau Report published as Senate Document: United States. Senate Document No. 176. Washington, D.C., January 1920.

29   "A kind of senile gravity": Samuel, Maurice. *Little Did I Know.* New York, 1963, pp. 242–43.

30   Jews produced "a struggle for existence" with Poles: Reznikoff, Charles, ed. *Louis Marshall: Champion of Liberty.* Philadelphia, 1957, Vol. 2, p. 590.

30–31   "[which would help] create a feeling of friendship and unity": Ibid., Vol. 2, p. 591.

31   "The Jews . . . most vehement enemies of our cause": Ibid., p. 99.

31   National minorities nearly one-fourth the population of Central-Eastern Europe: Macartney, Charles A. *National States and National Minorities.* London, 1934, p. 211.

32   Renner proposed that Austria create federation of autonomous nationalities. Renner, Karl. *Der Kampf der Österreichischen Nationen um den Staat.* Vienna, 1902.

33 Demand for a democratically elected American Jewish "Congress": Sachar, Howard M. *A History of the Jews in America*. New York, 1992, pp. 262–65.

33–34 "To judge the wisdom of this conception": Feinberg, Nathan. *La Question des Minorités à la Conference de la Paix de 1919–20*. Paris, 1929, p. 256.

34 "There will be hell to pay": Cohen, Naomi W. *Not Free to Desist: The American Jewish Committee: 1906–1966*. Philadelphia, 1969, p. 114.

35 "The business of the [Peace] Conference is to create a sovereign state for Poland": Levene, op. cit., p. 124.

35 Rejecting the very notion of Jewish "national" rights: Levene, Mark. "Britain, a British Jew, and Jewish Relations with the New Poland: The Making of the Polish Minorities Treaty of 1919," *Polin*, Vol. 8 (1994), p. 102.

36 "No lover of mankind will ever forget": Reznikoff, op. cit., Vol. 2, pp. 554–55.

37 Headlam-Morley did not demur on Jewish rights. Ibid., pp. 15–16.

37 Marshall and his colleagues would live with the compromise: Marcus, Joseph. *A Social and Political History of the Jews in Poland, 1919–1929*. New York, 1939, p. 297.

38 Interpreters to be provided for minority members in courts. Feinberg, op. cit., p. 43.

38 "Through the medium of their own language." Ibid.

39 "Desiring . . . to give a sure guarantee to the inhabitants of the territory": Macartney, op. cit., p. 213.

40 "Has led them to the conclusion that . . . special protection is necessary": Adler and Margalit, op. cit., p. 166.

41 "The whole policy would be fraught with disturbances": Adler, op. cit., p. 315.

42 "You, my friends, are celebrating an event": Reznikoff, op. cit., Vol. 2, pp. 545–46.

III. IN SEARCH OF A CONGLOMERATE IDENTITY (pp. 43–70)

43 Polish export market closed off in surrounding countries: Taylor, Jack. *The Economic Development of Poland, 1919–1950*. New York, 1952, p. 70.

43 Polish national budget deficit of 91 percent: Cienciela, Anna M., and Titus Komarnicki. *From Versailles to Locarno: Keys to Polish Foreign Policy, 1919–25*. Lawrence, Kansas, 1984, Introduction.

43 Poland's inflation rate was 50 percent: Taylor, op. cit., p. 70.

43–44 Poland's squirearchy controlled 38 percent of soil: Cienciela and Komarnicki, op. cit., Introduction.

44 Farm families average five acres a plot: Cang, J. "The Opposition Parties in Poland and Their Attitude to the Jews and the Jewish Problem," *Jewish Social Studies*, Vol. 1, No. 2, 1939, p. 247.

44 Poland's per capita income lowest in Europe: Marcus, Joseph. *Social and Political History of the Jews in Poland, 1919–1939*. New York, 1983, pp. 21–22.

44 Dmowski's priority agenda of enforced "amalgamation": Groth, A. J. "Dmowski, Pilsudski, and Ethnic Conflict in Pre–1939 Poland," *Canadian Slavic Studies*, Vol. 3, No. 1, 1969, pp. 71–82.

44 No other European state encompassed as large a proportion of minorities: Ibid., pp. 247–48.

45 Sixty thousand German farmers squeezed off Polish soil: Horak, Stepan. *Poland and Her National Minorities, 1919–1939*. New York, 1961, pp. 121–23.

46 Ukrainian school textbooks purged of Ukrainian historical material: Drozdowski, Marian M. "The National Minorities in Poland, 1919–1930," *Acta Poloniae Historica*, Vol. 14, No. 22, 1970, pp. 137–38.

46 Poland closed Ukrainian churches: Ibid., p. 139.

46 "[It is] not directed against individuals, but against a whole people": Horak, op. cit., p. 148.

47   Jews 10 percent of Polish population in 1931: Drozdowski, op. cit., p. 247.

47   "[I]n the character of this race so many different values": Groth, op. cit., pp. 73–74.

47   Of the influence of "unwelcome foreign elements": Groth, Alexander J., and Jerzy Holzer. "The Legacy of Three Crises: Parliament and Ethnic Issues in Prewar Poland," *Slavic Review*, Vol. 27, No. 4, 1969, p. 572.

48–49   Jews ranked proportionately second only to the Germans in medicine: Drozdowski, op. cit., pp. 367 ff.

49   Jews paying 40 percent of all direct taxes in Poland: Marcus, op. cit., p. 222.

49   United States government had opted out of European affairs: Reznikoff, op. cit., Vol. 2, p. 557.

49–50   Minority lobbies were the least effective: Levene, op. cit., pp. 103 ff.

51   Zionist network of schools and newspapers: Mendelsohn, Ezra. *On Modern Jewish Politics: The Jews in Poland*. New York, 1993, p. 70.

51   Autonomist variety of Jewish nationalism: Ibid., pp. 57–58.

51   Undereducated, pietistic village Jews of the Ukrainian districts: Rabinowicz, H. M. *The Legacy of Polish Jewry, 1919–1933*. New York, 1965, p. 118.

55   "[T]he Polish people have awakened to the realization": Fishman, Joshua, ed. *Studies in Polish Jewry, 1919–1939*. New York, 1974, pp. 153–54.

58   Jewish press output constituted 14 percent of the newspapers published in Poland altogether: Polonsky, Antony, Ezra Mendelsohn, et al., eds. *Jews in Independent Poland, 1918–1939*. London, 1994, p. 3.

58   Jewish privation related to Poland's economic underdevelopment: Marcus, op. cit., p. 321; See also Tomaszewski, Jerzy. "The Civil Rights of Jews in Poland, 1918–1929," *Polin*, Vol. 8 (1994), *passim*.

58   Jewish population growth climbing by 7 percent a year: Marcus, op. cit., p. 173.

58   Nondescript hole-in-the-wall operations: Polonsky, op. cit., p. 4.

58   Number of Jewish manual workers increased from 58 to 60 percent: Ibid., p. 4.

59   Cases not rare of Poles selling their children for adoption: Rabinowicz, op. cit., pp. 172–73.

59   "Will you permit this to happen to patriotic Poles?": Duker, Abraham. *The Situation of the Jews in Poland*. New York, 1936, p. 20.

59   Nearly a third of Poland's working-age Jews without employment: Sachar, Abram L. *Sufferance Is the Badge: The Jew in the Contemporary World*. New York, 1940, p. 186.

59–60   Jewish charity rolls approached two-thirds: Ibid., pp. 187–89.

60   Thousands of Jewish families clustered for shelter in single rooms: Janowsky, Oscar I. *People at Bay*. New York, 1938, p. 186.

61   "The . . . system of minority protection": Rabinowicz, op. cit., p. 37.

61   "The louse, the bedbug, the locust": Polonsky, Mendelsohn, et al., op. cit., p. 170.

61   "Whenever something is taking place which is harmful": Ibid., p. 171.

61   "A terrible gangrene has infiltrated our body": Polonsky, op. cit., p. 169.

61–62   "It is a fact that Jews oppose the Catholic Church": Polonsky, Mendelsohn, et al. op. cit., p. 170.

62   "[D]epriving the Jews of earning money": Buell, Raymond. *Poland: Key to Europe*. New York, 1939, p. 7.

62   Endeks mounted some three hundred separate attacks: Heller, Celia 5. *On the Edge of Destruction: The Jews of Poland Between the Two World Wars*. New York, 1977, p. 228.

63   "We accept the injunctions issued by . . . Cardinal Hlond": Cang, op. cit., p. 246.

63   "Fight for the complete elimination of Jews": Ibid., p. 248.

65   Of the nation's 49,967 university students: Mahler, Raphael. "Jews in Public Service and the Liberal Professions in Poland, 1918–1939," *Jewish Social Studies*, Vol. 6, No. 3, 1944, p. 341.

65   Wait not less than five years for licenses to practice: Rabinowicz, op. cit., p. 102.

66   "For Christ, too, belongs in the ghetto": Horak, op. cit., pp. 118–19.

66   Most Polish parties favor mass Jewish emigration: Polonsky, Mendelsohn, et. al., op. cit., p. 248.

66   Neither did a single member of Church hierarchy: Ibid.

67   Lipski promised to erect monument to führer: Polonsky, Mendelsohn, et al., op. cit., pp. 104–107.

67   "Hangs like a millstone around the neck of Poland": Rabinowicz, op. cit., p. 181.

67   "Solution to the Jewish problem . . . can be achieved above all": Marcus, op. cit., p. 394.

67   "Would do all in its power to obtain outlets for [Jewish] emigration": Rabinowicz, op. cit., p. 184.

68   Potocki said Poland will accept no further American Jewish investments: Fishman, op. cit., p. 199.

68   France's response on Madagascar was courteously negative: Cang, op. cit., p. 250.

68   Mouter acknowledged that limited Jewish immigration might be feasible: Yahil, Leni. "Madagascar—Phantom of a Solution for the Jewish Question," in Vago, Bela, and George Mosse, eds. *Jews and Non-Jews in Eastern Europe, 1919–1945.* Jerusalem, 1975, pp. 317–18.

69   "The Polish Government is following with interest the progress made": Marcus, op. cit., pp. 397–98.

69–70   Mainstream Zionist leadership condemned Jabotinsky's negotiations with Beck: Rabinowicz, op. cit., p. 192.

IV. HOSTAGES OF "LATIN" CIVILIZATION *(pp. 71–99)*

71   Known as "the Sphinx": Spector, Sherman D. *Rumania at the Peace Conference: The Diplomacy of Ioan I. C. Bratianu.* New York, 1962, p. 10.

72   "Like a pedlar in an Oriental bazaar": Ibid, p. 27.

73   Clemenceau responded to transformed diplomatic climate: Ibid, p. 137.

74   For minority composition of postwar Rumania, see Fischer-Galsati, Stephen. *Twentieth-Century Roumania.* New York, 1991.

75   Jews feared, reviled us infidels, aliens, leeches. Weber, Eugen, and Hans Rogger, eds. *The European Right: A Historical Profile.* Berkeley, Cal., 1966, p. 506.

75   Treaty of Berlin provisions on minorities' guarantees: Mair, Lucy P. *The Protection of Minorities: The Working and Scope of the Minorities Treaties under the League of Nations.* London, 1939, pp. 32–33.

76   "[U]ne monstrosité au point de vue international": Luzzatti, Luigi, ed. *God in Freedom.* New York, 1930, p. 469.

76   "Jews cannot be tolerated in the hospitals": Black, Eugene. *The Social Politics of Anglo-Jewry.* Oxford, 1988, p. 348.

76–77   Louis Marshall cited chapter and verse of Bucharest's unsavory record: Reznikoff, op. cit., Vol. 2, pp. 640–41.

77   "Iron-clad obligation on Rumania": Ibid, pp. 641–42.

77   Bratianu issued preemptive "decree" ostensibly extending Jews blanket citizenship: Ibid., pp. 542–43.

77   Bratianu would sign minorities treaty only if other major Powers did: Spector, op. cit., p. 176.

77   Wilson would not permit "disturbing elements" to threaten peace: Ibid., pp. 176–77.

78   "Rumania undertakes to recognize as Rumanian nationals": Starr, Joshua. "Jewish Citizenship in Rumania, 1878–1940," *Jewish Social Studies*, Vol. 3, No. 1, 1941, p. 66.

78   Peasantry subsisted as tenant farmers: Weber, Eugen. *Varieties of Fascism*. Princeton, N.J., 1964, p. 514.

78   Non-Rumanians dominated oil, banking, insurance sectors: Ibid., p 529.

78   Rumania ignored minorities treaty, discriminated: Cabot, J. M. *The Racial Conflict in Transylvania*. Boston, 1926, p. 102.

79   "The Allies have written the treaties": Sachar, Abram L. op. cit., p. 226.

79   "Dear Master and Friend: I am performing a duty to you": Luzzatti, op. cit., pp. 499–500.

79–80 Investigative commission studied fate of Jewish families lacking naturalization: American Committee on the Right of Religious Minorities. *Roumania Ten Years After*. New York, 1928, p. 47.

80   Minorities treaty provisions on Jews were ignored: Ibid, p. 63.

81   Nationalists characterized minorities as threat to Rumania's homogeneity: Volovici, Leon. *Nationalist Ideology and Antisemitism: The Case of Romanian Intellectuals in the 1930s*. Oxford, 1991, p. 3.

82   "It is a passion common to politicians of all parties": Iancu, Carol. *Jews in Rumania, 1866–1919: From Exclusion to Emancipation*. Boulder, Colo., 1996, p. 229.

82   Iorga an apotheosist of nostalgia: Volovici, op. cit., p. 66.

82   Iorga the spokesman for European racist doctrines: Volovici, op. cit., p. 6.

82–83 Prestigious cultural figures standard bearers of Rumanian antisemitism. Ibid, p. 9.

83   "[T]he Jews had as their father the Devil": Joint Foreign Committee of the Board of Deputies of British Jewry and the Anglo-Jewish Association. *The Jewish Minority in Roumania: Correspondence with the Roumanian Government Respecting the Grievances of the Jews*. London, 1927, p. 5.

83   "[A] form of transition to the . . . numerus nullus": Cuza, N. *Numerus Nullus*. Bucharest, 1923, qtd. in Volovici, op. cit., p. 23.

83   "[T]he only feasible solution . . . is the elimination of the *yids*": Volovici, op. cit., 26–27.

83   "[P]hilosophic old gentleman": Ibid., p. 25.

84   Codreanu was tall, handsome, eloquent: Ibid., p. 51.

84   For Codreanu, the Jewish issue was one of evil against good: Nagy-Talavera, N. *The Green Shirts and Others: A History of Fascism in Hungary and Rumania*. Stanford, Cal., 1970, p. 260.

84   "Brother, do not fear": Weber, op. cit., p. 522.

85   "Enough of politics, enough of talk": Ibid., pp. 101–102.

86   Codreanu's crusade burgeoned into nakedly Fascist movement: Volovici, op. cit., pp. 28 ff.

87   Filderman refused role of "show Jew": *Encyclopedia Judaica*, Vol. 6, Jerusalem, 1971, pp. 174–75.

87   "The Roumanian Government . . . intends to ensure to all the [religious communities]": Joint Foreign Committee, op. cit., pp. 6–7.

88   Wolf cited demands of antisemitic Rumanian deputies: Ibid., pp. 121–24.

88   "There have never been any pogroms in our country": Ibid., p. 19.

88   Lucien Wolf's indictment of Rumanian government: Ibid., p. 27 ff.

88–89 "Romania cannot expect moral or financial credit in the United States": Reznikoff, op. cit., Vol. 2, pp. 648–49.

89   Dilatory League of Nations' process on minorities' complaints: Claude, Inia. *National Minorities: An International Problem*. Cambridge, Mass., 1951, p. 27.

93   "One feels like crying with pity": Sachar, Abram L. op. cit., p. 225.

93–94 Carol forced to seek stopgap solution to Iron Guardist pressures: Volovici, op. cit., p. 70.

95   "[M]aintaining an attitude contrary to the interests": Sachar, Abram L. op. cit., p. 240.

95   "[A]nxiously watching developments": Ibid., p. 241.

V. BELA KUN AND THE LEGACY OF UTOPIANISM (*pp. 100–131*)

100   "Was of the Tatar type, with strong cheek bones": Fodor, M. W. *Plot and Counter-plot in Central Europe.* Boston, 1937, p. 136.

100   Another 740,000 [Hungarians] had been wounded: Tokes, Rudolf L. *Bela Kun and the Hungarian Soviet Republic.* New York, 1967, p. 49.

102   By 1840 . . . a [Jewish] population of some 240,000: McCagg, William O., Jr. "The Jewish Position in Interwar Central Europe: A Structural Study of Jewry at Vienna, Budapest, and Prague," in Don, Yehuda, and Victor Karady, eds. *A Social and Economic History of Central European Jewry.* New Brunswick, N.J., 1990, pp. 50–51.

102   Prewar Hungarian Jewish critical mass of 910,000: Janos, Andrew C. "The Decline of Oligarchy: Bureaucratic and Mass Politics in the Age of Dualism," in Mosse, George, and Walter Laqueur, eds. *The Left-Wing Intellectuals Between the Wars, 1918–1939.* New York, 1966, pp. 57–58.

102   Budapest Jewry second only to Warsaw's in size: Patai, Raphael. *The Jews of Hungary.* Detroit, 1966, p. 433.

102   Leading Jewish role in prewar Hungarian economy: Katus, Laszlo. "The Occupational Structure of Hungarian Jewry in the Nineteenth and Twentieth Centuries," in Silber, Michael K., ed. *Jews in the Hungarian Economy: 1760–1945.* Jerusalem, 1992, *passim.*

103   Jewish role in Hungarian professions: Lengyel, Gyorgy. "Jews in Hungarian Banking in the Interwar Period," in Silber, op. cit., p. 232.

103   Jews in prewar Hungarian government: Janos, op. cit., pp. 58, 79–80.

103   Tradition of Hungarian Jewish patriotism: McCagg, William O., Jr. "Jews in Revolutions: The Hungarian Experience," *Journal of Social History,* Vol. 6, No. 1, 1972, p. 79.

103   Jews in Hungarian armed forces: *Encyclopedia Judaica,* Vol. 8, p. 1091.

105   Bela Kun's family background: Tokes, Rudolf S. "Bela Kun: The Man and the Revolutionary," in Volgyes, Ivan, ed. *Hungary in Revolution, 1918–19.* Lincoln, Nebraska, 1971, p. 172.

105–106   Kun as Bolshevik POW in Siberia: Tokes, Rudolf S. *Bela Kun and the Hungarian Soviet Republic,* pp. 60 ff.

107   "Yesterday I heard Kun speak": Ibid., pp. 11–12.

108   Hungarians initially welcomed Communist regime: Koestler, Arthur. *Arrow in the Blue.* New York, 1952, pp. 53–55.

108   Kun a clumsy Bolshevik doctrinaire: Lowenthal, Richard. "The Hungarian Soviet and International Communism," in Mosse and Laqueur, op. cit., p. 177.

109   "Red Terror" claimed relatively few victims: Fodor, op. cit., p. 7.

109   Charges of "Jewish conspiracy" fell on receptive soil: Tokes, *Bela Kun and the Hungarian Soviet Republic,* p. 193.

109   Many Jews among victims of Red Terror: Patai, op. cit., p. 7.

109   "Personally, I do not think that anything on earth": Katzburg, Nathaniel. *Hungary and the Jews: Policy and Legislation, 1920–1943.* Ramat Gan, Israel, 1981, p. 35.

110   Kun sought treaty of military alliance with Moscow: Low, Alfred. *The Soviet Hungarian Republic and the Paris Peace Conference.* Philadelphia, 1963, p. 35.

111   "No one will be able to govern here": Tokes, *Bela Kun and the Hungarian Soviet Republic,* p. 204.

113–114   Jews were simply rounded up and gunned down: Katzburg, op. cit., p. 40.

114   Awakening Magyars extorted money from their victims: Sachar, Abram L., op. cit., p. 262.

114   Extensive Jewish conversions to Christianity: Ibid., p. 253.

114   British Labor Party investigation of Hungarian rightist excesses: British Joint Labour Delegation in Hungary: *The White Terror in Hungary.* London, 1920, p. 673.

114   "American sympathy for Hungary will depend": Katzburg, op. cit., pp. 54–55.

114   White Terror continued to focus heavily on Jews: Nagy-Talavera, op. cit., p. 54.

117   Jews represented 23 percent of Budapest population: Laszlo, Erno. "Hungary's Jewry: A Demographic Overview, 1918–1945," in Braham, Randolf, ed. *Hungarian Jewish Studies.* New York, 1968, Vol. 2, pp. 141–43.

117   Jews remained disproportionately involved in Hungarian industry: Veghazi, Istvan. "The Role of Jewry in the Economic Life of Hungary," in Braham, Randolf, op. cit., see also Lengyel, op. cit., p. 232.

117   Numbers of Hungarian unemployed swollen by new waves of university graduates: Nagy-Talavera, op. cit., p. 67.

117   Discrimination reduced numbers of Jewish engineers: Kovacs, Maria M. "Interwar Antisemitism in the Professions: The Case of the Engineers," in Silber, op. cit., p. 33.

117   Discrimination reduced numbers of Jewish professionals: Lengyel, op. cit., p. 232.

118   Hungarian government prepared numerus-clausus legislation for Jewish university students: Katzburg, op. cit., p. 62.

118–19   Wolf, Bigart invoked minorities treaty in appeal to League of Nations: Roucek, J. C. *The Working of the Minorities System Under the League of Nations.* Prague, 1929, p. 99.

119   Wolf, Bigart sought adjudication at The Hague: Ibid., pp. 110–11.

119   Klebelsberg promised numerus clausus to be "temporary": Katzburg, op. cit., p. 69.

119   League of Nations Council postponed appeal to The Hague: Roucek, op. cit., pp. 110–11.

119   Hungarian students protested revision of numerus-clausus law: Katzburg, op. cit., p. 75.

120   Jews still comprised high proportion of Hungarian millionaires, professionals, journalists: Lengyel, op. cit., pp. 232–33.

122   Gombos, Stern signed "protocol": Katzburg, op. cit., p. 86.

124–25   "[T]hat we create a just situation . . . and reduce the influence of Jews": Patai, op. cit., p. 519.

126   Arrow Cross membership rose from 20,000 to 100,000; Nagy-Talavera, op. cit., p. 141.

127   "Second Jewish Bill" to denaturalize large numbers of Jews: Katzburg, op. cit., p. 129.

127   Horthy, Bethlen regarded Imredy's Jewish bills as too extreme: Ibid., pp. 136–37.

127   Informed of his "Jewish" ancestry, Imredy resigned: Nagy-Talavera, op. cit., 150; see also Sachar, Abram L., op. cit., p. 264.

128   Kun fled, berated Hungarian working classes for neglecting "historical mission": Tokes, in Volgyes, op. cit., pp. 181–82.

129   Kun ordered mass execution of White Russian prisoners: Ibid., p. 183.

130   Lenin breathed "fire and flames" at Kun: Ibid., p. 188.

131   Veteran Jewish Communists returned to Hungary after 1945: Sachar, Howard M. *Diaspora: An Inquiry into the Contemporary Jewish World.* New York, 1985, p. 344.

VI. THE PROFESSOR AND THE PROPHET   *(pp. 132–60)*

132   "A German writer, little known among us": Bauer, Johann. *Kafka and Prague.* London, 1971, p. 177.

133   Population of Prague more than doubled, from 240,000 to 514,000: Carter, F. W. "Kafka's Prague," in Stern, J. P., ed. *The World of Franz Kafka.* New York, 1981, p. 41.

133   German proportion of Prague population dropped: Ibid., pp. 41–42.

133 "The hands of the ghetto clock": Apollinaire, Guillaume. *Les Alcoöls*. Paris, 1913.

134 Jewish proportion of German-speakers increased: Ibid.

134 "Cheek by jowl with the haunts of vice and debauchery": Bauer, op. cit., pp. 21–22.

134 Kafka conjured up atavistic images of Old Prague: Ibid., p. 11.

134–35 Golem tradition among Prague Jewry: Demetz, Peter. *Prague in Black and White*. New York, 1994, pp. 30–32.

135 Only 1 percent of Jews enrolled in Czech section of Karl-Ferdinand University: Carter, op. cit., p. 34.

137 "I once wrote of someone, accurately": Kafka, Franz. "Dearest Father," in *"Dearest Father" and Other Writings*. New York, 1954, p. 186.

138 "Miserable creature that I am": Brod, Max, ed. *The Diaries of Franz Kafka, 1914–1923*. New York, 1949, pp. 196–97.

139 Morally, "K" of *The Trial* is his own executioner: Neider, Charles. *The Frozen Sea: A Study of Franz Kafka*. New York, 1949, p. 49.

140 Growth of Czech cultural nationalism in nineteenth century: Sayer, Derek. *The Coasts of Bohemia: A Czech History*. Princeton, N.J., 1998, pp. 95–97.

140 Borovsky stigmatized Jews as opportunistic sycophants of German ruling minority: Dagan, Avigdor. "Jewish Themes in Czech Literature," in Society for the History of Czechoslovak Jews. *The Jews of Czechoslovakia*, Vol. 1. Philadelphia, 1968, pp. 457–58.

141 "Then why, for what reasons, was Agnes Hruza murdered?": Epstein, Binyamin, ed. *T. G. Masaryk and the Jews: A Collection of Essays*. New York, 1941, pp. 184–88.

142 Masaryk denounced blood–libel accusation: Ibid., pp. 193–94.

142–43 "[I]t is blasphemy for a Christian to state that ritual murder comes": Rychmovsky, Ernst. "The Struggle against the Ritual Murder Superstition," in Epstein, op. cit., pp. 150–51.

143 "I repeat what I have written on the blackboard": Ibid., p. 233.

143 A man "who had taken up the cause of a Jew": Herben, Jan. "Jews and Anti-Semitism," in Epstein, op. cit., p. 13.

143 "At [the time of the Hilsner trial] not only the student body but the whole . . . University was infected . . .": Ibid., 18–19.

146 "One part of this work of regeneration I see in Zionism": Weltsch, Felix. "Masaryk and Zionism," in Epstein, op. cit., p. 16.

146 "The Zionist movement appeals to me a great deal": Ibid., p. 17.

146–47 "Particularly in America the Jews helped me": Herben, op. cit., pp. 20–21.

147 "[I]n America the Jews are well treated": Ibid.

147 "If a man tells me he is a German": Weltsch, op. cit., pp. 6–7.

148 "The Jews as well as the other national minorities of this Republic": Ibid., pp. 8–9.

148 Jews opted for different "nationalities" in different parts of Czechoslovakia: *Encyclopedia Judaica*, Vol. 5, pp. 1190–92.

150 Kafka entered into study of Chasidic lore: Zohn, Harry. "Participation in German Literature," in Society for the History of Czechoslovak Jews, op. cit., Vol. 1, p. 485; see also, Brod, op. cit., p. 399.

150 "Kafka had been dying all his life": Grunfeld, Frederic. *Prophets Without Honor: A Background to Freud, Kafka, Einstein, and Their World*. New York, 1979, p. 189.

150 "A woman is punished when she displays too much intiative": Hüber-Neumann, Marete. *Kafka's Freundin Milena*. Munich, 1953, p. 134.

151 "The absence of any firm Jewish ground beneath my feet": Grunfeld, op. cit., p. 194.

151 Some have seen prototype for Josephine in a Yiddish-theater actress: Politzer, Heinz. *Franz Kafka: Parable and Paradox*. Ithaca, N.Y., 1979, p. 326.

153 Slang Czech term for Kafka's world is *kafkarna*: Bauer, op. cit., p. 180.

153 Eighty percent of Czechoslovak Jews lived in cities and towns: *Encyclopedia Judaica*, Vol. 5, p. 1189.

153   Thirty to forty percent of invested capital in 1930s was Jewish: Ibid., p. 1191.

155   "I feel an aversion toward the trial of a people trod": Hostovsky, Egon. "Participation in Modern Czech Literature," in Society for the History of Czechoslovak Jews, op. cit., Vol. 1, pp. 442–43.

156   Foreign Jews were admitted to Czech universities: Sachar, Abram L., op. cit., p. 112.

157   "The Jews may remain where they are, but they must understand": Weltsch, op. cit., p. 76.

157   Masaryk endorsed Zionist efforts to revive Jewish homeland: Ibid., p. 88.

158–59   "Jackals and Arabs" possibly Kafka's metaphor for Zionists in Palestine: Robertson, Ritchie. *Kafka: Judaism, Politics, and Literature.* Oxford, 1985, p. 165.

159   "Rotpeter" an ape who could only imitate a human being: Ibid., pp. 168–69.

160   "[A] prophet of calamities to come": Bauer, op. cit., pp. 173–74.

VII. NOTES FROM A SHATTERED DREAM *(pp. 161–204)*

161   "[R]otundly handsome at nineteen, carefully unkempt": Raabe, Paul, ed. *The Era of German Expressionism.* London, 1974, p. 53.

161   "I have done a good deed": Zohn, Harry. "Participation in German Literature," in Society for the History of Czechoslovak Jews, op. cit., Vol. 1, p. 491.

161   In 1910, Viennese Jewry numbered some 175,000: *Encyclopedia Judaica,* Vol. 3, pp. 895–97.

163   "The aristocracy would have nothing to do with such [cultural] things": Wassermann, Jakob. *Mein Weg als Deutscher und Jude.* Berlin, 1921, pp. 102 ff.

163   Jews transcended the stigma of "mere" commerce by cultural achievement: Zweig, Stefan. *The World of Yesterday [Die Welt von Gestern].* London, 1943, p. 20.

163   Jews one of every three students in Vienna's gymnasia: Goldhammer, Leo. *Die Juden Wiens: Eine statistische Studie.* Vienna, 1927, pp. 37 ff.; see also Rozenblit, Marsha L. *The Jews of Vienna, 1867–1914.* Albany, 1983.

163   Jews half of Vienna's doctors: Beller, Steven. *Vienna and the Jews.* Cambridge, England, 1989, pp. 34–35.

164   Important Jewish literary figures in Vienna: Zohn, Harry. "Fin-de-Siècle Vienna: The Jewish Contribution," in Reinharz, Jehuda, and Walter Schatzberg, eds. *The Jewish Response to German Culture.* Hanover, N.H., 1971, p. 144.

164   Sixteen Jews prominent in Jung-Wien group: Lothar, Ernst. *Das Wunder des Überlebens: Erinnerungen und Ergebnisse.* Vienna, 1961, p. 18.

164   "Sang the swan-song of old Vienna": Liptzin, Sol. *Arthur Schnitzler.* New York, 1932, pp. 137–38.

165   "Was promoted, nourished, or even created by Viennese Jewry": Zweig, op. cit., p. 22.

165   "Whoever wished to 'put something through' in Vienna": Wassermann, op. cit., pp. 102 ff.

165   Berlin could not match Vienna's Jewish intellectual elite: Beller, op. cit., p. 244.

165   "Gave to what was Austrian, and Viennese [culture]": Zweig, op. cit., pp. 28–29. See also Beller, Steven. "Why Was the Viennese Liberal Bildungsbürgertum Jewish?," in Don and Karady, op. cit., pp. 167–70.

166   Lueger's anti-Jewish political platform: Wistrich, Robert S., ed. *Austrians and Jews in the Twentieth Century.* London, 1992, p. 201.

166   Lueger's campaigning institutionalized white-collar antisemitism: Hamann, Brigitte. *Hitler's Vienna.* New York, 1999, p. 347.

168   "Schnitzler, he belongs here as much as Mozart and Schubert": Zohn, Harry. "Arthur Schnitzler and the Great Age of Vienna Jewry," in *Boston Jewish Advocate,* April 4, 1963.

168   Kafka rejected identification of himself as "psychoanalyst": Hoffman, Frederick J. *Freudianism and the Literary Mind.* Baton Rouge, La., 1957, p. 191.

170   Freud's views on sex influenced by Wilhelm Fliess: Sulloway, Frank J. *Freud: Biologist of the Mind.* Cambridge, Mass., 1992, p. 10.

171   "Freud . . . secularized Jewish mysticism": Bakan, David. *Sigmund Freud and the Jewish Mystical Tradition.* New York, 1958, p. 25.

171   Some sources see in Freud "deep ambivalence about his Jewish origins": Robert, Marthe. *From Oedipus to Moses: Freud's Jewish Identity.* Garden City, N.Y., 1976, pp. 6–7.

171   Freud described himself as an "absolutely irreligious Jew": Ibid., p. 7.

171   No "elusive Jewish quality . . . informed Freud's work": Gay, Peter. *A Godless Jew.* New Haven, Conn., 1987, p. 48.

172   Freud's analysis of Mahler: Jones, Ernest. *The Life and Work of Sigmund Freud.* New York, 1953–57, Vol. 2, p. 279.

173   "All my libido is given to Austria-Hungary": Punder, H. W. *Freud: His Life and Mind.* London, 1949, p. 161.

173   "[I]n spite of all my hatred and aversion for war": Prater, D. A. *European of Yesterday: A Biography of Stefan Zweig.* Oxford, 1972, p. 72.

173   Zweig signed antiwar petitions: Ibid., p. 106.

175   "Too small to live, too large to die": Sachar, Abram L. op. cit., pp. 73–74.

175   Viktor Adler suffered from antisemitism: Wistrich, op. cit., p. 239.

175–76   Prominence of Jews in Austria's Social Democratic party: Schwarz, Robert. "Antisemitism and Socialism in Austria, 1918–1962," in Fraenkel, Joseph, ed. *The Jews of Austria.* London, 1967, p. 445.

177   Jews a majority of "important" figures in Austrian socialism: Glaser, Ernst. *Im Umeld des Austromarxismus.* Vienna, 1981, pp. 371–91.

179   Half of Galician Jewish refugees remained in Vienna: McCagg, William O., Jr. "The Jewish Position in Interwar Central Europe: A Structural Study of Jewry at Vienna, Budapest, and Prague," in Don and Karady, op. cit., p. 72.

179   Jews prominent in Vienna's economy even in postwar: Andics, H. *Der ewige Jude: Ursachen und Geschichte den Antisemitismus.* Vienna, 1968, p. 292.

179   Few Jews employed in Gentile-owned businesses: Pauley, Bruce F. "Political Antisemitism in Interwar Vienna," in Oxaal, I., M. Pollak, and G. Botz, eds. *Jews, Antisemitism, and Culture in Vienna.* London, 1987, p. 156.

181   Schönberg prominent in "Second Vienna School" of music: Gradenwitz, Peter. "Jews in Austrian Music," in Fraenkel, op. cit., p. 24.

183   "[T]he unforgettable types which he created": Zohn, Harry, in *Jewish Advocate,* op. cit.

184   "More death and sickness will once again come into the world": Field, Frank. *The Last Days of Mankind: Karl Kraus and His Vienna.* London, 1967, p. 134.

184   "[T]he trouble is simply that we Austrian Aryans are not a match": Bettauer, Hugo. *The City Without Jews [Die Stadt ohne Juden].* New York, 1926, pp. 11–12.

186   Jung and Freud in first meeting: Freud, Martin. *Glory Reflected: Sigmund Freud—Man and Father.* New York, 1958, p. 240.

186   "[A]s a Christian and a pastor's son": Clark, Ronald W. *Freud: The Man and the Cause.* London, 1980, p. 252.

187   "I would . . . point [out] that your technique of treating your pupils": Ibid., pp. 328–29.

187   "Brutality and antisemitic condescension towards me": Ibid., p. 335.

190   Mussolini pressed Dollfuss to break Social Democrats: Fodor, op. cit., p. 217.

191   Christian Socialists sympathized with Hitler's boycott of Jewish businesses: Oxaal and Botz, op. cit., p. 162.

191   Social Democratic recriminations against Jewish members: Fodor, op. cit., p. 446; see also Schwarz, op. cit., p. 447.

192   How could one tell? The world was swarming with antisemites: Canetti, Elias. *Auto-da-Fé [Die Blendung],* New York, 1982, p. 197.

192   "The so-called Jewish 'self-hatred' ": Zweig, Arnold. *Caliban: oder Politik unter Lei-denschaft.* Potsdam, 1927, p. 199.

195   "[W]e [Jews] must do nothing now that involves": Prater, op. cit., p. 234.

195   "Ever since the giving of the Decalogue": Ibid., p. 191.

195–96 "Cured of the last shred of my predilection for the Aryan cause": Schultz, Duane. *Intimate Friends, Dangerous Rivals: The Turbulent Relationship Between Freud and Jung.* Los Angeles, 1990, p. 211.

196   "Would serve to make a sharp division between us": Diller, Jerry. *Freud's Jewish Identity.* Rutherford, N.J., 1991, p. 127.

196   "There is every reason to suppose . . . that the grand figure of Moses": Jones, op. cit., Vol. 2, pp. 364–65.

196   "Faced with the new persecution, one asks oneself": Yerushalmi, Yosef H. *Freud's Moses.* New Haven, Conn., 1991, p. 16.

197   "We know that Moses had given the Jews": Anna Freud's original presentation at congress of psychiatry, qtd. in Gay, Peter, *Freud: A Life for Our Time.* New York, 1988, p. 645.

197   "The hatred for Judaism is at bottom hatred for Christianity": Freud, Sigmund. *Moses and Monotheism [Der Mann Moses und die monotheistische Religion].* New York, 1938, pp. 116–17.

197   "[N]ow that everything is being taken from them": Clark, op. cit., pp. 523–24.

197   Freud sought to wean his wife from "religious prejudices": Diller, op. cit., pp. 85–86.

197   "I was born on May 6, 1856 . . . at Freiberg, Moravia": Freud, Sigmund. *Autobiographical Study.* New York, 1963, p. 12.

198   "Endangered the common interest": Gilman, Sander. *The Case of Sigmund Freud.* Baltimore, 1993, pp. 190 ff.

198   Freud cold to Werfel's flirtation with Christianity: Ibid., pp. 190–91.

198   "If you do not let your son grow up as a Jew": Graf, Max. "Reminiscences of Professor Sigmund Freud," *Psychoanalytic Quarterly,* Vol. 11, No. 3, 1942, p. 289.

198   "Only to my Jewish nature did I owe": Sachar, Howard M. *The Course of Modern Jewish History.* 3rd ed. New York, 1990, pp. 477–78.

198   Freud regarded Jews as better able to accept "subversive" ideas: Brunner, José. *Freud and the Politics of Psychoanalysis.* Cambridge, Mass., 1995, pp. 27–28.

199   "Once again our people is faced with dark times": Bakan, op. cit., pp. 48–49.

199   "So much better for psychoanalysis": Wortis, Joseph. *Fragments of an Analysis with Freud.* New York, 1958, pp. 144–46.

199   "The mighty deposit of ancestral experiences": Alexander, Franz, and Sheldon T. Selesnick. *The History of Psychiatry.* New York, 1966, p. 246.

199–200 "As a rule, the Jew lives in amicable relationship": Grossman, S. "C. G. Jung and National Socialism," *Journal of European Studies,* Vol. 9 (1979), p. 238.

200   Jung distinguished between German and Jewish psychology: Brome, Vincent. *Jung: Man and Myth.* New York, 1978, p. 217.

200   "[T]he Jew, a cultural nomad": Alexander and Selesnick, op. cit., p. 408.

202   Austrian antisemitism came on "rubber-soled shoes": Sachar, Abram L., op. cit., p. 89.

203   "[T]o conclude in good time and in erect bearing": Zweig, Stefan. op. cit., editor's note, p. 437.

204   "Two prospects present themselves in these troubled times": Freud, Martin, op. cit., p. 218.

VIII. THE AGE OF THE ASSASSINS *(pp. 205–254)*

206   Jewish population, affluence grew in prewar Berlin: Wistrich, Robert S. *Socialism and the Jews: The Dilemmas of Assimilation in Germany and Austria-Hungary.* London, 1992, p. 59.

206 Jewish women the first in Germany to practice birth control widely: Knodel, John E. *The Decline of Fertility in Germany, 1871–1939*. Princeton, N.J., 1974, p. 137.

207 One of Pappenheim's objectives was to address crises of "socially fallen": Pappenheim, Bertha. *Sisyphus Arbeit: Reisebrief aus den Jahren 1911 und 1912*. Leipzig, 1924, pp. 12–42, *passim;* see also, Sachar, Howard M. *A History of the Jews in America*. New York, 1992, pp. 164–67.

208 "[A]n Asian horde on the sandy plains of Prussia": Kessler, Harry. *Walther Rathenau: His Life and Work*. New York, 1944, pp. 37–38; see also Friedrich, Otto. *Before the Deluge*. New York, 1972, p. 112.

211 "What do you want with this particular suffering of the Jews?": Bronner, Stephen E., ed. *The Letters of Rosa Luxemburg*. Boulder, Colo., 1975, pp. 7–8.

211 "Help, for heaven's sake, help": Ettinger, Elzbieta. *Comrades and Lovers: Rosa Luxemburg's Letters to Leo Jogiches*. Cambridge, Mass., 1979, p. xix.

211 "I feel the way you do.... My golden one": Ibid., p. xix.

215 "Jewish influence in the press . . . is increasing steadily": Pulzer, Peter. *Jews and the German State*. Cambridge, Mass., 1992, p. 120.

215 "[T]he Jewish spirit has contributed especially to the degeneration:" Ibid., p. 120.

216 "Russian buffalo-Jews" Ibid., p. 162.

217 "[S]hamed, dishonored, wading in blood": Luxemburg, Rosa. *Der Krise der Sozialdemokratie*. 2nd. ed. Berlin, 1919, pp. 12, 16.

218 "Freedom only for the supporters of the government": Florence, Ronald. *Marx's Daughters*. New York, 1975, p. 14.

218 "[D]evote your resources to the Fatherland above and beyond": Pulzer, op. cit., p. 195.

218 "Germany is becoming a world power": Karlweiss, Manfred. *Jakob Wassermann*. Amsterdam, 1935, p. 241.

219 Lissauer's "Hassgesang gegen England": Poliakov, Léon. *The History of Anti-Semitism*. New York, 1977, Vol. 4, p. 138.

219 Haber's wartime scientific accomplishments: Stern, Fritz. *Einstein's German World*. Princeton, N.J., 1999, p. 119.

219 Rathenau pressed for complete German victory: Felix, David. *Walter Rathenau and the Weimar Republic*. Baltimore, 1971, p. 51.

220 Prewar German government consulted Rathenau on economic issues: Friedrich, op. cit., p. 100.

220 "Surrounded by the magic glitter of his wealth": Musil, Robert. *The Man Without Qualities [Der Mann ohne Eigenschaften]*. New York, 1995, p. 199.

221 "Rarely have I sensed the tragedy of the Jew": Zweig, Stefan, op. cit., p. 181.

221 "[S]omewhere within him he felt fear lurking": Kessler, op. cit., p. 26.

222 " 'Your Highness . . . before I am honored by the favor' ": Bülow, Bernhard von. *Denkwürdigkeitern*, Vol. 2, Berlin, 1930. Qtd. in Felix, op. cit., p. 45.

222 "Blood and steel-blue corn and air": Joll, James. *Walter Rathenau: Prophet Without a Cause*. London, 1960, p. 61.

222–23 Wartime frustrations turned against the Jews: Pulzer, op. cit., p. 196.

223 Rightists formulated plans for a Judenzählung: Zechlin, Egmont. *Die deutsche Politik und die Juden im ersten Weltkrieg*. Göttingen, 1969, pp. 518–19.

223 Only after the war did Jewish veterans groups publish statistics: Reichsverband Jüdischer Frontsoldaten. *Die jüdischen Gefallenen des deutschen Heeres, der deutschen Marine, und der deutschen Schutztruppen, 1914–1918: ein Gedenkbuch*. Berlin, 1932.

223 "We have become marked men . . . second-class soldiers": Zechlin, op. cit., p. 533.

223 "[R]eflected genuine popular attitudes": Ibid., p. 536.

224 Jews recovered from patriotic euphoria faster than most: Pulzer, op. cit., pp. 201, 202.

224 Jews anticipated better relationship with "new" Germany: Ibid., p. 207.

226   "[W]orse than the disease it was supposed to cure": Luxemburg, Rosa. *Die russische
       Revolution* (ed. Levi, P.). Berlin, 1922, p. 77.

226   "The Bolsheviks are welcome to keep their tactics to themselves": Ettinger, op.
       cit., p. 236.

227   "How could you? What about our program?": Friedrich, op. cit., pp. 40–45.

227   "Act quickly. The revolution demands it": Frölich, Paul. *Rosa Luxemburg, Her Life
       and Work.* London, 1990, p. 323.

228   "The revolution marches on—over the graves": Nettl, J. F. *Rosa Luxemburg.* Lon-
       don, 1966, Vol. 2, p. 71.

229   Jogiches moved to launch final strike: Friedrich, op. cit., p. 49.

229–30 Legend of a bloodthirsty Luxemburg altered: see Basso, Lelio. *Rosa Luxemburg: A
       Reappraisal.* New York, 1975, passim.

231   "Now that tsarism has attacked Germany": Mitchell, Allan. *Revolution in Bavaria,
       1918–1919.* Princeton, N.J., 1965, p. 60.

232   Eisner's "revolution" accepted by all major Bavarian parties: Ibid., p. 109.

232   "Authentic" socialism would have to wait: Toller, Ernst. *I Was a German: The Auto-
       biography of a Revolutionary.* New York, 1991, p. 149.

233   Jews prominent in Bavarian Socialism: Berghann, Klaus L., ed. *The German-Jewish
       Dialogue Reconsidered.* New York, 1996, p. 144.

233   Bavarian Jewish leaders protested role of Jewish Socialists: Ibid., p. 149.

233   "We want a Bavarian!": Watt, Richard M. *The Kings Depart: The Tragedy of
       Germany—Versailles and the German Revolution.* New York, 1968, p. 291.

234   "[Evidently] wanted to show that a half-Jew could perform such a deed": Berghan,
       op. cit., p. 150.

234   Elaborate funeral for Eisner: Mitchell, op. cit., p. 275.

237   "This Soviet Republic was a foolhardy *coup de main*": Toller, op. cit., p. 159.

237   "Pseudo-Soviet" was finished, Toller informed: Ibid., p. 173.

242   Jews in postwar German middle-class: Niewyk, Donald L. "The Economic and
       Cultural Role of the Jews in the Weimar Republic," *Leo Baeck Institute Yearbook*,
       Vol. 16 (1971), p. 13.

242   Jews hard hit by postwar German inflation: Ibid., p. 18.

243   Decline of parochial Jewish school system in postwar: Niewyk, Donald L. *The Jews
       in Weimar Germany.* Baton Rouge, La., 1980, pp. 114–16.

243   "If impoverished Germany cuts off immigration": Ibid., p. 116.

245   Decline of Jews in German political life: Pulzer, op. cit., p. 273.

246   Kaiser regarded Jews a "toadstool on the German oak": Ibid., p. 214.

247–48 Postwar growth of antisemitic movements, parties: Jochmann, Werner. "Die Austrei-
       tung des Antisemitismus," in Mosse, Werner E., and Arnold Paucker, eds. *Deutsches
       Judentum in Krieg und Revolution, 1916–1923.* Tübingen, 1971, pp. 456–60.

248   "If vindictiveness [to Germany] prevails": Kollman, Eric. "Walter Rathenau and
       German Foreign Policy," *Journal of Modern History*, Vol. 24, No. 1, 1952, p. 136.

249   Approving Rathenau's Erfüllungspolitik, Wirth appointed Rathenau foreign min-
       ister: Kessler, *Walther Rathenau*, pp. 291, 323.

249   "I really had to, Mama": Joll, op. cit., p. 118.

250   Rathenau conferred with Radek: D'Abernon, Edgar V. *The Diary of an Ambassador:
       Versailles to Rapallo.* New York, 1929, p. 270.

251   "[O]ften told me he is sure to be assassinated:" Ibid., p. 310.

251–52 "[Pacelli] informed me simply and soberly in a few sentences": Kessler, op. cit.,
       p. 362.

252   Nazis commemorated graves of Rathenau's assassins: Friedrich, op. cit., p. 117.

253   "In grief unspeakable I give my hand to you": Kessler, Harry. *In the Twenties: The
       Diaries of Count Harry Kessler.* New York, 1971, p. 381.

253   No resemblance to prewar Rathenau, "the social climber": Williamson, David G.

"Walther Rathenau: Patron Saint of the German Liberal Establishment," *Leo Baeck Institute Yearbook*, Vol. 20 (1975), p. 217.

253   Jews canonized Rathenau, overlooking his assimilationism: Ibid., p. 215.

253   "I am a German of Jewish descent": Friedrich, op. cit., p. 113.

254   "[I] thought of the first day of the war": Toller, op. cit., pp. 184–85.

IX. MINERVA'S OWL AT WEIMAR'S TWILIGHT *(pp. 255–282)*

255   When one thinks of Weimar Germany: Gay, Peter. *Weimar Culture*. New York, 1968, p. xiii.

255   "To its toughness of fiber": Ibid., pp. 5–6.

255   "Delightfully understated, cool . . . ambience": Haas, Willy. *Die literarische Welt: Erinnerungen*. Munich, 1960, p. 123.

255   Stefan Zweig professing to find Berlin a corrupt Babylon: Zweig, op. cit., p. 287.

255–56   Gottfried Benn saw Weimar's culture as forever identified with the Jews: Gay, *Weimar Culture*, p. 131.

256   "German cultural life seems to be passing increasingly into Jewish hands": Goldstein, Moritz. *Begriff und Programm einer jüdischen Nationalliteratur*. Berlin, 1913, p. 184.

257   Institut für Sozialforschung maintained influence in New York. Sachar, Howard M., *A History of the Jews in America*, pp. 750–51.

260   "A cheerful, impetuous jack-in-the-box": Marcuse, Ludwig. *Mein zwanzigsten Jahrhundert*. Munich, 1960, as qtd. in Grunfeld, op. cit., p. 272.

262   Lasker-Schüler's outstanding achievement was her lyric poetry: Grunfeld, op. cit., pp. 100, 105. Altogether, Grunfeld's evaluation of these literary eminences is magisterial.

266   "In the evening [I] saw Reinhardt's new production of *A Midsummer Night's Dream*": Kessler, *In the Twenties*, p. 399.

268   Reinhardt's mastery of production, direction: Eyman, Scott. *Ernst Lubitsch*. New York, 1993, p. 30.

268   "You sat . . . in thrall to the world Reinhardt had created": Ibid.

270   Schönberg's music seen as assault on German art: Ringer, Alexander L. *Arnold Schoenberg: The Composer as Jew*. New York, 1990, p. 56.

274   Stern delineates parallel careers of Haber, Einstein: Stern, Fritz. *Einstein's German World*. Princeton, N.J., 1999.

275   "Russian hordes allied with Mongols and Negroes": Brian, Denis. *Einstein: A Life*. New York, 1996, p. 89.

277   Germans regarded Jewish intellectuals as "Querulanten": Grunfeld, op. cit., p. 191.

277   "[T]he Jew conspicuously lacks understanding for the truth": Brian, op. cit., p. 142.

277   German scientists denounced Einstein's relativity theory: Ibid., pp. 105, 143.

278   Haber possibly in secret arms collaborations with Soviet Russia: Craig, Gordon, in *New York Review of Books*, Nov. 4, 1999.

278   "I can conceive of your inner conflicts": Stern, op. cit., p. 159.

278   German teachers politically rightist: Friedrich, op. cit., p. 240.

278   Einstein's visit to Palestine "greatest event of my life": Clark, Ronald W. *Einstein: The Life and Times*. Cleveland, 1971, p. 388.

279   "If anyone were to ask me among what people I had found the greatest understanding": Wassermann, op. cit., p. 109.

279   "Jews 'discovered' me, Jews published and propagated my reputation": Mann, Thomas. *Werke: Autobiographisches*. Frankfurt a/M, 1968, p. 55.

279   "But what is to become of the so-called host people?" Liptzin, Sol. *Germany's Stepchildren*. Philadelphia, 1944, p. 200.

279   Germans saw evidence of political, cultural Verjudung: Aschheim, Steven. "The

Myth of 'Judaization' in Germany," in Schatzberg, Walter, and Jehuda Reinharz, op. cit., pp. 238–39.

280 Hans Gunther's racial theories a merger of metaphysics and soul: Mosse, George. *Toward the Final Solution: A History of European Racism.* New York, 1978, pp. 189–90.

280 "[U]nder attack by Reason in all political parties": Ibid., p. 151.

281 The Weimar years a period of . . . communal and intellectual vitality: See Brenner, Michael. *The Renaissance of Jewish Culture in Weimar Germany.* New Haven, Conn., 1996.

281 Germany's Jews engaged in acrobatics of self-definition, self-justification: Bolkowsky, Sidney M. *The Distorted Image: German Jewish Perceptions of Germans and Germany, 1918–1938.* New York, 1975, p. 49.

281 "[T]he majority of the German people would continue along the democratic path": Ibid., p. 168.

282 "Germany and Germans will [not] abandon [our common national goals]": Ibid., p. 163.

282 "I have been fortunate to have been born and educated in the land of Kant": Oppenheimer, Franz. *Erleben, Erstrebten, Erreichten, Erinnerungen.* Berlin, 1931, p. 214.

X. IN SEARCH OF LOST SWANNS *(pp. 283–325)*

283 "No, it is no longer you, Schwarzbard": Imonti, Felix. *Violent Justice: How Three Assassins Fought to Free Europe's Jews.* Amherst, N.Y., 1994, p. 104.

284 In 1914, French Jewry had not exceeded 130,000: Sachar, Howard M. *Diaspora.* New York, 1985, p. 90.

286 " 'Your goodness toward me,' " " 'He is so kind to me' ": Clermont-Tonnère, Élisabeth. *Memoires,* Vol. I, p. 4, qtd. in Hayman, Ronald. *Proust: A Biography,* New York, 1990, pp. 58.

286 "He sometimes exaggerated his affability": Gregh, Fernand. *L'Âge d'or.* Paris, 1947, p. 179.

287 "My present unconscious memory . . . was sending [me] memories in floods": Hayman, op. cit., p. 100.

287 "For it was I who went to ask Anatole France": Painter, George D. *Proust.* Boston, 1959–65, Vol. 1, pp. 273–74.

287 Proust warned his aristocratic friends against antisemitic remarks: Ibid., Vol. 1, p. 279.

289 "The crowd always follows": Tannenbaum, E. R. *The Action Française.* New York, 1962, p. 75.

289 "The Jews are foreigners settled in France": Maurras, Charles. *La Démocratie religieuse,* Paris, 1921, p. 90.

289 By 1914, Action Française had emerged as a dynamic, powerful rightist organization: Rémond, René. *La Droite en France.* 2d. ed. Paris, 1982, p. 249.

290 "Our antisemitism consists in not being willing to let the Jews govern France": Poliakov, op. cit., Vol. 4, p. 266.

290 Among postwar immigrants, 185,000 were Jews: Dubief, Henri. *Le déclin de la Troisième République, 1929–1938.* Paris, 1976, p. 122.

290 By 1936, East Europeans constituted 60 percent of Jews in France: Sachar, Abram L. op. cit., p. 91.

291 "Without patriotism, how can there be a homeland?" Poliakov, op. cit., Vol. 4, p. 276.

291 "Russia is disappearing because it is infested with Jews": Ibid.

291 For Maurras, German Jews were "the masters in Moscow": Nolte, Ernest. *Three Faces of Fascism.* New York, 1965, p. 124.

291–92   "Gigantic boa whose constricting coils are tied around an agonizing world": Poliakov, op. cit., Vol. 4, p. 263.

292   Jewish army officers applying for early retirement: Ibid.

294   *Action française* attracted wide, prestigious readership: Weber, Eugen. *Action Française: Royalism and Reaction in Twentieth-Century France*. Stanford, Cal., 1962, p. 189.

295   Action française attracted members even among non-monarchists: Machever, Philippe. *Ligues et fascismes en France, 1918–1939*. Paris, 1974, p. 7.

295   Paramilitary ligues evinced growing receptivity to violence: Rémont, op. cit., pp. 278–79.

296   "[W]e shall descend into the street": Plumyène, J., and R. LaSierra. *Les Fascismes français, 1923–1963*. Paris, 1963, pp. 31–32.

296   "[A] gentleman among gangsters, and a gangster among gentlemen": Werth, Alexander. *France in Ferment*. 2nd ed. Gloucester, Mass., 1968, p. 80.

297   "[A]nthracite eyes, circled with green penumbra": Lorenz, Paul. *Les trois vies de Stavisky*. Paris, 1971, p. 9.

299   *L'Action française* urged a mass descent on the Chamber of Deputies: Werth, op. cit., p. 90.

299–300   Thousands of ligue partisans prepared to cross to Left Bank: Ibid., pp. 150–51.

300   Marshal Lyautey warned that Daladier must resign: Tint, Herbert. *France since 1918*. New York, 1970, pp. 54–55.

301   Reputation of great wealth clung to Blum: Logue, W. *Léon Blum: The Formative Years*. DeKalb, Ill., 1973, p. 12.

302   "Socialism wishes to bring social justice into accordance with reason": Judt, op. cit., p. 38.

302   "You will not make the revolution by consorting with gangs": Lacouture, Jean. *Léon Blum*. New York, 1982, p. 138.

303   "I am touched that the revolutionaries have chosen Blum": Ibid., p. 14.

303   "In the battle now engaged, we claim our place": Joll, James. "The Front Populaire—After Thirty Years," in Mosse and Laqueur, op. cit., p. 31.

304   Blum's *Du Mariage* attacked as "Jewish pornography": Lacouture, op. cit., p. 84.

304   "The virtues of the Jewish race are not French virtues": Gide, André. *Journals, 1889–1949*. London, 1967, p. 195.

305   "Nervous, feverish. . . . His eyes shone with a prodigious gleam": Bourgin, Hubert. *De Jaurès à Léon Blum*. Paris, 1938, pp. 508–509.

305   Yharnegary taunted Blum as a "Protestant Jew": Blumel, André. *Léon Blum: juif et sioniste*. Paris, 1951, p. 7.

305   Gaxotte urged that Blum, Jews be sent to Madagascar: Lacouture, op. cit., p. 181.

305   Blum regarded his Jewish ancestry as source of "nobility," "generosity": Blumel, op. cit., p. 5.

305   "He had within him a Jew of a great race": Ibid., p. 6.

306   "I am in fact a Jew. . . . I shall allow no one to remind me": Bloch, Marc. *Strange Defeat*. Oxford, 1949, p. 128.

306   "The rich Jews, the Jews of bourgeois means": Blumel, op. cit., p. 9.

306   "I would not see anything in the world as dolorous": Ibid.

306–307   Croix de Feu membership climbed to 160,000: Bernard, Philippe, and Henri Dubief. *Le Fin d'un monde, 1914–1929: Le Déclin de la IIIe République, 1929–1938*, Paris, 1975–76, Vol. 1, p. 292.

308   Wounded Blum carried to hospital, to undergo surgery: Boudrel, op. cit., p. 33.

309   "The Blums, the Kaisersteins, the Schweinkopfs": Lacouture, op. cit., p. 209.

309   "Hospitality of France . . . the sweetest of adoptive mothers": Soucy, Robert J. *French Fascism: The Second Wave, 1933–1939*. New Haven, Conn., 1995, pp. 154–55.

309   "The Abominable Kike, the traitorous Léon Blum": Lacouture, op. cit., p. 181.

310   "Your advent, M. le Premier, is without question a historic date": Sachar, Abram
       L., op. cit., p. 329.

310   Maurras's abuse of Blum and cabinet unrestrained: Judt, op. cit., p. 76.

310   Timorous French Jewish reaction to Blum's election: Birnbaum, op. cit.,
       pp. 88–89.

311   "[Blum's] silken moustache and his long hair were beginning to gray": Lacouture,
       op. cit., p. 227.

311   "[W]hen you see Blum, you sometimes imagine that Marcel Proust's Swann":
       Werth, Alexander. *The Twilight of France, 1933–40.* New York, 1942, p. 85.

312   Blum described Popular Front program as "French New Deal": Colton, Joel. *Léon
       Blum: Humanist in Politics.* New York, 1966, p. 161.

313   Croix de Feu's membership reached 600,000: Soucy, op. cit., p. 114.

313   Doriot's PPF reached 170,000 members: Ibid., pp. 116–17.

314   "I am a Marxist and a Jew. . . . but we cannot achieve anything": Larousse, Ernest.
       Léon Blum chef de gouvernement. Paris, 1967, p. 279.

314   Stanley Baldwin warned Blum against intervention in Spain: Greene, Nathanael.
       Crisis and Decline: The French Socialist Party in the Popular Front Era. New York,
       1969, p. 80.

314   News leaked of Blum's clandestine shipments to Spain: Boudrel, op. cit., p. 111.

314   "It is as a Jew that one must . . . destroy this Blum": Ibid., pp. 310 ff.

317–18 Widespread antisemitism in last years before World War II: Kingston, Paul. *Anti-
       semitism in France during the 1930s.* Hull, England, 1883, pp. 270 ff.

318   Maurras warned Jews against war-mongering: Micaud, Charles A. *The French
       Right and Nazi Germany, 1933–1939.* New York, 1964, p. 209; see also Pertinax
       (Geraud, André). *The Gravediggers of France.* New York, 1944, p. 415.

318   "I'd prefer a dozen Hitlers to one all-powerful Blum": Céline, qtd. in Vitoux,
       Frédéric. *Céline: A Biography.* New York, 1992, pp. 316–18; see also Poliakov, op.
       cit., Vol. 4, p. 467.

320   "[We have] reached the saturation point": Sachar, Abram L., op. cit., p. 486.

320   Bonnet sounded out Welles on Jewish resettlement in Madagascar: Marrus,
       Michael R., and Richard O. Paxton. *Vichy France and the Jews.* New York, 1981,
       p. 62.

323   "These are the ones who are responsible for this misery": Blum, Léon. *L'Histoire
       jugera.* Paris, 1945, p. 265.

323   Blum defended his record at Riom trial: Ibid., p. 273.

324   French authorities, citizens, collaborated in wartime Jewish tragedy: Sachar,
       Howard M., *Diaspora*, p. 90.

324   "What is important . . . is to go beyond . . . the liberation of the individual": Lacou-
       ture, op. cit., p. 495.

Bibliography

Some readings are listed, as relevant, in more than one chapter.

I. A MURDER TRIAL IN PARIS

Abramson, Henry. *A Prayer for Government: Ukrainians and Jews in Revolutionary Times, 1917–1920*. Cambridge, Mass., 1999.

Adler, Cyrus. *I Have Considered the Days*. Philadelphia, 1941.

——————, and Aaron M. Margalith. *With Firmness in the Right: American Diplomatic Action Affecting Jews, 1840–1945*. New York, 1946.

Altshuler, Mordechai. "Ukrainian-Jewish Relations in the Soviet Milieu in the Interwar," in Potichnyj, Peter J., and Howard Aster, eds. *Ukrainian-Jewish Relations in Historical Perspective*. Edmonton, Canada, 1988.

American Jewish Congress. *The Massacres and Other Atrocities Committed Against the Jews of Southern Russia*. New York, 1920.

Aster, Howard. *Jewish-Ukrainian Relations: Two Solitudes*. New York, 1983.

Bogen, Boris. *Born a Jew*. New York, 1930.

Chasanowitch, Léon, ed. *Les Pogromes anti-Juifs en Pologne et en Galicie en novembre et décembre 1918*. Stockholm, 1919.

Desroches, Alain. *The Ukrainian Problem and Symon Petlura (The Fire and the Ashes)*. New York, 1983.

Frankel, Jonathan. "The Dilemma of Jewish National Autonomism: The Case of the Ukraine, 1917–20," in Potichnyj, Peter J., and Howard Aster, eds. *Ukrainian-Jewish Relations in Historical Perspective*. Edmonton, Canada, 1988.

—————— et al., eds. *Studies in Contemporary Jewry*. vol. 4. New York, 1988.

Friedman, Saul S. *Pogromchik: The Assassination of Simon Petlura*. New York, 1972.

Gergel, N. "The Pogroms in the Ukraine in 1918–21." *YIVO Annual of Jewish Social Science*. Vol. 22 (1951).

Goldelman, Solomon I. *National Autonomy in the Ukraine, 1917–1920*. Chicago, 1968.

Grünbaum, Isaac. "Osias Thon: Statesman of Polish Jews," in Dawidowicz, Lucy, ed. *The Golden Tradition*. London, 1967.

Heifetz, Elias. *The Slaughter of the Jews in the Ukraine in 1919*. New York, 1919.

Horak, Stepan. *Poland and Her National Minorities, 1919–1939*. New York, 1961.

Hunczak, Taras. "A Reaprraisal of Symon Petlura and Ukrainian-Jewish Relations, 1917–1921." *Jewish Social Studies*, Vol. 31, No. 3, 1969.

——————. "Symon Petlura et les juifs." Paris, 1987.

——————. *The Ukraine: A Study of Revolution*. Cambridge. Mass., 1977.

Hyams, Edward. *Killing No Murder*. London, 1970.

Imonti, Felix. *Violent Justice: How Three Assassins Fought to Free Europe's Jews*. Amherst, N.Y., 1994.

Kenez, Peter. *Civil War in South Russia, 1919–1920*. Stanford, Cal., 1977.

Lichten, Joseph. "A Study of Ukrainian-Jewish Relations." *Annals of the Ukrainian Academy of Arts and Sciences in the United States*, Vol. 5, No. 7, 1956.

Manning, Clarence A. *Twentieth-Century Ukraine*. New York, 1951.

Margolin, Arnold. *The Jews of Eastern Europe*. New York, 1936.

Motyl, A. J. "Ukrainian Nationalist Violence in Interwar Poland, 1921–1939." *East European Quarterly*, Vol. 19, No. 1, 1985.

Pidhainy, Oleh S. *Syman Petlura: A Bibliography*. Toronto, 1971.

Potichnyj, Peter J., and Howard Aster, eds. *Ukrainian-Jewish Relations in Historical Perspective*. Edmonton, Canada, 1988.

Rechetar, John S. *The Ukrainian Revolution*. Princeton, N.J., 1952.

Rothschild, Joseph. *East-Central Europe Between the Two World Wars*. Seattle, 1974.

Schechtman, Joseph, ed. *The Pogroms in the Ukraine Under the Ukrainian Government (1917–1920)*. London, 1927.

Seton-Watson, Hugh. *Eastern Europe Between the Wars*. Cambridge, England, 1945.

Stephens, J. S. *Danger Zones of Europe: A Study of National Minorities*. London, 1929.

Stone, Norman. *The Eastern Front 1914–1917*. London, 1975.

Szajkowski, Zosa. "Symon Petliura and Ukrainian-Jewish Relations, 1917–21: A Rebuttal." *Jewish Social Studies*, Vol. 31, No. 3, 1969.

——————. *Jews, War, and Communism*. Vol. 1. New York, 1972. United States. Department of State. *Conditions in the Ukraine Respecting Treatment of Jews*. Washington D.C., 1920.

Vago, Bela, and George Mosse, eds. *Jews and Non-Jews in Eastern Europe, 1919–1945*. Jerusalem, 1975.

Watt, Richard E. *Bitter Glory: Poland and Its Fate, 1918 to 1939*. New York, 1979.

II. A MINORITY "BILL OF RIGHTS"
III. IN SEARCH OF A CONGLOMERATE IDENTITY

Abramsky, Chimen. *War, Revolution, and the Jewish Dilemma*. London, 1975.

——————, M. Jachimczyk, and A. Polonsky, eds. The Jews in Poland, Oxford, 1986.

Adler, Cyrus. *I Have Considered the Days*. Philadelphia, 1946.

——————, and Aaron M. Margalith. *With Firmness in the Right: American Diplomatic Action Affecting Jews, 1840–1945*. New York, 1946.

Alliance Israélite Universelle. *La Question juive devant la conference de la paix*. Paris, 1919.

Baron, Gershon C. "The Politics of Tradition: Agudat Israel in Polish Politics, 1916–1939." *Studies in Contemporary Jewry*. Vol. 2. Bloomington, Ind., 1986.

Beloff, Max. *Lucien Wolf and the Anglo-Russian Entente 1907–1914*. London, 1951.

Best, Gary D. *To Free a People: American Jewish Leaders and the Jewish Problem in Eastern Europe, 1880–1914*. Westport, Conn., 1982.

Black, Eugene. "Lucien Wolf and the Making of Poland: Paris, 1919." *Polin*, Vol. 2 (1987).

——————. *The Social Politics of Anglo-Jewry*. Oxford, 1988.

Bogen, Boris. *Born a Jew*. New York, 1930.

Bonsal, Stephen. *Suitors and Supplicants: The Little Nations at Versailles*. New York, 1946.

Brockmann, Albert, ed. *Germany and Poland in Their Historical Relations*. Munich, 1934.

Buell, Raymond. *Poland: Key to Europe*. New York, 1939.

Cang, J. "The Opposition Parties in Poland and Their Attitude to the *Jews and the Jewish Problem*." Jewish Social Studies, Vol. 1, No. 2, 1939.

Cienciela, Anna M., and Titus Komarnicki. *From Versailles to Locarno: Keys to Polish Foreign Policy, 1919–25*. Lawrence, Kansas, 1984.

Claude, Inis. *National Minorities: An International Problem*. Cambridge, Mass., 1951.

Cohen, Israel. *My Mission to Poland, 1918–1939*. New York, 1991.

Cohen, Naomi W. *Not Free to Desist: The American Jewish Committee: 1906–1966.* Philadelphia, 1969.

Comité des délégations juives auprès de la conférence de la paix. *Les Droits nationaux des Juifs en Europe orientale: Récueil d'études.* Paris, 1919.

Courtney, Daria T. "The Minorities Treaties: The Post–World War I Quest for Stability in East-Central Europe." *Maryland Historian,* No. 14, 1983.

Davies, Norman. *God's Playground—A History of Poland.* Vol. 2. Oxford, 1981.

—————. "Great Britain and the Polish Jews, 1918–1920." *Journal of Contemporary History,* Vol. 8, No. 2, 1973.

Dobroszcki, Lucjan. "The Fertility of Modern Polish Jewry," in Ritterband, Paul, ed. *Modern Jewish Fertility.* London, 1981.

Drozdowski, Marian M. "The National Minorities in Poland, 1919–1930." *Acta Polonoiae Historica,* No. 22, 1970.

Dybowski, R. *Poland and the Problem of National Minorities.* London, 1936.

Feinberg, N. *La Question des Minorités à La Conference de la Paix de 1919–20.* Paris, 1929.

Finney, P. B. " 'An Evil for All Concerned': Great Britain and Minority Protection after 1918." *Journal of Contemporary History,* Vol. 30, No. 3, 1995.

Fishman, Joshua, ed. *Studies in Polish Jewry, 1919–1939.* New York, 1974.

Frankel, Jonathan, et al., eds. *Studies in Contemporary Jewry.* Vol. 4. New York, 1988.

Goldstein, Joseph. "Jabotinsky and Jewish Autonomy in the Diaspora." *Studies in Zionism,* vol. 7, No. 2 (1986).

Goodhart, Arthur L. *Poland and the Minority Races.* London, 1920.

Greenbaum, Masha. *The Jews of Lithuania, 1916–1945.* Jerusalem, 1995.

Groth, A. J. "Dmowski, Pilsudski, and Ethnic Conflict in Pre-1939 Poland." *Canadian Slavic Studies,* Vol. 3, No. 4, 1969.

—————, and Jerzy Holzer. "The Legacy of Three Crises: Parliament and Ethnic Issues in Prewar Poland." *Slavic Review,* Vol. 27, No. 4, 1969.

Grunebaum, Yitzhak. *Milchamot Yehudei Polania, 1912/13–1939/40* [The Wars of Polish Jewry, 1912/13–1939/40]. Tel Aviv, 1941.

Gutman, Israel, Ezra Mendelsohn, Jehuda Reinharz, and Chone Smeruk, eds. *The Jews of Poland Between Two World Wars.* London, 1990.

Heit, Siegfried D. "National Minorities and Their Effect on Polish Foreign Relations." *Nationalities Papers,* No. 8. London, 1990.

Heller, Celia S. *On the Edge of Destruction: The Jews of Poland Between the Two World Wars.* New York, 1977.

Holzer, J. "The Political Right in Poland, 1918–1939." *Journal of Contemporary History,* Vol. 12, No. 3, 1977.

Horak, Stepan. *Poland and Her National Minorities, 1919–1939.* New York, 1961.

Janowsky, Oscar I. *The Jews and Minority Rights.* New York, 1966.

—————. *Nationalities and National Minorities.* New York, 1946.

—————. *People at Bay.* New York, 1938.

Johnpoll, B. K. *The Politics of Futility: The General Jewish Workers Bund of Poland, 1919–1943.* Ithaca, N.Y., 1967.

Kahn, Bernhard. *The Jews in Reconstituted Poland.* New York, 1940.

Kohler, Max. "The Origin of the Minority Provisions of the Paris Peace Treaty of 1919," in Luzzatti, Luigi, ed. *God in Freedom.* New York, 1939.

—————. "The Peace Conference and the Right of Minorities." *American Jewish Yearbook.* Vol. 22 (1920–21).

Korzec, Pawel. *Juifs en Pologne: La Question juive pendant l'entre deux-guerres.* Paris, 1980.

Laudynowa, Stefanja. *Jews, Poland, Humanity: A Psychological and Historical Study.* Chicago, 1920.

Lerski, George W. "Dmowski, Paderewski, and American Jews." *Polin,* Vol. 2 (1987).

Lestschinsky, Jacob. "The Industrial and Social Structure of the Jewish Population of Poland." *YIVO Annual of Jewish Social Sciences*, Vol. 51 (1956–57).

——————. *La situation économique des juifs depuis la guerre mondiale: Europe orientale et centrale*. Paris, 1934.

Levene, Mark. "Britain, a British Jew, and Jewish Relations with the New Poland: The Making of the Polish Minorities Treaty of 1919." *Polin*, Vol. 8 (1994).

——————. *War, Jews, and the New Europe: The Diplomacy of Lucien Wolf, 1914–1919*. Oxford, 1992.

Levine, Hillel. *Economic Origins of Antisemitism: Poland and Its Laws in the Early Modern Period*. New Haven, Conn., 1981.

Lewin, Isaac. *The Jewish Community in Poland*. New York, 1985.

Macartney, Charles A. *National States and National Minorities*. London, 1934.

Mahler, Raphael. "Jews in Public Service and the Liberal Professions in Poland, 1918–1939." *Jewish Social Studies*, Vol. 6, No. 4, 1944.

Marcus, Joseph. *Social and Political History of the Jews in Poland, 1919–1939*. New York, 1983.

Margolin, Arnold. *The Jews of Eastern Europe*. New York, 1936.

Mendelsohn, Ezra. *The Jews of East Central Europe Between the Wars*. Bloomington, Ind., 1983.

——————. *On Modern Jewish Politics: The Jews in Poland*. New York, 1993.

——————. *Zionism in Poland: The Formative Years, 1915–1924*. New Haven, Conn., 1981.

——————, and Chaim Shmeruk, eds. *Studies in Polish Jewry*. Jerusalem, 1987.

Morgenthau, Henry. *All in a Lifetime*. New York, 1922.

Netzer, Shlomo. *Ma'avak Yehudei Polin al Zekhuyoteihem v'Ezrachiyut v'ha'Leumiyut, 1918–1922* [The Struggle of Polish Jewry for Rights and National Citizenship, 1918–1922]. Tel Aviv, 1922.

Polonsky, Antony. *From Shtetl to Socialism: Studies from* Polin. London, 1993.

——————. *The Little Dictators: The History of Eastern Europe Since 1918*. Boston, 1974.

——————. *Politics in Independent Poland, 1921–1939*. Oxford, 1972.

——————, Ezra Mendelsohn, et al., eds. *Jews in Independent Poland, 1918–1939*. London, 1994.

Rabinowicz, H. M. *The Legacy of Polish Jewry, 1919–1939*. New York, 1965.

Reznikoff, Charles, ed. *Louis Marshall: Champion of Liberty*. 2 vols. Philadelphia, 1957.

Robinson, Jacob, et al., eds. *Were the Minorities Treaties a Failure?* 2d. ed., New York, 1993.

Rose, W. J. *Poland's Political Parties, 1919–1939*. London, 1947.

Rosenstock, Morton. *Louis Marshall: Defender of Jewish Rights*. Detroit, 1965.

Sachar, Abram L. *Sufferance Is the Badge: The Jew in the Postwar World*. New York, 1940.

Sachar, Howard M. *A History of the Jews in America*. New York, 1992.

Samuel, Maurice. *Little Did I Know*. New York, 1963.

Samuel, Sir Stuart. *Report by Sir Stuart Samuel on His Mission in Poland*. Cmd. 674. London, 1920.

Segal, Simon. *New Poland and the Jews*. New York, 1938.

Stephens, J. S. *Danger Zones of Europe: A Study of National Minorities*. London, 1929.

Sugar, Peter F. *Native Fascism in the Successor States, 1918–1945*. Oxford, 1971.

Taylor, Jack. *The Economic Development of Poland, 1919–1960*. New York, 1952.

Tomaszewski, Jerzy. "The Civil Rights of Jews in Poland, 1918–1939." *Polin*, Vol. 8 (1994).

United States Senate. *Report of American Mission to Poland [Morgenthau Report]*. Doc. No. 176. Washington D.C., 1920.

Vago, Bela, and George Mosse, eds. *Jews and Non-Jews in Eastern Europe. 1919–1945.* Jerusalem, 1975.

Wolf, Lucien. *The Myth of the Jewish Menace in World Affairs.* New York, 1921.

Wynot, Edward D. " 'A Necessary Cruelty': The Emergence of Official Anti-Semitism in Poland, 1936–39." *American Historical Review*, vol. 76, No. 4, 1974.

Yahil, Leni. "Madagascar—Phantom of a Solution for the Jewish Question," in Vago, Bela, and George Mosse, eds. *Jews and Non-Jews in Eastern Europe, 1919–1945.* Jerusalem, 1975.

IV. HOSTAGES OF "LATIN" CIVILIZATION

Adler, Cyrus. *I Have Considered the Days.* Philadelphia, 1941.

——————, and Aaron M. Margalith. *With Firmness in the Right: American Diplomatic Action Affecting Jews, 1840–1945.* New York, 1946.

Alliance Israélite Universelle. *La Question juive devant la conférence de la paix.* Paris, 1919.

American Committee on the Right of Religious Minorities. *Roumania Ten Years After.* New York, 1928.

Ancel, Jean, and Victor Eskenasy, eds. *Bibliography of the Jews in Romania.* Tel Aviv, 1991.

Balogh, Arthur de. *L'Action de la Société des Nations en Matière des Minorités.* Paris, 1937.

Barbu, Zev. "Rumania," in Woolf, S.J., ed. *Fascism in Europe.* London, 1968.

Bendiner, Elmer. *A Time for Angels: The Tragicomic History of the League of Nations.* New York, 1975.

Best, Gary D. *To Free a People: American Jewish Leaders and the Jewish Problem in Eastern Europe, 1880–1914.* Westport, Conn., 1982.

Black, Eugene. *The Social Politics of Anglo-Jewry.* Oxford, 1988.

Bonsal, Stephen. *Suitors and Supplicants: The Little Nations at Versailles.* New York, 1946.

Butnaru, I. C. *The Silent Holocaust: Romania and Its Jews.* New York, 1992.

Cabot, J. M. *The Racial Conflict in Transylvania.* Boston, 1926.

Clark, Charles U. *Racial Aspects of Romania's Case.* London, n.p., 1941.

Claude, Inia. *National Minorities: An International Problem.* Cambridge, Mass., 1951.

Cohen, Naomi W. *Not Free to Desist: The American Jewish Committee: 1906–1966.* Philadelphia, 1969.

Courtney, Daria T. "The Minorities Treaties: The Post-World War I Quest for Stability in East-Central Europe." *Maryland Historian*, No. 14, 1983.

Finney, P. B. " 'An Evil for All Concerned': Great Britain and Minority Protection after 1918." *Journal of Contemporary History*, Vol. 30, No. 3, 1995.

Fischer-Galati, Stephen. *Twentieth-Century Roumania.* New York, 1991.

Frankel, Jonathan, et al., eds. *Studies in Contemporary Jewry.* Vol. 4. New York, 1988.

Gelber, N. M. "The Problem of the Rumanian Jews at the Bucharest Peace Conference, 1918." *Jewish Social Studies*, Vol. 12, No. 2, 1950.

Hoisington, William A., Jr. "The Struggle for Economic Influence in Southeastern Europe: The French Failure in Roumania, 1940." *Journal of Modern History*, Vol. 43, No. 3, 1971.

Iancu, Carol. *Jews in Romania, 1866–1919: From Exclusion to Emancipation.* Boulder, Colo., 1996.

Janowsky, Oscar I. *The Jews and Minority Rights.* New York, 1966.

——————. *Nationalities and National Minorities.* New York, 1946.

Joint Foreign Committee of the Board of Deputies of British Jewry and the Anglo-Jewish Association. *The Jewish Minority in Roumania: Correspondence with the Roumanian Government Respecting the Grievances of the Jews.* London, 1927.

Kiraly, Bela, Peter Pastor, and Ivan Bandera, eds. *War and Society in East-Central Europe.* Vol. 2. New York, 1982.

Kohler, Max. "The Peace Conference and the Right of Minorities." *American Jewish Yearbook*, Vol. 22 (1920–21).

Lestschinsky, Jacob. *La situation économique des juifs depuis la guerre mondiale: Europe orientale et centrale*. Paris, 1934.

Levene, Mark. *War, Jews, and the New Europe: The Diplomacy of Lucien Wolf, 1914–1919*. Oxford, 1992.

Livezeanu, Ion. *Cultural Politics in Greater Romania*. Ithaca, N.Y., 1955.

Lungu, Dov. *Romania and the Great Powers*. Durham, N.C., 1989.

Luzzatti, Luigi, ed. *God in Freedom*. New York, 1930.

Macartney, C. A. *Hungary and Her Successors: The Treaty of Trianon and Its Consequences, 1919–1937*. London, 1937.

Mair, Lucy P. *The Protection of Minorities: The Working and Scope of the Minorities Treaties Under the League of Nations*. London, 1939.

Margolin, Arnold. *The Jews of Eastern Europe*. New York, 1936.

Mendelsohn, Ezra. *The Jews of East Central Europe Between the Wars*. Bloomington, Ind., 1983.

Nagy-Talavera, N. *The Green Shirts and Others: A History of Fascism in Hungary and Rumania*. Stanford, Cal., 1970.

Reznikoff, Charles, ed. *Louis Marshall: Champion of Liberty*. 2 vols. Philadelphia, 1957.

Robinson, Jacob, et al., eds. *Were the Minorities Treaties a Failure?* 4th ed. New York, 1993.

Rosenstock, Morton, *Louis Marshall: Defender of Jewish Rights*. Detroit, 1965.

Seton-Watson, Hugh. *A History of the Roumanians*. Boston, 1963.

Spector, Sherman D. *Rumania at the Peace Conference: The Diplomacy of Ioan I. C. Bratianu*. New York, 1962.

Starr, Joshua. "Jewish Citizenship in Rumania (1878–1940)." *Jewish Social Studies*, Vol. 3, No. 1, 1941.

Stone, Julius. *International Guarantees of Minority Rights*. London, 1932.

Sugar, Peter F. *Native Fascism in the Successor States, 1918–1945*. Oxford, 1945.

Vago, Bela. "Popular Front in the Balkans: Failure in Hungary and Roumania." *Journal of Contemporary History*, Vol. 30, No. 3, 1970.

————, and George Mosse, eds. *Jews and Non-Jews in Eastern Europe*. Jerusalem, 1974.

Volovici, Leon. *Nationalist Ideology and Antisemitism: The Case of Romanian Intellectuals in the 1930s*. Oxford, 1991.

Weber, Eugen. *Varieties of Fascism*. Princeton, N.J., 1964.

————, and Hans Rogger, eds. *The European Right: A Historical Profile*. Berkeley, Cal., 1966.

V. BELA KUN AND THE LEGACY OF UTOPIANISM

Bazany, George. "Magyar Jew or Jewish Magyar," in Vago, Bela, and George Mosse, eds. *Jews and Non-Jews in Eastern Europe*. Jerusalem, 1974.

Braham, Randolph, ed. *Hungarian Jewish Studies*. 2 vols. New York, 1968–69.

————. *The Tragedy of Hungarian Jewry*. Boulder, Colo., 1966.

British Joint Labour Delegation to Hungary [Wedgwood Report]. *The White Terror in Hungary*. London, 1920.

Carsten, F. L. *Revolution in Central Europe, 1918–1919*. Berkeley, Cal., 1972.

Don, Yehuda, and Victor Karady, eds. *A Social and Economic History of Central European Jewry*. New Brunswick, N.J., 1990.

Finney, P. B. " 'An Evil for All Concerned': Great Britain and Minority Protection After 1918." *Journal of Contemporary History*, Vol. 30, No. 3, 1995.

Fodor, M. W. *Plot and Counterplot in Central Europe*. Boston, 1937.

Frankel, Jonathan, et al., eds. *Studies in Contemporary Jewry*. Vol. 4, New York, 1984.

Gower, Sir Robert. *The Hungarian Minorities in the Succession States*. Budapest, 1929.

Hajdu, Tibor, and Zauzsa L. Nagy. "Revolution, Counterrevolution, and Consolidation," in Hanak, Peter, and Tibor Frank, eds. *A History of Hungary*. Bloomington, Ind., 1990.

Hanak, Peter, and Tibor Frank, eds. *A History of Hungary*. Bloomington, Ind., 1990.

Handler, Andrew. *From the Ghetto to the Games: Jewish Athletes in Hungary*. New York, 1985.

Ignotus, Paul. "Radical Writers in Hungary," in Mosse, George, and Walter Laqueur, eds. *The Left-Wing Intellectuals Between the Wars, 1919–1939*. New York, 1966.

Janos, Andrew C. "The Decline of Oligarchy: Bureaucrats and Mass Politics in the Age of Dualism," in Mosse, George, and Walter Laqueur, eds. *The Left-Wing Intellectuals Between the Wars, 1919–1939*. New York, 1966.

Janowsky, Oscar I. *Nationalities and National Minorities*. New York, 1945.

Jaszi, Oszkar. *Revolution and Counter-Revolution in Hungary*. London, 1924.

Jeszenszky, Geza. "Hungary Through World War I and the End of the Dual Monarchy," in Hanak, Peter, and Tibor Frank, eds. *A History of Hungary*. Bloomington, Ind., 1990.

Joint Foreign Committee of the Board of Deputies of British Jewry and the Anglo-Jewish Association. *The Jewish Minority in Hungary*. London, 1926.

Kaplan, Marion A. *The Making of the Jewish Middle Class*. New York, 1981.

Katzburg, Nathaniel. *Hungary and the Jews: Policy and Legislation, 1920–1943*. Ramat Gan, Israel, 1981.

—————. "The Jewish Question During the Inter-War Period: Jewish Attitudes," in Braham, Randolph, ed. *Hungarian Jewish Studies*. Vol. I. New York, 1968–69.

Kenez, Peter. "Coalition Politics in the Hungarian Soviet Republic," in Mosse, George, and Walter Laqueur, eds. *The Left-Wing Intellectuals Between the Wars, 1919–1939*. New York, 1966.

Kiraly, Bela, Peter Pastor, and Ivan Sanders, eds. *War and Society in East-Central Europe*. Vol. 4. New York, 1952.

Koestler, Arthur. *Arrow in the Blue*. New York, 1952.

Kovacs, Maria M. "Interwar Antisemitism in the Professions: The Case of the Engineers," in Silber, Michael K., ed. *Jews in the Hungarian Economy, 1760–1945*. Jerusalem, 1992.

Laszlo, Erno. "Hungary's Jewry: A Demographic Overview, 1918–1945," in Braham, Randolph, ed. *Hungarian Jewish Studies*. Vol. 2. New York, 1968–69.

Lengyel, Emil. *The Cauldron Boils*. New York, 1932.

Lengyel, Gyorgy. "The Ethnic Composition of the Economic Elite in Hungary in the Interwar Period," in Don, Yehuda, and Victor Karady, eds. *A Social and Economic History of Central European Jewry*. New Brunswick, N.J., 1990.

—————. "Jews in Hungarian Banking in the Interwar Period," in Silber, Michael K., ed. *Jews in the Hungarian Economy, 1760–1945*. Jerusalem, 1992.

Levin, Nora. *While the Messiah Tarried: Jewish Socialist Movements, 1871–1917*. London, 1978.

Low, Alfred D. *The Soviet Hungarian Republic and the Paris Peace Conference*. Philadelphia, 1963.

Lowenthal, Richard. "The Hungarian Soviet and International Communism," in Mosse, George, and Walter Laqueur, eds. *The Left-Wing Intellectuals Between the Wars, 1919–1939*. New York, 1966.

Macartney, Charles A. *Hungary and Her Successors: The Treaty of Trianon and Its Consequences, 1919–1937*. London, 1937.

McCartney, Charles A. *National States and National Minorities.* London, 1934.

McCagg, William O. Jr. *Jewish Nobles nad Geniuses in Modern Hungary.* Boulder, Colo., 1972.

——————. "The Jewish Position in Interwar Central Europe: A Structural Study of Jewry at Vienna, Budapest, and Prague," in Don, Yehuda, and Victor Karady, eds. *A Social and Economic History of Central European Jewry.* New Brunswick, N.J., 1990.

——————. "Jews in Revolutions: The Hungarian Experience." *Journal of Social History,* Vol. 6, No. 1, 1972.

Mendelsohn, Ezra. *The Jews of East Central Europe Between the Wars.* Bloomington, Ind., 1983.

Nagy-Talavera, N. *The Green Shirts and Others: A History of Fascism in Hungary and Rumania.* Stanford., Cal., 1970.

Nolte, Ernst. *Three Faces of Fascism.* New York, 1965.

Northedge, F. S. *The League of Nations: Its Life and Time, 1920–1945.* New York, 1986.

Ormos, Maria. "The Early Interwar Years," in Hanak, Peter, and Tibor Frank, eds. *A History of Hungary.* Bloomington, Ind., 1990.

Patai, Raphael. *Apprentice in Budapest.* Salt Lake City, 1988.

——————. *The Jews of Hungary.* Detroit, 1996.

Poliakov, Léon. *The History of Anti-Semitism.* vol. 4. Oxford, 1985.

Rothschild, Joseph. *East Central Europe Between the Two World Wars.* Seattle, 1974.

Roucek, J. C. *The Working of the Minorities System Under the League of Nations.* Prague, 1929.

Sachar, Abram L. *Sufferance Is the Badge: The Jew in the Postwar World.* New York, 1940.

Sachar, Howard M. *Diaspora: An Inquiry into the Contemporary Jewish World.* New York, 1985.

Sakmyster, Thomas. *Hungary's Admiral on Horseback: Miklos Horthy, 1918–1944.* New York, 1999.

Silber, Michael K., ed. *Jews in the Hungarian Economy, 1760–1945.* Jerusalem, 1992.

Sugar, Peter F. *Native Fascism in the Successor States, 1918–1945.* Oxford, 1971.

——————, ed. *A History of Hungary.* Bloomington, Ind., 1990.

Szajkowski, Zosa. *Jews, Wars, and Communism.* Vol. 1. New York, 1972.

Tokes, Rudolf L. *Bela Kun and the Hungarian Soviet Republic.* New York, 1967.

——————. "Bela Kun: The Man and the Revolutionary," in Volgyes, Ivan, ed. *Hungary in Revolution, 1918–19.* Lincoln, Neb., 1971.

Vago, Bela, and George Mosse, eds. *Jews and Non-Jews in Eastern Europe, 1919–1945.* Jerusalem, 1975.

Veghazi, Istvan. "The Role of Jewry in the Economic Life of Hungary," in Braham, Randolph, ed. *Hungarian Jewish Studies.* Vol. 2. New York, 1969.

Volgyes, Ivan, ed. *Hungary in Revolution, 1918–19.* Lincoln, Neb., 1971.

Wistrich, Robert S. *Revolutionary Jews from Marx to Trotsky.* New York, 1976.

——————. *Socialism and the Jews: The Dialectics of Emancipation in Germany and Austria-Hungary.* East Brunswick, N.J., 1984.

VI. THE PROFESSOR AND THE PROPHET

Bauer, Johann. *Kafka and Prague.* London, 1971.

Bonsal, Stephen. *Suitors and Supplicants: The Little Nations in Versailles.* New York, 1946.

Bradbury, Malcolm, and James MacFarlane, eds. *Modernism: 1890–1930.* New York, 1976.

Brod, Max. *Franz Kafka.* New York, 1963.

——————, ed. *The Diaries of Franz Kafka, 1914–1923.* New York, 1949.

Carter, F. W. "Kafka's Prague," in Stern, J. P., ed. *The World of Franz Kafka.* New York, 1981.

Dagan, Avigdor. "Jewish Themes in Czech Literature," in Society for the History of Czechoslovak Jews. *The Jews of Czechoslovakia*. Vol. 2. Philadelphia, 1983.

Demetz, Peter. *Prague in Black and Gold: Scenes from the Life of a European City*. New York, 1994.

Dinnage, Rosemary. "Under the Harrow," in Stern, J. P., ed. *The World of Franz Kafka*. New York, 1981.

Eisner, Pavel. *Franz Kafka and Prague*. New York, 1950.

Epstein, Binyamin, ed. *T. G. Masaryk and the Jews: A Collection of Essays*. New York, 1941.

Frynta, Emanuel. *Kafka and Prague*. London, 1960.

Gray, Ronald D. *Franz Kafka*. Cambridge, England, 1973.

Grunfeld, Frederic. *Prophets Without Honor: A Background to Freud, Kafka, Einstein, and Their World*. New York, 1979.

Hanak, Harry. *T. G. Masaryk*. London, 1990.

Herben, Jan. "Jews and Anti-Semitism," in Stern, J. P., ed. *The World of Franz Kafka*. New York, 1981.

Hoffman, Frederich J. *Freudianism and the Literary Mind*. Baton Rouge, La., 1957.

Hostovsky, Egon. "Participation in Modern Czech Literature," in Society for the History of Czechoslovak Jews. *The Jews of Czechoslovakia*. Vol. 1. Philadelphia, 1968.

Hüber-Neumann, Marete. *Kafka's Freundin Milena*. Munich, 1953.

Joll, James. *Three Intellectuals in Politics*. New York, 1960.

Kestenberg, Ruth. "The Jews Between Czechs and Germans in the Historical Lands, 1948–1918," in Society for the History of Czechoslovak Jews. *The Jews of Czechoslovakia*. Vol. 1. Philadelphia, 1968.

Kievel, Hillel J. *The Making of Czech Jewry: National Conflict and Jewish Society in Bohemia, 1870–1918*. New York, 1988.

——————. "Masaryk and Czech Jewry: The Ambiguities of Friendship," in Winters, Stanley B., ed. *T. G. Masaryk*. Vol. I. New York, 1990.

Kohn, Hans. "Before 1918 in the Historic Lands," in Society for the History of Czechoslovak Jews. *The Jews of Czechoslovakia*. Vol. 2. Philadelphia, 1983.

——————. *Living in a World Revolution: My Encounter with History*. New York, 1964.

Masaryk, Tomas. *The Making of a State*. London, 1927.

——————. *President Masaryk Tells His Story*. London, 1934.

McCagg, William O., Jr. "The Jewish Position in Interwar Central Europe: A Structural Study of Vienna, Budapest, and Prague," in Don, Yehuda, and Victor Karady, eds. *A Social and Economic History of Central European Jewry*. New Brunswick, N.J., 1990.

Neider, Charles. *The Frozen Sea: A Study of Franz Kafka*. New York, 1949.

Pascal, Roy. "Kafka's Parables," in Epstein, Binyamin, ed. *T. G. Masaryk and the Jews: A Collection of Essays*. New York, 1941.

Pawel, Ernst. *The Nightmare of Reason*. New York, 1984.

Peniza, Josef. "Masaryk and the Jewish Czechs," in Epstein, Binyamin, ed. *T. G. Masaryk and the Jews: A Collection of Essays*. New York, 1941.

Politzer, Heinz. *Franz Kafka: Parable and Paradox*. Ithaca, N.Y., 1979.

Rabinowicz, Aharon. "The Jewish Minority," in Society for the History of Czechoslovak Jews. *The Jews of Czechoslovakia*. Vol. 2. Philadelphia, 1983.

Robertson, Ritchie. *Kafka: Judaism, Politics, and Literature*. Oxford, 1985.

Rothkirchen, Livia. "Slovakia," in Society for the History of Czechoslovak Jews. *The Jews of Czechoslovakia*. Vol. 1. Philadelphia, 1968.

Roucek, J. S. *Central-Eastern Europe: Crucible of World Wars*. New York, 1941.

Rychmovsky, Ernst. "The Struggle Against the Ritual Murder Superstition," in Epstein, Binyamin, ed. *T. G. Masaryk and the Jews: A Collection of Essays*. New York, 1941.

Sachar, Abram L. *Sufferance Is the Badge: The Jew in the Postwar World*. New York, 1940.

Sayer, Derek. *The Coasts of Bohemia: A Czech History*. Princeton, N.J., 1998.

Slochower, Harry, et al., eds. *A Franz Kafka Miscellany*. New York, 1950.

Society for the History of Czechoslovak Jews. *The Jews of Czechoslovakia.* 3 vols. Philadelphia, 1968–84.

Sokel, Walter B. *Franz Kafka.* New York, 1966.

——————. "Freud and the Magic of Kafka's Writing," in Stern, J. P., ed. *The World of Franz Kafka.* New York, 1981.

Spann, Meno. *Franz Kafka.* Boston, 1976.

Stern, J. P., ed. *The World of Franz Kafka.* New York, 1981.

Tauber, Herbert. *Franz Kafka: An Interpretation of His Work.* Port Washington, N.Y., 1968.

Tramer, Hans. *Prague: City of Three Peoples.* New York, 1956.

Urzidil, Johannes. "The Recollections," in Stern, J. P., ed. *The World of Franz Kafka.* New York, 1981.

Vago, Bela, and George Mosse, eds. *Jews and Non-Jews in Eastern Europe.* Jerusalem, 1974.

Wegenbach, Klaus. "Kafka's Castle," in Stern, J. P., ed. *The World of Franz Kafka.* New York, 1981.

Weltsch, Felix. "Masaryk and Zionism," in Epstein, Binyamin, ed. *T. G. Masaryk and the Jews: A Collection of Essays.* New York, 1941.

——————. "The Rise and Fall of the Jewish-German Symbiosis: The Case of Franz Kafka," in Stern, J. P., ed. *The World of Franz Kafka.* New York, 1981.

Winters, Stanley B., ed. *T. G. Masaryk.* Vol. 1. New York, 1990.

Zohn, Harry. *Austria and Judaica: Essays in Translation.* New York, 1995.

——————. "Participation in German Literature," in Society for the History of Czechoslovak Jews. *The Jews of Czechoslovakia.* Vol. I. Philadelphia, 1962.

VII. NOTES FROM A SHATTERED DREAM

Alexander, Franz, and Sheldon T. Selesnick. *The History of Psychiatry.* New York, 1966.

Andics, H. *Der ewige Jude: Ursachen und Geschichte den Antisemitismus.* Vienna, 1968.

Arens, Hans. *Stefan Zweig—Der grosse Europäer.* Munich, 1960.

Aron, Willy. "Notes on Sigmund Freud's Ancestry and Jewish Contacts." *YIVO Annual of Jewish Social Sciences,* Vol. 9 (1956–57).

Badcock, C. R. *The Essential Freud.* New York, 1988.

Bakan, David. *Sigmund Freud and the Jewish Mystical Tradition.* New York, 1958.

Beller, Steven. *Vienna and the Jews.* Cambridge, England, 1989.

——————. "Why Was the Viennese Liberal Bildungsbürgertum Jewish," in Don, Yehuda, and Victor Karady, eds. *A Social and Economic History of Central European Jewry.* New Brunswick, N.J., 1990.

Bennet, Edward A. *C. G. Jung.* London, 1961.

Bergmann, Martin. "Moses in the Evolution of Freud's Jewish Identity." *Israel Annals of Psychiatry and Related Sciences,* 14 (March 1976.)

Berkley, George E. *Vienna and Its Jews: The Tragedy of Success, 1880s–1980s.* Lanham, Md., 1988.

Berliner, Arthur K. *Psychoanalysis and Society: The Social Thought of Sigmund Freud.* Washington D.C., 1983.

Bettauer, Hugo. *The City Without Jews [Stadt ohne Juden, Die].* New York, 1926.

Boyer, J. W. *Political Radicalism in Late Imperial Vienna.* Chicago, 1981.

Braunthal, Julius. *Viktor und Friedrich Adler: Zwei Generationen Arbeiterbewegung.* Vienna, 1965.

Brod, Max. "The Young Werfel and the Prague Writers," in Raabe, Paul, ed. *The Era of German Expressionism.* London, 1974.

Brome, Vincent. *Jung: Man and Myth.* New York, 1978.

Brown, J. A. C. *Freud and the Post-Freudians.* London, 1961.

Brunner, José. *Freud and the Politics of Psychoanalysis.* Cambridge, Mass., 1995.

Canetti, Elias. *Auto-da-Fé [Blendung, Die].* New York, 1982.

Carsten, F. L. *Revolution in Central Europe, 1918–1919.* Berkeley, Cal., 1972.

Clark, Ronald W. *Freud: The Man and the Cause.* London, 1980.

Cocks, Geoffrey. "The Nazis and C. G. Jung," in Maidenbaum, Aryeh, and Stephen Martin, eds. *Lingering Shadows: Jungians, Freudians, and Anti-Semitism.* Boston, 1991.

Craig, Gordon A., et al. *World War I: A Turning Point in Modern History.* New York, 1967.

Diller, Jerry V. *Freud's Jewish Identity.* Rutherford, N.J., 1991.

Don, Yehuda, and Victor Karady, eds. *A Social and Economic History of Central European Jewry.* New Brunswick, N.J., 1990.

Field, Frank. *The Last Days of Mankind: Karl Kraus and His Vienna.* London, 1967.

Fodor, M. W. *Plot and Counterplot in Central Europe.* Boston, 1937.

Forsyth, James. *Freud, Jung, and Christianity.* Ottawa, 1989.

Fraenkel, Joseph, ed. *The Jews of Austria: Essays on Their Life, History, and Destruction.* London, 1967.

Freeman, Lucy. *Freud and Women.* New York, 1987.

——————. *The Story of Anna O.* New York, 1972.

Freud, Ernst L., ed. *Letters of Sigmund Freud.* New York, 1960.

——————, and Hilda C. Abraham., eds. *A Psycho-Analytic Dialogue: The Letters of Sigmund Freud and Karl Abraham, 1907–1926.* New York, 1965.

Freud, Martin. *Glory Reflected: Sigmund Freud—Man and Father.* New York, 1958.

Freud, Sigmund. *Autobiographical Study.* New York, 1963.

——————. *Moses and Monotheism.* New York, 1939.

Gabriel, Yiannis. *Freud and Society.* London, 1983.

Gado, John E., and George H. Pollock, eds. *Freud: The Fusion of Science and Humanism.* New York, 1976.

Gastein, Heinz. *Jüdisches Wien.* Vienna, 1984.

Gay, Peter. *Freud: A Life for Our Time.* New York, 1988.

——————. *Freud, Jews, and Other Germans.* New York, 1978.

——————. *A Godless Jew.* New Haven, Conn., 1987.

Gehr, R. S. *Karl Lueger: Mayor of Fin-de-Siècle Vienna.* Detroit, 1990.

Gilman, Sander. *The Case of Sigmund Freud.* Baltimore, 1993.

——————. *Freud, Race, and Gender.* Princeton, N.J., 1983.

——————. *Jewish Self-Hatred, Anti-Semitism, and the Hidden Language of the Jews.* Baltimore, 1986.

——————. "Jews and Mental Illness: Medical Metaphors, Anti-Semitism, and the Jewish Response." *Journal of the History of the Behavioral Sciences,* Vol. 20, No. 2, 1984.

Glaser, Ernst. *Im Unfeld des Austromarxismus.* Vienna, 1981.

Gold, Hugo. *Geschichte der Juden in Wien.* Tel Aviv, 1966.

Goldhammer, Leo. *Die Juden Wiens: Eine statistische Studie.* Vienna, 1927.

Gradenwitz, Peter. "Jews in Austrian Music," in Fraenkel, Joseph, ed. *The Jews of Austria.* London, 1967.

Graf, Max. "Reminiscences of Professor Sigmund Freud." *Psychoanalyitic Quarterly,* Vol. 11, No. 3, 1942.

Grossman, S. "C. G. Jung and National Socialism." *Journal of European Studies,* Vol. 9, No. 4, 1979.

Grunfeld, Frederick. *Prophets Without Honor: A Background to Freud, Kafka, Einstein, and Their World.* New York, 1979.

Hannah, Barbara. *Jung: His Life and Work.* 1976.

Haymond, Robert. "On Carl Gustav Jung: Psycho-social Basis of Morality During the Nazi Era." *Journal of Psychology and Judaism,* Spring–Summer 1982.

Hoffman, Frederick J. *Freudianism and the Literary Mind.* Baton Rouge, La., 1957.

Hogenson, George B. *Jung's Struggle with Freud.* Notre Dame, Ind., 1983.

Iggers, Wilma Abeles. *Karl Kraus: A Viennese Critic of the Twentieth Century.* The Hague, 1967.

Jaffe, Walter. *Studies in Obsession: Otto Weininger, Arthur Schnitzler, Heimeto von Döderer.* Ph.D. dissertation, Yale University, 1979.

Jaffé, Aniela, ed. *C. G. Jung: Memories, Dreams, Reflections.* New York, 1963.

——————. "C. G. Jung and National Socialism." In Hull, R. F. C., and Murray Stein, eds. *From the Life and Work of C. G. Jung.* Einsiedeln, 1989.

Johnston, William M. *The Austrian Mind.* Berkeley, 1972.

Jones, Ernest. *The Life and Work of Sigmund Freud.* 3 vols. New York, 1953–1957.

——————. *The Life and Work of Sigmund Freud.* Edited and Abridged in one volume by Trilling, Lionel, and Steven Marcus. New York, 1961.

Jung, Carl Gustav. *Memories, Dreams, Reflections.* New York, 1962.

Kahler, Erich. *The Tower and the Abyss: An Inquiry into the Transformation of the Individual.* New York, 1957.

Keegan, Susanne. *The Bride of the Wind: The Life and Times of Alma Mahler-Werfel.* New York, 1992.

Kerr, John. *A Most Dangerous Method: The Story of Jung, Freud, and Sabina Spielrein.* New York, 1993.

Kirsch, James. "Carl Gustav Jung and the Jews: The Real Story," in Maidenbaum, Aryeh, and Stephen Martin, eds. *Lingering Shadows: Jungians, Freudians, and Anti-Semitism.* Boston, 1991.

Klein, Dennis B. *Jewish Origins of the Psychoanalytic Movement.* New York, 198.

Kobler, Franz. "The Contribution of Austrian Jews to Jurisprudence." in Fraenkel, Joseph, ed. *The Jews of Austria: Essays on Their Life, History, and Destruction.* London, 1967.

Loewenberg, Peter. " 'Sigmund Freud as a Jew': A Study in Ambivalence and Courage." *Journal of the History of the Behavioral Sciences,* Vol. 7, No. 4, 1971.

Lothar, Ernst. *Das Wunder des Überlebens: Erinnerungen und Ergebnisse.* Vienna, 1961.

Maidenbaum, Aryeh, and Stephen Martin, eds. *Lingering Shadows: Jungians, Freudians, and Anti-Semitism.* Boston, 1991.

Marcus, Steven. *Freud and the Culture of Psychoanalysis.* Boston, 1984.

Marius, Michael. *The Unwanted: European Refugees in the Twentieth Century.* New York, 1985.

Martin, Stephen A. "Introduction," in Maidenbaum, Aryeh, and Stephen Martin, eds. *Lingering Shadows: Jungians, Freudians, and Anti-Semitism.* Boston, 1991.

McGrath, William J. *Freud's Discovery of Psychoanalysis: The Politics of Hysteria.* New York, 1986.

Miller, Justin. "Interpretations of Freud's Jewishness, 1924–1974." *Journal of the History of the Behavioral Sciences,* Vol. 17, No. 3, 1981.

Mosse, George, and Walter Laqueur, eds. *The Left-Wing Intellectuals Between the Wars, 1919–1939.* New York, 1966.

Nelson, Benjamin, ed. *Freud and the Twentieth Century.* Gloucester, Mass., 1974.

Ostow, Mortimer, ed. *Judaism and Psychoanalysis.* New York, 1982.

Oxaal, I. "The Jewish Origins of Psychoanalysis Reconsidered," in Oxaal, I., M. Pollak, and G. Botz, eds. *Jews, Antisemitism, and Culture in Vienna.* London, 1987.

——————, M. Pollak, and G. Botz, eds. *Jews, Antisemitism, and Culture in Vienna.* London, 1987.

Paucker, Arnold. "Jewish Defense Against Nazism in the Weimar Republic." *Wiener Library Bulletin*, Vol. 26, No. 7, 1972.

Pauley, Bruce F. "Political Antisemitism in Interwar Vienna," in Oxaal, I., M. Pollak, and G. Botz, eds. *Jews, Antisemitism, and Culture in Vienna*. London, 1987.

Prater, D. A. *European of Yesterday: A Biography of Stefan Zweig*. Oxford, 1972.

Pulzer, Peter. *The Rise of Political Antisemitism in Germany and Austria*. New York, 1964.

Punder, H. W. *Freud: His Life and Mind*. London, 1949.

Rainey, Reuben M. *Freud as a Student of Religion*. Missoula, Mont., 1987.

Reichert, H. W., and Herman Salinger, eds. *Studies in Arthur Schnitzler*. Chapel Hill, N.C., 1963.

Rice, Emanuel. *Freud and Moses: The Long Journey Home*. New York, 1990.

——————. "The Jewish Fathers of Psychoanalysis," *Judaism*, Vol. 36, No. 1, 1987.

Roazen, Paul. *Freud: Political and Social Thought*. New York, 1968.

Robert, Marthe. *From Oedipus to Moses: Freud's Jewish Identity*. Garden City, N.Y., 1976.

Robertson, Ritchie. "Freud's Testament: *Moses and Monotheism*, in Timms, Edward, and Naomi Segal, eds. *Freud in Exile: Psychoanalysis and Its Vicissitudes*. New Haven, Conn., 1988.

Robinson, Paul A. *Freud and His Critics*. Berkeley, Cal., 1973.

Roth, Michael S., ed. *Freud: Conflict and Culture*. New York, 1999.

Rothschild, Joseph. *East Central Europe Between the Two World Wars*. Seattle, 1974.

Rozenblit, Marsha L. *The Jews of Vienna, 1867–1914*. Albany, 1983.

Sachar, Abram L. *Sufferance Is the Badge: The Jew in the Postwar World*. New York, 1940.

Schnitzler, Arthur. *The Road to the Open [Weg ins Freie, Die]*. New York, 1923.

Schorske, Carl E. *Fin-de-Siècle Vienna: Politics and Culture*. New York, 1980.

Schultz, Duane. *Intimate Friends, Dangerous Rivals: The Turbulent Relationship Between Freud and Jung*. Los Angeles, 1990.

Schur, Max. *Freud, Living and Dying*. New York, 1972.

Schwarz, Robert. "Antisemitism and Socialism in Austria, 1918–1962," in Fraenkel, Joseph, ed. *The Jews of Austria*. London, 1967.

Silberner, Edmund. "Austrian Social Democracy and the Jewish Problem." *Historia Judaica*, Vol. 13 (1951).

Simon, Ernst. "Sigmund Freud, the Jew." *Leo Baeck Institute Yearbook*, Vol. 2 (1971).

Singer, June. *Boundaries of the Soul: The Practice of Jung's Psychology*. Garden City, N.Y., 1972.

Steele, Robert S. *Freud and Jung: Conflicts of Interpretation*. London, 1982.

Stein, Richard. "Jung's 'Mana Personality' and the Nazi Era," in Maidenbaum, Aryeh, and Stephen Martin, eds. *Lingering Shadows: Jungians, Freudians, and Anti-Semitism*. Boston, 1991.

Storr, Anthony. *Jung*. New York, 1991.

Sulloway, Frank J. *Freud: Biologist of the Mind*. Cambridge, Mass. 1992.

Swales, Martin. *Arthur Schnitzler*. Oxford, 1971.

Talmon, Jacob L. *The Origins of Totalitarian Democracy*. London, 1952.

Thompson, Bruce. *Schnitzler's Vienna*. New York, 1990.

Timms, Edward. *Karl Kraus: Apocalyptic Satirist*. New Haven, Conn., 1986.

——————. and Naomi Segal, eds. *Freud in Exile: Psychoanalysis and Its Vicissitudes*. New Haven, Conn., 1988.

Vago, Bela. *The Shadow of the Swastika: The Rise of Fascism and Anti-Semitism in the Danube Basin, 1936–1939*. New York, 1975.

Wassermann, Jakob. *My Life as German and Jew [Mein Weg als Deutscher und Jude]*. London, 1934.

Wehr, Gerhard. *Jung: A Biography*. Boston, 1987.

Wistrich, Robert S., ed. *Austrians and Jews in the Twentieth Century*. London, 1992.

Wollheim, Richard. *Freud*. 2d ed. London, 1991.

Yerushalmi, Yosef H. *Freud's Moses*. New Haven, Conn., 1991.

Zohn, Harry. *Karl Kraus*. New York, 1971.

Zuckerkandl, Berta Szeps. *Erinnerungen 1892–1942*. Frankfurt, 1970.

—————. "Three Austrian Jews in German Literature: Schnitzler, Zweig, Herzl," in Fraenkel, Joseph, ed. *The Jews of Austria: Essays on Their Life, History, and Destruction*. London, 1967

Zweig, Arnold. *Bilanz der deutschen Judenheit 1933: Ein Versuch*. Amsterdam, 1934.

—————. *Caliban: oder Politik unter Leidenschaft*. Potsdam, 1927.

Zweig, Stefan. *The World of Yesterday [Welt von Gestern, Die]*. London, 1943.

VIII.   THE AGE OF THE ASSASSINS

Adler-Rudal, S. *Ostjuden in Deutschland, 1880–1914*. Tübingen, 1959.

Angress, Warner T. *Stillborn Revolution: The Communist Bid for Power in Germany, 1921–1923*. Princeton, 1963.

Arendt, Hannah. *Men in Dark Times*. London, 1970.

Aschheim, Steven. *Brothers and Strangers*. Madison, Wis., 1982.

—————. "The Myth of 'Judaization' in Germany," in Schatzberg, Walter, and Jehuda Reinharz, eds. *The Jewish Response to German Culture: From the Enlightenment to the Second World War*. Hanover, N.J., 1985.

Barkai, Avraham. *Jüdische Minderheit und Industrialisierung*. Tübingen, 1988.

Basso, Lelio. *Rosa Luxemburg: A Reappraisal*. New York, 1975.

Beer, Udo. *Die Juden, das Recht und die Republik, Verbandswesen und Rechtsschutz, 1919–1933*. Franfurt a/M, 1986.

Beradt, Charlotte. *Paul Levi: Ein demokratischer Sozialist in der Weimarer Republik*. Frankfurt a/M, 1969.

Berghahn, Klaus L., ed. *The German-Jewish Dialogue Reconsidered*. New York, 1996.

Berglar, Peter. *Walther Rathenau*. Bremen, 1970.

Bering, Dietz. *The Stigma of Names: Antisemitism in German Daily Life, 1812–1933*. Cambridge, England, 1992.

Bolich, Walter, ed. *Der Berliner Antisemitismus*. Frankfurt a/M, 1965.

Bolkolsky, Sidney M. *The Distorted Image: German Jewish Perceptions of Germans and Germany, 1918–1935*. New York, 1975.

Böttcher, Herlmuth M. *Walther Rathenau*. Bonn, 1958.

Brecht, Arnold. "Walther Rathenau and the Germans." *Journal of Politics*, Vol. 10, No. 2, 1948.

Bronner, Stephen Eric., ed. *The Letters of Rosa Luxemburg*. Boulder, Colo., 1978.

Bronsen, David, ed. *Jews and Germans from 1860 to 1933: The Problematic Symbiosis*. Heidelberg, 1979.

Carr, E. II. "Red Rosa, 1917: Before and After," in Carr, E. H. *Studies in Revolution*. London, 1969.

Carsten, F. L. *Revolution in Central Europe, 1918–1919*. Berkeley, Cal., 1972.

Carter, April. *The Politics of Women's Rights*. London, 1988.

Coper, Rudolf, *Failure of a Revolution: Germany in 1918–1919*. Cambridge, 1955.

Craig, Gordon O. *Germany, 1866–1945*. New York, 1986.

—————, et al. *World War I: A Turning Point in Modern History*. New York, 1967.

D'Abernon, Edgar V. *The Diary of an Ambassador: Versailles to Rapallo*. New York, 1929.

Don, Yehuda, and Victor Karady, eds. *A Social and Economic History of Central European Jewry*. New Brunswick, N.J., 1990.

Dunayevskaya, Raya. *Rosa Luxemburg, Women's Liberation, and Marx's Philosophy of Revolution*. Urbana, Ill., 1991.

Dunker, Ulrich. *Der Reichsbund jüdischer Frontsoldaten 1919–1938.* Düsseldorf, 1977.

Ettinger, Elzbieta. *Comrades and Lovers: Rosa Luxemburg's Letters to Leo Jogiches.* Cambridge, Mass., 1979.

——. *Rosa Luxemburg: A Life.* Boston, 1986.

Evans, Richard J. *Comrades and Sisters: Feminism, Socialism, and Pacifism in Europe, 1870–1945.* New York, 1987.

——. *The Feminist Movement in Germany, 1894–1933.* London, 1976.

Everett, Susan. *Lost Berlin.* London, 1979.

Eynern, Maximilian von. *Walther Rathenau in Brief und Bild.* Frankfurt a/M, 1967.

Felix, David. *Walther Rathenau and the Weimar Republic.* Baltimore, 1971.

Feuchtwanger, E. J. *From Weimar to Hitler: Germany, 1918–33.* New York, 1993.

Fischer, Ruth. *Stalin and German Communism.* Cambridge, Mass., 1948.

Fishman, Sterling. "The Assassination of Kurt Eisner," in Berghahn, Klaus L., ed. *The German-Jewish Dialogue Reconsidered.* New York, 1996.

Florence, Ronald. *Marx's Daughters: Eleanor Marx, Rosa Luxemburg, Angelica Balabanoff.* New York, 1975.

Frevert, Ute. *Women in German History: From Bourgeois Emancipation to Social Liberation.* New York, 1988.

Friedrich, Otto. *Before the Deluge.* New York, 1972.

Frolich, Paul. *Rosa Luxemburg, Her Life and Work.* London, 1990.

Geras, Norman. *The Legacy of Rosa Luxemburg.* London, 1976.

Gottgetreu, Erich. "Maximilian Harden: Ways and Errors of a Publicist." *Leo Baeck Institute Year Book,* Vol. 8 (1962).

Grab, Walter, and Julius H. Schoeps, eds. *Juden in der Weimarer Republik.* Stuttgart and Bonn, 1986.

Grossmann, Kurt. Deutsche Juden auf der Linken," in Strauss, Herbert, and Kurt Grossmann, eds. *Gegenwart in Rückblick.* Heidelberg, 1970.

Guérin, Daniel. *Rosa Luxemburg et la spontanéité révolutionnaire.* Paris, 1971.

Guettel, Charnie. *Marxism and Feminism.* Toronto, 1974.

Gumbel, E. J. *Vier Jahre politischer Mord.* Berlin, 1922.

Hamburger, Ernest. "Hugo Preuss: Scholar and Statesman." *Leo Baeck Institute Yearbook,* Vol. 20 (1975).

——. "Jews in the Public Service Under the German Monarchy." *Leo Baeck Institute Yearbook,* Vol. 9 (1964).

Howard, D., ed. *Selected Political Writings of Rosa Luxemburg.* London, 1971.

Ignotus, Paul. "Radical Writers in Hungary," in Mosse, George, and Walter Laqueur, eds. *The Left-Wing Intellectuals Between the Wars, 1919–1939.* New York, 1966.

Jochmann, Werner. "Die Ausbreitung des Antisemitismus," in *Deutscher Judentum in Krieg und Revolution, 1916–1923.* Tübingen, 1977.

Joll, James. *Three Intellectuals in Politics.* New York, 1960.

——. *Walter Rathenau: Prophet Without a Cause.* London, 1960.

Kallner, Rudolf. *Herzl und Rathenau: Wege jüdischer Existenz.* Stuttgart, 1976.

Kaplan, Marion A. *The Jewish Feminist Movement in Germany.* Westport, Conn., 1979.

——. *The Making of the Jewish Middle Class.* New York, 1981.

——. "Sisterhood under Siege: Feminism and Antisemitism in Germany, 1904–38," in Reinharz, Jehuda, and Walter Schatzberg, eds. *The Jewish Response to German Culture: From the Enlightenment to the Second World War.* Hanover, N.H., 1985.

Kapp, Yvonne. *Eleanor Marx.* 2 vols. New York, 1972.

Karlweiss, M. *Jakob Wassermann.* Amsterdam, 1935.

Kerr, Alfred. *Walther Rathenau.* Amsterdam, 1935.

Kessler, Harry. *In the Twenties: The Diaries of Count Harry Kessler.* New York, 1971.

Kessler, Harry. *Walter Rathenau: His Life and Work*. New York, 1944.

Knodel, John E. *The Decline of Fertility in Germany, 1871–1939*. Princeton, N.J., 1974.

Knütter, Hans-Helmuth. *Die Juden und die deutsche Linke in der Weimarer Republik 1918–1933*. Düsseldorf, 1973.

Kollman, Eric. "Walter Rathenau and German Foreign Policy." *Journal of Modern History*, Vol. 24, No. 1, 1952.

Lambert, M. *Jewish Activism in Imperial Germany*. New Haven, 1982.

Laqueur, Walter. *Russia and Germany, A Century of Conflict*. London, 1965.

—————. *Weimar: A Cultural History, 1918–1933*. London, 1974.

Létourneau, Paul. *Walther Rathenau*. Strasbourg, 1994.

Levin, Nora. *While the Messiah Tarried: Jewish Socialist Movements, 1871–1917*. London, 1978.

Levy, Richard S. *The Downfall of the Anti-Semitic Political Parties in Imperial Germany*. New Haven, Conn., 1975.

Looker, R., ed. *Rosa Luxemburg: Selected Political Writings*. London, 1972.

Lowenthal, Richard. "The Bolshevization of the Spartacus League," in Footman, David, ed. *International Communism*. Carbondale, Ill., 1960.

—————. *Der Krise der Sozialdemokratie*. Berlin, 1919.

—————. *Selected Works*. New York, 1976.

Marcus, A. "Jews As Entrepreneurs in Weimar Germany." *YIVO Annual of Jewish Social Studies*, Vol. 7 (1952).

Maurer, Trude. *Ostjuden in Deutschland, 1918–1933*. Hamburg, 1986.

Meinek, Hans Jürgen. *Walther Rathenau und die Sozialisierungsfrage*. Berlin, 1973.

Metall, Rudolf A. *Hans Kelsen, Leben und Werk*. Vienna, 1969.

Mitchell, Allan. *Revolution in Bavaria, 1918–1919*. Princeton, N.J., 1965.

Mosse, George. "German Socialists and the Jewish Question in the Weimar Republic." *Leo Baeck Institute Yearbook*, Vol. 16 (1971).

—————. *Germans and Jews: The Right, the Left and the Search for a "Third Force" in Pre-Nazi Germany*. New York, 1970.

—————. *Toward the Final Solution: A History of European Racism*. London, 1978.

Mosse, Werner E. *The German-Jewish Economic Elite, 1820–1935*. Oxford, 1989.

—————. "Wilhelm II and the *Kaiserjuden*," in Reinharz, Jehuda, and W. Schatzberg, op. cit.

Musil, Robert. *The Man Without Qualities [Mann ohne Eigenschaften, Der]*. New York, 1995.

Nettl, J. F. *Rosa Luxemburg*. 2 vols. London, 1966.

Niewyk, Donald L. "The Economic and Cultural Role of the Jews in the Weimar Republic." *Leo Baeck Institute Yearbook*, Vol. 16 (1971).

—————. *The Jews in Weimar Germany*. Baton Rouge, La., 1980.

—————. *Socialist, Anti-Semite, and Jew: German Social Democracy Confronts the Problem of Anti-Semitism, 1918–1933*. Baton Rouge, La., 1971.

Nye, Andrea. *Philosophia: The Thought of Rosa Luxemburg, Simone Weill, and Hannah Arendt*. New York, 1994.

Orth, Wilhelm. *Walther Rathenau und der Geist von Rapallo*. (East) Berlin, 1962.

Pappenheim, Bertha. *Sisyphus Arbeit: Reisebrief aus den Jahren 1911 und 1912*. Leipzig, 1924.

Pogge von Strandmann, Hartmut, ed. *Walther Rathenau: Industrialist, Banker, Intellectual and Politician: Notes and Diaries, 1907–1922*. Oxford, 1985.

Poise, Robert. "Walther Rathenau's Jewish Quandary." *Leo Baeck Institute Yearbook*, Vol. 13 (1968).

Poliakov, Leon. *The History of Anti-Semitism*. Vol. 4. New York, 1977.

Pore, Renata. *A Conflict of Interest: Women in German Social Democracy, 1919–1933*. Westport, Conn., 1981.

Pulzer, Peter. *Jews and the German State.* Cambridge, Mass., 1992.

——————. *The Rise of Political Antisemitism in Germany and Austria.* New York, 1964.

Quataert, Jean H. *Reluctant Feminists.*

——————. *Socialist Women.* New York, 1978.

Rabin, Else. "The Jewish Woman in Social Service in Germany," in Jung, Leo, ed. *The Jewish Library.* 1st. Ser. New York, 1934.

Rathenau, Walther. *An Deutschlands Jugend.* Berlin, 1918.

——————. *Ausgewählte Reden.* Ed. James T. Hatfield. New York, 1928.

——————. *Haputwereke und Gespräche.* Ed. Ernst Schulin. Munich, 1977.

——————. *In Days to Come.* New York, 1921.

——————. *The New Society.* Berlin, 1918.

——————. *Schriften und Reden.* Ed. Hans Werner Richter. Frankfurt a/M, 1964.

——————. *Tagebuch 1907–1922.* Ed. Hartmut Pogge von Strandmann. Düsseldorf, 1967.

Reichsverband Jüdischer Frontsoldaten. *Die Jüdischen Gefallenen der deutschen Heeres, der deutschen Marine und der deutschen Schutztruppen 1914-1918: ein Gedenkbuch.* Berlin, 1932.

Reinharz, Jehuda. *Fatherland or Promised Land: The Dilemma of the German Jew, 1893–1914.* Ann Arbor, Michigan, 1975.

——————, and Schatzberg, Walter, eds.*The Jewish Response to German Culture: From the Enlightenment to the Second World War.* Hanover, N.H., 1985.

Rosenbaum, E. "Walther Rathenau." *Leo Baeck Institute Yearbook,* Vol. 4 (1959).

Ryder, A. J. *The German Revolution of 1918.* Cambridge, Mass., 1967.

Sachar, Abram L. *Sufferance Is the Badge: The Jew in the Postwar World.* New York, 1940.

Salomon, Ernst von. *The Outlaws.* London, 1931.

Schatzburg, Walter, and Jehuda Reinharz, eds. *The Jewish Response to German Culture: From the Enlightenment to the Second World War.* Hanover, N.H., 1985.

Schorske, Carl E. *German Social Democracy 1905–1917.* New York, 1970.

——————. "Weimar and the Intellectuals: I," in *New York Review of Books,* May 7, 1970.

——————. "Weimar and the Intellectuals: II," in *New York Review of Books,* May 21, 1970.

Schreiner, Albert, ed. *Revolutionäre Ereignisse und Probleme während der Periode der grossen sozialistischen Oktoberrevolution 1917/1918.* Berlin, 1957.

Schulin, Ernst. *Walther Rathenau: Repräsentant, Kritiker, und Opfer seiner Zeit.* Frankfurt a/M, 1979.

Stern, Fritz. *Einstein's German World.* Princeton, N.J., 1999.

——————. *The Politics of Cultural Despair: A Study in the Rise of German Ideology.* Berkeley, Cal., 1961.

Tal, Uriel. *Christians and Jews in Germany.* Ithaca, N.Y., 1974.

Techow, Ernst-Werner. *Gemeiner Mörder?! Das Rathenau-Attentat.* Leipzig, 1933.

Thomas, Edith. *The Women Incendiaries.* New York, 1966.

Thönessen, Werner. *The Emancipation of Women: The Rise and Decline of the Women's Movement in German Social Democracy.* London, 1975.

Toller, Ernst. *I Was a German: The Autobiography of a Revolutionary.* New York, 1991.

Volkov, Shulamit. "The Dynamics of Dissimulation: Ostjuden and the German Jews," in Schatzburg, Walter, and Jehuda Reinharz, eds. *The Jewish Response to German Culture: From the Enlightenment to the Second World War.* Hanover, N.H., 1985.

Vollrath, E. "Rosa Luxemburg's Theory of Revolution." *Social Research,* Vol. 40, No. 1, 1973.

Waite, Robert G. L. *Vanguard of Nazism: The Free Corps Movement in Postwar Germany 1918–1923.* Cambridge, Mass., 1952.

Waldman, Eric. *The Spartakist Uprising of 1919.* Milwaukee, 1958.

Wasserman, Jakob. *My Life as German and Jew [Mein Weg als Deutscher und Jude].* London, 1934.

Watt, Richard M. *The Kings Depart: The Tragedy of Germany—Versailles and the German Revolution.* New York, 1968.

Wertheimer, Jack. *Unwelcome Strangers: East European Jews in Imperial Germany.* New York, 1987.

Williamson, David G. "Walther Rathenau: Patron Saint of the German Liberal Establishment." *Leo Baeck Institute Yearbook,* Vol. 20 (1975).

Willstätter, Richard. *From My Life.* New York, 1965.

Wistrich, Robert S. *Revolutionary Jews from Marx to Trotsky.* New York, 1976.

——————. *Socialism and the Jews: The Dilemmas of Assimilation in Germany and Austria-Hungary.* London, 1992.

Zechlin, Egmont. *Die deutsche Politik und die Juden im ersten Weltkrieg.* Göttingen, 1969.

Zinsser, Judith. *A History of Feminism: A Glass Half Full.* New York, 1998.

IX. MINERVA'S OWL AT WEIMAR'S TWILIGHT

Aschheim, Steven. *Brothers and Strangers.* Madison, Wis., 1982.

——————. "The Myth of 'Judaization' in Germany," in Schatzburg, Walter, and Jehuda Reinharz, eds. *The Jewish Response to German Culture: From the Enlightenment to the Second World War.* Hanover, N.H., 1985.

Austin, William W. *Music in the Twentieth Century.* New York, 1966.

Berghahn, Klaus L., ed. *The German-Jewish Dialogue Reconsidered.* New York, 1996.

Bolkolsky, Sidney M. *The Distorted Image: German Jewish Perceptions of Germans and Germany, 1918–1935.* New York, 1975.

Boretz, Benjamin, and Edward T. Cone, eds. *Perspectives on Schoenberg and Stravinsky.* Princeton, N.J., 1965.

Bradbury, Malcolm, and James MacFarlane, eds. *Modernism: 1890–1930.* New York, 1976.

Brenner, Michael. *The Renaissance of Jewish Culture in Weimar Germany.* New Haven, Conn., 1996.

Brian, Denis. *Einstein: A Life.* New York, 1996.

Bronsen, David, ed. *Jews and Germans from 1860 to 1933: The Problematic Symbiosis.* Heidelberg, 1979.

Carter, Huntley. *The Theatre of Max Reinhardt.* New York, 1964.

Clark, Ronald W. *Einstein: The Life and Times.* Cleveland, 1971.

Claus, Horst. *The Theater Director Otto Brahm.* Ann Arbor, Mich., 1981.

Craig, Gordon. Review of Fritz Stern's *Einstein's German World* in *New York Review of Books,* November 4, 1999.

Deak, Istvan. *Weimar Germany's Leftwing Intellectuals: A Political History of the Weltbühne und Its Circle.* Berkeley, Cal, 1968.

Don, Yehuda, and Victor Karady, eds. *A Social and Economic History of Central European Jewry.* New Brunswick, N.J., 1990.

Eisner, Lotte. *Fritz Lang.* New York, 1976.

——————. *The Haunted Screen: Expressionism in the German Cinema and the Influence of Max Reinhardt.* Berkeley, Cal., 1972.

Everett, Susanne, *Lost Berlin.* London, 1979.

Eyman, Scott. *Ernst Lubitsch.* New York, 1993.

Ferro, Marc. *Cinema and History.* Detroit, 1988.

Forman, Paul. "Weimar Culture, Causality, and Quantum Theory, 1918–1927: Adaptation by German Physicists and Mathematicians to a Hostile Intellectual Environment." *Historical Studies in the Physical Sciences,* Vol. 3 (1971).

Friedrich, Otto. *Before the Deluge: A Portrait of Berlin in the 1920s.* New York, 1972.

Gay, Peter. *Weimar Culture.* New York, 1968.

Goldstein, Moritz. *Begriff und Programm einer jüdischer Nationalliteratur.* Berlin, 1913.

Grab, Walter, and Julius H. Schoeps, eds. *Juden in der Weimarer Republik.* Stuttgart and Bonn, 1986.

Grunfeld, Frederic. *Prophets Without Honor: A Background to Freud, Kafka, Einstein, and Their World.* New York, 1979.

Haas, Willy. *Die literarische Welt: Erinnerungen.* Munich, 1960.

Hollinger, David A. *Science, Jews, and Secular Culture.* Princeton, N.J., 1996.

Ihering, Herbert. *Von Reinhardt zu Brecht.* 3 vols. Frankfurt am/M., 1958.

Jarman, Douglas. *Kurt Weill.* Bloomington, Ind., 1982.

Jensen, Paul. *The Cinema of Fritz Lang.* New York, 1969.

Karlweiss, M. *Jakob Wassermann.* Amsterdam, 1935.

Katznelson, Siegmund, ed. *Juden im deutschen Kulturbereich.* Rev. ed. Berlin, 1959.

Knütter, Hans-Helmuth. *Die Juden und die deutsche Linke in der Weimarer Republik 1918–1933.* Düsseldorf, 1973.

Koestler, Arthur. *Arrow in the Blue.* New York, 1952.

Kowalke, Kiim H. *Kurt Weill in Europe.* Ann Arbor, Mich., 1979.

Kracauer, Siegfried. *From Caligari to Hitler.* Princeton, N.J., 1947.

Laqueur, Walter. *Weimar: A Cultural History, 1918–1933.* London, 1974.

Liptzin, Sol. *Germany's Stepchildren.* Philadelphia, 1944.

Manvell, Roger, and Fraenkel, Heinrich. *The German Cinema.* New York, 1971.

Marcuse, Ludwig. *Mein zwanzigsten Jahrdundert.* Munich, 1960.

Maurer, Trude. *Ostjuden in Deutschland 1918–1933.* Hamburg, 1986.

Mosse, George. *Toward the Final Solution: A History of European Racism.* New York, 1978.

————, and Walter Laqueur, eds. *The Left-Wing Intellectuals Between the Wars, 1919–1939.* New York, 1966.

Murray, Bruce. *Film and the German Left in the Weimar Republic.* Austin, Tex., 1990.

Newlin, Dika. *Bruckner, Mahler, Schoenberg.* New York, 1947.

————. *Schoenberg Remembered.* New York, 1980.

Niewyk, Donald L. "The Economic and Cultural Role of the Jews in the Weimar Republic." *Leo Baeck Institute Yearbook,* Vol. 16 (1971).

————. *Jews in Weimar Germany.* Baton Rouge, La., 1980.

Oppenheimer, Franz. *Erlebten, Erstrebten, Erreichten, Erinnerungen.* Berlin, 1931.

Pais, Abraham. *"Subtle Is the Lord": The Science and the Life of Albert Einstein.* New York, 1982.

Paucker, Arnold. "Jewish Defense Against Nazism in the Weimar Republic." *Wiener Library Bulletin,* Vol. 26 (1972).

Payne, Anthony. *Schoeberg.* New York, 1968.

Peyser, Joan. *New Music: The Sense Behind the Sound.* New York, 1971.

Pulzer, Peter. *Jews and the German State.* Cambridge, Mass., 1992.

————. *The Rise of Political Antisemitism in Germany and Austria.* New York, 1964.

Reinhardt, Gottfried. *The Genius: A Memoir of Max Reinhardt.* New York, 1979.

Reinharz, Jehuda. *Fatherland or Promised Land: The Dilemma of the German Jew, 1893–1914.* Ann Arbor, Mich., 1975.

————, and Walter Schatzberg, eds. *The Jewish Response to German Culture: From the Enlightenment to the Second World War.* Hanover, N.H., 1985.

Ringer, Alexander L. *Arnold Schoenberg: The Composer as Jew.* New York, 1990.

Rosen, Charles. *Schoenberg.* New York, 1975.

Salzman, Eric. *Twentieth-Century Music: An Introduction.* 2nd ed. Englewood Cliffs, N.J., 1974.

Samuel, Richard, and Hinton Thomas. *Expressionism in German Life, Literature, and the Theater (1910–1924).* Cambridge, England, 1939.

Sanders, Ronald. *The Days Grow Short: The Life and Music of Kurt Weill.* New York, 1980.

Sayler, Oliver M. *Max Reinhardt and His Theatre.* New York, 1924.

Schatzberg, Walter, and Jehuda Reinharz, eds. *The Jewish Response to German Culture: From the Enlightenment to the Second World War.* Hanover, N.H., 1985.

Schorske, Karl. "Weimar and the Intellectuals: I," in *New York Review of Books,* May 7, 1970.

—————. "Weimar and the Intellectuals: II," in *New York Review of Books,* May 21, 1970.

Stern, Fritz. *Einstein's German World.* Princeton, N.J., 1999.

—————. *The Politics of Cultural Despair: A Study in the Rise of German Ideology.* Berkeley, Cal., 1961.

Stern, Rudolf. "Fritz Haber." *Leo Baeck Institute Yearbook,* Vol. 8 (1963).

Stuckenschmidt, Hans H. *Schoenberg: His Life, World, and Work.* New York, 1977.

Styan, J. L. *Max Reinhardt.* New York, 1982.

Tal, Uriel. *Christians and Jews in Germany.* Ithaca, N.Y., 1974.

Taton, René, ed. *Science in the Twentieth Century,* 2 vols. New York, 1963–66.

Taylor, Ronald. *Kurt Weill.* Boston, 1992.

Tucholsky, Kurt. *Deutschland, Deutschland über Alles.* Berlin, 1929.

Vollbach, Walther R. *Memoirs of Max Reinhardt's Theatres, 1920–1922.* Pittsburgh, 1972.

Walter, Bruno. *Theme and Variations.* New York, 1946.

Wassermann, Jakob. *My Life as German and Jew [Mein Weg als Deutscher und Jude].* London, 1933.

Weinberg, Herman. *The Lubitsch Touch.* New York, 1977.

Weinrich, Max. *Hitler's Professors.* New York, 1946.

Wellwarth, George W., Alfred G. Brooks, and Fraeda Pasish, eds. *Max Reinhardt: A Centennial Festschrift.* Binghamton, N.Y., 1973.

Weltsch, Felix. "The Rise and Fall of the Jewish-German Symbiosis." *Leo Baeck Institute Yearbook,* Vol. 1 (1956).

Whitaker, Andrew. *Einstein, Bohr, and the Quantum Dilemma.* Cambridge, England, 1996.

Willett, John. *Art and Politics in the Weimar Republic: The New Sobriety, 1917–1930.* New York, 1978.

—————. *The Theater of the Weimar Republic.* New York, 1988.

—————. *Weimar Years: A Culture Cut Short.* London, 1984.

Zuckermann, Carl. *Die deutschen Dramen.* Frankfurt a/M, 1951.

Zuckmayer, Carl. *A Part of Myself.* New York, 1966.

X. IN SEARCH OF LOST SWANNS

Allen, Luther A. "The French Left and Soviet Russia: Origins of the Popular Front." *Foreign Affairs Quarterly,* Vol. 30, No. 3, 1959.

Anderson, Malcolm. *Conservative Politics in France.* London, 1974.

Andreu, P., and F. Grover. *Drieu La Rochelle.* Paris, 1979.

Audry, Colette. *Léon Blum, ou la Politique du Juste.* Paris, 1965.

Barker, Richard H. *Marcel Proust: A Biography.* New York, 1968.

Bernard, Philippe, and Henri Dubief. *Le Fin d'un monde, 1914–1928; Le Déclin de la IIIe République, 1929–1938.* 2 vols. Paris, 1975–76.

Birnbaum, Pierre. *Un Mythe politique: La "République juive."* Paris, 1988.

Bloch, Marc. *Strange Defeat.* Oxford, 1949.

Blum, Léon. *L'histoire jugera.* Paris, 1945.

—————. *L'Oeuvre de Léon Blum.* 6 vols. Paris, 1955.

Blumel, André. *Léon Blum: juif et sioniste.* Paris, 1951.

Bodin, Louis, and Jean Touchard. *Front Populaire, 1936.* Paris, 1961.

Bonnefous, Édouard. *Histoire de la Troisième République: Les Années d'Illusions, 1918–1931.* Paris, 1960.

Bourdrel, Philippe. *La Cagoule.* Paris, 1970.

————. *Histoire des Juifs de France.* Paris, 1974.

Bourgin, Hubert. *De Jaurès à Léon Blum.* Paris, 1938.

Brogan, D.W. *France under the Republic: The Development of Modern France, 1870–1939.* London, 1940.

————. *French Personalities and Problems.* New York, 1947.

Burrin, Philippe. *La dérive fasciste: Doriot, Déat, etc.* Paris, 1986.

Buthmann, William. *The Rise of Integral Nationalism in France.* New York, 1939.

Byrnes, Robert F. *Anti-Semitism in Modern France.* New Brunswick, N.J., 1960.

Capitan, Charles. *Charles Maurras et l'idéologie de l'Action française.* Paris, 1972.

Carlton, David. "Eden, Blum, and the Origins of Non-Intervention." *Journal of Contemporary History,* Vol. 6, No. 3, 1981.

Carter, William C. *Marcel Proust: A Life.* New Haven, 2000.

Clermont-Tonnère, Élisabeth. *Mémoires.* Vol. 1. Paris, 1928.

Colton, Joel. *Léon Blum: Humanist in Politics.* New York, 1966.

Cot, Pierre. *The Triumph of Treason.* New York, 1944.

Curtis, Michael. *Three Against the Third Republic—Sorel, Barrès, and Maurras.* Princeton, N.J., 1959.

Dreifort, John. "The French Popular Front and the Franco-Soviet Pact 1936–37." *Journal of Contemporary History,* Vol. 2, Nos. 2–3, 1976.

Dubief, Henri. *Le déclin de la Troisième République, 1929–1938.* Paris, 1976.

Ducloux, Louis. *From Blackmail to Corruption: Political Crimes and Corruption in France, 1920–1940.* London, 1958.

Édito-Service. *Les Grandes Affaires Criminelles.* Geneva, 1975.

Fabre-Luce, A. *Pour en finir avec l'antisémitism.* Paris, 1979.

Favreau, Bertrand. *Georges Mandel.* Paris, 1969.

Ferro, Marc. *Pétain.* Paris, 1987.

Fraser, Geoffrey, and Thadée Natanson. *Léon Blum: Man and Statesman.* Philadelphia, 1938.

Gide, André. *Journals, 1889–1949.* London, 1967.

Goguel, François. *La Politique des partis sous la IIIe République.* Paris, 2d ed., 1958.

Green, Nancy L. *The Pletzl of Paris: Jewish Immigrant Workers in the Belle Époque.* New York, 1986.

Greene, Nathanael. *Crisis and Decline: The French Socialist Party in the Popular Front Era.* New York, 1969.

Gregh, Fernand. *L'Âge d'or.* Paris, 1947.

Griffiths, Richard. *Marshal Pétain.* London, 1970.

Guérin, Daniel. *Front Populaire—Révolution manquée.* Paris, 1976.

Halls, W. D. *Politics, Society, and Christianity in Vichy France.* Oxford, 1995.

Havard de la Montagne, Robert. *Histoire de l'Action française.* Paris, 1951.

Hayman, Ronald. *Proust: A Biography.* New York, 1990.

Herzog, Wilhelm. *From Dreyfus to Pétain.* New York, 1947.

Hindus, Milton. *The Crippled Giant: A Literary Relationship with Louis-Ferdinand Céline.* Hanover, N.H., 1986.

Horne, Alistair. *The French Army and Politics, 1870–1970.* New York, 1974.

Huddleston, Sisley. *Pétain: Patriot or Traitor.* London, 1951.

————. *The Obstructed Path: French Social Thought in the Years of Desperation.* New York, 1968.

Hyman, Paula. *From Dreyfus to Vichy: The Making of French Jewry, 1906–1939.* New York, 1979.

Ingram, Norman. *The Politics of Dissent: Pacifism in France 1919–1930.* Oxford, 1931.

Jackson, Julian. *The Popular Front in France: Defending Democracy.* Cambridge, England, 1988.

Jacomet, Robert. *L'Armament de la France, 1936–1939.* Paris, 1945.

Joll, James. "The Popular Front after Thirty Years." *Journal of Contemporary History,* Vol. 1, No. 2, 1966.

——————. *Three Intellectuals in Politics.* New York. 1960.

——————. "The Front Populaire—After Thirty Years," in Mosse, George, and Walter Laqueur, eds. *The Left-Wing Intellectuals Between the Wars.* New York, 1966.

——————, ed. *The Decline of the Third Republic.* St. Antony's Papers, No. 5, London, 1959.

Jordan, Nicole. *The Popular Front and Central Europe: The Dilemma of French Impotence 1918–1940.* Cambridge, England, 1992.

Judt, Tony. *The Burden of Responsibility: Blum, Camus, Aron, and the French Twentieth Century.* Chicago, 1998.

——————. *La Reconstruction du Parti Socialist (1921–1926).* Paris, 1976.

Kingston, Paul. *Antisemitism in France During the 1930s.* Hull, England, 1983.

Kolb, Philip, ed. *Marcel Proust: Correspondence.* Garden City, N.Y., 1989.

Lacouture, Jean. *Léon Blum.* New York, 1982.

Larmour, Peter J. *The French Radical Party in the 1930s.* Stanford, Cal., 1964.

Lebovics, Herman. *True France: The Wars Over Cultural Identity, 1900–1945.* Ithaca, N.Y., 1992.

Lefranc, Georges. *Histoire du Front Populaire.* Paris, 1963.

Logue, W. *Léon Blum: The Formative Years.* DeKalb, Ill., 1973.

Lorenz, Paul. *Les trois vies de Stavisky.* Paris, 1971.

Lottman, Herbert R. *Pétain: Hero or Traitor.* New York, 1986.

Machefer, Philippe. *Ligues et fascismes en France, 1918–1939.* Paris, 1974.

Maître, Jean. "Catholicisme d'extrême-droite et croisade anti-subversive." *Revue française de sociologie,* Vol. 2, No. 2, 1961.

Malino, Frances, and Bernard Wasserstein, eds. *The Jews in Modern France.* Hanover, N.H., 1985.

Marcus, John T. *French Socialism in the Crisis Years, 1933–1936: Fascism and the French Left.* New York, 1958.

Marrus, Michael R., and Robert O. Paxton. *Vichy France and the Jews.* New York, 1981.

Massis, Henri. *Maurras et notre temps.* 2 vols. Paris, 1951.

Maurras, Charles. *La démocratie religieuse.* Paris, 1921.

——————. *Mes idées politiques.* Paris, 1937.

Mayer, Daniel. *Pour une histoire de la gauche.* Paris, 1969.

McCarthy, Patrick. *Céline.* London, 1975.

McMillan, James F. *From Dreyfus to De Gaulle: Politics and Society in France, 1898–1969.* Baltimore, 1985.

Mehlman, J. *Legacies of Anti-Semitism in France.* Minneapolis, 1983.

Micaud, Charles A. *The French Right and Nazi Germany, 1933–1939.* New York, 1964.

Michel, Henri. *Le procès de Riom.* Paris, 1979.

Milza, Pierre, *Fascisme français, passé et présent.* Paris, 1987.

Moch, Jules. *Rencontres avec Léon Blum.* Paris, 1970.

Mourre, Michel. *Charles Maurras.* Paris, 1958.

Nolte, Ernst. *Three Faces of Fascism.* New York, 1965.

Osgood, Samuel. *French Royalism Under the Third and Fourth Republics.* The Hague, 1961.

Painter, George D. *Proust.* 2 vols. Boston, 1959–65.

Paxton, Robert O. *French Peasant Fascism.* New York, 1997.

——————. *Vichy France: Old Guard and New Order.* New York, 1972.

Pedroncini, Guy. *La défense sous la Troisième République.* Paris, 1989.

Pertinax (Geraud, André). *The Gravediggers of France.* New York, 1944.

Pierce, R. *Contemporary French Political Thought.* Oxford, England, 1966.

Plumiyène, J., and R. LaSierra. *Les Fascismes français, 1923–1963.* Paris, 1963.

Poliakov, Léon. *The History of Anti-Semitism.* Vol. 4: 1870–1933. New York, 1977.

Pougan, Jacques. *L'âge d'or du maurrassisme.* Paris, 1971.

Pujo, Maurice. *Les Camelots du Roi.* Paris, 1933.

Rémond, René. *La Droite en France.* 2d. ed. Paris, 1982.

Roblin, Michel. *Les Juifs de Paris: demographie—économie—culture.* Paris, 1952.

Rollin, H. *L'Apocalypse de notre temps: les dessous de la propagande allemande d'après des documents inédits.* Paris, 1939.

Roudiez, Léon S. *Maurras jusqu'à l'Action française.* Paris, 1957.

Sachar, Abram L. *Sufferance Is the Badge: The Jew in the Postwar World.* New York, 1940.

Sachar, Howard M. *Diaspora: An Inquiry into the Contemporary Jewish World.* New York, 1985.

Schor, Ralph. *L'opinion française et les étrangers en France, 1919–1939.* Vol. 1. Marseilles, 1980.

Sherwood, John M. *Georges Mandel and the Third Republic.* Stanford, Cal., 1971.

Soltau, Roger H. *French Parties and Politics, 1871–1930.* London, 1930.

Soucy, Robert J. *Fascism in France: The Case of Maurice Barrès.* Berkeley, Cal., 1972.

——————. *French Fascism: The First Wave, 1924–1933.* New Haven, Conn., 1986.

——————. *French Fascism: The Second Wave, 1933–1939.* New Haven, Conn., 1995.

Spengler, Joseph J. *France Faces Depopulation.* Paris, 1930.

Sternhell, Zeev. *Ni droite, ni gauche: L'Idéologie fasciste en France.* Paris, 1983.

Stone, Glyn. "The European Great Powers and the Spanish Civil War, 1936–1939," in Boyce, R., and E. M. Robertson, eds. *Paths to War.* London, 1989.

Tannenbaum, E. R. *The Action Française.* New York, 1962.

Tint, Herbert. *France Since 1918.* New York, 1970.

Touchard, Jean. *La Gauche en France depuis 1900.* Paris, 1977.

Tournoux, Jean-Raymond. *L'histoire secrète: La Cagoule.* Paris, 1962.

Viguier, Laurent. *Les Juifs à travers Léon Blum.* Paris, 1938.

Vitoux, Frédéric. *Céline: A Biography.* New York, 1992.

Wall, Irwin. "Socialists and Bureaucrats: The Blum Government and the French Administration, 1936–1937." *International Review of Social History,* Vol. 29, No. 3, 1974.

Wardi, Charlotte, *L'image du Juif dans le roman français.* Paris, 1973.

Warner, Geoffrey. *Pierre Laval and the Eclipse of France.* London, 1969.

——————. "The Stavisky Affair and the Riots of February 6th, 1934." *History Today,* June 1958.

Weber, Eugen. *Action Française: Royalism and Reaction in Twentieth-Century France.* Stanford, Cal., 1962.

——————. *Varieties of Fascism.* Princeton, N.J., 1964.

Weinberg, David. *Les Juifs à Paris de 1933 à 1939.* Paris, 1974.

Werth, Alexander. *France and Munich.* London, 1939.

——————. *France in Ferment.* Gloucester, Mass., 1968.

——————. *The Twilight of France, 1933–40.* New York, 1942.

Winock, Michel. *Nationalism, Anti-Semitism, and Fascism in France.* Stanford, Cal., 1998.

Zeldin, Theodore. *France 1848–1945.* Vol. 2. New York, 1977.

Ziebura, Gilbert. *Léon Blum et le parti socialiste.* Paris, 1967.

Index

A Note About the Author

Born in St. Louis, Missouri, and reared in Champaign, Illinois, Howard Morley Sachar received his undergraduate education at Swarthmore and took his graduate degrees at Harvard. He has taught extensively in the fields of Modern European, Jewish, and Middle Eastern history, and lived in the Middle East for six years, two of them on fellowship, the rest as founder-director of Brandeis University's Hiatt Institute in Jerusalem. Dr. Sachar has contributed to many scholarly journals and is the author of numerous previous books: *The Course of Modern Jewish History* (1958), *Aliyah* (1961), *From the Ends of the Earth* (1964), *The Emergence of the Middle East, 1914–1924* (1969), *Europe Leaves the Middle East, 1936–1954* (1972), *A History of Israel from the Rise of Zionism to Our Time* (1976), *The Man on the Camel* (1980), *Egypt and Israel* (1981), *Diaspora* (1985), *A History of Israel from the Aftermath of the Yom Kippur War* (1987), *A History of the Jews in America* (1992), *Farewell España* (1994), *A History of Israel from the Rise of Zionism to Our Time, Revised and Updated* (1996), and *Israel and Europe: An Appraisal in History* (1999). He is also the editor of the thirty-nine-volume *The Rise of Israel: A Documentary History*. Based in Washington, D.C., where he serves as Professor of Modern History at George Washington University, Dr. Sachar is a consultant and lecturer on Middle Eastern affairs for numerous governmental bodies and lectures widely throughout the United States and abroad. He and his family live in Kensington, Maryland.

A NOTE ON THE TYPE

This book was set in Janson, and composed by Creative Graphics, Allentown, Pennsylvania. Printed and bound by R. R. Donnelley & Sons, Harrisonburg, Virginia. Designed by Anthea Lingeman.